THE COMPLETE WORKS
OF THOMAS SHADWELL

THE COMPLETE WORKS OF THOMAS SHADWELL EDITED BY MONTAGUE SUMMERS ❧ VOLUME I

BENJAMIN BLOM, PUBLISHERS

First published London, 1927
Reissued 1968,
by Benjamin Blom, Inc. Bx 10452

Library of Congress Catalog Card No. 68 - 20247

Printed in U.S.A. by
NOBLE OFFSET PRINTERS, INC.
NEW YORK 3, N. Y.

Contents

Dedication

QVIDQVID SIT BONI
IN HOC LIBRO
ANIMAE IN MEMORIAM DVLCISSIMAE

PREFATORY NOTE.

WITH the possible exception of John Dryden, upon whose works I am, and have been for very many months, intensively engaged, there is certainly no writer of the Restoration period, and probably not more than three or four authors in English literature, who call for such detailed and ample annotation as Thomas Shadwell. Indeed if they are thoroughly to be appreciated and understood, the eighteen plays of Shadwell require notes and commentaries on an even more extensive a scale than is demanded by the theatre of his great antagonist himself. For Shadwell was above all a writer of intensest realism, and his crowded scenes which exactly and in veriest detail paint the life he saw all round about him, which present the typical figures and reproduce the typical conversations of the hour, consequently contain such numbers of topical allusions, such repeated references to passing, and often forgotten, events, as, I make bold to profess, are not to be met with elsewhere in his day outside the pages of Pepys and the political poems of Dryden.

It is, perhaps, owing to these difficulties that Shadwell has something fallen into the background, and by the irony of circumstance he is generally known not because of his own merits, which are very great, but because he was the chief victim of the finest and most terrible satires in the English tongue. Dryden, who was very well aware what he was about, and who fully realized in what consists the one unpardonable literary sin that will inevitably damn the sinner to oblivion, blackened Shadwell with this awful guilt when he dubbed him Dull. The shame has stuck ever since, but we hope that at last Shadwell will clear himself from this accusation, and show that in vitality and humour he is fully the equal of many who have been applauded and acclaimed as the brilliant and dazzling Wits of the Restoration.

If I have acquitted myself reasonably well of the task of editing Shadwell, this will be my (and his) reward. It is indeed singular what little recognition so important a figure as Thomas Shadwell has hitherto received. Not even Sir Edmund Gosse with one of his delightful essays has illumined our steps, and with his magic touch given new life to the dramatist whom the Revolution of 1689 crowned with the Laureate's wreath of bays.

Perhaps this neglect is to some extent generally due to the difficulty of obtaining Shadwell's works, and to the fact that there has hitherto existed no edition of our author. This, indeed, is the first time that the plays and poems of Shadwell have been collected, collated, and annotated. The very biography at once presented a multiplicity of difficulties. The brief "Account Of The Author and his Writings" which was prefixed to the poor reprint of seventeen of the plays in 1720 does not amount to half a dozen pages, and is of course hopelessly inadequate, as well as

(ix)

inexact. Literally no research in any direction had been essayed with regard to Shadwell, and the simplest facts, his birth-place, his age, the number and names of his children, were disputed and obscure. It has been necessary to piece together his biography entirely from original sources, from correspondence, some of which is yet unpublished; from official records, both in England and in Ireland, many of which had been unexamined; from local registers and tradition; from scattered notices in contemporary journals and newspapers; from Dedications to books of the last rarity; and, not least, from the mass of political and theatrical satire, much of which still remains in MS., most dangerous ground, where it has been my best endeavour to sift the false from the true.

The labour has been admittedly heavy, but it has been lightened and made happy owing to the ungrudging help which has been afforded me, and the interest which has been shown in my edition by many eminent and distinguished persons. In the first place I am deeply indebted to Sir Edmund Gosse, C.B., whose kind loans of Shadwell collections, rare quartos and other pieces from his magnificent library, immensely facilitated my work upon this most difficult of authors. Lord Sackville of Knole has not only permitted the facsimile reproduction of the Shadwell letter at Knole Park, but was so generous as to entrust me with the original, allowing me to retain it for some weeks so that it could conveniently be copied and photographed. Particularly do I desire to express my obligations and sincere thanks to V. Sackville-West, who has searched on my behalf the Knole Collections for papers by, or having reference to, Thomas Shadwell. I wish to record my very real gratitude to the Earl of Ossory, who most promptly and fully answered my inquiries concerning any documents relating to Shadwell which might have existed among the Ormonde MSS., and who himself was at the trouble to transcribe for me the letter, now preserved at Kilkenny Castle, in which Shadwell acknowledges the favour done to his son John by the second Duke of Ormonde. With his wonted generosity Professor Bensly was indefatigable in tracking down the obscurer quotations of which Shadwell is so fond. I venture to think that the Genealogical Table of Shadwell's family which is now printed for the first time will prove of especial interest. For this and a note upon Sir John Shadwell I am beholden to the very particular kindness of Mr. Archibald John Mackey.

Any further help I may have received in the elucidation of a technical point I have expressly acknowledged in my note upon such numerical passage.

THE TEXT.

THE text of the eighteen plays included in these five volumes is exactly given from the original quartos and has been collated with all reprints that appeared during Shadwell's lifetime, although as a matter of fact it is highly improbable that he troubled to revise the proofs of any second or third edition which came from the Press. The authority of any later issue than 1692 is, of course, negligible, and although I have compared such later copies as Epsom-Wells, 4to, 1704; The Tempest, 4tos, 1695 and 1701; The Libertine, 4tos, 1704 and 1705; The Virtuoso, 4to, 1704; Timon of Athens, 4tos, 1696 and 1703, and The Squire of Alsatia, 4to, 1699; I have not thought it worth while to record the minor variants and the many mistakes introduced by these unworthy texts. Within a year or two after the appointment of Shadwell as Poet Laureate, ten of his plays were reprinted, no doubt with a view to collecting his dramatic work in one volume, which was in fact actually done. These ten plays are as follows : The Sullen Lovers, 4to, 1693; The Royal Shepherdess, 4to, 1691; The Humourists, 4to, 1691, an edition which is for some reason excessively rare ; The Miser, 4to, 1691; Epsom-Wells, 4to, 1693; The Tempest, 4to, 1690; Psyche, 4to, 1690; The Virtuoso, 4to, 1691; The Lancashire Witches, 4to, 1691 ; and The Squire of Alsatia, 4tos, 1692 and 1693.

Shadwell's posthumous comedy, The Volunteers; or, The Stock-Jobbers, stands in a different category. It was published 4to, 1693, and is announced in the Term Catalogues for Trinity (June) of that year. This is altogether the poorest text of any one of Shadwell's plays, and it is difficult to suppose that as it passed through the printer's hand it was afforded any save the most superficial reading so great is the frequency of misprints and so gross are they.

Shortly after Shadwell's death James Knapton of the Crown in S. Paul's Churchyard hurriedly collected seventeen of the Shadwell quartos and bound them together in one volume with the title shown on p. xiii.

This was ready in the early summer of 1693. It is announced in the Term Catalogues for Trinity (June) of that year. It may be noticed that the plays in spite of the statement that they are arranged " in the method they were first published" are not even in any sort of order, as The Royal Shepherdess which should be No. 2 is No. 3 ; The Miser which should be No. 4 is No. 9 ; Epsom-Wells which should be No. 5 is No. 7 ; The Virtuoso which should be No. 8 is No. 4 ; and The Lancashire Witches first published, 4to, 1682, precedes The Woman-Captain, the first and only quarto of which play is dated 1680. In fact the whole collection bears every sign of carelessness, and was merely hurriedly *put out to catch the opportunity of the moment. The following editions were bound together by Knapton. (They are all quartos.)*

1. The Sullen Lovers, 1693 ;
2. The Humorists (*which Knapton misprints as* Humorist) ; 1691 ;
3. The Royal Shepherdess, 1691 ;
4. The Virtuoso, 1691 ;
5. *Psyche*, 1690 ;
6. The Libertine, 1692 ;
7. *Epsom*-Wells, 1693 ;
8. *Timon* of *Athens*, 1688 ;
9. The Miser, 1691 ;
10. A True Widow, 1689. (*This is merely the first 4to, 1679, with a new title-page, and a reissue of the page containing the Epilogue.*)
11. The *Lancashire* Witches, 1691 ;
12. The Woman Captain, 1680. (*This is the first 4to.*)
13. The Squire of *Alsatia*, 1693 ;
14. Bury-Fair, 1689. (*This is the first 4to.*)
15. The Amorous Bigotte, 1690. (*This is the first 4to. It will be noted that Knapton has a misprint* Biggotte.)
16. The Scowrers, 1691. (*First 4to.*)
17. The Volunteers, 1693. (*First 4to.*)

It will be remarked that The Tempest *is not included, but incidentally this must not be advanced as an argument against Shadwell's authorship of the operatic version, since it is obvious that the bookseller was at no great pains, but merely took what came to hand. It is, however, worth recording that nobody troubled to collect any of Shadwell's poetical pieces, which shows that he was regarded only as a dramatist.*

In 1720 these seventeen plays appeared in four badly-printed duodecimos, with a dedication to George I. by John Shadwell, which runs as follows : May it please Your *MAJESTY*, I beg Leave most humbly to present to Your *MAJESTY* the Works of a Man, who, I may say, (tho' my Father,) deserv'd the Patronage of a Good King, having in very troublesome-Times suffer'd for his good Wishes and Attempts to serve his Country, and for shewing on all Occasions, as far as lay in his Power, his Dislike to any Measures tending to give up the Laws and Liberties of the Nation. This can be no ill Recommendation of a Person to Your *MAJESTY*, who is so remarkable a Bulwark of both, and whose Counsels are indefatigably employ'd in securing Peace to Europe, and Freedom to your Subjects.

I know not, SIR, which is greatest, the Honour of being Your *MAJESTY'S* Servant, or the Happiness of being Your Subject : The good Fortune that I enjoy of being both, and the Honour of having had Access to Your *MAJESTY*, have given me the Opportunity of admiring my Master and revering my Sovereign ; and I may say, with the Numbers that have the Honour of approaching You, that Your *MAJESTY*, as You shew Your self more, must have as many Friends as Subjects.

THE
WORKS

OF

Tho. Shadwell, Esq;

Late Poet Laureat, and Historiographer Royal.

CONTAINING,

In One Volume, in the method they were first published,

1	*Sullen Lovers,*	10	*True Widow,*
2	*Humorist,*	11	Lancashire *Witches,*
3	*Royal Shepherdess,*	12	*Woman Captain,*
4	*Virtuoso,*	13	*Squire of* Alsatia,
5	Psyche,	14	*Bury-Fair,*
6	*Libertine,*	15	*Amorous Biggotte,*
7	Epsom *Wells,*	16	*Scowrers,*
8	Timon *of* Athens,	17	*Volunteers,*
9	*Miser,*		

LONDON,

Printed for *James Knapton,* at the *Crown* in St. *Pauls* Church-yard, 1693.

Where are also to be had all Mr. *Dryden*'s Works in 4 Vol. Mr. *Lee*'s, and Mr. *Otway*'s in one Volume each.

(xiii)

BUT I forgot that the Delicacy of Great Minds over-awes the Justice which is due to their exalted Virtues, and that my Gratitude had almost betray'd me into an Offence.

THE Dead Author of these POEMS is beyond the Sense or Advantage of Your MAJESTY'S Excellent Patronage; and Your Illustrious Name is prefix'd to his Writings chiefly as a Declaration of His Son's Happiness, as a most humble and a most dutiful Acknowledgment of Your MAJESTY'S Favours to him: And if this Dedication may remain as an entire Testimony of my Zeal for Your MAJESTY'S Service, and as a lasting Monument of my Father's Loyalty to Your Royal Ancestors; like him, I shall think I have liv'd like an Englishman, whose greatest Felicity is to be, as I am,

May it please Your *MAJESTY,*

Your *MAJESTY'S*

most Humble,

most Obedient,

and most Dutiful

Subject and Servant,

JOHN SHADWELL.

Since most of this edition was destroyed by fire the book now fetches a high price and is excessively scarce. From a textual point of view it is quite worthless; there are many errors, there are modifications and unpardonable omissions; and there has not, of course, been the slightest attempt at editing.

Four of Shadwell's plays (The Sullen Lovers, A True Widow, The Squire of Alsatia *and* Bury-Fair) *appeared in one volume in the Mermaid Series, as the " Best Plays of Thomas Shadwell," although it is difficult to see how any collection which omitted* The Virtuoso *and* Epsom-Wells *could be so ignorantly and ineptly named. Some five and thirty years ago the popular " Mermaid " Edition, for which we would not be ungrateful, proved an inestimable boon to many. The inception of these reprints originated, I believe, with Dr. Havelock Ellis, and whilst his was the guiding hand the familiar green or brown cloth books were of their kind excellent. The critical introductions and brilliant appreciations by such writers as Sir Edmund Gosse, John Addington Symonds, Arthur Symons, and Havelock Ellis himself it were impossible to better. Unfortunately the series fell on evil days, and some of the later volumes are altogether inadequate. But I believe the nadir is plumbed by the Shadwell, who, poor man! seems to have been doomed to misfortune all along the line. The editor (save the mark!) boldly says: " The text, which is fairly corrupt in the 1720 edition, has been corrected from the first edition where necessary." This sounds very conscientious and scholarly, but I am afraid it is a mere flam. Actually the text has been modernized and maltreated out of all recognition, and the general Introduction is on a par with the text. It is obvious that the gentleman who had the care of this volume was not merely unequipped for the task of editorship, but had no idea how to set about his work. He ventures* but one *statement that has sense or consequence, and this is :* " *Full annotation on Shadwell would have to be very full indeed.*" *True ; but he was not the man who could supply it, and I will at least do him the justice to say that he seemed to recognize the fact. I am afraid that in the Elysian Fields the spirit of Dryden must have chuckled when this Shadwell made its appearance.*

The Poems of Shadwell, which I have collected with no little research from various sources, are now for the most part reprinted for the first time. Two or three pieces, as I have remarked in the particular Textual Notes, appeared in the various editions of Poems On Affairs of State, *that vast miscellany which has become an exceedingly scarce book, and the bibliography of which is, incidentally, difficult to the last degree. Since then they were never reprinted, I have naturally had to go to the first editions for several poetical pieces, of which one at least,* The Tory-Poets, *is so rare that the sole survivor is believed to be the copy in the Dyce Library. With the* Letter from Mr. Shadwell to Mr. Wicherley *I have given the complementary* Answer. *These pieces are printed from the Dyce MS.*

The four Letters of Shadwell are now printed for the first time by the kind permission of their owners, to whom I have made my grateful acknowledgement in the Prefatory Note.

Introduction

"*THOMAS SHADWELL*[1] was of an ancient Family in *Stafford-shire*, the Eldest Branch of which has enjoyed an Estate there of at least five hundred Pounds *per Annum* for above three hundred Years, without any Honours or Publick Business. His Father was bred at *Caius* College in *Cambridge*, and from thence remov'd to the *Middle-Temple*, to study the Laws; but having more than a competent Fortune left him by an Uncle, he did not much trouble himself with the Practice. He had eleven Children to maintain in the time of the Civil Wars, wherein he was a great Sufferer for the King, which forc'd him to sell and spend good part of his Estate: He was in Commission for the Peace in three Counties in *England*, *Middlesex*, *Norfolk*, and *Suffolk*, and behav'd himself with great Ability and Integrity. He was afterwards Recorder of *Gallway* in *Ireland*, and Receiver there to the late King *James*, then Duke of *York*; he was sometime Attorney-General at *Tangier*, under the then Earl of *Inchequin*.

"Our Author was born at *Santon-Hall* in *Norfolk*, a Seat of his Father's, he was Educated at *Caius*-College, and was likewise, as his Father had been, plac'd in the *Middle-Temple*, to study the Laws; where after he had spent some Time, he went abroad to improve himself by travelling. Upon his Return home, he came acquainted with the most celebrated Persons of Wit and distinguish'd Quality in that Age, which was so given to Poetry and polite Letters, that it was not easie for him, who had so true a Relish and Genius, to abstain from the elegant Studies and Amusements of those Times. He apply'd himself chiefly to the Dramatick kind of Writing, in which he studied to serve his Country, rather than raise himself by the low Arts then in Practice; and he succeeded so well in his Design, as to merit the Honour of being made Poet *Laureat* and Historiographer Royal upon the Revolution by King *William* and Queen *Mary*, which Employments he enjoy'd 'till his Death 1692, in the 52d Year of his Age.

[1] The name is probably derived from "S. Chad's Well." There is a S. Chad's Well, which is yet a place of pilgrimage at Lichfield, Staffs. Mr. Walter Rye, the Norfolk antiquarian, points out that "not only is there a Shadwell on the Thames near London, and another place of the same name in the West Riding of Yorkshire, but we find that in Norfolk there was a little village called Schadewell in Rushworth from early times. At the end of the 12th Century, Philip de Schadewell owned a several fishery there, which was sold in 1362 by Adam de Shadwell." The name Shadwell often occurs in Norfolk. In 1334 Robert de Shadwell was presented to Intwood.

" His Principles were very Loyal and firm to the Interests and Laws of his Country, and to such good Princes as govern'd by their Authority; at once approving himself a good Patriot and a good Subject.

" He was allow'd by all who knew him to be an accomplish'd Gentleman; he had a great deal of ready Wit, and very quick Parts, improv'd by the best Advantages of Learning, the best Conversation and other Acquisitions; amongst which I might mention his Great Skill in Musick.

" He had not only a strict Sense of Honour and Morality, but likewise (particularly in his latter Days) a true Sense of Religion too.

" As to his Writings, *Langbain* has endeavour'd to do him Justice, in his View of the Stage; wherein he shews how free he is from the Barrenness of some other Poets, which made them turn Plagiaries, and copy from other Authors, what he, like a skillful Observer, drew to the Light from Nature. His writing thus his own unborrow'd Thoughts, what he had himself collected immediately from the World, (the most instructive Library for a Man of Genius and Observation,) accounts for that easie Turn of Conception and Language that graced every Thing he said or wrote. He is universally allow'd to have excell'd in Humour, which is a Talent almost peculiar to the *English* Nation."

Thus far " Some Account Of The Author *and his* Writings " which in Volume I. prefaces " The Dramatick Works Of *Thomas Shadwell*, Esq.; In Four Volumes," 12mo, 1720, " Printed for J. Knapton, at the *Crown* in Saint *Paul's Church-Yard;* and J. Tonson, at *Shakespear's Head* over-against *Katharine-Street* in the *Strand*." [1] This edition was dedicated in fulsome and nauseating adulation to George I. by John Shadwell, the son of the dramatist. All seems plain sailing here; it may be, and it has been, presumed that the son would have known the details of his father's life, particularly when that father was a public figure, but upon investigation it is found that there are certain discrepancies which call for a careful consideration. Not only the place of the poet's birth has been disputed, but also the precise date.

The arms which Thomas Shadwell claimed to bear were first granted to a Thomas Shadwell, of Linedon (Lyndowne) in Enville, Co. Stafford, on 2 June, 1537, by Sir C. Barker, Garter. They are Per Pale Or and Azure on a chevron between three annulets four escallop shells all counterchanged.[2] John Shadwell, the father of Thomas Shadwell, was the son of George Shadwell, of London,[3] and was born at Thetford, where either his father, George, or an uncle, his father's brother, whose name is

---

[1] Owing to the fact that most of this impression was destroyed in a fire the book has now become exceedingly rare and high prices are asked. It presents, however, a poor text; is incomplete; and of no intrinsic value.

[2] The right is disputed by Mr. Walter Rye in his *The Poet Shadwell*, pp. 287–292, *Some Historical Essays chiefly relating to Norfolk*, Part IV, 1927.

[3] Likelier Linedon.

believed to have been Thomas, had considerable property, and it was to this property as well as to the Broomhill and Santon Estates that John Shadwell succeeded upon the death of his uncle Thomas. It would seem that George Shadwell died whilst his son was yet young,[1] and accordingly John was brought up under the tutelage of his unmarried uncle as the acknowledged heir.

In the Middle-Temple Records [2] we have the following entry: " 16 May, 1639. Mr. John, son and heir of George Shadwell of London,[3] gent., deceased, generally; bound with John Pay and Thomas Shadwell, gents.; fine 3l 6s 8d." Here the word " generally " is used to indicate that John Shadwell was entered in the ordinary way, and paid fees amounting to £3 : 6 : 8. The fees have, of course, considerably increased since his time, even if we have regard to the proportionate value of money in the reign of Charles I. " Generally " applies to the admission of most members of the Inn; but some were admitted " specially " and without fine. Treasurers would sometimes admit notables, or their own sons " specially." Hence the distinction is employed.

Thomas Shadwell was dead before 1640,[4] and his nephew duly succeeded to his estates. As we have seen, he had already inherited from his father, and was now a considerable landed proprietor. John Shadwell never practised in the law, but he was a Justice of the Peace for no less than three counties, Middlesex, Norfolk, and Suffolk, and it was almost certainly he who in 1644 is recorded as being the King's Escheator at Wolverhampton.[5] There was a fine in Michaelmas 21 Charles I. (1645) between Robert Smyth, gent., and others and Jo. Shadwell, gent., and others in Methwold. The father of the future dramatist was more loyal than his celebrated son, and as a reward for his integrity he was heavily mulcted by the Parliament,[6] a portion of his estates being sequestrated. It was probably during his boyhood at Santon House or Broomhill Hall that young Tom met the old Cavalier Officers, " somewhat rough in Speech, but very brave and honest," who for their fidelity had been decimated by

[1] Before 1638.

[2] Ed. C. Honwood, II, p. 880.

[3] Mr. Rye well suggests that this is a transcriber's error for Linedon.

[4] His decease may probably be assigned to the early months of 1639. Another Thomas Shadwell, of the Inner Temple, a son of Edward Shadwell of Lyndon, in 1659 gave a clock to Enville of Stourbridge. There was yet another Thomas Shadwell, who, Mr. Rye notes, " in 1655 brought an action in the Exchequer against Thomas Toll and Doughty Wormall as to the execution of the office of Comptroller of the Customs at Lynn, Norfolk."

[5] *Collections for a History of Staffordshire*, 1886, &c., VII, ii, 110. It must be remembered that the Shadwell family were originally of Staffordshire.

[6] There was a John Shadwell, a Roundhead, for in 1656, John Shadwell, the well-known Tobias Frere, and other prominent Parliamentarians, were employed as Collectors of the Monthly Assessments in Norfolk. (Mason, p. 327.)

the rebels in power, and whose long-remembered conversation and figures, whose talk of Edgehill and Naseby Field, whose simple fruitless plotting, he was so vivaciously to reproduce well-nigh half-a-century after in his last comedy *The Volunteers*.

In addition to being spoiled and plundered by Parliament, John Shadwell had a long family of eleven children to educate and maintain. With great self-sacrifice, so affectionate a father was he, he determined that every one should be as well equipped as possible for the battle with the world, and accordingly he was compelled to dispose of much of his land, in those troublous times, at a great disadvantage. We are not surprised to find that Shadwell speaks with very sensible gratitude and sincerest affection of the efforts his father made on behalf of his family, and of the excellent education, with which, cost what it might, he ungrudgingly furnished them. Shortly after the Restoration John Shadwell and his family passed over to Ireland, a fact which gave Dryden the opportunity for a stinging couplet in *Mac Flecknoe* :

> In thy fellonious heart though Venom lies,
> It does but touch thy *Irish* pen, and dyes.

This, it may be remembered, called forth a loud protest from the victim.[1] In 1665 John Shadwell was elected Recorder by the Corporation of Galway, and he was also Receiver to the Duke of York, afterwards King James II.

We find an Order from King Charles, dated from Whitehall 21 September, 1671, to the Lord Lieutenant " Directing that when the Charter of the Corporation of Galway is renewed, John Shadwell, the Attorney-General of Connaught, who was elected Recorder by the said Corporation in 1665, be named Recorder at a reasonable salary." [2] The Duke of Ormonde, indeed, held John Shadwell in very high esteem, and afforded him no few marks of his patronage and goodwill. Dr. John Howley, the Librarian of University College, Galway, informs me that John Shadwell's appears in the lists of the old Corporation Books of Galway for 1666, 1668, and 1669, but the records for that period are very scanty. He succeeded Henry Whaling, and apparently in 1670 was succeeded by William Sprigge. Hence it would seem that Shadwell appealed to the King for reinstatement in this post whence Sprigge had dispossessed him, and the order of 21 September, 1671, allows his petition.

Early in 1675 [3] John Shadwell was recommended for promotion, and

---

[1] Dedication to *The Tenth Satyr of Juvenal*, 4to, 1687. Shadwell says that Dryden had no reason " for giving me the *Irish* name of *Mack*, when he knows I never saw *Ireland* till I was three and twenty years old, and was there but four months."

[2] *Calendar State Papers, Domestic*, 1671, *sub die*, p. 498.

[3] A Mrs. Elizabeth Shadwell who was buried 3 November, 1675, at S. Simon and S. Jude, Norwich, may have been some relative of John Shadwell.

shortly he was appointed to the important position of Attorney-General at Tangier. Owing to an illness, however, his departure was considerably delayed, and in a letter, 21 August, 1675, to the influential Sir Joseph Williamson, Secretary of State,[1] he formally presents his just apology. He writes: " In excuse of my tardy going to Tangier I beg leave to tell you that my first promise was not broken but prevented by a distemper which fell on me, and disabled me for travel, and I cannot but say the Yarmouth, which your courtesy designed for me on her second coming about to Portsmouth, did not play me fair, which will cost me about 50l. I am now at Deal and my family are in the Guinea Frigate, now a merchant, which conveys me to Cadiz. We wait the first fair wind, and it will be a favour if you will order Capt. Harman to call for me there and carry me to Tangier. I ask this with the more confidence on the relation and known kindness you have for Thetford, which gave me my first being." It will be readily remembered that Sir Joseph Williamson, in several Parliaments, represented Thetford and Rochester, both of which places benefited much by his excellent bounties, for he was a man of great wealth. Captain Harman, afterwards Admiral, and Sir John Harman,[2] had served with great reputation in several naval battles, and particularly distinguished himself against the Dutch. The "Yarmouth" in a list, of ships, 19 June, 1660, is catalogued as a man-of-war with 160 men and 44 guns.[3]

Early on the following morning, 22 August, 1675, John Shadwell went on board the "Guinea," and immediately from "The 'Guinea' in the Downs" he addressed a second letter to Sir Joseph Williamson: "Your kindness is the author of my boldness in begging your remembrance of me in the Irish establishment, whereof my Lord of Ormonde promised me to remind you, and I am sure the Duke, my Royal master, will own me so far as to take it kindly from you. After the slip the 'Yarmouth' gave me I have plied the first opportunity, and I hope it will not be many hours ere we sail. It would quicken my arrival at Tangier if Capt. Harman might have orders to take me in at Cadiz, which was my request to you in mine yesterday."

The Governor of Tangier, that most difficult and disturbed possession of the English Crown, at this time was William O'Brien, second Earl of Inchiquin. Born about 1638, he was the son of Murough O'Brien, sixth Baron and first Earl of Inchiquin. Most of his early life, during the Com-

---

[1] Sir Joseph Williamson, P.R.S., became eminent for his ability and services in the House of Commons. A considerable part of his fortune was devoted to charities or the promotion of learning. At his death he left £6,000 to Queen's College, Oxford, where he was educated, and at Rochester he founded a mathematical school. A whole-length portrait of Williamson still hangs in the Town Hall at this latter city.

[2] He is frequently referred to by Pepys, e.g., 16 June, 1665; 5 August, 1667; 9 September, 1667; 4 October, 1667; etc. His portrait was painted by Lely.

[3] See Pepys, 17 April, 1665.

monwealth, he had spent on foreign service, particularly in France and Spain. In the first month of 1674 he was created Captain-General of the English forces in Africa, Governor and Vice-Admiral at Tangier, which offices he held for six years; Colonel of the Tangier regiment, the Queen's Own; and on 5th March he was sworn of the Privy Council. He succeeded to his title as Earl of Inchiquin, 9 September, 1674. In spite of the honours which had been heaped upon him he proved a traitor, since in 1688 he welcomed the Prince of Orange to England. In the following year he was attainted by the King. However, in 1689–90 William appointed him Governor of Jamaica,[1] and here he died in January, 1691–2, only sixteen months after his arrival in the island, having proved himself utterly incapable of handling the reins. He was buried in the parish church there at San Jago de la Vega.

Tangier, which had been brought to us as part of the dowry of Queen Katharine of Braganza, was a colony the administration of which literally teemed with perplexities and entanglements of every kind; the smallest slip might lead to hostilities, which, breaking out in hazardous guerilla warfare, would presently become a prolonged and desperate struggle with the natives. It was the business of the Governor to avoid such conflicts at any cost, and with the Earl of Inchiquin at the helm the civil magistrates and syndics had their work cut out to prevent a disastrous shipwreck upon the pointed rocks. Utterly lacking in tact and diplomacy, almost daily the Earl of Inchiquin meddlesomely provoked the Moors and alarmed the English colony, treating, meanwhile, the tempered advice of the civil authorities, who had experience of local conditions, with a contempt he did not care to conceal, riding rough shod over their remonstrances. Disagreements broke out into open quarrels, the noise of which reached England, and the situation became intolerable. So dangerous a dictator did he seem that early in 1677 John Shadwell and other of the chief residents sailed for home to refer the whole matter to the King. The Earl of Inchiquin was not long before he busily followed them, and once in London both parties laid important information against each other. During the summer things came to a head, and on 6 August, 1677, Secretary Coventry wrote to Sir William Jones, the Attorney-General: "The Earl of Inchiquin having desired that you may be of counsel to him in the complaints brought against him by Mr. Shadwell and others of Tangier, His Majesty consents thereto." On the same date Coventry addressed a letter to Mr. John Creed, the secretary to the Tangier Commissioners,[2] as follows: "Whereas several complaints have

---

[1] Christopher Monck, second Duke of Albemarle, had been appointed Governor-General of Jamaica, 26 November, 1687. He died there early in the following autumn. Mrs. Behn celebrated his voyage to the West Indies with a Pindaric.

[2] There are constant references to Creed in the pages of Pepys.

been presented to His Majesty from the Earl of Inchiquin, Governor of Tangier, against Mr. Shadwell and other magistrates of the said city, and likewise from Mr. Shadwell and other the magistrates against the said Earl, and both the said Earl and Mr. Shadwell and those concerned with him are according to His Majesty's order now come to town, you are to give timely and official notice to both parties to appear before him in the Robes Chamber the first Monday after his return with their witnesses and evidences to justify the complaints on either side and to defend themselves against the informations mutually brought against each other." [1] The outcome was that John Shadwell did not return to Tangier, but less than three years afterwards the Earl of Inchiquin retired from the important post of Governor, for which he had given such ample evidence of being eminently ill-suited.

John Shadwell, weary by this continual bickering and legislation, now withdrew from public life, and took up his residence on his country estates. He died at his house in the parish of Oxborough,[2] Norfolk, and was buried there 2 March, 1684.[3]

Thomas Shadwell was "Born at Stanton Hall in Norfolk, 1640, his Father had 11 children. bred up at Bury School and Caius Coll in Cambridge. At the age of 23 years went over to Ireland at 4 months and return'd His Father bestowed the Learning and Address of a Gent. upon him as Musick &c wch himself tells us in his Dedication of his Translation of the Tenth Satyr of Juvenal. 4°. 1687 to Sr. Chr. Sidley. His Father was bred to the Law and had a Place of Profit & Distinction in his Profession in Ireland & wn Tom returned from Ireland he had Chambers in the Middle Temple." These are the MS. notes made by William Oldys in his copy of Langbaine,[4] and it will be noticed that he gives Santon Hall as the poet's birth place. The parish of Santon, Norfolk[5] is named in the Tithe Award " The Parish of Santon House," and the site is marked on the map about 100 yards west of the church. There was probably a house here from very early times, but at present no building is visible, and there can only be distinguished a grass-covered mound surrounded by a moat ; now dry, or partly so. No record of the year when Santon House was

[1] *Calendar State Papers, Domestic*, 6 August, 1677 (p. 295).

[2] John Brampton, of Oxnead, married Mary Bullen, the sister of Amy (or Anne) Boleyn, whose second husband was Nicholas Shadwell, of Broomhill. See Genealogical Table, *post*.

[3] The Rev. Walter Coombe, Rector of Oxborough, kindly furnished me with an official burial certificate. The age of the deceased is not stated, nor is it said by whom the ceremony was performed. The sepulture is unnumbered.

[4] *An Account of the English Dramatick Poets. . . .* By Gerard Langbaine. *Oxford, . . . An. Dom.*, 1691. British Museum, c. 28, g. 1.

[5] I have to thank the Rev. H. Tyrrell Green, Rector of Santon, for most courteously answering at length my ample inquiries, and for his kindness in furnishing me with these details concerning Santon House.

demolished is preserved, but the farm-house to the south-east of the church probably dates from the early part of the eighteenth century, and this took the place of the Santon House of Shadwell's days. Unfortunately the extant Registers of Santon commence as late as 1770, and Thomas Shadwell is not recorded as having been baptized at Weeting.[1]

There seems no doubt that this was actually the place of Thomas Shadwell's birth, and the statement that he was born at Broomhill Hall arose from a misreading, or rather from too precise an interpretation of the " Liber Matriculationis " as given in *Admissions to Gonville and Caius College* which records : " Shadwell, Thomas ; (eldest) son of John Shadwell, of Broomhill, near Brandon, Norfolk. Born there." It will be seen that this does not imply that Thomas Shadwell was born at Broomhill Hall, but merely in the district. Santon House, within a few miles of Broomhill Hall, was certainly the actual spot.[2] It is mentioned in the Lay Subsidy Rolls for the year 1673, its value being assessed at £100. The parish registers have no reference to Shadwell, but they tell us that in 1686 it was occupied by James Sargent and his wife, to whom no doubt the family had sold it after the death of John Shadwell two years before.

Thomas Shadwell died 20 November, 1692, and the monument which was erected by his son Sir John Shadwell in Westminster Abbey has *Ob. Nov. 20, 1692.*[3] *Ætat. Suæ* 52. With regard to the contemporary entry of Shadwell's admission to Gonville and Caius, the Bursar, Mr. J. F. Cameron, who at my request most courteously examined the original, writes to me as follows " The entry occurs in the half year ' a Computo Annunciationis 1656 '; the next half year being ' a Computo Michælis 1656.' The reference to age in the entry is . . . annos natus 14 admittitur in commeatum Baccalaureorum Decemb. decimo septimo . . . it would seem however that in the entry as first made a space was left for the date, for the words ' decimo septimo ' are crowded, and the whole date " Decemb. decimo septimo, though in the same hand writing as the rest of the entry seems to be in rather different ink. Also 17 December does not fall in the half year in question. The two preceeding entries are dated 12 April, 1656. I cannot explain these facts, but it seems to me that the date is more probably 17 December, 1655, than 17 December,

---

[1] Mr. Rye tells us that " The farm at Weeting, which belonged to the Priory of Broomhill was granted to Christ Church, Cambridge, and was afterwards held by the Pecks, Shadwells, Tooks."

[2] In *The Lives of the Most Eminent Literary and Scientific Men of Great Britain*, 1838, Vol. III, p. 155, Santon Hall (misprinted Lanton Hall) is given as Shadwell's birth-place. Austen and Ralph, *The Lives of the Poets-Laureate*, 1853, p. 183, say Santon Hall. As evidential these statements are, of course, of no importance, but they are valuable as maintaining and showing the continuity of the correct tradition.

[3] In *The Works of Thomas Shadwell, Esq.*, Vol. I, the transcription from the Monument gives *Ob. Nov. 19*. Under the portrait (*Saml. Gribelin Junr. Scul.*) we have *Ætat. 55*.

1656. If so he would be born in 1641. If ' æt. suæ 52 ' could mean in his 52nd year that would be right for the date of his death in November, 1692.'' This, I think, solves the difficulty, and after these researches we arrive at the conclusion that Thomas Shadwell was born at Santon House, Norfolk, in 1641.

In his earlier years his education was commenced at home, and for a space of five years his tutor was a Mr. Roberts. He then passed to Bury S. Edmund's School in 1654, where he remained for one year under Mr. Thomas Stephens, who was Head-Master from 1638 to 1645, and again from 1647 to 1663.[1] In the printed list of Grammar School pupils 1550–1900 reference is made to an undated school list which contains the following entry : " Johannes Shadwell filius Johannis Shadwell de Bromhill in Com. Norf. armigeri." It is, of course, just possible that this may be Thomas Shadwell, John having been written in error for Thomas, but, on the other hand, it is almost certainly John Shadwell, a brother of the dramatist.[2] It is, perhaps, not impertinent to remark that both Mr. Roberts and Mr. Stephens must have been classical scholars of no small attainments, for Shadwell, who passed through their hands shows every evidence of wide reading and a lively appreciation of Greek and Latin literature. That he should have stumbled, as was not infrequently the case, when he delved into his authorities for *The Lancashire Witches* is not surprising, and is no reflection at all upon his high standard of general culture, since the writings of the Fathers and Demonologists are technical in the highest degree and require an intimate knowledge of later Latin, which differs widely from Cicero or Horace; indeed, one might almost say without exaggeration, that to read these difficult and occult libraries with any facility demands a special and intensive training.

As we have already seen, Thomas Shadwell was admitted to Gonville and Caius College, Cambridge, 17 December, 1655, and was entered as a pensioner to the Bachelors' Table, his surety being Mr. William Naylore. With regard to his residence at Cambridge even tradition has nothing to tell us, and we only know that he enjoyed the name of being an excellent scholar, for in the Dedication, addressed to Sir Charles Sedley, which is prefixed to his translation of *The Tenth Satyr of Juvenal*, 1687, when explaining why he undertook a piece of work which was distasteful to him, namely, a translation, he says : " I was provoked to this first by the

---

[1] No doubt the unsettled events of the day account for this exceptional break.

[2] The editor of this printed list remarks : " As Thomas Shadwell did not go to Caius Coll. till Dec. 1655, he might be in this list ; and I expect that this is he, John being written instead of Thomas." This is improbable, but the editor would assuredly not claim to have made any particular inquiries with reference to this point. Mr. J. M. Wadmore, the present Head-Master of Bury School, after research in the original lists, informs me that in his opinion the entry is undoubtedly that of John Shadwell, brother of the dramatist.

supposed *Author* of *Mack-Fleckno*, who saies in another Pamphlet ; that to his knowledge, I understand neither Greek nor Latin, though in *Bury* School in *Suffolk*, and *Caius* Colledge in *Cambridge*, the places of my Youthful Education, I had not that reputation, and let me tell him he knows the contrary." The reason why Shadwell did not pursue a University career probably lay in the consideration that the times were so difficult and disturbed that the safest position open to any young man lay in the direction of the law, since here his father had influence, and his father moreover, owing to the losses he had suffered at the hands of the rebels, could not have held out much prospect of independent support for the sons of his family. Thomas Shadwell, then, left Cambridge without taking any degree, and entered the Middle Temple on 7 July, 1658. He seems to have applied himself diligently to his studies, and apparently as yet the thoughts of literature had hardly entered his head. He is said to have travelled abroad, which is exceedingly likely, although there is no indication that he journeyed far or for long. In any case we may be sure that he came back more of an Englishman than ever, for Shadwell was one of those hearty obtuse fellows, narrow and not to be converted, who have no tongue for any language save their own, and who find their paradise in the beef and beer and plum puddings of Britain. To them English discomfort is far more genial than foreign luxury or ease. We are informed that during 1664 he spent some four months in Ireland. In his reply to Dryden's satires, when he complains of being called the dullest of writers, he remarks that his opponent " has no more reason for that, than for giving me the *Irish* name of *Mack*, when he knows I never saw *Ireland* till I was three and twenty years old, and was there but four Months." Possibly his visit was connected with his father's appointment to various official positions under the Duke of Ormonde. We know that in 1665 John Shadwell succeeded Henry Whaling as Recorder of Galway, and probably the whole family had been resident in Ireland for at least two or three years previous to that date. According to Oldys, upon his return to England Shadwell had chambers in the Middle Temple.

Now that the dour domination of the Commonwealth was over, and the King had come back to his own again, London was once more alive with life and gaiety, a joy which, however severely dashed by the two appalling catastrophes of the Plague and the Fire, had within itself such powers of rejuvenation as almost immediately to recover, resolved not to let a moment of pleasure speed by untasted and unfulfilled. The town teemed with young men who were eager to make their mark in literature, to win their way into the society of the great. Among these there were few who so quickly gained a place and a position such as were achieved by Thomas Shadwell. He had neither rank nor money, and when it is remembered that he was known as a remarkable figure long before the production of his first comedy in the spring of 1668, it is interesting to inquire in what quality actually consisted the attraction which for his contemporaries his society undoubtedly had, and among his friends we number such brilliant names as Buckingham, Rochester, Buckhurst, Sedley, and Etherege. All accounts agree that he was a most gifted and brilliant conversationalist. It may seem strange to us that this should be the key to the highest and most intellectual circles of the land. The art of conversation, that is to say of being able to listen as well as able to talk, is long since dead. I suppose it survived its last in our two ancient Universities, where until fairly recent times a man who could enthral and entertain his auditors was always in great request. The lost art of conversation is extremely complex and subtle. It presupposes many gifts ; fluent and correct expression ; an elegant pronunciation ; the power of awakening and sustaining interest ; and, what underlies all these, the scholarship, unobtrusive but essential, which can cover wide fields of thought in the choice of subject. The great and grave Cicero has immortalized Volumnius for the felicity of his conversational powers, and in that agreeable satire *The Devil upon Two Sticks* Le Sage has drawn a picture not altogether exaggerated of the Graduate Donoso, who was " courted by all the nobility and city that make entertainments. Everyone strives who shall have him : he has a particular knack of making the guests merry, and is the very soul and light of entertainment ; so that he every day dines at some considerable man's table, and never returns till two in the morning. . . . About noon to-day there were five or six coaches at the graduate's door from different noblemen that all sent for him." Madelon called chairs " les commodités de la conversation " ;[1] and the novels of Mademoiselle de Scudéry abound in protracted conversations. Indeed this talented lady published books entirely made up of " conversations," which discuss at length such topics as pleasure, the passions, our knowledge of others, if we can know ourselves, and a thousand such niceties. These works were received with the greatest applause and read on every side. Madame de Sévigné highly praises them, and they were generously translated as : *Conversations upon several subjects* . . . " done into *English* by *Ferrand Spence*," 1683.[2] Nor must it be forgotten that the Duchess of Newcastle and her admirers spent many literary hours in these ingeniously embroidered conversations, some of which no doubt are reproduced for us in her folios, books now generally forgotten, but which yet for those who will search among them are not without a delicate, if somewhat faded fascination, long laid up in orris-root and lavender. It is not for a moment to be suggested that the " genial Nights " of the " taring Blades " with whom Shadwell mixed so freely were in any sense like the somewhat

[1] *Les Précieuses Ridicules*, Scene x.
[2] 2 vols., 12mo, London.

(xxvii)

solemn assemblies of the Duchess and her Lord. The libertines, no doubt, talked " beastly, downright bawdy, but with an infinite deal of wit." The laurelled optimates debated with " eloquent pleadings " and " romancicall " tales the lauds of virtue, " the muses leading her and the graces attending her," albeit her dress is spangled, her hair fruzzed, her cheeks bepatched and not wholly innocent of Spanish rouge.

The date of Shadwell's marriage unfortunately cannot be determined, but in his will he mentions " my beloved wife Ann ye daughter of Thomas Gibbs late of Norwich deceased, proctor and publick Notary." This lady was almost certainly the same person who married Thomas Gawdy, of Claxton, Norfolk, at S. Clement Danes, 12 July, 1662.[1] Anne Gibbs [2] was one of Davenant's earliest actresses, and we find that as Mrs. Gibbs she played Olivia and Julia in revivals of *Twelfth Night* and *The Dutchesse of Malfy* [3]; Mrs. Lucia in Cowley's amusing *Cutter of Coleman Street*, produced at Lincoln's Inn Fields, December, 1661; and in Sir Robert Stapylton's baroque *The Slighted Maid*, seen by Pepys at the same theatre on Monday, 1 February, 1662–3, Decio, " *The Slighted Maid;* Ericina, who (*to revenge her refusal by* Iberio) *assumes the person of her dead brother,* Decio." The name of Mrs. Gawdy does not appear in any printed list of casts, so far as I am aware, but in the quarto 1668 of Davenant's *The Rivals*, Licensed (for printing) 19 September, 1668, the name Mrs. Shadwell stands to the Princess Heraclia. *The Rivals*, however, was actually produced several years before that date; Pepys saw it on Saturday, 10 September, 1664, and although he makes no definite comment it is practically certain that not even this was the first performance. The cast of *The Rivals* was, for one reason or another, continually being changed,[4]

---

[1] *Marriage Allegations in Registry of Vicar-General of Archbishop of Canterbury, 1660 to 1679*; Harleian Society, XXIII, 23. Evelyn, 7 September, 1677, mentions a Sir John Gaudy whom he met at Euston, Lord Arlington's house.

[2] There was another Anne Gibbs the youngest daughter of Captain John Gibbs, 1645–1695, and his wife Elizabeth, *née* Pride, whose father was the famous Captain Thomas Pride of " Pride's Purge."

[3] Downes, *Roscius Anglicanus.*

[4] On Saturday, 10 September, 1664, Pepys writes : " to the Duke's House, and there saw ' The Rivalls,' which is no excellent play, but good acting in it ; especially Gosnell, comes and sings and dances finely, but, for all that, fell out of the key, so that the musique could not play to her afterwards, and so did Harris also go out of the tune to agree with her." On Friday, 2 December, 1664, he has : " After dinner with my wife and Mercer to the Duke's House, and there saw ' The Rivalls,' which I had seen before ; but the play not good, nor anything but the good actings of Betterton and his wife and Harris." In the quarto 1668, neither Mrs. Betterton nor Mrs. Gosnell appears in the printed cast. The three actresses are Mrs. Shadwell as Heraclia; Mrs. Davis as Celania; and Mrs. Long as Leucippe. From this it seems evident that Mrs. Shadwell in the revival of 1667 succeeded Mrs. Betterton; and that Mrs. Davis succeeded Mrs. Gosnell. Downes records : " All the Women's Parts admirably acted ; chiefly *Celia*, a Shepherdess, being mad for Love ; especially in singing several wild and mad songs;

and we can only say that Mrs. Shadwell was acting in this drama as Mrs. Shadwell in a revival of 1667.

We can narrow down the marriage of Shadwell to within some three years, 1663–1666, but owing to the lack of exact data it would be hazardous, at least, to venture more. It is very curious to note that Shadwell was once reported to have been married by a Catholic priest,[1] and as the poet did not promptly deny this, which there can be no doubt he would most emphatically have done had the statement been altogether without foundation, suggestions petrified into assurance, and it was definitely asserted that "our Poet hath owned himself . . . married by a Popish priest." [2]

On Thursday, 6 February, 1667–8, Mrs. Shadwell played Lady Cockwood in Etherege's *She wou'd if she cou'd*, that brilliant comedy which on its first production fared so ill owing to the fact that the actors were "extreamly imperfect in the action of it," and it may be noted that Mrs. Shadwell's rôle is the most important in the play. At the same theatre on Saturday, 2 May, 1668, she appeared as Emilia in her husband's *The Sullen Lovers; or, The Impertinents*.

Amongst other of Mrs. Shadwell's parts were Clarina in The Hon. Edward Howard's tragi-comedy *The Women's Conquest*, produced at Lincoln's Inn Fields in the winter of 1670; Joanna, maid of honour to the Princess of Muscovy in Crowne's *Juliana, or, the Princess of Poland*, produced at Lincoln's Inn Fields about June–July, 1671 [3]; Irene, friend and confidante to Cornelia, the widowed Queen of Cyprus, in the same author's heroic drama *The History of Charles the Eighth of France*, which was produced at Dorset Garden in November, 1671, being "the first new Play acted" at that theatre; "it was all new cloath'd, yet lasted but 6 days together, but 'twas acted now and then afterwards;" [4] Cælia in *The Fatal Jealousie*, a powerful tragedy by Henry Nevil (*alias* Paine), produced at

---

My Lodging it is on the Cold Ground, &c. She performed that so charmingly, that not long after, it rais'd her from her bed on the cold ground, to a Bed Royal." On 11 January, 1668, Mrs. Knepp gossiping with Pepys, told him how Moll Davis "is for certain going away from the Duke's house, the King being in love with her; and a house is taken for her and furnishing; and she hath a ring given her already worth £600." As Mrs. Davis originally attracted the King's attention by her acting in Celania; it is highly probable that she first filled this rôle in 1667.

[1] *Loyal Protestant*, 12 January, 1681. One may remember that in *Bury-Fair* the pseudo-Count suggests to Mrs. Fantast that they shall be married by a Catholic priest who will not heed Canonical hours. Olivia acknowledged to her father that the ceremony of her marriage with Squire Thornhill "was privately performed by a Popish priest." "What!" cried Dr. Primrose, "and were you indeed married by a priest in orders?" "Indeed, Sir, we were," replied she, "though we were both sworn to conceal his name."

[2] *Loyal Protestant*, 9 February, 1681.

[3] Licensed (for printing) 8 September, 1671.

[4] Downes, *Roscius Anglicanus*.

Dorset Garden early in August, 1672; Rose in the same author's *The Morning Ramble, or the Town-Humours*, performed in November, 1672, a somewhat sketchy comedy of considerable merit, which, we are told was "very well acted"; Lucinda, the daughter of old Paulo in *The Loving Enemies*, a play of complicated plot written by Lawrence Maidwell a schoolmaster, who was a personal friend of Shadwell himself [1]; the Queen in a revival of *Hamlet* [2]; and Goneril in Tate's *The History of King Lear*, which was originally produced at Dorset Garden in the early spring of 1681. About 1685 Mrs. Shadwell appears to have retired from the stage; and in 1693 with pathetic eloquence she dedicated her husband's posthumous play *The Volunteers; or, The Stock Jobbers*, to Queen Mary II. We know that she was living in 1709, for her husband had in his will left her "The Rent I purchased of ye Lady Davenant and Mr. Cave Underhill issuing out of ye Dayly proffitts of the sayd Theatre" (Dorset Garden), and in this year she and some twenty other persons complained that, after making heavy additional investments, they had drawn a total of £1000 a year from 1682 to 1695, since which time they "became yearly considerable losers." Eventually Mrs. Shadwell's share and others were absorbed by Christopher Rich owing to his shrewd sharp practice. She was her husband's sole executrix, and in his will he speaks of her in terms of the truest affection as "a diligent carefull and provident Woman and very indulgent to her children as ever I knew." In *A Satyr upon the Players*, [3] (1683), Mrs. Shadwell is very ungallantly derided:

> But antiquated *Shadwel* swears in Rage
> She knows not what's ye Lewdness of ye Stage,
> And I believe her, now her days are past
> Who'd tempt a Wretch that on meer force is Chast?
> Yet in her Youth, none was a greater Whore,
> Her Lumpish Husband, *Og*, can tell you more.

In D'Urfey's political comedy *Sir Barnaby Whigg*, 4to, 1681, which was produced at Drury Lane probably in August-September of that year, [4] there can be no doubt that the title-rôle is intended for Shadwell, and incidentally there are references to his wife's reputation, which seems to have been considerably blown upon during her career. *A Tryal of the*

---

[1] Lawrence Maidwell wrote a Latin poem of compliment to Pietro Reggio, the composer, which is published in the volume of Reggio's *Songs*, folio, 1680.

[2] Downes gives Mrs. Davenport as the actress who played the Queen in the first revival of *Hamlet* after the Restoration.

[3] MS. not printed.

[4] *Sir Barnaby Whigg; or, No Wit like a Womans. Term Catalogues*, Michaelmas (November), 1681.

Poets for the Bays,[1] thus coarsely introducing Shadwell, also alludes to the scandal :

> Next into the Crowd, *Tom Shadwell* does wallow,
> And swears by his Guts, his Paunch, and his Tallow,
> That 'tis he alone best pleases the Age,
> Himself and his Wife, have supported the Stage.

Between the years 1670 and 1680 there occurs in not a few casts the name of a Mrs. Gibbs, who was, we may fairly confidently suppose, a sister of Mrs. Shadwell. Unfortunately nothing definite is known of her, but on 2 December, 1672, she appeared as Lucia in *Epsom-Wells*. This if not actually her first effort must have been one of her earliest appearances, and it is perhaps not too speculative to suggest that this excellent part was entrusted to her owing to the influence of her brother-in-law, the author of the play. In June, 1676, she was Henrietta in Otway's *Don Carlos*, a small but effective rôle, and in the autumn of 1676 Beatrix in Ravenscroft's *The Wrangling Lovers*, a comedy founded upon the same romance whence Thomas Corneille has taken his entertaining *Les Engagemens du Hazard*. In the early autumn of the same year Mrs. Gibbs acted Mrs. Essence in *Tom Essence ; or, The Modish Wife*, a vacation play, which is ascribed by Langbaine to Rawlins, and which is in effect a wholesale plagiary from Molière and Thomas Corneille's *Dom Cesar d'Avalos*. A few weeks later Mrs. Gibbs was Arbella in D'Urfey's *Madame Fickle ; or, The Witty False One ;* early in 1677 Iras in Sedley's arid *Antony and Cleopatra*, and Clara in Otway's amusing farce *The Cheats of Scapin ;* in the summer of the same year Clarina in a vacation comedy *The Counterfeit Bridegroom ; or, The Defeated Widow*, which is, Langbaine truly says, " only an Old Play of Middleton's call'd *No Wit like a Woman's*, printed octavo," by some ascribed to Betterton, but far more likely to be a hurried alteration from the pen of Mrs. Behn ; in January, 1678, she played Maundy, Lady Fancy's pert woman in that capital comedy by Mrs. Behn, *Sir Patient Fancy ;* in the same month yet another Abigail, Chloe in *Timon of Athens ;* in April Victoria in Otway's mordant comedy *Friendship in Fashion ;* and during the following May Flora in John Leanard's *The Counterfeits*, of which Langbaine tersely says, " I believe it too good to be his Writing," and which was very largely borrowed by Colley Cibber in his *She wou'd and She wou'd Not ; or, The Kind Imposter*, produced at Drury Lane in November, 1702, a piece which kept the stage until well within the nineteenth century.[2]

His keen observation of human nature and his witty comments upon the panorama of life all about him must have made it obvious to his

[1] Printed as " By the Duke of Buckingham " in Buckingham's Miscellaneous Works, 1704, II, p. 41.
[2] Ada Rehan, the famous American actress, played Hypolita, a rôle which was originally created by Mrs. Mountford.

friends who had any discernment in such matters that Shadwell was exceptionally qualified for a dramatist. Such a man would be invaluable to the noble or wealthy amateurs of the day, and among these there was no more remarkable figure than William Cavendish, the Duke of New-castle. This great gentleman, who had extremely distinguished himself both by his literary talents and his heroic loyalty to his King, having been rewarded in part with well-deserved honours at the Restoration, with-drew from public life to the happy retreat of Wellbeck, " where he spent the evening of his days in calm repose, and in the indulgence of those studies, with which he was the most affected." His lady, " the Thrice Noble, Illustrious, and Excellent Princess," Margaret Cavendish, née Lucas, was " a most Virtuous and a loving and careful wife and was with her Lord all the time of his banishment and miseries : and when he came home never parted from him in his solitary retirement." In fact as a devotee of literature her conceptions and fancies were far more profuse than the authorship of her husband. She has, indeed, an extremely elegant address to her readers wherein with unusual self-depreciation she pro-claims herself but the silver moon reflecting all her life from the golden glories of the sun.

> A Poet I am neither born nor bred,
> But to a witty poet married
> Whose brain is fresh and pleasant as the Spring,
> Where Fancies grow and where the Muses sing
> There oft I lean my head, and listening, hark,
> To catch his words and all his fancies mark
> And from that garden show of beauties take
> Where of a posy I in verse may make,
> Thus I, that have no gardens of my own,
> There gather flowers that are newly blown.

It is not true positively that she had no gardens of her own ; they are vast in extent, they are full of bewildering beauties, and full of the most dis-concerting sterilities and ugly corrugations. We are now walking in some old English pleasaunce where the borders are bright with native flowers, the lawns are green as smoothest velvet, and the air is perfumed with damask roses ; the place is a little unkempt may be, but it is wanton Nature's own homely irregularities, which are fairer far than the refine-ments of art : we turn into another walk and we find ourselves in the square symmetry of a formal Dutch garth, the clipped trees are set in rigid ranks, the hedges of box or yew are tidy as a good housewife, broom and duster in hand, would have left them, there is a glow of myriad tulips, somewhat punctilious in their pageantry, of a gorgeous grace, but not without their own splendid loveliness ; another turn, and we find ourselves in the most neglected and decaying parterres, the flowers are dead and festering, the walks are tangled with nettles and dock, with thorns and brambles, through which it is difficult to push a way the old walls are crumbling, the cracked fountains covered with lichen and moss have forgot to play, all is desolate, disparting, and untrod. Such are the royaumes of the Duchess, and we may turn from one to another, from sunshine into shadow, from dark to light, with an abruptness that leaves us uncertain and perplexed. There are, I think, very few readers who to-day turn the vast folios she has left behind her, and yet for all her possessing faults of stiffness, of quaintness, of obscurity and euphuism, for all her allegories and catachreses, her profusion and luxuriance amounting to disorder, she has her lovers still. Some courtly flatterer told her that she had " pluckt feathers from the Universities," and even as a child she wrote upon philosophical subjects. A Fellow at Cambridge boldly attempted to render her transcendental theorizing in Latin, but is said to have given up the task almost in despair. Her readers—yes, I wonder how many there are to-day ?—have learned to know these " philosophical " dissertations, which she is prone to insert at random throughout her pages, and they have learned to pass them by without over close inquiry into their meaning.

Assuredly the Duchess was no dramatist ; in fact not only had she none of those faculties of concentration, observation, elimination, which are essential to the playwright, but she possessed every quality which would most unfit her for that particular field. In the two folio volumes of plays which she published, the first in 1662, the second in 1668, there is hardly one piece, which save by the most elastic stretch of the term can be called a play at all. They are allegories in dialogue, sometimes one might almost say in endless logomachy ; and an allegory is apt to be the most discomforting form of literature. The very names of the speakers—one cannot in truth call them the characters—at once give the key to the whole. Thus in *The Publique Wooing* we have Sir Thomas Letgo ; Sir William Holdfast ; The Lady Jealousie ; The Lady Parrot ; The Lady Gravity ; Mistress Parle ; Mistress Trifle ; Mistress Vanity ; Mistress Fondly. In *The Matrimonial Trouble*, which is in two parts, we have Sir Henry Sage and the Lady Chastity his wife ; Sir Thomas Cuckold and the Lady Wanton, his wife ; Sir Timothy Spendall and the Lady Poverty, his wife. *Nature's Three Daughters, Beauty, Love, and Wit*, which is also in two parts, shows us Monsieur Nobilissimo ; Monsieur Esperance ; Monsieur Phantasie ; Mademoiselle Amour ; Mademoiselle Grand Esprit ; Mademoiselle Bon ; Mademoiselle Tell-Truth ; Mademoiselle Spightfull ; Mademoiselle Detraction ; Mademoiselle Malicious ; and in *The Religious* we find Lord Melancholy and Sir Thomas Gravity ; Lady Perfection and Mistress Odd Humour. It will be seen at a glance that these names are mere labels, as numerical and as docketing as anything in a mediæval morality.

The Duke, at any rate, had a sense of the theatre, and his plays were acted upon the stage, meeting with a certain measure of success. They are only four in number, and of these two *The Country Captain* and *The Variety*, which had been produced at the Blackfriars before 1642, were published together at the Hague, 12mo, 1649, a little volume which has become excessively scarce. But the Duke sought professional assistance in his work, and he bestowed no inconsiderable fees upon those who helped him to polish and shape his comedies. Antony à Wood [1] says, when speaking of Shirley : " Our author *Shirley* did also much assist his generous Patrone *William*, Duke of *Newcastle*, in the composure of certain Plays which the Duke afterwards published," and there can be no doubt that much of these two plays must be attributed to the professional pen of the expert dramatist. It is remarkable that in 1833, A. H. Bullen, a scholar of acutest critical faculty, whom we may well call the last of the Elizabethans, since no man now has a tithe of his feeling for and knowledge of our great Elizabethan dramatists, when in 1883 in his second volume of *Old English Plays* (1st series), he printed from *Harleian MS.*, No. 7,650, a comedy which, following Halliwell, he dubbed *Captain Underwit*, he emphatically and confidently attributed this to Shirley, citing in proof of his ascription the many close parallels with Shirley's published work. He had indeed already spoken of its provenance as the discovery of " a lively comedy (quite unknown) by James Shirley." *Captain Underwit*, however, is none other than the Duke of Newcastle's *The Country Captain*. Although it is clear that Shirley had a very large hand in this piece we must not wholly deprive Newcastle of the credit of the sprightly scenes. *The Variety* also has distinct traces of Shirley's manner, and it seems pretty obvious that this play too had the benefit of his revision. It is equally certain that his patron very liberally rewarded the poet, who addressed him in an Ode which expresses something more than mere lip service or paid flattery. The last stanza is very agreeably turned :

> Great both in peace and war, thus fame
> Did honour *Sidney ;* on your name
>   Two laurels grow, and they
>   That speak them both, may say,
> Thus the fluent *Ovid* wrote,
> And thus, too, wise *Cæsar* fought ;
> For when your story shall be perfect, you
> May both deserve, and have their envies too. [2]

[1] Wood, 1691–1692, II, 262 ; cf. 1817, III, 739–740.
[2] Shirley's fine tragedy *The Traytor*, licensed 4 May, 1631 ; 4to, 1635 ; is dedicated in a most adulatory strain to the Duke (then Earl) of Newcastle by the author, " who

At the Restoration Shirley, who had then actually only attained the age of sixty-four, was a decrepit and prematurely broken man. "When the Rebellion broke out, and he (was) thereupon forced to leave *London*, and so consequently his Wife and Children (who afterwards were put to their shifts), he was invited by his most noble Patron, *William*, Earl (afterwards Marquess and Duke) of *Newcastle*, to take his fortune with him in the wars, for that Count had engaged him so much by his generous liberality toward him, that he thought he could not do a worthier act than to serve him, and so consequently his Prince. . . . After the King's cause declined he retired obscurely to *London*, where among other of his noted friends, he found *Tho. Stanley*, Esq., who exhibited to him for the present. Afterwards, following his old trade of teaching School, which was mostly in the *White Fryers*, he not only gained a comfortable subsistence (for the acting of plays was then silenced) but educated many ingenious youths, who afterwards proved most emminent in divers faculties." [1] It is to be doubted whether Shirley was in such easy circumstances as this roseate account would have us believe. A pensioner of Stanley, and a hard worked schoolmaster—for incidentally teaching boys is one of the most difficult and depressing of trades, and so in some measure it must have been even well-nigh three hundred years ago when boys were not nearly so stupid as they are to-day—Shirley was compelled to eke out his livelihood by the publication of his plays, which, at any rate, could be read even if they were not allowed to be acted. As an ardent Royalist, and as a once popular dramatist to boot, he was, moreover, an object of angry suspicion and continual annoyance. He truly passed through " various conditions." He lived in plenty and in poverty, in popularity and in forgetfulness, even in contempt.[2] "After his Majesties return to his Kingdoms, several of

confesseth his guilt of a long ambition, by some service to be known to you, and his boldness at last, by this rude attempt to kiss your Lordship's hands."

[1] Wood, 1691–1692, II, 261 ; cf. 1817, III, 737–738.

[2] Cf. Dryden's scornful allusion in *Mac Flecknoe* :

> From dusty Shops neglected Authors come,
> Martyrs of Pics and Reliques of the Bum.
> Much *Heywood, Shirley, Ogleby* there lay,
> But loads of *Sh[adwell]* almost choakt the way.

Oldham *A Satyr . . . Dissuading the Author from the Study of Poetry* has :

> And so may'st thou perchance pass up and down,
> And please a while th' admiring Court and Town,
> Who after shalt in *Duck-lane* Shops be thrown,
> To mould with *Silvester*, and *Shirley* there,
> And truck for pots of Ale next *Stour-bridg-Fair*.

Although this obloquy is, of course, some fifteen years after Shirley's death, already in his life-time he was neglected and outmoded.

his plays, which he before had made, were acted with good applause, but what office or employ he had confer'd upon him after all his sufferings I cannot now justly tell." [1] It would appear from Shirley's will [2] that he enjoyed a competency at least, to which it is reasonable to believe that his old patron the Duke of Newcastle contributed. The Duke who now devoted his whole time to literature had composed two or three comedies and a number of detached scenes and songs, which it was his intention to put into regular shape and then present in the public theatre. [3] As was his wont he looked around for somebody to lend him assistance in these labours, and his old ghost, Shirley, being in his opinion past such work, he determined to try what new blood would do. His choice fell upon that very remarkable young man, who was beginning to achieve such eminent social success, Thomas Shadwell. His Grace of Newcastle argued that so brilliant a conversationalist, so acute a critic of men and manners would assuredly infuse wit and vigour into any plays he might undertake to handle, accordingly Shadwell received what may be described as a command-invitation to Welbeck, and there he was employed upon the revision of the Duke's compositions in the dramatic kind, receiving the most princely remuneration for his services. Addressing the Duke, Shadwell definitely tells him : ' So vast was your Bounty to me, as to find me out in my obscurity, and oblige me several years, before you saw me at *Welbeck*.' [4] And again he says : ' I have been more obliged by my Lord Duke than by any man.' [5] Once more he tells his noble patron : ' Your Grace has, by so many and extraordinary favours, so entirely made me your own, that I cannot but think whatever is mine is so.' [6]

The two plays by the Duke of Newcastle in which Shadwell had a hand are *The Humorous Lovers*, quarto, 1677, and *The Triumphant Widow ; or, The Medley of Humours*, quarto, 1677. Incidentally the Jonsonian touch in each title, the reference to " humours " should not be passed unremarked. Although there is no record of the first performances both plays were produced at dates considerably earlier than their issue from the press. On Saturday, 30 March, 1667, Pepys notes " did by coach go see the silly play of my Lady Newcastle's, called ' The Humourous Lovers ' : the most silly thing that ever come upon a stage. I was sick to see it, but yet would not but have seen it, that I might the better understand her." Possibly

---

[1] Wood, 1691–1692, II, 261 ; cf. 1817, III, 739.

[2] Dated July, 1666. Shirley and his wife were buried at S. Giles in the Fields, 29 October, 1666.

[3] There is preserved at Welbeck a book containing sketches of plays, outlines of scenes, and appropriate songs, in the handwriting of the Duke.

[4] Dedication to *The Libertine*, 4to, 1676.

[5] Dedication of *The Humorists*, 4to, 1671, to the Duchess of Newcastle.

[6] Dedication of *Epsom-Wells*, 4to, 1673.

we should be right in assigning some day in March, 1667, as the date of
the first production of *The Humorous Lovers* at Lincoln's Inn Fields. On
Thursday, 11 April, 1667, Pepys retails some amusing gossip concerning
the Duchess of Newcastle. "The whole story of this Lady is a romance,
and all that she do is romantick. Her footmen in velvet coats, and herself
in an antique dress, as they say ; and was the other day at her own play,
' The Humourous Lovers ' ; the most ridiculous thing that ever was wrote,
but yet she and her Lord mightily pleased with it ; and she, at the end,
made her respects to the players from her box, and did give them thanks." [1]
For all this sharp criticism by Pepys *The Humorous Lovers* is a very lively
and entertaining comedy with several good and two excellent characters ;
Master Furrs, "An old Gentleman very fearful of catching cold," and
Mistress Hood, "An old School-Mistris, and a match-maker." Furrs,
who finds it " a Pilgrimage, a very Pilgrimage " from his bedroom to the
dining-room, and who " wears such a Turbant of Night-caps, that he is
almost as tall as *Grantham* Steeple," [2] lives in a perpetual alarm of draughts.
He begs a lady not to wave her fan when he is present as it stirs a deadly
cold blast of wind ; when his servant goes out of the door he exclaims that
there has been " let in wind enough to disperse a Navy " ; he cannot
endure the sight of a candied cake, " it puts me in mind of Winter," he
protests, " 'tis the very Emblem of a white Frost." In fact he is a remote
ancestor of Mr. Woodhouse, who it will be readily remembered when
admiring the likeness which had been drawn of Harriet Smith exclaimed :
" It is very pretty. So prettily done ! . . . The only thing I do not
thoroughly like is, that she seems to be sitting out of doors, with only a
little shawl over her shoulders—and it makes one think she must catch
cold." " But, my dear papa," remonstrated Emma, " it is supposed to be
summer ; a warm day in summer. Look at the tree." " But it is never
safe to sit out of doors, my dear," replied her father, setting the matter at
rest once and for all.

The second scene of the third act of *The Humorous Lovers* is in the theatre,
where a beautiful little Masque is played of Cupid and Venus, but this is
only a brief interlude and is not comparable to Shadwell's intensively
realistic sketch of a crowded audience in *A True Widow*. It may be remarked that each of these two comedies by the Duke of Newcastle contains songs, full as beautiful as anything the much-praised Sedley and

---

[1] It should be noted that the ascription of the play to the Duchess is erroneous ; this
comedy is the work of the Duke.

[2] The old rhyme says :

> O *Grantham* ! *Grantham* these wonders are thine
> A lofty steeple and a living sign.

A hive of bees once served as the sign of an inn at this town.

Rochester ever wrote, and there are, moreover, in his scenes lines of exquisite poetry.

The Triumphant Widow, which was probably produced, sooner or later, within a year or two of *The Humorous Lovers*,[1] is altogether a far better work. It were, of course, absurd to compare these pieces with anything of Jonson's, but it is no mean commendation to set them side by side with the theatre of Brome, whose plays indeed, to my mind, they very much resemble in many particulars. Langbaine, no easy critic, considers *The Triumphant Widow* " excellent," whilst his verdict on *The Humorous Lovers* is : " This Play equals most Comedies of this Age."

The lyric felicities of the Duke of Newcastle I have already praised, and in *The Triumphant Widow* the Footpad's songs when he is disguised as a pedlar, are extremely happy, whilst the whole scene is reminiscent, without being in the least degree imitative, of *A Winter's Tale*. As he goes on his way he trolls :

> Come maids what is it that you lack ?
> I have many a fine knack
> For you in my pedlar's pack ;
> Your sweethearts then kindly smack,
> If they freely will present you,
> And with trinkets will content you.
> Brushes, combs of tortoise shell,
> For your money I will sell ;
> Cambric lawn as white as milk,
> Taffeta as soft as silk :
> Garters rich with silver roses,
> Rings with moral, divine posies :
> Rainbow ribbons of each colour,
> No walking shop ere yet was fuller ;
> Various points and several laces
> For your bodies' straight embraces :
> Silver bodikins for your hair,
> Bobs which maidens love to wear :
> Here are pretty tooth-pick cases,
> And the finest *Flanders* laces,
> Cabinets for your fine doxies,
> Stoppers and tobacco boxes,
> Crystal *Cupid's*-looking-glasses,
> Will enamour all your lasses :
> Fine gilt prayerbooks, catechisms,
> What is orthodox or schisms,

---

[1] *The Triumphant Widow* was seen by the King on 26 November, 1674, but it cannot, of course, be argued that this was the first production.

Or for loyal faith defendant—
Presbyter or *Independant.*
Ballads fresh for singing new,
And more, the ballads all are true !

There are very many clever strokes in the play ; the Master-Cook who gives his bill of fare with fine poetic fury ; Crambo the heroic rhymster ; the Dogberry constable with his " Filly, fally, will you teach me Geogrecum ? " are all excellently done.

It would not be impossible to find traces of Shadwell's hand in *The Humorous Lovers,* but this perhaps is too finical an inquiry. When we consider *The Triumphant Widow,* however, we light upon a most curious point, namely, that Shadwell has conveyed two characters wholesale from this comedy for *Bury-Fair* which was produced at Drury Lane nearly twenty years later, in the spring of 1689, probably in April of that year. It is not a question of hints or suggestions, however ample, Shadwell's Mr. Oldwit and Sir Humphrey Noddy are utterly and at all points from *The Triumphant Widow,* nay, even their speeches and their quarter-quibbles are reproduced verbatim.

In *The Triumphant Widow* we have : Justice Spoilwit " *A foolish old Justice much affected with clinching,*" and Sir John Noddy, " *An arch Wag, a Coxcomb full of Monkey-tricks.*" In Act II, " *The Justice leans upon his Cane, Sir* John Noddy *strikes it away, and the Justice is ready to fall upon his Nose.*" This is precisely the trick Noddy plays on Oldwit in *Bury-Fair.* Again Sir John says : " Another time one of my Lords Men stood very soberly, I held my finger thus, and called him *Jack* of a sudden, and he turn'd suddenly, and hit his Nose such a bump, ha, ha, ha, I had almost died with laughing, and all that were by laugh'd so it was wonderful." In Act III when the company are at table Sir John repeats a vulgar jest and adds : " There was such laughing, the Ladies did so tihie under their Napkins, and could not eat a bit after it i'faith ; but when they look't most demurely, out went the Tihie again under the Napkin, ha, ha. I am a Villain, if the Tihie did not take a reverend old Gentlewoman when she was a drinking, and she did squirt the Beer out of her Nose, as an *Indian* does Tobacco, ha, ha." All this reappears in *Bury-Fair,* although we are glad to be spared the low joke. In Act V of Newcastle's play we have " A drunken Scene " of Sir John, the Justice, and others at a table, and as one of the company is about to sit, our prankster " *pulls the Chair from under him, and gives him a Fall.*" So Shadwell's Noddy " *plucks the Chair from under* Trim ; *and gives him a Devilish fall :* Oldwit *and he laugh immoderately.*" It is Crambo who recites the distich *Mittitur in disco* and the English " tendering " ; but the old Justice repeats his University verses, " an Elegy upon one Mr. *Murrials* Horse," and meanwhile Sir John pins him fast to his cricket.

Shadwell has much improved the jests and the fun, but the question arises with what salvo did he put upon the stage and print in one of his best-known and most applauded comedies characters from a play which had been acted only fifteen years before, even supposing there were no more recent revivals, a comedy, moreover, which had in the ordinary way been issued from the press in quarto a dozen short years since, and which must at least have been pretty widely known. Unless Shadwell were acknowledged to possess some indisputable right to these conceptions there can be no doubt at all that the whole host of his enemies, who had already accused him of plagiarism in more than one instance [1] would have attacked him mercilessly, and never have ceased to cast his borrowings from the Duke of Newcastle in his face. One can well imagine what capital the supreme satire and mordant wit of the great John Dryden would have made of such petty pilfering from the dead. It seems incontestable that these two characters are Shadwell's own originals, and there can be little doubt that when the Duke of Newcastle was composing *The Triumphant Widow* it was his coadjutor who wrote in Justice Spoilwit and Sir John Noddy, and who later with perfect propriety merely took back his own work which in his maturer experience he very much improved.

In spite of, perhaps in some measure because of, the fantasies that filled the head and filled the folios of Her Grace the Duchess, for King Charles himself held this princely pair high in honour for the nobility of their life and the heroic chivalry of their ideals, the patronage of so great an aristocrat as the Duke of Newcastle not only put gold into Shadwell's purse, but on his return to London from Welbeck established him that position in literary circles where even before his association with the great Duke he had been a welcome, nay more, a courted guest.

It is obvious indeed from his first play that Shadwell had mingled long and intimately with the wits and poets, ay, even with the wagtails and demi-poets of the time, and that there had for some time been a remarkably sharp " chiel amang them taking notes," and, faith, he printed it. He did more, he brought them all out on the stage, and a thronged theatre rocked with laughter to see Sir Robert Howard strutting and gasconading as Sir Positive At-all; his brother, Ned Howard, the most insufferable poetaster of the day, tormenting every character in the piece with impertinent discourses of poetry and the repetition of his own verses under the name of Ninny ; and Susanna Uphill, the pretty actress at the rival playhouse, with whose name not over-nice scandal had long and loudly con-

---

[1] We have Dryden's suggestions in *Mac Flecknoe*, and Shadwell in the preface to *The Tenth Satyr of Juvenal*, 4to, 1687, when he mentions *Epsom-Wells* and *The Virtuoso* particularly says " neither of which by the way are taken from a *Novel*, or stollen from a *Romance*."

nected that of Sir Robert,[1] as Lady Vaine, an arrant whore, taking upon herself the name of a lady, very talkative, and always pretending to virtue and honour. In truth Sir Positive and the rest were hardly caricatures, they were portraits; and society flocked to Lincoln's Inn Fields to see the picture of the Howards on the boards, in just the same way as they crowded the studios of the ingenious Mr. Peter Lely and the facile Mr. John Hales to see the features of their friends, drawn like, but perhaps a little improved, upon the glowing canvas.

We are not to suppose that Shadwell had any particular grievance against, far less that he had any personal quarrel with, the great Sir Robert Howard. Yet to anyone who was an observer of men and manners, to anyone who had a keen sense of humour, however coarse and robustious, Sir Robert Howard " conspicuous for the Lustre of his Birth, and the Excellency of his Parts," was almost equally conspicuous as a butt for irresistible satire. As for his brother, Edward Howard, who, " addicted himself to the Study of Dramatick Poetry," he flaunted all the extravagance of his elder brother without being able to boast a tithe of his intelligence and exceptional talents.

In spite of all his crazes and crotchets, his fine frenzies and thick-coming fancies, his rash weaknesses and ridiculous whims, his confidence and conceit, Sir Robert Howard was a strangely arresting and, indeed, even a noble figure. No man questioned his personal bravery. He seems to have had something of Bayard and something of Don Quixote; something of Cyrano and something of D'Artagnan. He would not have been out of place in the days of the Table Round, although, perhaps, he might never have caught even the most distant glimpse of the Holy Grail, and would have fallen an easy, nay, a willing victim to the wiles of Vivien or the magic of Morgan le Fay. He would have held his own as one of the heroes of Dumas, a gallant swashbuckler for whom Athos would have been a little too cold and precise; Porthos, a little too rampant and mundane; Aramis, a little too elegant and ecclesiastical. He was a fine cavalier, a noble knight, and among the Buckinghams and Rochesters and Sedleys of the Court of Charles II., he seems like some figure left over from a simpler and more honourable age, an armiger who might have scoured the plains of Ascalon with Cœur de Lion, or fought by the side of warlike Harry on the field of Agincourt.

[1] Evelyn, 18 October, 1666, writes: " This night was acted my Lord Broghill's tragedy, called *Mustapha*, before their Majesties at Court, at which I was present; very seldom going to the public theatres for many reasons now, as they were abused to an atheistical liberty; foul and undecent women now (and never till now) permitted to appear and act, who inflaming several young noblemen and gallants, became their misses, and to some, their wives. Witness the Earl of Oxford, Sir R. Howard, Prince Rupert, the Earl of Dorset, and another greater person than any of them, who fell into their snares, to the reproach of their noble families, and ruin of both body and soul."

Robert Howard, son of Thomas Howard, the first Earl of Berkshire, by Elizabeth, daughter of William Cecil, who was afterwards second Earl of Exeter, was born in 1626, and, according to Antony à Wood, he proceeded whilst quite young, to Magdalen College, Oxford. Cole, in his *Athenæ Cantabrigienses*, says that Sir Robert Howard was a member of Magdalen, Cambridge, but apparently this is a mistake, and the dramatist is being confused with his namesake and uncle, the Cantab Sir Robert Howard. Although only a mere lad at the outbreak of the Great Rebellion, young Howard enlisted in the Royalist forces, where he distinguished himself by his bravery among the brave, and as a recognition for his gallant action in rescuing Lord Wilmot on 29 June, 1644, when at Cropredy Bridge in North Oxfordshire the traitor Waller suffered a crushing defeat by the royal army, Howard, then only eighteen years old, was knighted upon the field. During the Commonwealth, Sir Robert was imprisoned in Windsor Castle, and he was regarded as so dangerous a malignant that it is somewhat surprising that he escaped with his life.

At the Restoration he was created a Knight of the Bath, returned member for Stockbridge in Hampshire, and appointed Secretary to the Commissioners of the Treasury. This post was certainly very lucrative, but the reward was no more than he deserved. As might have been expected, his enemies muttered that he was a mere creature of the King's, and, on Saturday, 8 December, 1666, Pepys, amongst other gossip, heard from Mr. Pierce of the Proviso to the Poll Bill, " brought in by Sir Robert Howard, who is one of the King's servants, at least hath a great office, and hath got, they say, £20,000 since the King come in." But Sir Robert was by no means just a honey-mouthed pickthank, when his play *The Duke of Lerma* was produced at the Theatre Royal on Thursday, 20 February, 1667–8, more than one of the audience expected a disturbance in the theatre. The King and the Court were present, and the drama was most palpably designed to castigate the looseness and licentiousness of Whitehall. The fact that a witty, but it must be confessed, impudent prologue was spoken by Mrs. Mary Knepp, the mistress of Sir Charles Sedley and of a good many other courtiers too, and by Nell Gwyn, in frankest *déshabillé;* a familiar dialogue, which both actresses delivered with the utmost sauciness and point, barbed the satire with no fortuitous aim.[1]

In 1677 Sir Robert Howard was appointed Auditor of the Exchequer, and Andrew Marvell to whom the mordant pamphlet " A Seasonable Argument to Perswade All the *Grand Juries* in *England*, to Petition for a New Parliament, Amsterdam, Printed in the Year, 1677 " under *Hant-*

[1] Pepys, Thursday, 20 February, 1667–8, says : " Knepp and Nell spoke the prologue most excellently, especially Knepp, who spoke beyond any creature I ever heard."

INTRODUCTION

Shire, notes Stockbridge[1] and roundly writes: "*Sir Robert Howard,*
Auditor of the Receipts of the Exchequer, with 3,000*l per annum :* many
great Places and Boons he has had, but his W—— *Uphill* spends all and
now refuses to Marry him." On 4 February, 1678–9, Howard was
returned member for Castle Rising, Norfolk, from which year, with the
exception of 1683, he sat in all Parliaments until 1692. In 1680 he purchased the fine property of Ashted, where Evelyn visited him on 10 May,
1684, and under this date he notes in his diary : " I went to visit my
brother in Surrey. Called by the way at Ashted, where Sir Robert
Howard (Auditor of the Exchequer) entertained me very civilly at his
new-built house, which stands in a park on the Down, the avenue south ;
though down hill to the house, which is not great, but with the out
houses very convenient. The staircase is painted by Verrio [2] with the
story of Astrea ; amongst other figures is the picture of the painter himself,
and not unlike him ; the rest is well done, only the columns did not at
all please me ; there is also Sir Robert's own picture in an oval ; the
whole in fresco. The place has this great defect, that there is no water
but what is drawn up by horses from a very deep well."

As years went on, more honours fell to Sir Robert's lot ; in February,
1688–9, he was admitted to the Privy Council, and early in June, 1690,
appointed " to command all and singular the regiments and troops of
Militia horse which are or shall be drawn together under the command of
John, Earl of Marlborough " throughout the whole of England.

26 February, 1692–3, Sir Robert took a fourth wife, Annabella Dives,
a girl of eighteen, one of the maids-of-honour to Queen Mary II. Sir
Robert's third wife presumably had been Susanna Uphill, for we know that
the lady rewarded his constancy by vouchsafing to accept his name. Tradition, which grows faint with time, speaks of her great beauty, and Downes
mentions her among our earliest actresses, but her theatrical talents cannot
have been remarkable, since we only find her name in very minor rôles ; for

[1] The population is now (1927) less than 900.
[2] Antonio Verrio, the celebrated Neapolitian painter, was born at Lecce, in the Terra
di Otranto, about 1639. His earliest pictures were done for ecclesiastics, the Jesuits'
College, Naples, the high altar in the Carmelite Church, Toulouse. His facility of
execution and rich colouring gained him fame, and Charles II. appointed him to direct
the royal tapestry works at Mortlake. Soon, however, Verrio was transferred to Windsor
to paint the walls and ceilings. Under Charles II. and his successor, Verrio was in high
favour. At the Revolution he threw up his office of surveyor of the royal gardens (a
sinecure) and refused to employ his pencil for William of Orange. He had, however,
many commissions from noble and private persons. His sight failing, Queen Anne
bestowed on him a pension of £200 a year. He died 1707. A list of Verrio's ceilings
will be found in Jesse's *Eton and Windsor.* Pope, *Windsor Forest,* has a couplet (307–9) :

from her roofs when *Verrio's* colours fall,
And leave inanimate the naked wall.

example, that of Erotion, an attendant, with one couplet to speak in the second act of Dryden's tragedy *Tyrannick Love; or, The Royal Martyr*, [1] produced at the Theatre Royal in 1669. She also played Artemis, a Court lady, in *Marriage A-la-Mode*, performed at Lincoln's Inn Fields about Easter, 1672; and Syllana, the confidante of Poppea, a part of only one line: "Oh Heav'ns how do you, Madam; what success?" in Lee's *The Tragedy of Nero*, produced at Drury-Lane in 1674. Her best opportunity seems to have been in Parthelia, daughter to the Doge of Venice, in Sir Francis Fane's *Love in the Dark; or, The Man of Bus'ness*, which was given in May, 1675. In Dryden's *Aureng-Zebe*, the last of this dramatist's heroic tragedies, produced at the same house during November, Mrs. Uphill played Zayda, the favourite slave of the Empress Nourmahal.

The second wife of Sir Robert was Lady Honora O'Brien, daughter of the Earl of Thomond, and widow of Sir Francis Inglefield. Sir Robert died the 3 September, 1698, "aged near eighty," says Luttrell, and he was buried in Westminster Abbey. His son, Thomas Howard, succeeded to the Ashted property. A daughter, born 28 December, 1653, Mary, under the assumed name of Talbot, was sent to Paris in her nineteenth year; for it is said that her beauty had unduly attracted the notice of Charles II., but her fortune was very different from that of the fair Bretonne La Querouille, or from the fame of Hortense Mazarin, since the closer to conceal her identity, as Mary Parnel, she entered the English convent of Poor Clares at Rouen, and, in that lonely grey cloister, Sister Mary of the Holy Cross wrote devotional works of exalted mysticism and spiritual symbolism. [2] Upon the resignation of Mother Winefrid Clare Giffard, who had held office since 1670, she was elected Abbess in 1702, and having governed the house with rare prudence and holy zeal, she died 21 March, 1735. Sir Robert Howard's portrait was painted by Sir Geoffrey Kneller, and a fine engraving of this, R. White Sculpsit, faces the general title-page [3] of the five new plays, folio 1692. It shows a remarkably fine face, alive with intellect and intelligence. The features are truly aristocratic, and are fittingly framed in the flowing luxuriance of a full-bottomed perriwig, whilst a steenkirk of richest point is clasped under the firm and determined chin. Sir Robert Howard was

---

[1] S. Catherine was played by Mrs. Hughes, and afterwards by Mrs. Boutel; Berenice by Mrs. Marshall; and Valeria by Nell Gwyn, who spoke the famous epilogue.

[2] Her *Chief Points of our Holy Ceremonies* was published in 1726, but her other books as yet all remain in MS. See Alban Butler's *Life and Virtues of the Venerable and Religious Mother, Mary of the Holy Cross*, London, 1767.

[3] Five new plays, viz. *The Surprisal, The Committee*, Comedies, and *The Indian-Queen, The Vestal-Virgin, The Duke of Lerma*, Tragedies. As they were acted by His Majesty's Servants at the *Theatre-Royal*. Written by the Honourable Sir *Robert Howard*. The Second Edition Corrected. London, Printed for *Henry Herringman*, and are to be sold by *Jacob Tonson, Daniel Browne, Thomas Bennet*, and *Richard Wellington*, 1700.

a great name, perhaps none greater in his day among Thespian folk and the sons of Literature. He held nine shares in the Theatre Royal (the first Drury-Lane), an equal number with Killigrew himself. He was a great arbiter in things theatrical, and when, in December, 1694, Betterton and the actors petitioned against Sir Thomas Skipwith and the patentees, the Lord Chamberlain took Sir Robert Howard into council, and all parties concerned were ordered " To attend Lord Dorset at Sr Robt Howards at Westmr Munday 17 Decr 94. betweene 10 & 11 a Clock." He was the brother-in-law of the great John Dryden, and under the name of Crites,[1] he is one of the interlocutors in the famous essay *Of Dramatick Poesie*. Dryden and he had even printed sharp strictures on each other's critical views.[2] As Bilboa, when Buckingham was penning the first draught of *The Rehearsal* in 1663–64, he was the original protagonist of the famous burlesque. His own plays won him applause and renown in his own day, and at least one of his comedies kept the stage for more than a hundred years, and, in an altered form as a farce, was still being acted late in the nineteenth century.[3] What matter if men laughed at him? Those who were wise did so when his back was turned. What matter if they paraded him on the stage? That was fair game, and he could return the compliment. The whole town was astir when Sir William Coventry was sent to the Tower for challenging the Duke of Buckingham in March, 1668-9.[4] Lord Bellassis told Pepys that the whole trouble arose " about a quarrel which Sir W. Coventry had with the Duke of Buckingham about a design between the Duke and Sir Robert Howard to bring him into a play at the King's House." Even Gerard Langbaine, who feared neither dramatist nor devil, is awed when he ventures to speak of Sir Robert Howard, and murmurs in reverent accents " Some Readers, who are strangers to the Excellent Tallents of Sir *Robert*, might expect from me some Discoveries of what he has borrow'd; but I am to Inform them,

---

[1] The identification of the " Colloquists in this Dialogue " is due to Malone, *Prose Works of John Dryden*, Vol. I, Part 1, pp. 62–68. However, Prior had already informed us (*Poems*, 8vo, 1709) that Eugenius was Buckhurst, and Mrs. Elizabeth Thomas in an Elegy on Dryden's death calls him Neander.

[2] In the preface prefixed to *The Great Favourite ; or, The Duke of Lerma*, 4to, 1668, Sir Robert Howard replied to certain of the arguments put forward in Dryden's *Of Dramatick Poesie*, which had just been published, whereupon the great poet rallied him very smartly in a new preface prefixed to the second edition of *The Indian Emperour* which appeared the same year. However, Dryden cancelled the preface and would not allow it to be reprinted during his lifetime. The breach was soon healed, and the two dramatists continued to live in friendship with each other to the close of their lives.

[3] *The Honest Thieves*, altered from the committee by Thomas Knight, produced at Covent Garden, 9 May, 1797 ; 12mo, 1797.

[4] Thursday, 4 March, 1668–69, Pepys notes : " I did meet Sir Jeremy Smith, who did tell me that Sir W. Coventry was just now sent to the Tower, about the business of his challenging the Duke of Buckingham."

That this Admirable Poet has too great a Stock of Wit of his own, to be necessitated to borrow from others."

The first of Sir Robert Howard's plays was a comedy, *The Blind Lady*, which was printed with his poems, 8vo, 1660. The scene lies in Poland, and the outline of the plot seems to be taken from Heylin's *Cosmography*. It must be confessed that the play is of no great value, whilst, as to the poems, even the kindly Sir Walter Scott judged them to be " a production of freezing mediocrity." They include " A Panegyrick to the King "; " Songs and Sonnets "; " The Fourth Book of Vergil "; " Statius his Achilleis, with Annotations "; " A Panegyrick to Generall Monck "; and although Dryden, in his complimentary address to Sir Robert " on his excellent poems," amongst other embroidered commendations, bravely remarks :

> We're both enrich'd and pleas'd, like them that woo
> At once a Beauty and a Fortune too,

I am sadly afraid that, with the best will in the world, one is bound to agree with the verdict of Sir Walter rather than echo the flattery of Dryden.

The Surprisal, the scene of which is laid in Siena, seems to me, of its kind, a capital comedy. The class to which it belongs is probably far more effective in the theatre than in the library, and it may be argued that there is a certain sameness in the ingredients of these dramas to which belong such typical plays as Dryden's *The Rival Ladies*, wherein sentiment and heroic love are emphasized : Fane's *Love in the Dark ;* Colley Cibber's *She Wou'd and She wou'd not* (largely conveyed from Leanard's *The Counterfeits*) ; Mrs. Centlivre's *The Wonder, a Woman keeps a Secret ;* in all of which pure comedy predominates. The action may take place in Venice or Palermo, in Salamanca or Seville or Madrid ; there must be plenty of quick intrigue and lively counter-intrigue, the incidents should hurry at one another's heels, there are complications and mistakes galore, the dialogue must always be vivacious and movement must never flag ; the result is always a very delightful entertainment, and often an eminently pleasing piece of literature. Whether it has any real relation to life in Venice or Madrid is a question. And yet, after all, if we call to mind the adventures of Thomas Killigrew on the Adriatic,[1] and thirty years before the escapades of the Duke of Buckingham at the Spanish capital, what time Charles, Prince of Wales, was wooing the Infanta Maria ; or to come nearer

---

[1] " To add to his evil nature as evil Arts, he went abroad, and in *Italy* studied the *Putana Errante*, the *Picaro*, in *Spain*, and the *Fripons* and *Friponeries* in *France*, till he had perfectly learnt all their Arts, and was completely qualified to deboish and couzen every one." *The Life of Tomaso the Wanderer*, by Richard Flecknoe, 1667 ; reprint 1925, edited by G. Thorn-Drury. The Venetian authorities certainly requested King Charles to withdraw " Resident Tom," as his more than ordinary lewdness caused resounding scandals.

home, the jaunt when Frances Jennings and Miss Price visited the haunts of the German fortune teller disguised as orange girls;[1] were these anglicized *comedias de capa y espada* so out of touch with life? At any rate their masks and cloaks and dark lanthorns thrilled with romance; they were not utterly sordid and vulgar and low as are the adventure plays of to-day, when some mean crook from 8.30 to 11, masquerading under the obvious disguise of a canny Scotch doctor with unspeakable accent, nightly succeeds in deluding the detective forces of two continents, but surely not the meanest intelligence in the audience who greet his triumphs with thunders of applause, whilst the management in imploring accents beseech those who have seen the play not to give away the secret to their friends intending to be present on the following evening.[2] In its day, *The Surprisal* had a considerable success, which was, perhaps, in some measure owing to the brilliant cast which interpreted it, since Nell Gwyn acted Samira, and Mrs. Knepp Emilia.

The Committee is probably the best-known of Sir Robert Howard's plays. It was a great favourite upon the stage, and remained for at least a century in the repertory of the theatre. Under Charles II. it owed some of its popularity, no doubt, to the political satire, if a photographic representation, without rancour and without prejudice, of proceedings under the Commonwealth can be called a satire.[3] The characterization is admirable.

[1] This frolic is related by Grammont. In 1670 various Court Ladies, and it was said the Queen herself, whilst staying at Audley End, visited a local fair. They all dressed themselves in scarlet petticoats as country girls, but both they and the gentlemen, disguised as rustic clowns, who attended them were recognized, and a curious mob escorted the party back to the mansion where they were guests.

[2] E.g., *The Ringer*, by Edgar Wallace.

[3] There are at least two other plays which give exact and personal pictures of the political situation on the eve of the Restoration. John Tatham's spirited comedy *The Rump; or, The Mirrour of the Late Times*, was acted at Dorset Court, probably in the summer of 1660 by Rhodes under Monck's licence. This was considerably altered and very much improved by Mrs. Behn in her amusing *The Roundheads; or, The Good Old Cause*, which was produced at Dorset Garden in the winter of 1681, or in January, 1682. Both these plays give a picture which is hardly exaggerated. There are a number of unacted pieces 1660–1661, many of which were obviously political pamphlets not intended for the stage. Thus we have *A Phanatique Play, The First Part, As it was Presented before and by the Lord Fleetwood, Sir Arthur Hasilrig, Sir Henry Vane, the Lord Lambert, and others, last night, with Master Iester and Master Pudding*, 1660; *The Tragical Actors, or, the Martyrdome of the late King Charles wherein Oliver's late falsehood, with the rest of his gang are described in their several actions and stations* (colophon, 1660); *Cromwell's Conspiracy. A Tragy-Comedy, Relating to our latter Times. Beginning at the Death of King Charles the First, and ending with the happy Restauration of King Charles the Second. Written by a Person of Quality.* 1660; *Hells Higher Court of Justice; or the Triall of the Three Politick Ghosts, Viz. Oliver Cromwell, King of Sweeden, and Cardinal Mazarine*, 1661; *Hewson Reduc'd; or, the Shoomaker return'd to his Trade*, 1661. It may be remarked that Hewson is a character in the topical comedies by Tatham and by Mrs. Behn.

In the same way Monmouth's rebellion and the Revolution produced a whole crop

Mr. and Mrs. Day are worthy to be named in the same breath as some of the minor characters of Dickens. The opening scene in particular shows the hand of the complete dramatist. The Irish footman, Teague,[1] who afforded infinite enjoyment to contemporary audiences, to me seems the weakest spot of the play. Probably we have been spoilt by Samuel Lover's sketches of Hibernian life.[2]

It is difficult precisely to determine what share Dryden had in the heroic tragedy of *The Indian-Queen*, which was produced on a scale of almost unexampled magnificence at the Theatre Royal in January, 1663-4, with the famous tragedienne Ann Marshall in the title-rôle. On Wednesday, 27 January of that year, Pepys observed " the street full of coaches at the new play ' The Indian Queene ' ; which for show, they say, exceeds ' Henry the Eighth.' " On Monday, 1 February, he visited the theatre and found that *The Indian-Queen* was " a most pleasant show, . . . but above my expectation most, the eldest Marshall did do her part most excellently well as I ever heard woman in my life." *The Indian-Queen* long remained popular in the theatre, and a later revival was made memorable by the music which Purcell [3] composed for that occasion.

Love and honour meet and conflict in true heroic fashion in *The Vestal Virgin; or, The Roman Ladies*, which was produced at the Theatre Royal in 1664,[4] probably in the autumn. Roman tragedies are apt to put on a certain dulness with the toga. *Coriolanus* is probably the most insipid of Shakespeare's plays ; Fletcher's *The False One* has always seemed to me rather a colourless piece; and in Restoration days, Sedley's *Antony and Cleopatra* is quite the poorest specimen of a drama in rhyme, a thing as dead as a door-tree. Roman tragedy was popular with Charles II.,[5] and *The Vestal Virgin* is a spirited enough specimen of its kind. One must not perhaps compare it with a great drama such as Lee's *Lucius Junius Brutus*, but it is infinitely better than the majority, and is untainted by that academic chilliness which so often freezes over five acts when Cæsar or a Senate or Lictors are mentioned. *The Vestal Virgin* is remarkable in possessing two

of semi-dramatic pamphlets, dialogues, and plays, which were happily neither fashioned for, nor given upon the stage.

[1] It is said that the character of Teague was drawn from an Irish servant of Sir Robert Howard's. Teague was originally played by Lacy, and afterwards by Antony Leigh, who on one occasion gave great offence to King James II. by some impudent gag which he introduced into a performance. Obadiah was acted by Underhill, of whom there is a portrait in this part.

[2] Especially that novel of rare humour *Handy Andy*.

[3] This was for a revival in 1691-2. Ismeron's *You twice ten hundred Deities* is especially famous.

[4] Folio, 1665.

[5] One might especially instance the gorgeous revival at the Theatre Royal on Friday, 18 December, 1668, of *Catiline* to which the King contributed a very considerable sum of money, no less than £500 for the dresses.

conclusions.[1] Originally it was acted as a complete tragedy, and " Just as the last Words were spoke, Mr. *Lacey* enter'd, and spoke the Epilogue," which commenced :

> *By your leave Gentlemen—*
> *After a sad and dismal Tragedy,*
> *I do suppose that few expected me.*

But it was also " *Acted the Comical way."* Alterations were made towards the end of Act IV. and a good deal of Act V. was rewritten. We then have " *Epilogue* Spoken by Mr. *Lacey,* who is suppos'd to enter as intending to speak the Epilogue for the Tragedy." Whilst he bustled forward to the front of the apron stage the actor began :

> *By your leave, Gentlem—How ; what do I see ?*
> *How ! all alive ! Then there's no use for me.*
> *'Troth, I rejoice you are reviv'd agen ;*
> *And so farewel, good living Gentlemen.*

As he retires, however, complaining that the poet has spoilt his epilogue, and like a quack physician brought all his characters back to life, the actors detain him, and with a shrug of his shoulders he declares that, since audiences enjoy variety he will " *turn* Rageu [2] *into a Tragedy."*

Sir Robert Howard's last play [3] is also his best. *The Great Favourite ; or,*

---

[1] Suckling's *Aglaura,* folio, 1638, was " First, a Tragedy, then by the said Sir Iohn turn'd to a Comedy." The author with " unheard-of prodigality, gave eight or ten new suits of clothes to the players." The Hon. James Howard altered *Romeo and Juliet,* " preserving Romeo and Juliet alive ; so that when the Tragedy was reviv'd again, 'twas play'd alternately, tragically one day, and tragicomical another, for several days together." It may be remembered that for political reasons *The Maid's Tragedy* was altered in various ways, and in one version at least the King remained alive till the end of the fifth act. In 1889 Sir Arthur Pinero was at production obliged to alter the ending of his play *The Profligate* (written 1887), as the death of the principal character was thought to be too tragical.

[2] *The Old Troop ; or, Monsieur Raggou* was probably produced at the Theatre Royal in 1664-1665. It is all broad farce and very amusing. On Friday, 31 July, 1668, Pepys went " to the King's House, to see the first day of Lacy's ' Monsieur Ragou,' now new acted. The King and Court all there, and mighty merry—a farce."

[3] In a letter of Dryden's dated 3 September, 1697, and addressed to his sons at Rome (Malone, *Prose Works of John Dryden,* London, 1800, Vol. I, Part 2, Letter xxi, pp. 55–56) he tells them : " After my return to town, I intend to alter a play of Sir Robert Howard's, written long since, and lately put by him into my hands ; 'tis called *The Conquest of China by the Tartars.* It will cost me six weeks study, with the probable benefit of an 100 pounds." In December, 1697, writing to Jacob Tonson he says : " I have broken off from my studies from *The Conquest of China,* to review Virgil, and bestow'd nine entire days upon him." Apparently, however, the play was never finished, but it is curious to notice that there exists a MS. (British Museum Add. MS. no. 28, 692), a small folio volume which in addition to a copy of *Valentinian,* comprising many of Rochester's alterations contains " A Scæn of Sir Robert Hoard's Play, written by the Earl of

INTRODUCTION

The Duke of Lerma[1] was produced at the Theatre Royal on Thursday, 20 February, 1667–8, before a crowded house including the King and the Court. " A well-writ and good play . . . altogether a very good and most serious play " was the judgement of Mr. Pepys, who was present, a verdict which may be most heartily endorsed. The plot is actually founded upon history, and although the poet has allowed himself certain liberties, such, for example, as the substitution of Donna Maria, Lerma's daughter, for the Duke of Uceda, the son of the historical Lerma,[2] who engineered his own father's downfall, these variants are not really excessive, and it must have been extraordinarily interesting to the audience to see upon the stage a foreign sovereign, who had actually been dead little more than two years.[3] In his address " To the Reader," [4] the poet tells us that a play called *The Duke of Lerma* was offered to the Theatre Royal, and handed to him by Charles Hart, the actor, with a request for his opinion upon it. The piece proved to be absolutely unsuitable for the stage, and was accordingly returned to its author. Sir Robert Howard, who was on the point of

Rochester." In spite of this ascription this scene may not impossibly be a portion of Dryden's work which was never completed.

In May, 1675, was produced at Dorset Garden Settle's *The Conquest of China, by the Tartars*, and perhaps since Settle had forestalled him Sir Robert Howard laid aside his tragedy, of which he had already composed several scenes, and when Settle's tragedy was forgotten he returned to these again with some idea of producing them on the stage.

[1] *The Duke of Lerma ; or, ye spanish Duke*, 1641, by Henry Shirley has not been preserved.

[2] Francisco De Rojas Y Sandoral, Duke of Lerma, was the favourite and chief minister of Philip III. of Spain, who raised him to the Dukedom in 1598, immediately upon his accession. In 1618 he was supplanted by his own son, and compelled to resign all his offices. He died in comparative obscurity in 1625.

[3] Philip IV. passed away just before dawn on Thursday, 17 September, 1665. It may be remembered that when a few years ago Laurence Housman's fine play, *Pains and Penalties*, was submitted to the censor to be approved for public production a licence was refused. The piece dealt with the divorce of George IV. in 1820, and it was considered that such an event in the life of a royal lady recently deceased must not be given upon the stage.

[4] *For the Subject, I came accidently to write upon it ; for a Gentleman brought a* Play *to the* King's Company, *call'd,* The Duke of Lerma ; *and by them I was desired to peruse it, and return my Opinion, whether I thought it fit for the* Stage : *After I had read it, I acquainted them, that in my Judgment it would not be of much Use for such a Design, since the Contrivance scarce would merit the Name of a Plot ; and some of that, assisted by a Disguise ; and it ended abruptly : and on the Person of* Philip *the* IIId *there was fix'd such a mean Character, and on the Daughter of the Duke of* Lerma, *such a vitious one, that I cou'd not but judge it unfit to be presented by any that had a Respect, not only to Princes, but indeed to either Man or Woman ; and about that time, being to go into the Country, I was persuaded by Mr.* Hart *to make it my Diversion there, that so great a Hint might not be lost, as the Duke of* Lerma *saving himself in his last Extremity, by this unexpected Disguise, which is as well in the true Story as the old* Play ; *and besides that and the* Names, *my altering the most part of the* Characters, *and the whole* Design, *made me uncapable to use much more ; though perhaps written with higher Stile and Thoughts, than I cou'd attain to.*

(1)

taking a holiday in the country, was persuaded by Hart to write a play on the same subject during his absence from London.

The same address is notable for Sir Robert Howard's strictures upon Dryden's *Of Dramatick Poesie*, 4to, 1668, a criticism to which the laureate replied in his *Defence of the Essay Of Dramatick Poesie*, which he prefixed to the second edition of *The Indian Emperour*, 4to, 1668, but which, since he was unwilling to allow this passage of arms with his brother-in-law to ripen into a formal quarrel, he suppressed in the third edition, 1670, of his tragedy, and which he would not suffer to be re-printed during his life-time. Although his works have been unduly neglected, and the last collected edition, 1722, is of considerable [1] rarity, Howard, in his five plays, has given exceptional proofs of a very fine talent, both in tragedy and in comedy. Had he not been absorbed in the maelstrom of politics and business, no doubt our stage would be all the richer from his ingenious and happy pen.

His historical essays are of value, but his best known non-dramatic work is doubtless *The Duel of the Stags*, 4to, 1668, a poem which was unmercifully parodied and burlesqued by the whole idle cabal of wits and witlings.

Side by side with Sir Robert, Shadwell has satirized his brother Edward Howard, a man of far meaner parts and lesser importance. Of the Honourable Edward Howard, the fifth son of the Earl of Berkshire, who was baptized at S. Martin-in-the-Fields, 2 November, 1624, little, save his literary activities, is certainly known, quite possibly because there is little to know, which is assuredly the case if his life at all resembled his plays, for these afford a monotonous lack of incident. As Dr. Doran says : " His characters ' talk,' but they are engaged in no plot." Lacy, the actor, roundly told him that he was " more a fool than a poet," whilst Rochester, Buckingham, Buckhurst, kept emphasizing the same unwelcome fact in yet more vigorous language, which nevertheless completely failed to convert him to their views. He is described as being insufferably conceited, and he was the one person in the world (they said) who took himself seriously. He would assume the liveliest and jauntiest air, and in order to show his light-hearted wit, he introduced a thousand silly affectations into his gait and gestures. But his long, foolishly-solemn face, and codfish eyes seemed set in a mask of frozen misery even whilst he was capering and jigitting like a Punch in a puppet-show. " There goes the Melancholy Knight ! " the maids and courtiers used to cry as Ned Howard stalked down the corridor at Whitehall.[2] Buckingham has immortalized

---

[1] *The Committee* was frequently reprinted with *The Indian Queen* in the eighteenth century. There is an edition for Tonson, 12mo, 1735, and acting editions " from the prompt book " are not uncommon. Of course from a textual point of view these have no value.

[2] See Rochester's satire *On Poet Ninny*.

Edward Howard at a rehearsal of one of his sterile plays. Ever restless, ever interrupting the actors, ever bragging, ever praising his own scenes, his mouth full of whimsical phrase and petty boast, he used to cry out to his friends in an excess of admiration : " Gad, it will pit, box, and gallery with any play in Europe." And if one of the assistants happened to commend an actor, and remark, " Sir, he does it admirably," " Ay, pretty well," the author grudingly replied, " but he does not hit me in't ; he does not top his part."

Perhaps the most celebrated of all Mr. Edward Howard's works was his " incomparable " heroic poem *The Brittish Princes*, 8vo, 1669, which, it was said, contained that admired couplet :

> A painted Vest Prince *Voltager* had on,
> Which from a Naked *Pict* his Grandsire won.

Alas ! this eloquent distich is a crusted old joke of Steele's,[1] and the original lines run :

> A vest as admir'd *Vortager* had on
> Which from this Island's foes his Grandsire won.

Edward Howard's plays that have come down to us are four in number : *The Usurper*, a tragedy, was produced at the Theatre Royal in December, 1663, and seen by Pepys, Saturday, 2 January, 1663–4. It is, as the diarist says, " a pretty good play," and it remained in the repertory for some eight or nine years.[2] The scene is laid in Sicily, and there is a political undercurrent which, at the time, must have proved extremely piquant, although to-day time has, of course, blunted the barb. Damocles, the usurper, represents Oliver Cromwell ; Hugo de Petra is his " parasite and creature"; whilst Cleomenes " a faithful, noble person " thinly veils General Monck.

[1] The Spectator, No. 43, Thursday, 19 April, 1711, " The *British Prince*, that Celebrated Poem, which was written in the reign of King *Charles* the Second, and deservedly called by the Wits of that Age *Incomparable*, was the effect of such an happy Genius as we are speaking of. From among many other Disticks no less to be quoted on this Account, I cannot but recite the two following lines :

> A painted Vest Prince *Voltager* had on,
> Which from a Naked *Pict* his Grandsire won.

Here if the Poet had been Vivacious, as well as Stupid, he could not, in the Warmth and Hurry of Nonsense, have been capable of forgetting that neither Prince *Voltager*, nor his Grandfather, could strip a Naked Man of his Doublet ; but a Fool of a colder Constitution would have staied to have Fleaed the *Pict*, and made Buff of his Skin, for the Wearing of the Conqueror."

[2] It was seen again by Pepys on Wednesday, 2 December, 1668, and on the following day the King was present at the theatre. The play was much liked, and on Monday, 7 December following a command performance was given at Court. *The Usurper* was printed 4to, 1668.

INTRODUCTION

The Six Days Adventure ; or, The New Utopia, was acted at the Duke of York's House in the spring of 1671, and printed 4to, the same year.[1] Upon the stage it was a complete failure, and although Howard had paid no less than three hundred pounds to have it produced, the play could not win through longer than a couple of nights.

> And it kept up the Second Night :
> And suddenly *Utopia* fell,
> Damn'd to the lowest pit of Hell.[2]

The author attributed his disaster to an angry clique, who seem to have caused something like a riot in the theatre, which practically prevented the performance. It is certainly the best of Edward Howard's extant comedies, so that the vivacious Aphra Behn and Ravenscroft were inspired to hail it with Pindarics [3] ; whilst Sam Clyat and a certain J. T. also contributed their quota of poetic laudation. *The Women's Conquest* acted at Lincoln's Inn Fields in the winter of 1670 is a dull disappointing play, the scene of which lies in some rococo Scythia. It is perhaps chiefly memorable as having afforded a hint to Mrs. Inchbald for her comedy *Every One has His Fault,* produced at Covent Garden, 29 January, 1793.

The only interest in *The Man of Newmarket* lies in the fact that the play gives us glimpses of a Restoration race meeting. Otherwise it seems to me a singularly vapid piece of work. *The London Gentleman* entered in the Stationers' Register, 7 August, 1667, was not printed, and is presumably lost. Edward Howard's output may seem mediocre, and something worse than mediocre, but it is hardly fair to judge him without taking into account *The Change of Crowns.* This may sound paradoxical enough, since we only know of the play from the pages of Pepys, but what Pepys has to tell us is exceptionally detailed : On Monday, 15 April, 1667, the diarist writes :

[1] *Term Catalogues,* Trinity (10 July), 1671.
[2] *On Three Late Marriages,* a satire, 1688 : unprinted MS.
[3] Mrs. Behn indulges in such adulation as :

> " Beyond the Merit of the Age,
> You have adorn'd the Stage ;
> So from rude Farce, to Comick Order brought,
> Each Action, and each Thought ;
> To so Sublime a Method, as yet none
> (But mighty *Ben* alone)
> Cou'd e'er arive, and he at distance too ;
> Were he alive he must resign to you :
> You have outdone what e'er he writ,
> In this last great Example of your Wit.
> Your *Solymour* does his *Morose* destroy
> And your *Black Page* does his *Barber's Boy ;*
> All his Collegiate Ladies must retire,
> While we thy braver *Heroins* do admire.

" I to the King's house by chance, where a new play : so full as I never saw it ; I forced to stand all the while close to the very door till I took cold, and many people went away for want of room. The King, and Queene and Duke of York and Duchesse there, and all the court, and Sir W. Coventry. The Play called ' The Change of Crownes ' ; a play of Ned Howards, the best that ever I saw at that house, being a great play and serious ; only Lacy did act the country-gentleman come up to Court, who do abuse the Court with all the imaginable wit and plainness about selling of places, and doing everything for money. The play took very much. . . . Then home, a little at the office, and then to supper and to bed, mightily pleased with the new play." On the morrow he made haste to escort his wife to the theatre, only to find that *The Change of Crowns* had been suddenly withdrawn, and *The Silent Woman* was being acted in its stead. Charles, Mrs. Knepp whispered in his ear, was furious at the galling satire. Lacy had been forthwith lodged in gaol, and, until intercession had been made on their behalf, the company were forbidden to perform again. " The King mighty angry " ; comments Pepys, " and it was bitter indeed, but very true and witty." To complete the actors' misfortunes, when the irate Lacy was released a couple of days later, he happened to meet the dramatist at the theatre and blows were actually exchanged. The bystanders wondered " that Howard did not run him through, he being too mean a fellow to fight with," but a complaint to the King proved perfectly effectual, and " Whereas John Lacy hath both in abusive words and actions abused the honourable Edward Howard Esquire," he was re-arrested, and the house was closed down in anger. A play the sting of which so sorely chafed the good-natured Charles, must have been particularly pungent, and we are bound to conclude that, in losing *The Change of Crowns*, we have lost a very remarkable drama.

None the less it cannot be denied that there are few names which have been handled so severely by their contemporaries as that of the luckless Ned Howard. So relentless, nay, so venomous is the vituperation that one is tempted to ask whether there was not something complacently uncouth and jarring in the man's actual personality, which ruffled and provoked those with whom he came in contact. " Thou damn'd Antipodes to common sense " Dorset calls him, and stupider folk have been more kindly treated, for Howard, although he wrote so much that is flat and featureless, had in some respects gleams of great intelligence. The Preface to *The Women's Conquest*, 4to, 1671, contains some very sound criticism. Of course among his great contemporaries, he did not shine ; but to-day, for example, in the field of dramatic criticism, he would hold no undistinguished position. He is infinitely more sensible, and an infinitely better writer of English for example, than the peevish Mr. St. John Ervine, who keeps telling us with wearisome reiteration how bad are the plays that he goes to see, and who, leaves us, or would like to leave us, under the impression that there is only one good dramatist, a certain Mr. Ervine, as there is only one good critic and his name forsooth is Ervine too.

Certainly *insanabile scribendi cacoethes* possessed the whole Howard family. The Honourable James Howard, the ninth son of the Earl of Berkshire, was, it may be remembered, the author of two capital comedies, *The English Mounsieur*, an exceedingly diverting piece, seen by Pepys, 8 December, 1666; " a mighty pretty play, very witty and pleasant "; and *All Mistaken; or, The Mad Couple*, " a pretty pleasant play," which Pepys applauded on Friday, 20 September, 1667.[1] James Howard also made *Romeo and Juliet* into a tragi-comedy, preserving the lovers alive, " so that when the Tragedy was reviv'd again, 'twas play'd alternately, tragically one day, and tragicomical another for several days together." [2]

Yet another brother, Colonel Henry Howard, " made a play called *The United Kingdoms*, which began with a funeral and had also two kings in it." [3] Practically nothing more is known of this drama, save that, probably for some purely personal reason, Buckingham and a noisy club of his friends banded together to hiss *The United Kingdoms* off the stage. Tradition says that they carried out their self-appointed task with so complete a thoroughness that Bedlam itself at the full moon was quiet to the row that took place in the theatre, and that in the fracas, amid the shouting and cat-calls which sang the poor play's requiem, Buckingham himself was within an ace of being marked for life. Writing in 1704 Briscoe tactfully sums up the event : *The United Kingdoms* " was acted at the Cockpit [4] in Drury Lane soon after the Restoration, but miscarrying on the stage, the author had the modesty not to print it."

In more ways than one we might compare the polygraphic Howards with the Gozzi family in their haunted old Palazzo a San Canziano, where although the doors were off their hinges, the casements broken, the floors uncarpeted, whilst the ancestral portraits had gone to the dealers and the magnificent furniture of former days had long been laid up in lavender,

[1] Hart acted Philidor and Nell Gwyn Mirida, " the Mad Couple." The fat and thin suitors, Pinguister and Leanman, seem to be borrowed from Lodam, a fat gentleman, acted by William Sherlock, and Rawbone, a thin citizen acted by William Robins, in Shirley's *The Wedding*, produced, according to Fleay (*Anglia*, VIII, 405), on 31 May, 1626. From Howard Sedley has taken Merryman and Cunningham for his best comedy *Bellamira*, which was given at the King's House in May, 1687. Charles Molloy in his farce *The Half Pay Officers* performed at Lincoln's Inn Fields 11 January, 1720, has likewise made use of these two contrasted *buffi*.

[2] Downes *Roscius Anglicanus*.

[3] This was parodied by the Duke of Buckingham in *The Rehearsal*.

[4] The Cock-pit, or Phœnix, was a small-roofed theatre, constructed in the cockpit in Drury Lane about 1617. It was dismantled in 1649, and last used in 1664. The site was afterwards known as Pit Court.

everybody in the house, from cock-loft to cellar, was occupied in writing, " writing abundantly, Songs, Elegies, Satires, Encomiums, Panegyricks, Lampoons, Plays, and Heroick Poems," as the lady in Congreve says. In one empty room the elder brother, Count Gasparo, dreaming all day long, slovenly but contented, was compiling commentaries and excursus which would never be printed ; in another his blue-stocking wife was translating French plays and entering up journals ; brothers and sisters were wandering up and down stairs improvising ballads, setting their own songs to music, reciting with magnificent gestures and resounding voice their own scenes to anyone who would listen ; and in the midst of all this huddle and rout and racket, Carlo Gozzi was conjuring the fairies back to earth, and penning those delightful plays *The Loves of the Three Oranges*, *The Beautiful Little Green Bird*, *Turandot*, *The Stag King*, *Zein Lord of the Djins*, and the rest of those exquisite fantasies, in comparison with which *The Blue Bird* seems a little gross in texture and mundane, whilst *Hansel and Gretel* is too sophisticate and point device.

All four brothers, Sir Robert, Colonel Henry, Edward and James, were satirized by Buckingham in *The Rehearsal*, produced at the Theatre Royal, 7 December, 1671, but here they are completely overshadowed by Dryden, who is, of course, caricatured as Mr. Bayes. Moreover, it is a school that is burlesqued, rather than any one particular person, although it is true that a quintessence of ridicule is concentrated upon Dryden as being the typical and chief exponent of that school. However, Shadwell came first, and on Saturday, 2 May, 1668, the audience at Lincoln's Inn Fields was fairly electrified when as Stanford was exclaiming, " Pray Sir, let me go, let me go, I will not stay," Henry Harris, dressed and perriwigged in exact replica of Sir Robert Howard, entered full on the unfortunate Stanford and caught him in the nick, waving a sheet of pricked music, and volubly exclaiming : " Ah Dear *Jack !* Have I found thee ? I would not but have seen you for twenty pounds : I have made this morning a glorious Corrant, an immortal Corrant, a Corrant with a Soul in't," whilst, on his other side, James Nokes, the ridiculous solemnity of whose features was enough to have set a whole bench of Bishops in a titter, [1] as he stood shutting up his mouth with a dumb studious pout, rolling his full eye with vacant amazement and palpable ignorance, the ideal copy of the melancholy Edward Howard, was clacking and blattering so quickly that the words tumbled one over the other " Sir *Positive* has a great Soul of Musick in him ; he has great power in Corranto's and Jiggs, and composes all the Musick to my Playes."

Pepys has left us the liveliest impressions of the first performance of *The Sullen Lovers* and of the sensation caused by Shadwell's saucy personalities. " To Hercules Pillars, and there dined, and thence to the Duke of York's

---

[1] Colley Cibber's *Apology*, Chapter V.

playhouse against the new play, and there set in a poor man to keep my place, I out, and spent an hour at Martin's, my booksellers, and so back again, where I find the house quite full. But I had my place, and by and by the King comes and the Duke of York; and then the play begins, called 'The Sullen Lovers; or, The Impertinents,' having many good humours in it, but the play tedious, and no design at all in it. But a little boy, for a farce, do dance Polichinelli, the best that ever anything was done in the world, by all men's report: most pleased with that, beyond anything in the world, and much beyond all the play." At first indeed Pepys criticizes *The Sullen Lovers* harshly, but we must remember that his opinion was often coloured by some extraneous event, the temper of his wife, the weakness of his eyes, some mishap at the office, some quarrel at home and in any case he was shortly to reverse his verdict on Shadwell's comedy. On Monday, 4 May, he is almost bitter in his disapproval, " to the Duke of York's house and there saw ' The Impertinents ' again, and with less pleasure than before, it being but a very contemptible play though there are many little witty expressions in it; and the pit did generally say that of it." None the less the very next day he was at the theatre again. Creed dined with him, " and after dinner he and I to the Duke of York's playhouse; and there coming late, he and I up to the balcony-box, where we find my Lady Castlemayne and several great ladies; and there we sat with them, and I saw ' The Impertinents ' once more, now three times, and the three only days it hath been acted. And to see the folly how the house do this day cry up the play more than yesterday! And I for that reason like it, I find, the better, too; by Sir Positive At-all, I understand, is meant Sir Robert Howard. My Lady pretty well pleased with it; but here I sat close to her fine woman, Willson, who indeed is very handsome, but, they say, with child by the King. I asked, and she told me this was the first time her Lady had seen it I having a mind to say something to her." The whole town was gossiping of Sir Positive, and it is interesting to note that even seventeen years later when Evelyn[1] dined with Sir Robert Howard he sums up his host as " a gentleman pretending to all manner of arts and sciences, for which he had been the subject of comedy, under the name of Sir Positive; not ill-natured but insufferably boasting."

On Friday, 8 May, 1668, Pepys was at a conference presided over by the Duke of York, and even the grave men of business interrupted their deliberations to gossip about the tremendous success of the new comedy, " But, Lord! to see how this play of Sir Positive At-all, in abuse of Sir Robert Howard, do take, all the dukes and every body's talk being of that, and telling more stories of him, of the like nature, that it is now the town and country talk, and, they say, is most exactly true. The Duke of York himself said that of his playing at trapball is true, and told several

[1] 15 February, 1685.

(lvii)

other stories of him." Pepys records that he saw Shadwell's comedy again on Wednesday, 24 June, 1668; "Busy till dinner, and then with wife, Mercer, Deb., & W. Hewer to the Duke of York's Playhouse, and there saw 'The Impertinents,' a pretty good play." On Saturday, 29 August the same year, during the excessive heat, when Henry Harris, the actor, had dined at noon with the diarist, Pepys "carried Harris to his playhouse, where, though four o'clock, so few people there at 'The Impertinents,' as I went out; and do believe they did not act,[1] though there was my Lord Arlington and his company there. So I out, and met my wife in a coach, and stopped her going thither to meet me; and took her, and Mercer, and Deb., to Bartholemew Fair." On Easter Wednesday, 14 April, 1669, Pepys notes "Out with my own coach to the Duke of York's Playhouse, and there saw 'The Impertinents,' a play which pleases me well still; but it is with great trouble that I now see a play, because of my eyes, the light of the candles making it very troublesome to me." The psychology of these entries by Pepys, is extraordinarily interesting in its simplicity and frankness. In spite of the fact that he judged *The Sullen Lovers* "tedious" at the first performance, he, nevertheless, sees it three days in succession, and when he finds that everybody is talking about the new comedy, it rises palpably in his estimation, and he discovers at each visit new springs of wit and humour.

Downes tell us: "this Play had wonderful success, being acted 12 days together, when our Company were commanded to *Dover*, in *May*, 1670. The King with all his Court meeting his sister, the Dutchess of *Orleans* there. This Comedy and *Sir Solomon Single*, pleas'd Madam the Dutchess, and the whole Court extremely."

Even before the production of the play Shadwell had taken care to send a holograph script of his comedy to his patron the Duke of Newcastle, and this MS. is still preserved at Welbeck.[2] It is inscribed "ffor His Grace the Duke of Newcastle," and after the list of Dramatis Personæ it has the note, "The plan of the ground London. The Time of the scene Aprill 68." It will be remarked that in the printed quarto it is: "The time. In the Moneth of *March*, 166⅞."

The Sullen Lovers is certainly a capital comedy, and it is far, very far, from being a mere adaptation of Molière,[3] indeed Shadwell speaks with absolute accuracy, not wont to be a virtue with writers in such circumstances, when he says that he only took a hint from *Les Fâcheux* and made

[1] It was sometimes announced that the play would be given, however small the audience.

[2] Mr. Richard W. Goulding, Librarian at Welbeck, kindly furnished me with tracings of notes from the MS.

[3] To say that *Le Misanthrope* " gave Shadwell the main theme of *The Sullen Lovers* and suggested part of the first act of *Bury-Fair*," as some silly dabbler has recently remarked, is merely to show ignorance both of Shadwell and Molière.

use of it in but two short scenes. Shadwell has drawn his characters excellently. Never was such a gang of busy bores, eternally chattering, eternally intriguing, eternally interfering and muddling with the best intentions both their own affairs and the affairs of all with whom they are brought in contact, or rather, of all whom they pester and beset with their importunities. They are no more to be shaken off than a cloud of locusts. They are pachydermatous as the muchocho whose hide no sword or spear may pierce. To convince them even by anger and insults that their society is not required were an impossible task. Sir Positive himself is the arch-priest and centre of the horde; they dance round him as thick as motes in a sunbeam; it is his colossal vanity which energizes them and sends them speeding on their way. He has declared his own infallibility; he has the confidence and assurance of a second-rate critic, or even of that more impudent and ignorant thing, a modern metropolitan school inspector. He will justify the grossest mistakes. Surely here is a character worthy of a place in the gallery of English literature. It may assuredly be questioned whether *The Sullen Lovers*, as a whole, is Shadwell's best play; *The Virtuoso, Epsom-Wells, Bury-Fair*, might all put in a strong claim for that place of honour, and there are other pieces which have detached scenes that Shadwell has not elsewhere excelled, but, as a character, Sir Positive is only equalled, I think, by Sir Formal Trifle, that immortal figure of sublime inconsequence and trivial eloquence. With reference to the greatest of English novelists, Jane Austen, Archbishop Whateley has shrewdly said, " it is no fool that can describe fools well," and we may with perfect truth apply this sentence to Thomas Shadwell.

In *The Comical Revenge* and *She wou'd if she cou'd* scenes are laid in Covent Garden, the New Exchange, the Mulberry Garden, a tavern, a gentleman's bed-chamber, and Etherege is praised to the skies as presenting the audience with the world they knew in a way that no other dramatist had attempted or approached.[1] Etherege had great parts; nobody would deny him wit and brilliance, even if it be something of a metallic lustre, but the lighter scenes of *The Comical Revenge*, at least, are by no means so intensively realistic; rather they seem a medley of manners and masquerade,[2] farce and the types of Middleton or Brome. I do not say that this renders them any the less delightful or vivacious, but I do contend that it is a mistake which hails " gentle George" as the first and completest master of realistic comedy whilst we have Shadwell in the field. Such a judgement, in truth, betrays a superficiality, a meagreness of view, a narrowness, which may almost certainly be diagnosed as arising from

[1] To talk of Dryden's " cumbersome improbabilities " and " lumbering unreality " is singularly inept.

[2] *E.g.*, III, 3, the " *Masque of the Link-boys, who are Dancing-masters, disguised for the Frollick.*"

too slender an acquaintance with Restoration comedy, and for which the medicine is simple, a more extensive and more sympathetic course of dramatic reading.

The scene of *The Sullen Lovers* is London; the time the month of March, 1667–8, and in a few moments we find ourselves literally surrounded by a whole throng of living men and women. They are not actors and actresses upon the stage; they are not characters in a printed play; they are so real that we feel them at our side, their velvet jumps and their silken petticoat brush our clothes and rustle about us, we hear their voices in our ears, sweet and shrill, harsh and low; they talk of persons and of places that are infinitely familiar. Sir Positive is boasting that he could design a ship more skilfully than Pett or Deane; Emilia is going off to write a letter to her sister at Bruges; Ninny is chattering of his barber, George; Woodcock boasting of his new lodgings over against the Rose in Covent Garden; Huffe is cursing his luck which has lost him twenty pounds at Spierings [1]; Lady Vaine is slyly slipping away to a merry party at the Setting Dog and Partridge in Fleet Street. This is real life.

The exceptional but richly-deserved success of his first play seems not only to have given Shadwell a secure position among the writers of

---

[1] Cf. Radcliffe's *The Ramble*, 8vo, 1682 :

> When Play was done I call'd a Link
> I heard some paltry Pieces chink
> Within my Pockets, how d'ee think
>   I employ'd 'em?
> Why, Sir, I went to Mistress *Spering*,
> Where some were cursing, others swearing
> Never a barrel better Herring,
>   *per fidem.*
>
> Seven's the Main, 'tis Eight God dam 'me,
> 'Twas Six, said I, as God shall sa' me,
> Now being true you cou'd not blame me
>   So saying.
> Sa' me! quoth one, what Shamaroon
> Is this, has begg'd an Afternoon
> Of's Mother, to go up and down
>   A playing?
>
> This was as bad to me as killing;
> Mistake not, Sir, said I, I'm willing,
> And able both to drop a Shilling,
>   Or two, Sir:
> Goda'mercy then, said Bully *Hec*
> With whiskers stern, and Cordubeck
> Pinn'd up behind, his scabby Neck
>   To shew, Sir.

the time, but also definitely to have turned his thoughts to the theatre as the means of his professional livelihood. It may at first sight certainly seem curious that in his second attempt he turned from a living London to a rococo Arcadia, but the explanation is, I think, to be found in the fact that Shadwell as a dramatist was trying his paces, that during the years immediately following the Restoration the pastoral play enjoyed no small vogue, and Shadwell had, ready made to his hand, a typical specimen, better indeed than most, in John Fountain's *The Rewards of Virtue*, which had never been acted. The most famous of all pastoral plays is undoubtedly *Il Pastor Fido* of Giovanni Battista Guarini,[1] which was originally written to rival the *Aminta* of his friend and contemporary Tasso. This pastoral tragi-comedy marks the culmination of the pastoral poetry of the Italian renaissance. In an age of dark intrigue and bloody politics men turned with pleasure from the tortuous turmoil around them to these artificial pictures of the gentle loves of nymphs and shepherds, and they found a refuge from reality in the sweetly sentimental world of an imaginary Arcadia. *Il Pastor Fido* is written with considerable dramatic power, but to-day its main charm lies in the exquisite lyrics which embellish the five acts. It was published towards the end of the year 1589, with a dedication to Carlo Emanuele I. of Savoy, and was frequently represented upon the stage with the greatest success. There are innumerable Italian editions, and an English translation by an anonymous member of the Dymock family saw the light in 1602, whilst a second humbly inscribed to Charles Prince of Wales, from the pen of Sir William Fanshawe, was published 4to, 1647. It may be worth remarking that Fanshawe turned

> With mangled Fist he grasp'd the Box,
> Giving the Table bloody knocks,
> He throws—and calls for Plague and Pox
>   T'assist him.
> Some twenty shillings he did catch,
> H'ad like t'have made a quick dispatch,
> Nor could Time's Register, my Watch,
>   Have mist him.

> As Luck would have it, in came *Will*,
> Perceiving things went very ill,
> Quoth he, y'ad better go and swill
>   Canary.
> We steer'd our course to *Dragon Green*,
> Which is in *Fleetstreet* to be seen,
> When we drank Wine, not foul, but clean
>   Contrary.

[1] 10 December, 1537, to 6 October, 1612. Giovanni Battista Guarini was a grandson of the eminent classical scholar of that name. For further details one may consult Rossi *Battista Guarini ed il Pastor Fido*, Torino, 1886; and Flamini *Il Cinquecento*, Milano, 1902.

Fletcher's *The Faithful Shepherdess*[1] into easy Latin verse[2] as *La Fida Pastoria, Comœdia Pastoralis,* and in the introduction he writes : " Enimuero quanti ego æstimo GUARINUM, & quantum ueneror, illum ipsum testor *Pastorem Fidelem,* qui ut semper fuit apud Italos celeberrimus, *Italumque* Fontem petentes ; sic nunc apud Nostrates etiam, uel bis coctus, & me Interprete, numeratur in deliciis." Fanshawe's translation gave Settle something more than a model for his pastoral in rhyme, *Pastor Fido ; or, The Faithful Shepherd,* which was produced at Dorset Garden in the spring of 1677, with Betterton and his wife, Smith, Mrs. Mary Lee and Mrs. Hughes in the cast.[3] Other pastoral plays of the period were Flecknoe's

[1] The most recent presentation of this exquisite Pastoral was by The Phœnix, under the special direction of Sir Thomas Beecham at the Shaftesbury Theatre, 24 and 25 June, 1923. The play was produced by Miss Edith Craig.

[2] Fanshawe's metres are often very beautiful. For example he turns thus the first speech of the Satyr,

> Thorough yon same bending plain,
> That flings his arms down to the main,
> And through these thick woods have I run . . .

> Illam planitiem per aestuosam
> Quæ curuat tremulo Mari lacertos,
> Hoc et spissicomum nemus cucurri,
> Cui nunquam iubar ima basiauit
> Ex quo Uer cupidum auspicatur annos.
> Ut *Pani* (domino meo) placerem,
> Hoc illuc sine fine cursitaui,
> Fructus propter eum legens, rogata
> Cui multa dape proximis tenebris
> Ipsius Domina est, corusca *Syrinx.*

That exquisite lyric *Come, shepherds, come !* is gracefully rendered as follows :

CANTIO

> Uenite, *Pastores, actutum,*
>   Uenite, uenite,
>   Dum statis in flore uitæ ;
>   Nemus uiride est mutum,
> Et nunquam feret illa cocleata
> Ulli Basia ; blandulis nec illos
> Nodos innumerabiles lacertis
> Qui dantur : mera suauitas, Facesque
> Queis accenditur impotens senectus,
> Et sanguis quoque uirginis rebellet !
>   Tunc, si unquam,
>   Nunc, aut nunquam
>   Sumite gratis
>   Id quod ego
>   Nulla nego
>   Quando petatis.

[3] Settle's *Pastor Fido* was well liked, and was revised in 1689 and 1694.

Love's Kingdom,[1] which was acted at Lincoln's Inn Fields probably in 1664; and the anonymous [2] *The Constant Nymph; or, the Rambling Shepheard*, which was produced at Dorset Garden about August, 1677. Thomas Forde's *Love's Labyrinth; or, The Royal Shepherdess*, the scene of which is laid in Arcadia, was printed 8vo, 1660, but was almost certainly not performed in the public theatre.

It was inevitable that pastorals should be popular in the theatre, so extraordinary a vogue had the pastoral romance in the library. One of the earliest of this kind, *Daphnis and Chloe*, is also one of the loveliest, and at the dawn of the Renaissance, the *Idylls* of Theocritus and Vergil's *Eclogues*, Moschus and Calpurnius, Hesiod and the *Metamorphoses* of Ovid all contributed their several elements to form the ideal of a pastoral Arcadia. What has been well termed *la volutta idillica*, " the sensuous sensibility to beauty, finding fit expression in the Idyll," was among the most prominent characteristics of Renaissance art and literature. Men dreamed of a golden age of rural simplicity tempered by a courtly elegance, and there came into existence a visionland of romance, a region called Arcadia, a realm of fairest maidens and courtliest shepherds, a wonder-world of chivalry and grace, where every reader might wander at his own sweet will by crystal purling streams that watered meadows fragrant with a thousand parti-coloured flowers, whose sweet breath was wafted gently on the balmy zephyrs in that Arcady of eternal spring. It was a land where every shepherd boy might prove a prince, stolen at birth from his royal cradle, and brought up at the bidding of a solemn oracle or at the mysterious hest of the Gods by some reverend councillor living disguised in a wattle hut 'neath the forest shade, or perchance tutored by an ancient priest of Diana, or some sage hermit devoted to the chapel of sylvan Pan. This then was the world which fascinated old and young alike, poet and warrior, man of business and monk, youth and maiden at Madrid and Naples, in the London of Elizabeth and the London of Anne, the world which Marie Antoinette created at Versailles whilst the very foundations of society were crumbling round the French throne. It was artificial, it was fanciful, it was fantastic, it was sometimes (be it whispered) not a little ridiculous, but do not let us laugh at it; let us refrain from treating it with contempt, for Shakespeare himself has trod its glades, Sidney has described its commonweal, Jacopo Sannazzaro is its cosmographer, Montemayor and D'Urfé [3] are its historians.

[1] Described as " a Pastoral-Tragi-comedy," being an alteration of the same author's *Love's Dominion*, " a Dramatick Piece, full of Excellent Morality; written as a Pattern for the Reformed Stage," 8vo, 1654. *Love's Kingdom* " had the misfortune to be hissed by the Audience."

[2] " Written by a Person of Quality."

[3] *L'Astrée* was published in various parts, the first of which appeared in 1608, and the fifth or last part of which was issued by Baro, the secretary and friend of D'Urfé in

" Que je regrette que ce sont là des fables ! " was the exclamation of a celebrated writer when he had finished the perusal of the *Astrée*. That pattern of a noble gentleman, Don Quixote de la Mancha, when he was perforce obliged to lay aside for a while the profession of arms, conceived a new and ingenious fancy, to buy a flock of sheep and tend them as the shepherd Quixotis, who with the shepherd Pansino would range the woods the hills and meadows singing and versifying. " The oaks, the cork trees, the chestnut trees, will afford us both lodging and diet, the willows will yield us their shade . . . the moon and stars, our tapers of the night, shall light our evening walks. Light hearts will make us merry, and mirth will make us sing. Love will inspire us with a theme and wit, and Apollo with harmonious lays. So shall we become famous, not only while we live, but make our loves eternal as our songs." In Paris, there were actually societies who tried to realize the pastoral life in practice. Country châteaux were fitted out as miniature Arcadias, and here many a marquis and marquise re-christened Mopsus and Mirtillo, Amaryllis and Galatea, played at the simplicity of artless loves, and the fidelity of rustic attachments. Gilt crooks, painted and beribboned, became a

1627. The whole was printed at Rouen in five volumes 1647. Exasperated by the extraordinary popularity of *Astrée* and the other Bergeries Charles Sorel composed *Le BergerExtravagant, où parmy des fantaisies amoureuses, l'on voit les impertinences des romans et de la poesie*, 1627. Lysis is crazed through reading pastoral romances, and adopts the life of a shepherd. This satire was translated into English 1653 and 1660 ; *The Extravagant Shepherd. The anti-romance, or the history of the shepherd Lysis*, Englished by John Davies of Kidwelly, folio, London. The extremes to which this pastoral mania had reached may be exemplified from the case of Des Yvetuax, who, with his Amaryllis, a young harp-player whom he found one day fainting at the door of his house in the faubourg Saint Germain, passed five and thirty years in the Arcadia into which he converted his house and grounds in Paris. Here, with lutes and crooks they sang poems of his own composing, and made believe that they were guarding a number of white-fleeced lambs and imaginary flocks of sheep. But after all he was realizing his dreams ; he was completely happy, and what can a man further ask ? His lot was more enviable than that of those who laughed at him.

Sorel was imitated by Du Verdier in his *Chevalier Hypocondriaque*, and by Clerville in his *Gascon Extravagant*. Thomas Corneille has a comedy " pastorale burlesque," 1653, *Le Berger Extravagant* which opens with the extravagant shepherd Lisis " *en équipage de Berger, chassant un Troupeau devant luy*." He speaks :

> Paissez, chères brebis, les fidelles compagnes,
> Paissez en liberté dans ces vertes campagnes,
> Où grace à ma Bergere, on voit regner encor
> Un siècle aussi doré que le feu siècle d'or.
> Mais ne vous repaissez que d'œillets et de roses,
> Qu'en ces lieux sous ses pas vous trouverez écloses.

Having finished his soliloquy of thirty lines, " *Il se sied sur l'herbe, et ayant tiré quelques fruits de sa Pannetiere, il se détourne et apperçoit Clarimond, qui surpris de voir un homme vestu comme les Romans nous dépeignent les Bergers, s'estoit arresté à le considerer*." Lisis greets the newcomer in the conventional way " Pan te garde, Berger. Où s'adressent tes pas ? "

INTRODUCTION

fashionable appendage to red-heeled shoes and flaxen perruques, to patched faces and silken petticoat. In Italy in particular, in Venice, in Parma, in Modena, the Arcadian Academies lasted long and counted among their members names still honoured in Italian literature. The *Pontificia Accademia degli Arcadi* dates back to February, 1656, when it arose under the auspices of Christina of Sweden, although it did not take on its definite form and official name until after the death of its patroness.[1] The *Arcadia* chose as its emblem the pipe of Pan with seven unequal reeds. *Pastorellerie*, that is to say, a definite sylvan note, must be regarded as an essential characteristic of the early academy, although, as the years went on, the members strove to keep in touch with the moving spirit of the times sans sacrifice of their traditional associations with an elegant rusticity. However, a reformed Academy, or what is practically a new foundation, was instituted in 1819, and its scientific, literary, and artistic conferences, given by the leading scholars of the day, are attended by large audiences. Since 1870 four sections of philology, Oriental, Greek, Latin and Italian, one of Philosophy and one of History have been established. The Academy issues the *Giornale Arcadico*, and the Holy Father himself is the foremost of its members.

Have we not ourselves seen here in England a revival of the Arcadian tradition, and that in all its most formal artificiality? In London, and in many of our big towns, we have shops devoted to the sale of peasant pottery, vessels which are obviously city-made, of the most bizarre contortions, daubed with the crudest colours. We have our mountebank country cottages of mediæval or Elizabethan appearance, black and white, gabled and timbered, deftly run up by some jerry contractor six months or a year ago, abodes of more than mediæval or Elizabethan discomfort. We have our small rooms, dark and naked and bare, whose few tables and chairs are arranged with the most odious simplicity. The pallet beds might have been slept upon with comfort by Cœur de Lion or Ivanhoe, but to modern limbs they are more full of torture than a miserere stall in a Gothic cathedral. All this affectation is but an endeavour to return to Arcadia, although the wrong path is being trod. Another symptom of that mental unrest whose only anodyne, as our ancestors knew so well, is the quest of the wonder-world of romance, has broken out in a neurotic craving for what is abruptly termed "the simple life." It were superfluous to recount the vagaries of its votaries, to remark upon the formless, colourless, sackcloth garments that are donned, the nut and sawdust foods that are eaten, the vegetable beverages that are drunk, the sleeping under trees, and maybe sleeping in the trees too, for there are few of us who have not had some experience of the apostles of this cult, which, if it is pushed to extremes, as is too often the case, makes men as mad as hares in March.

[1] Christina of Sweden died at Rome 19 April, 1689.

All these oddities and whim-whams are but an expression of this craving for Arcadia, as we may call it; the Arcadian complex, I imagine our neo-psychologists might label it, and it is, of course, a purely subconscious libido.

The Royal Shepherdess, Shadwell's sole contribution to pastoral drama, although realistic sketches [1] of country life and even a rural interlude occur in other of his plays, was produced at Lincoln's Inn Fields on Thursday, 25 February, 1668–9. Pepys, for whom pastoral plays had scant appeal, thus records the first performance: " At noon home and eat a bit myself, and then follow my wife and girls to the Duke of York's house and there before one, but the house infinite full, where, by and by, the King and Court come, it being a new play, or an old one new-vamped, by Shadwell, called ' The Royall Shepherdesse '; but the silliest for words and design, and everything, that ever I saw in my whole life, there being nothing in the world pleasing in it, but a good martial dance of pikemen, where Harris and another do handle their pikes to admiration; but never less satisfied with a play in my life." We may, however, largely discount this harsh sentence when we remember that the diarist was suffering from so violent a cold that his voice had entirely gone, and, in addition his throat was as sore as a Morris dancer's heels, whilst his eyes were putting him to considerable pain, which can hardly have been alleviated by the candlelight of the garish theatre. In fact the very next day he was obliged to stay late in bed and send his excuses for absence from an important meeting over which the Duke of York was to preside. Not that this prevented him from going to the theatre in the afternoon: " though I could not speak, yet I went with my wife and girls to the King's playhouse, to show them that, and there saw ' The Faithfull Shepherdesse.' But Lord! what an empty house, there not being, as I could tell the people as many as to make up above £10 in the whole house! The being of a new play at the other house, I suppose, being the cause, though it be so silly a play that I wonder how there could be enough people to go thither two days together, and not leave more to fill this house. The emptiness of the house took away our pleasure a great deal, though I liked it the better; for that I plainly discern the musick is the better by how much the house the emptier." There can be no doubt that the rival company had hastily put on Fletcher's *The Faithful Shepherdess* as a counter-attraction of the same kind to eclipse the new production at Lincoln's Inn Fields. For *The Faithful Shepherdess* [2] had been produced with the most lavish scenery and costumes, and as an

---

[1] E.g., *Epsom-Wells*, *The Lancashire Witches*, *Bury-Fair*. We have a pastoral interlude in *The Libertine*.

[2] On Saturday, 13 June, 1663, Pepys speaks of *The Faithful Shepherdess* at the Theatre Royal as " much thronged after, and often shewn, but it is only for the scenes' sake, which is very fine indeed and worth seeing."

extra attraction songs were introduced and executed by the celebrated Baldassare Ferri of Perugia,[1] a castrato of magnificent soprano voice, which had " an indescribable limpidity, combined with the greatest agility and facility, a perfect intonation, a brilliant shake, and inexhaustable length of breath."

Downes tells us that *The Royal Shepherdess* was acted for six days, which, it must be remembered, was a very fair success for the time.[2] There is no evidence, however, of any particular revival, and in his next play, Shadwell was to turn from romance to exploit his own particular vein.

Although Shakespeare and Fletcher were both immensely popular upon the Restoration stage, and although Ben Jonson's comedies, especially those masterpieces *The Alchemist, Volpone, The Silent Woman* and *Bartholomew Fair* [3] were continually given with the greatest applause, his Roman tragedies, as is not surprising, did not appear in the theatrical repertory. Great and magnificent poems as they are, one very practical reason stood in the way of their production, that of expense. To produce either *Sejanus* or *Catiline* in anything but a most haphazard fashion, which would not for one moment have been tolerated, must entail an enormous outlay. In his epilogue to the post-Restoration revival of *Every Man in his Humour*, the Earl of Dorset introduced Jonson's ghost, who, waving aside the actor who had commenced to address the audience, delivered some seventeen lines which doubtless voice Dorset's own opinions :

> Hold and give way for I myself will speak ;
> Can you encourage so much insolence,
> And add new faults still to the great offence
> Your ancestors so rashly did commit
> Against the mighty powers of art and wit,
> When they condemn'd those noble works of mine,
> *Sejanus*, and my best love, *Catiline*.

---

[1] 1610–1680.

[2] Eight days, which was the length of the runs of Davenant's *The Wits ;* of Betterton's *The Unjust Judge ;* of a revival of *The Dutchess of Malfey* and of many other favourite plays, Downes considers excellent. To continue acting twelve days, as was the success of *The Siege of Rhodes*, or ten days the life of Porter's immensely popular *The Villain* and Orrery's *King Henry the Fifth*, was very remarkable ; whereas the thirteen days of *The Adventures of Five Hours* and the fifteen days of the gorgeous pageantry of *King Henry the Eighth* were altogether exceptional and extraordinary.

[3] *The Alchemist* was revived with very great success by the Phœnix under my direction on 18 and 19 March, 1923. Similarly *Volpone* was presented on 30 January and 1 February, 1921, and again for one special performance 29 June, 1923 ; *Bartholomew Fair* was revived 26 and 27 June, 1921. There was a revival of *The Silent Woman* for two performances in November, 1924, and it had previously been given in May, 1905, by the Mermaid Repertory Theatre under the direction of Mr. Philip Carr.

Repent, or on your guilty heads shall fall
The curse of many a rhyming pastoral.
The three bold *Beauchamps*[1] shall revive again,
And with the *London 'Prentice* conquer *Spain*.
All the dull follies of the former age
Shall find applause on this corrupted stage.
But, if you pay the great arrears of praise,
So long since due to my much-injur'd plays,
From all past crimes I first will set you free,
And then inspire someone to write like me.

It is plain from these lines that the most influential patrons of literature of the day held *Catiline* in the highest estimation, as indeed well they might. Says Davies:[2] "The Duke of Buckingham and Lord Dorset were admirers of Jonson to a degree of idolatry; it is very probable that, by liberal promises, they encouraged the actors to bring forward this forgotten tragedy. Certain it is that the play was acted several times during the reign of Charles II. The action of Hart in *Catiline* was universally applauded." We know from Pepys that *Catiline* was produced at the Theatre Royal on Friday, 18 December, 1668, Hart played the title-rôle, Mohun, Cethegus; Burt, Cicero; Mrs. Corey, Sempronia; and the whole strength of the company, Kynaston, Beeston, Reeves, Wintershal, Cartwright, Gradwell and Richard Bell, helped to complete the cast. The King had granted the actors five hundred pounds for costumes; the battle was arranged with unusual care; the Senate scene had been mounted with a magnificence that almost foreshadowed Phelps and Charles Kean, Henry Irving and Tree, and no doubt the Jonson enthusiasts spared neither time nor money to make this splendid revival an intellectual and theatrical triumph. Shadwell was by this time widely known in Town as one of the most thoroughgoing, not to say fanatical, of the worshippers

---

[1] *The Bold Beachams*, which is not extant, has been doubtfully attributed to Thomas Heywood, who is the author of *The foure Prentises of London*, to which reference is here also made. *The foure Prentises* was acted at the Red Bull about 1599–1600, and printed 4to, 1615; also 4to, 1632. In this play Godfrey visits Spain. Both these pieces were immensely popular with the groundlings and cits.

Cf. the Induction to *The Knight of the Burning Pestle*, where the Citizen's Wife cries: 'I was ne'er at one of these plays, as they say, before; but I should have seen Jane Shore once, and my husband hath promised me any time this twelvemonth, to carry me to the Bold Beachams, but in truth he did not."

[2] *Dramatic Miscellanies*, London, 1783, Vol. II, pp. 88–89. Davies also adds: "The duke of Buckingham has found room in his Rehearsal to give praise to Ben Jonson, though he nowhere mentions Shakespeare. But the duke, it seems, conversed with Ben when his grace was a boy of about thirteen, and the poet was near his grand climacterique, and thence conceived such a veneration for him, that it never left him afterwards."

at Jonson's shrine. He had already acquired a name among men of letters, and he was now defiantly waving aloft the banner of rare Ben, and provoking the critics to tread on the tail of his coat. In the preface to *The Sullen Lovers*, he had loudly extolled " the practice of *Ben Johnson*, whom I think all Dramatick Poets ought to imitate, though none are like to come near ; he being the onely person that appears to me to have made perfect Representations of Humane Life." He even goes so far as to say that he never saw in any comedy any character, except that of Falstaff, " comparable to any of *Johnson's* considerable Humours : You will pardon this digression when I tell you he is the man of all the World, I most passionately admire for his Excellency in Drammatick-Poetry." Dryden, who had dared to say that Jonson did not want wit but was frugal of it, and that Shakespeare was the greater wit, is severely rapped over the knuckles for such audacity.[1] And yet Dryden and Shadwell were fast friends in these early days, there was not even the shadow of the cloud upon that horizon which in but a few years was so black as night, fierce as ten furies, and terrible as hell in the hurricane of political passions. Such was Shadwell's worship of Jonson that he set himself to imitate his idol in every respect, and Nature indeed seems to have done her part to help him, for, as he grew in years, he increased in bulk, until he almost rivalled the titanic girth of his mighty original. On Saturday, 19 September, 1668, Pepys, being at the Theatre Royal, saw *The Silent Woman*, " The best comedy, I think, that ever was wrote ; and sitting by Shadwell the Poet he was big with admiration of it."

The following day, Sunday, Pepys notes that he stayed dinner till past one o'clock for Henry Harris, the young actor, " whom I invited, and to bring Shadwell the Poet with him ; but they come not, and so a good dinner lost, through my own folly." There is one other reference to Shadwell in the diary. On Friday, 16 April, 1669, Pepys went to the first performance of *Guzman* [2] at the Duke of York's theatre, and after the performance was over, whilst he was loitering in the pit " I did meet with Shadwell, the Poet, who, to my great wonder, do tell me that my Lord of Orrery did write this play, trying what he could do in comedy, since his heroique plays could do no more wonders. This do trouble me ; for it is as mean a thing, and so he says, as hath been upon the stage a great while ; and Harris, who hath no part in it, did come to me, and told me in discourse that he was glad of it, it being a play that will not take." Downes, on the contrary, says that it took very well, and, although one can quite understand that it would not commend itself to Shadwell's

---

[1] *Of Dramatick Poesie*, 4to, 1668. " As for *Johnson* . . . One cannot say he wanted Wit, but rather that he was frugal of it. . . . If I would compare him with *Shakespear*, I must acknowledge him the more correct Poet, but *Shakespear* the greater Wit."

[2] Not printed until 1693, folio.

taste, being a broad farce founded upon a Spanish plot, yet it has its amusing scenes, particularly the astrological interviews, and worse plays [1] have been received with tolerance, if not with favour.

But the Jonsonians did not have matters entirely their own way. Shadwell's insistent admiration aroused opposition among his contemporaries, and Mrs. Behn, in her Epistle to the Reader, which prefaces *The Dutch Lover*, 4to, 1673,[2] a Spanish play, the scene of which lies in Madrid, and which was probably as severely criticized by Shadwell as had been Orrery's comedy, very plainly attacks her fellow-dramatist. She writes : " Plays have no great room for that which is men's great advantage over women, that is Learning ; we all well know that the immortal Shakespeare's Plays (who was not guilty of much more of this than often falls to women's share) have better pleas'd the World than Johnson's works, though by the way 'tis said that Benjamin was no such Rabbi neither, for I am inform'd that his Learning was but Grammar high ; (sufficient indeed to rob poor Salust of his best orations) and it hath been observ'd that they are apt to admire him most confoundedly, who have just such a scantling of it as he had ; and I have seen a man the most severe of Johnson's sect, sit with his Hat remov'd less than a hair's breadth from one sullen posture for almost three hours at *The Alchymist ;* who at that excellent Play of *Harry the Fourth* (which yet I hope is far enough from Farce) hath very hardly kept his Doublet whole ; but affectation hath always had a greater share both in the action and discourse of men than truth and judgement have ; and for our Modern ones, except our most unimitable Laureat, I dare to say I know of none that write at such a formidable rate, but that a woman may well hope to reach their greatest heights. Then for their musty rules of Unity, and God knows what besides, if they meant anything, they are enough intelligible and as practible by a woman ; but rarely methinks that they disturb their heads with any other rule of Playes besides the making them pleasant, and avoiding of scurrility, might much better be employed in studying how to improve men's too imperfect knowledge of that ancient English Game which hight long Laurence : And if Comedy should be the picture of ridiculous mankind I wonder anyone should think it such a sturdy task, whilst we are furnish'd with such precious Originals as him I lately told you of ; if at least that Character do not dwindle into Farce, and so become too mean an entertainment for those persons who are us'd to think." Mrs. Behn was very friendly with the Howards,[3] and here then

---

[1] The verdict of Sir Adolphus Ward that it is " an uninteresting comedy " seems too severe.

[2] Produced at Dorset Garden in February, 1672–1673. Edward Angel, a leading comedian, played the title-rôle Haunce van Ezel.

[3] She addressed a copy of complimentary verses to the Hon. Edward Howard upon his comedy *The Six Days Adventure* which when produced at the Duke of York's House

we have a direct attack upon Shadwell. Her personal vehemence is wholly exceptional, for she was a good-natured hussy, and only once or twice in her later years when she was worn out with work, sick and racked with pain, does she permit her pen any overt reproach or detraction of individuals.[1] But Thomas Shadwell, as is very evidently shown throughout the whole of his career, was not a figure who could be ignored or disregarded; by sheer heavy weight and burly solidity he forced himself and his opinions upon the notice of his contemporaries. There must have been something very remarkable in the man's personality, almost a certain brute force which compelled consideration from friend and foe alike. His views, which are extreme and exaggerated on any subject, religious, political, or literary, are voiced with tremendous thumps and explosive gusto; his dogmatism exhibits the utmost intolerance; to right and left he delivers great swashing blows, and although his bludgeon often strikes out blindly it never fails to fall with a mighty thud. Prejudice and passion often make him beat the air, whilst his agile opponents with their shining lances wound him in a thousand places. For he is particularly vulnerable, but nevertheless, in spite of his bluntness and wrong-headedness, there is, fortunately, much in this leviathan of literature which, now that the din and dust of the fray is over, we can both enjoy and admire.

As we have said, Shadwell was in the front rank of the Jonsonian enthusiasts, and loyalty to Jonson was with him a conviction as rigid as the unbending laws of the Medes and Persians. There are I imagine, none with any literary apperception who would deny that Ben Jonson's masterpieces are among the greatest things in English literature. The homely old couplet is true which runs:

> The Fox, the *Alchemist*, and *Silent Woman*,
> Done by *Ben Jonson*, and outdone by no man.

And what other author is there who may reach the excellencies of *Bartholomew Fair, Every Man in his Humour, Catiline, The Poetaster*, to name but a few? Yet it cannot be denied that there was a certain decay in Jonson's dramatic powers, and of his last plays one or two at least must I fear be ranked among his 'dotages,' as Dryden has termed them, surely with reason and respect.

But in the ears of the Jonsonian fanatic this would have sounded as rank blasphemy. It were treason to suggest that any line, any hemistich

in the spring of 1671 was a failure. In Mrs. Behn's Miscellany of 1685 is included " a Pindaric by the Honourable *Edward Howard* to Mrs. B. Occasioned by a Copy she made on his Play called the *New Eutopia*."

[1] Her ungenerous *Satyr on Dryden* was written when she was ill, and rather represents bad temper and failing nerves than any true opinion of her own.

written by Ben Jonson were anything other than impeccable. The un-reasoning extent to which this idolatry, harmful both to the god and the worshipper, was carried would seem almost incredible had we not to-day an exact parallel in the fanaticism with which the cult of Shakespeare is pushed by certain monomaniacs. Such intemperance can but defeat its own ends. It is no exaggeration to say that there are zealots who regard Shakespeare as a person almost divine. To suggest that any play of his is not peerless perfection, to criticize any speech or line, to write that Shakespeare is sometimes dull, sometimes faulty, that we are weary of the *Merchant of Venice*, that the braggadocio of *Henry the Fifth* in spite of some splendid rhetoric, is unhealthy ; that *Coriolanus* is tedious to a degree ; to hint at any one of these truths is to excite a whirlwind of vituperation, nay, even personal abuse and actual calumny, gusts of malice which leave the critic astounded and amazed. Reviewers have been hectored into silence or rather into praise. Shakespeare has, with some, literally assumed the same position as that in which the *Authorised Version* was held by Biblical literalists, and these bigots would treat the man who dared to suggest that sometimes Shakespeare nods and sleeps in the same way as the Puritan fathers would have dealt with one who denied the inspiration of Holy Writ. What is perhaps the saddest feature of all is that this movement does not include the true lovers of Shakespeare, but merely a number of disingenuous persons who are utilizing the fashion for purposes of their own, and who, by means of insipid essays, asinine associations, worthless performances, and pseudo-educational stunts, contrive their own self-advertisement and braggart glorification.

The Jonsonian enthusiast under Charles II. was at least sincere and honest. In the preface to *The Sullen Lovers* Shadwell had emphatically stated that the highest aim of all dramatists must be the imitation of Ben Jonson. There are certainly several characters in this, his first comedy, which are wholly in the Jonsonian vein ; and in his third play, his second comedy, *The Humorists*, he swerves not a hairbreadth from the models of his master, and emphatically lays down as a postulate : " I am so far from thinking it impudence to endeavour to imitate him, that it would rather (in my opinion) seem impudent in me not to do it."

The very title of Shadwell's play, *The Humorists*, strikes the keynote. Mediæval physiology had formulated a theory of " humours," the four elements which composed the body and determine the temperament of the individual. Fire is hot and dry ; air is hot and moist ; water is cold and moist ; earth is cold and dry. In the human system fire produced choler ; air produced blood ; water, phlegm ; and earth, melancholy. An equal or equivalent admixture of the four humours produced the well-balanced normal [1] individual. In *Cynthia's Revels* " a creature of a most

---

[1] Actually, of course, there is no such thing as a normal individual.

perfeét and divine temper " is " neither too fantaétically melancholy, too slowly phlegmatic, too lightly sanguine, or too rashly choleric." But in the ordinary everyday individual one of these humours (or a variant of one of these humours) ſtrongly predominated, and so the type was determined. This physical theory loomed large in English literature towards the end of the sixteenth century. It seems to have made a special appeal to the Elizabethan imagination, which was ever prone to concentrate upon certain traits, and to exaggerate. In a leéture at Florence on Ariſtotle about the year 1586, the head of the *Accademia della Crusca*, Lionardo Salviati, gave as his definition of humour " a peculiar quality of nature according to which every one is inclined to some special thing more than to any other." It is, of course, exceedingly doubtful whether Jonson had any knowledge of such an exaét interpretation, but, none the less, one might very well accept it as entirely applicable to the Jonsonian canon. Nowadays probably we should call a " humoriſt " a " type." They are often cranks, persons who are (as we say) " Mad upon such-or-such a thing." A man may be " mad " upon aéting, or dancing, or the cinematograph, or bridge, golf, football, or a thousand other trivialities.[1] All these men are humoriſts, and if a humour were pushed to an extreme, the man would be a monomaniac. In literature the humoriſt is very closely conneéted with those extremely popular " Charaéters," which are moſtly modelled upon the work of Theophraſtus,[2] the favourite pupil of the Stagirite philosopher, the famous Ἠθικοὶ Χαρακτῆρες. This served as a pattern in English literature to Overbury, Earle, Samuel Butler ; in French to La Bruyère and many other minor names. The Elizabethan conception of Humour and Humoriſts is summed up by Samuel Rowlands in an epigram of the moſt trenchant direétness :

> Aske *Humors* why a Feather he doth weare ?
> It is his humor (by the Lord) heele sweare.
> Or what he doth with such a Horse-taile locke ?
> Or why vpon a Whoore he spends his stocke ?
> He hath a Humor doth determine so.
> Why in the Stop-throate fashion doth he go,
> With Scarfe about his necke ? Hat without band ?
> It is his humor, sweete sir vnderſtand.

[1] For if they were concerns of importance he could not be said to be " mad " upon them, but rather laudably, if somewhat intensively, intereſted.

[2] 278 B.C. is generally given as the date of his death. The *Charaéters* are in thirty chapters. Various theories have been advanced as regards the composition of the book. Some hold that it was designed by Theophraſtus as we now have it ; others consider that it is a colleétion of fugitive sketches, which were put together by his friends after his death. It has even been thought that it is a set of extraéts from two treatises which he wrote upon moral philosophy.

What cause his Purse is so extreame diſtreſt,
That often times t'is scarcely penny bleſt?
Onely a Humor: If you queſtion why?
His tongue is nere vnfurnish'd with a lye:
It is his Humor too he doth proteſt.
Or why with Serjants he is so oppreſt,
That like to Ghoſtes they haunt him e(u)rie day?
A rascall Humor, doth not loue to pay.
Obieƈt, why Bootes and Spurres are ſtill in season?
His Humor answeres; Humor is his reason.
If you perceiue his wittes in wetting shrunke,
It commeth of a Humor, to be drunke:
When you behould his lookes pale, thin, and poore,
Th' occasion is, his Humor, and a Whore:
And euery thing that he doth vndertake,
It is a vaine, for sencelesse Humors sake.[1]

Although Shadwell was by far the moſt important exponent of Humours upon the Reſtoration ſtage, there were several other dramatiſts who carried on the tradition. One of the moſt remarkable plays of this school is John Wilson's capital comedy *The Cheats*, which was produced at the Theatre Royal in Vere St. March, 1662–3, and which is thoroughly Jonsonian in atmosphere and charaƈterization. In a letter of the 28th of that month Abraham Hill writes: "the new play called *The Cheats* has been attempted upon the ſtage; but it is so scandalous that it is forbidden." Although there is in exiſtence [2] a MS. copy of the play in which Sir Henry Herbert, the censor, has marked those passages that did not meet with his approval, we are ſtill left wondering what can have given offence. The play itself is certainly an innocent harmless thing. There is a good deal of satire, of course, in the charaƈter of Scruple,[3] who is willing to conform "reform, transform, perform, deform, inform, and form" for "£300 a year, and a goodly house upon't," and who quotes the delightful example of our brother Fox "that had so little wit as to write his Book of Martyrs, yet had enough to keep himself from being one of the number," and who finds that in conscience he muſt forsake his flock under the inspiration of a higher call, and who cannot be tempted even by Friday night suppers and purifying dinners, jellies, venison and white fowl, but who, when the siſters offer him £40ɔ a year, feels that he has a call from on high to remain with them, and promises never to forsake his lambs. The piƈture, however, seems exaƈtly true to life, and, in any case, it is not a whit more

---

[1] Epigramme 27, *The Letting of Humours Blood in the Head-Vaine.* 1600.
[2] At Worceſter College, Oxford.
[3] Admirably aƈted by Lacy, of whom there exiſts a portrait in this part.

cynical than the Chadband and Stiggins, the Rev. Melchisdech Howler of
Charles Dickens, or even Trollope's Obadiah Slope. The other characters,
Alderman and Mrs. Whitebroth, Mopus the astrologer and his wife ; the
Major and the Captain ; Double Diligence, the Puritan constable, are all
excellently drawn, and would have delighted rare Ben himself. A second
comedy by Wilson, *The Projectors*,[1] which probably was never acted, presents us with a complete assembly of humours, where Sir Gudgeon Credulous bears something more than an accidental likeness to Fabian Fitz-
dotterel in *The Devil is an Ass.*

With regard to other Restoration plays that utilize this tradition it must
be sufficient to name but a few. It is certainly marked in the work of
the Duke of Newcastle, who, however, was writing whilst Jonson was
still alive, and who had been a patron of the great dramatist. *The Town-
Shifts ; or, the Suburb-Justice,* by Edward Revet, produced at Lincoln's Inn
Fields in 1671, which Langbaine commends as an " Instructive " comedy,
introduces several notably Elizabethan characters of this type, Clowt the
Constable, Mold the Sexton, and Goody Fells. *Tunbridge-Wells ; or, a Day's
Courtship,*[2] acted at Dorset Garden in 1678, assuredly owes something
more than a hint to *Bartholomew Fair,* and we are not surprised to meet
with Parson Quibble, Paywel, and Owmuch. It is perhaps just worth
remarking that the second title of a comedy called *The Morning Ramble,*
acted at Dorset Garden in November, 1672, is *The Town-Humours*,[3] and
the author completely neglects the course of his plot to devote himself to
the delineation of individuals. *Mr. Turbulent ; or, The Melanchollicks,*
Dorset Garden early in 1682 ; and *The Rampant Alderman ; or, News from
the Exchange,* " a Farce patcht up out of several plays," 4to, 1685 ; both
clearly evince their Jonsonian source, and this is also unmistakable in
Henry Higden's *The Wary Widdow ; or, Sir Noisy Parrat,* produced at Drury-
Lane, February, 1692–3, which, although furnished with a prologue by
Sir Charles Sedley, miscarried [4] in the action. Of the same school is *The
Braggadocio,* printed 4to, 1691, but seemingly not performed. It is said to be

---

[1] 4to, 1665.

[2] Langbaine says, " I have been told it was writ by Mr. *Rawlins.*"

[3] " This Play is said to be written by One Mr. *Pane,* and may be accounted a good
Comedy." Langbaine. Henry Nevil *alias* Payne was also the author of *The Fatal
Jealousie,* acted at Dorset Garden in August, 1672, and *The Siege of Constantinople,* acted
at the same house in November, 1674. Perhaps he is even better known for his gallant
loyalty than as a dramatist.

[4] The old story, reported by Whincop, that Higden had introduced such generous
tippling into his scenes that the performers were fairly raddled by the end of the third
act, and accordingly the house was obliged to dismiss amid hisses and catcalls would
seem to be a canard. Yet Tom Brown has two or three epigrams on the event, one of
which is entitled to Mr. Higden " *upon his Play's being damn'd, for having too much Eating
and Drinking in it.*" Also " *Upon persecuting it with Cat-calls* " ; and " Henrico Higden,
Arm. Cum. infeliciter ipsi Comoedia cesserit, 1693."

written by that very elusive individual " a Person of Quality," and it contains at least one well-drawn character, Flush, who, through discontent, never ceases to rail against his university, and, tradition avers, was closely drawn from somebody living at that time. Stock humours appear in the three comedies written by young Thomas Dilke of Oriel, who held a lieutenant's commission under Lord Raby, afterwards Earl of Strafford. The best is perhaps the first, *The Lover's Luck*, produced at Lincoln's Inn Fields late in 1695. Here we at once recognize such old friends as Sir Nicholas Purflew, " a formal Herald and Antiquary," and Alderman Whim, " a Projector and Humourist." Dilke indeed may be said to be a close follower of Shadwell himself. Unfortunately the town seemed tired of humours at second hand. His *The City Lady; or, Folly Reclaim'd*, met with a cool reception at Lincoln's Inn Fields in the spring of 1697; whilst *The Pretenders; or, The Town Unmask'd*, acted at the same house in the following year, was an even more decided failure.

It may be remarked that many of D'Urfey's comedies contain characters which are distinctly humours, and this is particularly the case with those which were produced between 1680 and 1703, for D'Urfey was often clever enough to forestall the taste of the town, although he had not sufficient acumen to realize when a fashion was beginning to get stale, and he rides his poor foundered horse to death. In *The Virtuous Wife; or, Good Luck at Last*, which was produced at Dorset Garden late in 1679, Sir Frolick Whimsey is described as " a humorous old Knight," whilst in *The Intrigues at Versailles; or, A Jilt in all Humours*, produced at Lincoln's Inn Fields in the spring of 1696-7, Sir Blunder Bosse is described as " a dull sordid brute and Mongril whose Humour is, to call every Body by Clownish Names," and in the Dedication, speaking of his many plays, D'Urfey says, " some have pleased more, some less, according as the Town Humour eb'd and flowed." Again, in the letter prefixed by Charles Gildon to *The Marriage-Hater Match'd*, this critic compliments D'Urfey and declares " Such a variety of Humours and Characters I have seldom seen in one Play; and those so truly drawn, that they all look like Principal Parts; and that, which is more, they are all *New*, and so worthy observation, that indeed I admire the humour of Madam *La Pupsey* has been so long neglected, since grown to be so general a custom, that the Lap-Dog takes up all the thoughts of the fair Sex, whilst the faithful Lover sighs in vain and at a distance unregarded." He also singles out for particular approbation the fact that " the humour of *Van Grin* is new "; and a little later he applauds " the pleasant Humour of *Bias*." That clever lampoon *Poeta Infamis; or, A Poet not worth Hanging*, 1692, tells us how D'Urfey personally taught the actor Anthony Leigh the humours of the rôle of Van Grin, and how he prided himself upon the novelty La Pupsey. Shadwell's self-gratulation will be readily remembered when he proclaimed that in *The True Widow* three of the humours "*are wholly new, not so much as touch'd upon before, and the following ones are new in the greatest part.*"

With deliberation Shadwell chose as the title for his second comedy *The Humorists*, for thereby he was boldly enunciating to the world his literary creed. The great success of *The Sullen Lovers* had brought him so warm and particular an invitation to Welbeck that the soul of the rising young dramatist was vastly gratified and rejoiced. Here he was encouraged to make a lengthy stay and daily admitted into Newcastle's public and private conversation. "When I had the favour daily to be admitted to your Grace's more retired Conversation, when I alone enjoyed the honour, I must declare I never spent my hours with that pleasure, or improvement; nor shall I ever enough acknowledge that, and the rest of the Honours done me by your Grace as much above my condition as my merit," writes the ecstatic poet. The fact is Shadwell was now received at Welbeck on the footing of an intimate friend, "having had nothing to recommend me," he modestly assures his patron, "but the Birth and Education, without the Fortune of a Gentleman, besides some Writings of mine, which your Grace was pleased to like."

In the spring (April), 1669, Shadwell was in London, but shortly afterwards he seems to have gone to Welbeck, where he spent several months, working meanwhile at his new comedy, scene by scene of which he used to submit to his noble host as it was composed. When he returned to London he formally read the script of the play to Betterton, to his close friend Henry Harris, and to the other actors of the Duke's company. It was received with compliments and congratulations, for Shadwell was now of some standing in the theatrical world, and this hearty and spontaneous welcome must have been no ordinary encouragement, since he was mainly relying upon this comedy, in which he had (so to speak) proclaimed his gospel, effectually to establish his position as a dramatist. The warning then that grave exception had been taken to his comedy, a work sponsored by Newcastle's august approval, must have come literally as a bolt from the blue. In the original copy of the play, there was a good deal of satire on particular persons, and it was quite unmistakably intimated to Shadwell that all this must be deleted in its entirety. It is barely possible to guess at the identity of the persons who took such umbrage at the play, but it is scarcely hazardous to suppose that the Howards had something to do with this prohibition. Presumably the aggravated parties were persons of some considerable standing, else they would hardly have had the power to compel (albeit indirectly) such drastic changes; they must, moreover, have been persons who were in touch with, and possessed influence in, the theatre; persons, probably, whom the censor was unwilling to disoblige, and to whom he had shown, or sent, a report upon Shadwell's new play.

The Howards would fulfil all these conditions. Although, no doubt, extremely mortified at the caricature in *The Sullen Lovers*, once the thing was public property, Sir Robert Howard seems to have had the good sense to conceal his displeasure under a mask of indifference, but it only stands to reason to suppose that he would prevent any repetition of the annoyance, and that he would keep a sharp eye upon the future productions of the young dramatist. It is not probable that the original version of *The Humorists* again scarified his actual victims of a little more than two years before, but they, no doubt, were not slow to ensure that the script of the new comedy should be seen by those individuals whom it burlesqued, and accordingly, Shadwell was obliged to make the most drastic alterations in his completed piece, for, as he somewhat plaintively deplores, "the Sting was taken out" of his scenes. Nor was this all, a clique banded together, and on the day of the first performance assembled in force to hiss him from the stage. Yet another misfortune supervened, and, what was the more galling, this last accident could easily have been prevented. The actors "were extremely imperfect in the Action of it," that is to say in modern parlance "they fluffed all over the place." Anyone who knows the agony of a final rehearsal when half the cast cannot remember a word must sympathize with the martyrdom of the unhappy dramatist. Perhaps the performers had really made up their minds not to know a line,[1] and Shadwell's sensations can only have been comparable to a bout of seasickness on a rough Channel crossing. There is actual physical nausea ; there is a sinking fear that each coming moment may be worse than the last ; and there is an utter helplessness almost amounting to prostration.

Such we can well believe were Shadwell's feelings on that December afternoon of 1670, when the actors stumbled through his mutilated comedy. It certainly would not have survived after the second performance had not one of the actresses, probably Mrs. Johnson, who was famous for her dancing, introduced "the most excellent Dancings that ever has been seen on the Stage." This *bonne bouche* did not fail to attract audiences, who, for the sake of the lady, tolerated the play, and as, meanwhile, the conscience-stricken actors, ashamed of their delinquencies, had got their parts tolerable, the poor comedy was something better "understood, and liked, than at first." But it seems never fully to have recovered, and it did not remain in the repertory of the theatre.

Invaluable as a realistic picture of London life in 1670, it is in truth so topical a satire that it hardly bears the qualities of permanency. The plot, the return of Sir Richard Loveyouth, supposed dead, who remains incognito

---

[1] At a recent production of *Othello*, during the last rehearsal the producer was bound to inquire of the actor who was playing the Moor if he had really quite made up his mind that he would not know his part.

as his wife's gentleman-usher, the better to obtain first-hand evidence of her lascivious pranks and to satisfy his own eyes with the daily spectacle of her malice and lewdness, completely falls into the back-ground, when, as the title of the play proclaims, we have a series of very lively portraitures, rakes and fantasts, common women of the town, an errant bawd, a wanton city wife. All these are treated in the typical Jonsonian manner; stroke follows stroke; detail is heaped upon detail; until the very mass of observation builds up, as it were, the figure before our eyes.

To the modern reader the most amazing thing in the whole play is the character of Crazy, who is represented as grievously afflicted with the pox, and yet this terrible disease which we have learned to pity and to dread is treated with a flippancy that is bound to jar, nay, even in its ugly and painful description to revolt and oppress. Yet Crazy is obviously intended, and was received, as a legitimate figure of comedy. The fact is that venereal disease,[1] although rampant in those days, could yet be made a subject of jesting. Again and again is it alluded to with puns and laughter.[2] The Prologue, " *spoken by* Mrs. Ellen, *and* Mrs. Nepp," to Sir Robert Howard's *The Great Favourite ; Or, The Duke of Lerma*, produced at the Theatre Royal, Thursday, 21 February, 1667-68, craving a happy deliverance for the poet, concludes :

> *Nepp.* Deliver him from you that nothing spare ;
> Nay, you that would fain seem worse than you are,
> Out-talk your own Debaucheries, and tell
> With a fine Shrug, *Faith*, Jack, *I am not well.*
> *Nell.* From you that with much Ease, and little Shame,
> Can blast a Poet's, and a Woman's Fame ;
> For at first sight a well-bred Trick y'have got,
> Combing your Wiggs, to Cry, *Dam me, She's naught.*
> *Nepp.* Prithee let's say no more, but run away,
> For they'll revenge themselves on the poor Play.
> *Nell.* No matter, we have here our Party fast,
> I mean the Gentlemen we spoke of last :
> Though they deny't the Poet, yet we know,
> On us they freely wou'd their Claps bestow.

[1] It is, of course, ridiculous ignorance to say, as a recent book upon the theatre of Charles II. avers, " Sexual disease had been carried over from France," meaning presumably that the Restoration brought the pox to England. Henry VIII. died of syphilis ; and Cardinal Wolsey was at one time grievously afflicted with the pox. The common Restoration name "French disease" (*Morbus Gallicus*) which may have given occasion for the error in question does not really mean very much, certainly not that the disorder originated in, and was only spread from, France.

[2] I do not conceive that the exclamation " Pox " or " Pox on't " conveyed, or was intended to convey, anything more than our " damn." For as chairs, tables, events, are damned to-day—which is absurd—so were they in the days of Charles II. poxed.

INTRODUCTION

In the Epilogue to Duffett's rhyming comedy, *The Spanish Rogue*, produced at Lincoln's Inn Fields whilst Killigrew's company was playing
there in 1673, Mrs. Knepp, again, had the following lines :

> *Poets, from* France, *fetch'd new Intrigue, and Plot,*
> *Kind Women, new* French *Words, and Fashions got :*
> *And finding all* French *Tricks so much did please,*
> *T'oblige ye more, They got—ev'n their Disease.*
> *That too did take—and as much Honour gets*
> *As breaking Windows, or not paying debts.*
> *O 'tis so gente ! So modish ! and so fine !*
> *To shrug and cry, Faith* Jack ! *I drink no Wine :*
> *For I've a swinging Clap this very time————*

With this one may compare the Prologue, spoken by Smith, to D'Urfey's
Madam Fickle ; or, the Witty False One, produced at Dorset Garden in
November, 1676 :

> *The Stages Ruine unconcern'd you see,*
> *And Dam th' Original of Gallantry.*
> *Shou'd we leave off then, we shou'd hear you say,*
> *Dam 'em what Drones are these, why don't they Play ?*
> *'Sblud I shall never leave this Wenching vein,*
> Jack, *my last swinging Clap's broke out agen.*
> *And if we do Play—then you Censure raise,*
> *And to encourage us, Dam all our Playes.*

As we appreciate the fatal ravages, the loathly horror and suffering of
the disease such reference may well seem shocking in the last degree. But
are we so clear of flippancy ourselves ? I trow not. The word " clap "
will raise a horse-laugh in most junior common-rooms at Oxford ; more
than one obscene limerick which is heard with avidity and retailed with
applause turns for its point upon the symptoms of gonorrhœa or " syph,"
—the very abbreviation denotes some degree of familiarity, in converse
at least. Schoolboys and other unthinking creatures yet regard a quip
that plays with venereal disorders as the salt of Attic wit. I was
told by a friend that when on one occasion he happened to have hurt his
leg and walked to his office with something of a limp, various porters and
warehousemen with whom he was on excellent terms, as he crossed the
great yard, sympathetically, and yet with an undercurrent of admiring fun,
consoled him for his " bite from the old dog," which is, it seems, their
antic phrase for the malady of Venus.

Let us not forget these things when we come to judge our Restoration
dramatists. I myself, with pain, once saw young men and women

sniggering at a performance of *Damaged Goods* as the English version of *Les Avariés* was called, that fine moral lecture by Brieux, which is essentially dramatic, a sermon on the stage, sheer monkery in fact, and yet which one hesitates, perhaps, to call a play.

The prevalence of the disease in King Charles's days may be judged by the many treatises which were written upon the subject, nor do I think matters had much improved a hundred years later. At any rate, Hogarth's harlot is represented as expiring of the disorder incident to her profession. It is impossible to forget the scene in that wretched garret. Swathed in flannels, propped in a chair, the unhappy victim of lust and depravity, closes her dying eyes without solace or compassion. A blazing fire roars up the chimney ; a table falls with the crash of china ; the pot boils over hissing and bubbling ; two quacks, one of whom is known to be Dr. Misaubin, a celebrated nostrum-monger of the day and a notorious pretender to the speedy alleviation of venereal complaints, are disputing with no small vehemence about the efficacy of their pernicious drugs ; and in vain does the servant entreat them to suspend their vociferations at this serious moment. The confusion, as Mr. Ireland has justly remarked, is admirably represented. " The noise of the two enraged quacks, disputing in bad English,—the harsh vulgar scream of the maid-servant,—the table falling—and the pot boiling over, must produce a combination of sounds, dreadful and dissonant to the ear. In this pitiable situation, without a friend to close her dying eyes, or soften her sufferings by a tributary tear;—forlorn! destitute! and deserted, the heroine of this eventful history expires :—her premature death being brought on by a licentious life, seven years of which had been devoted to debauchery and dissipation, and attended by consequent infamy, misery, and disease."

In the third plate of *Marriage A la Mode* we find the hero of the piece in the apartment of a quack, where he would not have been but for his lewdness. A quarrel has arisen between him and an infamous procuress, and the subject thereof appears to be the bad condition, in point of health, of a young girl, from a commerce with whom he has received an injury.

Again in *The March to Finchley* Hogarth shows us a soldier the distortions in whose countenance betray him to be suffering from an indelicate malady, whilst near him appears a bill of Dr. Rock's for relief in such unhappy cases. Such examples show us only too clearly what inroads this scourge, owing to ignorance, to carelessness, to culpable neglect, had made in England during the eighteenth century.

Of the treatises upon the disorder, which were published in Shadwell's day, amongst others I have consulted, Gideon Harvey's *Little* Venus *unmasked ; or, A perfect discovery of the French Pox*, 12mo, 1671 ; the same author's *Great* Venus *Unmasked ; or, A more exact Discovery of the French*

Disease, 8vo, 1672; both of which ran into several editions; Everard Maynwaring's *The History and Mystery of the Venereal* Lues, 8vo, 1673; *New and Curious Observations on the Art of Curing the Venereal Disease*, Englished by Dr. Walter Harris from the French of de Blegny, 8vo, 1676; *Tuta, ac Efficax Luis Uenereae saepe absque Mercurio, ac semper absque saliuatione Mercuriali curandae Methodus, Authore Dauide Abercromby, M.D.*, 1684; William Salmon's *A New Method of Curing the French Pox*, 1689; as well as various Latin tractates and discussions. Although the arrangement is unsystematic the great work of Aloysius Luisini, a celebrated physician of Udine, is important, *De morbo Gallico omnia quæ extant apud omnes medicos cuiuscumque nationis, qui uel integris libris, uel quoque alio modo huius affectus curationem methodice aut empirice tradiderunt, diligenter hinc inde conquisita, sparsim inuenta, erroribus expurgata et in unum tandem hoc corpus redacta. In quo de ligno Indico, Salsa Perillia, Radice Chyne, Argento uiuo, ceterisque rebus omnibus ad huius luis profligationem inuentis diffusissima tractatio habetur. Cum indice locupletissimo rerum omnium scitu dignarum, quæ in hoc uolumine continentur. Opus hac nostra aetate, quo Morbti Gallici uis passim uagatur, apprime necessarium.* Two volumes, Venice, 1567. This was reprinted " Editio longe emendatior et ab innumeris mendis repurgata " at Leyden, in 1728, a huge tome of nearly 1,400 pages with a valuable preface by Boerhave. The *De Lue Uenerea*, 1594, of Jerome Capivacci, a famous physician of Padua, was much commended in the seventeenth century. In 1736 Jean Astruc published his *De Morbis uenereis libri sex*, Paris, and in 1789 appeared at Jena the *Aphrodisiacus siue de lue uenerea* of Christian Gruner, which he followed up with similar exhaustive treatises.

Julius Rosenbaum's *Geschichte der Lustseuche im Alterhume* is a work of immense erudition, but some of his conclusions must be received with extreme caution, and in particular those sections which discuss the νοῦσος θήλεια of the Scythians. Had the extraordinary, I will say the terrible, figure of Crazy in *The Humorists* excited in the smallest degree the same feelings of repugnance and pity which we now feel at any presentation of venereal disorders, Shadwell could not have dedicated his play to the Duchess of Newcastle, nor would that great and noble lady not merely have generously accepted the homage but richly rewarded him for the compliment.

Shortly after the failure of *The Humorists*—for we cannot disguise that the play was a failure—Shadwell spent some two months in the country, and meantime, his piece was passing through the press. The printed quarto is dedicated to the Duchess of Newcastle, and when the poet returned to London in April, 1671, he received the preliminary copy of his comedy. On 20 April of that year he writes both to the Duke and to the Duchess forwarding them copies of the printed play.[1] The letters are as follows:

[1] It appears in the *Stationers Register*, 9 February, 1670–71; *Term Catalogues*, Easter (30 May), 1671.

INTRODUCTION

To the Duke:

MY LORD,

HAd I not been out of Town a great part of the last Summer, and almost all this Winter, I had written to your *Grace* long since. The Town might have furnish'd me with occasions of writing that had not been impertinent. For only to say that I am the humblest of your *Graces* Servants, and that no man has a greater Honour for you than I have, would be Impertinent, since all that know me, know it of me already, and I hope your *Grace* believes it. But (my Lord) the Printing of the *Humourists* has given me a new occasion of troubling you, and desiring your Favour to be an Advocate, for me, to my Lady Dutchess, to procure me her Pardon, and a favourable reception of that little Comœdy. My Lord, (as long as you are so great a *Mecænas*) it will be impossible to defend your self from the Importunate Addresses of Poets : And Poetry is in such a declining condition, that it has need of such Noble Supporters as are at *Welbeck :* Your *Grace* saw this *Comœdy* (before the Sting was taken out) and was pleased to approve it, which is to me more than the Plaudit of a Theatre : As it is, it stands more in need of Pardon, and Protection, which I hope your *Grace*, and my Lady Dutchess will have the Mercy to afford it. I have (in this Play) only shown what I would do if I had the liberty to write a general Satyr, which (though it should really reflect upon no particular persons, yet) I find the Age is too faulty to endure it. If, for this reason, I were not tyed to too great a strictness for a Poet, I should not despair of presenting you with something much more worth your view than this mangled Play ; but all that I can do can never make any proportionable return to the favours, received from you, by,

London, *April* 20. 1671.

My LORD,
Your Graces most Obliged
Humble Servant,
Tho. Shadwell.

To the Duchess:

MADAM,

I Am to beg your *Graces* Pardon for my self, and this imperfect Piece, for which I have borrowed the Patronage of your Name ; I am not ignorant of the disadvantage that Name might appear with (before such a Trifle as this Play) if it were not too well known, and had been too often prefixt to excellent Pieces of your own, to suffer any detraction now : This Dedication will only in some measure express the Honour that the Humblest of your Servants has for your *Grace*, and the Power you have to protect so defenceless a Poem. But (*Madam*) I confess it is too great a Presumption, for me, to hope that your *Grace* (that makes so good use of your time with your own Pen) can have so much to throw away as once to read this little offspring of mine : And (but that before I found not only Pardon for an Offence of this kind but encouragement) I should despair of having this forgiven. When none of all the Nobility of *England* gives encouragement to Wit, but my Lord Duke and your excellent self, you are pleased to receive favourably and encourage the very endeavours towards it : and under that notion this poor Play begs your Pardon and Reception. Though it met with opposition from the Malice of one party, yet several men of Wit were kind to it. But whatsoever opposition threatens that, or me, it can never prejudice either, if that be Protected by your *Grace*, and I be thought what I really am,

London, April 20. 1671.

MADAM,
Your Graces most Humbly
Devoted Servant,
Tho. Shadwell.

(lxxxiii)

Almost immediately after the dispatch of these letters Shadwell went on a visit to his friend Edmund Ashton, a young fellow of twenty-four, the owner of Chadderton Hall, which is some two miles west from Oldham market-place, Lancashire.

Edmund Ashton, the host of the poet, was a Gentleman of the Bed-chamber to the Duke of York, and Lieutenant-Colonel in the Horse Guards. Chadderton Hall was granted *circa* 1260 by Richard de Trafford to his younger son Geoffrey, who forthwith adopted the local surname. The ultimate heir of the Chadderton estate was Edmund Ashton's younger brother, William (born *circa* 1649), who sold the family inheritance to Joshua Horton, of Saverly, Yorkshire. Chadderton Hall is now a brick Georgian house.[1] Of the appearance of the old hall, where Shadwell stayed, nothing is known, since it was entirely rebuilt about the middle of the eighteenth century by Sir William Horton.

If we may believe Shadwell's jesting letter to Wycherley,[2] they spent their time in the rather coarse pleasures and rough pursuits of the old English country squires. Hunting; interminably talking of dogs, and hawks, and horses; stealing a snap at local whoring; and then drinking the wholesome native ale " Nappy, clear and stale," in the village inn, where the neighbouring justices might be found always ready to forgather and generously down their tipple, or, it may be, carousing at home, and here the local rector, although his Latin was somewhat far to seek, could drink the lustiest toper of them all under the table. Whilst Shadwell was at Chadderton, upon the 23 or 24 May, a letter reached him from his wife to inform him that the Duchess of Newcastle had acknowledged the com-pliment of the dedication of *The Humorists* with a handsome present of golden guineas. He immediately replied to this bounty in a courtly but

---

[1] An illustration may be found in the *Victoria County History of Lancaster*, Vol. V, p. 118.

[2] It may be remarked that Wycherley in his *Answer* says " Duke's a Widdower," and speaks of the formal condolences sent by Louis XIV. on that occasion. Anne Hyde, the first wife of the Duke of York (James II.) died 31 March, 1671. Both her husband and Queen Catherine were present at the final scene, when the last Sacraments were administered. The Duchess of York was received into the Church in August, 1670, by Father Christopher Davenport (Franciscus a Sancta Clara), 1598–1680, a Minorite friar, who had been chaplain to Queen Henrietta Maria, and after the Restoration served the consort of Charles II. in the same office. He is the author of many treatises, of which the best generally known is *Paraphrastica Expositio Articulorum Confessionis Anglicanae* (1634), a great authority in the early days of the Oxford Movement, since it endeavours to show that the XXXIX *Articles* are patient of an interpretation more in accordance with Catholic teaching than is usually supposed. Upon publication this tractate gave sore offence in many quarters; in Spain it was put on the Index; but Mgr. Gregorio Panzani, the Pope's nuncio in London, averted any official condemnation at Rome.

clever letter, expressing his very real obligations to his noble patrons, and this gave her Grace such satisfaction that it was printed after her death, being found some two years later among the papers she had carefully preserved. His acknowledgement is as follows:

MADAM,

BEing an Hundred and fifty Miles from *London*, at a place called *Chaddeston*, near *Manchester* : I had an account, but the last Post, of the receit of your *Graces* Noble present : otherwise you had received a more early Acknowledgment with my humble Thanks ; which are all the return I can make for that, and many other Favours I have received from *Welbeck* : It had been Bounty enough (and as much as I could have expected) for your *Grace* to have Pardoned the presumption of my Dedication, which intituled you to the Patronage of so sleight a thing : but to reward my Crime, is beyond expression Generous. Thus your *Grace*, like Heaven, rewards the intention without considering the imperfection of the Act. My Design was, in some measure, to testify my Gratitude, and the Honour I have for your *Grace* : but even this Acknowledgment has run me more in debt. Your *Grace* is thus resolved to be beforehand with all your Servants. Let them be never so dilligent, your Benefits will out-go their Services ; and they can never over-take your Bounty. I, for my part, am in despair of ever coming near it : But nothing shall ever hinder me from making use of all occasions, I can lay hold on, to testify the great Honour I have for my Lord Duke, and your *Grace*, and that I am,

MADAM,
Your Graces most Humble,
and most Obedient Servant
Tho. Shadwell.

May 25. 1671.

No doubt Shadwell was glad to leave these rustic delights, and to return to London to the society of William Wycherley and Henry Harris, of Sir Charles Sedley and Lord Dorset, all of whom appear to have been his close intimates at this period. His skill in music, for he was an accomplished musician in an age of accomplished musicians, and above all the charm of his conversation, made him the best and most welcome of companions. Rochester, than whom (when he would) there was no acuter judgement in these matters, tersely remarked : " If Shadwell had burnt all he wrote, and printed all he spoke, he would have had more wit and humour than any other poet " [1]

It is plain that his constant companionship with the wits and men of quality did not allow him much time for writing, and, according to

[1] It is true that a writer in *The Gentleman's Magazine* of 1745 says · " Shadwell in conversation was a brute," but this in any case must have been in his later years when he was coarser and grosser. Moreover, it is possible that these reminiscences are spurious. I have no doubt, however, that he was bawdy enough in his talk. The younger men were often shocked by the freedoms of the Restoration rakes. It may be remembered that Gwinnet, writing from Bath, 15 September, 1709, to Elizabeth Thomas, expresses his distaste of Wycherley's society : " Yesterday Mr. *Wycherley* dined with Sir *John* [Guise], whose Conversation I find like his Poetry, is very much decayed; unless plain fulsom Obscenity (not to be borne with in a Young Man, but unpardonable in an Old one) may pass for Wit and good Breeding."

Rochester again, he wrote hurriedly and carelessly,[1] so that when he next took up his pen, he was glad to avail himself of Molière's *L'Avare* which had been acted in Paris some three years before, and he ingenuously says, " 'tis not barrenness of wit or invention, that makes us borrow from the *French*, but laziness; and this was the occasion of my making use of *L'Avare*."

Molière's Harpagon is a thorough Parisian, from whom social amenities have slipped away gradually, and by degrees. There is more than a suggestion that during the lifetime of his wife, the mother of Cléonte and Élise, a reasonable show of gentility seems to have been aimed at, although no doubt he was always extremely close-fisted, and his griping avarice grew upon him when there was no longer any restraint put upon his niggardly ways. At any rate, his son has a manservant, and he himself is obliged to keep up his coach and horses. Both these points, and there are others in the play, seem to indicate that his miserliness has waxed with the years, and that although his household was always, no doubt, conducted upon a most ungenerous scale, yet where he once used to skimp and grudge, he now screws and starves.

Harpagon is an unpleasant follow enough, selfish, sordid, shabby, capable of infinite meannesses and tyrannies, but Shadwell's Goldingham is far worse, coarser and more brutal, more odious and offensive, malicious and vindictive; and in his sentiments, as indeed in his actions, he shows that he would not, upon occasion, shrink from absolute villainy. The other characters too have taken on a rougher cast. Cléonte is extravagant and careless almost to unscrupulousness, but Theodore in the English play is a shameless young rakehell, and it is difficult to believe that his affection for Isabella will make any great change in him when a month or so has passed. Rant, Hazard, and the more than dubious society of strumpets and bawds with whom he mixes, will probably welcome him back after the briefest interim of respectability, but I think that Madam Isabella is prepared to give him as good as she gets and plant his forehead with a fine crest of antlers. Frosine, never ultra-respectable perhaps, is in her London guise as brazen as Bennet or Betty Buly; La Flèche was a bit of a rogue, but Robin is a bit of a ruffian too.

---

[1] *An allusion to Horace : the Tenth Satir of the First Book.*

> Of all our Modern Wits none seems to me
> Once to have toucht upon true Comedy,
> But Hasty *Shadwell*, and slow *Wicherley*.
> *Shadwell*'s unfinish'd works do yet impart
> Great proofs of force of Nature, none of Art;
> With just bold strokes he dashes here and there,
> Shewing great Mastery with little Care,
> And scorns to varnish his good touches o'er,
> To make the Fools and Women praise him more.

That part of *The Miser* which is Shadwell's own is by no means the least important in the English play. These original scenes present us one of those vivid pictures of Restoration life which are perhaps not to be found elsewhere depicted with such vividness as by this robust and observant dramatist. Dryden, it is true, gives us more of the intellectual atmosphere, the philosophy, so to speak, of the day ; but with one single exception or two even his comedies are romantic and do not provide so photographic a presentation of the actual life around him, although it were impossible that his individuals should be more skilfully drawn. Of his plays *Secret Love* has its story in Sicily, and the lighter episodes gratefully relieve a poignant situation, which nearly touches upon tragedy. *The Mock Astrologer* takes place in Madrid during a carnival, the very time when every person high and low, great and small, is trying to forget the monotony of his daily life, of business and affairs, and is eager for all kinds of adventure. In *Marriage A-la-Mode* we have adventures so romantic that it has been suggested that the play was originally intended as an heroic piece, and that the comedy was only introduced when the great success of *The Rehearsal* had made it inadvisable immediately to stage a drama of the type therein satirized, by the very author who was the chief butt of Buckingham's ridicule. Delightful as the comedy is, full of wit and exquisite persiflage, no one would claim that it was a realistic picture of ordinary town life, realistic, that is to say, as a canvas by Hogarth, or a novel by Zola or Joyce. Later plays of Dryden, *The Assignation; The Spanish Fryar*, which was one of his greatest successes ; his last piece, *Love Triumphant*, which was a sad failure, have their scenes in Italy and Spain, in Rome and Saragossa. Of his comedies, the action of which takes place in London, *The Wild Gallant*, his first effort for the theatre, although it certainly has episodes of contemporary life, subordinates these to the main theme of somewhat fantastic adventure, so fantastic indeed that I suspect a Spanish original, and in the Spanish theatre, so long as the interest did not flag, all varieties of ingenious surprises and extraordinary (not to say impossible) coincidences were not only allowed, but applauded and approved. *Sir Martin Mar-All*, the locale of which is indicated as Covent Garden, has minor episodes which prove what Dryden could have done in realism had he been so minded, the imbroglio of Lord Dartmouth, Lady Dupe, and her young niece Mrs. Christian. This, indeed, is portrayed with unerring skill, and here the hand of the complete master is at once observed. The remainder of the piece is frankly farcical, but what glorious fun it is ! *Mr. Limberham*, which was produced at Dorset Garden in March, 1677–78, takes place in " A Boarding House in Town," and now Dryden, who has for once shown what he can do when he elects to give a simple picture of Restoration life, easily beats Shadwell on his own ground. Indeed, so true and so bitter was the sketch that even a contemporary audience could not endure to see its own follies mirrored with such vigour and life ; they winced, and the play, which was intended " for an honest Satyr," " was permitted to be acted only thrice." [1] It is interesting, however, to remark that the King was present at one of these performances on 11 March, 1677, and although he himself is hit pretty hard, but very covertly, with his rare sense of humour he must have appreciated the neat thrusts, and thoroughly have enjoyed the discomfiture of the courtiers and the ladies round about him. When Dryden published his play 4to, 1680, with rare wit he has put two quotations upon his title-page. The one from the Greek Anthology runs :

Κᾶν με φαγῇς ἐπὶ ῥίζαν, ὁμῶς ἔτι καρποφορήσω.

the other from Horace :

Hic nuptarum insanit amoribus ; hic meretricum ;
Omnes hi metuunt uersus ; odere Poetas.

And this remains as true to-day as it was when Horace wrote it, and when Dryden marked it as the motto to *Mr. Limberham*.

Save in this one instance, where Dryden has, it must be confessed, shown himself infinitely the superior, these two great dramatists and two great antagonists, Dryden and Shadwell, are hardly to be compared, and yet one cannot but think with a sigh what a fine thing Dryden would have made of *Psyche*, with what stores of wit and humour he would have dressed *The Amorous Bigotte*, and have made this capital comedy even more rich and entertaining.

The miser has always been a favourite study in fiction and upon the stage. The Euclio of Plautus had his prototype in Greek comedy, and he reappeared throughout the satires and songs of the Middle Ages. Avaritia has been declaimed against again and again by the Fathers and Doctors of the Church, by pagan moralists of every century, as one of the cruellest and hardest of vices. Coheleth proclaims : " Est et alia infirmitas pessima, quam uidi sub sole : diuitiae conseruatae in malum domini sui. Pereunt enim in afflictione pessima."

Theologians say that a desire of, or a pleasure in, riches for the comforts and conveniences that they bring is a natural feeling not in itself blame-worthy, since by the proper and orderly spending of wealth many persons are usefully and diligently employed, and much good may be done. It is reasonable to think that money, even very large sums of money, com-

---

[1] Dryden *good Man thought* Keepers *to reclaim*
Writ a Kind Satyr, *call'd it* Limberham.
This all the Herd of Letchers *straight alarms,*
From Charing-Cross *to* Bow *was up in Arms ;*
They damn'd the Play all at one fatal Blow,
And broke the Glass that did their Picture show.

monly called capital, should be in the hands of those whose intelligence and industry have acquired it, and who are best qualified to make use of it. If lakhs and lakhs of money, however many, are distributed among a great number of people, each individual will find himself only in possession of a trifling modicum, and such is the spirit of the age, in the vast majority of cases he will argue, as the man with one talent said to himself, that no profit can accrue from so insignificant an amount, and that therefore he may as well spend it at once. He promptly proceeds to squander it unprofitably.

The inordinate love of riches for riches' sake, that is to say, to accumulate and hoard them up, apparently for the mere desire to gloat over them is in itself a grievous vice. The particular incentive seems to be the sense of power which is derived from the arid possession, not necessarily the utilization, of great wealth. The special malice of avarice lies in the injustice of the fact, and this inevitably makes the miser brutal and even savage in all his relations and social dealings. It is noticeable how Shadwell in his Goldingham developed the roughness, the harshness, even the violence and vulgarity of the covetous nature, which has been coarsened and degraded by penurious habits. Many English dramatists had brought avarice upon the stage. In Massinger's *A New Way to Pay Old Debts* we have the tremendous figure of Sir Giles Overreach; in Middleton's *A Trick to Catch the Old One* appear Lucre, Hoard and Moneylove; in Brome's *The Damoiselle; or, The New Ordinary* among the characters are Vermine, an old usurer and his son Wat; in the same author's *The English Moor; or, The Mock Marriage* we meet Quicksands, " an old usurer "; in *The Scornful Lady* Morecraft was the delight of Restoration audiences; in *Eastward Hoe* Security, " an old usurer," plays no unimportant part; in that very Jonsonian comedy, *The Projectors*,[1] by John Wilson, which was published 4to, 1665, Suckdry the usurer is excellently drawn, and according to Genest " a better character of that description is not to be found in any play." But this is excessive praise. However well they may be portrayed, and in some cases the sketches are exceedingly clever, with the exception of Sir Giles Overreach, the rest are rather types than individuals, and hardly to be compared with Shadwell's Goldingham, who has a distinct, if very unpleasant, individuality. In some ways he reminds one of Dickens's Ralph Nickleby, who, it will be readily remembered, gave a " discounting dinner," much in the same way as Goldingham was to give a supper, a sprat to catch many whales. The miser, in truth, often appears in the pages of Dickens; we have Ralph Nickleby's colleague Arthur Gride, and the immortal Scrooge, Antony and Jonas Chuzzlewit (who has many traits very like Goldingham), *cum multis aliis*. Sir Walter Scott introduces a miser in his *Old Mortality;* and again in *The Fortunes*

---

[1] Probably unacted.

(lxxxix)

of Nigel, large portions of which romance incidentally owe their vivid atmosphere to Shadwell's *Squire of Alsatia*, for Scott was a great admirer of Shadwell, and wisely drew much from these unknown and almost inexhaustible mines. It has been suspected, and perhaps not without truth, that Harrison Ainsworth's *The Miser's Daughter*, which formed the principal feature of the opening volumes of *Ainsworth's Magazine*, 1842,[1] was to some extent suggested by Wilson's *The Projectors*, since in any case in both play and novel we have the incident of the suitor for the hand of the miser's daughter disguising himself in mean habiliments, so as to make it appear that he was of a thrifty nature, and in accord with the lean ideas of the father. In speaking of his romance Ainsworth has said that he intended to show the " Folly and wickedness of accumulating wealth for no other purpose than to hoard it up, and to exhibit the utter misery of a being who should thus voluntarily surrender himself to the dominion of Mammon." The moral the author wished to point was " all high and generous feelings, all good principles, and even natural affection itself will become blunted, and in the end completely destroyed, by the inordinate and all-engrossing passion for gain . . . the sin carries its own punishment with it ; and is made the means of chastising the sinner. Dead to every feeling except that of adding to his store, the miser becomes incapable of enjoyment except such as is afforded by the contemplation of his useless treasure . . . distrust of all around him darkens his declining days." This is well observed, and it is entirely exemplified in the personality of Shadwell's miser.

It was probably owing to his ill success at Lincoln's Inn Fields with *The Humorists* that Shadwell gave his next piece, to which at first he refrained from subscribing his name, to Killigrew's company, but the fatal fire which broke out between seven and eight o'clock on Thursday evening, 25 January, 1671–2, destroying the Theatre Royal and doing terrible damage in Russell Street and Vinegar Yard, cut short the run of the new play in very tragic fashion.

If, however, his hopes were thus sadly dashed for any success with *The Miser*, he had no reason to complain of the reception of his following comedy. In *Epsom-Wells* Shadwell had a theme, life at a fashionable resort, exactly suited to his genius, and the result is that he has written a comedy, which in its own day proved a most triumphant and lasting success, and which even now gives extraordinary pleasure in the library, and would, I am convinced, afford infinite entertainment upon the stage. Epsom, partly no doubt because it lay at a convenient distance from London, partly because of the rural beauties of its surroundings and approach, and in great measure, of course, owing to the medicinal springs,

---

[1] Towards the end of its serial appearance the first book edition was published in three volumes 1842 with the fourteen fine illustrations by George Cruikshank.

had immediately after the Restoration become an exceedingly fashionable resort. It may be noticed that the waters had been discovered about 1618, but their vogue does not seem to have been of any consequence until after the return of King Charles II. It is true that the more fashionable courtiers preferred perhaps to journey a little further afield and to visit Tunbridge, "the place of all Europe, the most rural and simple, and yet, at the same time the most entertaining and agreeable,"[1] which was brought into the very height of fashion by the famous sojourn of Queen Catherine. If the company at Epsom, however, was more mixed it was certainly merrier, and no doubt it was just this freedom which attracted even the wits and the gallants who were content to leave Tunbridge to the staid and respectable folk; for it was at Epsom in July and August, 1667, that Lord Buckhurst and Sir Charles Sedley were lodging with Nell Gwyn in a house [2] next to the King's Head, and, says Pepys, they "keep a merry house."

Epsom was the grand rendezvous of the wealthier Cockneys, whose wives, at a distance from Cornhill and Cheapside, were able to affect the airs of countesses, to gossip about their vapours and spleen,[3] and drink the waters to assist their robust and cheery good health. As early as Saturday, 25 July, 1663, Pepys on his way down to Epsom was amazed to find "the road full of citizens going and coming towards Epsum, where, when we came, we could hear of no lodging, the town so full." Indeed, they had to be content with what quarters they could get, and

[1] Rochester has a famous satire *Tunbridge Wells*. Burr's *History of Tunbridge Wells* will be found valuable.

[2] Local tradition says that this was the two-storied building with two windows, still standing next door to the King's Head Inn. It is now the Nell Gwyn Restaurant. The interior has been wholly modernized.

[3] In Colley Cibber's *The Double Gallant; or, The Sick Lady's Cure*, produced at the Haymarket in November, 1707, much of which is borrowed from Charles Burnaby's two capital comedies *The Reform'd Wife* and *The Ladies Visiting Day*, together with suggestions from Mrs. Centlivre's *Love at a Venture*, the scenes of the fashionable hypochondriac Lady Dainty (created by Mrs. Oldfield), which open Act III., are excellently done. The lady says: "No Woman of Quality is, or shou'd be in perfect Health. . . . To be always in Health, is as vulgar as to be always in Humour, and wou'd equally betray one's want of Wit and Breeding; 'tis only fit for the clumsy State of a Citizen. I am ready to faint under the very Idea of such a barbarous Life." The same lady is so elegant that she would not have her ailments "prophan'd by the Crowd: The *Apoplexy*, the *Gout*, and *Vapours*, are all peculiar to the Nobility." "I could almost wish," she sighs, "that *Colds* were only ours; there's something in 'em so genteel,—so agreeably disordering."
As the mistake has often been made, it may be worth remarking that in spite of the similarity of title Cibber's comedy owes nothing to Thomas Corneille's *Le Galand Doublé*, and the error arises from the fact that *Love at a Venture* derives its main plot from the French play. It is certain that Cibber made no use of, in all probability he did not know, Calderon's *Hombre pobre todo ez traças*.

these were small enough, although the fare was excellent, since Pepys "among another meats had a brazed dish of cream"; "the best I ever eat in my life," he cries in ecstatic content. On Sunday morning he visited the Wells "where great store of citizens, which was the greatest part of the company, though there were some others of better quality. I met many that I knew, and we drank each of us two pots and so walked away." In the afternoon, they resolved to return home if they could not find other accommodation, "and so rode through Epsum, the whole town over, seeing the various companys that there were there walking; which was very pleasant to see how they are there without knowing almost what to do, but only in the morning to drink waters. But, Lord! to see how many I met there of citizens, that I could not have thought to have seen there, or that they had ever had it in their heads or purses to go down thither." Might we not apply this pregnant comment to almost any seaside or inland resort in the very present year of grace?

There are many references in the Diary to Epsom Wells and the drinking of Epsom water, and this pleasant spa remained popular until well within the eighteenth century. The Derby and the Oaks were as yet unknown, but John Toland, in his description of Epsom, says that on a Sunday evening he often counted seventy and more coaches in the Ring, the present race-course on the Downs. In fact, it was not until towards the end of the eighteenth century that the throngs of holiday makers and pleasure seekers began to leave the enjoyment of this delightful town to the residents, whose mansions formed so striking a feature of the neighbourhood.

Writing in 1672, Shadwell could have chosen no more topical title for his new comedy than the name of this favourite spot. The very opening of the play, the company drinking at the Wells in the early morning, bragging of the number of pints they have already swallowed, talking of last night's adventures, making plans for the coming day, and finally dispersing in small groups or singly about their various occupations and affairs, at once strikes the right note, and is, we might even venture to say, something new in English comedy. The interest, moreover, is well sustained until the very end of the play. The country magistrate, Clodpate, with his hearty dislike of London and London ways, is in particular most admirably portrayed, and was a source of unfailing delight to Shadwell's audiences. It is impossible to believe that the character is not drawn from the life. The excellence of the original representative, Cave Underhill, has passed into a theatrical tradition, and when we read Cibber's lively description of this comedian it requires little imagination to see Clodpate as he actually was upon the candle-lit boards. "He seemed the immovable log he stood for. A countance of wood could not be more fixed than his when the blockhead of a character required it; his face was full and long;

from his crown to the end of his nose, was the shorter half of it, so that the disproportion of his lower features, when soberly composed, with an unwandering eye hanging over them, threw him into the most lumpish, moping mortal, that ever made beholders merry ; not but, at other times, he could be wakened into spirits equally rediculous. In the coarse rustic humour of justice *Clodpate*, in *Epsom-Wells*, he was a delightful brute." According to all accounts the drinking scene with which Act IV. opens would not have come amiss to this gentleman, for Davies [1] tells us " Under-hill was a jolly and droll companion, who divided his gay hours between Bacchus and Venus with no little ardour ; if we may believe such a story as Tom Brown. Tom, I think, makes Underhill one of the Gill-drinkers of his time, men who resorted to taverns, in the middle of the day, under pretence of drinking Bristol milk [2] (for so good Sherry was then called) to whet their appetites, where they indulged themselves too often in ebriety. Underhill acted until he was past eighty, he was so excellent in the part of Trinculo, in the Tempest that he was called Prince Trinculo. He had an admirable vein of pleasantry and told his lively stories, says Brown, with a bewitching smile. The same author says, he was so afflicted with the gout, that he prayed one minute and cursed the other. His shambling gait, in his old age, was no hindrance to his acting particular parts."

Mrs. Betterton, an admirable actress, was no doubt excellent as the London cyprian who gulls worthy Justice Clodpate. The society of ladies of the profession that Mrs. Jilt adorned could be very frequently enjoyed at Epsom Wells, and is with reason ruthlessly exposed in *The Female Fire-Ships*, a satire of 1691 :

> There are a sort of *Cloyster'd Punks* beside,
> Who to be Vertuous thought, will take a Pride ;
> Reserv'd they live, in mighty State and Fashion,
> And who dares scandalize their Reputation ?
> At *Tunbridge* and at *Epsom Wells* each year,
> Like people of *best Quality* appear :
> Blush when they hear a word they judge obscene,
> Whilst thousand lewd Ideas lurk within.
> With *Artful Wiles* they take a Pride to vex,
> And bid defiance to the other *Sex* :
> But if at last betraid by *Inclination*,
> Or overcome by your too Foolish *Passion* ;

---

[1] *Dramatic Miscellanies*, 1784, Vol. III., pp. 133–135.

[2] This excellent old brown sherry is still drunk, but I believe that the genuine Bristol Milk is very hard to come at, and there are possibly imitations. There was also a more potent tipple yet styled Bristol Cream. I note that Messrs. Harvey, the well-known wine merchants, still advertise both Bristol Milk and Bristol Cream.

Or if by *Presents* moſt *magnetick Charms,*
You are at length conducted to her Arms ;
Not *Fleet ſtreet Cracks* who on young Striplings prey,
Are half so Lewd and Impudent as they.

Epsom-Wells was produced at Dorset Garden 2 December, 1672, before a crowded theatre, King Charles himself being present at the performance. Shadwell's friends had for many weeks paſt been praising the new comedy at every time and in every place, and general expectation was on tiptoe. For the dramatiſt it muſt have been an anxious hour indeed, since by this teſt his reputation was to be made or marred. He was known to his friends, and they included the gayeſt wits of the town, as a brilliant conversationaliſt, it now remained to be seen whether he could convey the sallies of his genius to a wider public. There were present, no doubt, the Duke of Buckingham, as high an authority in the world of letters as he was influential in the arena of politics ; Lord Buckhurſt, Shadwell's especial patron ; Sir Charles Sedley, one of the dramatiſt's closeſt and oldeſt friends,[1] who had himself, as we have noted, cut a brilliant if deboshed figure at the Wells when he deigned to visit the modeſt little town, and who had set the seal of his approval upon the new comedy by equipping it with a prologue of his own enditing. Doubtless there were also present the Earl of Rocheſter, who, Dryden was presently to tell him, " would not suffer the leaſt Shadow of [his] Wit to be contemn'd in other men " ; Sir George Etherege, in Shadwell's opinion, the author of " the beſt Comedy written since the Reſtauration of the Stage " ; Sir Car Scroope ; Henry Savile ; William Wycherley, a brother dramatiſt ; Sir George Hewit ; Henningham, and the reſt ; whilſt fop-corner fairly hummed with the chatter of flaxen-haired beaux eager to see which way the cat might jump before they ventured an opinion upon the piece, and solemn critics already resolved to bless or to damn whatever the merits or faults of the new play, for that race has never altered. One cannot but suppose that Edward Howard and his clique were agog to censure and dispraise, all with a month's mind for a miscarriage. *The Sullen Lovers* had made Shadwell enemies and they were not prone to forget.

The caſt entailed the full ſtrength of the company. The three young men " of Wit and Pleasure," Belvil, Rains, and Woodly, who had their counterparts a hundred times over in the thronging audience, were played by the great Betterton ; " incomparable " Henry Harris, himself " as very a rogue as any in the town " ; and handsome Will Smith, the leading actors of the Duke's company ; Bisket muſt have been truly admirable as interpreted by Nokes, who scarcely ever made his firſt entrance without

[1] In the Dedication of *The Tenth Satyr of Juvenal*, 1687, addressed to Sir Charles Sedley, Shadwell says " I have from my Youth Lived " in your friendship.

being received " by a general laughter, which the very sight of him provoked, and Nature could not resist; yet the louder the laugh, the graver
was his look upon it." Fribble was safe and more than safe in the hands
of Edward Angel, " the Poets Darling," " the best of mimiques," who
indeed made so great a name in this character that the author of the *Elegy* [1]
upon his death exclaims :

> No more to *Epsom ;* Physicians try your skills,
> Since *Frible* now has ta'n his leave o' th' Wells.

The actresses too were particularly well suited in their parts, and Downes,
who is not frequently given to special commendation, singles out Mrs.
Johnson for his warmest applause. This lady's admirers, whom she did
not love to disappoint either in the theatre or in yet more familiar trifling
abed, had gathered in full force. She was indeed one of the loveliest
women upon the stage, and Etherege, writing to Middleton nearly
twenty years later, when he wishes to emphasize the beauty of his own
fascinating Julia, describes her as " a Comedian no less handsom and no
less kind in Dutchland, than Mrs. Johnson was in England." It would
seem, indeed, that Etherege had once laid his easy heart at Mrs. Johnson's
feet, and after a dozen years had flown could not forget her charms, for in
November, 1686, he had in recounting the arrival of " a Company of
Strolers, who are lately come from Nurenberg to divert us here " in
Ratisbon, been warm in his praises of " a Comedian in the Troop as handsom at least as the faire made of the West, wch you have seen at Newmarket,
and makes as much noise in this little Town, and gives as much jealousies
to ye Ladys as ever Mrs. Wright, or Mrs. Johnson did in London."

From the very first there was no doubt with regard to the success of
Epsom-Wells. The King expressed himself delighted with the piece, and
not only paid a second visit [2] to the theatre upon 4 December, but commanded a performance at Whitehall two days after Christmas. The
Queen was then present, and there was spoken a special prologue, written
for the occasion, which directly addressed their Majesties, and, in the name
of the dramatist, boasted of the entertainment this comedy had already
given his royal patron.

Shadwell's detractors, none the less, had been busy, and it was openly
being gossiped about the town that *Epsom-Wells* was not the work of the
supposed author at all, but a composite play, written by the whole society

---

[1] Printed by Mr. G. Thorn-Drury in *A Little Ark*, 1921, pp. 38–39.

[2] Steele in *The Guardian* (No. 82, 15 June, 1713), reminding his readers that D'Urfey's
A Fond Husband was to be acted that evening for the benefit of the author, says : " This
comedy was honoured with the presence of King *Charles* the Second, three of its first
five nights." The original production of this play took place at Dorset Garden in the
spring of 1676. It was licensed (for printing) 15 June, 1676.

of Court wits, with whom he was known to be a prime favourite. Amongst others the Hon. Edward Howard was very active in spreading these rumours, and in lending them his authority, beneath which every disappointed dramatist, and envious rival, who had been failures in the theatre, were glad to shelter themselves when they circulated the news. Even if Shadwell had penned certain scenes of the play the major part, they said, was the work of others' brains more intelligent than he. At any rate, his friends, especially Sir Charles Sedley, had furbished and polished the dialogue. There can be no doubt that Shadwell, as well he might, exceedingly resented these imputations. He declares that they " left an impression upon few or none," but this does not seem borne out by the facts. No doubt his enemies were glad to believe anything that might disparage his intellectual powers ; no doubt they were glad to exaggerate the most trifling suggestions into a present of whole episodes and scenes, nay even entire acts ; but there is plenty of evidence to show that the accusation had its sting, though possibly it had no truth. In any case, little more than three weeks after the original production Shadwell is at the trouble to contradict these rumours, and this on a most important occasion, in the Prologue spoken before the command performance at Whitehall. Personally, I believe that the help Shadwell received may resolve itself into very little. He was a keen observer of life with eyes and ears ever wide open, and it is impossible that at some of those combats of wit, those brilliant suppers at the French House, or the Rose, or the Setting Dog and Partridge, he should not have picked up many a useful hint, many a merry jest, many a lively design, and indeed whole snatches of conversation which might be admirably well utilized in his realistic comedies. No doubt, too, Buckingham or Buckhurst would spare an idle hour to overlook the script of the next new play, but these great gentlemen were far too careless to do more than to add at most a prologue or a song as a garniture—to write plays might be thought mechanic.[1] In the dedication to *A True Widow*, 4to, 1679, Shadwell addressing Sir Charles Sedley certainly says : " No Success whatever could have made me alter my Opinion of this Comedy, which had the benefit of your Correction and Alteration, and the Honour of your Approbation " ; [2] but he goes on to add, and this is important, " And I heartily

[1] In Crowne's *Sir Courtly Nice*, Act III., Sir Courtly remarks that he only writes for his diversion, " Like a gentleman, soft and easy." " Does your Honour write any Plays ? " asks his valet. Sir Courtly repudiates the idea : " No, that's Mechanick ; I bestow some Garniture on Plays, as a Song or Prologue."

[2] Dryden, in his dedication of *Marriage A-La-Mode*, 4to, 1673, to the Earl of Rochester writes : " My Lord, I Humbly Dedicate to Your Lordship that Poem, of which you were pleas'd to appear an early Patron, before it was Acted on the Stage. I may yet go farther, with your Permission, and say, That it receiv'd amendment from your noble Hands, ere it was fit to be presented. You may please likewise to remember, with how

wish you had given yourself the Trouble to have review'd all my Plays, as they came incorrectly and in haste from my Hands." [1] Dryden in *Mac Flecknoe*, 1682, has a famous couplet:

> But let no alien *S-dl-y* interpose
> To lard with wit thy hungry *Epsom* prose,

but then each pungent point of this great satire must not be pressed too far. There had been gossip which had annoyed Shadwell, and Dryden, of course, makes splendid capital out of that. Again, Oldys, in his MS. notes on the article Thomas Shadwell in his copy of Langbaine,[2] says: " I have heard that Dorset, Sedley and others of those idle Wits would write whole Scenes for him." This is very interesting as showing that the tradition survived, but actually it does not add anything to our knowledge, and, without any undue emphasis, it should be borne in mind that Oldys definitely asserts he is only repeating hearsay.

Personally, I find it difficult to believe that Shadwell could have had much help from Sir Charles Sedley. It is well known that Sedley enjoyed in his day, and has left, an immense reputation as a wit,[3] and some of his songs, such as " Love Still has Something of the Sea," and " Phyllis is my only Joy," are exquisitely turned; his three elegies from Ovid, too, are very happy. But in truth the man himself is far more interesting than his work. *Bellamira* is easy and gallant, an amusing comedy, which I have always enjoyed in the reading, and which I should no doubt find a yet more agreeable entertainment upon the stage. Complaisance can hardly do more than echo Pepy's opinion of *The Mulberry Garden*, " here and there a pretty saying and not very much neither, yet the whole play has nothing extraordinary in it at all, neither of language or design." [4] I would not go so far as to call it " worthless," but with the exception of a good sentence or two (and they are few enough) in the lighter scenes, it seems to me that the piece is intolerably dull, whilst the heroic characters express

---

much favour to the Author, and indulgence to the Play, you commended it to the view of His Majesty, then at *Windsor*, and by His Approbation of it in Writing, made way for its kind reception on the *Theatre*."

[1] It is surely excessive, and indeed erroneous, to assert: " There is abundant evidence that Sedley gave Shadwell considerable help in his writings, and the flashes of wit that lighten up the scenes of some of his best comedies are, no doubt, often due to the Baronet's pen." V. De Sola Pinto, *Sir Charles Sedley*, 1927, p. 108. In truth, there is no foundation whatsoever for so sweeping a statement.

[2] *An Account of the English Dramatick Poets*, 1691 (British Museum, C. 28, g. i.).

[3] The world has recently been obliged with a study of Sir Charles Sedley by Mr. V. De Sola Pinto, *Sir Charles Sedley*, 1927.

[4] It is true that in the Dedication of *A True Widow* Shadwell says to Sir Charles Sedley: " You have in the *Mulberry-Garden* shewn the true Wit, Humour, and Satyr of a Comedy," but this eulogy is very interested, and even Mr. Pinto feels bound to discount it. *Op. cit.*, p. 248, note 3.

fuſtian sentiments in a hobbling doggerel of which Settle or Pordage would have been not a little ashamed. Sedley's one tragedy *Antony and Cleopatra* is beſt forgotten, for it is the dulleſt, drabbeſt thing of its kind conceivable; it has not sufficient spirit even to rant.[1] To sum up the matter, so far as the theatre is concerned, Sedley has left us one sprightly comedy, and unless some malevolent fairy at his cradle endowed him with the gift of sparkling diamonded wit in his talk which was inevitably to turn into lack-luſtre rubble whensoever the pen touched his hand for a play, I do not see how a writer entirely lacking in dramatic sense can have been of any material use to an accomplished dramatiſt such as Thomas Shadwell. Incidentally, the popularity of *Epsom-Wells* in the theatre is atteſted by a reference in Sam Vincent's *Young Gallant's Academy*, which was published in the spring of 1674.[2] Chapter V. of this little book gives " Inſtruƈtions for a young Gallant how to behave himself in the Playhouse." Here the advantages of making a conspicuous figure in the pit of the theatre are ſtrongly urged upon the fop of fashion, who is told : " By sitting in the *Pit*, if you be a Knight, you may happily get you a Miſtress ; which if you would, I advise, you never to be absent when *Epsome Wells* is plaid : for,

> *We see the* Wells *have ſtoln the* Vizard—masks *away.*
> *Empress of Morocco, in the Prologue.*

In his *Mixt Essays*, St. Evremond, writing " Of the English Comedy," remarks : " As they scarcely ever ſtick to the unity of aƈtion, that they may represent a principal person who diverts them by different aƈtions : so many times also they quit that principal person, that they may shew what various things happen to several persons in public places ; *Ben Johnson* is much for that in his *Bartholomew Fair*. The same thing hath been done in *Epsom Wells*, and in both these Comedies the ridiculous adventures of these publick places are comically represented."

It should be noticed that when *Epsom-Wells* was published early in 1673 Shadwell, who was firm in his loyalty to his firſt patron the Duke of Newcaſtle, dedicated his popular play with grateful, but not fulsome compliment, to that eminent nobleman.[3]

---

[1] Sir Adolphus Ward's criticism is not one whit too severe : " Nothing more frigid and feeble than this ' heroic tragedy ' (in rimed couplets) could well be imagined."— *English Dramatic Literature*, 1899, Vol. III., p. 447.

[2] *Term Catalogues*, Eaſter (26 May), 1674.

[3] So Dryden in *Mac Flecknoe* writes with a sneer :

> Sir *Formal*, though unsought, attends thy quill,
> And does thy *Northern Dedications* fill.

It will be remembered that *The Virtuoso* is dedicated to the Duke of Newcaſtle, to whom Dryden had inscribed *An Evening's Love ; or, The Mock Aſtrologer*.

It was at this time that the vogue of the heroic tragedy was at its height. The town, it is true, had rocked with laughter at the Duke of Buckingham's famous burlesque *The Rehearsal*, which was produced at the Theatre Royal, Drury Lane, on 7 December, 1671, but it is none the less true that the same town thronged to suffocation the same house whenever there was acted Mr. Dryden's " famous play, called *The Siege of Granada*," with " very glorious scenes and perspectives, the work of Mr. Streeter," a tragedy which even so nice a critic as Mrs. Evelyn found " so full of ideas that the most refined romance I ever read is not to compare with it ; love is made so pure and valour so nice, that one would imagine it designed for an Utopia rather than our stage." Not the least industrious of the purveyors of rhyming plays was young Elkanah Settle, who had recently come down from Trinity College, Oxford, without taking a degree, and who was beginning to make some noise in the world. His first play, *Cambyses, King of Persia*,[1] which had been produced at Lincoln's Inn Fields, probably in January, 1666–67, is an omnium gatherum of the most approved materials ; a long distant age and country, an exotic atmosphere of impossible emotions and ambitions ; a " young Captive Prince " ; a villain Prexaspes, acted by Henry Harris ; a lovely lady, Mandana, acted by Mrs. Betterton ; prisons ; ghosts ; and numberless kindred attractions. The result was a tremendous success, and jealousy began to burn aflame in the hearts of rival dramatists.

Here was fair game for the freakish young Rochester, whose monkey mischief and " a disposition to extravagant mirth "[2] made him, for the sake of " some ill-natur'd Jest,"[3] love to embroil his associates, were they peers or poets, and then, as soon as the fracas he had fomented inevitably resulted, amid the dust and noise he would rub off out of the arena and stand fleering at the combatants. When called to account for his tricks, as more than once happened, he was too much of a craven—doubtless his nerves were shattered with drink and every other excess—too sneaking to see the thing through, and carelessly enough he was wont to " put it off with some Buffoon conceit."[4] The whimsical earl, then, resolved that Settle should experience the sweets of his patronage, and accordingly this poet's second play, *The Empress of Morocco*, was by Rochester's

---

[1] " The first new Play that was acted in 1666 was the Tragedy of *Cambyses*, King of *Persia ;* wrote by Mr. Settle ; *Cambyses* was performed by Mr. *Betterton ; Prexaspes,* the General, by Mr. *Harris ;* Prince *Smerdis*, Mr. *Young ; Mandana*, by Mrs. *Betterton ;* all the other parts being perfectly well acted, succeeded six days with a full audience." Downes, *Roscius Anglicanus. Cambyses* was not printed until 1671.

[2] Burnet, *Some Passages of the Life and Death of the Right Honourable John Earl of Rochester, Who died the 26th of July*, 1680. 8vo, 1680, p. 13.

[3] Sir Car Scroope, *Defence of Satire.*

[4] *Ibid.*

influence performed at Court,[1] " and by persons of such Birth and Honour, that they borrow'd no Greatness from the Characters they acted." Rochester even went so far as to furnish a prologue. There is some difficulty about precisely fixing the exact date of public production, but *The Empress of Morocco* was probably given at Dorset Garden in the early autumn of 1673, perhaps during the first weeks of October.[2] The play had been very carefully cast, and the actors were all seen to the greatest advantage. Henry Harris appeared as Muly Labas ; Smith Muly Hamet ; Betterton Crimalhaz, the robustious villain of the play, who was particularly distinguished by the immense plume of feathers which crowned his peruke ; Matthew Medbourne Hametalhaz, the villain's " confident and creature " ; and Crosby, a young actor who was soon to attain considerable distinction and popularity as a handsome juvenile, Abdelcader. The three female parts were taken by the three leading actresses of the company : Laula, Empress of Morocco, by Mrs. Betterton ; the Princess Mariamne by Mrs. Mary Lee, who afterwards became Lady Slingsby, our first titled actress ; and Morena by the beautiful Mrs. Johnson. With such a galaxy of brightest stars the artistic presentation must have been indeed superb. Moreover, there were further attractions ; newly painted scenery and prospects, dances, pseudo-native music, " a very fierce Fight," and above all an elaborate masquerade, although it must be confessed that Pluto, Proserpine, and Orpheus, are rather out of place, to say the least, in the Court of Barbary. But what matter so long as they wore magnificent habits, and their voices were harmonious and clear. In any case the play achieved an extraordinary success. In the preface to Dennis's *Remarks upon Mr. Pope's Translation of Homer* (1717) we learn that it ran " a month together," which, however, can hardly mean upon successive days, for this would have been altogether so exceptional that it seems impossible there should not be some contemporary mention of so striking a circumstance. One of the most brilliant of all English comedies, *Love for Love*, which was produced on 30 April, 1695, " took 13 days successively," and this was esteemed so wonderful that it passed as a proverb into theatrical tradition.

Whatever the exact length of the initial run of *The Empress of Morocco*, there can be no doubt that Settle's play won a veritable triumph, and this good success was by no means undeserved, for it certainly is a most

---

[1] The Epilogue commences :

> *This play like Country Girle come up to Town,*
> *Long'd t'appear fine, in Jewels, and rich Gown ;*
> *And so,*
> *Hoping it's Pride you Courtiers would support,*
> *To please You, lost its Maiden-head at Court.*

[2] The quarto is in the *Term Catalogues*, November, 1673.

effective melodrama, a kind which, whatever half-educated people may say, is extremely attractive.[1] Moreover, Settle's verse, always fluent and facile, which even Dryden was bound to allow,[2] not infrequently is vigorous and within measure of some inspiration.

The favour shown to Settle by the Town and the enthusiasm of his admirers proved a source of considerable annoyance to the rival theatre. The older actors promptly called in the aid of Thomas Duffett, who extravagantly burlesqued the popular tragedy in his farce *The Empress of Morocco*. Although it is inevitable that for us this skit must have lost nearly all its point, that its happiest hits fall lifeless and dull, yet there is some rough humour in the metamorphosis of Settle's begums and bashaws into apple-women and scullions. To us, undoubtedly, the most interesting part of it is the Epilogue, "a new Fancy, after the old and most surprising way of *Macbeth*." Hecate and Three Witches commence "the most renowned and melodious Song of *John Dory*," and presently "Three Witches fly over the Pit Riding upon Beesomes," which, of course, parodied the "flyings for the witches" that had been so great a feature of the recent revivals of *Macbeth*. Duffett then introduces two Spirits, who serve the company with a kind of snapdragon, which the weird sisters appear to relish so exceedingly that they burst forth into carol and song, lustily chanting the praises of the daughters of Sir Pandar to the tune of *Haste to the Ferry*.

> *A health, a health to Mother* C——
> *From* Moor-fields *fled to* Mill-bank *Castle*
> *She puts off rotten new-rig'd Vessel,*

they sing, as they quaff bumpers of brandy to the bawd. Mother Cresswell, who had recently transferred her vaulting-school to new quarters, was living in Moorfields as early as March, 1659, since we find in a pleasant squib of that date, *The Proceedings, Votes, Resolves, and Acts of the late Half-quarter Parliament Called the Rump*, the following entry: "*Ordered,*

---

[1] As I write, *Maria Marten; or, The Murder in the Red Barn* is drawing all London to the Theatre Royal, Elephant and Castle, where, incidentally, some of the best acting in London is to be seen.

[2] *Absalom and Achitophel*, the Second Part:

> *Doeg*, though without knowing how or why,
> Made still a blund'ring kind of Melody;
> Spurd boldly on, and Dash'd through Thick and Thin,
> Through Sense and Non-sense, never out nor in;
> Free from all meaning, whether good or bad,
> And in one word, Heroically mad,
> He was too warm on Picking-work to dwell, ⎱
> But Faggoted his Notions as they fell, ⎰
> And, if they Rhim'd and Rattl'd, all was well. ⎰

That the Earl of *Pembroke* does very well in going to Mistress *Creswels* in Moor-fields to mortifie his pamper'd flesh, and that it is no sin for a Quaker to go a whoring after strange women, provided he did not go a whoring after strange gods." Mother Gifford, Mother Temple, and Betty Buly, three notorious procuresses, whose names occur again and again in satire and ballad, are next celebrated ; and the pæan soars to its height when Shaftesbury's particular *lena anus*, as Ovid has it, Mother Moseley receives her meed of gratulation. There is a good deal more in similar strain, and the whole concludes with a trio by the Three Witches :

> *Rose-mary's green, Rose-mary's green !*
> > derry, derry, down.
> *When I am King, thou shalt be Queen.*
> > derry, derry, down.
> *If I have Gold thou shalt have part.*
> > derry, derry, down.
> *If I have none thou hast my heart.*
> > derry, derry, down.

These tomfooleries for all their lewdness and vulgarity immensely diverted the Town, although it is very certain that they in no way interfered with the applause that was being given both to *The Empress of Morocco* and to *Macbeth*. This latter, indeed, was almost first among the most popular of Shakespeare's [1] plays upon the Restoration stage. Moreover, when *The Empress of Morocco* was published in 1673, it was issued " With Sculptures. The like never done before . . . in Quarto. Price, stitcht, 1s.," an edition which nowadays commands a very high price owing to the fine old copper plates, five in number, together with an engraved frontispiece showing the exterior of the Duke's Theatre. These illustrations, which have often been reproduced, are as follows : Act I., The Interior of the Prison, a very fine stage set; Act II., The Prospect of a large River, with a glorious Fleet of Ships ; the third, in the same Act, shows the Moorish Dance about the " Artificial Palm Tree " ; Act IV., the Masque of Pluto and Proserpine ; Act V., the Scene of the gaunches, which is really rather ghastly.

An illustrated play was quite a novelty, and it was a novelty which roused the other dramatists to something very like fury. Dryden, who was the master of the heroic play, seems to have been particularly annoyed, and, if we consider the circumstances, his vexation was not unreasonable. In 1674 there appeared a quarto of seventy-two pages, *Notes and Observations on the Empress of Morocco*, which it was unkindly suggested might be printed in the next edition of the play instead of the Sculptures. Adopting the mode of the old theological fighters who in their controversies would accumu-

[1] In the alteration by Davenant, who greatly elaborated the scenes with the witches.

late huge folios, answering their opponents line for line, almost word for word, this pamphlet examines Settle's tragedy in minutest detail. Sometimes fairly, sometimes very unfairly, but always very cleverly and caustically enough it analyses line after line, every speech and almost every sentiment, and it succeeds in making fine rubbish of the whole. So severe a castigation must have been almost unendurable, and the volubly petulant Settle was not the person to suffer in silence. That the attack was anonymous did not throw him off the scent. He soon penetrated the secret, perhaps those concerned made no great mystery about it, and forthwith proceeded to retaliate in kind. His talent did not lie towards originality, and one cannot help feeling that his *tu quoque* does not rise very much above the imagination and ingenuity of the schoolboy who retorts upon his fellow " So are you ! " Early in 1675 [1] Settle published *Notes and Observations on the Empress of Morocco Revised with Some few Errata's to be Printed instead of the Postscript with the next Edition of the Conquest of Granada,* a pamphlet of ninety-five pages, quarto. In the Preface he thus ruthlessly raises the veil : " With very little Conjuration, by those three remarkable Qualities of Railing, Boasting, and Thieving I found a *Dryden* in the Frontispiece. Then . . . I consider'd that probably his Pamphlet might be like his Plays, not to be written without help. And according to expectation I discover'd the Author of *Epsome-Wells,* and the Author of *Pandion and Amphigenia* [2] lent their assistance. Had I Three to me thought I ? and Three Gentlemen of such disagreeing Qualification in one Club ; The First a Man that has had Wit, but is past it ; the Second that has it, if he can keep it ; and the Third that neither has, nor is ever like to have it. . . . The Second I suppose only puting his Comical hand to the Work, to help forward with the mirth of so ridiculous a Libel." It must be confessed that this answer misses fire, although Dennis says that Mr. Settle " according to the opinion which the town then had of the matter, (for I have utterly forgot the controversy) had by much the better of them all." No doubt Dryden's was the chief hand in the attack upon Settle, and Crown was eager enough, one may well suppose, as the laureate's lieutenant. But it can easily be seen that Shadwell had very little to do with the attack. [3] True Jonsonian that he was, he contemned the heroic play, and although he complimented Dryden upon that great poet's excellence in tragedy, he was not likely to be over much disturbed at the success of *The Empress of Morocco,* save in a general way as misliking that the town

---

[1] *Term Catalogues,* Hilary (15 February, 1675).

[2] *Pandion and Amphigenia ; or, the History of the Coy Lady of Thessalia,* adorned with sculptures, London, 8vo, 1665.

[3] After full consideration I decided not to reprint this piece in an edition of Shadwell's works. Shadwell had the smallest hand in the piece, and the pamphlet is hardly to be understood, for it would in fine be quite useless, unless a reprint of *The Empress of Morocco* were to accompany it.

should follow "the concupiscence of Gigges, and daunces" and so "runne away from Nature." No doubt he added a few smashing blows, for in all controversy and offensive criticism his weapon was ever the Protestant flail rather than the tempered Toledo. Perhaps for us one of the most interesting features of the whole discussion is that it serves to show that Dryden and Shadwell were on very friendly terms.

On Thursday, 7 November, 1667, there was produced at Lincoln's Inn Fields *The Tempest; or, The Enchanted Island*, the famous alteration of Shakespeare's play by Dryden and Davenant. This was published in 1670, with a preface signed by Dryden, dated "1st December, 1669." Pepys, who was present at the first performance, notes that "a great many great ones" were among the audience. "The house mighty full; the King and Court there." All, Pepys tells us, "were mightly pleased with the play." As is well known, the most important variations, and these are truly material enough, were the supplying of Miranda with a sister, Dorinda; the "*excellent contrivance*" of "*the Counterpart to Shakespear's Plot, namely, that of a Man who had never seen a Woman,*" the character of Hippolito; and the very important amplification of the lighter scenes. Of these latter Dryden expressly says that Sir William Davenant was the author: "*The Comical parts of the Saylors were also of his Invention, and for the most part his Writing.*" Whatever one may think of the other changes, surely these new scenes are extremely amusing, and one cannot but be grateful to find that the exceptionally dull and prolix conversations between Alonso; Sebastian; Antonio; that impossible old bore, Gonzalo; and those dummy attendants, have been entirely eliminated.

However modern literary criticism may regard the alteration of *The Tempest*, the fact remains that theatrically it was very effective; with some slight modifications it kept the stage until well within the nineteenth century; and at its first production it proved a tremendous success, indeed it would hardly be an exaggeration to say that it was the favourite play of the Restoration stage.[1] No doubt some of the original popularity was due to the music, the effects, the scenery and costumes,[2] and the shrewd managers of the theatre were quick to recognize this. They argued, with unimpeachable knowledge, that if these attractions were elaborated, a greater success yet might be attained, but to go even a little

[1] Constant references and allusions attest the exceptional popularity of this play. One may consult the *Shakespeare Allusion Books*, and particularly *Some Seventeenth Century Allusions to Shakespeare and his Works Not Hitherto Collected*, 1920, and *More Seventeenth Allusions to Shakespeare and his Works*, 1924, both compiled by Mr. G. Thorn-Drury. It may be remarked that the majority of the references are to "the Comical parts of the Saylors," and that the character of Trincalo was especially popular.

[2] On Monday, 11 May, 1668, Pepys went behind the scenes whilst *The Tempest* was being acted, and "had the pleasure to see the actors in their several dresses, especially the seamen and monster, which were very droll."

further along these lines would mean that they would have to turn *The Tempest* into that species of entertainment which upon the Restoration stage was known as an " Opera," a term which it is somewhat difficult exactly to define, since it was used in a vague way to cover very many varieties. In the preface to *Albion and Albanius*, folio 1685, Dryden remarks : " An *Opera* is a Poetical Tale, or Fiction, represented by Vocal and Instrumental Musick, adorn'd with Scenes, Machines, and Dancing." This is sufficiently elastic, and it leaves us something in doubt as to what the essentials which constituted an Opera exactly were. Music certainly ; but then music formed a prominent feature in most Restoration plays. Music was widely cultivated and admired, and many spirits in the audience, such as old Pepys or D'Urfey, were excellent amateur musicians. Dancing is another important feature ; but then there are few Restoration plays into which a dance, often even a formal masquerade, is not introduced. Downes considered *The Lancashire Witches* " a kind of Opera," since it had " several *Machines* of Flying for the Witches," and *Macbeth* because of " flyings for the witches, with all the singing and dancing in it," was most assuredly " in the nature of an Opera." Dryden, in the Preface which has been quoted above, discusses the opera at great length, and with his usual acuteness to some extent refines upon the several definitions, endeavouring to give the word a concise and accepted interpretation. Incidentally, and the passage is very important, he makes mention of *The Tempest ;* " which is a Tragedy mix'd with *Opera ;* or a *Drama* written in Blank Verse, adorn'd with Scenes, Machines, Songs: and Dances : So that the Fable of it is all spoken and Acted by the best of the Comedians ; the other Part of the Entertainment to be perform'd by the same Singers and Dancers who are introduc'd in this present *Opera*. It cannot properly be call'd a Play, because the Action of it is suppos'd to be conducted sometimes by supernatural Means, or Magick ; nor an *Opera*, because the Story of it is not sung. . . . When *Opera's* were first set up in *France*, they were not follow'd over eagerly ; but they gain'd daily upon their Hearers, 'till they grew to that Height of Reputation, which they now enjoy. The *English*, I confess, are not altogether so Musical as the *French ;* and yet they have been pleas'd already with *The Tempest*, and some Pieces that follow'd."

Little indeed was required to turn *The Tempest* " altered by Sir William Davenant and Mr. Dryden, before 'twas made into an Opera," wholly into a Restoration opera, and accordingly the change was made, and Downes records : " The year after in 1673, *The Tempest, or Inchanted Island ;* made into an Opera by Mr. *Shadwell :* having all new in it ; as Scenes, Machines ; particularly, one scene painted with myriads of *Ariel* Spirits ; and another flying away with a table furnisht out with fruits, sweat-meats, and all sorts of viands just when Duke *Trinculo* and his companions were going to dinner ; all things perform'd in it so admirably well, that not any succeeding opera got more money." The chief differences between the comedy *The Tempest* and the opera *The Tempest* very briefly may be summed up as,—new songs, dances, and spectacular effects, in particular the gorgeous masque of Neptune, fair Amphitrite, Oceanus, Tethys, the Tritons and Nereides. In order to allow of all this extra pomp and diversion there has been some excision of dialogue, perhaps not always very neatly contrived. For the opera, Act II. of the comedy has been rearranged. This was a practical necessity to allow of the shifting and setting of the scenery. It must be emphasized, how-ever, that the alterations which prevailed in the opera are all planned and carried out with deliberate care upon very definite lines.

The question arises to whom are the changes to be attributed ? The text of the comedy, *The Tempest*, by Davenant and Dryden, was printed quarto, 1670, and it should be noted that there are two issues. It again reappears in the folio Dryden, two volumes, Tonson, 1701. It was very perfunctorily given in a privately printed American edition, which is of no account whatsoever, and finally it was edited for the first time by myself in *Shakespeare Adaptations*, 1922.

The edition of *The Tempest* in the collection called " English Plays " (Neatly and Correctly printed, in small volumes fit for the pocket, & sold by *T. Johnson*, Bookseller in the *Hague*), and advertised under Shakespeare's name, " altered by *Davenant* and *Dryden*," contains more of the comedy than most editions supply, although the elaborate scenic directions of the opera are here freely given, and the text is faulty to a degree, frequent lines and whole speeches having been carelessly dropped.

The operatic *The Tempest* was printed quarto 1674; 1676 (bis); 1690; 1695; and 1701. Moreover, this is the text which has been given in all reprints of Dryden's work.

It would seem that these difficulties and discrepancies had escaped attention until March, 1904, when that complete authority upon matters theatrical, Mr. W. J. Lawrence, published an article in *Anglia* discussing this crux. In his *The Elizabethan Play-house and other Studies*, 1912, Mr. W. J. Lawrence republished this article, which he had amplified and revised as *Did Thomas Shadwell Write An Opera On The Tempest?* Incidentally it must be remarked that Sir Ernest Clarke contributed to *The Athenæum* of 25 August, 1906, an article on *The Tempest as an Opera*, in which he maintains Shadwell's authorship. Sir Ernest Clarke, who had not seen Mr. Lawrence's article in *Anglia*, had independently evolved his theories, but he adds nothing very essential to the arguments of our great Irish scholar. It will be well as concisely as possible to summarize Mr. Lawrence's conclusions, although it must be borne in mind that so curtailed a conspectus must necessarily fall far short of conveying the full force and weight of his detailed exposition. In the first place, Mr. Lawrence acknowledges : " The sole authority for the ascription of an opera on *The Tempest* to Thomas Shadwell is the *Roscius Anglicanus* of John Downes, a rambling stage record published in 1708, when the quondam prompter who penned it was in the decline of his years and his interest." We can make amplest allowance for the blunders and unconscious errors, the tricks of senile memory, which only too frequently occur in this valuable monograph. But Downes is least likely to have gone wrong when he recorded matters which came directly under his own notice, that is to say, productions at his own theatre. The mistake into which he has fallen with regard to the date of the operatic *Tempest*, which he assigns to 1673, whereas it was produced in the spring (probably 30 April), 1674, I make of no account whatsoever ; nothing is easier than to go astray with regard to a date, and Downes is only a few months out in his reckoning. Indeed, if we consider that he was counting by the old computation, and taking 25 March to be the dividing date of the year, he is only five weeks at fault. This point has been overlooked, and although a small detail it certainly weighs in the balance.

Mr. Lawrence does not neglect to consider that no quarto of *The Tempest* ever bore Shadwell's name, that neither Winstanley, Langbaine, nor Gildon so much as hint that Shadwell had a hand in the operatic version of *The Tempest*. A small detail, which has not, I think, been adduced, is that *The Tempest* was not included in the volume of Shadwell's plays, quartos of various dates, which in 1693 James Knapton, the publisher, hurriedly bound together with a special title-page as " the Works of *Tho. Shadwell*, Esq. ; Late Poet Laureat, and Historiographer Royal " ; nor yet does it appear in the duodecimo edition, four volumes, which appeared in 1720. But nothing must be argued from this omission ; neither Knapton's edition, if edition it may be called, nor the collection of 1720, if collection it may be called, has the slightest vestige of authority, or even bearing with regard to such a point as that immediately under discussion.

Again, Mr. Lawrence points out that in the operatic *Tempest* we find a song " Arise, arise ! ye subterranean winds," which we know is Shadwell's, since the music for these words was published in 1680 by Pietro Reggio in his folio collection of songs and music, and here " Arise, arise " is definitely by name given to Shadwell, and, what has not hitherto been recorded, complimentary verses by Shadwell, together with an Italian sonnet addressed to Shadwell by Reggio, are prefixed to this sumptuous volume. Further, Mr. Lawrence considers that the " Prologue and Epilogue to the Tempest " which are preserved in the Egerton MSS. in the British Museum were written by Shadwell for his opera.[1]

---

[1] This Prologue and Epilogue are now for the first time correctly printed in the present edition of Shadwell.

These then, very roughly, are the main grounds of Mr. Lawrence's statement, and I believe I am correct when I say that they have been generally received. My late friend Mr. W. Barclay Squire, who was one of the most learned and cautious of investigators, told me that he confidently accepted Mr. Lawrence's conclusions. He frankly allowed that the arguments were not demonstrative ; but then, what arguments ever are ?

So the matter rested, until that very eminent authority Mr. G. Thorn-Drury published an article, or rather a lengthy note,[1] in which with the wealth of the research at his command he controverted the accepted opinion, and gave it as his decision that Dryden himself was responsible for the operatic version of *The Tempest*. His line of reasoning is, as we should expect, very strong. He first points out that it is somewhat extraordinary, to say the least, that if Shadwell is responsible for the operatic version of *The Tempest* neither he himself publicly claimed it, nor did anyone claim the credit on his behalf. Mr. Thorn-Drury certainly admits that Shadwell may " have had a hand in *The Tempest* as it proceeded on its successful career." In 1674 " Shadwell was a friend of Dryden and also of Reggio, the composer, and he was, which Dryden was not, a musician though only an amateur." " In these circumstances," remarks Mr. Thorn-Drury, " I see nothing of moment in the appearance of the words of a song by him in the 1674 text."

The Prologue and Epilogue from the Egerton MSS. are then discussed. It is, of course, obvious that nobody can definitely pronounce them to be Shadwell's ; and it is true that scant reliance can be placed upon internal opinion, which seems to be Mr. Lawrence's main ground for his attribution.

In Settle's *Notes and Observations on the Empress of Morocco* revised, Dryden is thus addressed : " Prethe dear heart set up for *Operas*." Mr. Thorn-Drury reads this as an allusion to the " successful issue of *The Tempest* opera venture," but he candidly allows that it may be " construed as a chaffing invitation to try an entirely new field," and to my mind, at any rate, this is the obvious interpretation. When Tom Brown in *The Reasons of Mr. Bays Changing his Religion* makes Dryden say that " poor Tragedy itself was swallowed up in an opera," he may well be alluding only to one acknowledged opera by Dryden, *Albion and Albanius*.

These, then, are in outline the arguments which two great authorities have produced for and against Shadwell's authorship of the operatic version of *The Tempest*.[2] If I may venture to say so, I regard the opinions of both these gentlemen with the profoundest respect. They themselves, I think, would be the first to acknowledge that there are weak joints in

[1] *The Review of English Studies*, Vol. I., No. 3, July, 1925, pp. 327–330.
[2] One or two callow sophomores from minor academies have tried to rush into this perplexing dispute, where scholars fear to tread, but their silly chatter is negligible.

both suits of armour. We have arrived at an impasse, and after having given the matter the most careful consideration for more than two years, my own opinion, since I recognize the amazing difficulties and ambiguities of the argument, is so indeterminate that I would prefer, as Herodotus says, to keep it to myself. But this is shirking the issue, and accordingly I am bound to confess I believe that Shadwell is responsible for the operatic version of *The Tempest*. It is certainly with no dogmatism that I venture to state this, but with a more than ordinary diffidence.

The success of *The Tempest*, which was produced *circa* 30 April, 1674, was, as we have emphasized, beyond anything great, and very promptly Thomas Duffett's pen was again called into action. His travesty, *The Mock-Tempest; or, The Enchanted Castle*,[1] was produced at Drury Lane in November, 1674, probably on 19 November, which day it was seen by the King. It was, Langbaine tells us, " writ on purpose to draw Company from the other Theatre, where was great resort about that time, to see that reviv'd Comedy call'd *The Tempest*, then much in vogue." Duffett, who was, " before he became a Poet, a Milliner in the New Exchange," certainly had a sense of humour, and although those blind idolaters of Shakespeare may express themselves shocked at a parody of their divine poet, many wits of to-day tell me that they have found *The Mock-Tempest* infinitely entertaining. It must be remembered, too, how much we are bound to lose in every parody and burlesque. So far as I am aware, there has been no revival of Duffett's farces, and when in our libraries we turn the fading quarto pages more than half the spirit of these merry scenes has already vanished and for ever gone.

There is a good deal of rollicking, if not very refined, fun in this skit, the note of which was struck at once when that arch-rogue Joe Haines appeared as if to speak the Prologue and summoned Ariel, whereupon there entered upon the stage Betty Mackarel, a well-known bona-roba of the Town, who had commenced her career of gallantry as an orange-wench at Drury Lane, and the dialogue which followed, if lively enough, is a little broad, a trifle risky. The actual storm is parodied in a Shrove Tuesday attack upon a brothel and all is noise and confusion. The whores and the mother-bawd scuttle to and fro with their bingo-blades and apple-squires, shouting and whooping as they bar the doors against the rabble, who at length break through, and the scene ends in a regular Armageddon. We are then transported to Bridewell; Prospero and Miranda are pretty roughly parodied, and in their turn the masques and songs of the opera are not forgotten. Some of the burlesque is amusing enough even to-day, but there is a good deal to which we realize we have lost the key. Allusions and topical speeches full of point and meaning to the Restoration audiences for us must be almost unintelligible.

[1] Reprinted for the first time in my *Shakespeare Adaptations*, 1922.

It was no doubt Shadwell's tremendous success with the operatic version of *The Tempest*, from which he must have derived great financial profit, even if his reputation was not actually enhanced thereby, since this theatrical revision of *The Tempest* appeared without a name, that decided him to venture his hand again upon another opera, a project in which he was much encouraged, and indeed even aided by the power behind the theatre, "infallible *Tom*," [1] the great Thomas Betterton. This plenipotentiary of Dorset Garden—a house especially adapted, it must be remembered, for elaborate production and spectacular show—had recently, at the King's own behest, paid a visit to Paris in order that he might study upon the spot the French methods of production, and the *mise-en-scène* of their operas and more elaborate performances. In January, 1671, a "tragédie-ballet" *Psyché*, upon which the greatest geniuses of the day employed themselves, had been produced with the utmost magnificence at the theatre of the Palais des Tuileries, and at the theatre of the Palais-Royal upon 24 July following. Molière, Corneille, Quinault, and Lulli all joined forces to make the new piece a success, and the result exceeded the liveliest anticipations. There were no less than eight and thirty consecutive performances, to thronging houses, and in the following year also there took place two remarkable revivals.

Betterton was deeply impressed by what he saw, and bearing in mind London's love for spectacle, a craving which incidentally has lasted until the very present day, the great actor, who was also a remarkably clever man of business, visualized in the liveliest colours the furore that *Psyché* would create at home. The whole material, "variety of Musick, curious Dancing,[2] splendid Scenes and Machines," lay ready to his hand. The only question was to whom should *Psyché* be entrusted to trick her out in English attire and native ornament? Dryden was writing for the rival

---

[1] A satire upon the production of *Albion and Albanius*, 1685, has these stanzas:

> *Betterton, Betterton*, thy decorations,
>   And the machines, were well written, we knew ;
> But all the words were such stuff, we want patience,
>   And little better is Monsieur *Grabu*.

> Damme, says *Underhill*, I'm out of two hundred
>   Hoping that rainbows and peacocks would do ;
> Who thought infallible *Tom* could have blundered ?
>   A plague upon him and Monsieur *Grabu*.

The "rainbows and peacocks" allude to the gorgeous pageantry of the performance. In Act I " Juno *appears in a Machine drawn by Peacocks ; while a Symphony is playing, it moves gently forward, and as it descends, it opens and discovers the Tail of the Peacock, which is so large that it almost fills the opening of the Stage between Scene and Scene.*" Presently " Iris *appears on a very large Machine.*" Such elaborate and detailed directions give us some idea of the gorgeousness with which the opera was mounted.

[2] In the French *Psyché* there were nearly 100 dancers.

company; Settle and D'Urfey had no great claims to be considered in this connexion; ſtarch Johnny Crowne was wholly absorbed in his masque *Caliſto; or, The Chaſte Nymph* which he was preparing for performance at Court; it was obvious that the choice muſt fall upon the dramatiſt who had recently made such a tremendous hit with his operatic *Tempeſt*, and accordingly Betterton communicated his design to Shadwell, urging him to undertake the subjeſt. Juſt at firſt Shadwell was not over enthusiaſtic. " I had rather be author of one scene of comedy, like some of Ben Jonson's, than of all the beſt plays of this kind that have been, or ever shall be written," he bluntly replied. However his artiſtic scruples were soon overcome by the very efficacious consideration of pecuniary profit. Moreover, although his name should publicly appear as the author of *Psyche*, yet when the libretto was printed he could vaunt his disdain of such a trifle and boldy wave the Jonsonian flag in the preface. After all, *Psyche* was from a Latin classic, and rare Ben himself would not have scorned to have taken his theme from the pages of the philosopher of Madaura. The admirers of French poetry were already sounding the praises of *Psyché* on this side of the Channel, and soon gossip began to spread about the town that London too was to have its *Psyche*, which Mr. Betterton had been heard say would prove a far rarer entertainment than even the Parisian opera. Dryden, who perhaps considered that he should have been approached to supply the words, and who was juſt then extremely mortified, since not he, the poet Laureate, but Crowne had been commissioned to write a masque for performance at Court, showed himself offended in the higheſt degree; and there was every excuse, nay reason, for his vexation. Without any undue vanity of conceit he muſt have known that as a poet he was a giant towering high in ſtrength and ſtature above a crowd of pigmy minikins.[1] Dryden would have made something infinitely great of *Psyche*, he would have set it aflame with the fire of his own genius, he would have wrought a poem very exquisite and very rare, not far from the exotic beauty of Apuleius.

The authorities at Dorset Garden did not pursue the policy of letting their new venture burſt suddenly upon the town; they were so sure that they could overtop all expeſtation, that they were content their opera should be talked about and advertised a great while in advance. On

---

[1] So in *Mac Flecknoe* we have :

> Thou art my blood, where *Johnson* has no part ;
> What share have we in Nature or in Art ?
> Where did his wit on learning fix a brand
> And rail at Arts he did not underſtand ?
> Where made he love in Prince *Nicander*'s vein,
> Or swept the duſt in *Psyche*'s humble ſtrain ?
> Where sold he Bargains, Whip-ſtich, kiss my Arse,
> Promis'd a Play, and dwindled to a Farce ?

22 August, 1673, James Vernon, writing a letter from London to Sir Joseph Williamson at Cologne, announces as a fine piece of news " that the Duke's house are preparing an Opera and great machines. They will have dansers out of France, and St. André comes over with them." [1] Betterton was a busy man in those days, and we may suppose that Shadwell himself did not fail to boast of the extraordinary expense which was being lavished upon the new production. This must have been gall and wormwood to Dryden, for not even the most patient soul can bear to see an inferior promoted above him and winning a charlatan reputation in matters of this kind. The offence is not merely personal, but also there is an artistic crime. Such situations are rendered none the less poignant by the fact that personal considerations so often play a part in these affairs. An ignorant patronage ; brazen presumption and self-advertisement will often push a fellow forward into the limelight. How frequently do we not see this to-day ! A scholar will devote the best years of his life to concentration upon a certain subject, he will publish some treatise of authority, or well-considered review. Almost immediately a swarm of locusts from the minor universities, and their humming parasites from college and conservatoire, will seize upon his suggestions ; in their sedulous predacity they rush into print with ill-informed hand-lists and histories (save the mark !), dialogues, developments, surveys, introductions to theory, and what not beside ! Naturally these leeches of literature fasten upon original figures, and although I am far from suggesting that Shadwell was one of these cuckoo-clowns,—he was too robust and virile for that—yet when in the circumstances he undertook to furnish the English libretto of *Psyché*, Dryden must have felt that a lesser man was poaching upon his own particular reserves.

Psyche was produced at Dorset Garden on 27 February, 1674-75. It had every advantage of music, composed by Draghi ; of scenery painted by Stephenson ; of ballet arranged by St. Andrée ; and the consequence was that it was followed with the most enthusiastic applause. Downes, although, it must be remarked, the old man mistakes the actual year, well sums up the reception in a few words : " In *February*, 1673, the long-expected Opera of *Psyche* came forth in all her ornaments ; new scenes, new machines, new cloaths, new French dances ; this Opera was splendidly set out, especially in scenes ; the charge of which amounted to above 800£. It had a continuance of performance about 8 days together ; it prov'd very beneficial to the company."

Although, of course, obvious faults may be remarked without much difficulty, to me *Psyche* is very pleasing. There are, it is true, roughnesses, as there are in all Shadwell's verses, for confessedly he was not a polished poet, but none the less much of the dialogue is elegant and agreeable ; it

[1] Letters to Sir Joseph Williamson at Cologne (*Camden Society*), 1, 179.

is far easier than anything we should have expected from Shadwell's pen.
It is, perhaps, mediocre melody, yet 'tis harmonious withal, and we must
remember that it was, as it were, but a framework to be dressed and draped.
In order to appreciate it at its true and proportionate worth, we should
compare it with the libretti of other operas, not with any great or even
with any felicitous poem. But set *Psyche* by the side of the English words
of *Il Pirata*, *La Somnambula*, *Norma* (the text of which by Romani is ranked
as a classic among Italian poetry), *I Puritani*, or *Anna Bolena;* of *L'Elisir
d'Amore*, *Gemma di Vergy*, and *La Favorita ;* or even *Il Trovatore* and *La
Traviata*, or wellnigh any other opera that was translated in the little
books we used to buy at Covent Garden, and I venture to think that
Psyche will prove to be possessed of no inconsiderable merit, perhaps of
its kind even to boast a certain charm.

The exquisite fiction of *Cupid and Psyche*, which is told by the old woman
in the robbers' cave to the captive damsel, has captured the imagination
of the world. Variants and parallels abound. In the collection of Indian
stories called *Somadeva Bhatta* there is a legend which is extremely similar
to the old Latin romance, and here the wood-cutter's daughter, Tulisa,
plays the part of Psyche. The story reappears among other Oriental
legends, in Persia, in Arabia, in China, it is said, and even yet further afield
among the folk-lore of Zululand. It has been treated as an allegory by
Fathers and Divines, the most famous interpretation in this kind being
perhaps that of S. Fulgentius (468–533). *Psyche* passed into the realms
of fairy, for to mention but a few stories out of very many there can be no
doubt that Madame D'Aulnoy's *Serpentin Vert* was directly, and *Gracieuse
et Percinet*, *Le Mouton*, together with Madame de Villeneuve's *La Belle et
la Bête*, were indirectly, suggested by the story. In poetry Marino in his
exquisite epic *L'Adone* has devoted the fourth canto to a most beautiful
recital of the legend. He has, however, made it symbolic, for he says :
" La Favola di Psiche rappresenta lo stato dell' uomo. La Città, dove
nasce, dinota il Mondo. Il Re, e la Reina, che la generano, significano
Iddio, e la Materia. Questi hanno tre figliuole, cioe la Carne, la Libertà
dell' arbitrio, e l'Anima." But all this means nothing to the poet. In
French there is a well-known poem by La Fontaine ; and in Polish
literature Andrew Morsztyn's *Psyche* holds a high place. In 1637 Shacker-
ley Marmion printed his *Cupid and Psiche, or an Epick Poem of Cupid, and
his Mistress*,[1] which has often been praised, and yet gives great pleasure in
the reading. The romantic *Cupid and Psyche* by Hudson Gurney, which was
anonymously published in 1799, is not altogether without merit, but a far
better piece of work is *Psyche ; or, The Legend of Love*, a poem in six cantos,
written in the Spenserian stanza by Mrs. Henry Tighe, which when first
printed in 1805 went through three editions, and which has been re-issued

---

[1] London, 4to 1637 ; also 1638 ; and 16mo as *Cupid's Courtship*, 1666.

as late as 1866. We also have the fair and gracious opening of the second part of William Morris's *Earthly Paradise ;* as also *Eros and Psyche* by the present poet Laureate, Mr. Robert Bridges. Nor must I let to praise, as is its meed, the sadly sweet *Legend of Eros and Psyche* of J. Redwood-Anderson. Boccaccio, *De Genealogia Deorum*, V, 22, says, that a whole volume would be required adequately to explain the allegory of Cupid and Psyche, and certainly yet another volume would be required to enumerate the multifold appearances of the legend, either under its own name or in some transparent disguise.[1]

The earliest rendering of Apuleius into English was that of William Adlington, which first appeared in 1566, and was reprinted at least four times before the end of the century, and as often since. In 1579 Stephen Gosson, who was violently attacking the theatre, mentions *The Golden Ass* amongst the books which had " been thoroughly ransackt to furnish the Play-houses," and it seems that a dramatization of *Cupid and Psyche* had been " played at Paules," although there is, I believe, no reliable evidence that any other part of the book had been seen upon the stage, beyond the fact that the incidents in the various tales which are introduced into the longer narrative had been utilized by the Elizabethans, as later they were often utilized by Restoration writers. But this does not in any sense amount to a play upon the adventures of Lucius.

Heywood's *Loves Mistris ; or, The Queene's Masque* was performed in 1634, and within the space of eight days was presented at Court no less than three times before King Charles I and his Queen. In fact Henrietta Maria, who had probably first seen the play at one of the private theatres, was so well pleased that she bade Inigo Jones embellish it with " rare decorements," and thus beautified she presented it as a fitting entertainment for the King on his birthday, 19 November, at Denmark House. Heywood's play was a favourite upon the stage both before and after the Restoration. It was seen by Pepys no less than five times, and upon his visit, Saturday, 15 August, 1668, he found it " full of variety of divertisement." This masque does not touch the heights of genius which inform the laurelled masques of Ben Jonson, and it is without those exquisite broideries of poetical prose, those silver liquid periods and courtly compliments of which Lyly is so bounteous in his Elizabethan pageantry ; indeed when in his prologues and epilogues to *Love's Mistris* Heywood would flatter his royal patron he becomes fulsome and servile-spoken ; but nevertheless it has a vein of lyric fancy which gives some of the scenes no inconsiderable beauties and charm. Apuleius, the refined thinker, and Midas, supply a running commentary throughout the whole play. " Apuleius explains the allegory as the action proceeds ; Midas remains

---

[1] See Friedlander's *Darstellungen aus der Sittengeschichte Roms. Anhang.,* I, pp. 509-548, 4th edition ; and also Creuzer, *Symbolik und Mythologie*, III, 6.

to the end the dull unappreciative boor, who ' stands for ignorance,' and only cares for dancing clowns, or the coarse jests of buffoons. Apuleius is the type of the enthusiastic poet, whose wit is ' aimed at inscrutable things beyond the moon.' Midas is the gross conceited groundling, who, turning everything he touches to dross, prefers Pan's fool to Apollo's chorus, and drives the God of life indignantly away. Both of them wear ass's heads ; Midas, because he grovels on the earth ; Apuleius, because all human intellect proves foolish if it flies too far."

Nor have the fine arts less contributed to the representation of the exquisite legend. Many monuments of ancient sculpture represent Cupid and Psyche in the various circumstances of their many adventures. The Eros in the British Museum has been ascribed to Praxiteles, and the Psyche in the museum at Naples is one of the finest examples of Græco-Roman virtu. Of more recent date are Canova's Psyche and Cupid, a composition of the most ethereal grace (1793), and the delicate Psyche and Cupid of the Louvre (1797). Nor must the intaglio, a gem of rarest loveliness, the Cupid and Psyche of Luigi Pichler [1] be forgotten.

The history of Psyche, twelve frescoes in the large gallery of the Villa Farnesina at Rome, can but be regarded as among the masterpieces of Raphael. It is true that this series of paintings owes something to the pupils of this great genius, notably to Giulio Romano, none the less the sketches and designs are his, and he directed the execution of such as he was unable himself to complete. Even after Raphael, the " Psyche received into Olympus " of Caravaggio,[2] now in the Louvre, Paris, compels admiration ; and there is a most daintily graceful canvas by David of Eros and his bride.

John Addington Symonds in a very illuminating essay has suggested that Heywood's *Love's Mistris* may from one point of view be regarded " as a very early attempt at classical burlesque," and although this must not be unduly emphasized, yet there are humorous situations that certainly seem a faint foreshadowing of those classical extravaganzas which delighted so many audiences in the nineteenth century, but which nowadays appear to be obsolete and wellnigh forgotten. Such were Robert Brough's *Medea ; or, The Best of Mothers* (1856) ; *The Siege of Troy* (1858) ; William Brough's *Perseus and Andromeda* (1861) ; *Hercules and Omphale ; or, The Power of Love* (1864) ; *Endymion ; or, The Naughty Boy who Cried for the Moon* [3] ; Gilbert's excellent *Thespis ; or, The Gods Grown Old* (1871) ; and many of Planché's pantomimes, which were initiated by his *Olympic Revels ;*

---

[1] 1773–1854.

[2] Polidoro Caldara, 1492 (or 1495)—1543.

[3] Produced at S. James's Theatre, London, on 26 December, 1860, with Miss M. Taylor as Endymion, Miss Herbert as Diana, Miss Kate Terry as Poldora, and Miss E. Romer, Miss C. St. Casse, Dewar, Emery, Belmore, and Charles Young in the cast.

or, Prometheus and Pandora, that proved so remarkable a success when produced at the Olympic, 3 January, 1831, under the management of Madame Vestris. The strictly correct classical costumes of the performers were wrought with a beauty that caused a furore of delight and crowded the theatre to see the spectacle. As early as May, 1733, this vein had been exploited, for Breval's [1] *The Rape of Helen*, a mock-opera which was acted at Covent Garden that month, shows us the gods of Greece as walking the earth awhile. All these, of course, are far more thorough-going parodies than anything which Heywood has suggested. His fun is very simple, and is exemplified in such a scene as that where Vulcan, with so vast an influx of orders on hand that he is unable to cope with the stress, appears at his forge very overworked and muttering to himself in a worried tone of voice :

> There's half a hundred thunder-bolts bespoke ;
> Neptune hath broke his mace ; and Juno's coach
> Must be new mended, and the hindmost wheels
> Must have two spokes set in.

Far more in the vein of the extravaganzas of Planché and the brothers Brough is the skit with which the indefatigable Duffett travestied Shadwell's *Psyche*. The wits were already laughing at the elaborate splendours of the opera, and no doubt Dorset and the rest would not hesitate to let Shadwell know very clearly that such libretti did not fall within his province. Rochester, who never missed an opportunity of being caustically ill-natured, in an Epilogue (spoken by Joe Haines), which he wrote for his friend Sir Francis Fane's *Love in the Dark ; or, The Man of Bus'ness*, produced at Drury Lane in April–May, 1675, hit at *Psyche* with a dry bob as follows :

> As Charms are Nonsense, Nonsense seems a Charm,
> Which hearers of all Judgment does disarm ;
> For Songs, and Scenes, a double Audience bring,
> And Doggrel takes, which *Smiths* in Sattin sing.
> Now to Machines, and a dull Mask you run,
> We find that Wit's the Monster you would shun,
> And by my troth 'tis most discreetly done
> For since with Vice and Folly Wit is fed,
> Through Mercy 'tis, most of you are not dead.
> Players turn Puppets now at your desire,
> In their Mouth's Nonsense, in their Tail's a Wire,
> They fly through Clouds of Clouts, and Showers of Fire.

[1] The authorship is uncertain, but the attribution to John Durant Breval is accepted by the *Biographia Dramatica*.

A kind of loseing *Loadum* [1] in their Game,
Where the worst Writer has the greatest Fame.
To get vile Plays like theirs, shall be our care ;
But of such *awkward* Actors we *despair*.[2]
False talked at first—
Like Bowls ill byass'd, still the more they run,
They're further off, than when they first begun.

  . . . .

Could they—
Rage like *Cethegus*, or like *Cassius* die,[3]
They ne'er had sent to *Paris* for such Fancies,
As Monster's Heads and *Merry Andrew*'s Dances.
Wither'd, perhaps, not perish'd we appear,
But they were blighted, and ne'er came to bear,
Th'old Poets dress'd your Mistress Wit before,
These draw you on with an old painted Whore,
And sell, like Bawds, patch'd Plays for Maids twice o'er.
Yet they may scorn our House and Actors too,
Since they have swell'd so high to hector you.
They cry, Plague o' these *Covent-Garden* Men,
Plague 'em, not one of them but keeps out ten.
Were they once gone, we for those thund'ring Blades
Shou'd have an Audience of substantial Trades,
Who love our muzzled Boys, and tearing Fellows,
My Lord, great Neptune, and *great Nephew* Æolus.
O how the merry Citizens (are) in Love
With—
Psyche, the Goddess of each Field and Grove.
He cries I'faith, me thinks 'tis well enough ;
But you roar out and cry, 'Tis all poor stuff.
So to their House the graver Fops repair,
While Men of Wit find one another here.

In these mordant lines the " *Smiths* in Sattin," of course, have reference
to the opening of Act III in *Psyche*, where the Cyclops are at work at their
forge, fashioning great vases of silver. It is interesting to note that these
Titan craftsmen were dressed by the theatrical costumier in tinsel and
brocades ; whilst the " Monster's Heads " allude to the huge and grotesque

---

[1] A very popular old card game at which, as in reversi, the loser won, the object
being to gain no tricks. Cf. Cotgrave (1611) ; " Coquimbert qui gaigne pert. A game
at cards like our losing Lodam."
[2] It is unfortunate that the cast of *Psyche* has not been preserved.
[3] Alluding to Michael Mohun, who excelled in these two rôles.

masks which were worn by the Furies and Devils in the scene of Hades, and which are familiar to those of us who have the happiness of belonging to Victorian days from the pantomimes of our boyhood, when pantomimes were pantomimes indeed. It will be noticed that "*Merry Andrew's Dances*" is aimed at the ballet which was designed and superintended by St. Andrée; whilst "*My Lord, great* Neptune," and "*great Nephew* Æolus," and "Psyche, *the Goddess of each Field and Grove*," are actual quotations from *The Tempest*, the terminal masque, which was Shadwell's original work, and from *Psyche*, Act I, the recitative of Pan. Perhaps it would be over-strained to emphasize this little point as an additional tittle of evidence that Rochester, at any rate, who is fleering at Shadwell all through, and who would have certainly have known the truth, regarded Shadwell as the author of the operatic version of *The Tempest*. "Muzzled Boys" refers to the line "Muzzle your roaring Boys" which Neptune addresses to Æolus, and there is also a hit at these ogrish pantomime heads, for "muzzled" is equivalent to "masked," and is so used by Pitcairn in his *Criminal Trials*,[1] where when describing the sabbat at North Berwick in 1590, he records that seven score witches "danced end-long the Kirk yard. *John Fian*, missellit led the ring." Satires such as these were what would be known to-day as "high-brow," but they did not in any way affect the popular success of operatic spectacle at Dorset Garden. Duffett delivered an even more direct attack. About Easter, 1675, hard on the heels of *Psyche*, followed his mock opera *Psyche Debauch'd*,[2] the cleverest and most amusing of his burlesques. When it was produced at Drury Lane several of the male characters were acted by women, just as they would have been in the days of Mrs. Keeley and Nellie Farren, or of the pantomime princes forty years ago. Thus Mrs. Corbett, who played Narcissa in Lee's *Gloriana*, and Monima in *Mithridates, King of Pontus*, appeared as King Andrew; Nicholas, a prince in love with None-so-fair, was taken by the sprightly Mrs. Mary Knepp, who is so familiar to us from the pages of Pepys; whilst Philip, the rival suitor, was acted by Charleton, the original Jerry Blackacre in *The Plain-Dealer*, a young player whom death robbed from the theatre at an early age. Bruin, the White Bear of Norwich, was performed by William Harris, a very useful actor in farce, and a clever exponent of the First Witch in the burlesque epilogue to Duffett's *The Empress of Morocco*; Apollo, A Wishing-Chair, was sustained by Lydall; and Jeffrey, Bruin's man, by Coysh,[3] an actor of

---

[1] Edinburgh, 1833.

[2] Publication was delayed as *Psyche* was not printed until 1678.

[3] He played Plautus in Lee's *The Tragedy of Nero*, 1674; Aristander in *The Rival Queens*, 1676–7; Sir Robert Malory in Leanerd's *The Country Innocence*, 1677; Bramble in the same author's *The Rambling Justice*, 1677–8; the Second Physician in D'Urfey's *Trick for Trick*, 1678; and Swift, a servant, in the same author's *Sir Barnaby Whigg*, August–September, 1681.

inferior rank, " ſtrowling *Coiſh*," he is called in *A Satyr upon the Players* (unprinted MS.), about 1683.

On the other hand, Coſtard, a Country-man, and Gammer Redſtreak his wife were safe in the hands of Martin Powell, and that inimitable comedian the great Mrs. Corey. John Wiltshire, who had made a marked success by his rendering of Sir Robert Howard's song " Washed with Sighs," [1] which was introduced into a revival of *The Chances,* perhaps had little opportunity for his talents in the rôle of Juſtice Crabb (for the God Mars). Of King Andrew's three daughters, Wou'dhamore, Sweet-lips, and None-so-fair ; Mrs. Rutter, " tall, and fair, and bonny," who was accounted an admirable exponent of Mrs. Crossbite in *Love in a Wood,* and Old Lady Squeamish in *The Country-Wife* [2] played the eldeſt, whilſt the youngeſt, None-so-fair, a name very reminiscent of Madame d'Aulnoy, and a direct parody of Psyche, fell to the lot of that graceless buffoon Joe Haines, who old Aston says was " more remarkable for the witty, tho' wicked, Pranks he play'd, and for his Prologues and Epilogues, than for Acting." [3] Nevertheless so elegant a dancer and so famous a farceur in his green ſtockings, silken petticoat and new mantoplicee, his curls, powder and patches, muſt have been a fine figure of fun as the Princess who enters murmuring with an affected lisp to her attendants, Twattle and Glozy, in rude burlesque of Psyche's

How charming are these Meads and Groves !

the following lines :

O *Glozy* ! What a crumptious place is here ?
Where one can see one play with ones own Dear.
Under each bush kind Sun doth warm ;
Here one may kiss, and laugh, and think no harm :
For Countrey Love has neither joyes nor fears,
And Bushes break no Truſt, though Walls have ears.

Glozy. No Missy *None-so-fair,* they are not of *Oatalian* mind.

Many of Duffett's scenes are extremely happy. And even now there is good fun when None-so-fair, in parody of Psyche and the two Zephyri

[1] The music was by John Eccles.

[2] Among other of her rôles were Emilia in *Othello ;* Lady Haughty in *The Silent Woman ;* Dame Pliant in *The Alchemiſt ;* Martha in *The Scornful Lady ;* Olinda in *Secret Love ; or, The Maiden Queen ;* Lady Malory in Leanerd's *The Country Innocence ; or, The Chamber Maid Turn'd Quaker ;* and Alicia, Confidante to the Princess Matilda, in Ravenscroft's *King Edgar and Alfreda.*

[3] Joe Haines with Betty Mackarel, a flaming ſtrumpet as common as tobacco, delivered the saucy Introduction to Duffett's *The Mock-Tempeſt* (produced in November, 1674), which Haines followed up with a smart prologue. On 18 June, 1677, Haines was actually arreſted " for reciteinge . . . a Scurrilous & obscoene Epilogue."

is whewed away by the enchanted Wishing-Chair to " an Arbour dress'd up with gaudy Play-games for Children," the realms of Bruin, who is her Cupid. This extremely resembles Madame de Villeneuve's [1] *La Belle et la Bête*, or perhaps, to speak by the card, that pretty little nursery tale for juvenile readers which Madame Jeanne Leprince de Beaumont constructed out of one of the most ingenious of fairy chronicles.

In the Prologue to *Psyche Debauch'd*, we have some very sharp bobs at Shadwell :

> *But Sirs, free harmless Mirth you here condemn,*
> *And Clap at down-right Baudery in them.*
> *In* Epsom-Wells *for example—*
> *Are they not still for pushing Nature on,*
> *Till Natures feat thus in your sight is done.*
> *Oh Lord !—*
> *Take off their* Psyches *borrow'd plumes awhile*
> Hopkins *and* Sternhold *rise, and claim your style ;*
> *Dread Kings of* Brentford ! *leave* Lardellas Herse, [2]
> Psyches *despairing Lovers steal your verse :*
> *And let* Apollo's *Priest restore again*
> *What from the nobler* Mamamouchy's [3] *ta'n.*
> *Let 'em restore your Treble prices too,*
> *To see how strangely still they bubble you,*
> *It makes me blush ; and that I seldom do.*
> *Now* Psyche's *strip'd from all her gay attire,*
> *TE DE POLUKAGATHOI, Behold the Fire !*

The masque of Pan is burlesqued by " Enter *a Countrey* Crouder, *followed by a Milk-maid with her Payl dressed up as on* May-day. *After them a company*

[1] Gabrielle Susanne Barbot, daughter of a gentleman of Rochelle, and widow of Monsieur de Gallon, Seigneur de Villeneuve, Lieutenant-Colonel of Infantry, died at Paris, in the house of Crébillon père, the tragic writer, 29 December, 1755. This is practically all that is known of the writer of one of the most popular of all fairy tales.

[2] In allusion to *The Rehearsal*, IV, 1, the scene of the Funeral, where a Paper of Verses which has been pinned to Lardella's coffin, is read. The lines are a parody of a speech of Berenice in *Tyrannick Love*. They commence :

> Since death my earthly part will thus remove
> I'l come a Humble Bee to your chaste love.
> With silent wings I'll follow you, dear Couz ;
> Or else, before you, in the Sun-beams, buz.
> And when to Melancholy Groves you come,
> An Airy Ghost, you'l know me by my Hum ;
> For sound, being Air, a Ghost does well become.

[3] Ravenscroft's *The Citizen turn'd Gentleman*, produced at Dorset Garden, July, 1672 ; 4to, 1672 ; and reissued as *Mamamouchi*, 1675. The scene to which reference is here made is the burlesque investiture of old Jorden as a mamamouchi. Much of Ravenscroft's comedy is from *Le Bourgeois Gentilhomme*.

of Morris-dancers, a Sylvan, *and a* Dryad." Presently: " *Enter* Ambition, *an Alderman's Wife;* Power, *Schoolmistress;* Plenty *an Ale Wife, and* Peace *a Zealot."* Venus is burlesqued by Woossatt, acted by young Clarke, and Bruin " *the White Bear of* Norwich " is her son. The three Princesses visit the Wishing-Chair (Apollo, *A Wishing-Chair*). There is an elaborate parody of the Oracle scene in *Psyche*, and after a dance we have:

The Invocation.

2 *Priest.* James Naylor,[1] *Pope Joan, Wat-Tyler, Mall Cutpurse,[2] Chocovelly.[3]*
All Answer. Help our *Opera*, because 'tis very silly.
2 *Priest.* Massaniello, Moseley,[4] *Jack-straw, Jantredixco, Pimponelli.*
Answer. Help our *Opera*, because 'tis very silly.
2 *Priest.* Hocus-pocus, Don-Quixot, Jack Adams,[5] *Mary Ambry,[6] Frier Bungey,[7] William Lilly.[8]*
Answer. Help our *Opera*, because 'tis very silly.
2 *Priest.* Carpentero, Paintero, Dancero, Musickero, Songstero, Punchanelly.
Answer. Help our *Opera*, because 'tis very silly.

The satire upon the elaborate accessories which made *Psyche* so great a success, and the hit at their foreign origin should not be overlooked.

[1] The mad fanatic, born at Ardsley in Yorkshire, 1616. In his frenzies he proclaimed himself the Messiah, and was severely punished, further being imprisoned in Bridewell. He was liberated in 1660, which year he died.

[2] Mary Frith, a rampant virago, born in 1584, or rather later in Aldersgate Street. Probably nowadays she would have passed muster without comment. She distinguished herself by donning male attire, " and to her dying day she would not leave it off." Her sluttish and indecent pranks are told in a *Life* which was published in 1662. Middleton and Dekker have a comedy *The Roaring Girl*, in which she is a conspicuous figure. It was produced at the Fortune and printed 4to, 1611. She also appears in Field's *Amends for Ladies*, acted at the Blackfriars, 4to, 1618.

[3] Coviello, a mask in the *Commedia dell'Arte*.

[4] Bawd en titre to the Earl of Shaftesbury, and chief agent for his debaucheries. Amongst other references she is mentioned in the " Macbeth " Epilogue to Duffett's skit *The Empress of Morocco*.

[5] " A Person very notorious for his prodigious Science and dexterity in Counterfeiting all manner of Hands and Writing, who being at last detected, performed the Exercises used in those Cases, and through the Pillory over-saw several Markets according to his Sentence in the Court of King's Bench, when he lately died." (1685.)

[6] A frampold jade, often alluded to as a typical Amazon. She is said to have " fought at the Siege of Ghent," 1584. Jonson frequently mentions her, *e.g.*, *The Silent Woman*, IV, 1, when Morose cries to Mrs. Otter, who is chastising her husband : " Mistress Mary Ambree, your examples are dangerous." She is mentioned in Field's *Amends for Ladies*, with Long Meg of Westminster. In Percy's *Reliques* there is a ballad of her exploits.

[7] The companion of Friar Bacon in the adventure of the Brazen Head. Cf. Greene's play *The Honorable Historie of frier Bacon, and frier Bungay*, 4to, 1594, which is founded on the old chap-books.

[8] The famous astrologer, 1602–1681.

None-so-fair is carried off to the abode of Bruin. She is said to be a morsel for Jupiter " himself in his Altitudes [1] . . . that's drunk as David's sow, with *Nectar* and *Ambrosia*, which is stout Mum, and Brandy; the Gods drink upon Holy-dayes." The scene, as we have before noted, next changes to " *an Arbour dress'd up with gaudy Play-games for Children*," where None-so-fair enters and is courted by Bruin.

> *Oh fair Maid ! be not affraid : For I am come a wooing*
> *Thou art mine, and I am thine own sweet heart, and* Bruin.

After, " *A dance of Bears, amongst which is the white Bear of* Norwich, *and at the end of the Dance his shape flyes off, and he appears dressed like a* Cupid." In the next act we have a good deal of fooling with Costard and Redstreak, some of which when Redstreak apes the lady of quality is amusing enough, and at length in Act V we find " A common Prison confused " which appropriately represents the Hades of the opera. Cries of " Garnish, garnish," are heard; there is some close burlesque of the original story, and the whole concludes with bacchanalian revelry.

Of Duffett's *Psyche Debauch'd*, Langbaine says : " This *Mock Opera* was writ on purpose to Ridicule Mr. *Shadwell's Psyche*, and to spoil the Duke's House, which, as has been before observ'd, was then more frequented than the King's." The *Biographia Dramatica* tells us that Duffett's farce " soon met with the contempt it merited." I know not upon what authority this statement is made. From the very nature of the thing any parody of a particular piece cannot be long lived. When the original play falls out of the repertory, the travesty must also expect to be discarded. Moreover, this lightest of light fare must be stuffed with topical carwichets and clinches, and these can but endure a very little time. In fine, any burlesque, save the very greatest, which are informed by genius, and of these I take the comedy of the Greek poet, Aristophanes, to be the most excellent, must soon wholly be laid aside, and to point this out seems a superfluous comment.

It might have been expected that after two operas Shadwell would have returned to his Jonsonian comedy, but such was not immediately the case. Rochester called him " hasty Shadwell " [2] and his output at this juncture certainly merits that epithet. In June, 1675, probably on the 15th day of that month, when the King was present in the theatre, The Libertine was produced at Dorset Garden, and Shadwell has told us that Acts I, II and III were put together in a fortnight, no one several act having occupied him for more than five days, whilst the last two acts together, since Betterton was urging him to complete the script at breakneck speed, were both

---

[1] Cf. *Dictionary of the Canting Crew* : " *Altitudes, the Man is in his Altitudes,* he is Drunk."

[2] *An Allusion to Horace, The Tenth Satire of the First Book.*

penned in the amazingly short time of four days. True, the way was well chalked out for him, but none the less it is an extraordinary feat to have accomplished so much in so short a time and to have accomplished it so well. The legend of Don Juan has become one of the sagas of the world. In his complex psychology Don Juan is a modern type, because he has thought out a philosophy by which he models and defends his conduct and his code. Possibly the love of change, in some state or stage, exists in us all; the pleasures that we know so well and can repeat at will tend to become tedious and utterly boring. Familiarity breeds ennui. But the whole question is not nearly so simple as that. Honour, gratitude, comfort, security, all have their claims, and it is just these claims which Don Juan refuses to recognize. Many of us too, are, or use to be, frankly domesticated; Don Juan is not a domestic animal. There is often something very magnificent about him, as there is something very magnificent in the black and yellow body, the polished claws, the gleaming teeth, the lithe grace and swift spring of a tiger. But the ordinary mortal would shrink from consorting with a tiger however lovely a creature he may be, and so I think the mortal who values peace and happiness may well shrink from a meeting with Don Juan.

Don Juan proclaims himself as " the man of reason," he does not realize that reason without romance will ruin the world. Reason is cruel, reason is ethical, reason is sordid, reason is dangerous, unless there be a very large admixture of passion and poetry. Don Juan claimed to be an individualist, he was in reality not an individualist, but utterly and entirely selfish. The true individualist is the man who recognizes his superiority, and whose logic deduces thence that it is for the best that his ideas and his will should override the will and the ideas of those who are in every way his inferiors. The individualist is the true aristocrat of intellect. He is supremely unselfish, and supremely great. The real Don Juan is the rationalist; ineffably vain, inordinately self-centred, a vulgarian in his ideas and in his practical exposition of them. He is, in truth, a small man. Poet, philosopher, and musician have tried to dress him in the robes of dream-land and jewels of fancy, but they fit him ill. They have metamorphosed him with a change the reverse of that effected by Circe's charms, for they have turned the animal into a man, the wallowing swine into a picturesque hero. Sometimes he is not a human being at all, at any rate no such human being as could be suffered to exist in a world of peace and truth and comely order. He is a cold calculating machine. There may be such men, bred by the corruption of modern social theory and modern politics, but really they do not belong to this world at all, and they strike one as being something sub-normal; something very ugly and terrible; something which has no decent right to exist. We kill dumb animals who are far more pleasing to God than they.

Don Juan is of the type which does not realize that in the face of the eternal realities man's reason is a worthless guide, and if he blindly follows it, it is not so much that he will deserve punishment, as that punishment must inevitably come. There was more wisdom in the little finger of another Spanish John, S. John of the Cross, than in Don Juan's whole heart.

The legend of Don Juan as we know it does not seem to have taken shape earlier than the seventeenth century, when it was developed by the teaching of religion, which embodied a psychology that is as old as the world in the person of one particular individual. It is not to be denied that many traits of Don Juan are to be found in the Greek deity Zeus. When we think of the beauty of the Greek religion, of the splendour of the Attic poets, of the chivalry of their heroes, of the romance of their wanderings, we are apt to forget that there is a very sombre and a very unlovely side to all this, features by no means trivial or insignificant, essential traits of which S. Augustine has spoken in no uncertain voice. The mysteries of Hecate, " Queen of the Phantom-World," " the nameless one," " all terrible," are wrapt in dread and darkness ; the very sight of Pan drove the traveller mad ; there were hideous spectres and ghosts who at night haunted lonely houses, the deserted highways and four cross-roads, there were the Empusas, Cercopis, and the ghoul Mormo.[1] So the Greek divinities and demigods were not always those who sat in their celestial halls upon the snow-clad heights of Olympus and drank immortal nectar to the sweet songs of lyric Apollo.

Don Juan is not merely, as the vulgar believe, and the thing has passed into a common proverb, the wanton philanderer,[2] he is much more than that. He is the protagonist of reason and natural law in the eternal conflict against the divine law and the supernatural, in fact Don Juan is the " natural man." [3] The ancient world could only conceive one side of his psychology ; it was not until later that we had the complete Don Juan. He is the enemy of the ideal, of the sentimental, of romance, of all that rises above mere materialism ; he is anti-social, and he would, I imagine, be at home in Moscow to-day ; he is somewhat more dangerous than a mad tiger suddenly let loose. One may observe, and the point has deep

---

[1] See my *Geography of Witchcraft*, 1927, pp. 6–8.

[2] One might almost say that the ancient world had its typical philanderer in Zeus (Jupiter), a masterpiece of incontinence, whose amours were legion. Such a legend as that of Theseus, who deserted Ariadne, and Antiope, who married Phaedra, who carried off Helen, and attempted to rape Proserpine, is pregnant in this connexion.

[3] " But the natural man receiveth not the things of the Spirit of God : for they are foolishness unto him : neither can he know them, because they are spiritually discerned." I *Corinthians*, 11, 14 (*A.V.*). The Vulgate has : " Animalis autem homo non percipit ea, quae sunt Spiritus Dei ; stultitia enim est illi, et non potest intelligere : quia spiritualiter examinatur." Don Juan is exactly " animalis homo " of the Apostle.

significance, that the two great legends of the modern world, Faust and Don Juan, could not have existed before Christianity came.

The original Don Juan is Spanish, and it were well to inquire whether there is any actual foundation for the story. Although the details may be obscure, it certainly seems that an individual, from whose history the germ of the legend took its rise, once existed. Viardot, in his *Études sur l'histoire des institutions, de la littérature, du théâtre et des beaux-arts en Espagne*, 1835, remarked: " Tirso de Molina was the first who wrote a play upon the story of Don Juan . . . when I was in Spain last year, I made it my business to endeavour to discover whether any actual fact is contained in the legend, and I found out that the incidents which gave rise to this famous tale undoubtedly occurred. Don Juan Tenorio was born in Seville, and his family, who are still represented there, have always been accounted persons of the highest quality. Their names are registered among the *veinticuatro ;* and the name Tenorio is actually to be found in the municipality to-day. Don Juan belonged to this house, and much that we see in our plays of his adventures is recorded in his life. One night he killed the Commander d'Ulloa, whose daughter he had violently carried off some little time before. The Commander was buried in a chapel of the church attached to a monastery, San Francisco, where was the family vault. This chapel and the marble statue might be seen until the beginning of the eighteenth century, when they were destroyed in a terrible fire. The Franciscan friars, an order very prominent and powerful in Seville, determined to put a stop to the scandals to which Don Juan gave rise, for owing to his noble birth he imagined he could indulge his lewdness and brutality unchecked, and indeed commit any excess with perfect impunity. Accordingly he was privately arrested within the precincts of the cloister, brought before a close tribunal, and for his crimes condemned to death. Since he thus disappeared the story arose that one day he had violently forced his way into the chapel, and was insulting the statue of the man whom he had slain, when the earth opened and he was swallowed up quick. This legend is actually recounted in certain old chronicles of the city, and hence Tirso de Molina derived the story of his play, to which he gave this curious but telling title [1]; *No hay plazo que no llegue ni deuda que no se pague, o El convidado de piedra* (*A day of reckoning always arrives, and debts must be paid ; or, the Guest of Marble*)."

Castil-Blaze,[2] and A. de Latour,[3] regard this story as authentic ; whilst the latter adds that in 1855 there was a street in Seville which bore the

---

[1] Viardot in his *Études sur l'histoire des institutions, de la littérature, du théâtre et des beaux-arts en Espagne*, 1835, has confused the title of Tirso's play with the title of the piece by Zamora.

[2] *Molière musicien*, I, p. 221.

[3] *Études sur L'Espagne*, II, p. 99 *et sqq.*

name Ulloa, the family of the Commander. Arvède Barine,[1] Koch,[2] Zeidler,[3] don Manuel de la Revilla,[4] have all investigated the sources of the legend, and are satisfied that it had its origin in an actual history.

It is true there are some difficulties, and it is no easy matter precisely to identify the Don Juan Tenorio who is the figure in the saga. A great many interesting theories have been put forward which it were impertinent to investigate here, and it may further be said that the Franciscans would have been little likely to publish the affair abroad or to remember it in their records. One thing is certain, the names Don Juan Tenorio and the Commander d'Ulloa are strictly historical.

El Burlador de Sevilla y convidado de piedra was printed in 1630, and the composition of this play is generally ascribed to a date not more than three or four years before publication, nevertheless there is a tradition, which is reported amongst others by Castil-Blaze, that in the fifteenth and sixteenth centuries there was performed an " auto-sacramental " entitled *El Ateísta fulminado* which dealt with the same subject as the *Burlador*, and which probably inspired the later piece. As yet nothing definite concerning this " auto-sacramental " has been discovered, but so vast are the collections of dramatic manuscripts in the libraries of Spain that it is quite possible the script, or some scenario, may come to light. In the Preface to his Tragedy, *The Libertine*, Shadwell says : " I have been told by a worthy Gentleman, that many years ago (when first a Play was made upon this Story in *Italy*) he has seen it Acted there by the name of *Atheisto Fulminato*, in Churches, on *Sundays*, as a part of Devotion." M. Simone Brouwer found in a Roman library eight and forty *lazzi*, that is to say drafts or outlines of plays, and among these was one called *Il Ateísta fulminato*, the author and date of which are quite unknown. This drama has been judged to be a work of the later decades of the seventeenth century, but it may well prove a much earlier composition ; and, in any case, in its present form it is undoubtedly a redaction from an older drama. It is highly probable, nay, almost certain, that the tradition of this " auto-sacramental " is correct, and from Catholic Spain the legend, no doubt, soon passed into Catholic Italy.

The Italian scenario shows us the adventures of a certain Count Aurelio, who carries off from the convent, where she is enclosed, a young maiden named Leonora. When he is pursued by her brother, jealous for the family honour, he disguises himself as a hermit, and, secure from recognition, in this habit he escapes from the vengeance which threatens him. But eventually a terrible punishment overtakes him, for the statues of the

---

[1] " Les Origines de Don Juan " ; *Revue politique et littéraire*, 15 October, 1881.
[2] *Zeitschrift für vergl. Litter.*, 1887, p. 392 *et sqq.*
[3] *Ibid.*, 1896, p. 89 *et sqq.*
[4] *El Tipo leyendario de Don Juan Tenorio y sus manifestaciones en las modernas literaturas.*

father and mother of Leonora, animated by some awful life, as he mocks them for senseless things, suddenly overwhelm him, and he is swallowed up in the earth whilst the thunder growls and mutters over his doom. It will be seen that here we have in detail the theme of the drama of Don Juan.

Various parallels to the *Burlador*, some tolerably close, some exceedingly far fetched, have been adduced, and it would not be impossible to cite yet more from the legends and folk-lore of many countries, from Portugal and Sicily, from Brittany and Gascony, from Germany, from Denmark, from distant Scandinavia. Dio Chrysostom, the famous sophist (100 A.D.),[1] and Pausanias [2] tell the story of the statue that the people of Elis raised to the athlete Theogenis of Thasos, and how one night some envious rival lashed it insultingly with a whip. The figure suddenly moved, and with its full weight of bronze limbs leaped upon its enemy, crushing him to the earth. Aristotle [3] relates that the murderer of the Argive Mitys was slain by the statue of the man whom he had killed.

To return to Spain itself, we have in the theatre of Lope de Vega and Juan de la Cueva figures who are not unlike the character of Don Juan. There is, for example, Leonido the hero of the *Fianza satisfecha* of Lope ; and again Leucino in the *Infamador* of Cueva.

However, the gallant adventures of Don Juan, his rapes, adulteries, and fornications, for he is lecherous as a polecat, are perhaps the least important part of his legend. The essential feature is not so much the punishment of the libertine, as the punishment of the philosopher and propagator of evil, and the supernatural character of that vengeance which thus proclaims itself divine. *El Burlador de Sevilla* is the work of Gabriel Tellez,[4] who is better known by his pseudonym of Tirso de Molina. He was born at Madrid about the year 1571, and, actually, comparatively little is known in detail of his life. The exact date of his ordination to the priesthood, and of his entry into the Mercedarians,[5] have not been precisely ascer-

---

[1] *Orationes*, XXXI.

[2] Ἑλλάδος Περιήγησις. Elis ; VI. c. xi.

[3] *Poetics*, XI, 6.

[4] It is true that A. Farinelli, *Don Giovanni. Noti critiche*, in the *Giornale storico della letteratura italiana*, 1896, t. xxvii, fasc. 79 and 80, questions the authorship, but I believe that he is alone in so doing, and as the point has never before been disputed, and his arguments, or rather his hypotheses, seem baseless, we may confidently say that the *Burlador* is from the pen of Tirso de Molina.

[5] The Celestial, Royal, and Military Order of Our Lady of Mercy was founded in 1218 by S. Peter Nolasco, who was bidden by the Mother of God Herself to institute a Religious Order devoted to the ransom of captives. S. Peter was the first Superior with the title of Commander-General. The Order spread widely, and those members who accompanied Columbus formed no less than eight provinces in Latin America. At present the Order has houses in Palermo ; Spain ; Venezuela ; Peru ; Chile ; Argentina ; Ecuador ; and Uruguay. The Mercedarians of Cordova publish a *Revista*

tained. He was a very prolific writer, and, as well as other works, is credited with having written no less than four hundred plays, but only some eighty are now available. In 1620 Tellez was living in the monastery of his order at Madrid, and here he remained for several years; in 1645 he was appointed prior of the Mercedarian house at Soria in Aragon, where he died 21 March, 1648. Although Spanish critics are not agreed that *El Burlador de Sevilla* is the best of Molina's dramas, it is certainly the most famous, and, generally speaking, the most interesting. The psychology is very complex and admirably observed, whilst the author ingeniously raises certain theological problems, which are not altogether easy to resolve.[1]

Very early did the *Burlador* pass into Italy. Probably the legend was already current there, and had been no doubt presented in some rough dramatic form, but now it appeared as fashioned with complete artistry. Riccoboni tells us that a *Convitato Di Pietra* was known as early as 1620, and this may be one of those scenarios which we have mentioned, or, on the other hand, the dramatic historian may have dated this play ten or fifteen years too soon, and it may actually be a translation of the *Burlador* to which he alludes. At any rate before 1650, the probable date of the death of the author, there appeared *Il Convitato di pietra, opera esemplare del signor Jacinto Andrea Cicognini*. One of the most notable features of this piece is that here we meet the servant Passarino, who has all the features of Shadwell's Jacomo. In the Spanish dramatist, Catalinon is a very different type; he supplies some lighter touches, but he is by no means a mere buffoon. Passarino is a clown who is there to make merriment; he is a coward and greedy; if he dared, he would betray his master to those who are seeking revenge; he is always wishing to leave Don Juan's service, but he is too cowardly to run away. Not that he has any scruples about attending upon the worst villain in the world, he is only alarmed for his own skin, lest one day when the end comes he shall be involved in the penalties and disgrace.

There is, further, a *Convitato di pietra* by Onofrio Giliberto, which

---

Mercedaria. Of recent years the church of San Adriano al Foro, where was the Roman house, has unfortunately been demolished. The habit is white, and the badge the coat armour of James *el Conquistador*, 4 pallets, and in chief a cross *pattee*. The great feast of the Order is 24 September, Our Lady of Mercy.

[1] The Don Juan of Tirso is far from being an atheist or a free-thinker. He knows that he must answer for his crimes, but he is young and he counts upon having time to clear his conscience. His last cry is:

> Deja que llame
> Quien me confiesa y absuelva.

The catastrophe of the play is certainly open to criticism; but *El Condenado por desconfiado* must also be considered in this context.

appeared at Naples in 1652,[1] but of this we know no more than the name, and that the play dealt with the legend. Yet another *Convitato di pietra* was acted for the first time in France early in 1658 by the Italian players, who were presenting their pieces at the Petit-Bourbon. This was one of the repertory of the *Commedia dell' arte*, that is to say those impromptu or half-impromptu plays with the traditional masks of which the Italians alone seem completely to have held the secret. We have, it is true, a scenario which was given at the same theatre by the Italians in 1662, and which has been transmitted to us owing to the incomplete and ill-arranged notes of the famous Dominico Biancolelli, who succeeded Locatelli in the rôle of the valet of Don Juan, at first acted as Trivilino, and a little later as Harlequin.

Of far greater importance are the two plays by Dorimon [2] and De Villiers, *Le Festin de Pierre ; ou, Le Fils Criminel.* Of Dorimon practically nothing is known beyond the facts that he wrote seven dramas, and that he belonged to the company patronized by Mademoiselle de Montpensier, the daughter of Gaston of Orleans. As an actor he seems to have enjoyed a considerable reputation, and it is said that his wife, Marotte Ozillon (or Marie du Mont-Ozillon, the name is uncertain), who was a performer of most mediocre talents, was tolerated in leading rôles on his account. Curiously enough, the career of De Villiers is almost equally obscure. We only know that he and his wife were playing at the Marais theatre, and that the famous Mondory attempted to engage the lady in an intrigue, but found his advances despised. When Mondory retired in 1637, De Villiers and his wife went to the theatre of the Hôtel de Bourgogne, where they were entertained for a considerable time. As an actor high in the second rank, he enjoyed considerable success, and among the parts he created was that of Thésée in the *Œdipe* of Pierre Corneille. His wife, who attained to real excellence, and played the heroines in tragedy, died in December, 1670. At this time, although he had not actually left the stage, the appearances of De Villiers were very infrequent. In 1674 he is spoken of as an old actor, drawing a pension from the theatre, after very many years of good service. He died 23 May, 1681, leaving a son Jean,[3] who excelled as the marquis and the fop in light comedy, and who is often confused with his father. The bibliography of De Villiers is very difficult. There are four plays, of which *Le Festin de Pierre* is one, that are undoubtedly his work. There are some half-a-dozen comedies, including *Zélinde ; ou, la Véritable critique de l'École des Femmes,* and a few minor pieces of criticism, which are generally considered to be from his pen, but which, on the other hand, may be the work of Donneau de Vise, since the initials D.V. represent either of these two authors.

[1] Allacci, *Drammaturgia*, p. 87.
[2] The name is indifferently spelled Dorimon, Dorimont, or Dorimond.
[3] Who died in 1702.

The *Feſtin de Pierre* of Dorimon, which was acted at Lyons in November–
December, 1658, and at Paris in 1661, extremely resembles the synonymous
play of De Villiers, not only as regards the names of the characters, the
conduct of the plot, the sequence of scenes, but even in actual expressions
and turns of phrase. It is plain that both have a common original, and
this was certainly the *Convitato di pietra* of Giliberto. There is, indeed,
not a great deal to chose between them. In his Dedication, De Villiers
speaks rather slightingly of " un imparfait Original," which was acted in
the French provinces—an unkind hit at Dorimon's play—and by the
Italian troop at Paris, but this, he adds, " noſtre Copie surpasse infiniment."
One muſt not take all this too literally ; probably the scenes of De Villiers
are something more than a mere copy, at leaſt so they appear to us, and
his talents do not seem to be more markedly brilliant than those of the
rival poet. Both pieces are intereſting ; both pieces have their patent
faults ; and both pieces are not without elegance and vigour.[1]

[1] In Dorimon's drama a few moments before his deſtruction, Don Juan replies to
L'Ombre, who bids him " Demande au Ciel pardon de tes faits criminels," as follows :

> Ne parle point du Ciel, qu'il punisse, ou pardonne,
> Je ne me repens point, il n'eſt rien qui m'eſtonne,
> Et quiconque a le cœur aussi bon que le mien,
> Ne peut s'espouvanter pour toy qui n'eſt qu'un rien.
> M'oses-tu proposer cett' action infame ?
> Je ne repentirois pour prolonger ma trame !
> Mon deſtin eſt escrit, mesme des le berceau,
> Et l'endroit eſt marqué qui fera mon tombeau.
> Si je voyois icy ma Sepulture ouverte,
> Et qu'un sot repentir peut differer ma perte,
> J'affronterois la mort, je ne le ferois pas,
> Et voilà ce qui peut retarder mon trespas.
> Ouy, ce fer armeroit ma main contre un Tonnerre,
>   *Luy montrant son eſpée.*
> Si le Ciel m'attaquoit, je luy ferois la guerre,
> Tout au moins je mourrois dans cette volonté.

The Don Juan of De Villiers, *Le Feſtin de Pierre*, V, 7, thus sums up and juſtifies
himself when the Ghoſt of Don Pierre reproaches him for his wickedness :

L'Ombre.	Au Ciel crois-tu tant d'injuſtice,
	Qu'il voulut d'un moment diferer ton suplice ?
	Quoy ! ton Père meurtry, moy-mesme assassiné,
	L'un traiſtrement surpris, et l'autre empoisonné,
	Celle-cy violee, et cette autre enlevée,
	L'une perduë, et l'autre a la mort reservée,
	Après ces beaux effets de ta brutalité,
	Tout cela se feroit avec impunité ?
	Ne le presume pas, ô cœur que rien ne touche,
	C'eſt un Arreſt du Ciel prononcé par ma bouche.
D. Juan.	Auras-tu bien-toſt fait ? te veux-tu déspecher ?
	Certes ! je suis bien las de t'entendre prescher ;

INTRODUCTION

On Sunday, 15 February, 1665, at the Théâtre du Palais-Royal, Molière and his company produced *Don Juan; ou, Le Festin de Pierre*. At the moment things did not look particularly promising; *Tartuffe* had been prohibited, and *L'École des Femmes*, when acted before Madame de Sully on 6 January, had been much disliked. It was necessary to find some especial attraction, but the suggestion that La Grange and his comrades proposed the subject of Don Juan seems superfluous. However that may be, Molière originally intended to write his play in verse, and then, just as in the case of Shadwell, "the Play-house having great occasion for a Play," he hurriedly completed and introduced his drama as a prose work.[1] The success of the new piece was very considerable, and although it was withdrawn on Friday, 20 March, after fifteen performances, and did not again appear in the theatre during the author's lifetime, it is entirely misleading to count it as a failure.

The reason why it was taken off was the fact that it caused a resounding scandal.[2] Even after the second performance Molière was obliged to suppress certain passages in the dialogue. The scene with the Beggar was thought particularly outrageous; the passage concerning "le moine bourru" when Don Juan tersely sums up his creed by saying that two and two make four, and four plus four are eight, was considered abominable, although it must be acknowledged that this opinion is wholly con-

> Trop ennuyeux Esprit, aussi bien qu'hypocrite,
> À quoy bon entasser redite sur redite ?
> Ne t'ay-je pas fait voir quels sont mes sentimens ?
> Penses-tu par tes vains et sots raisonnemens,
> Que Dom Juan soit jamais capable de foiblesse ?
> Et qu'il se laisse aller à la moindre bassesse ?
> Non, non, ce parler grave, et cet air, at ce ton,
> Ne sont bons qu'a prescher les Esprits de Pluton :
> Apprens, apprens, Esprit ignorant et timide,
> Que le feu, le viol, le fer, le parricide,
> Et tout ce dont tu m'as si bien entretenu,
> Passe dans mon esprit comme non advenu ;
> S'il en reste, ce n'est qu'une idée agreable,
> Quiconque vit ainsi ne peut estre blâmable,
> Il suit les sentimens de la Nature ; Enfin,
> Soit que je sois ou loin, ou proche de ma fin,
> Sçache que ny l'Enfer, ny le Ciel ne me touche,
> Et que c'est un Arrest prononcé par ma bouche.

[1] There are distinct traces of the original verse as, for example, in the rhythmic speech of Don Louis, IV, 6.

[2] Tom Brown in his *Laconics* has a curious error concerning *Don Juan*, the very name of which he mistakes: "When *Molière's Tartuff* was acted in *France*, all the churchmen complain'd of it. The *Festin de Saint Pierre*, tho' a lewd beastly piece, went down without the least wry face. At so much an easier rate may a man expose religion than hypocrisy!"

siſtent with the mentality of the rationaliſt, and it is difficult to see how he could have spoken otherwise. The greateſt indignation, however, was aroused by the final passage of the play, when after Don Juan has disappeared amid the red blaze of lightning and horrid peals of thunder whilſt ghoſtly sulphurous flames are flickering from the mouth of the darkly yawning pit which has suddenly gaped wide to swallow him up alive, Sganarelle cries aloud for the wages he has loſt. " Mes gages, mes gages, mes gages ! " This was judged horribly impious, and although Molière might have argued that in Cicognini's *Convitato di pietra* Passarino utters the same lament,[1] nay, that there is, moreover, an extra scene of hell itself,[2] and that he has modified rather than exploited the situation, it muſt be confessed these concluding phrases in *Don Juan* do border upon the profane, and we can hardly be surprised at the annoyance which they caused in certain quarters. Several pamphlets attacked the new play with an undue measure of violence, and although there was no official prohibition,[3] yet Molière was possibly wise when he withdrew his drama from the theatre. In faċt *Le Feſtin de Pierre* was not published until 1682, in volume vii of the *Œuvres*, and even then the complete text is only found in the very earlieſt impressions, of which no more than three are supposed to have survived. In France there were unhappy mutilations of the script, and one is obliged to have recourse to the Amſterdam edition of 1683, and the Brussels edition of 1694, to find a copy which has not been tampered with and injured.

Any detailed examination of so famous a play as Molière's *Don Juan* were entirely superfluous here. Suffice to say that he presents his protagoniſt as a mixture of evil, cruelty, hypocrisy, courage, and a certain chivalry.[4] He is unscrupulous and unprincipled to a degree ; he has some traits of the savage, but he is always perfeċtly genteel ; truly, in

---

[1] Atto III, Scena IX, where Passarino cries : O pover al me Patron, al me salari, è andà a cà del Diavol. Auit, soccors, ch'al me Patron è precipità. O là zent, a'n gh'è ngun che al soccorra ?

[2] Scena Ultima. Inferno. Don Giovanni laments " Quando terminaran queſti miei guai ! " and the demons howl " Mai."

[3] Louis XIV. himself favoured *Don Juan*, but he did not wish to come into conflict with his mother, and she was scandalized at the play. Anne of Auſtria was greatly diſturbed because his elder son was, as she considered, lax in his religious duties, and not infrequently she urged him to confess and communicate. *Mémoires de Fouquet*, II, p. 169.

[4] In III, 2, Don Juan exclaims : " Mais qui vois-je là ? Un homme attaqué par trois autres ! la partie eſt trop inégale, et je ne dois pas souffrir cette lâcheté." Whereupon *il met l'épée à la main, et court au lieu du combat*. Thus he saves the brother of Elvire, Don Carlos, who with Don Alonse is seeking his life. However, this episode is not original. It is from *Obligados y offendidos y gorron de Salamanca* of de Rojas, whence it was borrowed by Boisrobert for his *Généreux Ennemis*. Scarron also transferred it to his *Écolier de Salamanque*, and Thomas Corneille reproduced it in *Les Illuſtres Ennemis*.

spite of ourselves, we find that now and again we cannot but admire his frankness and his bravery, so much so that I fear that in spite of the catastrophe *Don Juan* is a very immoral play. Had he been converted by some hermit, some holy Hieronymite, or had he, paying due heed to the terrible warning, repented and buried himself in monastic seclusion to expiate his crimes by cilice and scourge, ethically the lesson of the piece would have been far nobler, although artistically it might have suffered in some small degree. For all its faults, the drama of Molière is immortal. Notwithstanding the fact that it disappeared at so early a date in its career it was inevitable that *Don Juan* should make a great impression. As we have seen, the legend was immensely popular, and this new exposition of the theme gave occasion to various imitations and new tragedies dealing with the same subject. In 1673 Thomas Corneille turned Molière's play into verse, and this alteration was represented with considerable success at the theatre in the Rue Guenegaud in 1677. It is a clever piece of work, and the younger Corneille has in his *Avis* candidly pointed out the line which he felt it prudent to adopt. " *Cette Pièce, dont les Comédiens donnent tous les ans plusieurs representations, est la mesme que feu Mr. de Molière fit jouër en Prose peu de temps avant sa mort. Quelques Personnes qui ont tout pouvoir sur moi, m'ayant engagé à la mettre en vers, je me reservay la liberté d'adoucir certaines expressions qui avoient blessé les Scrupuleux.*" [1] This alteration kept the stage for more than a century and a half. It was not until 17 November, 1841, that the original play by Molière was revived at the Odéon.

In 1669 the actor Rosimond presented at the Théâtre au Marais his

---

[1] Thomas Corneille concludes his *Festin de Pierre* thus :

La Statue.	L'Arrest en est donné ; tu touches au moment Où le Ciel va punir ton endurcissement. Tremble.
D. Juan.	Tu me fais tort, quand tu m'en crois capable ; Je ne sçay ce que c'est trembler.
Sganarelle.	Détestable !
La Statue.	Je t'ay dit dès tantost que tu ne songeois pas Que la mort chaque jour s'avançoit à grands pas. Au lieu d'y refléchir, tu retournes au crime, Et t'ouvres à toute heure abysme sur abysme. Après avoir en vain si long-temps attendu, Le Ciel se lasse ; prens, voilà ce qui t'est dû. *La Statue embrasse D. Juan, & un moment après tous les deux sont abysmez.*
D. Juan.	Je brûle, & c'est trop tard que mon âme interdite . . . Ciel !
Sganarelle.	Il est englouty, je cours me rendre Hermite ; L'exemple est étonnant pour tous les Scélerats ; Malheur à qui le voit, & n'en profite pas. *Fin du cinquième & dernier Acte.*

(cxxxiii)

verse drama *Le Nouveau Festin de Pierre, au l'Athée foudroyé.* In his preface the author says that he was induced to undertake the work owing to the fact that his was the only company in Paris which had not given a play on the subject of Don Juan. This was to be very unfashionable; this was to lose money. The comicalities of Passarino, Briguelle, Philipin, Sganarelle, or whatever name Don Juan's valet might be called; and above all the theatrical machinery, the blaze and roar of the doom of Don Juan, if the first rôle was in the hands of a capable comedian and the grand finale in the hands of a clever stage-carpenter, were sure draws to attract all Paris. As was natural, Rosimond has introduced into his drama all kinds of hints and incidents from both the French and the Italian writers who had already treated this theme. His play opens with the desertion of Léonor (Molière's Elvira), when the valet Carrille directly informs the lady of his master's treachery. As she reproaches Don Juan he tells her quite brutally that his love is dead. Then in the company of two friends he seeks new adventures in new lands, thus evading the vengeance which his crimes in Seville are about to bring down on his head. A shipwreck follows, and upon his escape from the storm, Don Juan promptly seduces two peasant girls, Paquette and Thomasse. Presently he helps one of his friends to carry off a young girl who is enclosed in a nunnery, and in order to effect this he conceives the atrocious idea of setting fire to the cloister.[1] When he is pursued by the city watch, he is able to put them to flight, and they withdraw discomfited for the moment, to rally their strength. Next he comes to the monument of the Commander whom he has killed but a short time before. With bitter mockery he invites the statue to supper, and that evening whilst he is drinking with his two friends, there is a hollow knock, the door flies open, and the terrible figure of cold white marble appears on the threshold. Very solemn and very fearful are the punishments with which this messenger from Heaven threatens Don Juan. His two companions in crime are destroyed before his eyes, but he remains firm and unmoved. He promises that he will in his turn accept the hospitality of the ghost, and without a shadow of fear he taunts him anew. From the bowels of hell the voices of his friends cry horribly, imploring him to repent, but he dies unconquered and unconquerable, a stoic and a veritable colossus of evil, almost admirable in the depth of his wickedness. Here indeed we have the Don Juan who has been portrayed for us by the dark genius of Baudelaire.

> Quand don Juan descendit vers l'onde souterraine
> Et lorsqu'il eut donné son obole à Charon,

---

[1] In De Sade's *Justine*, somewhat similarly, a prison is fired by the confederates of la Dubois, who amid the conflagration, in which many perish, escapes from durance with Justine.

Un sombre mendiant, l'œil fier comme Antisthène,
D'un bras vengeur et fort saisit chaque aviron.

Montrant leurs seins pendants et leurs robes ouvertes,
Des femmes se tordaient sous le noir firmament,
Et, comme un grand troupeau de victimes offertes,
Derrière lui trainaient un long mugissement.

Sgnarelle en riant lui réclamait ses gages,
Tandis que don Luis avec un doigt tremblant
Montrait à tous les morts errant sur les rivages
Le fils audacieux qui railla son front blanc

Frissonnant sous son dueil, la chaste et maigre Elvire,
Près de l'époux perfide et qui fit son amant,
Semblant lui réclamer un suprême sourire
Où brillât la douceur de son premier serment.

Tout droit dans son armure, un grand homme de pierre
Se tenait à la barre et coupait le flot noir ;
Mais le calme héros, courbé sur sa rapière,
Regardait le sillage et ne daignait rien voir.

For us the Don Juan of Rosimond is particularly interesting as being the principal source whence Shadwell drew his Libertine. It may be noticed that in Molière Don Juan veils his wickedness with a certain delicate art, although this if anything makes it all the worse, since he thereby hides the more brutal deformities of his practice and philosophy. The Don Juan of Rosimond is so truculently cynical that he does not trouble to disguise his vilest motives, and he stands naked and unashamed in all his native hideousness. When the Don Juan of Molière wishes to excuse his desertion of Elvire, he talks of conscientious scruples in politest phrases, he reminds the lady that he has taken her from a cloister, and he declares that he is very uneasy to think that she has broken her vows, in fine he points out to her that quite the best course for them to pursue is that they should endeavour to forget one another, so that she may resume her former obligation.[1] It is true that this flam does not deceive the lady for a moment. She turns upon him, and tells him roundly that now for

---

[1] " Il m'est venu des scrupules, madame, et j'ai ouvert les yeux de l'âme sur ce que je faisais. J'ai fait réflexion que, pour vous épouser, je vous ai dérobée à la clôture d'un couvent, que vous avez rompu les vœux qui vous engageaient autre part, et que le ciel est fort jaloux de ces sortes de choses. Le repentir m'a pris, et j'ai craint le courroux céleste. J'ai cru que notre mariage n'était qu'un adultère déguisé, qu'il nous attirerait quelque disgrâce d'en haut, et qu'enfin je devais tâcher de vous oublier, et vous donner moyen de retourner à vos premières chaînes." *Don Juan*, I, 3.

the first time she realizes how utterly base and dishonourable he is, and, " Heaven," she cries, " that Heaven which you mock will avenge me for your perfidy." Don Juan does not trouble to wear the mask a minute longer, he turns to his man and says with a sneer, " Sgnarelle, le ciel ! " It is worth noting that this expression gave extraordinary offence in the theatre. When Rosimond's Don Juan abandons Léonor he is not sufficiently concerned even to offer an excuse ; he tells her bluntly that he has had quite enough of her ; he is weary of her ; her body is stale to him, and

> Le bien dont on jouit ne cause plus d'ardeur.

And when the poor wretch in faltering accents reminds him of his protestations and the oaths that he swore, he bluntly retorts that had it been necessary he would have sworn as many again, that she is a fool ever to have imagined that he had the slightest intention of keeping his word. This ruffian will not be at pains to soften his cruelties, even though it be by a few untruths which cost him nothing.

If possible, Shadwell's Don Juan is uglier still. He has all the cynical philosophy of Molière, and all the savagery of Rosimond, he carries his wickedness to an extreme, and the result is a picture which, although exceedingly licentious in its details, is in its end remarkably moral and even didactic. Perhaps it may not be impertinent here to remark that we are not in the slightest degree concerned as to whether morality should, or should not enter into a play, as a question of artistic theory. We merely state a fact, that Shadwell's *The Libertine* is a most edifying drama. It must, I think, be accorded a very high place among Shadwell's work. There are evident signs of haste ; here and there there is a little botching, which some small attention might easily have set in order. But with all its faults *The Libertine* is a powerful play, and it is a good play. Upon the stage it must undoubtedly have been extremely effective. The first act which opens with so frank an exposition of the philosophy of Don Juan and his friends, concludes in the midnight imbroglio where the sweet serenades are stilled by the angry clash of steel. The second act paints the libertine and his friends in darker, yet darker colours, and there is hardly a stroke which can be deemed superfluous. The rage of the storm and the horror of the shipwreck in Act III are agreeably succeeded by the charming picture of the old hermit's retreat, a peace soon to be marred owing to the irruption of the three villains, who have escaped the waters, and whose brains are already busy with new plans for evil. The light and thoughtless gaiety of Clara and Flavia, two characters to whom misfortune alone can give solidity, their idle chatter and silly modern ideas, prepare us for the tragedy that is to overwhelm their house. The gentle pastoral of the shepherds and their lasses is a welcome refreshment before the welter of crime into which the madmen plunge when the shadow of the horror of the end begins swiftly to lower as the inevitable Nemesis is hard at their heels. That the story of Don Juan was a great success upon the stage is obvious from the fact that in many variants it has continued to be a favourite theatrical entertainment until the present day.[1]

However interesting a task, it is impossible to follow Don Juan in his many wanderings, and to track his later adventures, in every country of Europe. Briefly it must suffice to say that Molière's drama was translated and was printed at Nuremberg in 1694 as *Das steinerne Gastmahl;* and in the following year as *Das Don Pedro Gastmahl.* In 1684 the famous actor, Johannes Velthen, played at Dresden before the Elector Johann-Georg III, Molière's *Festin de Pierre* under the curious title *Die stadua der Ehre.* In many versions and adaptations the legend became extremely popular on the German stage, and towards the middle of the eighteenth century the celebrated Schrœder was particularly applauded in the part of Don Juan. The verse play of Thomas Corneille, *Le Festin de Pierre* was also well known in Germany, and between the years 1730 and 1743 it was one of the favourite performances of the French company which was established at Mannheim whilst the Palatine Court remained in residence there. Moreover, those little pieces known as *Hauptactionen* and *Puppenspiele* carried the play throughout the length and breadth of the land. These are for the most part mere scenarios, and their titles all bear a close similarity ; *Don Pedro's Gastmahl ; Das steinerne Gastmahl ; Das steinerne Todtengastmahl ;* with very many more.

Curiously enough in 1674 the Elzevirs at Amsterdam printed Dorimon's *Le Festin de Pierre* under the name of Molière. The mistake appears to be quite genuine, and the play was reissued more than once with this erroneous attribution. There are several Dutch pieces which owe their source to the various French dramas. Some of these are separate adaptations ; some are an admixture of scenes from Molière and Dorimon, from De Villiers and Rosimond. Van Maater in his *Don Jan of de Gestrafte Vrygeest,* follows Molière pretty closely ; whilst Adriaan Peys, in his *De Maeltyt van Don Pederos Geest of de Gestrafte Vrygeest,* Amsterdam, 1699, is obviously inspired by Dorimon and De Villiers. F. Seegers, again, in his *De Gestrafte Vrygeest,* has combined Molière and De Villiers. There is one rather amusing scene in this play, wherein the author has invented a device to reveal the hypocrisy of Don Juan, which for some reason he did not dare to expose as frankly as Molière had shown it. Don Juan is at an inn, and when the host sets a dish of meat before him at dinner, he rejects it, remarking that it is an Ember Day. "We have not forgotten," Boniface replies,

---

[1] As I write, in the Picture-Houses a Film of Don Juan "The Great Lover"— which he was not—is being shown with extraordinary success. I understand that John Barrymore sustains the rôle of Juan.

" but, sir, travellers are allowed to eat meat at any time." "I dare not avail myself of the dispensation," Don Juan unctuously remarks, and at the same time demands fish and vegetables to be served. A drama by Ryk, *Don Pedroos Geest of de Gestrafte Baldaadigheid*, Amsterdam, 1721, is mainly a copy of Seegers. In 1721 was published *De Gestrafte Vrygeest* by Ryndorp, a drama which had been acted with very great success at Leyden and the Hague. Although these many pieces are interesting as showing the extremely wide diffusion of the story of Don Juan in its dramatic form, and although many of them have their quota of vigour and humour, they can hardly be considered as of any particular value from a purely literary point of view. To return to France, we may notice that throughout the eighteenth century the legend of Don Juan was a great favourite at the theatres of the foire Saint-Germain and the foire Saint-Laurent. In 1713 Le Tellier produced a *Festin de Pierre* which had an extraordinary success, and which was the inspiration of more than an hundred such pieces, many of them burlesques and extravaganzas, which year after year drew crowds to be thrilled by, or to laugh at, their ingenious representation of the popular story.

In Spain Molina's *El Burlador de Sevilla* still held the stage, and throughout the seventeenth and eighteenth centuries there appeared to be only two plays of any importance which dealt with the same theme. The first, *La Venganza en el sepulcro*, by Alonso Cordiva y Maldonado, belongs to the last decade of the seventeenth century. Since the many adventures of Don Juan are not shown us, but are merely related in a rapid narrative when the hero tells the story of his life, the consequence is that only some half-a-dozen characters appear, and it must be acknowledged that the result is very frigid and tame. The latter part of the play follows the accepted legend. Don Juan goes to sup with the statue of the Commander, and is destroyed in the traditional manner, whilst Colochon, his servant, vows that he will enter a Carthusian monastery.

About the year 1735, or it may be even a little earlier, Don Antonio de Zamora, an official of great importance in the secretariat of the colonial governments, who was in his leisure hours a patron of the fine arts and himself a dramatist of no mean order, a passionate admirer and close imitator of the great Calderon, brought upon the stage a drama which not only in its title closely resembles former plays upon the subject of Don Juan, but also marks the author's intention of emphasizing these moral lessons upon which Tirso de Molina has particularly insisted. *No ay deuda que no se pague, y Combidado de piedra* was printed at Madrid in 1744, although assuredly it appeared in the theatre at least ten years before actual publication. The scenes of Don Alonso Cordova are empty and thin; in the drama of Don Antonio de Zamora the boards are always crowded, and the incidents follow one another with breathless speed. The result

INTRODUCTION

is that the play certainly has a movement and a vigour the colder and more academic *La Venganza en el sepulcro* entirely lacks, and these certainly give it life and interest. Ladies fair and wanton courtezans, bullies and pimps, students, nobles of high estate, the King, and his own father, there is not an individual whom Don Juan does not in some way outrage, insult, and offend, as he heaps crime upon crime with the violence of a maniac or demon incarnate.

Turning from the stage it would be impossible here to follow Don Juan through all the poems and romances of which he has been the hero during the past one hundred and fifty years. The fact is that we have to deal not with one person, but with many, not with one legend, but with a multiplicity, some of which are so far remote from the original as to have absolutely nothing in common with the Spanish and French theatres, with Shadwell's *Libertine*, save the bare name. Even so famous a poem as Byron's *Don Juan* which, as he wrote to Moore, is a gentle satire upon everything [1] must only receive a passing notice. It was begun at Venice, 6 September, 1818, and the earlier cantos, at any rate, have something of the cynical frankness, the tinsel and glitter, and the charm of the decadence of its birthplace. As a confession, as a biography, one may in some sort compare Byron's poem [2] with the great work of Casanova. Both have so much in common ; both are extraordinarily witty, extraordinarily clever, and extraordinarily interesting. Both are at times a little too human ; both are at times a little inhuman and cruel. Both concentrate upon one and the same changeless theme, and the result is—dare one say it ?—one becomes just a little tired of both. Both were surrounded with lewd and foolish mystery ; both were damned as obscenities not to be named ; both are yet admired by the uninformed as rare pornography, and in neither case could itching prurience have gone further astray. Both are great books, and there is no reason at all why instead of being regarded as ware for the bawdy-baskets, they should not calmly and quietly take their places upon the open shelves of the library, only in this event it is to be feared that much of their cryptic fascination would be gone.

It must suffice barely to name Adam Lang's *Don Juan* (1820) ; Pouchkine's drama (1830) ; Alexandre Dumas' *Don Juan de Marina ; ou, la chute d'un ange*, which was speedily parodied in the very year of its production, 1836 ; Creizenach's poem *Don Juan* (1836–37) ; the nine tragedies, all having the same title, *Don Juan*, by Wiese (1840) ; by Braun von Braunthal (1842) ; Levavasseur (1848) ; Wilde (1850) ; R. Hornick (1850) ; Spiesser (1857) ; E. Jourdain (1857) ; Hauch (1864) ; and by Julius Hart

---

[1] 19 September, 1818.

[2] In 1866 a French author, M. Genty, published his continuation of Byron, *Suite de Don Juan*. The hero visits Ireland, France, Switzerland, and Rome. He has many adventures, and the poem breaks off, unfinished, when he is on his way to Sicily.

(1881); as well as Heyse's *Don Juan's Ende* (1883); Haraucourt's *Don Juan de Manara* (1898); Durel's pantomime *Pierrot Don Juan* (1905); and such comedies as Henri de Regnier's *Les Scrupules de Sganarelle* (1908). There are numerous novels too; Hesekiel's *Faust und Don Juan* (1846); Ferrand's *Le Mariage de Don Juan* (1883); Montegut's *Don Juan à Lesbos* (1892); Marcel Barrière's *Le nouveau Don Juan* (1900–1909); C. Debans' *La vieillesse de Don Juan* (1905); Bruni's *Les deux nuits de Don Juan* (1907); and Fidao-Justiniani's *Le mariage de Don Juan* (1909). Most striking of all is Barbey d'Aurevilly's *Le plus bel amour de Don Juan* in his *Diaboliques;* but unfortunately Flaubert did not carry out his idea of a novel to be called *Une nuit de Don Juan*, and Baudelaire's drama *La fin de Don Juan* is also unwritten.

There are two English plays which, since they have been widely discussed, call for particular consideration. It is said that it was Mr. A. B. Walkley who asked Shaw to write a " Don Juan " play, and the result of this suggestion proved to be *Man and Superman*. As one might expect, the Don Juan of history and legend has quite disappeared, and *Man and Superman* is, in Shaw's own words, " a stage projection of the tragic-comic love chase of the man by the woman." Of course this has been done before upon the English stage. For example, Fletcher's *The Wild-Goose Chase* [1] which was first acted at Court in 1621, presents the same problem. Mirabell, the Wild-Goose,[2] a travelled young man who is a somewhat heartless philanderer is at last brought to matrimony by Oriana, his fair betrothed, " and wittie follower of the Chase." The comedy is brisk and vivacious enough, but I think it is very far from being among Fletcher's best comedies, although it has always enjoyed a great reputation.[3] It compares very favourably indeed with *Man and Superman*, which seems to me mechanical and artificial to a degree. The ideas are those of a schoolboy in the playground when well out of his master's hearing; coxcombical boasting of which he is half ashamed as he utters it, and which he only parades to impress those who are smaller and more ignorant than himself. The prolix and tedious dream in Hell reaches an extremity of bathos and boredom. The fact is that the whole thing lacks spirituality, that is to say, it lacks life, it is " nothing but a cold, dull mass . . . a dwarfish thought dress'd up in gigantick words, repetition in abundance, looseness of expression, and gross hyperboles; the sense of one line expanded pro-

---

[1] It was revived by the Renaissance Theatre for the John Fletcher Tercentenary, on 19 and 20 July, 1925.

[2] Originally acted by Joseph Taylor. Oriana was first played by Stephen Hammerton.

[3] Pepys who was present at a performance at Drury Lane, Saturday, 11 January, 1668, notes that he had " long longed to see it, being a famous play." Upon the stage *The Wild-Goose Chase* gave way to Farquhar's *The Inconstant; or, The Way to Win Him*, which was produced at Drury Lane in February or March, 1702, and which is a wholesale conveyance from Fletcher.

digiously into ten : and to sum up all, uncorrect English, and a hideous mingle of false (Philosophy), and true nonsense." If Ann were alive she would be repulsive ; as it is she is merely a smudge, a blur. I have, it is true, sat through parts of this banal play with pleasure ; but, *distinguo*, my pleasure arose from the very excellent acting of Mr. Esmé Percy, and the genius of Mr. Percy could, I verily believe, put life and beauty into the pages of a blue-book.

James Elroy Flecker's *Don Juan* was first published in October, 1925, and seems to have been composed in the winter of 1910 and the spring of the following year. In November, 1910, he wrote : " I shall portray *Don Juan* utterly disappointed in his grande passion seeking refuge from sickly and decadent despair first in the world and in the passion for humanity and justice, then questioning religion, then ordinary morality, until finally he becomes an utter sadist. Then comes the statue which is the miracle, to make him doubt reason itself, and he dies bravely." What on earth does all this mean ? I very much doubt if it means anything at all, and I frankly confess that I can find no solution in reading the play, which seems to me commonplace to ineptness. There are a few lines of real poetry ; we have a scantling of ideas, which once or twice are near to being very tolerably expressed. It is a sadly disappointing piece ; one feels that the author is at least striving after something that he has to say, only he is not at all clear exactly what he wishes to express, and even if he could formulate his thought, he would certainly not be able to convey it. Whilst reading the book I had the idea that I was standing at a door which was just going to be opened, and then when the door was flung wide, the room beyond was naked, empty, cold and bare.

Perhaps one is old-fashioned enough to take greater pleasure in the traditional treatment of the theme. After all, however hackneyed it became, it did mean something. At its best it was a piece of profoundest philosophy often informed with exquisite poetry ; even at its tritest it had not lost its spiritual message, however roughly delivered. That was for the modern to cast away. I do not wish to compare Shadwell and Shaw, but I infinitely prefer Shadwell.

It has been observed, and with some truth, that one of the most remarkable events of the reign of Charles II. was the development of the Royal Society, which not only gave a tremendous impetus to scientific research, but, as it were, safeguarded it to some extent at any rate from charlatanry and abuse, and sealed it with the official approval of the responsible and the wise. Since both Evelyn and Pepys were members, much of its early history may be read in their pages. It is only natural that however cautious and learned was this august and most respectable body, their aims and ideas were at first liable to be burlesqued and misunderstood, for perhaps some of their experiments may have afforded the uninitiated cause for mirth and wonder. It must be remembered, too, that a number of quacks and medicasters pressed forward eager to gain admittance into that distinguished corporation, and by the advertisement of their fool-hardiness and ignorance, by their boasting and self-praise, they did excite unmeasured ridicule from those who were too careless to distinguish between the substance and the shadow. These parasites loudly published their claims to recognition, and these claims were so grotesque that they afforded the wits infinite matter for jest and satire. The King himself, who was greatly interested in the work of the Royal Society, and who could boast himself no mean chemist, liked to have his joke.[1] " Gresham College he mightily laughed at, for spending time only in weighing of ayre,[2] and doing nothing else since they sat." Samuel Butler has a fine satire *The Elephant in the Moon*, which is frankly a hit at the Royal Society. But it has been well observed that the poet's real intention " was not to ridicule real and useful philosophy, but only that conceited and whimsical taste for the marvellous and surprising which prevailed so much among the learned of that age ; and though it would be ungrateful not to acknow-ledge the many useful improvements then made in natural knowledge, yet, in justice to the satirists, it must be confessed that these curious in-quirers into Nature did sometimes, in their researches, run into a super-stitious and unphilosophical credulity, which deserved very well to be laughed at." [3] To an observation so keen as that of Shadwell, the pre-tenders to learning, and even the mistakes of the learned themselves, offered an irresistible subject for a satirical comedy. In such a theme Jonson would have delighted, and one can well imagine it might have inspired a masterpiece comparable to *The Alchemist*. No higher compli-ment can be paid Shadwell than to say that certain scenes of *The Virtuoso* and certain figures actually do come within measurable distance of Jonson's

---

[1] Monday, 1 February, 1663–1664.

[2] One may compare *The Virtuoso*, IV, where Sir Nicholas says ; " I employ Men all over *England*, Factors for Air, who bottle up Air, and weigh it in all places, sealing the Bottles Hermetically : they send me Loads from all places. . . . I have sent one to weigh Air at the Picque of *Teneriff*, that's the lightest Air ; I shall have a considerable Cargoe of that Air. *Sheerness* and the Isle of *Dogs* Air is the heaviest. Now, if I have a mind to take Countrey Air, I send for maybe, forty Gallons of *Bury* Air, shut all my Windows and doors close, and let it fly in my Chamber." A little later they are seen enjoying the Bury air in this fashion. In a letter " *To Sir* John Sands " printed in Tom Brown's works, we have : " To expect fidelity from a female that has been rais'd up in that hot bed call'd a play house, is to expect honesty from an evidence. 'Tis a folly not to be excus'd : 'Tis to bottle up air, like *Shadwell*'s virtuoso : 'Tis to wash a blackmoor : 'Tis to make Dr. Oates *rectus in curia* : 'Tis, in short, to grasp at more than attaining an impossibility ; for 'tis impossible to secure any other woman to yourself, but much more an actress."

[3] In this connexion Mrs. Behn's excellent extravaganza *The Emperor of the Moon* should not be forgotten, for her Doctor Baliardo is a true virtuoso.

great play, and this is a high meed of praise when we consider that *The Alchemist*, which Dryden regarded as the finest effort of Jonson's genius, is one of the very greatest of English comedies. If in *The Virtuoso* the quartette of lovers, Longvil and Bruce, Clarinda and Miranda, are perhaps just a trifle stereotyped in their affection and in their expression thereof, if we feel that we have met them, or met figures very like them, more than once before, we must remember that they are probably just the ordinary young men and young women of the day, and that in London social circles, which were, comparatively speaking, small and confined, very possibly one did not encounter any great variety of character and outlook. It is true that the Lovels, the Raymunds, the Bellamours, the Carolinas, Theodoras and Isabellas of Shadwell have not the wit and vivacity of Dryden's Lovebys, Wildbloods, Bellamys, Constances, Jacinthas and Mrs. Tricksys, but he has created them with a fund of solid common sense, of hearty English sentiment, and he has endowed them with a certain shrewdness, which may be taken to reflect his own individuality. They are not infrequently a trifle rough, especially the men, and they have few delicate scruples, but they are capable of, and they are often guided by, the dictates of a very hearty affection. One can see them settling down, good allowances being made on both sides, into comfortable married couples. They are not mere lay figures as are the Harry Modish and Jack Wildish of *The Mulberry Garden*, or even emptier labels like the futile Eugenio and Philander in the same play.

Sir Nicholas Gimcrack[1] and his lady, and even the minor characters, Hazard and Flirt, are very well drawn; but the three glories of the piece are Sir Samuel Hearty, old Snarl, and Sir Formal Trifle, and the greatest of these is Sir Formal. Sir Samuel we can meet any day; the eternally idle, eternally busy, good-natured, frankly conceited fribble, whose chief occupation in life seems to be to waste his own time and the time of all those unfortunates whom he can buttonhole and compel to listen to his drivelling stories. He has always just come from watching a football match, or dancing at some dance-tea, or seeing the latest revue, and he is never happy until he has told all his acquaintance—he has no friends—the amplest details of these exciting and important adventures. His dialect largely consists of clipped English, sporting terms, and the American language, so that it is quite unintelligible to the ordinary person

---

[1] Steele in *The Tatler*, Nos. 216, 221, where he has an elaborate hit at Virtuosi, gives the will of Sir Nicholas Gimcrack. This type of philomath is everlastingly the subject of dramatic satire. In *Three Hours after Marriage*, printed as by Gay, but written by Arbuthnot, Pope, and Gay, and produced at Drury Lane in January, 1716–17, Fossile was known to be intended for Dr. Woodward, Professor of Gresham College. One may compare the " mere antiquary " Mr. Rust in Foote's *The Patron*, 8vo, 1764. Peter Pindar's Sir Joseph Bank is a virtuoso of the Gimcrack school. One of his experiments is to boil fleas in order that he may ascertain if they will turn from black to red like lobsters.

who has little or no acquaintance either with the foreign tongues or the temporary graces of fashionable conversation.

Uncle Snarl is a true *laudator temporis acti*, and I respect him uncommonly for it. In my opinion he was very right not to tolerate the ill-manners of his nieces, and there is as tang agreeably honest and direct about the candid way in which he speaks his mind. He is a little testy and a little magisterial as old fellows are wont to be, but his criticism of the age is excellent, and we might very well echo it ourselves to-day. Why should we be such coxcombs as to go to modern plays where they act like poppets, we that have seen Henry Irving and Tree and Charles Wyndham?

It is true that Mr. Snarl's private pleasures are something odd, but then 'tis monstrous ill-bred to break in upon a gentleman's retirement. In a rare little piece, *Fashionable Lectures*,[1] we have the following : " It was very well known in the incontinent reign of Charles the Second, and, in a comedy of Shadwell's called *The Virtuoso*, there is a courtezan with a rod going to castigate a gentleman of this order before the audience, but is happily prevented by the introduction of another person. It was supposed, in many of the writings of that day, that Otway was the very person thus satirized, and in one of the many thousand political squibs published at that time in which this great writer flourished the following distich appears :

> *Tom Otway* loves birch in his heart, and *Nat Lee*
> With a rod and his *Chloris* will ever agree.

If the strain of Otway's writings, and Lee's in particular when woman is the subject, did not strengthen this assertion, it would be right to place a doubt upon the matter." [2] That Mr. Snarl is aimed at Otway I cannot for a moment believe. Shadwell and Otway were then intimate friends, and even had they been at daggers drawn I fail to see how old Snarl has any traits which can remind one of young Otway. In *Venice Preserv'd* we have, it is true, the famous scene where the Greek courtezan Aquilina lashes the fumbling dotard Antonio into ecstasies of lust, but this great tragedy was produced half-a-dozen years later. Antonio, moreover, is a portrait of Shaftesbury, whose masochism was notorious.[3] There had, I think, been some resounding flagellation scandal about the year 1675, or perhaps a series of scandals, since there are frequent references in prologue and play [4] of that date to this particular mobidity. Mother Cresswell, Jenny Crom-

---

[1] London. Printed for G. Peacock, No. 66, Drury Lane, *circa* 1785.

[2] *Op. cit.*, pp. 18, 19.

[3] Shaftesbury's aberration is very keenly satirized in *The Siege of Constantinople* by Henry Nevil (Paine), given at Dorset Garden in November, 1674 ; 4to, 1675.

[4] *E.g.*, the Introduction, spoken by Joe Haines and Betty Mackarel, to Duffett's *The Mock-Tempest*, acted at Drury Lane in the winter of 1674 ; also the epilogue, spoken by Haines, to Lee's *Gloriana ; or, The Court of Augustus Caesar*.

well, and Betty Buly were all singularly famed for their skilful compliance in giving satisfaction of this kind to their patrons. In later days the tradition was amply sustained by Mrs. Collet, Mrs. James, Emma Lee, Mrs. Shepherd, Mrs. Chalmers, Mrs. Noyau, Mrs. Price, and Mrs. Sarah Potter. Above all Mrs. Theresa Berkley,[1] who resided at 28, Charlotte Street, was especially renowned. She died in September, 1836, and so numerous was her clientèle that in the eight years between that date and 1828 she had netted considerably more than ten thousand pounds. Well might a French writer cry : " L'Angleterre, la terre classique du flagellantisme sexuel ! "[2]

Sir Formal Trifle, the sententious florid speaker is surely an immortal figure. He is literally hypnotized by the eagre of his own verbosity ; he is one who knows the magic of words ; a man of silver eloquence, equal to any occasion. He pours forth such excess of nonsense that he would have rivalled the Bishop of Birmingham in the pulpit, or the President of some scientific Assembly on the platform. Yet what could be finer than his resolve to confront the angry rabble, alone and unarmed, and to conquer them by his Demosthenic periods ? What could be more gracious, what could be more superb than his morning salutations ; what could be neater than his desire to be both " concise and florid " ? Even when he pays irregular addresses to a lady, what gallantry, what ardour, what urbanity and breeding !

One is not surprised to find that the figure of Sir Formal Trifle became proverbial, for we may, I think, almost set him beside the humours of Dickens himself. In its day *The Virtuoso*, as it well deserved, was immensely successful in the theatre. Our only wonder is that it fell out of the dramatic repertory so soon, for it is obviously an excellent acting play, and pieces of far inferior merit have maintained a considerably longer lease of life. Capital comedy as *The Sullen Lovers* is, one can appreciate the reason why after thirty years or so it did not retain so complete a hold on popular favour. It is eminently topical, and as time went on the significance of Sir Positive At-All must inevitably have been to some degree obscured, since he is a parody, or rather a portrait, of one numerical person. But Sir Formal is an immortal type, and an individual as well.

It seems most probable that after his great success, Shadwell would have followed up *The Virtuoso* with another comedy of the day, but his friends and patrons were determined that he should carry out their ideas, and a suggestion from the most influential and remarkable of the aristocrats of

---

[1] Her correspondence which she left to her executor, Dr. Vance, comprised letters from the highest in England. All these papers were afterwards destroyed.

[2] The library of flagellation literature, English and foreign, is enormous. A useful study of this aberration in England will be found in Chapter VI, " Die Flagellomanie," of Dr. Eugen Dühren's (Iwan Bloch's) great work *Das Geschlechtsleben in England*.

the day, the Duke of Buckingham, was not to be ignored. The Duke, who was a warm admirer of Shakespeare, directed Shadwell's attention to *Timon of Athens*, a drama which almost certainly had not been revived after the Restoration, but which His Grace was pleased to praise in the most enthusiastic terms. Shadwell, presumably, must have been working at his version of *Timon of Athens* during the autumn and winter of 1677, and the play was probably put into rehearsal in November of that year. By that somewhat curious, but no doubt necessary, arrangement which gave the monopoly of certain old plays to Killigrew's company, and again the sole rights in others to the Duke's Theatre, Shakespeare's *Timon of Athens* appears among " the list of the playes allowed to His Royall Highnesse Actors and none other has right to them, Aug. 20th, 1668," which was endorsed by the Earl of Manchester.[1] Accordingly Shadwell's *The History of Timon of Athens* was produced at Dorset Garden, either in December, 1677, or early in the following January. Downes records: " *Timon of Athens*, alter'd by Mr. *Shadwell*, was very well acted, and the musick in't well performed; it wonderfully pleas'd the Court and City, being an excellent moral." [2] Thus it was one of those few pieces which pleased every kind of play-goer, for the City was not always friendly to the theatre; the good folk within the sound of the bells of Bow were too often cuckolded and ridiculed upon the stage, their politics denounced, their affected decorum exposed; so, when the City distinguished a play by loud applause, it was a mark of exceptional favour, and as such the old prompter has thought it worthy of particular note. The wording of the quarto, 1678, *The History of Timon of Athens, The Man-Hater . . . Made into a Play. By Tho. Shadwell*, has aroused a certain amount of rather vapid criticism from those who did not stop to think exactly what this expression intended, and who possibly had not been at the trouble to read Shadwell's version. If we regard the matter without any prejudice there is certainly one sense, an artificially theatrical sense it may be, in which Shakespeare's

[1] Edward Montagu, second Earl of Manchester, Lord Chamberlain of the Royal Household, K.G., a Privy Councillor, and Chancellor of the University of Cambridge. He died in 1671.

[2] Several of the writers who answered Collier quote *Timon of Athens* as an apt illustration. Thus Edward Filmer in his *A Defence of Dramatick Poetry*, 8vo, 1698, p. 73, says: "Thus we pity *Timon of Athens*, not as the Libertine nor Prodigal, but the *Misanthropos*: When his Manly and Generous Indignation against the Universal Ingratitude of Mankind makes him leave the World and fly the Society of Man; when his open'd Eyes and recollected Virtue can stand the Temptation of a Treasure he found in the woods, enough to purchase his own Estate again: When all this glittering Mine of Gold has not Charm to bribe him back into a hated World, to the Society of *Villains*, *Hypocrites*, and *Flatterers*." And John Dennis *The Usefulness of the Stage . . .* , 8vo, 1698, p. 117, has: "Thus *Don John* is destroy'd for his libertinism and his impiety; *Timon* for his profusion and his intemperance; *Macbeth* for his lawless ambition and cruelty."

Timon of Athens is not " a play," that is to say it is not a drama well adapted and well contrived for the scenic stage. Moreover, a play which had only two female characters, and those of the smallest,[1] was in the reign of Charles II. eminently unsuitable to a theatre where actresses, who were yet something of a novelty in England, had shown histrionic genius of the highest order, and were universally flattered and admired, from whose ranks the mistresses of the King himself were the mothers of noble houses. From the point of view of his time, by the introduction of two female characters of the first importance, as well as of Chloe, the saucy Abigail, by the development of the character of Alcibiades, by the writing up of the parts of the Senators (who incidentally were assigned to some of the leading performers, Sandford, Underhill, and Anthony Leigh), Shadwell has made Shakespeare's drama " into a Play." Personally I feel pretty well assured that those who have so freely condemned Shadwell simply have not troubled to study the question, and I am confirmed in my opinion by the very careful judgement of Professor Odell,[2] who has certainly given the matter closest attention and is fully qualified to express an opinion. He writes of Shadwell's *Timon* : " This play was revived constantly and perhaps deserved to be. Thoughts of Shakespeare aside, it is an excellent acting-medium. Perhaps I shall incur ridicule in admitting it, but I believe Shadwell was not far out when he asserted in his Epistle Dedicatory to George, Duke of Buckingham, that his play ' has the inimitable Hand of Shakespeare in it, which never made more masterly Strokes than in this. Yet I can truly say, I have made it into a Play.' The character of Melissa alone makes me doubtful." There can be no doubt that Shadwell's *Timon* is a first-rate acting play, and there is proof thereof in the fact that with certain revisions it kept the stage until the beginning of the nineteenth century. Myself, since I consider *Timon of Athens* to be one of the greatest of Shakespeare's plays, so as an alteration I must needs dislike Shadwell's *Timon* perhaps more than any other adaptation from Shakespeare made during the Restoration period. On the other hand, I prefer to think of Shadwell's version as an entirely new piece, which indeed it is. Although I much disrelish the character of Evandra, the introduction of whom, in my opinion, entirely destroys the unity of the theme and palpably weakens the savage nobility of Timon, an intrusion which is in fact a deformity throughout the whole of the five acts, yet setting this blemish aside I find Melissa for instance extremely happy, and there are many other excellent individual strokes.

The only two female characters of Shakespeare's tragedy, Phrynia and Timandra, who have been taken over by Shadwell [3] as Thais and Phrinias,

[1] Since they only appear in one scene of Act IV and speak but nine lines.
[2] *Shakespeare from Betterton to Irving.* Two volumes, 1921.
[3] Curiously enough Odell is in error here. When reviewing Shadwell's *Timon of*

were at Dorset Garden played by Mrs. Seymour and Mrs. Le Grand, two actresses of inferior rank whose names occur very seldom in printed casts. Mrs. Seymour played Sabina, "Confident to Laura Lucretia," in Mrs. Behn's *The Feign'd Curtizans; or, A Nights Intrigue* produced at Dorset Garden in 1678-9; Lettice, a maid, in Otway's *Friendship in Fashion*, given at the same house early in April, 1678[1]; Lucinda, woman to Christina, in D'Urfey's *Squire Oldsapp; or, The Night-Adventurers*, produced at Dorset Garden in May, 1678[2]; and Lidia, Beverly's sister in the same author's *The Virtuous Wife; or, Good Luck at Last*, produced at Dorset Garden in the autumn of 1679.[3] Mrs. Le Grand played Eugenia in *The Counterfeit Bridegroom; or, The Defeated Widow*, a vacation play performed at Dorset Garden in August, 1677, which is but a slight alteration of Middleton's *No Wit, No Help, like a Woman's*, generally attributed to Mrs. Behn.

I know not what the reason may be, but Shakespeare's magnificent tragedy, *Timon of Athens*, is so infrequently given upon the stage—one of the most notable productions during the nineteenth century was the very splendid performance at Sadler's Wells by Phelps on 15 September, 1851, revived in 1856,—that it is worth remarking I have seldom seen a drama of such power and such interest. Small as the two female characters are, they break out with extraordinary effect, and should only be entrusted to actresses who are talented in a very high degree. *The History of Timon of Athens* must have added very considerably to Shadwell's reputation,[4] but at this period he seems to have spent as freely as he earned, which was perhaps inevitable considering the brilliant and extravagant society with whom he continually mixed. We get an interesting glimpse of this in a letter dispatched to Laurence Hyde,[5] Envoy Extraordinary to The Hague, by Nell Gwyn, who appears to have written in August, 1678, and whilst retailing the news that Rochester has gone into the country, that Henry Savile is ill,[6] whilst Lord Beauclerk is on the point of setting out for

Athens he writes (*op. cit.*, I., p. 45): "Of course, the mistresses of Alcibiades are omitted."

[1] Probably on the 5th of that month.

[2] Licensed (for printing) 28 June, 1678.

[3] 4to, 1680.

[4] This drama was very popular. In *The Innocent Mistress*, a comedy by Mrs. Mary Pix, produced at Lincoln's Inn Fields in the early autumn of 1769, Lady Beauclair cries: "Divartions! what Divartions? Yes, you had me to the Play-house, and the first thing I saw was an ugly black Devil kill his Wife, for nothing; then your *Metridate* King o' the *Potecaries*, your *Timon* the *Atheist*, the Man in the Moon, and all the rest—Nonsense, Stuff, I hate 'em."

[5] *Camden Miscellany*, Vol. V; *Notes and Queries*, 4th Series, vii. 2.

[6] Henry Savile, writing from "Leather Lane in Hatton Garden," on 2 July, 1678, to Rochester, says: "Here I have chosen to finish the last act of a long tedious course of physic which has entertained me ever since December last. . . . I confess I

France, she adds : " My lord of Dorseit apiers wonse in thre munths, for he drinkes aile with Shadwell & Mr. Haris at the Dukes House all day long." Henry Harris, a gay young dog, was, we know, continually in difficulties, and amongst other demands he was being constantly sued by his wife for maintenance. One of these petitions is dated as late as 2 November, 1677. From a social standpoint his good looks, his wit, his talents, made him one of the most popular companions of the day, and on Wednesday, 29 April, 1668, Pepys, who had been present at a performance of Etherege's *Love in a Tub*, in which the young actor played the excellent comic part of Sir Frederick Frollick,[1] notes " after the play done, I stepped up to Harris's dressing-room, where I never was, and there I observed much company come to him, and the Witts, to talk, after the play is done, and to assign meetings." Shadwell and Harris, as we have remarked before, were friends very early, for on Sunday, 20 September, 1668, Harris was to have taken the dramatist to dinner with Pepys, but they disappointed their host and lost an excellent meal.

It is curious that after having obtained such great success with a play which he did not consider altogether in his own particular vein, when Shadwell returned to that kind of Jonsonian comedy he so especially cultivated, he should for no cause that we can divine save the cold caprice of the audience, meet with discomfiture and defeat. *A True Widow*, produced at Dorset Garden in the winter of 1678, probably in December, was a failure, and there seems to be every reason why it ought to have enjoyed a most favourable reception, at any rate such was the opinion of the wits and the writers, but very clearly such was not the opinion of the town. And yet it is a capital comedy, the dialogue is vivacious, the characters are well individualized and amusing, the interest well sustained until the end,[2] and even if the trick by which Lady Cheatly abuses her creditors is artificial, it would not have appeared so in the Restoration theatre, and are we

---

wonder at myself and that mass of mercury that has gone down my throat in 7 months, but should wonder more were it not for Mrs. Roberts for behold, a greater than I, she is in the same house."

[1] Downes enthusiastically breaks into a rough couplet :

> *Sir* Nich'las, *Sir* Fred'rick ; *Widow and* Dufoy,
> *Were not by any so well done,* Mafoy.

[2] The incidents in Act IV, behind the scenes, where Lady Cheatly whistles and two mock-Devils descend to fly away with Lump, and also where Prig and young Maggot are carried up in their chairs and hang in the air until they are let down by the carpenter, may be thought somewhat farcical. They can be paralleled with an episode in Lacey's *The Dumb Lady; or, The Farrier Made Physician*, produced at Drury Lane in 1669, Act IV, when the Conjurer " *whistles, Elizium opens ; many Women's voices sing* '*John, come kiss me now* ' ; *after that a dance ; they draw up* Squire Softhead *with a devil, and he cries out.*"

to-day to declare that it is overdrawn when we remember the case of Madame Humbert and her empty safe?

One feels that the delightful scene with which Act IV opens, the Playhouse, should alone have been sufficient to secure success for this comedy. Strictly speaking, the idea was, perhaps, not entirely new. In *The Knight of the Burning Pestle* [1] acted in 1607, the citizen and his wife appear from the audience upon the stage, and keep up a running commentary upon the play, which they do not hesitate to interrupt with their criticisms and ejaculations; Jonson in *The Staple of News*, acted in 1625, introduces "four Gentlewomen, lady-like attired," who enter upon the stage immediately as the prologue begins and who gossip to each other between the acts, although it must be confessed that the business is rather clumsily managed. Other fairly close parallels might be cited, but Shadwell may have taken his most direct hint from the Duke of Newcastle's *The Humorous Lovers*, in which, Act III, scene ii, the characters appear in the theatre where a little mask is played,[2] but this is only an interlude, and in no way comparable to Shadwell's realistic scene, which is so admirably detailed and so true to life that it may, I think, be justly termed original, if even not unique in the English drama. It will readily be remembered that in the first act of Rostand's *Cyrano de Bergerac* [3] a theatre is represented. This is the only scene I know which in detailed observation parallels Shadwell's picture of a contemporary audience. It is excellently done, and the opening at least must be quoted in full.

" Premier Acte. Une Représentation à l'Hôtel de Bourgogne.

La salle de l'Hôtel de Bourgogne en 1640. Sorte de hangar de jeu de paume aménagé et embelli pour des représentations.

La salle est un carré long : on la voit en biais, de sorte qu'un de ses côtés forme le fond qui part du premier plan, à droite, et ça au dernier plan, à gauche, faire angle avec la scène qu'on aperçoit en pan coupé.

Cette scène est encombrée, des deux côtés, le long des coulisses, par des banquettes. Le rideau est formé par deux tapisseries qui peuvent s'écarter. Au-dessus du manteau d'Arlequin les armes royales. On descend de

---

[1] It is now generally ascribed to Beaumont alone.

[2] Very many examples might easily be quoted of masques introduced into Elizabethan plays. Shakespeare's *The Tempest* will at once be remembered; there is an elaborate masque in Middleton's *Women Beware Women*; and again in *The Maid's Tragedy*. The catastrophe of Tourneur's *The Revenger's Tragedy* is arranged by a masque. In the Restoration Theatre we have a masque in Dryden's *The Rival-Ladies*, where it is germane to the action of the play. There are masques in Settle's *The Empress of Morocco*, and again in *The Counterfeit Bridegroom ; or, The Defeated Widow*, an alteration of *No Wit, No Help Like a Woman's*, generally considered to be by Mrs. Behn. In Massinger's fine tragedy *The Roman Actor*, licensed by Sir Henry Herbert, 11 October, 1626, there is a play within a play, and even a scene of another play is commenced, but none of these can in any way compare with Shadwell's realistic picture of an actual theatre.

[3] Produced at the Porte Saint-Martin, 28 December, 1897.

l'estrade dans la salle par de larges marches. De chaque côté de ces marches, la place des violons. Rampe de chandelles.

Deux ranges superposés de galines laterales : le rang supérieur est divisé en loges. Pas de sièges au parterre, qui est la scène même du théâtre ; au fond de ce parterre, c'est-à-dire à droite, premier plan, quelques bancs formant gradins et dont on ne voit que le départ, une sorte de buffet orné de petits lustres, de vases fleuris, de verres de cristal, d'assiettes de gâteaux, de flacons, etc.

Au fond, au milieu, sous la galerie de loges, l'entrée du théâtre. Grande porte qui s'entrebaille pour laisser passer les spectateurs. Sur les battants de cette porte, ainsi que dans plusieurs coins et au-dessus du buffet, des affiches rouges sur lesquelles on lit : *La Glorise*.

Au lever du rideau, la salle est dans une demi-obscurité, vide encore. Les lustres sont baissés au milieu du parterre, attendant d'être allumes."

The arrival of the audience who drop in gradually may be compared in detail with Shadwell's picture. We have : *Un cavalier entre brusquement.*

Le Portier, (le poursuivant.) Holà vos quinze sols !

Le Cavalier. J'entre gratis !

Le Portier. Pourquoi ?

Le Cavalier. Je suis chevau-léger de la maison du Roi !

Le Portier, (à un autre cavalier qui vient d'entrer.) Vous ?

Deuxième Cavalier. Je ne paie pas !

Le Portier. Mais . . .

Deuxième Cavalier. Je suis mousquetaire.

Premier Cavalier, (au deuxième.) On ne commence qu'a deux heures. Le parterre

Est vide. Exerçons-nous au fleuret.

(*Ils font des armes avec des fleurets qu'ils ont apportés.*)

Un Laquais, (entrant.) Pst . . . Flanquin ! . . .

Un Autre, (déjà arrivé.) Champagne ? . . .

Le Premier, (lui montrant des jeux qu'il sont de son pourpoint.) Cartes. Dés.

(Il s'assied par terre.)

Jouons.

Le Deuxième, (même jeu.) Oui, mon coquin.

This is precisely Shadwell's :

" *Door-keeper.* Pray, Sir, pay me, my Masters will make me pay it.

3 *Man.* Impudent Rascal ! Do you ask me for Money ? Take that, Sirrah.

2-Door-keeper. Will you pay me, Sir ?

4 *Man.* No : I don't intend to stay.

2-Door-keeper. So you say every day and see two or three Acts for nothing.

4 *Man.* I'll break your Head, you Rascal.

1-*Door-keeper.* Pray, Sir, pay me.

3 *Man.* Set it down, I have no Silver about me, or bid my Man pay you,"
whilst the gambling between the two lackies closely resembles Prig's :
" A Pox on't, Madam ! What should we do at this damn'd Play-house ?
Let's send for some Cards, and play at Lang-trillo in the Box."

Presently in *Cyrano de Bergerac* all is ready to commence, and then
Montfleury " parait en scène, énorme, dans un costume de berger de
pastorale, un chapeau garni de roses penché sur l'oreille, et soufflant dans
une cornemuse enrubannée." He plays Phédon, who begins Act I :

> *Heureux qui loin des cours, dans un lieu solitaire,*
> *Se prescrit à soi-même un exil voluntaire,*
> *Et qui, lorsque Zéphire a soufflé sur les bois.* . . .

The burlesque *Cyraunez de Blairgerac,*[1] by Gerny and Briollet, parodies
this scene by a *cabaret-restaurant.*

The prologue to *A True Widow*[2] is by Dryden, and so as late as the
spring of 1679, at least, Shadwell and Dryden were yet on friendly terms.

Shadwell made haste to retrieve his disappointment of *A True Widow*
with another comedy, and in the autumn of the same year, 1679, *The
Woman-Captain* was produced at Dorset Garden and rewarded with that
applause which indeed so lively and amusing a piece thoroughly deserved.
In the first act we have the influence of Jonson at its fullest. When Sir
Humphrey Scattergood and his two friends in Act I discuss the pleasures
of the table, they give us a most amazing catalogue of flesh, fish, fowl, and
every conceivable dish, exhausting the vegetable kingdom, and reciting a
vinous litany of the contents of a wine-merchant's cellar. Shadwell must
have been at infinite pains to collect all these hard names, and the result
is that such tremendous speeches smell of the lamp rather than conjure
up any vision of good tipple and brave cheer. The half is greater than
the whole, said the wise old Greek poet, and rich field as all these dainties

---

[1] Concert Eldorado, 12 February, 1898.

[2] This prologue appears again, printed as the prologue before Mrs. Behn's *The
Widdow Ranter ; or, The History of Bacon in Virginia,* 4to, 1690. But from an entry in
the *Stationer's Register,* 20 November, 1689, it is certain that Dryden wrote both a
Prologue and an Epilogue for Mrs. Behn's play. Unless they should be discovered in
manuscript, or as a broadside, it seems that this Prologue and Epilogue must be lost.
They were the property of Jacob Tonson, and as James Knapton published *The Widdow
Ranter* it is probable that Tonson withheld the right to print these, and accordingly the
Prologue and Epilogue as they now stand were inserted to fill the gap. The Epilogue
printed with *The Widdow Ranter* does not belong to that play. It appears, probably for
the first time, in *Covent Garden Drollery,* 1672, as the prologue to *The Double Marriage.*
After it had been printed in 1690 as the Epilogue to *The Widdow Ranter,* it again did
service as a Prologue to the second edition of *Abdelazer ; or, The Moor's Revenge,* 4to,
1693. The first edition of *Abdelazer,* 4to, 1677, has no prologue.

and beverages are for a commentator, one does not feel that such an exposition is very dramatic. It is true that Ben Jonson poured out from his learned cornucopia similar details with equal profusion, but in his case they are delivered with all the roll of mighty verse, not in periods of plain prose. To use such extended lists of words produces the most remarkable results when it is well done, and certainly can create a most pregnant atmosphere, but this is the gift of consummate art. It demands a peculiar genius, and this was not Shadwell's quality. In that wonderful study, *A Rebours*, Huysmans has told us of the music of a thousand liqueurs, and made us see the colour of a myriad perfumes, whose names decorate his pages like some strange arabesque. The mere sound of the words evokes extraordinary emotional pictures. All this was far outside Shadwell's ken.

Were *The Woman-Captain* to be acted once more, it would probably prove advisable to cut down these excessive catalogues, and to suggest rather than to detail. However, this is a very trifling blemish, and if the rest of the play is rather too farcical, what first-rate farce it all is! Old Gripe is excellent, and his ludicrous apprehensions when he finds himself enlisted for a soldier—rare fun in the reading—must have made a merry audience hold aching sides. In the hands of a comedian of genius, such as was Anthony Leigh, it requires little imagination to see that such a character cannot but have been memorable in the annals of laughter.

In the winter of 1679 was produced at Dorset Garden Lawrence Maidwell's comedy *The Loving Enemies*, which was furnished with an Epilogue by Shadwell, whose acquaintanceship with the author seems to have begun owing to their similar taste in music, and their admiration of the same master, Reggio. Of Maidwell[1] Langbaine, writing in 1691, has the following account: "An Ingenious Person, still living (as I suppose) in *London*; when some time ago he undertook the Care and Tuition of young Gentlemen, and kept a Private School; during which Employment, besides some other Performances, (with which he has obliged the World) he has borrow'd so much time as to write a Play, stiled *Loving Enemies*, a Comedy."

The Loving Enemies was produced with the following cast: Lorenzo and Marcello, "Two Noblemen Enemies to one another from a long fewd in their families," Betterton and Smith; Antonio, "In love with *Lucinda*, but pretends to the Widow," Joseph Williams; Paulo, "A brisk old Gentleman in love with the Widow," Leigh; Circumstantio, "A formal *Valet de Chambre* very troublesome with impertinent Rhetorick," Underhill; Albricio,[2] "Servant to *Lorenzo*," Richards; Julia, "Sister to *Lorenzo*,

---

[1] Whom he mistakenly calls John Maidwel; unless, indeed, Maidwell had this second Christian name. *An Account of the English Dramatick Poets*, Oxford, 1691, p. 335.

[2] *Albricias*: a gratuity; a tip.

in love with *Marcello*, yet never seen by him," Mrs. Mary Lee ; Camilla, " Sister to *Marcello*, in love with *Lorenzo*, yet never seen by him," Mrs. Barry ; Lucinda, " Old Paulo's daughter, in love with *Antonio*," Mrs. Shadwell ; Paulina, " A rich Widow," Mrs. Leigh ; Nuarcha, " An old Maid almost undone for want of a Husband," Mrs. Norris. The scene is laid in Florence. Inasmuch as Julia, Lorenzo's sister, loves Marcello, whilst Camilla, Marcello's sister, loves Lorenzo, and these two cavaliers are here-ditary enemies. This amorous circumstance causes many mistakes and intricate confusion, but eventually leads to a happy ending. It is not a bad play on the whole, and the characters of Circumstantio, the garrulous valet, and Nuarcha are particularly good. He is, however, obviously con-veyed from Sir Formal Trifle, as Shadwell must have recognized. Some of the strokes are very exactly borrowed, as for example in Act IV, Scene 1, where Circumstantio kissing Nuarcha very formally cries : " There's *Nectar* and *Ambrosia* on thy Lips," and when he shows an " occasional Reflection which *Melitetique* Paper contains some small Diversion of my Thoughts . . . Upon a *Magpy* sucking of an *Hen's* Egg." Use has also been made of a few hints from Mrs. Behn. *The Loving Enemies* was published, quarto, 1680,[1] with a Dedication to the Hon. Charles Fox.

Shadwell, who had always cultivated music, was well known as an admirable lutanist, a fact in which he took considerable pride, and a boast of which the satirists were soon to make tremendous capital. When in 1680 the celebrated musician Pietro Reggio published his magnificent folio of *Songs* [2] he included therein his setting of Shadwell's " Arise, arise ! ye subterranean winds," which is sung in the terminal masque of the operatic version of *The Tempest*. Reggio was one of the most celebrated musicians of the day,[3] famous, Evelyn [4] tells us, " for playing on the harpsicord, few if any in Europe exceeding him." He had long been on intimate terms with Shadwell, who studied for several years under this distinguished master, and upon the publication of his compositions, the

[1] *Term Catalogues*, Easter (May) ; 1680.

[2] In the *London Gazette*, 1680, is advertised " A choice collection of songs set by Signior Pietro Reggio to be engraved on copper in an extraordinary manner in very large folio, most of them out of Mr. *A. Cowley's* excellent Poems." The delightfully rococo title-page has a copper engraving of Arion on a dolphin, a favourite subject. Henry Goldingham represented " Arion on a dolphin's back " in the pageantry exhibited at Kenilworth when Queen Elizabeth was entertained there ; Thoms's *Anecdotes and Traditions*, 1839, p. 28. On Friday, 4 September, 1663, at Bartholomew Fair Pepys saw : "some German Clocke works, the Salutation of the Virgin Mary, and several Scriptural stories ; but above all there was at last represented the sea, with Neptune, Venus, mermaids, and Ayrid on a dolphin, the sea rocking, so well done, that had it been in a gaudy manner and place, and at little distance, it had been admirable."

[3] Reggio died 25th July, 1685, and was buried at S. Giles in the Fields.

[4] 25 July, 1684.

poet addressed him in a copy of complimentary verses[1]: "To my Much Respected Master, and Worthy Friend, Signior PIETRO REGGIO, On the Publishing his Book of Songs." To this Reggio replied with a sonnet, *Al' Signor Tomaso Shadwel, Poeta Dignissimo, per li suoi bellissimi Versi scritti in lode del' Autore*, haling him as "Immortal Swan." The lines are certainly graceful with a pretty precious elegance:

> Cigno Immortal, chi col'tuo nobil' canto
> Radolciresti al più crudo Aspe il core:
> Ben tu di Preggio avanzi il Gran Cantore,
> Che placò t' fra del' Eterno pianto:
>
> Egli co i dolci accenti, impetrò tanto
> Che ñtrasse il suo Ben dae' cieco horrore,
> Tu con là Cetra, à le CASTALIE suore
> L'alme rapisci: onde, è maggiore il vanto.
>
> Sono lè rime tue Rivi correnti,
> Che di Eloquenza in sen' chiudon tesori
> Riechi viè più dè gl' Indian Torrenti.
>
> Su i bei Colli di PINDO a coglier Fiori
> M'invita l'Harmonia dè tuoi concenti:
> Mentre APOLLO t'intreccia il' crin di Allori.

Already in the Dedication to *A True Widow*, which is signed "16th February 1678-9," Shadwell had given as his opinion that one of the reasons for the failure of his comedy was "*the Calamity of the Time, which made People not care for Diversions*," and indeed by this time the country was in a state of such bitter religious and political turmoil as has seldom, if ever, been paralleled in the chronicles of English history. This crisis is so closely connected with the career of Shadwell, and so essentially the basis of his quarrel with the great John Dryden, that it seems necessary to give, what must at best be a very meagre and perfunctory sketch of the trend of events.

In the first place, however, not to break the sequence of the historical narrative, I would point out a fact which hitherto seems to have escaped observation. It was not until somewhat late in the day that Shadwell came forward as the champion of the Whigs, although we hasten to add that once he had taken the plunge it was, as we should fully have expected, of such a violent and robustious creature, in for a penny in for a pound, and when his satires are launched he attacks his opponents with an explosion and a fierceness that are almost fanatical in the excess of their fury. Yet it would appear that by the beginning of 1681 he had not taken

---

[1] To the folio is also prefixed a Latin encomiastic poem by Maidwell.

up any definite stand, at least he had not committed himself openly to any party. He is even mentioned as still being on friendly terms with Dryden, and in the spring of this very year, 1681, we find their names coupled together in a pamphlet entitled *A Modest Vindication of the Earl of S———y, In a Letter to a Friend concerning his being Elected King of Poland*,[1] in which Dryden is with biting irony represented as being of Shaftesbury's faction, and actually one of the officers of the new Polish monarch : " *Jean Dryden-urtzitz,* our Poet Laureate, for writing Panegyricks upon *Oliver Cromwel* and Libels against his present Master, King *Charles II* of *England ; Tom Shadworiski,* His Deputy."

Very shortly, however, after the publication of this pasquil Shadwell boldly proclaimed his adherence to the Whig cause, and consequently thrust himself into prominence as a mark for the shafts of the loyal Tory writers. One of the earliest of these satires was D'Urfey's comedy *Sir Barnaby Whigg ; or, No Wit Like a Woman's,* produced at Drury Lane in the early autumn of 1681.[2] It is obvious that the title-rôle, Sir Barnaby Whigg, "*A Phanatical Rascal, one of Oliver's Knights ; one that always pretends to fear a change of Government yet does his best to cause one,*" is intended as a complete portrait of Shadwell. When in the development of the piece is exhibited the easy villainy of Sir Barnaby Whigg, who changes from Whig Dissenter to Catholic and then to Mahometan, with a view of bettering his fortune by his rapid vacillations, it seems certain that such transilience trounced Shadwell's wavering, his procrastination in taking a definite stand and at the last his swaggering adherence to Shaftesbury's reckless camarilla.

In the course of D'Urfey's comedy, which is incidentally a clever and entertaining piece of work, there are many quite personal hits at Shadwell, and to those who knew him, if only by sight and reputation, each jest must have been full of point and application. He is described as being one

---

[1] The ambitious Shaftesbury actually aimed at the Crown of Poland, since this was an elected monarchy. There are innumerable references to this, and in Mrs. Behn's lively comedy *The City Heiress* produced at Dorset Garden in 1681–2 there is an amusing scene in which a mock ambassador arrives at the house of Sir Timothy Treat-all and announces : " The *Polanders* by me salute you Sir, and have in this next new Election prick'd ye down for their succeeding King." They then measure his head for the diadem. In the prologue to Otway's *Venice Preserv'd* produced at Dorset Garden 9 February, 1681–2, we have

> O Poland, Poland ! *had it been thy Lot,*
> *T'have heard in time of this* Venetian *Plot ;*
> *Thou surely chosen hadst one King from thence,*
> *And honour'd them as thou hast* England *since.*

Prose pasquils, and versified squibs such as *The Last Will and Testament of Anthony, King of Poland,* were infinitely numerous.

[2] *Term Catalogues,* Michaelmas (November), 1681 ; 4to, 1681.

who will " In all turns of State, change his Opinion as easily as his Coat, and is ever zealous in Voting for that party that is most Powerful." He fears a famine more than any other calamity, and when rated for his treasonable sentiments, bawls out : " Ha—what the loud Traytor to a man of my kidney ? a Portly, Jolly, Fat man ; a man of Fat and Belly : Away fool, 'tis your lean, your scraggy fellows that Plot mischief ; if the Pope himself had been a fat fellow, he had been honest." " I am plump, plump, a man of kidney," he asseverates when called " swoln and bloated." When a lute is introduced Sir Barnaby is said to play on it to a miracle ; " I have observ'd, (Gentlemen) that your thick squab-hand and short thumb-like fingers always become a lute extremely," says Sir Walter Wiseacre. Sir Barnaby uses *Tace*, Sir Samuel Hearty's cant phrase, and perhaps the sharpest hit of all is when Benedick says : " If I mistake not, this fellow values himself extremely by playing on the Musick." " Oh, yes," answers Wilding, " but the Town of late has us'd him so unkindly, that he has left it off, and now sets up for a grand Politician."

Shadwell was furious at the satire, and did his utmost to damn the play. " *As to this Comedy*," says D'Urfey, " *it had the Honour to please one party, and I am only glad, that the St. Georges of Eighty-one got a Victory over the old hissing Dragons of Forty-two ; 'tis a good Omen, and I hope portends future successes, though some fat Whiggs of Sir Barnaby's tribe made all the interest they could to cry it down.*"

Even more precisely is Shadwell ridiculed in the following song, which, were it not for the sake of the trenchant sarcasm, might seem rather superfluously introduced, but which is full of vigour and highly significant as sung by Sir Barnaby Whigg in Act III, scene i :

I

Farewell my Lov'd Science, my former delight,
Moliere is quite rifled, then how should I write ?
My fancy's grown sleepy, my quibbling is done ;
And design or invention, alas ! I have none.
But still let the Town never doubt my condition ;
Though I fall a damn'd Poet,[1] I'le mount a Musician.

II

I got Fame by filching from Poems and Plays,
But my Fidling and Drinking has lost me the Bays,
Like a Fury I rail'd, like a Satyr I writ,
Thersites my Humour, and *Fleckno* my Wit.

[1] In particular reference to the recent failure of *A True Widow*.

> But to make some amends for my snarling and lashing,
> I divert all the Town with my Thrumming and Thrashing.[1]

Although the rebels were yet active and anarchy was still in the air by the autumn of 1681 light had begun to break through the dark threatening clouds, and it may be said that the worst of the danger was over. On 22 June, 1678, Titus Oates, after various wanderings over the Continent, during the course of which he had been expelled from two colleges, Valladolid and S. Omers, returned to London. Here he renewed his acquaintance with a half-crazed fanatic and scaremonger, Dr. Ezrael Tonge, Rector of S. Michael's in Wood Street, and together they spawned that monstrous fabrication which is generally known as Oates's Plot.[2] Systematically they reduced their wild imaginings to a series of eighty-one articles, and, owing to the instrumentality of one Christopher Kirkby, who held some small appointment in the royal laboratory, they were able to convey a wild tale to the King. The death of Charles had been resolved upon instantly. He was to be poisoned in the Italian fashion by Sir George Wakeman, the Queen's physician. He was to be shot with silver bullets as he walked in S. James's Park. Four Irish ruffians had received considerable sums of money to dispatch him at Windsor. A mysterious person named Coniers, a Jesuit of course, of whom nothing was known and who could never be traced, had consecrated with solemn ceremonies a knife a whole foot in length, to stab him to the heart. Great largesse was to be bestowed from abroad to whomsoever should accomplish the work. If the Duke of York did not consent to his brother's immediate assassination, he himself was to be forthwith removed by venom or dagger. King Charles, with his usual fund of shrewd commonsense, waved all this folly aside. He did not, and he could not realize the powerful forces in the background who were working so singly and so steadily for evil. A detailed and an unprejudiced examination of the available records leaves little doubt that the Plot was a deliberate concoction by Oates and Dr. Tonge. It is true that the former was the greater villain and the latter the

---

[1] Cf. *Mac Flecknoe* :

> Sometimes, as Prince of thy Harmonious band,
> Thou wield'st thy Papers in thy threshing hand.
> *St. André*'s feet ne'er kept more equal time,
> Not ev'n the feet of thy own *Psyche*'s rhime.

[2] It is a pity that there is no reliable history of Oates's Plot. Sir George Sitwell's *The First Whig* is valuable, and probably the best thing on the subject. There are a few useful but slight monographs upon several particular points and events. T. Seccombe's chapter on Titus Oates in *Twelve Bad Men* (London, 1894), is well done, but an extended study is greatly needed. John Pollock's *The Popish Plot*, 1903, if employed, must be used with the utmost caution. The book is so unconsciously falsified, prejudiced, and biased as to be gravely erroneous.

greater fool, but their combination proved dangerous in the highest degree. The authority of L'Estrange and Simpson Tonge may be taken fairly to establish this fact. L'Estrange was in the position of an impartial inquirer, in fact he was attacked by both sides for his moderation ; as the circumstances turned out, Simpson Tonge had every inducement to speak the unvarnished truth, and when in the winter of 1680 L'Estrange definitely challenged Oates to prosecute young Tonge for defamation of character, and publicly urged him to take up the case, Oates was literally afraid to move in the matter. If it seems surprising that two men such as Oates and Tonge, however bold and however wicked, could have set England aflame, we must remember that behind them directing their movements, giving them constant information and valuable suggestion, financing them in every direction, was a figure of undoubted, if most demoniacal and crooked genius, the Earl of Shaftesbury, who stood as the leader and energizer of a band of malcontents and anarchists, whose ramifications and secret intrigues extended far and wide on every hand.

It was probably Shaftesbury who suggested Sir Edmund Berry Godfrey as the magistrate before whom Oates should swear to the truth of his information. On 6 September, 1678, Oates, Tonge and Kirkby entered the magistrate's office and formally required him to take the affidavit of Oates concerning the information which had been in detail committed to paper. In his public capacity it was impossible for Godfrey to refuse such a request, and from this initial move he was implicated in their proceedings. He was known as an austere and resolute Justice of the Peace, a man who would do what he conceived to be his duty at all costs, and one who had gained an exceptional reputation for integrity by his resistance to the Court and even upon occasion to the King. To have involved so prominent and respectable a personage in their proceedings was a masterstroke. It seems probable, however, that Godfrey was able to detect this tissue of lies, and had he used the weight of his impartial evidence against the conspirators, which is what would inevitably have happened, not only must all their schemes have crumbled to nothing, but they would have been in danger of the most severe punishment for their perjuries, and it is highly possible that Godfrey's penetration might have reached Shaftesbury himself. In fact so far from Godfrey being an advertisement and an ally, as they had hoped, his perception and his honesty made him a most dangerous opponent. Accordingly on 12 October, Sir Edmund Berry Godfrey was missing. Carefully circulated rumours and well-organized gossip began to create something like a panic, and when on 17 October the body of the murdered magistrate was found among the fields at the foot of Primrose Hill there ensued a period of frenzied terror. With pale faces and trembling limbs men asked each other whose turn was coming next. The most contradictory, the wildest, reports were instantly believed.

It was instantly bruited that certain Jesuits had enticed Godfrey into Somerset House and there made away with him, under the shades of night conveying the body into the country and throwing it down among the brambles by a ditch. London was to be set on fire at various points, and in the confusion on the same evening a number of prominent citizens were to have their throats cut as they lay sleeping in their beds. How all this was to be effected does not seem very clear, but certain it is that no story was too extravagant to be swallowed. Even men of no rank, of no profession, of no importance, persuaded themselves that they were marked down owing to some mysterious reason for instant destruction. Nobody dared to stir abroad unless he were fully armed. A cutler sold no less than three thousand daggers in one day. Men carried these unsheathed beneath their cloaks; ladies concealed them amid their furbelows and point lace. Another favourite weapon of defence was the Protestant flail, a kind of knuckle-duster, very serviceable at close quarters; the Countess of Shaftesbury had a pair of pistolets made for her muff, and not a few of her friends copied her example. In most houses as the families retired to rest, with the bedroom candles there were served out life-preservers and poniards to be kept under the pillows in case of some sudden midnight attack. When the corpse of Godfrey, after having lain in state, was on 31 October borne to S. Martin-in-the-Fields for burial the streets through which the very pompous and theatrical mourning procession had to pass were thronged with excitable and terrified crowds. The church itself, as one might have expected, was packed from an early hour. Dr. Lloyd, afterwards Dean of Bangor and Bishop of S. Asaph, a Herculean divine, roared forth an inflammatory discourse from the text: "Died Abner as a fool dieth?" London literally went mad, and howled for blood. Wholesale arrests followed, and at the moment there was not the slightest chance for any one of the accused. Oates, proclaimed the Saviour of the Nation, came forward and swore away life after life of innocent men. Seldom in history has there been so extraordinary and abject a manifestation of mob-mania. The most glaring contradictions of this perjured man were glozed over, and it is no exaggeration to say that prisoners were condemned on his word alone. The King recognized that he was powerless to stem the fury of the populace; any action on his part would have jeopardized, it might well have lost him, his throne. On 26 November, 1678, William Staley, a young man of promise and fair repute, was executed at Tyburn on the evidence of two witnesses, who bore the worst possible reputation as perjurers and false swearers. They declared that he had spoken treasonable words whilst dining in a Covent Garden ordinary. The fact that it would have been very difficult to catch and very easy to mistake the drift of a sentence in so crowded a place unless one were personally in the speaker's company, and, moreover, the admission by the evidence that the language used was French, with which it does not appear that the informers were even imperfectly acquainted, all went for nothing. On 3 December, 1678, Edward Coleman was put to death for high treason, chiefly it would seem on account of his correspondence with Père la Chaise, the confessor of Louis XIV., letters in which, as was quite natural, he expressed his hopes for the spread of the Faith in England, but which are perfectly innocent of any dark design or projected conspiracy. It was in November, 1678, that Titus Oates had reached such a height of impudence that he actually accused the Queen at the bar of the House of Commons. However, this was going too far, and Charles so strongly showed his displeasure that the accusation was very quickly dropped and forgotten. In 1679 there was a melancholy tale of executions. To name but a few : Father Ireland, S.J., and William Grove, a temporal coadjutor, were put to death on 24 January; Thomas Pickering, a Benedictine lay-brother, on 25 May; on 21 February Robert Green and Lawrence Hill were hanged as the murderers of Godfrey; on 28 February Henry Berry was executed on the same charge.

Who killed Godfrey has been a much disputed question, and many elucidations, including suicide, have been put forward.[1] A careful study of the period, which is, it may be remarked, a task not to be lightly or briefly undertaken, can lead to only one conclusion. Sir Edmund Berry Godfrey was murdered by Oates and his associates in crime. Not merely was it wholly to their interest that this upright if severe Justice of the Peace should have his mouth closed, since in applying to him they had made a false step, but unless he were silenced they would pay no light penalty for their plots and perjuries, nay, almost the whole party might be blown to destruction. Moreover, the death of Godfrey, who, if anything, was supposed to believe in and favour their story, would give a fearful impetus to popular fanaticism, and could be utilized as a proof of their integrity. This, indeed, is exactly what happened ; they were not men to stick at trifles, and so the unfortunate magistrate was entrapped in one of their dens and put out of the way. It is not known whose hand actually struck the blow, but the onus of the guilt falls upon Oates and upon Shaftesbury, although perhaps in the case of two such atrocious villains it will not stand for much, as it certainly does not stand singly, in their black account.

The first faint symptoms of sanity flickered in July, 1679, when there came a few acquittals. Sir George Wakeman ; Dom Marshall, O.S.B. ; Rumley and Corker were charged with conspiracy to poison the King. However, Scroggs instructed the jury that they might disbelieve the evidence for the prosecution. Oates was at last contradicted in his lies,

---

[1] Any reader of Pollock must be warned against his theories upon this point, which are not merely guesswork but frankly impossible.

and the jury promptly returned a verdict of not guilty. However, it must not be supposed that the tide had actually turned. The mob were primed to believe that Court influence had secured the acquittal; there were still executions in the provinces.[1] On 17 November, the anniversary of the accession of Queen Elizabeth, there was organized by the Green Ribbon Club, a hotbed of Whiggish activities, that elaborate and spectacular show which is so often ridiculed in contemporary satire.[2] On 9 December, 1679, a petition of seventeen Whig peers marked the beginning of the contumacious practice of petitioning, whilst the declaration of the Scottish Privy Council, 26 February, 1680, expressing their abhorence of seditious petitions, gave to the Tories the name " Abhorrers," as they were popularly known. They were, in fact, the loyal party, true to their King and the rightful succession, whilst the petitioners were the revolutionaries and runagates who to serve their own bad ends strained every resource to plunge the country into anarchy and civil war. On 11 June, 1680, Mrs. Cellier was tried for high treason and acquitted; and on 23 June the Earl of Castlemaine was also declared innocent of the same charge. None the less, at York on 29 July, Thomas Thwing, a secular priest, was convicted on the most discreditable evidence and suffered the extreme penalty, 23 October, 1680. Affairs were indeed still in a very perilous condition, and there was as yet no sense of security at all. 2 November, 1680, the Exclusion Bill was voted, but a fortnight later it was rejected by the House of Lords. Notwithstanding the madness of the mob was again seen at its worst on 17 November, when the Green Ribbon Club with desperate energy once more, and as it proved for the last time, organized their city bonfires and tomfool processions. Lord Stafford was beheaded on Tower Hill, 29 December, 1680, but the time had come when the King was able to strike the blow which would end these long black months of terror and blood. A parliament was summoned at Oxford. Thither on 17 March Shaftesbury and other Whig leaders set out in the most truculent manner, flaunting in their hats their badge, a big blue rosette, girt with wide blue sashes, armed to the teeth with dags and great horse pistols, some even wearing helmets, old murrions, and freshly scoured brigandines. Bands of steel-clad retainers followed them as if for war, and this, no doubt, was their ultimate intention. On 21 March Parliament met. The Commons sat in the Convocation House; the Lords in the Geometry School. The lower house boasted and bragged apace, vociferating disloyalty, and giving free tongue to the vilest treason. With great glee and much self congratulation the leaders were busily hurrying through a Third Exclusion

---

[1] Especially in Yorkshire. See Father Parkinson's " The Yorkshire Branch of the Popish Plot," *The Month*, xviii., 393.

[2] *E.g.*, Dryden's Prologue to Southerne's first play, *The Loyal Brother; or, The Persian Prince*, produced at Drury Lane in the early spring of 1681-2.

Bill. They felt confident that they had won the fight, and that the King would be a mere puppet in their hands. On the eighth day the Commons were summoned to the upper house, and thither they rushed in tumult and disorder, eager to hear the King announce his surrender. A decent silence was proclaimed; Charles suddenly appeared in his full robes of State, the royal dress in which alone he could utter the formula of dissolution. He spoke the words, and retired. Parliament was at an end. In vain did Shaftesbury send his creatures round the town, imploring the Whigs to combine and make a stand. A great panic seized the traitors, they were only too conscious what punishments they had deserved, and escape was their one thought. It is said that in an hour or two the price of horses and the hire of coaches doubled, nay trebled, whilst in every direction the roads were black with men flying to their country manors and distant homes, happily to evade that just retribution they had so long invited and deserved. And, indeed, in perfect equity the King might honourably have wreaked a sudden and terrible vengeance, but he was merciful, and soon they were to repay his generosity by plotting against him again, and planning his destruction.

Unhappily more innocent blood was yet to be shed, and on 11 July, 1681, the Blessed Oliver Plunket,[1] Archbishop of Armagh and Primate of all Ireland, was executed at Tyburn. In the following month, however, a fearful incendiary Stephen College, the Protestant joiner as he was dubbed, who whilst the last Parliament had been in session at Oxford was wont to parade the streets armed with a huge broadsword and pistols, persistently making use of the most opprobrious expressions regarding the King, and openly inciting to revolt, had been put on his trial. He was found guilty in the face of accumulated evidence, and executed 31 August. On 24 November, 1681, a bill of indictment for high treason was presented against Shaftesbury to the grand jury, but these packed and disloyal men threw out the bill with an Ignoramus, an event which occasioned the last Whig demonstration of the period. In 1682 the Whigs were hatching the Insurrection and Assassination Plots, but even in their own ranks all was wrangling and confusion. The ridiculous pageant of 17 November of that year was prohibited by Government, a detail, which however small in itself was so ominous that Shaftesbury fled beyond the seas to Holland. The Insurrection came to nothing and the Rye House Plot was betrayed. Mercy could not with safety to the King's own life overlook these repeated attacks, and when the conspirators who were most deeply dyed in guilt had met their just doom, peace was at length, for a few years at any rate, restored to the English nation.

Since actors " are the abstracts and brief chronicles of the time " it was inevitable that the political situation should be mirrored in the theatre,

---

[1] His shrine is at Downside Abbey near Bath, where his Relics are venerated.

and not only do Prologues and Epilogues teem with topical allusions, but there were produced a large number of plays which under the thinnest veils reproduced both actual situations and living individuals. Political and religious controversy may be regarded as having reached an extreme in the theatre during the period of years from 1679 to the death of Charles II., and the whole position is bewilderingly complicated by the fact that for some while many of the poets do not seem definitely to have decided for one party or the other, although this is not altogether strange if we realize how at first there were many shades of disagreement, and men's opinions had not instantly taken on so pronounced and violent a colouring. It must be remembered also that writers who depended upon their output for their livelihood were by no means eager to commit themselves beyond retraction either with one party or with the other, so that whether Court or City eventually gained the upper hand—and the issue long seemed doubtful—they could not if the situation required promptly identify themselves with the victors. As months went by it became impossible to sit on the hedge, but even so we find that authors who had more or less definitely taken one course, in a very short time veer on to another tack, and seem flatly to contradict themselves. This does not merely apply to small and insignificant Grub-Street chapmen, whose pens were at the service of any purchaser, but also to writers of standing and repute, and even to eminent names. Nor need we censure this change of front and expression, for as the mind acquires more knowledge it may easily perceive that it has been mistaken, and then on surer grounds arrive at certain truths. A reasonable change of opinion, to advance from error to verity is a sign of strength and courage, not a mark of weakness and vacillation. Thus we find that John Dryden whose *The Spanish Fryar ; or, The Double Discovery*,[1] a play prohibited under James II.,[2] which was produced at Dorset Garden in March, 1679–80, had *The Duke of Guise* ready for production in July, 1682,[3] and in 1687 expresses his settled convictions in that fine poem *The Hind and the Panther*.[4] Dryden was great enough and noble enough to

[1] Father Dominic, be it observed, is a ludicrous but surely not malicious caricature, he is a common enough figure in the Italian *novellieri;* and the lighter scenes of *The Spanish Fryar* are of the first order of comedy. It seems a pity that it was necessary for it to be banned, but the times were perilous and those in authority must have known best. When Mary II. assumed the crown she selected this play to be given on a particular occasion when she was present, but there were so many passages which, as it happened, could easily be applied to her own unfilial conduct that before the piece was done she had betrayed the utmost confusion and had heartily repented of her indecency.

[2] By an order dated 8 December, 1686, which commands " that ye play called ye Spanish Friar should bee noe more Acted."

[3] Lee joined with Dryden in this fine drama, but it was no doubt the master hand which gave the colour to the whole play. It was banned on 18 July, 1682, but allowed to be acted later in the year, and produced at Drury Lane 1 December, 1682.

[4] There is more than one issue of the first edition.

proclaim and hold fast to his creed, but there were others who were more pliant and pliable, and although they might urge that they were wholly dependent upon their writings for their very bread and that therefore sheer necessity forced them to truckle, yet the same excuse could be put forward in the case of Dryden. Crowne, for example, showed a lamentable falling off, when after that capital comedy *City Politiques*,[1] which was produced at Drury Lane in January, 1682-3, he brought out at the same house in the spring of 1689-90 his unworthy *The English Frier ; or, The Town Sparks*. Perhaps Elkanah Settle, although probably the most insignificant, is in some ways the most striking example of a political Vicar of Bray. An extreme and fanatical Whig,[2] in support of which party he drove the busiest and dullest of pens, later he turned Tory, and whereas in 1681 he had written *A Character of a Popish Successor*, a virulent libel upon the Duke of York,[3] two years later he issued *A Narrative of the Popish Plot*,[4] which is in effect an exposure of Shaftesbury, Titus Oates, and all his former associates. In the same year, 1683, he indited *A Panegyrick On The Loyal and Honourable Sir George Jefferies, Lord Chief Justice of England*, and when the opportunity offered he was not slow to publish a *Heroick Poem on the Coronation of the High and Mighty Monarch James II.*,[5] and in all probability he received ample albricias for his compliment. But hardly had that great and excellent King been driven into exile, " Recanting Settle," as he was already known, openly expressed his readiness to turn Whig again. By now, however, he was so extremely discredited that nobody thought it worth while to employ his little talents, which were notoriously as venal as they were mediocre, and when Matthew Taubman died, he was thankful to obtain the reversion of his post as City Poet. After some eight years' silence he returned to the stage with *Distress'd Innocence ; or, The Princess of Persia*,[6] which seems to have been a fair success. It was produced at Drury Lane in the autumn of 1690 and published quarto with date 1691 and dedicated to the Right Honourable John Lord Cutts, Baron of Gowran. In the Preface Settle bitterly re-

---

[1] This comedy was banned 26 June, 1682, and the order which gave leave for its production did not reach the theatre until 18 December of that year, so it is reasonable to suppose that it was produced in the following January.

[2] He is described as " poet laureate and master of ordnance to the *Whig* party, who would vindicate Lucifer's rebellion for a few guineas." *Heraclitus Ridens*, 50.

[3] He afterwards declared that Shaftesbury had furbished the thing, and added much of the venom and many of the lies. This was probably the case.

[4] Folio, 1683.

[5] 4to, 1685.

[6] " This Tragedy was kindly receiv'd by the Audience, as the Poet gratefully acknowledges, and owns likewise his Obligations to Mr. *Betterton*, for his several extraordinary Hints, to the heightning of his best Characters ; and to Mr. *Montford*, for the last Scene of his Play, which he was so kind to write for him : To which may be added the Epilogue." Langbaine, *English Dramatick Poets*, 1691, *The Appendix, sub nomine* Settle.

marks : " Alas I was grown weary of my little Talent in Innocent *Dramaticks*, and forsooth must be rambling into *Politicks*, and much have I got by't, for, I thank 'em, they have undone me." Langbaine, also, noticing Settle in 1691 speaks of him as " An Author who has forsaken the Banners of *Mars* and *Pallas*, to return to the *Theatre*, the Seat of the *Muses* : One, (to use his own Expression) ' Who after all his repented Follies, is resolv'd to quit all Pretentions to *Statecraft*, and honestly skulk into a Corner of the *Stage*, and there dye contented.' "

When such turncoats as Settle were supplying the theatres, and there were others as versatile, not to say corrupt, as he, although owing to accident he made a louder noise, it will be seen that one can at best only roughly divide the dramatists into two classes, the loyalists and the Whigs. Davies says : " On the side of loyalty were listed the poets of genius : Dryden, Lee, and Otway, were an over match for Shadwell, Settle, and others. The audiences, divided in political principles, fell often into riot and tumult. One side of the theatre loudly applauded what the other with violence exploded." [1] To amplify this list we may say that the best known writers on the Tory side were Dryden, Lee, Otway, Rochester,[2] D'Urfey, Mrs. Behn, Southerne, Crowne, Ravenscroft,[3] Tate, and Henry Nevil (*alias* Paine), but it would be difficult to mention any other names save those of Shadwell and Settle who were active in the faction of the Whigs. To give even a bare list with briefest comments of the political plays of this period would mean to write a detailed account of many busy years of the Restoration theatre, and it must suffice here barely to mention just one or two of the more notable satirical scenes which may be taken as typical of many, not unimportant but not here described because a selection, and that of the smallest, must necessarily be made.

The arch villain Shaftesbury himself appears as the Chancellor in *The Siege of Constantinople*, which was produced at Dorset Garden in November, 1674, a spirited tragedy by Henry Nevil (Paine), who compliments the Duke of York (James II.) as Thomazo. In Otway's *The History and Fall of Caius Marius*, acted at Dorset Garden in the autumn of 1679, when Romeo and Juliet are presented alongside Sulla and Sulpitius in a Roman setting, Shaftesbury is the elder Marius, a most apposite presentation, as the characters of the two politicians were remarkably alike, both were crooked, cruel, unscrupulous, bloody, seditious, treacherous, consumed with extreme ambition and mad jealousy. In that fine tragedy *The Loyal Brother ; or, The Persian Prince*, Southerne's first introduction to the stage, Shaftesbury is Ismael, " a villainous Favourite." [4] The play, which is

[1] *Dramatic Miscellanies*, III., p. 218.
[2] *Valentinian*.
[3] The epilogue to *Dame Dobson ; or, The Cunning Woman*, produced at Dorset Garden in the autumn of 1683, is a spirited attack upon the Whigs.
[4] Acted by Michael Mohun.

founded upon a novel, *Tachmas, Prince of Persia*,[1] is a respectful compliment to the Duke of York, and it was received with much applause when it was given at Drury Lane in the spring of 1681-2. Mrs. Behn's delightful comedy *Sir Timothy Treat-all; or, The City Heiress*, which was produced at Dorset Garden probably before Easter, 1681-2, has in the title-rôle an extremely happy satire upon the Revolutionary politician. Nat Lee has twice drawn us full-length portraits of Shaftesbury. In that effective melodrama *Cæsar Borgia, the Son of Pope Alexander the Sixth* performed at Dorset Garden in the autumn of 1679 he appears as Ascanio Sforza, " a Buffoon Cardinal "[2]; and again in *Constantine the Great* he is perhaps even more clearly distinguished as Arius, the plotter and the atheist.[3] In yet another historical play, *Vertue Betray'd; or, Anna Bullen*, by John Banks, produced at Dorset Garden in the autumn of 1682, a "distrest Domestick Tale," he is Cardinal Wolsey, the villain of the tragedy, who has of course no relation at all to the chief Minister of King Henry VIII.[4] In addition to his immortal satires *Absalom and Achitophel* and *The Medal* Dryden has at least twice brought his enemy upon the stage. That loyal opera *Albion and Albanius*, which was produced with elaborate splendour at Dorset Garden in June, 1685, is wholly directed against the Association and its chief. At the conclusion of the piece: "*Fame rises out of the middle of the Stage, standing on a Globe; on which is the Arms of England; The Globe rests on a Pedestal: On the Front of the Pedestal is drawn a Man with a long, lean, pale Face, with Fiends Wings and Snakes twisted round his Body: He is encompass'd by several Phanatical Rebellious Heads, who suck Poison from him, which runs out of a Tap in his Side.*" The allusion here is to a certain physical infirmity from which Shaftesbury suffered, to wit, an abscess, that in order to preserve his life had to be kept continually open by a silver pipe. This, and his foolish ambitions in Poland, got him the nickname of Count Tapsky. In *Don Sebastian, King of Portugal*, performed at Drury Lane in December, 1689, Shaftesbury

---

[1] " An Historical Novel; which happened under the *Sophy Soliman*, who Reigns at this day. Rendered into *English* by P. *Porter* Esquire." *Term Catalogues*, Michaelmas (22 November), 1676.

[2] Created by Anthony Leigh.

[3] Originally acted by Gillow.

[4] It is insisted that the play is not political. The prologue says:

> I'm sent to plead the Poet's Cause, and say,
> There's not one Slander in his modest Play:
> He brings before your Eyes a modern Story,
> Yet meddles not with either Whig or Tory.

And the Epilogue commences:

> Well, Sirs, your kind Opinion now, I pray,
> Of this are neither Whig nor Tory Play.

is Benducar, Chief Minister to the Emperor of Barbary, the perfidious murderer and tortuous traitor to his lord.

Although, naturally enough, Shadwell's violent partisanship, as soon as he had overtly joined himself to the Whig factions showed itself in many of his scenes, and he was consistently to maintain his aggressive truculency until the end of his career, he has more particularly concentrated his political and religious rancour in a play which for accidental reasons was among the longest lived and most popular of all his pieces.[1] There can be no doubt that the great success upon the Restoration stage of *Macbeth* " altered by Sir William Davenant ; being drest in all its finery, as new cloaths, new scenes, machines, as flyings for the witches, with all the singing and dancing in it " [2] that gave Shadwell the idea of introducing similar magical properties into his next production. He was shrewd enough to see that—although masterpieces have been inspired by both— politics and religion alone, so far as it lay within his power to represent them, that is to say by bias and railing, were not sufficient matter for five acts, at least not for such a drama as might have any hope of passing the Censor. Accordingly he had to find extraneous attractions, and it was with no little acuteness that he selected the Sabbat and witchcraft, since these things have not only always had a great fascination for the curiosity even of the man in the street, but they were also (as he had certain proof) admirably adapted for theatrical attempt. So he mounted his Whig sedition upon a broomstick, launched it forth and wished it an easy flight. He himself tells us : " *All run now into Politicks, and you must needs, if you touch upon any humour of this time, offend one of the Parties. The Bounds being then so narrow, I saw there was no scope for the writing of an intire Comedy, (wherein the Poet must have a relish of the present time ;) and therefore I resolved to make as good an entertainment as I could, without tying my self up to the strict rules of a Comedy ; which was the reason of my introducing of Witches.*"

When the script of the new comedy was sent to Charles Killigrew, the Master of the Revels, he could not but note how full of inflammable matter the dialogue was. With an inadvertence, which some might deem highly culpable, and which no doubt was induced in him by the apprehension of noisy recriminations from the revolutionary party, who, although scotched by the dissolution of Parliament upon the previous 28 March (1681), had still to be reckoned with and were still dangerous,

---

[1] *The Lancashire Witches* was played as late as 1736, and this revival met with considerable favour. In this year was published, *J. J. and P. Knapton,* an edition in 12mo, with an engraved frontispiece. *The Squire of Alsatia,* which lived longest of Shadwell's plays, was given at Covent Garden in 1766.

[2] Downes ; *Roscius Anglicanus.* *Macbeth* was burlesqued by Duffett in the elaborate and extraordinary epilogue, " Being a new Fancy, after the old and most surprising way of *Macbeth* Perform'd with new and costly Machines," which concludes his skit *The Empress of Morocco* produced at Drury Lane in the spring of 1674.

INTRODUCTION

Charles Killigrew—to use Walpole's expression—only "chastised" the play by cutting out a number of the more flagrant indecorums. Shadwell ingenuously says that at the first reading there were struck out about a dozen lines. The piece then went into rehearsal, but the actors began to feel more than a trifle nervous; there can be no doubt that they would not keep silent with regard to such grave misgivings, moreover, others who were on occasion present in the theatre must certainly have caught snatches and speeches of the new play which could not but arouse their worst suspicions as to its integrity. Dryden, for example, who as the leading dramatist of the day must have frequented the play-house, since he held an official position under the King would justly and from a sense of duty, have inquired into the matter. The result of these anxious rumours, and it would seem of direct and very proper representation to Charles Killigrew, was that he suspended the rehearsals until he had re-examined the manuscript. It was obvious that the Whigs were losing ground, and by now he felt strong enough to take a firmer stand, and consequently he excised a very great deal more of the play, all that in the printed copies is given in the italic letter; and even so, some of us will think that he left a great deal too much which might more decently have been deleted and disallowed. It is nothing less than amazing to read such a criticism as that of Genest: "Shadwell has no profaneness, whereas Dryden is at times scandalously profane." [1]

As was only to be expected, a considerable part of the audience heartily hissed the piece; however, the Whigs, who could always be relied upon, then as throughout their whole history, to collect together a regular rabble, packed the theatre with their gladiatorial hirelings, and so the play won through the first opposition. Above all, the pantomimic accessories preserved it, and these indeed continued to give it life when the political travesty, if not negligible, had at least largely fallen into the background and become an unimportant feature. There is good reason to suppose that later the witch scenes were elaborated, and that the political portion of the play was reduced to the barest minimum. In August, 1711, *The Lancashire Witches* is advertised [2] as "carefully revised," and from what Steele tells us it is quite plain that practically the whole entertainment consisted of the magic, the dancing, the broomsticks, and the flights through the air. [3]

[1] Genest, *History of the English Stage*, Vol. II., p. 41.

[2] *Spectator*, cxxxii., Wednesday, 2 August, 1711.

[3] In *The Guardian*, No. LXXXII, we have a supposed bill from Will Peer for properties, etc. Three of the items are:

For boarding a setting dog 2 days to follow Mr. Johnson in Epsom Wells	o o 6d.
For blood in Macbeth	o o 3d.
Raisons and almonds for a Witch's banquet . .	o o 8d.

As Steele again has pointed out, the moral of the piece is extremely bad. The two heroines, if we may dignify two gillfirts by such a name, Isabella and Theodosia, have become secretly engaged to Bellfort and Doubty, in spite of the fact that their hands are pledged elsewhere, and that they are on the eve of their weddings, for which every preparation has been made. In neither case do they seem to have represented to their parents that they are not agreeable to the matches proposed. Of the two, Isabella is considerably the more objectionable character. It may be urged that Theodosia is the daughter of Sir Jeffrey, who is simple and silly and very much under the domination of his lady. Even if she were to express her disinclination for her intended bridegroom it might not avail her very much, but she would at any rate have done the honest thing, and this hardly seems to enter her mind. On the other hand, the father of Isabella is expressly described as a " true *English* Gentleman, of good understanding, and honest Principles," but although throughout he shows her the most considerate affection, and she surely might give him her confidence, so base is her nature that she prefers to deceive him, and were one to take the thing seriously, one cannot help thinking that he would be very well justified had he packed her rous out of doors. Pert and clownish Sir Timothy, to whom she is engaged, plainly appears, but she treats him with callous cruelty ; and no amount of foolishness on his part, clumsy dizzard and drumbelo that he is, can justify the rudeness with which this young drab handles him. The two fellows who are rewarded with the hands of these two ladies are eminently suitable for such partners. Owing to an accident they obtain admission to the house of Sir Edward Hartfort ; they are welcomed with the utmost kindness, and proceed at once to abuse their host's trust in a very ugly and discreditable manner. Disloyal and treacherous in their actions ; huffing and dinging ; impudent and irreverent in their conversation ; with so far as one can see not a single thing to recommend them, these two worthies were, so Shadwell tells us, intended to be gentlemen " well bred and of good sense," but he has given us, we will take leave to tell him, two full-length portraits of thorough-paced ruffians and blackguards. In fact both the ladies and the gentlemen closely resemble the principal characters in a certain modern novel which has achieved some notoriety, the main theme of which entertains us with the amours of an atheist and a whore. The author lingers lovingly over his protagonist's loss of faith, and lusciously over the intrigue. Had the romance ended by the rascal being whipped at the cart's tail, and the drab being sent to the house of correction, religion and morality would have gained, and artistry would not have suffered. As it stands, these two beastly characters conclude in an aureole of sloppy sentimentality, which is not merely trivial but disgusting.

The fact is that in *The Lancashire Witches*, by a paradox which may seem strange, the two characters whom the author considers knaves, Smerk and Tegue O'Dively, are the two best gentlemen in the play.

The name Smerk is derived from Etherege's *The Man of Mode ; or, Sir Fopling Flutter*, produced at Dorset Garden 11 March, 1676, and published in the July of the same year. Among the Dramatis Personæ we have " Mr. *Smirk, a Parson*," a name which Andrew Marvell picked up in his pamphlet *Mr. Smirke ; or, The Divine in Mode ; being Certain Annotations upon the Animadversions on the Naked Truth*, a violent attack upon Francis Turner, Master of S. John's College, Cambridge, whose *Animadversions on . . the Naked Truth*, 1676, answered Herbert Croft's *The Naked Truth ; or, The True State of the Primitive Church. By an Humble Moderator*, 1675. Marvel draws a parallel between Turner and " my Lady *Biggots* Chaplain," who " will serve for the flesh as well as the spirit," and cries out that he is " huff'd up in all his Ecclesiastical fluster " to " out-*boniface* an *Humble Moderator*. So that there was more to do in equipping of Mr. *Smirke* than there is about *Doriman*, and the *Divine in Mode* might have vyed with Sir *Fopling Flutter*."

Shadwell is at some pains in his address " To The Reader " to declare that as " *for reflecting upon the Church of* England " why, he " *intended nothing less.*" This is too ingenuous, and he must not expect to be believed. He has depicted Smerk as, according to his ideas, " *a Fool and Knave* " " *an infamous Fellow* " " *exposed for his Folly and Knavery, and expell'd the Family*," a pretty type forsooth of the Anglican clergy.[1] It is extremely surprising to find that Jeremy Collier in his *A Short View of the Immorality and Profaneness of the English Stage*, 1698, has not had a throw at Shadwell, and especially in his chapter *The Clergy abused by the Stage*, has not trounced him roundly for Sneak, Mr. Smerk, Father Tegue O'Divelly, and the Alsatian divine, ay, even for the Priest in *The Royal Shepherdess*. The satire in Smerk is extremely particular, and, according to Collier's principles, loudly calls for reproof. *The Spanish Fryer, Amphitryon, The Country Wife, The Orphan, Don Sebastian, The Old Batchelour, Cleomenes, The Relapse, The Provok'd Wife, Don Quixote*, and other pieces are rebuked as " horribly Smutty and Profane," but not a word of *The Lancashire Witches*, which, I venture to think, is as rampant and ruttish as any. Again, to name but a few, *The Double-Dealer, The Mock-Astrologer, Love for Love, Love Triumphant*, are numerically corrected for their profaneness, whilst Collier roundly rattles me up Dryden, D'Urfey, Congreve, and Vanbrugh as lewd and immodest to the last degree. It is inexplicable that Shadwell should not have been docked with the delinquents, and incidentally not a word of

---

[1] It may be remarked that Etherege rails coarsely at clerics. In a letter from Ratisbon 19 December, 1687, he pertly writes : " 'tis not amiss to see an humble clergy," and again in a letter to Jephson some three months later he execrates " the mischief they dayly do in the world " and " their pride, their passion, and their covetousness."

reproof is administered to Mrs. Behn, whom we should have expected to have been well firked for her freedoms, which are after all harmless enough.

In what, we may ask, consist Smerk's folly and knavery? Having observed that Sir Edward Hartfort, his patron, is spleenful and melancholic, he civilly inquires into the cause of his heaviness, so that he may perchance relieve it by counsel and sympathy, a very courteous motion, as I take it. He is not only rebuffed with an extreme of boorishness and acrimony, but his kindliness earns him a regular jobation. He offers— somewhat sillily I allow—his hand to Isabella, who deals him a box on the ear as her answer. A fine-spirited wench to reply thus to a suitor. Had he attempted to debauch her it had not been amiss, perhaps. He very truly informs Young Harfort that there is no Popish Plot and that none but wild fanatics believed such an invention, and he adds that the Jesuits died innocent, which was the case. All this is very honest and very sensible save the wooing of the lady, which is a little awkward. And yet he is knave and infamous, and all sorts of big bug words. If such is the fact, we must take Shadwell's word therefor; Smerk does not exhibit these bad qualities; I would call him a green hick where women are concerned, but I do not know any worse of the fellow.

It may be noted that Smerk is far from being a Catholic, he is not even a High Anglican. He denies Purgatory, and boggles at Transubstantiation.

In drawing Tegue O'Divelly, Shadwell has overreached himself. 'Tis not to the life; 'tis a mere mock-moppet. I am afraid it was meant maliciously, but the caricature is too gross. He is lecherous and lewd, and much of his talk is scandalously profane, but I do not think he will do any harm, for he is as unreal as a pantomime head whose pasteboard cheeks and huge rolling eyes do not frighten even the littlest children. They laugh at his antics and japeries, and are ready to tweak the ogre's nose. Tegue O'Divelly is just such a figure of fun as that fascinating Jesuit Father Ritzoom,[1] who " impressed you with his air of mystery, as one who delighted to deal in secret things," who had an " unspeakable face " (whatever that may be) " like the face of the sphinx," " a mocking smile " and " mysterious, dark, deep-set, impenetrable eyes "; and whose adventures never fail to thrill me. Alas! in a workaday life the English Jesuits are so far less interesting and entertaining; they are commonplace to a miracle. I much prefer Miss Sinclair's Father Eustace and Mr. Talbot and Mrs. Lorraine " the Jesuitess " [2]; or Father O'Toole, Mr. Tractate, and Ricci *alias* Aubrey de Vere in *Nightshade* [3]; or the two French priests

[1] *The Scarlet Woman* (1899), and other novels by Mr. Joseph Hocking.
[2] *Beatrice, or the Unknown Relatives*, a romance once immensely popular. " Mrs. Lorraine is a Jesuit, or, what is ten times worse, a Jesuitess; " Chapter XIV.
[3] By Mr. William Johnston, M.P., 1857; second edition 1895.

in *The Story of a Pocket Bible* [1] who—not before they were required—appeared at the merchant's bedside with vehement language and many signs and tokens; or Margaret S. Comrie's [2] Father Alphonso Gesparo "a tall black figure who glided with noiseless steps"; or Miss Augusta J. Evans Wilson's [3] Father Mazzolin in whose countenance "a large amount of Jesuit determination was expressed in his iris, blended with cunning, malignity, and fierceness"; or even poor "Padre Guiliamo [*sic*] who was a monk of one of the Dominican orders—at least he gave himself out as such, though he was, in fact, a Jesuit." [4] All these good folk are intensely amusing, but that any save a disordered brain can for a moment suppose they bear the slightest resemblance to reality I refuse to believe. Tegue O'Dively is just as grotesque a figure as they.

Most probably the best picture of the ordinary secular priest will be found in the novels of Monsignor Hugh Benson:—Father Maples,[5] Father Mahon,[6] the ineffable Father Richardson,[7] and the priest of the prim Yorkshire village.[8] They are all so well-meaning; such good fellows; most conscientious and correct; meritorious, hard-workers, clean livers; but all so obtuse, clumsy, half-educated, crusted lower middle class, second rate, tactless, unmystical,[9] and painfully true to life. Paradoxical as it may seem one wishes that they had the apperception of Father Tegue, who did at any rate realize that he was waging war "aduersus principes, et potestates, aduersus mundi rectores tenebrarum harum, contra spiritualia nequitiae, in coelestibus."

To what extent Shadwell himself accepted the facts of witchcraft is a curious point.[10] He boasts that he is "*somewhat costive of belief*," and it is true that if one scratches a Whig one finds an atheist. None the less I am very much inclined to think that he was far too sensible a fellow to dismiss these things lightly, and although there is, of course, much grotesque folk-lore, old wives' charms and mummery, it appears to me that he recognized the underlying and horrible truth. It is worth remarking that

---

[1] *The Sunday at Home*, Vol. II., 1855, Nos. 44 (1 March)—61 (28 June). Nos. 59 and 61 are embellished with most felicitous wood-cuts of these admirably zealous abbés.

[2] *The Lord of that Land; or, Margherita Brandini's Deliverance.*

[3] *Inez, a Tale of the Alamos.*

[4] *Jessie's Bible, or the Italian Priest*, by Mrs. S. Kelly.

[5] *The Sentimentalists.*

[6] *The Necromancers.*

[7] *Initiation.*

[8] *None other Gods*, Part I, c. v., 4.

[9] As wise old Mr. Cathcart in *The Necromancers* observed: "I've hardly ever met a priest who takes these things seriously. In theory—yes, of course; but not in concrete instances. . . . And the worst of it is that the priesthood has enormous power, if they only knew it."

[10] E. Ammann's dissertation *Analysis of Thomas Shadwell's Lancashire Witches*, Bern, 1905, is worthless.

the last execution for sorcery in England was that of three witches, Temperance Lloyd, Mary Trembles, and Susanna Edwards, who were hanged at Exeter 25 August, 1682,[1] about a year after the production of Shadwell's play.

Although Shadwell, taking his goetry from authority, has in his " Notes upon the Magick " given us quotations from half a hundred writers, and this at first sight appears the cream of very considerable and most recondite research, as I have shown in my Excursus it is pretty evident that Shadwell often takes his citations at second-hand or even third-hand, and that sometimes he has gone astray in the understanding of his authors. So vast an array of names has impressed many, and until now the point escaped examination, owing to the simple fact that in order adequately to investigate this an extensive and concentrated study of the demonologists is an essential equipment, and this was a task not likely to be undertaken nor yet to be accomplished in the space of a few months or even years. Such occult studies are of the most difficult, and to embark upon them seriously is without exaggeration the devotion of a lifetime. Shadwell, of course, intended nothing less; but as his great master Jonson had on every occasion amazed men by his encyclopædic knowledge, so must Shadwell parade a mighty display of learning in his turn. He has certainly read some authoritative books, although not near so many as he would have us think, and a good deal of his erudition comes from a tainted source, the egregious Reginald Scot, whose *Discoverie of Witchcraft*,[2] originally issued in 1584, was reprinted quarto 1651, and folio 1665.

Shadwell has further laid under contribution Ben Jonson's *Masque of Queens*, celebrated at Whitehall 2 February, 1609; and he has also taken something from Heywood and Brome's play *The Late Lancashire Witches*, " A Well Received Comedy " produced at the Globe in 1634.

There were two famous trials of witches in Lancashire; the one in 1612; the second in 1633. *The Late Lancashire Witches* and Shadwell's play are to some extent alike in combining the two events, taking incidents from both. It is probable that in 1612 Heywood had written a topical play dealing with the first prosecution, which made a great noise at the time, and that when some twenty years later practically the same events repeated themselves in the same area and created an equal sensation, Heywood called in the facile Brome to help him refit his scenes for the Globe Theatre. To combine the circumstances as Shadwell has done seems a perfectly legitimate piece of stagecraft.

Of the two prosecutions the first is the most famous. Among the hills of eastern Lancashire, in the forest of Pendle, there dwelt a miserable old blind beggar of some eighty years, a " wicked firebrand of mischiefe,"

---

[1] See my *Geography of Witchcraft*, c. II., pp. 151—153.
[2] There is a modern edition by Brinsley Nicholson, London, 1886.

who was by common repute " a genrall agent for the Deuill in all those partes." Elizabeth Southernes, or Demdike as she was more generally known, had been a witch from her earliest years, and she had dedicated her whole race, children and grandchildren to the service of Satan. Her bitter rival in influence and evil was a hag named Anne Whittle, or rather Chattox, " a very old, withered, spent, and decrepid creature, her sight almost gone ; a dangerous witch of very long continuance ; always opposite to old Demdike ; for whom the one fauoured the other hated deadly ; and how they curse and accuse one another in their examinations may appear. In her witchcraft always ready to doe mischief to men's goods than themselves ; her lippes ever chattering and talking ; but no man knew what. She lived in the Forest of Pendle amongst this wicked company of dangerous witches . . . from these two sprung all the rest in order ; and even the children and friendes of these two notorious witches." [1] In addition to the usual petty quarrels which so continually persisted amongst ignorant country folk in small villages, disputes concerning strayed chicken ; pilfering ; silly slanders ; and what not beside, a deadly feud had long embroiled the two families, and in their fearful striving for the mastery in evil terrible was the mischief they wrought throughout the whole country-side. Even a third family of superior station was involved. A squireen of the district, gay young Robert Nutter, quarrelled with Mother Chattox, whose daughter he had attempted to seduce, and the terrible old crone was not slow in taking her revenge. A curious ailment which baffled the skill of the doctors drained Master Nutter's life, and in less than three months he was in his grave, having with his latest breath accused old Chattox of contriving his illness by her charms. Moreover, this was not the only death laid to her account. As for Demdike, the rankest hag that ever troubled daylight, the tale of her crimes was appalling. The rumour of the " many strange practises " that were almost the boast of these wretched creatures became so resounding a scandal justice was bound to interfere, and in the person of Master Roger Nowell, a strict and energetic magistrate who suddenly swooped down upon the community, the law promptly secured Elizabeth Demdike and three other of the most kakodaimoniacal witches, who were placed under durance in Lancaster Castle.

The rest of the gang summoned a hurried meeting at Malking Tower, a remote and haunted spot where many a Sabbat had been held. Numbers of wild schemes for the release of the prisoners were hastily discussed, and they began to brew a plot to blow up the castle with gunpowder, an atrocity which it would have been easier to effect than it may to us appear. There is no doubt that these wretches were ready for any violence, but

[1] Thomas Potts' *Wonderfull Discoverie of Witches in the countie of Lancaster*, London, 1613.

before they could carry out their bad designs the whole coven was seized, and they were shortly put on their trial before Sir Edward Bromley and Sir James Altham, the Justices of the Northern circuit, who reached Lancaster on 16 August. Mother Demdike had died in prison, but various members of the rival Pendle clans bore the most damning witness against each other. In their rage and revenge they did not care how they jeopardized their own lives so that they might destroy their enemies. Much, no doubt, may have been exaggerated; much seems fantastic, although that is no reason why it should be any the less true; but even when every allowance is made, when their ignorance and their horrid passions are alike discounted to the full, enough remains to show that the charges of sorcery were proved up to the hilt. Ten persons were executed,[1] including one Alice Nutter, "a rich woman of a great estate," who had many times and oft assisted old Demdike in her charms, and who had attended countless Sabbats, including the last meeting at Malking Tower.

The prosecutions of 1633 were mainly instituted owing to the stories of Edmund Robinson, a boy of eleven years of age, who dwelt with his father, a woodcutter and poor mason, in Pendle Forest. He deposed upon oath that one Hallowmas he saw in a lonely field two dogs, one black, the other brown. Close at hand was a hare, but strangely enough the dogs refused to course, and presently they swiftly vanished from sight, whereupon he met an old woman whom he recognized as Mother Dickenson, a notorious and defamed witch, in the company of a little boy whom he did not know. It was they who had appeared as the two dogs, and they offered him money to buy his silence, but he refused. Thereupon she took from her pocket something like a bridle "that gingled" and threw it over the head of the little boy who seemed to be transformed into a white horse. Upon this steed she conveyed young Robinson to a large house where a numerous company was assembled. Tables bore a mighty spread of roast meat, puddings, white bread, and all manner of dainties, of which Robinson was asked to partake. He rejected such hospitality, when so formidable and threatening did the attitude of those about him become that with a great effort he broke away and took to flight. Several persons pursued him, and among them he saw a woman of ill-repute for her dark practices, who was much resorted to in the district as a diviner and fortune-teller, a certain Mother Lloynd. Just as he gave himself up for lost two horsemen came riding by, at the sight of whom the company scattered and fled, thus enabling him to reach home in safety. It is obvious that the story has been embroidered out of all recognition, and not very skilfully embroidered at that, but in spite of this, and in spite of the fact that Robinson when thoroughly frightened recanted the whole, I suspect a

---

[1] As the mistake is still perpetuated it may be worth while emphasizing that in England witches were hanged, and not burned at the stake.

substratum of truth, by which I mean no more than that there did exist a coven of witches in Pendle Forest, who were carrying on the bad old tradition, and that young Robinson, whilst wandering far abroad as boys will, did catch some glimpse of their meetings and mysteries.

However that may be, after his deposition had been taken at Padham on 10 February, 1633, before Richard Shuttleworth and John Starkey, Esqs., two of his Majesty's Justices of the Peace within the County of Lancaster, a number of arrests followed. At the Lancaster Assizes, " there were seventeen found guilty by the Jury, but the Judge not being satisfied with the Evidence, they were reprieved ; and His Majesty and his Council being informed of the Matter by the Judge, the Bishop of *Chester* was appointed to examine them, and to certify what he thought, which he did ; and four of them, viz. *Margaret Johnson, Frances Dicconson, Mary Spender,* and *Hargrave's* wife, were sent for up to *London,* and committed to the *Fleet,* great sums of money were gotten there by showing of them, and publick Plays were acted thereupon. They were viewed and examined by his Majesty's Physicians and Surgeons ; and after, by His Majesty, and the Council ; and no Cause of Guilt appearing, but great Presumptions of the Boys being subborned to accuse them falsely ; it was resolved to separate the Boy from his Father, and put them in several Prisons. Soon after this, the Boy confessed, that he was taught and encouraged to say those things by his Father, and some others, whom Envy, Revenge, and hope of Gain had prompted. Besides the Notoriety of such a publick Fact, Mr. *Webster* adds, that he himself had had the whole Story from *Edmund Robinson's* own Mouth, more than once." [1] All the accused were pardoned, but none the less there were many, and some shrewd heads, who thought that however false the evidence might be on this occasion Mother Dickenson did truly commerce in occult arts, and that she had escaped owing to the fact of her enemies having got hold of the wrong story. This seems exceedingly probable, and is only natural that young Robinson being thoroughly frightened should under a promise of forgiveness deny even the little truth upon which he, or rather others for him, had built these fabrications, and that in after years he should stick to it that his tale had been false, since he knew exactly what he was expected and required to say.

The Late Lancashire Witches was produced at the Globe in 1633, immediately after the Lancaster Assizes, whilst four of the accused who had been sent up to London were in the Fleet. A good many incidents from Robinson's actual narrative are introduced. For example, we have the boy and the two dogs. He is carried off against his will " to a brave

---

[1] *An Historical Essay concerning Witchcraft,* by Francis Hutchinson, D.D. Second Edition, 1720, pp. 270–271. The Webster to whom reference is made is John Webster, author of *The Displaying of Supposed Witchcraft,* 1677.

feast." Living individuals appear; such were Goody Dickenson, Mal Spencer, Mother Hargrave, Granny Johnson, Meg, and Mawd, all of whom were incriminated before the magistrate. A fictional character, Mistress Generous, the wife of an honourable country gentleman, is a witch. When Robin, the serving man, refuses to saddle her a horse she shakes a bridle over his head and makes him act as her steed to the assembly. Again a soldier, who undertakes to watch in a haunted mill, is at midnight beset by a number of fierce cats. In the confusion whilst he is defending himself with drawn sword he strikes off a tabby's paw. Next morning a hand is found whose long tapering fingers shine decked with costly jewels and golden rings. These are recognized as belonging to Mrs. Generous, and upon inquiry she is said to be ill in bed. By force they tear back the clothes, and see that one of her hands has been lopped off from the wrist. In their drama there can be no doubt that Heywood and Brome regarded the accusations as essentially true, and they seem to look forward to the execution of those who had been found guilty. Both implicitly believed in witchcraft.[1]

Shadwell has adopted various incidents from *The Late Lancashire Witches*, but his play can in no sense be said to be taken from the earlier authors.[2] He has, it is true, followed them in his conflation of the two prosecutions, but we should naturally expect any dramatist to chose the most striking features from each and fit them into one piece. The minor details which are similar in both plays seem to be derived from original sources. Shadwell's witches are Mother Demdike, Mother Dickenson, Mother Hargrave, Mal Spencer, Madge, and others unnamed. Elizabeth Demdike and Jennet Hargrave belonged to the first Lancashire trials of 1612; Frances Dickenson, Mal Spencer, and Madge were involved in the Robinson disclosures of 1633.

The Lancashire Witches is a sombre and shadowed play, and it seems to me a misnomer to call it, as the author has done, a comedy. There is no humour; there is no laughter to clear the air as nothing else will. The Sabbat of evil may be crude, but it is horrible and murky; the atmosphere is stifling, stale, and befogged; we feel ourselves soiled and grimed by

---

[1] See Heywood's famous *Gunaikeion*, folio, 1624, the discourse, *Lib*. viii, of witches; and especially pp. 414–15, the story of his neighbour a "woman of good credit and reputation, whom I have knowne above these foure and twenty yeares and is of the same parish where I now live" (Clerkenwell), who had related to him "upon her credit with manie deepe protestations" her experience with a witch of Amsterdam.

[2] In 1853 James Halliwell issued (80 copies for Private Circulation only) *The Poetry of Witchcraft Illustrated by Copies of the Plays on The Lancashire Witches by Heywood and Shadwell*. The texts are very poor,—in Shadwell's play the italicized speeches have been printed in the same roman character as the rest of the piece,—there is no attempt at editing, there are no notes, the format is intolerably heavy and clumsy, and one wonders why the thing was done.

the dirt, the paltriness and meanness of these sorceries which are none the less potent for bitter mischief as the village hags gather round the charmed pot with its carrion contents like some dark flight of obscene birds.

The mockeries which Shadwell intended have missed their mark. Sir Jeffery and Lady Shacklehead, and their assessor Father O'Dively, are all in deadly earnest at the examination of the witches. The rustic witnesses tell their unvarnished simple stories—the sow has cast her farrow, the butter will not come from the churn, the cow is drained dry and gives no milk, the good wife at home is groaning with pain ; there is no note of deep tragedy, just the everyday talk of sorrows and sickness which befall poor country folk, the pathetic happenings which make their humble lives sour instead of sweet. And then the miserable wretches whose malice has wrought these ills are dragged away struggling and yowling to Lancaster gaol, to the dungeon and the gallows.

There were even more bitter and more rancorous attacks than Shadwell's *The Lancashire Witches*, although these perforce were clandestine, or, at any rate, semi-secret. Such a one is *Romes Follies; Or, the Amorous Fryars*, " A Comedy, As it was lately Acted at a Person of Qualitie's House," which was " Printed for *N. Nowell*," and published 27 January, 1681–2. It is a supremely foolish farce, blasphemous and lewd. Although equipped with Prologue and Epilogue it was certainly only given privately. Among the characters are Marforio, an old rich Neapolitan Doctor of Physic who is in love with Florimel, the daughter of Senior Ronsard ; Father Turbin, " a Lascivious Fryer, but Hath the Vogue of the Holy, in Love with *Florimel*" ; Father Lupin, " His Comrade, in Love with *Isabella*," Florimel's maid ; the Pope, Cardinals and Bishops ; Oldcross, " a Jesuit and great *Negromancer*," who raises the ghosts of Clement I., Boniface VIII., Gregory III., Innocent III., and Pope Joan ! There is a good deal of indecency between Turbin and Lupin, Florimel (who is described as " An Airy Young Lady," which she assuredly is), and Isabella, but there is no vestige of plot in this gallimaufry. In the incantation scene we have : " *Enter the Ghost of Pope* Joan *in long dishevell'd hair like an* Amazon." This mythical personage proceeds to deliver a violent harangue which serves up all the old lies and scandals, a rant like a Protestant lecturer brawling in Hyde Park on a Sunday afternoon.

This pretty piece was dedicated to the Earl of Shaftesbury, and to Lord Howard of Esrick by a fellow who signs himself N.N., and there is one passage of the Epistle Prefatory which is not without interest : " My Lords, it may be thought a great presumption in me, to offer you a Play which never run the Risk of an hiss on either of the Theaters ; some will say it ought not to pass Muster for that very reason : But my Lords, I can boldly affirm say [*sic*] that this is not the first Play that hath been published and not Acted on the publick Stage. Mr. *Dryden's Fall of Man* tho' an excellent Poem, yet never appeared there. I could name many more, had I not other reasons perhaps more important for the non-acting of it at either of those places, the Subject being not a little Satyrical against the Romanists, would very much hinder its taking, and would be far more difficult to get play'd than *Cæsar Borgia*[1] was : or if it should chance to have been played, might have found a colder entertainment than *Tegue O'Divelly*, The Irish Priest, at the Duke's Theatre, merely for the Subjects sake. The Reason I have humbly offered your Lordships, will, I hope, gain your approbation in the necessity of its not having been offered to be Acted at either of the Houses."

With regard to the success of *The Lancashire Witches* upon the stage[2] Downes tells us : " *The Lancashire Witches*, acted in 1681, made by Mr. *Shadwell*, being a kind of Opera, having several *Machines* of Flyings for the Witches, and other diverting Contrivances in't; All being well perform'd, it prov'd beyond expectation very beneficial to the Poet and Actors."[3] It is very plain then, as we have noted above, that the vogue of the play was entirely due to the spectacular magnificence and the surprising effects with which it was produced. No doubt Shadwell derived considerable profit from so popular a performance, but none the less he does not appear to have been in assured circumstances, for there is evidence that he depended upon help from his friends, and in particular that he was regularly subsidized by the Earl of Dorset, since in a letter of 24 January, 1682–3, he applies to that nobleman for the last Christmas quarter of his pension.[4] Again in a

---

[1] *Cæsar Borgia, the Son of Pope Alexander VI.*, a tragedy by Nathaniel Lee, produced at Dorset Garden in the autumn of 1679 with Betterton as Cæsar Borgia ; Joseph Williams, the Duke of Gandia ; Smith, Machiavelli ; Anthony Leigh, Cardinal Sforza ; and Mrs. Mary Lee, the heroine, Bellamira.

[2] In *The Vindication of the Duke of Guise*, 4to, 1683, Dryden says : " The *Lancashire Witches* were without doubt the most *insipid* Jades that ever flew upon a Stage ; and even *These*, by the Favour of a *Party*, made a Shift to hold up their Heads."

[3] It was even to descend to the Fairs, and there is extant a little bill : " John Harris's BOOTH in Bartholomew-Fair *between the* Hospital-gate *and* Duck-lane-end, *next the Rope-dancery, is to be seen,*

> The Court of *King Henry* the *Second ;* And the Death of Fair *Rosamond :*
> With the merry Humours of *Punchinello*, and the *Lancashire* Witches.
> As also the famous History of *Bungy* and Frier *Bacon :*

With the merry Conceits of their Man *Miles*. And the Brazen Speaking Head ; wherein is represented the manner how this Kingdom was to have been walled in with *Brass*. *Acted by Figures as large as Children two years old. Mistake not the Booth ; you may know it by the* Brazen Speaking Head *in the Gallery*."

[4] The letter is printed in Volume V. Cf. the Dedication of *The Squire of Alsatia* addressed to Dorset, when Shadwell says : " *You are ever obliging, and seeking out occasions of doing good, and exerting Your Charity and Generosity. . . . I must acknowledge my self infinitely oblig'd to your Lordship every way.*"

MS. (not printed) *Satyr on the Poets*, which I should refer to the same date, we have :

> Mac Fleckno, for the Mirth of Mankind framd,
> For Magic Broom-sticks, and for Witches fam'd,
> In vain to thrive by Poetry Essay'd ;
> His Muse, and wife, e'ne spoyld the Poets Trade :
> Yet he Joggs on, in Measure hard and Rude ;
> A wretched Rhimer, Pennyless, and lewd.

There can be no doubt that owing to its violent, and one might without exaggeration say venomous, attack not only upon principles, but also upon individuals, *The Lancashire Witches* made a great noise. Dryden's *The Medall*, the subject of which is said to have been suggested by the King himself,[1] was published about the middle of March, 1681–82, and almost immediately afterwards appeared *A Lenten Prologue refus'd by the Players*, a slight satire, which may be pretty certainly ascribed to Shadwell. By this time there is little doubt that *Mac Flecknoe* was in circulation in MS., although perhaps not in its perfect and polished form, and a good many people, including the victim must have seen it. It is indeed probable that D'Urfey's idea of linking Shadwell's name with Flecknoe's as in the song introduced in *Sir Barnaby Whigg* was derived from Dryden's poem, which in this case would have been handed about, in part at any rate, as early as the autumn of 1681. Again in *The Loyal Protestant* of Thursday, 9 February, 1681–2, there is an attack upon Shadwell in the course of which the following significant passage occurs : " He would send him (Shadwell) his Recantation next morning, with a *Mac Flecknoe*, and a brace of Lobsters for his Breakfast ; All which he knew he had a singular aversion for." It is probable that the date of the publication of *Mac Flecknoe* was 4 October, 1682, at least this is the day inscribed on the title of his copy by Narcissus Luttrell, and although, perhaps, we must not insist that the day upon which Luttrell bought the poem was inevitably the very day it was issued from the press, it is not likely that such an indefatigable collector would not purchase so important a satire at the earliest opportunity, and we are surely safe in saying that *Mac Flecknoe* was published on one of the first days in October, 1682, not later than the fourth. From the same authority I take it that *The Medal of John Bayes* was published some six months before,

---

[1] " One day as the King was walking in the Mall, and talking with Dryden, he said, ' If I were a poet, and I think I am poor enough to be one, I would write a poem on such a subject in the following manner.' He then gave him the plan of *The Medal*. Dryden took the hint, carried the poem as soon as it was written, to the King, and had a present of a hundred broad pieces for it." This is told by Spence, who relates that the anecdote " was said by a priest whom I often met at Mr. Pope's : who seemed to confirm it."

as upon the title-page of his copy [1] of this satire he has noted : " *6d.* By Thomas Shadwell. Agt Mr. Dryden very severe 15 May." Malone unhesitatingly accepts this ascription,[2] but recently it has been argued that Shadwell was not the author of this ribald assault. *The True Protestant Mercury*, 22–26 July, 1682, advertises *The Satyr to His Muse by the Author of Absalom and Achitophel,* a piece which Oldys positively ascribes to Shadwell ; and on 4 September of the same year was published *The Tory Poets* which, Malone says, " Has always been attributed to the same person." We have then three satires, the first published in May, 1682, the second in July of the same year, and the third in the following September, all of which violently attack the Tories and in particular Dryden as the champion of the Tories, and all of which are ascribed to Shadwell. It is argued that " it is to the last degree improbable that within the short period covered by the appearance of the three (just mentioned above) which can be dated with approximate accuracy, any one man should have produced them all and should have returned three several times to the attack upon Dryden." [3] For my part, however, when regarding the circumstances I can see nothing at all unlikely in the supposition that within a very short space of time Shadwell should have thus fiercely beset Dryden on no less than three occasions, and when this supposition is supported by a contemporary authority, a man who would have been interested to inquire into, and who would have had exceptional facilities to discover the facts, although his be but a single statement, the suggestion seems to me practically to resolve itself into certainty. *Mac Flecknoe* had been for some months in circulation, and Shadwell was not the man to take an attack lying down ; we know that he wrote hastily and roughly ; his language, especially as regards his political opponents was intemperate to a degree ; he had a certain bulldog pertinacity which would have made him return to the onslaught again and again ; every one of these qualities and particulars may be found strongly marked in the three poems under discussion. It is generally perilous to argue from internal evidence, but it cannot escape notice that the *Epistle to the Tories* is precisely similar in spirit and expression to the address " To the Reader " which prefaces *The Lancashire Witches.* Again, in the speeches excised from that play there are close resemblances to the language used by the author of *The Medal of John Bayes.* It is impossible to read the two and not conclude that they came from the same pen. To quote but one example : in Act III of the play when Smerk refuses to believe in a Popish Plot, Bellfort says, " This is great Impudence, after the King has affirm'd it in so many Proclamations, and three Parliaments

---

[1] Now in the Dyce Library.
[2] *Prose Works of John Dryden*, Vol. I., Part I., p. 165, and p. 168.
[3] " Some Notes on Dryden," by Mr. G. Thorn-Drury. *The authorship of The Medal of John Bayes,* pp. 190–192 ; *The Review of English Studies,* Vol. I., No. 2, April, 1925.

have voted it, *Nemine contradicente.*" In the " Epistle to the Tories " we have :
" *Yet ye have the face to deny a Popish Plot . . . after* Coleman's *letters, and
. . . a multitude of other convincing Circumstances, which were of that force, that
there were at least ten of the Kings Proclamations that affirmed it, a publick Fast
was enjoyned for it, and three successive Parliaments,* nemine contradicente, *and
upon a full hearing of the Evidence, reading all the Letters, and weighing all the
Circumstances, declared it to be a horrid Conspiracy against the Kings Life and
Government. What impudence or stupidity is this, let the world judge ! "* Other
parallel passages might be cited, but these will, I think, be obvious to
every reader.

In *The Tory-Poets* we have in reference to Dryden :

> Can'st thou abuse that youthful *Hero's* fame,
> That wide as the vast World hath spread his name ?
> When he from *Mastricht* warlike Trophies bore,
> Vollies of Praises eccho'd on the Shoar.

" The youthful Hero," is, of course, Monmouth, to whom Shadwell
in the Dedication of *Psyche,* 4to, 1675, addresses this fulsome flattery :
" When *Mastrick* shall be a heap of Rubbish, and the name might otherwise be swallow'd in the Ruine, it will be remembered by the greatest
Action in the World, done there by the Greatest and the Earliest Hero."

The Duchess of Monmouth (named Annabel in *Absalom and Achitophel*)
to whom Dryden had dedicated *The Indian Emperour,* is thus spoken of in
The Tory-Poets :

> So when to *Damn* was in her *graces* power,
> She kindly smil'd on th' *Indian Emperor.*

The Medal of John Bayes has :

> Sweet *Annabel* the good, great, witty, fair ;
> (Of all this Northern Court, the brightest Star)
> Did on thee, *Bayes,* her sacred beams dispence,
> Who could do ill under such influence ?

This same satire, *The Medal of John Bayes,* alludes to Dryden's nickname :

> How truly *Poet Squab* would'st thou appear !

With a foot-note : " *The Name given him by the Earl of* Rochester."
We may compare *The Tory-Poets :*

> 'Cause *Rochester* Baptis'd him *Poet Squab.*

The allusion to Jonson in *The Tory-Poets* is wholly in Shadwell's vein :

> Did but *Ben. Johnson* know how Follies rise . . .

If Shadwell was not the author of these three poems, or of any one of
these three poems, he did not, so far as I am aware, reply to *Mac Flecknoe*

(clxxxiii)

save by such mild remonstrance as his protest in the epistle before his translation of *The Tenth Satyr of Juvenal*, quarto, 1687, which would have been singularly unlike the man from what we know of his inclinations and character. Again, if Dryden had not been greatly provoked there seems little reason why, when he had already pulverized his opponent in *Mac Flecknoe* he should return to the charge, and brand him forever with even more relentless vigour as Og in the second part of *Absalom and Achitophel*, which was published 10 November, 1682, and which was undoubtedly inspired by Shadwell's rampant and outrageous aggression.

To sum up the matter, in my opinion Shadwell was certainly the author of these three virulent satires, *The Medal of John Bayes*, *The Satyr to His Muse*, and *The Tory Poets*, and so far from Dryden's *Mac Flecknoe* having been provoked by the first of these, as some writers seem to think, it is more correct to assume that the three satires were provoked by *Mac Flecknoe*, and that Dryden's answer to this torrent of abuse may be found in the second part of *Absalom and Achitophel*.

More than twenty years before, when the theatres opened their doors at the Restoration of King Charles, there naturally arose a general and instant demand for new plays. Dryden, who even in those early days was beginning to enjoy a reputation as poet and critic, naturally turned his thoughts in the direction of the stage, and commenced work upon a tragedy, the subject of which was to be the history of the Duke of Guise, in which he thought he could give some representation of recent events. However, acting upon the advice of Sir Robert Howard and other of his friends he did not pursue his theme to an end, but laid by in his desk the scenes which he had written, among them being an episode of the return of the Duke to Paris against the positive command of Henri III. Dryden then essayed comedy, when the first piece he produced was *The Wild Gallant*, which proved unsuccessful, and was not liked even upon a later revision, the form in which we now have it.

In 1678 there was produced at Drury Lane a drama dealing with the very subject, some scenes of which Dryden had sketched and left incomplete, *Henry The Third Of France Stabb'd by a Fryer. With The Fall of the Guise*,[1] a tragedy in heroic verse by Thomas Shipman. This dramatist was born at the little village of Scarrington, two miles from Bingham, Notts, and was baptized there in November, 1632. Dr. Thoroton alludes to him as " a good Poet, and one of the Captains of the Train Bands of this County." [2] He was a member of S. John's College, Cambridge, and in addition to this play he is the author of a number of poems, which were collected and published posthumously as *Carolina; or, Loyal Poems*, 8vo,

---

[1] 4to, 1678. The Epistle Dedicatory addressed to the Marquess of Dorchester is dated 30 August, 1678.
[2] He is termed by Flatman " a Man every way accomplish'd."

1683. He married a daughter of John Trafford, Esquire, Margaret, by whom he had twelve, if not thirteen, children. He died at Scarrington, and was buried there 15 October, 1680.

Henry the Third is not a bad tragedy of its kind, although often very unhistorical, absurdly so in fact.[1] King Henry, Henry of Navarre, the Guise, and Grillon " Collonel of the Guards," all love " Gabriel de Estree, *Mistress to* Henry *the fourth.*" There is a very florid Incantation scene, when the Guise and his brother the Cardinal consult a Friar, who is a conjurer, and in a cave amid a wood this worthy evokes various astral spirits of Endor. The mage comes of stanch old warlock lineage, for he tells us :

> Thrice fifty years ago, one *Gyles-de-Raiz*
> (*Marshal of France*) my great Grand-father was,
> 'Twas he who first with Necromantick art,
> Taught *Joan of Orleans* to act her Part.
> Whose pow'rful charms made th' *English* quit the Field ;
> No mortal force else could have made 'em yield.
> 'Twas he (as by my bloody Roll appears)
> Who hir'd two Spirits for two Hundred Years.

It is curious here to meet with this foul and dark tradition concerning S. Joan, which had already been so abominably exploited on the English stage in *Henry VI, Part I.* Shipman is very robustious not to say violent, for we are shown the assassination of Guise, and a few moments later the murder of the Cardinal. The original cast has not been preserved, and there is no record of any revival of this drama.

Early in 1678–9, the tragedy of *Œdipus*, in which Dryden collaborated with Nathaniel Lee, had proved a great success at Dorset Garden, and the younger dramatist obtained a promise that they should join together on another play. This he claimed during the spring of 1682, and although Dryden, having only just finished the first part of *Absalom and Achitophel*, would (as he himself tells us) have been glad of a little rest, his good nature was so anxious not to disoblige his friend that he made no difficulty about setting to work at once. He had been turning over in his mind as a fit subject for tragedy the Sicilian Vespers,[2] but apparently Lee had recently composed several scenes dealing

---

[1] V, 2 ; and the whole characters of Commolet and Burgoin. Yet the plot is said to be founded on Davila, and a life of D'Epernon by Girard.

[2] The traditional name given to the insurrection which broke out at Palermo on Easter Tuesday, 31 March, 1282, against the domination of Charles of Anjou. See Amari, *La guerra del Vespero Siciliano*, ninth edition, 3 vols., Milan, 1886. This history has more than once been taken as a theme for drama. *The Vespers of Palermo* by Mrs. Hemans, given at Covent Garden, 12 December, 1823, with Charles Kemble, Young, and Miss Kelly in the cast did not meet with favour, although a performance in Edinburgh was more successful. There is a tragedy by Kenney, *The Sicilian Vespers*, 1840.

with S. Bartholomew's Day (24 August, 1572), which he submitted for
the approval of Dryden, who although he judged the subject might be a
little daring, and at a moment of such intense political excitement liable
to be wrongly interpreted and applied, was by no means willing that such
excellent poetry should be thrown away.[1] He bethought him of the
material which he himself already had in hand ; the story of the Duke of
Guise was most eminently suited for drama, and what he and his colleague
had written could very aptly be fitted together in a play on this theme.
Accordingly both began in good earnest, and before long they had completed their task. Dryden wrote the first scene ; the whole of Act IV[2] and
rather more than the first half of Act V ; the rest belongs to Lee. Meanwhile spies in the enemy's camp were not idle, and such disquieting
rumours reached the Lord Chamberlain to the effect that Charles II. was
openly satirized as Henri III., and the Duke of Guise was but the thinnest
veil for the Duke of Monmouth, that in some alarm he sent for a copy of
the play. A few days afterwards Dryden waited upon him, and respect-
fully pointing out that the ticklish scene, the return of the Duke to Paris
against the King's command (Act IV, 1), had been written a great many
years before, ventured to hand him Sir Charles Cotterel's *History of the
Civil Wars of France*,[3] a translation from the Italian of Enrico Caterino
Davila.[4] " This was before *Midsummer ;* and about two Months after, I
receiv'd the Play back again from his Lordship, but without any positive
Order whether it *should* be Acted or *not ;* neither was Mr. *Lee,* or *my self*
any way sollicitous about it : But this indeed I ever said, That it was
intended for the *King's Service ;* and *His Majesty* was the best *Judge,* whether
it answer'd that End or no ; and then I reckon'd it my Duty to submit,
if his Majesty, for any Reason whatsoever, should deem it unfit for the
Stage. In the *Interim,* a strict Scrutiny was made, and *no Parallel* of the
Great Person design'd, could be made out. But this Push failing, there
was immediately started some terrible Insinuations, that the *Person* of His
Majesty was represented under that of *Henry the Third ;* which if they could

Delavigne wrote *Les Vepres Siciliennes,* 1819, and Verdi's opera of the same name was
produced at Paris in 1855.

[1] Lee afterwards introduced several scenes from Act II. of *The Duke of Guise* into
Acts I. and IV. of his fine drama *The Massacre of Paris,* produced at Drury Lane in November, 1689. Marlowe's *The Massacre at Paris, with the Death of the Duke of Guise* is a breathless fragment. It will be remembered that Talma made a great success in M. J. de
Chénier's tragedy *Charles IX., ou l'École des Rois,* 1789. Charles de Rémusat's posthumous play *Saint-Barthélemy* was published in 1878. Meyerbeer's grand opera *Les
Hugenots,* produced in Paris March, 1836 (London, 1842), concludes with S. Bartholomew. Nor among romances must we forget the *Reine Margot* of Dumas.

[2] This contains the scenes of the Citizens to which great exception was taken by the
Whigs as so trenchantly exposing the disloyalty of the Londoners.

[3] Folio, 1678. *Term Catalogues,* Hilary (28 February), 1678.

[4] 1576–1631.

have found out, would have concluded, perchance, not only in the *ſtopping* of the *Play*, but in the *hanging up* of the *Poets*. But so it was, that His Majeſty's *Wiſdom* and *Juſtice* acquitted both the *One*, and the *Other ;* and when the *Play it ſelf* was almoſt *forgotten*, there were Orders given for the *Acting* of it."

On 18 July, however, *The Duke of Guiſe* had been prohibited,[1] and the ban was not lifted until November, so that actually it was produced at Drury Lane on 1 December, 1682. Dryden ſays : " In the Repreſentation it ſelf, it was perſecuted with ſo notorious Malice by one Side that it procured us the Partiality of the other; ſo that the Favour more than recompens'd the Prejudice ; And 'tis happier to have been ſav'd (if ſo we were) by the Indulgence of our good and faithful Fellow-Subjects, than by our own Deſerts ; becauſe thereby the Weakneſs of the Faction is diſcover'd, which in us, at that Time, attack'd the Government ; and ſtood combin'd, like the Members of the Rebellious League, againſt the Lawful Sovereign Authority." [2] The play was a great ſucceſs : " It *ſucceeded*," ſays Dryden, " beyond my very *Hopes*, having been frequently Acted, and never without a conſiderable Audience." [3] As is usual in hiſtorical dramas, there are a goodly number of characters, and the caſt was very ſtrong. Henri III. was played by Kynaſton ; the Duke of Guiſe, Betterton ; Grillon, Smith ; Alphonſo Corſo, Mountfort ; the Curate of St. Euſtace, Underhill ; the two City Sheriffs, Bright and Sandford ; Catherine de' Medici, Lady Slingsby (formerly Mrs. Mary Lee, *née* Aldridge) ; and Marmoutiere, Mrs. Barry. There were a couple of weak ſpots, and it is very unfortunate that these two characters required the moſt excellent performance. Thomas Percival as the magician Malicorne, and Gillow as the familiar Melanax, ſeem to have been totally inadequate, and Dryden ſays that the very fineſt ſcene in Act IV, which is one of the beſt in the tragedy, " was murder'd in the Acting." For the original Epilogue, which had been compoſed in the ſummer, there was provided a new addreſs, more topical and yet more pointed, which was given fulleſt effect by Sarah Cooke, one of the favourite actreſſes of the time. The Prologue ſpoken by Smith commences :

> Our Play's a parallel ; The Holy League
> Begot our Cov'nant ; Guiſards got the Whigg.

The Duke of Guiſe takes a very high rank in Reſtoration tragedy, and it is a fine example of a play in which the political motives—for there can hardly be any doubt that the parallel may be puſhed further than Dryden thought proper to concede—are entirely ſubſervient to the dramatic

---

[1] Public Record Office, L.C. 5–16, p. 101.
[2] Dedication of *The Duke of Guiſe*, 4to, 1683.
[3] *The Vindication of The Duke of Guiſe*, 4to, 1683.

quality. That is to say, it is a piece which in itself has even to-day lost none of its interest, although at the date it was produced it certainly had the additional attraction of contemporary application. In the library it is most moving, and upon the stage it must be, I can well picture, very great indeed. The play opens with a meeting of the Council of Sixteen;

> the whole Sixteen,
> That sway the Crowd of *Paris*, guide their Votes,
> Manage their Purses, Persons, Fortunes, Lives,
> To mount the *Guise*, where Merit calls him, high;
> And give him a whole Heaven, for Room to shine.

After some factious talk and plotting the Duke appears, and is enthusiastically greeted by his followers as their Lord and Champion:

> The King, like *Saul*, is Heav'n's repented Choise;
> You his anointed one, on better Thought.

In the following scene the wizard Malicorne appears, and his Spirits warn him that Guise must "By Blood resolve to mount to Pow'r." Marmoutiere, whom Guise loves, endeavours to persuade him to submit to the King, but his ambition tugs the other way. Meanwhile Polin, who is one of the Sixteen, keeps the Queen-Mother informed of the progress of the plot, and she urges Henri to take sudden measures. The second Act concludes with a quarrel between the uncle of Marmoutiere, Colonel Grillon, and the Duke, and in Act III. we have an encounter between the Colonel and the City Sheriffs, where there is some very trenchant satire on the disloyalty of London and the Whig civic officials. In spite of the King's command, the Duke forces his way to Paris, and even into the royal presence. It was this episode in particular which gave great offence to the revolutionary party, because, although strictly historical, the entry of the Duke of Guise into Paris certainly did bear a close resemblance to Monmouth's return to England in 1679 in defiance of the King. Some extremely well-written speeches show the disorders of the mob, and it must be allowed that this rioting was very like the turbulence that set bonfires ablaze and made the bells peal from every steeple in their factious and fatuous devotion to the son of Lucy Walters. There is an extremely fine scene between Melanax and Malicorne, when the fiend appears to demand the unhappy wretch's soul, now forfeit by his bond with hell. We are soon at Blois, and events hasten swiftly to their end. On 23 December, 1588, as in the historical narrative, Henri de Guise is summoned by the King, and cut down in the corridor before he can enter the private apartments. The play concludes with the monarch's enunciation of the royal prerogative.

As might have been expected, although they had been foiled in their attempts to suppress the piece, the Whigs were very hot to protest, and endeavoured, if possible, to raise a resounding scandal. But it is clear that they are thoroughly disheartened, and their onsets have not the tang and virulence of twelve months before. No less than three direct attacks upon the play appeared in 1683. *The true History of the Duke of Guise* was "Published for the undeceiving such as may perhaps be imposed on by Mr. *Dryden's* late Tragedy of the 'Duke of *Guise*.'[1]" *Sol in Opposition to Saturn; or, A Short Return to the Tragedy call'd The Duke of Guise* is merely a folio broadside. More important is the pamphlet *Some Reflections Upon The Pretended Parallel In The Play Called The Duke Of Guise,* to which Dryden felt compelled to answer in *The Vindication; Or, The Parallel Of The* French *Holy League, And The* English *League and Covenant, Turn'd into a Seditious Libell against* the King and His Royal Highness, By Thomas Hunt *and the Author's Of the Reflections upon the Pretended Parallel in the Play call'd The Duke Of Guise.* Thomas Hunt,[2] a busy and factious hireling of the revolutionary party, fiercely attacked Dryden in his tract *A Defence of the Charter, and municipal rights of the City of London, And the rights of other municipal Cities and Towns of England. Directed to the Citizens of London,* wherein he had a sharp bob at the play :

"They have already condemned the Charter and City, and have executed the Magistrates in effigie upon the stage, in a play called the Duke of Guise; frequently acted and applauded; intended most certainly to provoke the rabble into tumults and disorder. The Roman Priest had no success (God be thanked) when he animated the people not to suffer these same Sheriffs to be carried through the City to the Tower prisoners. Now the Poet has undertaken for their being kicked three or four times a week about the Stage to the Gallows, infamously rogued and rascalled, to try what he can do toward making the Charter forfeitable by some extravagancy and disorder of the People, which the authority of the best governed cities have not been able to prevent sometimes under far less provocations."

But it was pretty common knowledge that the *Reflections* might justly be ascribed to Shadwell alone, since the work was for the most part his, although even the negligible Settle had a finger in the pie. Dryden soon discovered the triumvirate. "I have done with mannerly Mr. *Hunt,*" he cries, "who is only *magni nominis umbra;* the most *malicious,* and withal, the most *incoherent ignorant Scribler* of the whole Party. . . . Now for my *Templar* and *Poet* in *Association* for a *Libel,* like the Conjunction of *Saturn* and *Jupiter* in a *fiery Sign.* What the *one* wants in *Wit,* the *other* must supply in *Law.* As for Malice, their Quota's are indifferently well adjusted : The *rough Draught,* I take for granted, is the *Poet's,* the *Finishings* the *Lawyer's.* They begin, that in Order to one Mr. *Friend's* Commands, one of them

---

[1] 4to, *Term Catalogues,* Trinity (June), 1683.

[2] His disloyalty became so rampant that eventually he was obliged to fly to Holland.

went to see the Play. This was not the *Poet*, I am certain, for Nobody saw him there, and he is not of a *Size* to be *conceal'd*. But the *Mountain*, they say, *was deliver'd of a Mouse ;* I have been *Gossip* to many such *Labours*, of a *dull Fat Scribler*, where the *Mountain* has been *bigger*, and the *Mouse less*." It could not escape notice that Dryden is here hitting at the huge girth of Shadwell, who by now he rivalled in bulk his master Ben Jonson, whom he also imitated in the deepness of his potations, thus rendering himself peculiarly vunerable to the satirists who were not likely to spare either his corpulence or his bibacity. In fact in his *Vindication* Dryden again attacks, and heaps unsparing ridicule upon, Shadwell for these very reasons. Speaking of Thomas Hunt he says : " Yet even this their Celebrated Writer knows no more of *Style* and *English* than the *Northern Dedicator*. As if *Dulness* and *Clumsiness* were fatal to the name of TOM. 'Tis true, he is a *Fool* in *three Languages* more than the *Poet*, for they say, he understands *Latin*, *Greek*, and *Hebrew*, from all which, to my certain Knowledge, I acquit the other. *Og* may write against the King, if he pleases, so long as he *drinks* for him, and his *Writings* will never do the Government so much *Harm*, as his *Drinking* does it *Good :* For true Subjects will not be much perverted by his *Libels ;* but the Wine-*Duties* rise considerably by his *Claret*. He has often call'd me an *Atheist* in Print ; I would believe more charitably of him ; and that he only goes the *broad Way*, because the other is too *narrow* for him. He may see by this, I do not delight to meddle with his Course of *Life*, and his *Immoralities*, though I have a long *Bead-Roll* of them. I have hitherto contented my self with the *Ridiculous* Part of him, which is enough in all Conscience to employ one Man : even with the Story of his late fall at the *Old Devil*,[1] where he *broke no Ribs*, because the hardness of the *Stairs* could reach *no Bones ;* and for my Part I do not wonder how he came to *fall*, for I have always known him heavy ; the Miracle is, how he got *up again*. I have heard of a *Sea-Captain* as *fat* as he, who to 'scape Arrests, would lay himself flat upon the Ground, and let the *Bailiffs* carry him to *Prison* if they cou'd. If a Messenger, or two, nay, we may put in three or four, should come, he has friendly Advertisement how to 'scape them. But to leave him, who is not worth any further Consideration, now I have done laughing at him, Wou'd every Man knew his own Talent, and that they who are only born for *drinking*, wou'd let both *Poetry* and *Prose* alone." [2] It would appear that at this period Shadwell was given the cold shoulder in the theatre. " The *Players* have but *little Communication with him*," Dryden observed in 1683. Politically he had compromised himself beyond all hope, and the actors were by no means anxious to perform in

---

[1] Between Temple Bar and the Inner Temple Gate. The Young (or Little) Devil was in Fleet Street, on the south side, adjoining Dick's Coffee House.

[2] *The Vindication of the Duke of Guise*, 4to, 1683.

his plays. For two or three years at all events his name was very unpopular; almost ostentatiously his pieces were not revived, and it was intimated to him that for the present no new comedy from his pen would be acceptable. This must indeed have been a severe blow, but we can at least give him this meed of praise; mistaken and bad as his principles were he was consistent in his adherence to them, an obstinacy which was, of course, part of his essentially British character, and we may charitably suppose that he was sincere in his errors. "By God, my Lord," he complained to the Earl of Dorset, "those Tory-Rogues will act none of my Plays."

Shadwell's three satires, *The Medal of John Bayes*, *The Satyr to his Muse*, and *The Tory-Poets* have been wholly and for ever over-shadowed by the immortal poems of his great antagonist. They are coarse and rough, brutal and sometimes obscene; the metre is wont to hobble awhile; but none the less they cannot be denied a certain vigour and strength; he is lunging with all his force and some of the lines have the punch of a swashing blow. They bruise, but they do not annihilate as does the conscious power, the divine scorn of *Mac Flecknoe* and *Absalom and Achitophel*. From the starlit peaks Dryden looks down upon his opponents with a contempt that is not unmixed with a certain impersonal pity; they must be destroyed and he is all ready for the task; but he takes up the pen with a sigh; as cold as ice and fiercer than fire he sweeps them into oblivion with his ruthless words, writing as S. Augustine wrote against the Donatists and Pelagians long ago.

The invectives upon Otway in *The Tory-Poets* should be particularly noticed, for Otway and Shadwell had been close friends. In *A Tryal of the Poets for the Bays, in Imitation of a Satyr in Boileau*, written in the winter of 1676,[1] which is printed [2] in the Duke of Buckingham's *Miscellaneous Works*, two volumes, 1704, Otway is described as "*Tom Shadwell's* dear Zany," and the success of *Don Carlos*, produced at Dorset Garden in June, 1676, is made the occasion of some ribald personalities. Shadwell himself is roughly handled:

> Next into the Crowd, *Tom Shadwell* does wallow,
> And swears by his Guts, his Paunch, and his Tallow,
> That tis he alone best pleases the Age,
> Himself, and his Wife, have supported the Stage:
> *Apollo* well-pleas'd with so bonny a Lad,
> T'oblige him, he told him, he should be huge glad
> Had he half so much Wit, as he fancy'd he had.

---

[1] There is mention of Settle's *Ibrahim The Illustrious Bassa* produced at Dorset Garden in the summer of 1676, and other indications point to this year.

[2] Vol. II., pp. 41–46.

At this time (1676) Shadwell is obviously still contemptuous of Settle, for when Elkanah appeared

> And humbly desir'd he might give no Offence ;
> Dam him, cried *Shadwell*, he cannot write Sense.

In an earlier *Session of the Poets*, " to the tune of *Cook Laurel*,"[1] Etherege and Shadwell are treated with scant courtesy :

> *Ethridge* and *Shadwel*, and the Rabble appeal'd
>   To *Apollo* himself in a very great Rage ;
> Because their best Friends so freely had deal'd,
>   As to tell them their Plays were not fit for the Stage.

In *The Laurel*, 4to, 1685, a poem in praise of Dryden, which is sometimes attributed to Robert Gould, the anonymous author does not forget to rally " *Shadwell* and his Lute " pretty severely. He writes :

> But let thy stubborn *Ogg* be ne're forgot,
> Whose drowsie Verse lurks deep, as still their Plot
> In something's understood, in something's not.
> He from Wits Empire, and his Princes flew,
> Or rather, Wit asham'd from him withdrew.
> Hail Mighty *Gutts !* for Drink the Standard made,
> Thou swilling Pensioner to the Brewers Trade.
> Go with thy Masters Horses, feed on Grains,
> As theirs thy Massy Gutts, as theirs thy Brains.
> We envy not thy Greatness ; still drink on,
> 'Till two-legg'd Hogshead swell up to a Tun,
> And Famous *Heidelberg* it self out-done.
> Go then invoke thy rotting Patrons Tap,
> Instead of Muse, to vent the flowing sap.
> Thy better Midwife, and with lesser Pain,
> Brings forth both Excrements, of Gutts, and Brain ;
> You wou'd swear to see him sordid Satyr write.[2]
> The Poet Rhym'd, but Doctor did indite,
> *Tom*, and his *Titus*, both one Province chose,
> This Rascals it in Verse, and that in Prose.
> If not to both disabled, Whore and Fight,
> Or any thing wee'll grant him but to write.
> Let him sing well his Dogrells, play them too ;
> Wee'll give to him, as to the Devil his due.
> But who with docile Beasts would Art dispute,

---

[1] Written *circa* 1669. *Poems on Affairs of State*, the Sixth Edition, 1710, Vol. I., pp. 206–211.
[2] Surely an allusion to *The Medal of John Bayes*.

The Bear and Fiddle, *Sh--ll* and his Lute.
Such rugged Monsters in a *Smithfield* Booth,
(Where ought to be the Poets Stage in Truth.)
Act, show at every Fair, for usual price,
And Tuneful *Sh---lls* seen for Pence a piece.
But as in every kind we something see,
Grac't with Perfection in more high Degree.
His frighten'd Dam, ran trembling from her kind,
And left the shapeless Lump unlickt behind:
The forc't Neglect beyond all natural Care,
Made him the more compleat, and better Bear;
To Dulness damn'd, and Faction since he fell,
To perfect all the Punishment of Hell,
His stubborn Error, is incurable.
His spungy, sappy Soul, would yield to thee,
But's body'd up by Trunk of sturdy Tree.
Your Loyal Pen attempts with fruitless stroke,
With Spriggs of Bays, for to chastise an Oak.
Your too keen Satyr, does oblige your Foe,
As harmless *Tom*'s, kind dulness still does you.
Your *Fleckno*'s kind, (tho' still severe enough)
It Arms him Cap-a-pe with Nonsense Proof.
He fears no more, of harden'd dulness full,
He is not, will not, can't be made more dull.

Leave then the Mud, that can't be made more mean,
And praise, what can't be prais'd enough, agen;
Search, mighty *Pan*, round all your tuneful Plain,
Try the sweet Pipe, of each Melodious Swain.
Let the fair *Sylvia* Judg, and kindly prove,
If her dear *Damon*'s Lays she more could love.
Shee'll make her self his Prize, and him her choice,
Her Eyes, her Heart, her Soul too, for his Voice.
In your own rural Eclogue he excells,
'Tis all *Arcadia*, wheresoere he dwells,
Say God of Verse, Judg of Immortal Wit,
Say, who of all your inspir'd Men more fit,
To have the highest place, and next you sit?
Speak, envious God, tho he your Rival be,
For if you're Just, you'll boldly say 'tis he.

Had not Shadwell at this time been very considerably assisted by his good friends he must have found himself in very pressing and straitened circumstances for several years together.[1] Men have been apt to censure the wits and the rakes of the Restoration hardly enough, and not only are they ready to condemn more obvious follies and indecorum but also, which is a far more serious inculpation, to brand them as callous, heartless, and dishonourable. Perhaps Buckingham and the mischievous Rochester might justly be accused of these horrid traits, but most certainly the Earl of Dorset and Sir Charles Sedley, whose names have been written very black by the ignorance of prejudice and priggishness, do not deserve so harsh a judgement. Foolish they undoubtedly were ; selfish and unfriendly, two far uglier vices than mere folly, they were not. At any rate their patronage of Shadwell shows them both in a very estimable and praiseworthy light. The former, Dorset, although under no obligation save that of amity, as we have seen, kept Shadwell supplied with a regular pension ; whereas the latter, Sir Charles Sedley,[2] constantly placed his purse at Shadwell's disposal,[3] and in the spring of 1687 presented him with the profits of a new comedy, no inconsiderable gift, and had it been possible would have presented him with the authorship and reputation too. In the course of convalescence after a serious illness[4] in order to pass the time began to draft some rough scenes of a new comedy. He had been reading Terence, who has been found by many more than he an excellent companion in hours of depression and unrest, and he began, not to translate, but to turn some scenes of the great Latin dramatist into a Restoration comedy. He says that whilst he was at work upon the first act, a friend came into his chamber and " seemed to approve the design." The result was that Sedley finished the play and made him the offer of it if " he could get it Acted under his own or another's name." The piece in question, *Bellamira ; or, The Mistress*, is by far the better of Sedley's two

---

[1] Rochester in a *Poem to Julian*, 1679–80, writes :

> from their num'rous Party thou may'st hope
> More than *Prance*, *Oats*, or *Bedloe* from the *Pope* ;
> *Thirsis* has gain'd Preferment by a Song,
> While *Hudibras* does starve amidst the Throng ;
> Nay, Minion *Shadwell* cannot hold out long.

[2] It will not be forgotten that Sedley was reported to revise Shadwell's comedies. In *Timon*, a satire by Buckingham and Rochester, the bore

> Pulls out a Libel of a Sheet or Two,
> Insipid, as the praise of th' Fairy Queens,
> Or *S[hadwell's]* unassisted former Scenes.

[3] In the Dedication, addressed to Sir Charles Sedley, of *The Tenth Satyr of Juvenal*, 4to, 1687, Shadwell writes : " You have so many years together pursued me with your Favour and Bounty."

[4] British Museum. Add. MS. 2869. " 25 March, 1686 : Sir Charles Sedley is very ill and some think he will scarcely wether his disease." On 13 April following he was reported to be dead.

comedies.[1] The " friend " to whom reference was made may almost certainly be identified with Shadwell, who was, however, unable, owing to the disfavour in which he was held, to get the play accepted at the theatre under his own name. Sedley therefore frankly produced the piece as by himself, " or my friend would have lost his third night." [2]

Bellamira was produced at Drury Lane in May, 1687, and achieved a very great success. The theme is directly derived from the *Eunuchus*, one of the wittiest of Terentian comedies,[3] which is itself borrowed from Menander's Εὐνοῦχος. Sedley has very cleverly fitted the original into his contemporary London ; the dialogue is brisk and amusing, although I cannot myself distinguish that supreme excellence of prose which some are pleased to praise in these scenes. The wanton Bellamira is certainly modelled upon the Duchess of Cleveland, but I do not think that Merryman was in any sense suggested by Shadwell himself, as has been fancied. The character is rather taken (and improved) from James Howard's *All Mistaken ; or, The Mad Couple*,[4] and Howard had him from Shirley's fat gentleman, Lodam [5] in *The Wedding*. It is, methinks, *nihil ad rem* that Keepwell should mock Merryman by the lilt of a song Clodpate trolls in *Epsom-Wells* [6] :

> *Her Breasts of delight*
> *Are two Bottles of white,*
> *And her Eyes are two Cups of Canary.*

The lines were apt, and in every man's mouth.

The compliment, which was far from being an empty one, that Sir Charles Sedley had bestowed upon Shadwell by presenting him with this lively comedy was returned by the latter in his dedication before *The Tenth Satyr of Juvenal, English and Latin*,[7] addressed to the knight in a most laudatory strain, which, contrary to the normal strain of such adulations, was not, perhaps, entirely undeserved. Shadwell at once commences : " Sir, You have so many years together pursued me with your Favour and Bounty, that I ought to have been alwaies upon the Watch for an

---

[1] *The Mulberry Garden* is a poor piece.

[2] When the receipts went to the author.

[3] And one of the most popular. Donatus says : " Acta est tanto successu ac plausu atque suffragio, ut rursus esset uendita, et ageretur iterum pro noua : proque ea pretium, quod nulli ante ipsam fabulam contigit, octo milibus sestertium numerarent poetae." Suetonius tells us : " Eunuchus quidem bis die acta est : meruitque pretium quantum nulla antea cuiusdam comoedia, id est, octo milia nummum, propterea summa quoque titulo ascribitur."

[4] 4to, 1672, but acted some five or six years earlier and seen by Pepys, September, 1667, which was perhaps the date of production.

[5] Acted by William Sherlock.

[6] IV., 1.

[7] Licensed 25 May, 1687.

opportunity of Publishing my Gratitude. Your late great obligation in giving me the advantage of your Comedy, call'd *Bellamira*, or the *Mistress*, has given me a fresh subject for my Thanks; and my Publishing this *Translation* affords me a new opportunity of owning to the World my grateful resentments to you. . . . It is honour enough for me, that I have from my *Youth* Lived in yours, and, as you know, in the *favour* of the *wittiest men of England*, your familiar *friends and acquaintance*, who have encouraged my Writings; and suffer'd my Conversation." There is not, I think, very much to say about Shadwell's translation from Juvenal. His metre is rough although informed with a certain stolid vigour, as Hannibal won his way through the Alps with vinegar. His rendering of this famous poem is not for a moment to be compared with Dryden's version, and when Dryden translates he is so great a master that his genius produces an original. Nor would we mention Shadwell's adaptation in the same breath as Dr. Johnson's *The Vanity of Human Wishes*,[1] a fine work, scarcely if at all inferior in power to its Latin model, a piece the excellences of which are even now generally unrecognized, such is the perversion of the present age, but which I have no hesitation in pronouncing as among the great poems of the English language. It is interesting to note that Shadwell's version was dedicated to Sir Charles Sedley, and *The Vanity of Human Wishes* contains the famous couplet :

> Yet *Vane* could tell what ills from beauty spring ;
> And *Sedley* cursed the form that pleased a King.

Although at a distance, Gifford's translation of the Tenth Satyr deserves commendation even after Dryden and Johnson, but Hodgson and Badham must be content to take a second place, which is no disparagement to their talents when we consider with what superlative writers they had to vie. Although forgotten now, in its day Shadwell's translation seems to have enjoyed no small popularity.

It was owing to the influence of his constant patron the Earl of Dorset that in May, 1688, Shadwell was able to bring on the stage his comedy *The Squire of Alsatia*. No doubt Sedley had directed his friend's attention to Terence, and as *Bellamira* was taken from the *Eunuchus*, so the main theme of *The Squire of Alsatia* is derived from the *Adelphi*. This new comedy was indeed a lucky hit, and by its extraordinary success Shadwell recovered his position in the theatrical world; and, what is more, he seems to have filled his empty pockets. When printed the piece, as was due, was dedicated to the Earl of Dorset, at whose seat Copped Hall,[2] near Epping,

---

[1] 1749.

[2] Etherege writing from Ratisbon 25 July, 1687, to Dorset says : " I wou'd gladly be a witness of the Content you enjoy at Copt-Hall now, and I hope to surprise you there one ay (your gravity lay'd aside) teaching my Lord Buckhurst how to manage his Hoby-horse."

the whole of the first act and a good portion of the remainder had been composed. In his dedication Shadwell says that Dorset, reading the play in MS. " thought it a true, and diverted Comedy." He continues : " This, I must confess, made me hope for success upon the Stage, which it met with, but so great, as was above my expectation (in this age which has run mad after Farces) no Comedy, for these many years, having fill'd the Theatre so long together : And I had the great Honour to find so many Friends, that the House was never so full since it was built, as upon the third day of this Play ; and vast numbers went away, that could not be admitted." Downes also tells us : " This Play by its excellent acting being often honour'd with the presence of Chancellour *Jefferies*, and other great persons ; had an uninterrupted run of 13 days together. . . . *Note*, The Poet receiv'd for his third day in the House in Drury-Lane at single Prices 130£. which is the greatest receipt they ever had at that house at single prices."

Etherege, writing to Jephson from Ratisbon 27 February—8 March, 1687-8, says : " tho' I have given over writing plays I shou'd be glad to read a good one, wherefore pray lett Will. Richards send me Mr. Shadwells, when it is printed, that I may know what follies are in fashion ; the fops I knew are grown stale, and he is likely to pick up the best collection of new ones." In a later letter, dated 21 October of the same year, he has : " By my last Pacquet from England, among a heap of nauseous Trash, I received the *Three Dukes of Dunstable*, which is really so monstrous and insipid, that I am sorry *Lapland* or *Livonia* had not the Honour of producing it ; but if I did Pennance in reading it, I rejoyced to hear that it was so solemnly interr'd to the Tune of Catcalls. The '*Squire of Alsatia* however, which came by the following Post, made me some amends for the cursed impertinence of the *Three Dukes* ; and my witty Friend Sir C—S—y's *Bellamira* gave me that intire Satisfaction that I cannot read it over too often."[1] D'Urfey's *A Fool's Preferment ; or, The Three Dukes of Dunstable*, which was produced at Dorset Garden in the spring of 1688, probably in April, is an adaptation from Fletcher's *The Noble Gentleman*, and although undeserving of the brutal censure of Etherege is too farcical to be called a good comedy, howbeit not without some vigorous and amusing scenes. The songs were set by Henry Purcell. There is some pretty sharp satire upon the game of Basset, which had just become fashionable among persons of quality, and it is to this cause that D'Urfey in the Dedication [2] attributes the ill-success of his play. It is worth remark

[1] Printed in *Miscellaneous Works, Written by His Grace, George Late Duke of Buckingham,* 1704, Vol. II, pp. 131-140, as addressed to the Duke by Etherege. But there must be a mistake here since the Duke of Buckingham died 18 April, 1688. D'Urfey's comedy was not licensed for printing until 21 May of that year. It is more than unlikely that Etherege received a MS. copy. *Bellamira* was produced in May, 1687.

[2] To Charles Howard Viscount Morpeth, later third Earl of Carlisle.

that Justice Grub,[1] " An old Peevish County Justice, an hater of the Town and its Fashions," is largely drawn from Shadwell's Clodpate, and some of the language (especially the references to the Mare) is very exactly borrowed. Toby, Clodpate's man, appears as Toby, servant to Cocklebrain.[2] We may add that if Etherege truly preferred *Bellamira* to *The Squire of Alsatia*, if this is not mere compliment, his friendship was better than his taste.

The original title of Shadwell's play was to have been *The Alsatia Bully*,[3] and perhaps the alteration was suggested by a couple of lines in the prologue to Elkanah Settle's pastoral, *Pastor Fido ; or, The Faithful Shepherd*,[4] produced at Dorset Garden in the winter (probably December), of 1676 :

> And when poor Duns, quite weary, will not stay ;
> The hopeless Squire's into *Alsatia* driven.

It may be noted that No. 50 of Tempest's *Cries of London* (drawn and published in the reign of James II.), is called " A Squire of *Alsatia*," but it seems to represent a fashionable young gallant of the period. In addition to its own intrinsic merit Shadwell's new comedy had every advantage of cast. It is true that Betterton himself and Mrs. Barry did not appear, although one might have thought that the latter who half a dozen years later was to play Lady Touchwood in *The Double-Dealer*, would have made a fine thing of Mrs. Termagant. Indeed the reason why she did not sustain this part was illness. Not many days before, she had been suddenly seized with a fever whilst about to appear as the Princess Barzana in Crowne's tragedy *Darius, King of Persia*, and was still confined to her bed. In the dedication to the printed play [5] Crowne tells us : " A misfortune fell upon this play, that might very well dizzy the judgements of my audience. Just before the play began, Mrs. *Barry* was struck with a very violent fever, that took all spirit from her, by consequence from the play ; the scene she acted fell dead from her ; and in the fourth act her distemper grew so much upon her, she cou'd go on no farther, but all her part in that act was wholly cut out, and neither spoke nor read ; that the people went away without knowing the contexture of the play, yet thought they knew all." Accordingly the rôle of Mrs. Termagant was given in some

---

[1] Created by Anthony Leigh.

[2] Acted by Thomas Jevon.

[3] In Otway's comedy *The Souldiers Fortune*, produced at Dorset Garden early in 1680, I, 1 Courtine says : " 'Tis a fine Equipage I am lik'd to be reduc'd to ; I shall be e're long as greasy as an *Alsatia* Bully ; this a flopping Hat, pin'd up on one side, with a sandy weather-beaten Perruque, dirty Linen, and to compleat the Figure, a long scandalous Iron Sword jarring at my Heels."

[4] Based upon Guarini.

[5] 4to, 1688. See also Sir William Leveson's letter to Lord Granville, 5 May, 1688.

haste to Mrs. Boutel, a most accomplished actress, but hardly suited for such virago scenes, since with her blue eyes and chestnut hair she was " celebrated for the gentler parts in tragedy such as Aspasia in the Maid's Tragedy, Statira in Alexander." [1] In the *History of the Stage*, which Curll, in 1741, published under the name of Betterton, she is spoken of as follows : " Mrs. *Boutel* was likewise a very considerable Actress ; she was low of stature, had very agreeable Features, a good Complexion, but a Childish look. Her Voice was weak tho' very mellow ; she generally acted the young Innocent Lady whom all the Heros are mad in Love with ; she was a Favourite of the Town."

It should be remarked that for some reason which is not apparent after the first two or three performances that great comedian Mr. Nokes retired from the cast, and resigned the part of Belfond Senior to Tom Jevon, who is said to have acquitted himself very admirably, thereby winning the applause of the Town.

The cant name Alsatia had been given to the precinct of Whitefriars before 1623. The Carmelites, whose Order may fairly be said to be the oldest and most venerable of all communities since it traces back its origin to the prophet Elias [2] and his successor Eliseus, first came to England in 1241, when certain brethren of British nationality accompanied the Barons de Vesey and Grey on their return journey from the Crusading expedition of Richard, Earl of Cornwall. Foundations were made at Hulne, Alnwick, in Northumberland ; Bradmer (Norfolk) ; Aylesford ; Newenden (Kent) ; and in London near Fleet Street. This latter house was regarded as a place of especial sanctity, and enjoyed peculiar privileges. Even when the monastery was suppressed and the religious dispersed at the dissolution, the traditional privileges remained, and the consequence was that this quarter became a refuge for rogues and masterless men, and for all persons who for any reason were desirous of escaping from justice. It was here if anywhere that arrests could be successfully evaded, and naturally before long the whole district became of notorious ill repute. The particular portions of Whitefriars forming Alsatia were Ram Alley, Mitre Court, and a lane called in the local slang Lombard Street. It may to us seem extraordinary that such a state of things was allowed, but we must remember that at a far later date there were similar rookeries in London, and that until well within the nineteenth century S. Giles was festering with vice and open crime. [3] The evil privileges of Alsatia were

---

[1] Davies, *Dramatic Miscellanies*, 1783, Vol. II, p. 404.

[2] A statue of S. Elias was placed in the year 1725 in the Vatican Basilica, S. Peter's, among the Founders of Orders.

[3] Harrison Ainsworth's *Auriol*, which made its first appearance in *Ainsworth's Magazine*, 1844-45, under the title of *Revelations of London*, contains a description of S. Giles as it existed in the London of 1830.

abolished by the Act 8 and 9 William III., c. 27 (1697), and Steele, *Tatler* (No. 66), 10 September, 1709, speaks of Alsatia as " now in ruins."

Joseph Moser in Nichol's *Literary Anecdotes* [1] has the following note: " The George Tavern was situated in a *Liberty* divided betwixt *Puritanism*, *Pleasure*, and *Profligacy ;* which had, during the reign of Charles II, like *Ram-alley* in a former age, obtained a kind of *infamous celebrity*. The *George* was not only the temple of dissipation and debauchery ; but contained under its ample roof the recesses of *contrivance* and *fraud*, the nests of *perjury*, and the apartments of *prostitution*. Shadwell, who has been much too lenient with respect to his reprobation of *The Friars*, has laid several scenes of his comedy of ' The Squire of Alsatia ' in this house. How such a nuisance as this district was suffered so long to exist, is unaccountable. It did, however, at length, attract the notice of the Legislature, and was, with several other places of the like nature, *purified* by the Stat. 8th and 9th William III. c. 27, enacted for the suppression of *pretended* privileged places."

There are very many contemporary references to Alsatia, its vagabond rabble, and its bullies, who used to congregate at the George Tavern in Dogwell Court. In Mrs. Behn's comedy *The Luckey Chance ; or, An Alderman's Bargain*, produced at Drury Lane in the winter of 1686, when Gayman has fallen upon evil times he takes a lodging in this low part of the town, and one scene is laid in his miserable room, where we witness his interview with " Gammer *Grime*, Landlady to *Gayman*, a Smith's Wife in *Alsatia*." [2] To-day Alsatia is probably best known from Sir Walter Scott's masterly description in *The Fortunes of Nigel*, and it may be remarked that for his material he has drawn largely from Shadwell, nor would it be difficult to point out an occasional anachronism, but these are trifling and in no way do they detract from the genius which informs these chapters. Another description of Alsatia, which is possibly not so widely known, but which fairly equals Scott upon his own ground, may be read in *Whitefriars ; or, The Days of Charles the Second*, a masterpiece of romance by Emma Robinson. Originally published in 1844 it has attained a curious one-sided fame. Those who know and appreciate this fine historical novel unhesitatingly place it in the very first rank, and it seems strange that Miss Robinson's other works *Whitehall* and *Caesar Borgia* should not have won an equal reputation. *Whitefriars*, of course, has its faults ; the character of Charles II., for example, is quite unreal, but nevertheless this is balanced by the extraordinarily just and life-like portraits of Titus Oates, Shaftesbury and their colleagues. Moreover, the scenes in Alsatia are extraordinarily well done, and Mervyn's wanderings in the

[1] 1844, Vol. VIII, p. 353.
[2] Acted by Mrs. Powell.

haunted old mansion, whilst the conspirators are plotting below, should thrill the most jaded reader.

The Squire of Alsatia [1] has often been regarded as the best of Shadwell's work, and such a brilliant picture of contemporary life certainly makes a considerable claim to that distinction. It is true that it does not present us with so lively a figure as Sir Positive At-all, and upon the whole I cannot prefer it to the exquisite humour of *The Virtuoso*, a comedy which seems to me to be distinguished by some rare strokes of genius. *Bury-Fair*, again, runs it pretty close, and in some respects is certainly superior, although I do not know that one may extend this verdict to the entire piece. Indeed I think that perhaps *The Virtuoso* alone in Shadwell's theatre can be ranked higher than *The Squire of Alsatia*. Upon the stage this latter comedy must be extraordinarily entertaining, and we are not surprised to find that it remained in the theatrical repertory until the reign of George III.,[2] indeed the only wonder is that it did not continue much later. With regard to the use of the Cant there is little to say beyond the fact that in representation it must have proved extremely effective, and in the printed copy it affords rare opportunities for the philologist. At Drury Lane in August, 1731, was presented a pastoral play of little significance, *The Triumphs of Love and Honour*, by Thomas Cook, who when he published his piece, 8vo, in the same year, added thereto certain essays, " Considerations on the Stage, and on the Advantages which arise to a Nation from the Encouragement of Arts." These are assuredly worth attention, and are interesting from more than one point of view. They deal mainly with *King Lear*, *The Squire of Alsatia*, and *Rosamund*. It will not be impertinent here to give Chapter III of this critique, which is an exceptionally sound and sensible piece of work.

CHAP. III.　On *COMEDY*.　*A Criticism on* the Squire of ALSATIA.

I SHALL make some few Observations on *Shadwell*'s Comedy called *the Squire of ALSATIA*, with the same Candour with which I examined into the Tragedy of *King LEAR*, confining myself, as in that, chiefly to the moral Part. In the first Act we see a young Fellow who had been reared up in the Country under a rigid Father in a servile Manner, restrained from every Pleasure that Youth might reasonably expect, and never allowed any Money to dispose of according to his own Will. The Father being obliged to go to *Holland*, the Son takes the Advantage of his Absence, and goes to *London ;* where he falls into the Hands of Sharpers,

---

[1] It is perhaps worth remarking that on 14 January, 1926, the Liverpool Welsh Operatic Society produced at Liverpool an opera, *A Tale of Alsatia*, the book of which was by E. M. Carnforth, and the music by Vincent Thomas.
[2] The latest revival seems to have been in 1766.

who know him to be Heir to an Estate of three thousand Pounds a Year, which is entailed on him; on the Credit of which they supply him with Money, and lead him into Scenes of Drunkenness, and Leudness, and make him their Prey, by raising Sums at exorbitant Interest on the Reversion of the Estate. The Father, Sir *William Belfond*, returns from *Holland* six Weeks sooner than expected; and, coming to *London* before he goes into the Country, he treats with Mr *Scrapeall*, a Usurer, whose Niece has twenty thousand Pounds in his Hands, he being appointed her Guardian, about a Match for his Son, whom he supposes employed, as he left him, in his country Affairs at Home. Mr *Scrapeall* agrees to sell her to him for five thousand Pounds, and is at the same Time furnishing his Son with Money and Goods at unreasonable Interest, and endeavouring to get deep into the Reversion of the Estate. Sir *William* meets his Brother Sir *Edward Belfond*, talks of his own Happyness in a hopeful Son, whom he had brought up according to his Desire. He complains greatly of his younger Son, whom Sir *Edward*, who is a Bachelor, had adopted, and bred from his Childhood. Sir *Edward* gave him a liberal Education, and sent him to the polite Parts of the World to improve by Travel, and at his Return treated him with the Freedom and Candour of a Friend, and not with the Authority of a Parent; he layed no Restraint on his Inclinations, nor stinted him in his Expences. This Behaviour made the Nephew desirous of concealing no Part of his Conduct from him, and careful not to act to his own Dishonour nor to the Uneasyness of his Uncle. He enjoyed his Friend, his Glass, and his Mistress; all which Sir *Edward* knew, and reasonably accounted for the Levitys of Youth to his Brother, when he complained of his Son.

BEFORE I relate any more of the Busyness of the Play, let us enquire into the Consequence of the Manners in which these two Gentlemen educated their Sons. Sir *William* debarred his Son from all Kinds of Pleasure, and used him rather like a Slave; we are not therefore to wonder if he embraced the first Opportunity to taste, what makes Life most worth preserving, Liberty, and when he found the Sweets of it, if he was for maintaining it at any Rate. Sir *Edward*'s Son, who had no Restraint layed on him, had no Occasion to use any little Arts, or to watch an Opportunity, to deceive a rigid Father. The Busyness of his Days was to indulge his Inclinations; which he did in a moderate Way, and soon purged himself of the few Levitys to which the Fire of Youth subjected him. I shall now point out some particular Dangers which such an Education as Sir *William Belfond* gave his elder Son often throws Youth into, and which are well represented in this Play. The first Step which his elder Son took, after he came to *London*, was to get Money, without considering the Consequence of his Manner of getting it, not thinking how the Reversion of the Estate might be swallowed up by the Principal, and the Exorbitance of the Interest. In such a Condition as this he was liable to be imposed upon, to the Ruin of the Peace of all his future Life, by marrying a Whore whom his Brother had cast off, the Sharpers about him bringing her to him for a great Fortune; and Accidents like these we often see, as the Effects of a too severe Education. The younger Son comes to the Knowledge of his Brother being in the Hands of Cheats; and freeing him from them, he restores him to his Father; who, convinced of his Error in being too austere, settles five hundred Pounds a Year on him for his Expences. Young *Belfond* marrys the Usurer's Niece, who went from her Uncle, and deluded his Hopes of having five thousand Pounds for marrying her to the elder Brother. The Cheats are all punished for their Roguery; and the Women, whom young *Belfond* had made subservient to his Pleasures, have Reparation in a reasonable Fortune which the Uncle gives them; and young *Belfond* makes this Inference from his passed State, and present Condition, *there is no Peace but in a virtuous Life.* An Audience, which is convinced of the good Effects of Sir *Edward Belfond's* prudent Management of his Son, will not go contrary to it when they have Occasion to follow the Example; nor is the Consequence of Sir *William's* Manner of Behaviour any Encouragement to follow it. The Lenity of Sir *Edward*, and his taking proper Opportunitys to instill such Maxims into his Son as these, *young Fellows will never get Knowledge but at their own Cost, there's Nothing but Anxiety in Vice, and every drunken Fit is a short Madness, that cuts off a good Part of Life*, made his Son reflect on his Actions, and profit from every Reflection; but the Severity of Sir *William* made his Son eager in Pursuit of what he had been tyrannically restrained from, and had so blunted his Understanding that he was scarcely capable of enjoying the Benefit of Reflection, till Destruction, the Product of Vice and Folly, stared him in the Face.

WHERE can Youth more properly go than where they are not only taught, but have presented to their Eyes, what are the Rewards of Virtue, and what the woeful Fruits of Vice? The Wit and Humour of a Comedy may be the chief Inducements to the greater Part of the Audience to come to the Representation of it; and if so, the Argument for this Sort of dramatic Poetry is very strong; because the Objects of Pleasure are made the Lures to Instruction. The same Argument serves for those who are charmed to the Theatre by the Sublimity of the Diction, or any other Excellence, in Tragedy.

A STORY regularly told, full of various and surprising Circumstances, and dressed with all the Ornaments with which a great Genius is able to adorn it, must, without Dispute, be allowed to gain Attention more than a mere Discourse of moral Precepts; and when the same Story is presented to the Eye, with the Advantages of Action, the Attention which it gains must be greater, and the Impression which it makes in the Minds of the

Spectators much deeper, than when related only. This last Remark is just both on Tragedy and Comedy.

Although probably it would not have thus appeared to a contemporary audience, in my opinion the one grave blot upon the play lies in the character of Belfond Junior and his treatment of Lucia. It is worth while inquiring why an attitude which in the rakes of Etherege and Wycherley we should accept without comment as perfectly in keeping with the atmosphere of their comedies, should in Shadwell's hero shock us not a little. It is the cruelty, be it marked, which revolts us, not, of course, the gallantry. In such a play for example as Dryden's *The Kind Keeper ; or, Mr. Limberham*, the figure of Woodall does not arouse the slightest indignation, and yet he is in every way a far greater scapegrace than Shadwell's Belfond. If we pause to ask ourselves why this should be the answer is very clear. The persons with whom Woodall comes in contact are as gay and easy as he, there is no heart, no emotion, and it is a question of " When Greeks join'd Greeks, then was the Tug of War." But in *The Squire of Alsatia* Lucia, tender and loving, is very different from Dryden's Paphian Mrs. Tricksy or wanton Mrs. Brainsick, or even from the lively Mrs. Pleasance.

It is notable that here, for the first time, we have Sentimentalism in Shadwell.[1] Sir A. W. Ward was altogether mistaken when he supposed that Steele was the founder of sentimental comedy, and that *The Lying Lover*[2] is " the first instance of Sentimental Comedy proper." [3] Bernbaum, who is never very reliable, apparently would regard Colley Cibber's *Love's Last Shift ; or, The Fool in Fashion*, produced at Drury Lane in January, 1695–6, as the first sentimental comedy.[4] Curiously enough although he devotes a couple of pages to *The Squire of Alsatia* he entirely fails to see the significance of Shadwell's play, and 'tis mere empty talk he gives us. As a matter of fact sentimental comedy goes back at least as far as Sir Samuel Tuke's *The Adventures of Five Hours*,[5] produced at Lincoln's Inn Fields on Thursday, 8 January, 1662–3, and if we wish to consider the theatre before the Restoration such a dramatist as Shirley would afford us some very excellent specimens of this genre.[6]

---

[1] Of course I except *The Royal Shepherdess, The Libertine*, and *Timon*.

[2] Produced at Drury Lane, December, 1703.

[3] *English Dramatic Literature* (1899) III, p. 495.

[4] " Much of Colley Cibber's *Love's Last Shift*, with the production of which, in January, 1696, the rise of sentimental begins, was written in the manner of Restoration comedy." Bernbaum, *The Drama of Sensibility*, 1915, Chapter V, p. 72.

[5] See the recent edition, 1927, edited by Mr. B. Van Thal, with an Introduction by the present editor.

[6] To write as Bernbaum has done (*op. cit.*, pp. 70–71) that " a sentimental comedy was written by Etherege " is nonsense and betrays a more than ordinary opacity.

It is worth remarking that scenes which would admirably have suited the French *comédie larmoyante*, are found in Dryden's heroic plays, as for example the contentions of Honoria and Angelina in *The Rival-Ladies;* the whole character of the Queen of Sicily in *Secret Love; or, The Maiden Queen;* the episode of Ozmyn and Benzayda in *The Conquest of Granada;* the exquisite dialogue between Leonidas and Palmyra that concludes Act II of *Marriage A-La-Mode;* which examples might be considerably amplified. Mrs. Behn has scenes of sensibility that rival Richardson himself in *The Town-Fopp; or, Sir Timothy Tawdrey*, and again ten years later in *The Luckey Chance.* Since both the author and his plays are continually misunderstood and misinterpreted one is hardly surprised to find the fact generally unrecognized that so rollicking a comedy as Vanbrugh's *The Provok'd Wife*, has a sentimental character which goes far to balance the riot of the more deboshed scenes. I well remember that as the curtain fell upon a performance of this excellent comedy,[1] Sir Edmund Gosse remarked to me how admirably Miss Margaret Halstan had brought out the tenderness and sentiment which Vanbrugh introduced for those who had the wit to see it into the character of Lady Brute.

The triumph which he had won with *The Squire of Alsatia* regained Shadwell his place upon the stage, and he at once set to work upon another comedy. However, disappointment and disregard, which he had doubtless endeavoured to assuage and forget, took their toll of his health, and accordingly when he dedicated his next play *Bury-Fair* to his constant and unfailing patron, the Earl of Dorset, he felt obliged to crave indulgence, " since it was Written during eight Months painful Sickness, wherein all the several Days in which I was able to Write any part of a Scene, amounted not to one Month, except some few which were employ'd in indespencable Business." This illness, we may reckon, seized him in the early summer of 1688, and he does not seem to have recovered until the spring of the following year. Certain it is that during the winter he was confined to his house at Chelsea, and he could not even stir forth to pay his respects to his honoured patron, the second Duke of Ormonde, on so important an occasion of a signal favour being shown his son John by that nobleman. Upon the death of his distinguished grandfather at Kingston Hall, Dorsetshire, on 21 July, 1688, James Butler succeeded as second Duke of Ormonde, and two days later was elected Chancellor of Oxford, a dignity with which the first Duke had been invested at the decease of Archbishop Sheldon, 9 November, 1677. On 15 May, 1685, John Shadwell at the age of fourteen had entered All Souls College, Oxford, and now through the good influences of the Chancellor, who very particularly recommended his protégé to the Warden, this young scholar was granted on 3 November, 1688, a Fellowship of that eminent Society.

[1] Produced at the King's Hall, Covent Garden, 14 January, 1919.

(ccv)

The dramatiſt was warm in his expressions of gratitude, and returned thanks to the Duke in the following letter : [1]

My Ld,

Were I not a Cripple I would assume yᵉ boldness to wait upon yʳ Grace and give yᵘ my moſt humble thanks for yᵉ extraordinary favour yᵘ have shewn to my son who is elected a fellow of All-souls [2] wch I muſt wholly attribute to yʳ Graces commands to yᵉ worthy Mr. Warden who has been juſt to yʳ Grace and very favourable to my son. I have nothing to return to yʳ Grace for soe great a benefitt but my moſt humble acknowledge-ments and my continuall prayers for yʳ long health and prosperity in all yʳ affaires I presume yʳ Grace does not confer benefitts with any prospect of returne but to follow yᵉ Dictates of yʳ great minde wch yᵘ derive from yʳ moſt illuſtrious Grandfather and moſt renowned Father who were ever doeing good and may yʳ Grace live as long and bee as much eſteemed and Reverenced by all good men as both of them. I know yʳ consciousness of haveing done a bountiful or charitable action is a very great satisfaction to a generous nature especially where hee who receives it is or may by that make himself worthy of it hereafter. I have my Ld. taken already and shall if God lends mee life take yᵉ farther care in yᵉ inſtructions of my son here-after that I hope yʳ Grace will have no reason to blush when in time to come yᵘ may reflect upon yʳ . . .[3] bee a reſtorer of a drooping family wch my fathers losses for Kg. Charles yᵉ firſt his multitude of children mis-fortunes, and some unthriftiness had almoſt left naked to yᵉ world. But if my son proves a virtuous honeſt man and an eminent Scholler I am confident it will please yʳ Grace when ever yᵘ should remember who raysed him to a condition of beeing soe and if hee does not ſtudy all hee can to make himself such a man I am sure I shall wish this undone as well as yʳ Grace may juſtly. For I am sure hee shall bee noe longer mine than while hee endeavours to make himself worthy to bee yʳ Graces. For my part my Ld I will never while I have breath loose my gratefull resentments for this great favour and I had been equally gratefull had hee not had success I am.

My Lᵈ
Yʳ Graces
Moſt obliged & moſt
humble Servᵗ

Novemb. 5   THO. SHADWELL.
    88

[1] This letter which has not before been printed is preserved in the Collection at Kil-kenny Caſtle, and the Earl of Ossory moſt kindly transcribed it for me from the original.

[2] In the original " of of All-souls."

[3] One line of some eight or ten words is here illegible, owing to the fold of the paper on which the letter is written.

In February or March, 1689, the script of the new play muſt have been in the hands of the actors, since, although unfortunately we have no definite record, one may almoſt certainly date the production of *Bury-Fair* in April of that year. There can, I think, be little doubt that for his health's sake Shadwell had spent some weeks in the country, and as the Fair was held on 2 October it is not hazardous to suppose that he was actually sojourning at Bury S. Edmunds at this time, when he had an excellent opportunity of observing all those characters and episodes of which he has made such excellent use. Upon his return to London he was, as we have seen, proſtrated by a severe attack of the gout.

Meantime events had been moving faſt, and although fortunately it is not our sad task to give even in outline the ſtory of that unhappy cataſtrophe, yet since it played so important a part in Shadwell's career, and so ameliorated his fortunes, bringing him into sunshine from shadow, it seems essential to rehearse as briefly as may be the order of a few of the chief happenings. For many months rank disloyalty had been undermining the throne of James II. ; and on 30 June, 1688, seven traitors [1] actually signed a letter to the Prince of Orange inviting him to England. After four months of complexity, during which that good and gracious king made every concession compatible with his royal prerogative and sovereign dignity, open rebellion broke forth with the landing of the Dutchman at Torbay on 5 November, 1688. Guardian as he was of the honour of the English crown, it was impossible for King James to accept the terms which were impudently dictated to him by a foreign enemy on English soil. Accordingly, at the risk of every slander and misrepresentation, in December, 1688, he retired to France, and the King of England was entertained by Louis XIV. with brotherly hospitality at the palace of St. Germains.

An informal assembly hurriedly voted both the civil and military adminiſtration into the hands of the Prince of Orange. Various projects were feverishly discussed ; in his ambition William refused to become regent, and the Princess Mary declined to reign by herself. There was, of course, only one fitting solution of the whole bad business, the inſtant recall of the King with humbleſt submission ; but so many and so powerful had the Whigs become that this way was impossible. Finally William and Mary were proclaimed together on 13 February, 1689, and it was provided that the husband should hold office during his life. The Whigs had swept away the divine character of the throne, and the door was opened to the worſt disorders.

[1] Shrewsbury, Devonshire, Danby, Lumley, Russel, Sidney, and Compton, the Bishop of London. It will hardly be believed that even in comparatively recent years a violent partizan has written of these fellows as " risking their lives in legitimate rebellion ! "

INTRODUCTION

When the Earl of Dorset was appointed Lord Chamberlain on 14 February, 1688–9,[1] Shadwell's star was truly in the ascendant. He had already smoothed the way to his advancement by publishing *A Congratulatory Poem On His Highness the Prince Of Orange His Coming into England*, and as was natural he was ready and eager to use his pen on behalf of the intruders. On the afternoon of 12 February, Mary, the wife of William of Orange, landed at Whitehall Stairs. Various accounts are given of her behaviour that day ; according to some she was diffident and conscience-striken ; according to others she behaved with the most indecent levity. However that may have been, on 20 February, 1688–9, Shadwell rushed into print with *A Congratulatory Poem To the Most Illustrious Queen Mary Upon Her Arrival In England*, than which fulsome adulation and untruth have possibly never sunk lower.[2] His reward was soon to come. By a statute I William and Mary, c. 8, every person holding any office was obliged to take the oaths of allegiance, supremacy, and abjuration, before 1 August, 1689 ; otherwise his office was to be void. That Dryden should swear fealty was impossible, and so loyal a heart rejected the oaths with a dignity that has won him the admiration of all good men. The office of Poet Laureat was now formally vacant, and Dorset made haste to appoint Shadwell to that position. Among the Lord Chamberlain's records is the following entry : " A Warrant to sware Thomas Shadwell Esqr into the place and quality of poet-Laureat to His Matie March 9, 1688–9." [3] In the dedication to *Bury-Fair*, addressing his patron, Shadwell says, I " cannot be silent of the late great Honour you have done me, in making me the King's Servant." *Bury-Fair* appears in the *Term Catalogues* for Trinity (June), 1689, and upon the title-page Shadwell terms himself " Servant to His Majesty." It was not uncommon that a certain amount of delay should occur between the issue of a warrant for an appointment and the drawing up of the patent, especially when, as in the successive appointments to the laureateship, the pension was made payable from the death of the predecessor. Shadwell's patent (Patent Roll 1 Wm. & Mary, Part 5 [4]) was drawn up on 29 August, and is as follows : " D' Con. Offic' Tho Shadwell Ae. William and Mary by the Grace of God &c. To the Lords Commissioners of Our Treasury Treasurer Chancellor Under Trea-

[1] " The Rt. Hono. Charles Earle of Dorsett received the staffe of Lord Chamberlaine of His Maties Househould from His Mae at Whitehall February the 14th 1688." Public Records, LC, 5149.

[2] Rymer had been even more alert, for a day or two previously he issued " A Poem on the Arrival of Queen Mary, February 12th, 1688–9." There were, of course, many such copies of verses, including, I regret to say, a poem by Mrs. Behn *To Her Sacred Majesty Queen Mary on her Arrival in England*.

[3] Public Records, LC, 5149, p. 99.

[4] Record Office, c. 66/3329, No. 6, but *rectius* 16, as the number of this enrollment is preceded by 14, and 15, and followed by No. 17.

surer Chamberlains and Barons of the Exchequer of Vs Our Heires and Successores now being and that hereafter shall be and to all other the Officers and Ministers of Our said Court and of the Receipt there now being and that hereafter shall be and to All others to whom these presents shall come Greeting Knowe yee That Wee for and in Consideration of the many good and acceptable Services by Thomas Shadwell Esquire to Vs heretofore done and performed And taking Notice of the Learning and eminent Abilities of him the said Thomas Shadwell and of his great Skill and Elegant Stile both in Verse and Prose And for diverse other good Causes and Considerations Vs therevnto especially moving have Nominated Constituted Declared and Appointed And by these presents Doe Nominate Constitute Declare and Appoint him the said Thomas Shadwell Our Poet Laureat and our Historiographer Royall Giveing and Granting vnto the said Thomas Shadwell All and singular the Rights Priviledges Benefitts and Advantages therevnto belonging as fully and Amply as Sir Geoffry Chaucer Knight Sir John Gower knight John Leland Esquire William Camden Esquire Beniamin Johnson Esquire James Howell Esquire Sir William Davenant Knight John Dryden Esquire or any other person or persons having or exerciseing the Place or Employment of Poet Laureat or Historiographer or either of them in the time of any of Our Royal Progenitors had or received or might lawfully Clayme or Demand as incident or belonging vnto the said Places or Employments or either of them And for the further and better Encouragement of him the said Thomas Shadwell diligently to Attend the said Employments Wee are gratiously pleased to Give and Grant And by these presents Doe Give and Grant vnto the said Thomas Shadwell One Annuity or yearely Pension of Three Hundred Pounds of Lawfull Money of England during Our Pleasure To have hold and yearely to receive the said Annuity or Pension of Three Hundred Pounds of Lawfull Money of England by the yeare vnto the said Thomas Shadwell and his Assignes The first Payment thereof to beginn from the ffeast of the Annunciation of the Blessed Virgin Mary last past and to be forthwith made for One Quarter ended at the ffeast of St. John the Baptist now last past And the subsequent quarterly Payments to be made from time to time as they shall become due and payable for and during Our Pleasure at the Receipt of Our Exchequer out of Our Treasure from time to time there remaineing By the hands of the Treasurer or Treasurers and Chamberlaines there for the time being at the ffour most vsuall Termes of the yeare (that is to say) At the ffeast of the Nativity of St. John Baptist St. Michaell the Archangell the Birth of Our Lord Christ and the Annunciation of the Blessed Virgin Mary by even and equall Portions to be paid The ffirst Payment thereof to be made forthwith for the Quarter ended at the ffeast of the Nativity of St. John Baptist last past Wherefore Our Will and Pleasure is And Wee do by these presents

Require Command and Authorize the (said) [1] Lords Commissioners of Our
Treasury Treasurer Chancellor VnderTreasurer Chamberlaines and Barons
and other Officers and Ministers of the said Exchequer now and for the
time being not only to pay or cause to be paid vnto the said Thomas Shadwell and his Assignes the said Annuity or yearely Pension of Three Hundred Pounds of Lawfull Money of England according to Our Will and
Pleasure herein before expressed   But also from time to time to give full
Allowance of the same according to the true meaning of these presents
And these presents or the Inrollment thereof shall be vnto all men whom
it shall concerne A sufficient Warrant and Discharge for the Paying and
Allowing of the same accordingly without any further or other Warrant
to be in that behalfe procured or obteyned   And further know yee That
Wee of Our more especiall grace certaine knowledge and meer motion have
Given and Granted and by these presents do Give and Grant vnto the said
Thomas Shadwell and his Assignes One Butt or Pipe of the best Canary
Wine yearely To have hold receive pceive and take the said Butt or Pipe
of Canary Wine vnto the said Thomas Shadwell and his Assignes during
Our Pleasure out of Our Store of Wines yearely and from time to time
remaineing at or in Our Sellars within or belonging to Our Palace of
Whitehall And for the better effecting of Our Will and Pleasure herein
Wee do hereby Require and Command All and singular Our Officers and
Ministers whome it shall or may concerne or who shall have the Care or
Charge of Our said Wines That they or some of them do Deliver or cause
to be delivered the said Butt or Pipe of Wyne yearely and once in every
yeare vnto the said Thomas Shadwell or his Assignes during Our Pleasure
at such time and times as hee or they shall Demand or Desire the same
And these presents or the Inrollment thereof shall be vnto all Men whom
it shall concerne A sufficient Warrant and Discharge in that behalfe In
Witnesse &c' Witnesse Ourselves at Westminster the nyne and twentieth
day of August. By writ of Privy Seale, &c'."

This appointment can but have gratified Shadwell intensely, in spite of
the fact that he must have known he was destitute of poetic inspiration. [2]
Perhaps there are few stories more familiar than that of the answer which
Dorset gave to the very reasonable expostulation upon this appointment.
It was pointed out that Shadwell was no poet. "I will not pretend to
determine how great a poet Shadwell may be," replied the Minister, " but
I am sure that he is an honest man," which perhaps is not the most eminent
qualification for such a position. At any rate, however dull and however
drudging Shadwell's official effusions appear, they could not sink lower
than the Odes of Eusden, which contain " as much of the Ridiculum and

---

[1] Interlineated.
[2] He certainly seems to acknowledge this in his poem to Pietro Reggio.

Fustian in them as can well be jumbled together " [1] ; or Cibber's " out-doing his past out-doings " [2] in such a birthday ode as *Let there be Light !* which was performed on 28 October, 1732, and presents an almost inconceivable admixture of bathos and banality. The following stanzas—although I hardly expect to be believed—are not the worst in this poem :

> The word that form'd the world,
> In vain did make mankind ;
> Unless, his passions to restrain,
> Almighty wisdom had design'd
> Sometimes a WILLIAM, or a GEORGE should reign.
> Yet farther, *Britons*, cast your eyes,
> Behold a long succession rise
> Of future fair felicities.
>
> Around the royal table spread,
> See how the beauteous branches shine !
> Sprung from the fertile genial bed
> Of glorious GEORGE and CAROLINE.

When after this rubbish we read the Pindarics of Shadwell, we feel that we are indeed upon the rarefied heights of Parnassus.

To Shadwell's work as a Laureate must be added the *Song for S. Cecilia's Day*, since this composition is at least indirectly connected with his official effusions. Of its kind it is tolerable, and the sentiments are far more reverent and far better expressed than we might have expected from a Whiggish pen. It must not, of course, be mentioned in the same breath as Dryden's two great lyric poems, pæans of divine ecstasy, but it compares very favourably with the strains of D'Urfey, Tate,[3] and Thomas Yalden. Tate, in particular, who could write such a Christmas carol as, *While Shepherds Watched their Flocks by Night*, when he celebrates S. Cecilia is sugary, simpering, and mincing with almost incredibly bad taste. His gauche fopperies commence with the following stanza :

> Tune the viol, touch the lute,
> Wake the harp, inspire the flute,
> Call the jolly swains away,
> Love and Musick reign to-day.

---

[1] Oldmixon, *Arts of Logick and Rhetorick*, London, 1728, pp. 413–14.

[2] In the Preface to the first edition of *The Provok'd Husband ; or, A Journey to London*, 8vo, 1728, speaking of Mrs. Oldfield's excellent performance as Lady Townly, Cibber wrote : " It is not enough to say, that she outdid her usual outdoing." The phrase was afterwards amended, and in his *Apology* he frankly confesses that 'twas florid nonsense. But the wits did not forget, nor for many a long year did they fail to pay it public honours.

[3] He wrote the Ode for 22 November, 1685.

Let your kids and lambkins rove,
  Let them sport or feed at will,
  Grace the vale, or climb the hill;
Let them feed, or let them love:
Let them love, or let them stray,
Let them feed, or let them play;
    Neglect them, or guide them,
    No harm shall betide them,
On bright *Cecilia*, bright *Cecilia's* day.

In comparison with this we feel that Shadwell was almost a poet.

S. Cecilia was a noble Roman lady who lived in the reign of the Emperor Alexander Severus (222–235). Her parents, who were secretly Christians, educated her in the Faith, and from her childhood she was remarkable for her piety and purity. She had early taken a vow of chastity, devoting herself to heavenly things, and delighting to praise God with sweet music and psalmody, so that even the Angels were seen listening to her, and their voices were heard softly joining with hers. Hence it is said that she invented the organ, and dedicated it to the solemn service of the Church. When she was about sixteen she was given in marriage to a young Roman, rich, handsome, and of noble birth, named Valerian, who was, however, yet a pagan. That night, as he was about to embrace his bride, she stayed him, saying that she had a guardian Angel who watched her always and would suffer no earthly lover to approach: " Est secretum, Ualeriane, quod tibi uolo dicere: Angelum Dei habeo amatorem, qui nimio zelo custodit corpus meum." [1]

I have an Angel which that loveth me,
That with great love, wher-so I wake or slepe,
Is redy ay my body for to kepe.[2]

Whereupon Valerian asked to see this Holy Angel, and Cecilia sent him to Pope S. Urban, who was concealed from the heathen persecutors in the catacombs. Under instruction the young noble was converted and baptized. Returning to his wife he beheld in her chamber the Angel who was standing near her, and holding in his hands two crowns of roses gathered in Paradise. Now Valerian had a brother whom he dearly loved, and accordingly he did not rest until his Tiburtius also was brought to a knowledge of the truth. O beata Cecilia, quae duos fratres conuertisti! [3] Before long the three Christians, owing to their good works, attracted the attention of the Prefect of Rome, Almachius, before whom they were

---

[1] Antiphon to Magnificat, First Vespers of the Feast.
[2] Chaucer: the " Seconde Nonnes Tale."
[3] Second Responsory, First Nocturn of Matins of the Feast.

brought and commanded to sacrifice to Jupiter. Upon their refusal the two brothers were put to death, Cecilia was taken back to her house to be stifled in a boiling bath. Since this failed, the executioner was summoned to strike off her head. He struck awry, and left her bleeding from terrible wounds. She lingered three days, with her latest breath desiring S. Urban that he would consecrate her house as a place of worship for Christians.

This was done, but afterwards, in the troubles and invasions of the barbarians, the ancient sanctuary fell into ruin, and was largely rebuilt by Pope S. Paschal I, who reigned 817–824.[1] The present basilica of S. Cecilia in Trastevere contains under the High Altar the bodies of S. Cecilia, SS. Valerian and Tiburtius, S. Maximus, Pope S. Urban, and Pope S. Lucius, all of which were placed here by S. Paschal in 820. In 1599 Cardinal Sfondrato restored the church, and recent excavations have been undertaken at the expense of Cardinal Rampolla. The lower church, which His Eminence decorated with fine mosaics, is the original house of the saint, whilst in the upper church is the famous recumbent statue of the saint by Carlo Maderna, representing the body as it was found when the tomb was opened at the end of the sixteenth century. High holiday is kept here on 22 November, the feast of S. Cecilia, which is preceded by a solemn novena.

When the Academy of Music was founded at Rome in 1584, S. Cecilia was made patroness of the institute, and she is regarded as the patroness of all church music, indeed of music in general. The greatest painters have vied with their genius to depict her beauty. Cimabue, Raphael, Lucas van Leyden, Moretta, Giulio Campi, Zurbaran, Giulio Procaccino, Luini, Riminaldi, Lorenzo Costa, Lionello Spada, are only a few of those who have drawn her on famous canvases, whilst the series by Domenichino is celebrated in the history of Art. Nor are poets slow to sing her praises, in England we have the " Seconde Nonnes Tale " of Chaucer, Dryden's great Odes, and Tennyson's exquisite stanzas.

The formal celebration of S. Cecilia's Day in England by a musical entertainment, seems to have begun in the year 1683 when the Musical Society inaugurated a " Musick Feast," for which three Odes were written, the music for all three being composed by Henry Purcell. It may be said without exaggeration that these words are among the most miserable of their kind; they sink to such a bathos as almost to preclude even a smile. On 22 November, 1684, was performed *An Ode For an Anniversary of Musick on S. Cecilia's Day*, by Oldham, of which I have not

---

[1] The discovery of the Relics in the Catacomb of Prætextatus, whence they had been transferred from the Catacomb of Callistus, and their translation are described in *Liber Pontificalis*, ed. Duchesne, II., 52 *sqq.* See also Marucchi *Basiliques et églises de Rome*, Rome, 1902 ; and especially T. P. Kirsch, *Die hl. Cäcilia in der römischen Kirche des Altertums*.

much good to report. It was set by Dr. John Blow. In the following year William Turner composed the accompaniment to Nahum Tate's effusion, from which a stanza has just been quoted. In 1686 Flatman provided the words, and Isaac Blackwell the music.[1] In 1687 we have Dryden's magnificent piece, set by Draghi. It would appear that the performances were interrupted during 1688 and 1689, and when resumed in 1690 the new Poet Laureate was complimented by being asked for a contribution, and, as we have seen, he acquitted himself very fairly. His Song was set by Robert King. In 1691 Dr. Blow composed the music to D'Urfey's words, and in the following year Nicholas Brady provided the Ode, which " was admirably set to music by Mr. Henry Purcell, and performed *twice* with universal applause, and particularly the second stanza, which was sung with incredible graces by Mr. Purcell himself." [2] It would appear that Oxford vied with London in paying honour to S. Cecilia, and that this year at the University was performed an Ode by Addison. In 1693 the poem was written by Theophilus Parsons,[3] and set by Finger. The poets of the next three years seem to be unknown, although the Ode of 1694 is ascribed with authority to Samuel Wesley. 1697 was glorified by the finest of all, *Alexander's Feast*, the music being by Jeremiah Clarke. It is interesting to notice that in future years D'Urfey, (1700); Congreve (1701); Hughes (1703), and Pope (1708), all contributed to the celebration of this Festival, for full accounts of which one may consult Malone [4] and W. H. Husk.[5]

As might have been expected, at the Revolution Shadwell could not let slip the golden advantage of crowing loudly over his old antagonist, and in *The Address of John Dryden to the Prince of Orange* (1689), and *To the King* (1689), he tried to repay old scores. Probably because he felt more secure in his superiority, certainly not because it was below the dignity of an Orange Laureate, these two pasquils lack the vigour and violence of ten years before. Dryden treated them with silent contempt. But there was now another way in which Shadwell could vex and annoy the great poet. Having lost so considerable a part of his income, Dryden was constrained to turn once more to the stage, and accordingly, after a silence of several years, in December, 1689, there was produced at Drury Lane that fine tragedy *Don Sebastian, King of Portugal*. But just as Dryden had in the past censured and prevented the representation of disloyal and

---

[1] Malone, *Prose Works of John Dryden*, Vol. I., Part 1, p. 277, says : " The author being then extremely young, and a student at Oxford, it probably was not performed in London. It might perhaps have been sung at Oxford."

[2] *The Gentleman's Journal*, November, 1692.

[3] Printed in *The Gentleman's Journal*, November, 1693, p. 377.

[4] Malone, *op. cit.*, pp. 254–307.

[5] *An Account of the Musical Celebrations on S. Cecilia's Day*, London, 1857.

factious dramas, so Shadwell was all agog to turn the tables, and he narrowly watched everything, whether play or prologue, that his adversary produced to see if by some chance he might not be able to lodge an information against these performances as being likely to stir up party feeling, and so obtain their prohibition in the theatre.

When a man is eager to make mischief of this sort his opportunity is bound soon to come. In November, 1690, there was produced with considerable splendour at Dorset Garden an alteration from Beaumont and Fletcher's drama *The Prophetess*, a dramatic opera, *The Prophetess ; or, The History of Dioclesian*. This, the work of Betterton,[1] was equipped with a prologue by Dryden, who very smartly laughed at the Irish campaigns.

"This Prologue was forbidden to be spoken the second night of the representation of the *Prophetess*. Mr. *Shadwell* was the occasion of its being taken notice of by the Ministry in the last Reign. He happen'd to be at the House on the first night, and taking the beginning of the Prologue to have a *double meaning*, and that meaning to reflect on the *Revolution*, he told a Gentleman, *He wou'd immediately put a stop to it.* When that Gentleman ask'd, Why he would do the Author such a Disservice ? He said, *Because while Mr. Dryden was the Poet Laureat, he wou'd never let any Play of his be Acted.* Mr. *Shadwell* informing the Secretary of State of it, and representing it in its worst colours, the Prologue was never Spoken afterwards, and is not Printed in Mr. *Dryden's* Works, or his Miscellanies.[2] Whatever was the meaning of the Author then, had he liv'd to have seen the Happy Effects of the Revolution in Her present Majesty's Triumphant Reign, he wou'd have blush'd at his Poor Politicks, and Vain Malice. Tho' we say this with some warmth, we wou'd not be understood to mean anything derogatory to Mr. *Dryden's* merit ; to which, as a Poet, we pay as much deference as any one, and think the *British* Muse indebted to him for his admirable versification, as much as to all the writers who went before him. Indeed, he has so refin'd our Numbers, that he has taught all who follow him, to do really better in that kind, than those who were famous for their excellence in it in the last Century." [3]

This prohibition caused no little stir, and it has been said that Queen Mary II. expressed her displeasure at Dryden's raillery in very warm and lively terms.[4] The pother was even well remembered many years after,

[1] It is attributed to him by Gildon and others, and was printed, 4to, 1690.

[2] The Prologue was not printed with *The Prophetess*, 4to, 1690, but seems to have been first given, anonymously, in *Poems on Affairs of State*, Part III., 1698. The second issue was that in *The Muses Mercury*, January, 1707.

[3] *The Muses Mercury ; or, Monthly Miscellany*, January, 1707 (Vol. I., No. 1). This interesting and rare miscellany was edited by J. O., who is probably John Oldmixon. He claims to have printed most of the pieces which he includes from the authors' MSS.

[4] Miss Strickland's *Queens of England*, 1847, Vol. XI., p. 277.

and Cibber in his *Apology*, 4to, 1740,[1] recalled the incident : " A Prologue (by *Dryden*) to the *Prophetess*, was forbidden by the Lord *Dorset*, after the first day of its being spoken. This happened when King *William* was prosecuting the war in *Ireland*. It must be confessed that this prologue had some familiar, metaphorical sneers at the Revolution itself ; and as the poetry of it was good, the offence of it was less pardonable."

Similar trouble arose with regard to *Cleomenes, the Spartan Heroe*, a tragedy upon which Dryden had been engaged during the summer of 1691,[2] and which was to have been acted in April, 1692, when it was suddenly prohibited on the eve of production.[3] It was alleged that the figure of Cleomenes in exile at Alexandria might be too lively a reminder of King James at St. Germains, and this parallel was strongly urged by Shadwell to Dorset. In *The Gentleman's Journal* for April, 1692, Peter Motteux writes : " I was in hopes to have given you in this Letter an account of the acting of Dryden's *Cleomenes* : it was to have appeared upon the stage on Saturday last, and you need not doubt but that the town was full of the expectation of the performance ; but orders came from her Majesty to hinder its being acted ; so that none can tell when it shall be played." In the following month the same writer adds : " I told you in my last that none could tell when Mr. Dryden's *Cleomenes* would appear. Since that time, the innocence and merit of the play have raised it several eminent advocates, who have prevailed to have it acted ; and you need not judge but it has been with great applause." The fact was that Lord Dorset had sent for a copy of the play, and when he had read it with some care returned it to Dryden, of whose genius he was, as is very well known, a great admirer, affirming that in his opinion there was nothing to prevent its appearance upon the stage. The Earl of Rochester, also, to whom the tragedy was dedicated when it was issued from the press,[4] spoke very warmly on Dryden's behalf ; whilst Antony, Viscount Falkland, informed Queen Mary that to his certain knowledge Dryden had sketched out a rough plan of the play some seven or eight years before, and had for so long a time entertained the idea of treating this subject. As was inevitable, the postponement, and the reasons for the postponement, being very widely discussed, only served to rouse new interest in the drama, which, when it came upon the stage, was received by crowded houses with those thunders of applause it so entirely merited and deserved. Accordingly the malice of Dryden's enemies only added to the lustre of his reputation.

[1] p. 200.
[2] Part of the fifth act of this tragedy was written by Southerne, to whom Dryden, who had been ill, entrusted it for completion.
[3] See Luttrell's *Brief Relation*, Vol. II., pp. 413 and 422 ; 9 and 16 April, 1692.
[4] 4to, 1692.

Shadwell, what time he was busy in performing the function of a political censor in the theatrical world, was himself providing the actors with some excellent comedies. In fact, in spite of ill health, the last three years of his life were by far the most active and the most crowded. His official duties as Poet Laureate, too, which he seems to have taken seriously enough, most inappropriate as they were, must have occupied a certain amount of his time. Since his output in this direction requires so little consideration it may be well to dismiss the subject presently. The sheaf is both small in quantity and weak in quality. It is interesting to remark that his contemporaries fully recognized his lack of poetic inspiration, since his official Odes and Pindarics are simply ignored, and in their appreciation of his genius they very justly concentrate upon those comedies in which it is so amply evident. We can only say that Shadwell's Odes are worthy of their themes, and, even if they were far more pedestrian than they actually are, they would do well enough to celebrate such occasions as the birthday of William of Orange, and the return from Ireland. To consider the unctuous adulation which was paid to this Prince is a task extraordinarily nauseating, since the fashion of the day demanded an obsequiousness which even when rendered to great and good men sometimes seems a little exaggerated, and when such a strain is dictated by servility to an intruder, it becomes ineffably distasteful and disgusting. Although probably he by no means designed them to bear this complexion, more than once Shadwell's sentiments and his expression of them in these Odes addressed to William and Mary are horribly blasphemous in their intended application.

Gladly do we return to his dramatic work. In spite of the fact that he was, as he tells us, suffering from a long and languid illness, *Bury-Fair*, which he composed on a bed of sickness, is a comedy of the first rank. Something it is true is owing to Molière, but Shadwell has not conveyed much more than a mere hint, and this he has so amply elaborated as to make the characters of La Roch and Mrs. Fantast entirely his own. We have already discussed the relation between *Bury-Fair* and the Duke of Newcastle's *The Triumphant Widow*, and we have said that it is wellnigh certain that when Shadwell introduced Mr. Oldwit and Sir Humphrey Noddy into his Suffolk comedy he was but reclaiming his own. The pictures of provincial culture—and one must bear in mind at what a great distance the provinces then were from London—the bustle and rustic jollity of the fair, the crowds, the traffic and the noise show Shadwell at his best. The characters of Oldwit and his family, of that dull joker Sir Humphrey, and of Mr. Trim are exceedingly happy. In the hands of a good actor La Roch would become truly comic, although in the library he may not perhaps prove so entertaining, but we must endeavour to visualize him upon the stage, a thing which is not altogether easy, save for the expert who is trained to read dramatic work from the point of view of actual representation. It is interesting to notice the sentimentality of the character of the female page Charles, or rather Philadelphia, a figure who very easily becomes coldly conventional and a somewhat arid type, but who has been rendered by Shadwell both pleasing and individual. Perhaps Gertrude is sketched upon somewhat commonplace lines, but this very formality contrasts well with the preciosity and vagaries of the rest of the house. Even Bellamy and Wildish have far more personality than the ordinary run of young men of that time, and the consequence is that in the aggregate we have drawn for us a most exact picture which, without dullness, contains no notable exaggeration of or deviation from ordinary life. This capital comedy is certainly entitled to the warmest praise, and must be accorded a high place among Shadwell's works.

Now that the times had so altered that the sentiments which ten years before would have been frowned upon and heartily hissed were received with smiles of approbation and warmest applause Shadwell, who had by no means forgotten the prohibition of *The Lancashire Witches* and the controversy which had surrounded that play, resolved to have a fling at his opponents, once so powerful but now helpless, if not by any means silenced. Accordingly he made up his mind that Tegue O Divelly should again walk the stage, and he conceived the idea of transporting that gentleman to Madrid and giving us some further episodes from his Guzman history. *The Amorous Bigotte : With the Second Part of Tegue O Divelly* was produced at Drury Lane early in 1689-90, possibly in March. We are in the Spanish capital, and the Irish Friar is surrounded not by yokels and witches but by dons and duennas. The caricature, although, of course, sufficiently grotesque and out of all nature, is in some respects not so outrageous as the Rawhead of a decade before. The comedy is one of a type, plays of Spanish or Italian intrigue, which gave ample scope for all kinds of gallantries, mistakes, adventures, serenades, and night-walking when any event seemed possible. Of this kind are Sir Francis Fane's *Love in the Dark ;* Sir Robert Howard's *The Surprisal ;* Richard Rhodes' *Flora's Vagaries ;* Ravenscroft's *The Wrangling Lovers ;* Mountfort's *The Successful Strangers,* and very many pieces of the school of Cibber and Mrs. Centilivre. Such plays are generally full of bustle and business, distinguished by adroit construction with lively dialogue, and although by no means negligible from a literary point of view more entertaining upon the stage than in the closet. *The Amorous Bigotte* is an exceedingly amusing piece, and it met with a most favourable reception. Indeed so popular did it prove that a little novel *The Irish Rogue ; or, The Comical History of the Life and Actions of Teague O'Divelley* which was issued in 1690 achieved a certain success owing to the fact that it had borrowed and flaunted a character from Shadwell's play. It is, however, a dull little fiction, and although read by many at the moment before twelve months had passed it fell into obscurity.

Shadwell was now living at Chelsea [1] in his own house, and since he was a man whose opinion carried considerable weight, whose good word for a rising young dramatist might prove of the best recommendations at the theatre, just as he had it in his power to show himself extremely obstructive and vexatious, he was soon surrounded by a number of persons endeavouring to win his favour. Amongst his friendships it is interesting to notice that with Gerard Langbaine, who when reviewing Shadwell's plays in 1691 wrote: "I am willing to say the less of Mr. *Shadwell*, because I have publickly profess'd a friendship for him: and tho' it be not of so long date, as some former Intimacy with others; so neither is it blemished with some unhandsome Dealings, I have met with from Persons, when I least expected it." Shadwell's elevation to the Laureatship, however, did not place him at once in such a pecuniary position as he might reasonably have expected. For the first two years neither his fees (£100), as Laureate nor his salary (£200) as Historiographer Royal was promptly forthcoming. At the end of 1691 the Report of the Accounts Commissioners set forth: " 2 years salary £600 due to Tho. Shadwell, Esq., Poet Laureat." [2] The Report for the following year [3] shows that he received £300 just before his death. Moreover, his salary as both Laureate and Historiographer was paid to his executors for the year following his decease,[4] a bounty which was most gratefully acknowledged by his widow in her dedication to Queen Mary of the posthumous play *The Volunteers ; or, The Stock-Jobbers*, 4to, 1693. Anne Shadwell writes: " Madam, The little Wit of our poor *Family*, as well as the best part of the *Subsistance*, perish with my Husband ; so that we have not where withall, worthily to express our great Acknowledgment due for the *Support* and *Favour* we have already received, . . . This Consciousness of our own *Disability*, will much shorten your Majesties Trouble, we shall only therefore, without more word, and with all Humility and Profound Respect, throw this our last Play at Your Majesties Feet, begging Your Acceptance of it."

Owing to these financial delays Shadwell found it useful to keep the theatre well supplied, and very wisely for his next comedy he returned to London, and drew in his own intensely realistic way a vivid and vivacious picture of contemporary life. During the summer his two old and intimate friends, who both enjoyed a great reputation for their comic genius, the celebrated actor Anthony Leigh and his wife Elinor, had been

---

[1] The air of Chelsea was considered particularly good, and St. Evremond mentions it as fine and invigorating.

[2] *Historical MSS. Comm.*, 13th Rep., V. 373.

[3] *Ibid.*, 14th Rep., VI. 166.

[4] *Historical Comm. MSS.*, *House of Lords*, Vol. I., new series, p. 90.

Staying in lodgings at Chelsea from 24 August to the end of September, and when Shadwell read them his new comedy *The Scowrers* they expressed themselves as highly delighted with it. They must indeed have been especially pleased with the two rôles they were called upon to interpret, old Tope and Lady Maggot.

The Scowrers is an excellent comedy, somewhat rough and boisterous perhaps, but eminently deserving of far greater attention than it has hitherto received. It is very difficult for us to-day to realize the dangers of the London streets two centuries and a half ago, when " a man could not go from the *Rose Tavern* to the *Piazza* once, but he must venture his life twice." From Juvenal to Johnson writers deplore the perils of venturing abroad after dark. A whole attendance of armed footmen with flambeaux was necessary to escort a coach or My Lord going on foot through the London streets ; humbler passengers had to be content with the link-boy, who as often as not might lead them into some trap and decoy them by a route where footpads were lurking in the shadows.

> Nec tamen haec tantum metuas : nam qui spoliat te
> Non deerit, clausis domibus, postquam omnis ubique
> Fixa catenatae siluit compago tabernae,
> Interdum et ferro subitum grassator agit rem.

Seventeen hundred years later we find the same tale [1] :

> Prepare for death, if here at night you roam,
> And sign your will before you sup from home.
> Some fiery fop, with new commission vain,
> Who sleeps on brambles till he kills his man ;
> Some frolic drunkard, reeling from a feast,
> Provokes a broil, and stabs you for a jest.
> Yet e'en these heroes, mischievously gay,
> Lords of the street, and terrors of the way ;
> Flush'd as they are with folly, youth, and wine,
> Their prudent insults to the poor confine ;
> Afar they mark the flambeaux's bright approach,
> And shun the shining train, and golden coach.

Even Greek and Roman scowrers were not unknown, and the disorders of the streets in Athens became notorious owing to the nocturnal riots of a number of young debauches of quality, at the head of whom was Alcibiades. They had long been a nuisance and a danger, until at length breaking all bounds they not merely profanely travestied the sacred Mysteries, but mutilated the Hermæ, that is to say, the heads of the god placed on a quadrangular pillar, and set up in the Attic streets before

[1] Dr. Johnson's *London*, 1738.

houses, temples, gymnasia, and other buildings, statues venerated as being of extraordinary sanctity. A thrill of horror ran through the whole city. The affair was immediately inquired into by the Assembly, and " During this Examination, *Androcles*, one of the *Demagogues*, produc'd certain Slaves and Strangers before them, who accus'd *Alcibiades* and some of his friends for defacing other Images in the same manner, and for having prophanely acted the sacred Mysteries at a drunken Meeting." [1]

Andocides, *On the Mysteries*,[2] tells us that Teucer denounced by name twenty-two persons, and that of these four at once took to flight, whilst eighteen were arrested and put to death as guilty of the most heinous offence.

The emperor Nero was wont to indulge in nocturnal riots in the streets, and Suetonius [3] gives a very vivid account of the proceedings on such occasions, when Cæsar's conduct may be pretty closely paralleled with that of Shadwell's Sir William Rant, Crowne's Young Ranter [4] and other Scowrers of the later decades of the seventeenth century. Of Nero Suetonius says : " Post crepusculum statim arrepto pileo uel galero, popinas inibat : circumque uicos uagabatur ludibundus, nec sine pernicie tamen. Siquidem redeuntes a coena uerberare, ac repugnantes uulnerare, cloacisque demergere assueuerat : tabernulas etiam effringere et expilare : quintana domi constituta, ubi partae et ad licitationem diuidendae praedae pretium assumeretur. Ac saepe in eiusmodi rixis, oculorum et uitae periculum adiit, a quodam laticlauio, cuius uxorem attrectauerat, prope ad necem caesus. Quare nunquam postea se publico illud horae sine tribunis commisit, procul et occulte subsequentibus."

In the London streets these nightly riots did not merely proceed from the casual disorders of footpads and shabberoons, or from the brawling of gallants on their way home from the taverns where they had supped too well, but they were the result of organized bands of idle rakeshames, who actually adopted curious titles and particular insignia, who had their extraordinary and elaborate rictual of initiation into their ranks, whose nightly revels in the street were a regular business and a part of their profession, and who deliberately sallied forth from their headquarters in some bowsing-ken or brothel to terrify and assault the passers-by, to beat the watch, and to cause hideous clamour and confusion. In his diary [5] John Manningham tells us that his cousin informed him there was " a company of young gallants sometyme in Amsterdame which called them-

---

[1] *The Second Volume of Plutarch's Lives. Translated from the Greek by Several Hands.* Tonson, 1684, pp. 33–34.

[2] LII, LIX, LXVII.

[3] *Nero Claudius Cæsar*, XXVI.

[4] *The English Frier ; or, The Town Sparks*, produced at Drury Lane early in 1689–90; 4to, 1690.

[5] Camden Society, pp. 142–3.

selves the Damned Crue. They would meete togither on nights, and vowe amongst themselves to kill the next man they mett whosoever;" and the editor of the diary says that a similar band, under the leadership of a notorious profligate, Sir Edmund Baynham, plagued the streets of London almost without let or hindrance.[1]

The author of *The Secret History of the Reign of King James I.*[2] paints a a terrible picture of the insecurity of the streets, for "divers sects of vicious persons, under particular titles, pass unpunished or regarded, as the sect of Roaring Boys, Bravadoes, and such like, being persons prodigal and of great expense, who, having run themselves into debt, were constrained to run into faction to defend themselves from the danger of the law; these received maintenance from divers of the nobility, and not a little (as was suspected) from the Earl of Northampton; which persons, though of themselves they were not able to attempt any enterprise, yet faith, honesty, and other good arts being little set by, and citizens through lasciviousness consuming their estates, it was likely that the number would rather increase than diminish; and under these pretences they entered into many desperate enterprises, and scarce any durst walk the streets in safety after midnight."[3]

Contemporary literature is full of allusions to this abominable rowdyism, and towards the end of the reign of James I. these gangs became so formidable as to attract the notice of the authorities, who suspected that an assumption of reckless conviviality and dissipation could cover dark political schemes, and that their meetings might strike something deeper into such matters than was generally supposed. In particular a certain society called the Order of the Bugle, and a fraternity whose members dubbed themselves Tityre tues [4] engaged the serious attention of His Majesty's council, although upon examination it could not be shown that any conspiracy or other subversive movement was on foot. The leaders of the Bugle Men wore a black bugle as a badge, and their followers pinned blue ribbons on to their doublets or yellow favours in their hats. An absurd oath was imposed with Bacchic ceremonies when a recruit was made free of the fraternity. Chamberlain says that the members were "young gentlemen who use to flock to taverns, thirty or forty in a company," and he adds: "What mischief may lurk under the mask, God knows." It is certain that the King, at least, was very suspicious, and the Venetian ambassador remarked in a letter to Italy that although the

---

[1] Camden Society, pp. 142–3.
[2] Generally dated before 1615.
[3] Edited J. O. Halliwell, pp. 324–5.
[4] This Vergilian tag is continually quoted by Elizabethan writers. In *The Merry Devil of Edmonton* (*circa* 1598), I, 2, the Host salutes Bilbo: "I serve the good Duke of Norfolke. Bilbo, *Titere, tu, patulæ recubans sub tegmine fagi.*"

INTRODUCTION

Tityre tues appeared to be harmless persons, " it is feared that they may have more extensive designs." [1]   It may be remembered that nearly one hundred years later Swift was not alone in thinking that the Mohocks of his day were a menacing political organization.

Whether the Bugle Men and similar gangs were political or not, they became so great a nuisance in London that to us it appears extraordinary how they could have been tolerated, and their continuance certainly throws a somewhat untoward light upon the manners of the time.   The references to their boisterous behaviour are innumerable, and Shirley in his famous comedy *The Gamester*, licensed 11 November, 1633, gives the following description of such nocturnal exploits :

> I do not all this while accompt you in
> The list of those are call'd the blades, that roar
> In houses, and break windows ; fright the streets
> At midnight worse than constables, and sometimes
> Set upon innocent bell-men,[2] to beget
> Discourse for a week's diet ; that swear, damn-mes
> To pay their debts, and march like walking armories,
> With poniard, pistol, rapier, and batoon,
> As they would murder all the King's liege people,
> And blow down streets.

Sir John Suckling, the poet, seems to have been regarded as a leader among these losels, and there is a contemporary broadside, 1641, *The Sucklington Faction ; or, (Sucklings) Roaring Boyes* which very pointedly reprimands their lewd way of life.   The writer sharply chides these " prodigall children, the younger brothers (Luk. 15. 12.) acting ye parts of hotspur Cavaliers and disguised ding-thrifts. . . . What with wine and women, horses, hounds and whores, dauncing, dicing, drabbing, drinking, may the prodigall man say : I am brought unto a morsell of bread, yea unto the very husks of Swine.   Pride of spirit makes him scorne an Alehouse, and therefore with greater eagernesse hee daily haunts Tavernes : where sometimes he sits by his Liquor, and bloud of the Vine, and the spirits of the Celler, exhausting, and infusing them unto mad ebriety : thus drinking ad modum sine mensura, whole ones, by measure without measure, like the Elephant through the juice of Mulberries, he is enraged unto bloud, and most damnable resolutions and designes, terminated in the

---

[1] *Calendar of State Papers, Venice,* 1623–25, p. 175.

[2] In the Gifford-Dyce *Shirley* (1833), III, p. 199, is the following note : " The watch, who, at this period, carried a bell.   The *blades,* who occur in the preceding line, are bravoes, bullies.   They were the predecessors of the Mohocks, and other pestilent disturbers of the peace, who continued to infest the streets down to the beginning of the last century."

death and destruction of the next man he meets, that never did neither thought him harme. . . . This notorious good-fellow (corruptly so called) being a confederate of the Greeks, *Titere tris*, or joviall roaring Boyes, is of the Poets mind, when he said;

Facundi calices quem non fecere disertum ? "

In Richard Brome's comedy *The Weeding of the Covent-Garden, Or the Middlesex-Justice of the Peace*, acted in 1632, there is a tavern scene (III, 1) where Clotpoll, a foolish gull, is initiated by Captain Driblow into the Order " *Philoblathicus* and *Philobatticus*," that is to say, "the Blade and the Battoon," a ceremony which involves an oath to be true to every member of the Order, and faithfully to observe their laws. When he has kissed the book Clotpoll cries : " So, now I am a Blade, and of a better Rowe then those of *Tytere tu*, or *Oatmeal hoe*." [1]

In Wilson's comedy *The Cheats* which was acted at the Theatre Royal in Vere Street, March 1662-3, he has introduced two characters, Bilboe and Titere Tu, " Two Hectors ; the one usurping the name of a Major the other of a Captain ; whereas, in truth, and as may be gather'd from their discourse, they never were either, or scarcely anything like it,— a humour that can be no wise strange to any man that knew this town between the years '46 and '50." [2]

Other fraternities who specialized in nocturnal street rows were the Circling-Boys, the Twibills, the Huffs,[3] the Muns, the Swashes,[4] the Tuquoques, and the Lords of the Sword, all of which societies enlisted ruffians of the type that Wilson has depicted. Edmund Gayton in his *Notes on Don Quixote* [5] has preserved for us the names of similar rowdy covens, some of whom, at any rate, must have been small in numbers. Speaking of the creation of a Knight Errant, he says : " This Ceremony, I say, is farre short of those of the Garter, or of the Golden Fleece (though of the same continent with this latter) or those of the Knights of Malta. If the Formalities were well compared, they would more resemble these new Orders of the Tityrie-Tues, the Fellow Cues, the Confederates, the Dead Boyes, the Tories, the John Dorians, or the late Ranters, or the Hectors whose rites and customes were never fully executed (like those of

---

[1] Folly's catch (I, 1), in Dekker and Ford's *The Sun's Darling* sings of " Roaring-boys and Oatmeals." The Oatmeals are also mentioned in Cartwright's *The Ordinary*.

[2] " The Author to the Reader." *The Cheats*, 4to, 1664.

[3] In Tatham's *The Scots Figgaries ; or, A Knot of Knaves*, 4to, 1652, I, Trapheir is admitted into the Huffs' company.

[4] In Southerne's *The Maid's Last Prayer ; or, Any Rather than Fail*, produced at Drury Lane in January, 1692-93, II, 2, Captain Drydrubb says : " I remember your Dammee-Boyes, your Swashes, your Tuquoques, and your Titire-Tues : have us'd the *Fleece* and *Speering's*." Shadwell mentions this latter gaming-hell in *The Sullen Lovers*.

[5] 1654, pp. 11, 12.

(ccxxiv)

the Don) without a Tolosa, or a Molinera, in plaine English, a whore or so, for creature-comfort, as they call it ; or as the Hectors, for Carnelevation."

Of all these the Hectors or Knights of the Blade were the most famous, and there are continual allusions to this gang, whom no doubt Milton had in mind when he wrote of

> luxurious cities, where the noyse
> Of riot assends above thir loftiest towrs,
> And injury and outrage : And when Night
> Darkens the streets, then wander forth the Sons
> Of *Belial*, flown with insolence and wine.
> Witness the Streets of *Sodom*, and that Night
> In *Gibeah*, when hospitable Dores
> Yielded thir Matrons to prevent worse rape.

The Hectors seem to have arisen 1648–1650,[1] for although the word hector had long been in use meaning a bully, actual organizations calling themselves by this name appeared towards the middle of the century, and were only merged in the Scowrers about 1690, and later in the Mohocks of the days of Queen Anne. There were, of course, of Hectors " several Gangs or Companies, some meaner, and some higher," and whilst the lower sort were no better than common robbers and highwaymen, a number of swaggering debauches joined their ranks for the sake of the mad excitement and the gross adventure. It is not necessary, I think, to give any detailed description of their aims and pursuits, which briefly included violence and roguery of every kind, fighting in taverns, picking quarrels abroad—often with the idea of extorting " composition "—duelling, and every conceivable outrage. The Scowrers, perhaps, usually confined their riots to the night-time, and as we might expect burglars and professional criminals were not slow to take advantage of the opportunity afforded by the brawls and depredations of such comrades. In their turn Scowrers were succeeded by the Nickers and the Hawcubites, but both these gangs were quite eclipsed by the Mohocks, whose exploits under the moon and stars caused something like a reign of terror in the London streets at the beginning of the eighteenth century. " A race of rakes," Swift calls them, " that play the devil about this town every night." On 14 March, 1712, Lady Wentworth wrote : " I am very much frighted with the fyer, but much more with a gang of Devils that call themselves Mohocks ; they put an old woman into a hogshead, and rooled her down

---

[1] A pamphlet, 1652, *A Notable and Pleasant History of the Famous renowned Knights of the Blade, commonly called Hectors, or St. Nicholas Clerkes* gives a full account of the origin and practices of these fellows.

a hill,[1] they cut of some nosis, others hands, and several barbarass tricks, without any provocation. They are said to be young gentlemen, they never take any mony from any; insteed of setting fifty pound upon the head of a highwayman, sure they would doe much better to sett a hundred upon their heads."[2] In 1712 John Gay published anonymously *The Mohocks. A Tragi-Comical Farce. As it was Acted near the Watch-House in Covent-Garden. By Her Majesty's Servants. Printed for Bernard Lintott. 8vo.* Contemporary literature teems with allusions to these blackguards, but it were impertinent to follow the chronicle of street rowdies further,[3] to pursue it until the days of Tom and Jerry and their brushes with the Charlies, to the spring-tide of the gay lads in *London Assurance*, and the period of Nicholas Nickleby when Miss Petowker thought it very aristocratic for Lords to " break off door-knockers and beat policemen, and play at coaches with other people's money, and all that sort of thing." I suppose the last pale reflection of street revelry may be seen on University Boat Race Night in London, or at some season of special jollity at Oxford and Cambridge, but the boys to-day have milk in their veins not red blood, a reflection which seems strange in the mouth of an eremetical and rigid old Victorian like myself. With regard to the Scowrers one may recall scenes in Shadwell's own *Miser* and *The Woman-Captain*. A band of Scowrers, shouting " Hay, hay, scour, scour," rescue Ramble from the Watch at the end of Act II of Crowne's *The Countrey Wit* and " *All go off scuffling and roaring*," and in the same author's *The English Frier; or, The Town Sparks*, we have Young Ranter, Old Ranter, and Dullman who enter with " *Bullies, Whores, Fiddlers; the Fiddlers playing, the rest singing and dancing*." Beaugard's Father in that capital comedy by Otway *The Atheist*, when disguised as a fanatic preacher, rebukes Daredevil for " Drunkenness, and burning of Houses; thy Whoredoms and Adulteries; Blasphemy, and Profaneness; thy Swearing, and Forswearing; thy rubbing out Milk-scores and lamb-blacking of Signs in *Covent-Garden;* thy breaking of Windows, killing Constables and Watchmen, Beadles, Taylors, Hackney-Coachmen and Link-boys." In Mountfort's *Greenwich-Park*, III, 4, Sir Thomas Reveller describes a watch-man as " a Midnight Rakehell-Driver, that has crack'd more skulls, than ever Pavier thump'd Flints; there's not a Scowrer of any Reputation, whose facetious Noddle

---

[1] Cf. Gay, *Trivia*, III, 326, etc.

> How matrons, hoop'd within the hogshead's womb,
> Were tumbled furious thence.

[2] *Wentworth Papers*, 1883, pp. 277–78.

[3] For the Mohocks see *inter alia, The Town-Rake; or, The Frolicks of the Mohocks or Hawkubites*, 1712; *The Spectator*, No. 324 (Steele), Wednesday, 12 March, 1712; No. 347 (Budgell) Tuesday, 8 April, 1712, and *passim;* Ashton's *Social Life in the Reign of Queen Anne*.

has not had the Honour of being dub'd with his Quarterſtaff." Sir John Vanbrugh in *The Provok'd Wife* has shown us Sir John Brute scowring Covent Garden with Lord Rake, Colonel Bully and their gang. In Mrs. Behn's poſthumous comedy *The Younger Brother ; or, The Amorous Jilt,* Sir Merlin sings " *a Song in praise of a Rake-hell's Life,*" [1] which pretty plainly details the amusements of a Scowrer who, when he has taken his three flasks at the Rose,

> *At Houses of Pleasure breaks Windows and Doors ;*
> *Kicks Bullies and Cullies, then lies with their Whores.*
> *Rare work for the Surgeon, and Midwife he makes.*
> *What Life can compare with the Jolly Town-Rake's ?*

Many another example from play and poem describing these rowdy royſtering gallants might be quoted, but in truth the piĉture which Shadwell has drawn is as complete as any.

The Scowrers is a comedy of well-suſtained intrigue and incident, and as an exaĉt representation of certain phases of contemporary life it can hardly fail extremely to have diverted the audience. Although Sir Richard Maggot is made no wiser than the Mayor of Banbury, who would prove that Henry III. was before Henry II., perhaps politics are not unduly ſtressed. At any rate, D'Urfey the loyaliſt, who in 1682 was satirizing the Whigs and lampooning Shadwell himself as the unprincipled Sir Barnaby, in 1689 had very roughly attacked the Tories in his *Love for Money ; or, The Boarding-School,*[2] so that in some quarters this comedy met with an Arĉtic reception ; indeed, by a considerable party it was much hissed, and when it came to be printed the author had to defend himself in his Preface from these censures, for which, in truth, there was only too obvious ground, and it muſt be allowed that the plea he so ingenuously puts forward fails to convince.

Langbaine says, I believe truly, that *The Scowrers* is " wholly free from *Plagiary,*" and although the *Biographia Dramatica* will have it that Eugenia is copied from Harriet in *The Man of Mode,* for my part I do not imagine that there was any such borrowing, since it is but natural that the portraits of two witty and lively young ladies should have a good deal in common, juſt as Lady Maggot might be said to resemble other cursed and scolding shrews who with their sharp tongues rattle up the scenes of many an amusing play.

During the following year, 1691, Shadwell was in ill health and capable of very little exertion. Always of a full habit and corpulent, a faĉt of which

---

[1] Written by Motteux.

[2] 4to, 1691. D'Urfey says that he wrote the play in June, 1689, and it was probably performed in the winter of that year.

his opponents did not fail to make fine capital in their satires,[1] but which he rather boasted as marking even a physical resemblance to his idol, Ben Jonson, by now Shadwell had grown exceeding gross, mountain-bellied, and unwieldy. His prolonged sickness of a year or two before seems completely to have broken down his health, and he also began to suffer from frequent and violent attacks of gout. Since he could rarely stir from the house men came to seek him at home, and among his many visitors was an Irish divine, Nicholas Brady, with whom he became very intimate. Brady was born at Bandon, Cork, 28 October, 1659. Being sent to England at the early age of twelve, he matriculated at Christ Church, Oxford, 4 February, 1678-9; and proceeded B.A. in Michaelmas Term, 1682. Upon his return three years later he graduated B.A. and M.A. at Dublin, and was ordained in 1688, when he obtained several fat preferments, and amongst other advancements was appointed Chaplain to the Duke of Ormonde. Being an enthusiastic adherent of the Whigs, when William and Mary obtained the throne he came to London, as an official representative of the Orange party, to present them with an address, desiring certain compensations. As he had already made several essays in poetry it was of course natural that whilst in London he should seek the acquaintance of the Poet Laureate, whose views, both political and religious, so nearly coincided with his own. The warm recommendation of the Duke of Ormonde was enough and more than enough freely to open to him Shadwell's house, and before long a very close friendship was struck up between the two. Brady did not return to Ireland, as he attracted considerable attention by his eloquence in the pulpit, and was appointed as a lecturer in S. Michael's, Wood Street. On 10 July, 1691, he was instituted to the rectorship of S. Catherine Cree (or Christ) Church, which is on the north side of Leadenhall Street, in Aldgate Ward, London.[2] After

---

[1] Cf. *Mac Flecknoe*, 195-6 :

> A Tun of Man in thy large Bulk is writ,
> But sure thou'rt but a Kilderkin of wit.

And *Absalom and Achitophel*, II., 457 :

> Now stop your noses, Readers, all and some,
> For here's a tun of Midnight work to come,
> *Og* from a Treason Tavern rowling home.
> Round as a Globe, and Liquored ev'ry chink,
> Goodly and Great he Sayls behind his Link ;
> Withall this Bulk there's nothing lost in *Og*,
> For ev'ry inch that is not Fool is Rogue :
> A Monstrous mass of foul corrupted matter,
> As all the Devils had spew'd to make the batter.

[2] The present edifice was consecrated by Archbishop Laud (when Bishop of London), 16 January, 1630-1. Stow tells us that the old church was built on the cemetery of the priory of the Holy Trinity, an Augustinian foundation.

a long career, during which he held several good livings and was chaplain to William and Mary and Queen Anne, Brady died 20 May, 1726, at Richmond, Surrey, of which place he was rector, and is buried there in the parish church of S. Mary Magdalene.

In his desk Brady when he came to London had some scenes of a tragedy, which he showed to the Laureate, and received the warmest persuasion to proceed with them. When they were completed during the autumn of 1690, Shadwell with every encouragement sent the script of the play to Drury Lane, assuring his friend that it would not be long before it was acted. The period of the piece is somewhere roughly in the fifth century, or the earlier part of the sixth, the characters are Goths and Vandals, and Shadwell, who had gone so far as to discuss the costumes, decided that the dresses should be those pseudo-classical habits and Roman mantles which the theatrical convention of the day dictated for these remoter histories. To his surprise the actors did not exhibit that interest which Shadwell thought his good word should have secured. No doubt Dryden, though covertly, was still a power in the theatre, and as both governors and actors were very much guided by his advice, although a play by Shadwell himself must be readily accepted, they did not consider themselves called upon to be equally complacent with regard to his protégé. In any case several weeks passed, and after the impatient Laureate had once or twice reminded Thomas Davenant of the matter he began to feel bitterly aggrieved and wrote in so peremptory a strain that Davenant angrily replied that if the play were to be acted at all it must wait its time, whilst as for costumes they would have to be content with what was already in the wardrobe, certainly no new dresses would be provided. To make matters worse, Mrs. Barry, who had only been disposed to take her rôle since she had been informed that the production would be with splendid scenes and newly dressed, threw up her part, whereupon Davenant in a rage curtly told Shadwell that he was not going to bother his head any more about the play. We can well understand the intense mortification of the elder dramatist in being so slighted and that before a younger man, hsi friend, to whom he had boasted of his power in the world theatrical. He at once wrote to the supreme arbiter in these matters, but Dorset, as might have been expected, was exceedingly full of business, and did not immediately reply, so before many days Shadwell followed up his letter with yet a second appeal.

My Ld
I wrott a complaint to y^r Lp against ye players & governers and again I renew it and humbly beg if y^u ever had any favour for mee to right mee in it by commanding that ye Innocent Impostors bee the next new play to bee acted. I would have had it acted in Roman habits and then wth a

Mantle to have coverd her hips Mrs Barry would have acted ye part but Tho Davenant has with a great slight turnd mee of and sayes he will trouble himself noe more about ye play : I beseech y^u my Ld bee pleasd to favour the Auther and mee. they have putt Durfeys play before ours and this day a play of Drydens is read to them and that is to bee acted before ours too.[1] I never was soe much concerned in any thing in my life or soe much surprisd at ill usage when I deserve none but good pray pardon mee that I putt yr Lp in mind of this once more for this is ye onely time to right.

Chelsea Jan 19
    91

        My Ld
            y^r L^{ps} most obliged
                humble Servt
                  Tho Shadwell.

Mr Cooling knows this to
    have been practisd by y^r Lps predecessours and I have twice his bond against mee in a contest between Mr Crown and mee twice.

This missive had the desired effect, and Dorset sent Thomas Davenant an enjoinder requiring that Brady's tragedy should be put in train for production. Such a command was not to be disputed, although even so the resentful Thespians contrived all sorts of subtle shifts and delays—no season could be worse than Lent for an important production—and it was not until some weeks after Easter that the piece came upon the stage. On 2 May, 1692, Shadwell writes from Chelsea to Lord Dorset, sending a copy of *The Rape*[2] for his patron's acceptance. Incidentally it will be noted he complains of a sad attack of the gout, which was flying about his system.

For ye Ld Chamberlain
    at ye Cockpitt
        Whitehall.

My Ld
    I should have presented this play of Mr Brady's to y^r Lp but I am layd up with a very painfull fitt of the Gout : I told him w^t you commanded mee when last you did mee the honour to see mee at my house viz that you would get him a turn to preach at Court which has been the occasion of a letter of thanks to yr Lp. I hope yr Lp has read over my comeedy and I should bee very glad to heare of my faults in time if I were able to wait on yr Lp. bee pleasd to order yr servant to deliver it to

---

[1] The two plays which Shadwell complains had been so signally preferred were D'Urfey's *The Marriage-Hater Match'd*, produced in January 1691-2 ; and Dryden's *Cleomenes, The Spartan Heroe*.

[2] *Term Catalogues*, Trinity (June), 1692. The quarto is dedicated in grateful strain to Dorset.

Know all men by these presents that revookeing
all other wills & Testiments whatsoever by mee
formerly made I doe declare and oppoint this
to bee my last will and Testament in manner
and forme following. Imprimis I desire to bee
buried in flannell wth the least charge that may
bee. Item I give and bequeath to yᵉ Earl of Dorsett
Sr Charles Sedley, William Jephson Esq and Coll
Edmund Ashton my most deare friends by whom
I have been extreamly obliged and to each of
them one Ring of Gold weighing twenty shillings
wth this motto. Memor esto tui:
Item I give one ring to my Mother at the discretion of my Executrix as to yᵉ price wth yᵉ same
motto
Item I give to my son John five pounds for
mourning and my latine & philosophicall bookes
wth mr Hobbes workes warning him to have
a care of some ill opinions of his concerning
government but hee may make excellent use of
what is good in him I doe allsoe charge and comand
my sayd son to bee obedient to his mother.

Item I doe by these presents constitute and appoint
my dearly beloved wife Ann ye daughter of Tho
Gibbs late of Norwich deceased proctor and publick
notary my Executrix of my last will and Testamt
above declared to whom I give and bequeath
my lease of two tenements holden by mee in Dorset
Garden alias Salisbury Court in London by the Theatre
as allsoe yᵉ rent I purchased of yᵉ Lady Davenant
and mr Cave Underhill issuing out of yᵉ sayd
proffitts of the sayd Theatre viz out of yᵉ sayd Lady
Davenants & Cave Underhills several proportions
of Rent for yᵉ sayd Theatre Item I give and bequeath
to my sd Executrix all mony and summes of mony of
whatsoever putt out upon mortgage bond or any
other way and all my interest in annuall rents

or houses whatsoever: Item, I give and bequeath
to my sd Executrix all my plate and houshold stuff
and all my goods and chattells whatsoever as
I have declared in a deed intrust for her & Charles
Sedley and William Jephson Esqs being her trustees in ye
deed mentioned

Lastly I give my sd Executrix all ye money goods and
chattells which I shall dye possest of or wch shall bee
due to mee at ye time of my death intreating her
to preserve all for my children after her death as I
doubt not but shee will haveing been a diligent carefull
and provident woman and very indulgent to her
children as ever I knew for wch reason I intrust
her wth ye disposall of what I shall leave behind
mee to my children in what proportions shall
please her but principally recommend my poore
little daughter Ann the greatest comfort to mee of
all my children to her particular care wch I doubt
not but shee will not employ to ye utmost in her education
I desire her to pay my just debts & performe this
my last will to wch I have sett my hand & seale
this

                                                Thomas Shadwell

Declared signd
and seald in ye
presence of

Anthony Leigh

Richard Guilford

Ellenor Leigh

Probatu London Coram venli viro Dno
Thoma Pinfold Milite Legu Dtore Surroge-
dcimo tertio die mensis Decembris Anno
Dni 1692 Justo Anna Shadwell Relicta
Relcea et Extrix &c &c &c &c Jurat

13 Decemb: 1692

Which Day appeared personally Ellianor Leigh
(wife of Anthony Leigh of the parish of St Bridgett
als Brides London Gent) And deposed upon the
holy Evangelists That she was present when Mr
Thomas Shadwell did ~~signe~~ seigne and execute his
                    in his owne house at Chelsea
last Will and Testament, begining thus, Know all
men by these presents that , And ending thus,
To which I have sett my hand and Seale this,
Which was betweene Bartholomew=tide and Michaelmas 1690. And this she doth the better remember
because that she tooke Lodgings at Chelsea some
few dayes before Bartholomew-tide in the yeare
1690. and left the said Lodgings at Michaelmas
following, And she further deposed that the said
~~Deced~~ was at such his ~~being in~~ sealeing and
publishing his said Will of perfect mind and
memory and did soe execute his said Will
in the presence of this Deponent, her said husband
Anthony Leigh, and Richard Guilford who all
subscribed their names as witnesses to the said
Will in the presence of the said Thomas Shadwell
deced.

Ellenor Leigh

Eodem die.
Dicta Ellianora Leigh
jurata fuit
coram me

Jno: Pinfold Esqr.

the Bookkeeper or when one from him call for it : Ther is a very foolish omission befor this dedication of Mr Bradys to yr Lp of yr Titles but I doubt not but yr Lp will forgive it since I am sure hee that dedicates it wants noe respect to you

I am
My Ld
yʳ Lps
Most obligd humble
sevᵗ
Tho Shadwell

Chelsea May 2
1692

In compliment to his friend, Shadwell had himself penned the Epilogue, and he was able to secure that the leading actors should support the production. Betterton and his wife, Joseph Williams—Smith, upon a certain disgust, had retired, not to return until three years later [1]—Charlotte Butler, Shadwell's own friend, Mrs. Elinor Leigh, and the fascinating Anne Bracegirdle, to whom was entrusted the delivery of the Epilogue, were all in the cast. The piece was, as it indeed deserved, accorded a very favourable reception.

The plot is complicated, but not inextricably so, and it does not lack interest. The Vandals wellnigh twenty years before have conquered the Goths, and as the play opens King Gunderic, acted by Betterton,

> fights o're his Battels
> Of 20 Years, and numbers all his Conquests ;
> Whilst the base Herd of Fawning Courtiers screw
> Their servile Looks to seeming Admiration,
> And cry him up a second *Alexander*.

Being anxious for a son, Gunderic had sworn to destroy his next child if a girl, whereupon his Queen Amalzontha (Mrs. Betterton) in terror brought up Elisimonda as a boy, Agilmond (Mrs. Butler). The Queen of the Goths, Rhadegonda (Mrs. Leigh), to save the life of her son Ambiomer, has educated him as a girl, Valdaura, acted by young Michael Leigh. King Gunderic intends to secure the obedience of the Goths by giving Agilmond in marriage to Eurione (Mrs. Bracegirdle), Rhadegonda's daughter. Genselaric, Gunderic's nephew (Joseph Williams), one night ravishes Eurione in an arbour, when she has been walking in the gardens of the palace.[2] Agilmond's dagger, which had been accidentally dropped near

---

[1] At the instance of Betterton and Mrs. Barry this admirable actor came back to the boards to create Scandal in *Love for Love*, produced at Lincoln's Inn Fields, 30 April, 1695.

[2] For the circumstance of the rape one may remember that fine drama *The Queene of Corinth*, in which Fletcher is now generally thought to have been aided by Massinger, but although Brady doubtless knew the play there is, I think, no conscious plagiarism.

the spot, is found, and so it is presumed it is he who has forcibly enjoyed the princess. Queen Rhadegonda assembles the Goths and reveals that Valdaura is in truth her son. When Agilmond comes to visit Eurione he is detained as a prisoner, and meanwhile Valdaura appears as Ambiomer, King of the Goths, entrenched in the citadel. The Vandal hosts are quickly marshalled, but when Gunderic advances at their head Ambiomer from the ramparts threatens :

>   soon as your Forces
> Attempt our Strength, the Head of *Agilmond*,
> Reeking with Blood, shall be thrown over to you !
> And the first hour of your Assault shall be
> His last of life.

Mad with rage Gunderic retorts :

>   Perish ten thousand Sons,
> Rather than I'll endure Affronts like these :
> Though *Agilmond* should fall, my Noble Vengance
> Shall, like another Son, keep up my Fame,
> And make my Name Immortal.

A piercing shriek from the Queen attracts all eyes. Throwing herself upon her knees she confesses that Agilmond is a woman :

>   *Agilmond* is not
> What he appears, nor could commit a Rape
> On fair *Eurione*.

Genselaric is discovered to be " the Actor of this horrid Rape," and meets his fate at the hand of Ambiomer. Eurione, in shame refusing to live, stabs herself

> Since nothing more is to be lost or gained ;
> My Honour gone, and my Revenge obtain'd.

The nuptials of Ambiomer and Elisimonda unite Goths and Vandals in firmest friendship.

The Rape ; or, The Innocent Impostors is a good tragedy, and I conceive that with strong acting it could be singularly impressive.

It was revived with some alterations, the Vandals and Goths being turned into Spaniards and Portuguese, at Lincoln's Inn Fields 25 November, 1729. Quin, Lacy Ryan, Boheme, Walker, Chapman, Mrs. Younger, Mrs. Buchanan, and Mrs. Bullock, were the principals of an exceptionally brilliant cast.

During the summer and autumn of 1692 Shadwell was occupied with the composition of a new comedy, which as events proved did not appear upon the stage until after his death. *The Volunteers ; or, The Stock-Jobbers* was in full rehearsal and indeed upon the eve of production early in November. Shadwell had for many months been suffering very acutely, since although only just turned fifty years of age, in his youth he had made such terrible inroads upon his constitution, of the hardiest and most robust as it was, by his profligacy and potations[1] in the reckless company of the wits of King Charles's day, that now past excesses began to take a terrible toll of his health, spirits, and vitality. The pain which he endured induced periods of deep depression, and in order to alleviate his gout he had even more frequent and copious recourse than before to the palliative of opium, to which apparently he had been long and notoriously addicted, since ten years ago Dryden in that scathing portrait contained in the Second Part of *Absalom and Achitophel* published 10 November, 1682, wrote with mordant censure :

> Thou art of lasting Make, like thoughtless men,
> A strong Nativity—but for the Pen ;
> Eat Opium, mingle Arsenick in thy Drink,
> Still thou mayst live, avoiding Pen and Ink.

It is noticeable that other accusations Shadwell traverses with scorn, even such a harmless and half-meant jest as attributing to him an Irish origin, but the blame of being a votary of the poppied sedative, which one might have well thought he would have repudiated, he was never at the trouble to contradict, and we may be very certain that he would loudly have disputed this allegation had it not been too well founded and too widely known for any denial to be either possible or accredited. As we might suppose, Shadwell latterly found himself obliged to increase his narcotic doses, although he fully realized that he was running immediate and very considerable risk each time he had recourse to this medicine. On the morning of 20 November, 1692, after an unusually severe bout of pain, he had recourse to the opium for the last time, for he absorbed so exceptional a quantity of the drug that when some hours later his wife and attendant entered the room it was found he had passed away in his sleep. The loss of her husband only three years after their fortune had taken a stable turn for the better, and when their position seemed secured by his appointment as Poet Laureate, must have been a terrible blow to Anne

---

[1] Cf. *A Session of the Poets, circa* 1682, where when Shadwell claims recognition—

> *Apollo* well pleas'd with so bonny a lad,
> To oblige him, he told him, he should be huge glad,
> Had he half so much wit as he fancied he had.
> However, to please so jovial a wit,
> And to keep him in humour, *Apollo* thought fit
> To bid him drink on, and to keep his old trick
> Of railing at poets, and——.

Shadwell. He was buried at S. Luke's,[1] old Chelsea Church, four days later, on 24 November, and a devout and eloquent sermon was preached upon that occasion by Dr. Nicholas Brady, but no monument has been erected to the Laureate who is interred within those sacred walls.

The matter was debated, but upon consideration there did not appear sufficient reason to postpone the production of *The Volunteers*, indeed there was very ample cause why the piece should be given forthwith, since were it fortunate Mrs. Shadwell would notably benefit by the fees accruing therefrom, especially the receipts of the third day. The prologue which the author himself was known to have written, could not at the moment be found among his papers, and so the facile D'Urfey quickly supplied an appropriate substitute to be spoken by Mrs. Bracegirdle,[2] whilst the epilogue was delivered " by one in deep Mourning." In the cast were Shadwell's friends Anthony Leigh and his wife. Both had excellent parts, and probably Major-General Blunt was the last of Leigh's original rôles, for " upon the unfortunate death of Mountfort, Leigh fell ill of a fever, and died in a week after him, in December, 1692." [3]

The Volunteers is a capital comedy, and shows no falling off in Shadwell's powers. His observation of the life round about him is as acute, and his picture of contemporary follies is as clear cut, as in the jolly old days of *A True Widow* and *The Woman-Captain*. Perhaps some of the scenes between Hackwell Junior, his friend Welford, Eugenia and Clara, are a little inclined to dawdle, but here was always Shadwell's weakness. On the other hand, Colonel Hackwell and his wife, the old Cavalier Officer and his comrades, who fall out because one says that fifty years since " he was nearer being hang'd for Plots . . . and more, and better Plots than any other man in the company, are superlatively well done, whilst the two beaux afford some extremely amusing scenes. That the comedy did not keep a place in the usual repertory was no doubt owing to the death of Leigh, but when it was revived in 1711, " Not acted these Twenty Years," it seems to have been received with considerable favour, although, of course, the more topical hits had by that time lost much of their piquancy and point.

Shortly before Shadwell's death he had been paid his salary as Laureate and Historiographer Royal, £300; and, as we have already noticed, this salary was generously bestowed upon his executors for the year following his decease. Some little difficulty arose about his will—drawn up two years previously—which was undated, but on 3 December, 1692, appeared

---

[1] This edifice of red brick and stone dates from the fourteenth century. The Blessed Thomas More added a chapel to the church, which was extensively repaired between the years 1667 and 1671.

[2] Who created Clara.

[3] Colley Cibber, *Apology*, c. v.

INTRODUCTION

Ellenor [1] Leigh, wife of Anthony Leigh, of S. Bride's, London, Gent., and made oath that she was present when Mr. Thos. Shadwell did seal and execute his will in his own house at Chelsea, some time between Bartholomew Tide and Michaelmas, 1690, for that she took lodgings at Chelsea at Bartholomew Tide and left the same at Michaelmas aforesaid. "Probate granted the same day (3 December, 1692), to Anne Shadwell, widow and relict, the sole executrix." [2] Shadwell's last will and testament, which he wrote out fair with his own hand, is as follows :

Know all men by these presents that revoaking all other wills & Testaments whatsoever by mee formerly made I doe declare and appoint this to bee my last will and Testament in manner and forme following : Imprimis I desire to bee buried in flannell wth the least charge that may bee. Item I give and bequeath to ye Earl of Dorsett Sr Charles Sedley William Jephson Esqr and Coll Edmund Ashton my most deare friends by whom I have been extreamly obliged and to each of them one Ring of Gold weighing twenty shillings wth this Motto Memor esto tui :

Item I give one ring to my Brother at the discretion of my Executrix as to ye price wth ye same Motto.

Item I give to my son John five pounds for mourning and my latine & philosophicall bookes wth Mr Hobbes his workes warning him to have a care of some ill opinions of his concerning government but hee may make excellent use of what is good in him. I doe allsoe charge and comand my sayd Son to bee obedient to his Mother.

Item I doe by these presents constitute and appoint my dearely beloved wife Ann ye Daughter of Tho Gibbs late of Norwich deceased proctor and publick Notary my Executrix of my last will and testam^t Above

[1] This is how she spelled her own name. See her signature affixed to Shadwell's will. She has mistakenly been called Mrs. Elizabeth Leigh, and in the printed cast of Porter's *The French Conjuror*, 4to, 1678, she appears as Mrs. Eliz. Leigh, an error which perhaps gave rise to this inexactitude.

[2]   3, December 1692.
Which day appeared personally Ellianor Leigh (wife of Anthony Leigh of the Parish of St. Bridgett als Brides London Gent) and deposed upon the Holy Evangelists that she was present when Mr Thomas Shadwell did seale and execute his last will and testament in his owne house at Chelsea beginning thus Know all men by these presents that and ending thus To wch I have sett my hand and seale this which was betweene Bartholomew Tide and—Michaelmass 1690 and this shee doth the better remember because that shee tooke lodgeings at Chelsea some few dayes before Bartholomew Tide in the said yeare 1690 and left the said lodgings at Michaelmas following And she further deposes that the said deceased was at such his sealeing and publishing his said will of perfect mind and memory and did soe execute his said will in the presence of this deponent her said husband Anthony Leigh and Richard Guilford who all subscribed their names as witnesses to the said will in the presence of the said Thomas Shadwell deceased—ELLENOR LEIGH Eodom die dicta Ellianora Leigh Jurata fuit Coram un^d —THO PINFOLD Surr.
Proved December 3rd 1692.

INTRODUCTION

declared, to whom I give and bequeath my lease of two tenements holden by mee in Dorset Garden alias Salisbury Court in London by the Theatre as alsoe yᵉ rent I purchased of yᵉ Lady Davenant and Mr Cave Underhill issuing out of yᵉ Dayly proffitts of the sayd Theatre. viz out of yᵉ sayd Lady Davenants & Cave Underhills severall proportions of Rent for yᵉ sayd Theatre Item I give and bequeath to my Sᵈ Executrix all mony and summes of money whatsoever putt out upon mortgage bond or any other way and all my interest in annuall rents or houses whatsoever: Item, I give and bequeath to my Sᵈ Executrix all my plate and household stuffe and all my goods and chattells whatsoever as I have declared in a deed in trust for her Sʳ Charles Sedley and William Jephson Esqre being her trustees in tᵗ deed mentioned.

Lastly I give my Sᵈ Executrix all yᵉ money goods and chattells which I shall dye possessd' of or wᶜʰ shall bee due to mee at yᵉ time of my death intreating her to reserve all for my children after her death as I doubt not but shee will haveing been a diligent carefull and provident Woman and very indulgent to her children as ever I knew for wᶜʰ reason I intrust her with yᵉ disposall of what I shall leave behind mee to my children in what proportions shall please her but principally I recommend my poore little daughter Ann the greatest comfort to mee of all my children to her particular care wᶜʰ I doubt not but shee will Employ to yᵉ utmost in her education I desire her to pay my just debts & performe this my last will to wᶜʰ I have sett my hand & seale this

Thomas Shadwell
(L S)

Declared signd' and seald' in yᵉ presence of Anthony Leigh Richard Guildford Ellenor Leigh.

It will be noticed that even at the last Shadwell did not forget to express his gratitude to his " most deare friends " and constant patrons the Earl of Dorset and Sir Charles Sedley. William Jephson, who is co-trustee with Sedley for the widow, had been Secretary to the Treasury, but pre-deceased the testate, for he died on 7 June, 1691.[1] A close companion of Buckingham, Rochester, and the Restoration rakes, he was a figure of considerable importance, an official with whom Etherege, when Resident at Ratisbon,[2] was careful to maintain a correspondence. We hear of him in connexion with riot and rowdiness at Epsom in the summer of 1676. On 29 June of that year Charles Hatton wrote to his brother: " Mʳ Downs is dead. Yᵉ Lᵈ Rochester doth abscond, and soe doth Etheridge,

[1] Luttrell, II, 242, in June, 1691, says: " The 7th, William Jephson, esq., secretary to the Lords of the treasury, died."

[2] At which town he arrived in November, 1685, and whence he took his departure in 1689.

and Cap[t] Bridges who ocasioned y[e] riot Sunday sennight."[1] A letter written on the same day by John Verney,[2] adds further particulars : " Mr. Downes, who (with Lord Rochester, Mr. William Jepson, and Geo. Etheridge) skirmisht the watch at Epsom 12 days since, died last Tuesday of his hurts received from the rustics." In a letter to Will Richards, Etherege writes from Ratisbon : " I have heard of the success of y[e] Eunuch,[3] and am very glad the Town has so good a tast to give the same just applause to S[r] Charles Sidley's writing, w[ch] his friends have always done to his conversation ; few of our plays can boast of more wit than I have heard him speak at a supper.[4] Some baren sparks have found fault with what he has formerly done on this occasion onely because the fatness of the soile has produc'd to big a Crop. I dayly drink his health, my Lord Dorsets, Mr. Jepsons, Charles Godfreys, your own & all our friends."[5]

Colonel Edmund Ashton was one of Shadwell's oldest intimates. In 1671, and no doubt often before and after, he was the host of the poet at Chadderton Hall, his seat near Oldham, comitatu Lancaster. As we have noticed before he was a Lieutenant-Colonel in the Horse Guards, and had acted as a Gentleman of the Bedchamber to the Duke of York. On 5 July, 1673, Sir Charles Sedley had been accepted as a good " surety " for Ashton, then " Receiver of Hearth-money " for the County of Lancashire.[6] At the time of Shadwell's death he was five and forty years of age.

Ellenor Leigh, who had witnessed Shadwell's will and came forward to make her affidavit, was an actress of the very first rank in her own line, and during the long period of nearly forty years that she was upon the stage she filled an immense number of parts. Colley Cibber, having spoken of the famous comedian Anthony Leigh, says : " Mrs. Leigh, the wife of Leigh already mentioned, had a very droll way of dressing the pretty foibles of superannuated beauties. She had, in herself, a good deal of humour, and knew how to infuse it into the affected mothers, aunts and modest ladies ; the coquette prude of an aunt, in Sir Courtly Nice, who prides herself on her beauty, at fifty ; and the languishing Lady Wishfort, in The Way of the World. In all these, with many others, she was extremely entertaining, and painted, in a lively manner." Mrs. Eliz. Leigh (an error)

---

[1] Hatton Correspondence, 1878, I, 133–4.
[2] To Edmund Verney. Historical MSS. Commission. Appendix to Seventh Report, p. 457b.
[3] Sedley's Bellamira ; or, The Mistress, produced at Drury Lane in May, 1687.
[4] From the Dedication, 16 February, 1678–9, of A True Widow, 4to, 1679, to Sir Charles Sedley : " My Comedies have had his [Sedley's] Approbation, whom I have heard speak more Wit at a Supper, than all my Adversaries, with their Heads joyn'd together, can write in a Year." It may be noted that Etherege for his expressions here borrows from Shadwell, who has been too often accused of plagiarizing She wou'd if she cou'd and The Man of Mode.
[5] Letter Book, 23 May/2 June '87 : f. 94 b.
[6] Col. Treasury Papers, IV (1672–5), p. 367.

stands to Scintillia in Porter's *The French Conjuror*, produced at Dorset Garden in 1677, and in Betterton's comedy *The Revenge; or, A Match in Newgate*, which was produced at Dorset Garden in 1680, she appears in the printed cast as Mrs. A. Lee. It is possible only to give a very few of her more famous rôles, among which were Beatrice, a waiting-woman in Ravenscroft's *The Careless Lovers*, March, 1672–3; Isabella, Christina's maid in Crowne's *The Countrey Wit*, January, 1675–6; Lady Woodvil in Etherege's *The Man of Mode*, March of the same year; Moretta, the Courtezan's woman, in Mrs. Behn's *The Rover; or, The Banish'd Cavaliers*, 1677; Paulina, a rich Widow, in Maidwell's *The Loving Enemies*, autumn of 1679; Tournon's in Nat Lee's *The Princess of Cleve*, 1681; Engine, Arabella's woman, in Ravenscroft's *The London Cuckolds*, November of the same year; Mrs. Closet in Mrs. Behn's *The City Heiress; or, Sir Timothy Treat-all*, spring of 1682; Mrs. Prudence in Ravenscroft's *Dame Dobson; or, The Cunning Woman*, during the autumn of 1683; the Aunt, " an old, Amorous, envyous Maid," in *Sir Courtly Nice; or, It Cannot Be*, 1685; Clara, Erminia's woman, in Southerne's second play, *The Disappointment; or, The Mother in Fashion*, in the winter of 1689; Oyley in D'Urfey's *Love for Money; or, The Boarding-School;* and Johayma, Chief Wife to the Mufti, in Dryden's *Don Sebastian, King of Portugal;* in December of that year; Lady Pinch-gut, a rich covetous widow, in Crowne's *The English Frier; or, The Town Sparks*, in the spring of 1690; in the winter of the same year Lady Maggot in Shadwell's *The Scowrers;* Rhadegonda, in Brady's *The Rape; or, The Innocent Impostors*, April, 1692; in November–December, 1692, Mrs. Hackwell in *The Volunteers; or, The Stock-Jobbers;* Lucy in *The Old Batchelour*, January, 1693; and a few weeks later Siam, an Indian woman (one who keeps a house for Oriental goods, china, silk, teas, and the like), in Southerne's *The Maid's Last Prayer; or, Any, Rather than Fail;* and also Marmalette, An old ridiculous Waiting-woman . . . very desirous of a Husband, and contriving all she can to get one, in D'Urfey's *The Richmond Heiress; or, A Woman Once in the Right;* in March of the same year Mrs. Sneaksby, " A Woman of an Eternal Tongue," in George Powell's *A Very Good Wife;* and in April, Lady Meanwell, " An imperious Wife; great Pretender to Wit," in Thomas Wright's *The Female Virtuoso's*, which is largely conveyed from *Les Femmes Savantes;* early in November, 1693, Lady Plyant in *The Double-Dealer;* in February, 1693–4, the Nurse to Biron, in Southerne's great tragedy, *The Fatal Marriage; or, The Innocent Adultery;* in 1694, Teresa Panza, Wife to Sancho, a silly credulous County Creature, in D'Urfey's *The Comical History of Don Quixote*, Part I (Part II the same year; in Part III, 1696, Mrs. Powell acted Teresa); in April, 1695, at Lincoln's Inn Fields, the Nurse in *Love for Love;* in the winter of that year, Plackett, " Waiting-Woman to Lady Dorimen," in *The She-Gallants*, by George Granville,

Lord Lansdowne; and Vesuvia, a woman of the town, in Dilke's *The Lover's Luck*; in 1696 Betty in Dogget Gloucestershire comedy, *The Country-Wake*; the Doctor's Wife in Ravenscroft's farce, *The Anatomist*, March, 1697; in 1697 Madam de Vandosme's maid, " a Finical Jilt," in D'Urfey's *The Intrigues at Versailles; or, A Jilt in all Humours*; in the same year Secreta, " An old Intelligencer, a Seller of Essences," in Dilke's *The City Lady; or, Folly Reclaim'd*; in 1698 Sweetny, " Sister to *Nickycrack*; a Boarding-Landlady. A fawning dissembling Hypocrite, pretending to much Piety and Devotion; " in the same author's *The Pretenders; or, The Town Unmaskt*; in 1700 Lady Wishfort in *The Way of the World*; in 1701 Lady Autumn in Burnaby's *The Ladies Visiting-Day*; and Sophia, the old Empress, in *The Czar of Muscovy*, by Mrs. Pix; and Lady Rakelove, an amorous old woman, in *The Gentlemen Cully* by Charles Johnson; in 1702 Mrs. Plotwell, in Mrs. Centlivre's *The Beau's Duel; or, A Soldier for the Ladies*; in 1703 Marama in Trapp's *Abra-Mule* and Chloris in Charles Boyle's *As You Find It*; and in November of the same year, Dromia in Burnaby's *Love Betray'd; or, The Agreeable Disappointment*; in that winter Widow Bellmont in *The Different Widows; or, Intrigue All-A-Mode*, by Mrs. Pix; in December, 1704, Lady Stale, " an affected amorous old Widow," in Rowe's solitary comedy *The Biter*, and Peeper, Mrs. Dowdy's woman, in Mrs. Centlivre's *The Platonick Lady* in November, 1706. To these rôles we must add her many parts in revivals, such as Emilia in *Othello* to the Moor of Betterton and Desdemona of Mrs. Bracegirdle [1]; Goneril in *King Lear* (Tate) to the Lear of Powell, with Verbruggen as Edgar, Husbands the Bastard, Mrs. Bowman Regan, and Mrs. Bracegirdle Cordelia; the Hostess to Betterton's Falstaff in that great actor's version of *King Henry IV*; Lady Clare in *The Merry Devil of Edmonton* (1690–1) [2]; Mrs. Day in *The Committee*; Lady Wou'd be in *Volpone*; the Aunt in Steele's *The Tender Husband*; Mrs. Sentry in *She wou'd if she cou'd*, to the Lady Cockwood of Mrs. Barry; Lady Laycock in *The Amorous Widow*; Marcellina (more probably Ardellia) in a revival of Rochester's *Valentinian*, about 1689–90 [3]; and the Bawd in *The Chances*. After 10 June, 1707, when she acted Lady Sly in Carlile's *The Fortune Hunters; or, Two Fools*

---

[1] In the British Museum copy of the 1695 4to, a contemporary hand has recorded that *Othello* was acted at the Theatre Royal, " 21 May, Fryday 1703." Othello, Betterton; Cassio, Powell; Iago, Verbruggen; Roderigo, Pack; Desdemona, Mrs. Bracegirdle; Emilia, Mrs. Lee [Leigh]. In early Restoration days Mrs. Rutter had played Emilia to the Othello of Burt; Cassio, Hart; Iago, Mohun; Roderigo, Beeston; and Desdemona, Mrs. Hughes.

[2] Betterton, Sir Ralph Jerningham; Mountfort, Raymond Mounchensey; Nokes, Sir John; Leigh, the Host; Kynaston, the warlock Fabel; Mrs. Bracegirdle, Millicent; the Abbess of Cheston, Mrs. Corey.

[3] From a MS. cast. Powell is Valentinian; Betterton Æcius; Nokes Balbus; Leigh Chylax; Mountfort Lycias; Mrs. Barry, Lucina; Mrs. Boutell, Celandia.

well Met, a rôle she had created upon the first production of this comedy at Drury Lane in the spring of 1689, her name no longer appears in the bills, and in October, 1707, Mrs. Powell, who would certainly have been her successor, is playing her parts.[1] We know that Mrs. Leigh was alive in 1709, when, with other performers, she signed a petition to Queen Anne.

We may note that after the death of her husband Mrs. Shadwell continued to reside at Chelsea, and although the actual date of her decease is not traced she was living there as late as 1710. Of her three children the daughter Anne, evidently the father's favourite and so lovingly mentioned in his will, married Anthony Oldfield. Concerning Charles Shadwell [2] little is definitely known, but the absence of his name from his father's testamentary depositions would lead one to suspect that there had been a quarrel, which unhappily was never adjusted. Charles, who in 1710 was surveyor of the excise in Kent, saw active service in Portugal, and later enjoyed a post in the revenue in Dublin, in which city he died on the 12 August, 1726. Although he had not his father's dramatic genius he was at any rate gifted with very exceptional talents in that direction. His first play *The Fair Quaker of Deal; or, The Humours of the Navy* was produced at Drury Lane on 25 February, 1710, and received with great applause.[3] Leigh acted Commodore Flip; Pack, Captain Mizen; Booth, Captain Worthy; Powell, Rovewell; Bickerstaff, Sir Charles Pleasant; Elrington, Cribbage; Mrs. Moore, Belinda; Mrs. Bradshaw, Arabella Zeal; and Miss Santlow Dorcas Zeal, in which rôle she achieved a most brilliant triumph. "I cannot," says Shadwell, "omit mentioning the extraordinary Performances of Mrs. *Bradshaw*, Mrs. *Santlow*, Mr. *Pack*, and Mr. *Leigh*, who are the only People, on the *English* Stage, that could have acted those Parts so much to the Life." [4] Shadwell concludes the Preface by saying "I am call'd in haste to my Duty in *Portugal*." In the Prologue there is the following allusion to the dramatist's father:

> *Under these Terms of Grace young* Bays *has writ,*
> *With double Title to be dubb'd a Wit,*
> *First, 'cause* Poeta nascitur, non fit.
> *From a fam'd Stock our tender* Cyon *grows,*
> *And may be Laureat too himself, who knows?*

---

[1] Mrs. Powell had acted such rôles as: Gammer Grime, a Smith's Wife in Alsatia, in Mrs. Behn's *The Luckey Chance*, produced at Drury Lane in the winter of 1686; Lady Blunder in *The Younger Brother*, Drury Lane, December, 1696; Teresa, Sancho's wife, in D'Urfey's *The Comical History of Don Quixote*, 1696 (Mrs. Leigh had created Teresa in Parts I and II); Miss Hoyden's Nurse in *The Relapse*, 1697; Bulfinch a landlady, in Farquahar's *Love and a Bottle*, 1699; old Lady Darling in *The Constant Couple*, 1699.

[2] Jacob erroneously says that he was nephew to the Poet Laureat, a mistake hardly worth notice had it not been repeated.

[3] *The Success of it has been wonderful.* Preface to the Play, 4to, 1710.

[4] *Ibid.*

INTRODUCTION

In his *Apology* Cibber tells us : "During the trial of *Sacheverel*, our audiences were extremely weakened, by the better rank of people's daily attending it : while, at the same time, the lower sort, who were not equally admitted to that grand spectacle, as eagerly crowded into Drury-lane, to a new comedy, called the *Fair Quaker of Deal*. This play, having some low strokes of natural humour in it, was rightly calculated for the capacity of the actors who played it, and to the taste of the multitude, who were now more disposed, and at leisure to see it : but the most happy incident in its fortune was the charm of the *fair Quaker*, which was acted by Miss *Santlow* (afterwards Mrs. *Booth* [1]) whose person was then in the full bloom of what beauty she might pretend to : before this she had only been admired as the most excellent dancer [2]; which, perhaps, might not a little contribute to the favourable reception she now met with, as an actress, in this character, which so happily suited her figure and capacity. The gentle softness of her voice, the composed innocence of her aspect, the modesty of her dress, the reserved decency of her gesture and the simplicity of the sentiments that naturally fell from her, made her seem the amiable maid she represented : in a word, not the enthusiastic maid of *Orleans* was more serviceable of old to the *French* army, when the *English* had distressed them, than the *fair quaker* was, at the head of that dramatic attempt, upon which the support of their weak society depended."

The Fair Quaker of Deal was very frequently revived in subsequent seasons. In 1730 at Drury Lane Mrs. Cibber was acting Dorcas, a rôle played by Mrs. Hale (Covent Garden, 1748), Mrs. Davies (Drury Lane, 1755, to the Mizen of Woodward), Miss Wilford (Covent Garden, 1766), and other favourite actresses. On 9 November, 1773, at Drury Lane an alteration by Captain Thompson, was produced and well liked. Dorcas Zeal was played by Miss Pope. The scene has been shifted from Deal to Portsmouth, and the character of Binnacle, played by Weston, is largely new. It seems that prudery dictated many changes since the adapter says " the seasoning of the original play may be too high for the palates of the present age." This version kept the stage for some ten or fifteen years.

The Humours of the Army,[3] Charles Shadwell's second comedy, was produced at Drury Lane, 29 January, 1713, and the author says : "*The Success of this Play was much beyond what the Author could expect, and as much as*

---

[1] It is said by Dennis that when this lady, who had been kept by the Duke of Marl-borough and Mr. Secretary Craggs, gave her hand to Barton Booth, the great tragedian was admonished by his friends for bestowing his name upon a strumpet, whereupon he replied with an oath : " If she be so I like her the better for it." One may remember Sir Positive's " he's a Wise Man that marries a Harlot, he's on the surest Side ; who but an Ass would marry at uncertainty ? "

[2] " Far off from these, see *Santlow*, fam'd for dance." Gay ; *Mr. Pope's welcome from Greece*.

[3] Suggested by F. Carton Dancourt's *Les Curieux de Compiègne*.

any one that writes to the Stage can hope for." [1]   He especially praises Wilks who acted Major Young Fox, and Mrs. Mountfort who played Belvedera, the Female Officer.   There is a long cast, twenty-nine characters, which entailed the whole strength of the company, Doggett, Colley Cibber, Bullock, Bowen, Booth, Mills, Powell, Pinkethman, Leigh, Bickerstaff, Bowman, Pack, Spiller, Johnson, Mrs. Knight, Mrs. Oldfield, Mrs. Porter and Mrs. Younger.   Norris and young Bullock in daggled petticoats and tattered justacorps afforded great merriment as the two trulls. The detail of Belvedera having followed Wilmot, whom she feigned to scorn, to Portugal, and disguising herself as a man, when he has enlisted, seems borrowed from *The Woman-Captain*.   Clara, her maid, attends her, in the breeches of a footman.   In the Fourth Act she drills some soldiers under the direction of Serjeant File-Off, for she has obtained a lieutenant's commission.   The scene of the play is the Camp near Elvas, and the time six hours.   The piece was revived at Drury Lane, 23 April, 1746, for Mrs. Macklin's benefit, and announced as "Not Acted 30 years."   Peg Woffington played "the Female Officer" (Belvedera), "new dress'd with an Epilogue."   Henry Brooke's [2] *The Female Officer*, a comedy [3] in two acts, is taken from the play.

When printed, 4to, 1713, it was dedicated to Major-General Newton, Governor of Londonderry.   Shadwell says : "The Honour of serving under You in *Portugal*, when You commanded the *British* Forces there, let me so far into Your Favour and Friendship, as now to beg You would take the following scenes into Your Protection as You have always done the Author of 'em."

The Merry Wives of Broad Street, a farce "by the author of *The Humours of the Navy*," was played at Drury Lane on Tuesday, 9 June, 1713.

The insistence upon "Humours" in the titles of his two comedies should be remarked.   He was thoroughly in the family tradition, and even the most casual reader could not but note that he was his father's own son. Both pieces have something of the robust quality of *A True Widow* and *Bury-Fair*, thinned, of course, and weaker, but yet distinctive and not to be mistaken.   Other dramatists, too, were following at a distance in the steps of rare Ben ; Thomas Baker, William Phillips, John Leigh, James Miller, all proclaim themselves of the "humours" school, whilst Welsted, after applauding Jonson as the one exemplar and pattern, wrote :

> Shadwell, *at Distance, the great Model Views,*
> *And with unequal Steps his Sire pursues ;*
> *But few beside the happy Mark have hit.*

---

[1] Whincop is mistaken in thinking it a failure.
[2] Died 10 October, 1783.
[3] Printed in the collected *Works*, 4 vols, 8vo, 1778.   Vol. IV.

INTRODUCTION

Charles Shadwell also wrote five pieces for the Irish stage, *The Hasty Wedding, or, The Intriguing Squire; The Sham Prince, or, News from Passau; Rotherick O'Connor, King of Connaught, or, the Distress'd Princess; The Plotting Lovers, or, The Dismal Squire;* and *Irish Hospitality, or, Vertue Rewarded.*[1] Although by no means devoid of considerable merit, they are certainly inferior to his lively English comedies. *The Hasty Wedding* and *Irish Hospitality* are good genre-pieces, which were received with favour in the theatre. *The Sham Prince*, acted in 1719, was written in five days; rehearsed and produced in ten more. It mainly owed its striking success to a recent circumstance, when a cunning impostor had deceived a number of Dublin residents and netted no mean sum from their pockets. *The Plotting Lovers* is a farce founded upon *Monsieur de Pourceaugnac*. It proves indeed to be no more than the *Squire Trelooby* of 1704, reduced to one act, and the concision is by no means an improvement. *Rotherick O'Connor* is a robustious " Buskin Tale," which was warmly greeted owing to the native theme from Irish history. The Epilogue was written by the author, but there was also provided an Epilogue by " Hercules Davis, Esq ; Design'd to have been spoke by Mr. Griffith, if all the Persons in the Play had been kill'd." It commences :

> *What, are they all destroy'd, pray look around,*
> *Can none to speak the Epilogue be found.*
> *Not one by Jove ! Hey day—Then I must try,*
> *How far will reach my Stock of Poetry.*[2]

In the Dedication of his *Collected Works*, 2 vols, 1720, to Lady Newtown, Shadwell writes : " I should say something in behalf of my Scribling Performances, but Your Ladyship knows, that it was change of Circumstances that drew me in to be a Poet, in order to help out a small Income towards the support of my Family. . . . Poetry is a Science I do not, nor dare not Value my self upon ; I may say with my Father, ' It was not a Harbour I chose, but a Rock I split upon.' "

John Shadwell, Charles' brother, was a more prominent person. On 15 May, 1685, he matriculated at Oxford from University College, whence he migrated to All Souls. He graduated B.A. on 1 June, 1689 (3 November, 1688, according to the All Souls Register); M.A. on 26 April, 1693 ; M.B. on 19 April, 1697 ; and M.D. on 5 June, 1700. His was a most distinguished career, for as physician in ordinary to Queen Anne he was created a Fellow of the College of Physicians on 22 December, 1712. On 30 November, 1701, he was elected a Fellow of the Royal Society, being

---

[1] I have used the Dublin edition, 2 vols, 1720. These include a Prologue and Epilogue, and a couple of slight songs.
[2] The hint of this may not improbably be taken from Lacy's Epilogue to Sir Robert Howard's *The Vestal Virgin ; or, The Roman Ladies*, for which see *supra*, pp. xliv–xlv.

admitted on 3 December following. He read at least one learned paper before the Society, " An Account of an Extraordinary Skeleton," *Philosophical Transactions*, 1741, xli, p. 820. He was appointed physician-extraordinary to Queen Anne on 9 November, 1709, and on 9 February, 1712, was sworn one of the physicians in ordinary in room of Dr. Martin Lister, who had died at Epsom on 2 February of that year, and was buried in Clapham Church. The famous Dr. (afterwards Sir) Hans Sloane succeeded Shadwell in his former office. The accounts of Queen Anne's illness in December, 1713–14, given in Boyer's *History of the Reign of Queen Anne*, are wholly derived from Shadwell's letters to the Duke and Duchess of Shrewsbury. Boyer has even recorded Shadwell's opinion that the cause of the Queen's death was " gouty humour translating itself upon the brain." Shadwell continued physician in ordinary to George I. and George II., and was knighted on 12 June, 1715. He long resided in Windmill Street, but in 1735 retired from practice and withdrew to France, where he remained until 1740. He died at his house in Windmill Street on 4 January, 1747. On 8 January he was interred at Bath Abbey, which fane is adorned by a monument with a somewhat rhetorical epitaph to his memory.

Sir John Shadwell was twice married, his first wife Elizabeth, daughter of Arnold Coldwall, Esq., dying on 14 April, 1722. He married, secondly, Ann Binns, daughter of Colonel John Binns, at Somerset House chapel on 12 March, 1725, and on 29 June, 1731, he made his will in her favour. Lady Shadwell survived until 1777.

In *The Gentleman's Journal* of November, 1692,[1] there appears, from the pen of Motteux, the following notice of the deceased Laureate :

" We have lately lost *Thomas Shadwell* Esquire, Poet Laureat and Historiographer Royal. His Works are so universally known, particularly his Comedies, that none can be a Stranger to his Merit ; and all those that love to see the Image of humane Nature, lively drawn in all the various Colours and Shapes with which it is diversifyed in our age, must own that few living have equall'd that admirable Master in his Draughts of Humours and Characters. 'Tis true that his greatest excellence lay in treating Comic Subjects ; yet none ought to wonder either at the Reputation or Honours it gained him : Since, that a Painter may deserve the name of Famous, it is not always necessary he should paint Lofty Palaces, and only employ

---

[1] This number must have been published after 10 December, 1692, as Mountfort died that day and immediately following the account of Shadwell is this paragraph :
" The Stage hath had another mighty Loss ; 'Tis that of Mr. *William Mountfort*, one of its best and most usefull Actors, unfortunately kill'd in his prime. As the Circumstances that caused his Death are variously reported, I shall forbear giving you an account of them : I shall only say, that if he could have given us such Comedies to which his Name is prefix'd, call'd *Greenwich-Park*, I should lament as is that loss of him almost equally in the double capacity of Author and Actor."

his Pencil to draw the Pictures of Princes and Monarchs : A homely Shed well drawn is sometimes more esteem'd, if by the hand of a good Artist, than a Marble Palace by that of a bad one ; and the Picture of a King which hath nothing to recommend it, but the Name of the Person it represents, is less admired than that of a Clown, when it wants nothing of what may cause it to be look'd upon as a good Piece. The most animated Figures of our Painters are only dumb Pictures, if compar'd with those in the Works of that Author. His Genius was inexhaustible on those sorts of matters : Neither were its Productions less usefull than diverting ; since the best way to reform us is, to lay before us our Faults ; thus observing *Horace*'s Rule ; which the Comic Glass doth often : And so, even those whose Characters he hath wrote are oblig'd to him ; for by showing the Picture of Avarice he hath sham'd Misers into Liberality ; by exposing Bullying Sparks and Prodigal Squires, he hath made the first tamer and the other wiser ; how many contented Cuckolds has he not hindred from taking their Gloves, and going out, when their Wives Gallants came in to visit them ? how many Maids hath he not sav'd from ruin by the Picture of that in others ? how many Hypocrites, Coquetts, Fops, Gamesters, has he not reclaim'd ? and in short, what store of Fools and Madmen did he not reform ? The Comedy which, as I told you, he design'd for the Stage, was acted since his decease : 'Tis call'd the *Volunteers ;* and though that Orphan wanted its Parent to support it, yet it came off with reasonable success."

There were a number of most regrettable, and even scurrilous squibs and lampoons upon the deceased Laureate. The great and dignified Dryden was, of course, silent upon the occasion, uttering neither praise nor blame, which was indeed the only correct and honourable attitude. They had been friends once, and no doubt he felt that another link with old times had snapped. Hard words, yes, even abuse had passed, but his old opponent was gone, let him rest in peace. Not so the smaller fry, who showed a more than ordinary lack of decorum. A few couplets by Tom Brown [1] may serve as sufficient, and perhaps more than sufficient, sample of many. In Obitum *T. Shadwell*, pinguis memoriae, 1693.

> Conditur hoc tumulo Bauius, grauis esse memento
> Terra tuo Bauio, nam fuit ille tibi.[2]

> Tam cito miraris Bauii foetere cadauer ?
> Non erat in toto corpore mica salis.

> Mors uni Bauio lucrum ; non iugera uates
> Qui uiuens habuit nulla, sepultus habet.

---

[1] *Works*, Vol. IV, 1744 ; pp. 92–93.
[2] This epigram was borrowed with a slight variation for Sir John Vanbrugh.

Porrigitur nouus hic Tityus per iugera septem,
  Nec quæ tondebit uiscera deerit auis.

Dicite (nam bene uos noſtis) gens critica, uates
  An fuerit Bauius peior, an Hiſtoricus.

Militiam sicco Wilelmus marte peregit,
  O clemens Cæsar ! consulis hiſtorico.

Tom writ, his readers ſtill slept o'er his book ;
For *Tom took opium*, and they opiates took.

In Tom Brown's *Works*,[1] *Miscellanies*, is also printed " *An* Impromptu *to* Shadwell's *Memory, by Dr.* B——— " :

And muſt our glorious laureat then depart !
Heaven, if it please may take his loyal heart ;
As for the reſt, sweet devil, fetch a cart.

Tom Brown seems heartily to have disliked Shadwell, for in another place he has the following ill-natured sneer : " Mr. *Shadwell*, in one of his laſt plays,[2] is so honeſt as to own that he had ſtole a few hints out of a *French* comedy, but pretends, 'twas rather out of laziness than want. This confession, inſtead of mending matters, would have hang'd him at the *Old Bailey ;* and why it should save him in *Parnassus*, I can't tell."

It was a hard fate, but perhaps we can hardly wonder, so superlative is the genius of *Mac Flecknoe*, that Shadwell's name was, absolutely without juſtification, preconized as a type of dullness and oblivion. So in *The Dunciad* Cibber apoſtrophizes his works juſt before he applies the blazing brand for their deſtruction :

Oh pass more innocent, in infant ſtate,
To the mild Limbo of our Father *Tate :*
Or peaceably forgot, at once we bless
In *Shadwell*'s bosom with eternal Reſt.

And Pope's note upon the lines is : " Two of his predecessors in the Laurel."

The faĉt is men took and continue to take their impressions from Dryden alone, they are angry with Shadwell for having dared to cross swords with the great poet, and there had been no reprint of Shadwell's works to show that although he was in truth no poet, and he had provoked his own condemnation by incurring the wrath of one of the greateſt

---

[1] Vol. IV, p. 93. The Eighth Edition, carefully correĉted, 1744.
[2] " To the Reader " before *The Miſer*, 4to, 1672 : " 'Tis not barrenness of wit or invention, that makes us borrow from the *French*, but laziness : and this was the occasion of my making use of *L'Avare*."

(ccxlvi)

names that English literature boasts, yet in his own line, as a master of realistic comedy, he had very considerable parts, and some of his characters could not have been drawn without genius. But the eighteenth century was too nice; it had very little use for realism upon the stage, in comedy at all events, and when we remember that Goldsmith's *The Good Natured Man* was voted " low," we can well imagine what treatment would have been accorded to the robuster scenes of Shadwell. Shadwell was not read, partly, as we have just pointed out, because there was no opportunity of reading his works. The edition of 1720 is negligible. It is very poorly produced, and most of the impression was destroyed in a disastrous fire.

Collier, it is true, in his *Dictionary*, Supplement (by another hand), 1705, has the following : " SHADWELL (Thomas) Esq ; was a Gentleman of a Good Family in the County of *Norfolk ;* and taking early to the Company of the Muses became a great Proficient in the Art of Poetry, and so was well received by the Noblemen of Wit, especially the present Earl of Dorset, the late Duke of *Newcastle,* &c. Mr. *Dryden* having in King *James'* time, Complied too far with that Prince's Religion, upon the Revolution in 1688, was put out from being Laureate, and Mr. *Shadwell* Preferred into his Place ; which he held till his Death, which happened, as I take it, in 1694. His Comedies, at least some of them, show him to understand Humour, and if he could have drawn the Character of a Man of Wit, as well as that of a Cockscomb, there would have been nothing wanting to the Perfection of his Dramatick Fables." There follows a list of Shadwell's plays, but this is very inaccurate, since the first item is inscribed as *The Royal Scepter,* a Tragedy, 4to, 1669, which is obviously a mistake for *The Royal Shepherdess : The Tempest* is omitted ; *The Libertine* is described as " A Comedy " ; and there are other errors.

But generally Shadwell was regarded with a distaste which was in truth founded upon prejudice and ignorance of his work, but which did not care to enlighten itself. This is marked in a clever essay which appeared in *The Gentleman's Magazine*, May, 1738.[1] In *The Apotheosis of Milton, A Vision*, the writer imagines himself present at a shadowy assembly of all the poets. The company are annoyed at the entrance of Shadwell. " Here my Conductor (who had been very justly praising *Dryden,*) was interrupted by an indignant Murmur which run through the whole company, who turned their Eyes towards the Door. Soon I preceived a bloated Figure enter, who seemed rather to be fit for a Midnight Revel, than to be a Member of that august Body. He used a thousand ridiculous Gestures, sometimes he affected a polite, easy Air, sometimes he appeared to aim at the *French* Grimace; but all was forced, unnatural, and ungraceful, soon he relapsed into his *Bacchanalian* Fits, and it appeared that the Part cost him nothing : He wore on his Brow a Branch of withered Ivy, bound up in form of a

[1] Vol. VII, p. 232.

Garland, which seemed to be pulled down from the Door of an Alehouse ; When he came up to take his Seat, all the Assembly looked at him with a contemptuous Eye especially when with an Air of Triumph, he seated himself opposite to *Dryden. That person so unlike the other awful Form*, said my Guide, *is* Shadwell ; *he has a Seat here by the Indulgence of a Tasteless Court, who bestowed on him the Laurel in prejudice of the Great* Dryden. I had scarce Time to testify my surprise, when a Young Man of a divine Aspect [1] appeared ; and to my great Amazement, went up to *Shadwell* in a familiar manner. My Amazement was changed to the utmost Concern, when I saw him affect the same Airs and Motions with him : But there was a remarkable Difference betwixt them, for that abandoned Deportment seemed as unnatural in him, as the Airs of Wit and Politeness appeared in the other."

It may be that our estimate of Shadwell will to some extent depend upon our just appreciation of his model and pattern, Ben Jonson. The author of *A Comparison between the two Stages* [2] has a penetrating sentence : " *Fletcher* and *Beaumont* are everywhere irregular, but always gentile and easy ; their Tragedies are moving, and their Comedies diverting ; *Shakespear* sublime in the first, and always natural in the latter ; *Jonson* humourous in one, and very correct in both : I descend to no others, only I can't omit *Shadwel*, whose Comedies are true Copies of Nature." [3] If we realize how supreme a master in drama is the titanic figure of Jonson, and how acute an apprehension Shadwell had of his own very remarkable powers in proposing to himself this mighty genius as an exemplar, we shall, perhaps, be able with truer and clearer judgement more definitely to assign the Orange laureate that very high place in the English theatre to which he is undoubtedly entitled.

For, as has already been emphasized, Shadwell must be regarded as a playwright alone. His contemporaries, Langbaine and the rest, who wished to estimate him fairly, simply disregarded the satires and the Pindarics, and although it may be objected that this partiality is unallowable—and in most instances it would certainly be an inadmissible indulgence—yet I think that with Shadwell it is warranted, since his occasional pasquils, violent and vigorous as they are, he never cared to father, and his Whitehall Odes were necessitated by the obligations of his Office.

His political views were, it is only too plain, atrocious ; and it is to be feared that his religious sentiments—for the greater part of his days at all events—were gravely reprehensible. It is well to read that towards the end Dr. Brady found he had " (however the World may be mistaken in

---

[1] Otway.

[2] Generally, but upon no authority, ascribed to Gildon, who almost certainly was not the author.

[3] P. 57.

him) a much deeper Sense of Religion, than many others have, who pretend to it more openly." We trust that much which is blameworthy in *The Lancashire Witches* is but the extravagance and exaggeration of angry prejudice and obliquity lashed to fury at an hour when bitterest passions had full play on every side. Yet even in calmer moments he can commend, with a reservation it is true, the philosophy of Hobbes, and his praise of the philosophy—be it well marked I do not say the poetry—of Lucretius is highly suspicious. " Thou great *Lucretius !* Thou profound Oracle of Wit and Sense ! thou art no Trifling-Landskip-Poet, no Fantastick Heroick Dreamer, with empty Descriptions of Impossibilities, and might sounding Nothings. Thou reconcil'st Philosophy with Verse, and dost, almost alone, demonstrate that Poetry and Good Sence may go together." [1] This is very bad. It was not for nothing that Cardinal Melchior de Polignac [2] wrote his fine work *Anti-Lucretius* [3] in nine books, a complete refutation of Lucretius and of Bayle too, as well as offering an attempt to determine the nature of the Supreme Good, of the soul, of motion, of space. As a poet Lucretius was a proud and brilliant genius, and it is in " passages of profound and majestic broodings over life and death, that the long rolling weight of the Lucretian hexameter tells with its full force." [4] But the *De Natura Rerum* is a didactic poem, and not only didactic but argumentative, nay, more, highly controversial. And here lurks the poison, nor is the venom less deadly because proffered in a cup of gold. The terrible pessimism, the nihilism of Lucretius can have but one logical end. The influence of the Roman poet was not negligible in Restoration days, and unfortunately it persists, though in a thinner stream, to-day.[5] The *De Natura Rerum* was translated, and well translated, in 1682 by Thomas Creech, a Fellow of All Souls, Oxford, who also published a *Commentary* on the Poem, 1695. In June, 1700, after he had been missing for five days, his body was discovered in a garret at the house of Mr. Ives, an apothecary with whom he lodged. He had committed suicide very deliberately, but at the coroner's inquest he was found *non compos mentis*.

[1] *The Virtuoso*, I, 1. It may be argued that this speech is put into the mouth of a character, Bruce, a gentleman " of wit and sense," but the voice is the voice of Shadwell.

[2] 1661–1742.

[3] Paris, 1745.

[4] Mackail, *Latin Literature*, p. 49.

[5] Dr. Inge, the Dean of S. Paul's, is wont to dismiss abstruse and difficult theological questions by a quotation from Lucretius. Cf. *Christian Mysticism*, 1899, p. 265, where he seems to imagine that the phenomena of Mysticism can all be dismissed by urbanely murmuring with a courtly wave of the hand :

> Hunc igitur terrorem animi, tenebrasque necessest
> Non radii solis, neque lucida tela diei
> Discutiant, sed naturæ species ratioque.
>
> *De Natura Rerum*, I, 147–49.

John Hoyle, of Gray's Inn and the Inner Temple, a well-known figure in the town, professed himself " a great admirer of *Lucretius*." [1] Hoyle was " an Atheiſt, and a Blasphemer of Chriſt."

We shall do well then, and we shall aĉt juſtly, if in our appreciation of Shadwell we concentrate upon the plays, and here we shall find much, very much to admire. In the firſt place, if we would review his faults and have finished with 'em, these are obvious and may be considered at a short rate. Too often the scenes are ill hewn ; there is a certain roughness, a certain coarseness of fibre and texture, which will perhaps be infinitely surprising to those who know the Reſtoration theatre by the polished Congreve alone, but by no means so surprising to those who compare Shadwell with Wycherley and with Vanbrugh. For Shadwell has something of the cynicism, almost of the experienced brutality, of Wycherley ; and assuredly his plays are often in their technique very like the rather rough and tumble irregular episodes of *The Relapse* and *The Provok'd Wife*. It appears as if Shadwell saw his scenes separately, that in his mind each charaĉter ſtood by itself, and he was at no trouble to compose them into a proportionate and balanced whole. For all his worship of Jonson, for all his " Duration of the Scene 24 Hours," no man cared less about the Unities than he. This gives his comedies a quality of realism which otherwise they might lack, for in our everyday round events do happen in somewhat fortuitous and indiscriminate fashion, as it humanly seems to us, and accidents of luck or mishap are not nicely graduated or consecutive and arranged in apple-pie order.

It has been said by a writer who is himself an archetype of flaccid inanition and triteſt vacancy that Shadwell is flabby and commonplace. This opinion may be delivered through ignorance or from a mere exigency of ideas. In any case " flabby " and " commonplace " are the moſt unfitting epithets that well could be employed. When Dryden dubbed Shadwell " dull " and mislead the world for two and a half centuries, he knew very well what he was about, but then glorious John had superlative genius, and lightly commanded a consummate cleverness of description. He did not throw about meaningless words at random. Shadwell's scenes are all beef and brawn, solid fare. To an appetite that craves to glut itself with the rather rancid excitement of ſtale romance and cheap thrills *Epsom Wells*, *The Virtuoso* and *Bury-Fair* will, of course, seem flat and unlively, " commonplace," since they are merely exaĉt representations

---

[1] " A Letter to Mr. *Creech* at *Oxford*, Written in the laſt great Froſt." Mrs. Behn's *Miscellany*, 1685 :

> To Honeſt H——*le* I shou'd have shown ye,
> A Wit that wou'd be proud t'have known ye ;
> A Wit uncommon, and Facetious,
> A great admirer of *Lucretius*.

of life ; a day at an inland spa ; a few hours of London, a luncheon party, a dance ; an old-world fair in a country-town.

Even if Shadwell had no dramatic value, and a writer who is almost notoriously deficient in his apprehension of stagecraft assures us that Shadwell could not " treat a situation," his work would yet be incalculably important as a picture of his times. In Etherege, in Wycherley, and above all in Congreve, we have the fine gentlemen and the ladies of quality not as they were but as they would like to have been, and as we too should like them to have been. Their converse and their adventures are wit and gallantry raised to the most refined and polished degree. Shadwell gives us the world in which he walked and talked exactly as it moved and spoke about him, without exaggeration, without veneer. That is to say his people are real living folk with all their defects of awkwardness, and sincerity, and unreason, and self-consciousness and conceit. This, I think, is why his Theodosia, his Miranda and Clarinda, his Isabella, by their frivolity and selfishness vex us and provoke, whereas the very same sentiments and the very same motives in Etherege's Emilia and Ariana and Gatty merely arouse a certain intellectual interest, no personal feeling at all. This is because in the latter case we are contemplating literature— exquisitely wrought literature be it said—in the former case we are contemplating life.

It were superfluous to defend Shadwell against Dryden's charge. The best answer to that is the comedies themselves. Here we have the whole tribe of fops, virtuosos, debauches, cuckolds, coarse country clowns, crooked politicians, business men, minor poets, sportsmen, loose wives, whores, puritans, cavaliers, the whole kaleidoscope of Restoration life, and he who is not interested in them is interested in nothing worth a moment's consideration.

In some ways Shadwell had he lived a century later, or two centuries later, would have made an admirable novelist. His theatre is very exuberant, his stage is never empty. There is no great refinement, his method was too hasty to allow of any nice and long-considered artistry, there is— let us frankly admit—a good deal which we might very well wish away, but with all his faults he does give us humanity ; his strokes are vigorous and vital ; he, at least, shows us life as it presented itself to him, which is one facet of truth, and this, I take it, when the world is sick of confectionery and cloyed with sham, is that plain but hearty fare to which it will always be glad yet once more to return.

MONTAGUE SUMMERS.

San Zenone, Verona—London.

Chronology

Thomas Shadwell born at Santon House, Norfolk . . 1641.
He enters Bury St. Edmund's School . . . . 1654.
Admitted to Gonville and Caius College, Cambridge . . 17 December, 1655.
Enters the Middle Temple . . . . . . 7 July, 1658.
Is in Ireland for four months . . . . . 1664.
Marries Anne Gawdy, *née* Gibbs . . . . . *circa* 1663–66.
The Sullen Lovers produced at Lincoln's Inn Fields . . 2 May, 1668.
   Stationer's Register, 9 September, 1668. Term Catalogues,
    Michaelmas (November), 1668, 4to, 1668.
The Royal Shepherdess produced at Lincoln's Inn Fields . . 25 February, 1668–69.
   Stationer's Register, 8 June, 1669. Term Catalogues,
    Michaelmas (22 November), 1669, 4to, 1669.
The Humourists, produced at Lincoln's Inn Fields . . December, 1670.
   Stationer's Register, 9 February, 1670–71. Term Cata-
    logues, Easter (30 May), 1671, 4to, 1671.
Shadwell stays at Chadderton Hall, near Oldham . . . April–May, 1671.
The Miser, produced at the Theatre Royal in Bridges Street . January, 1671–72.
   Term Catalogues, Trinity (24 June), 1672, 4to, 1672.
The Theatre Royal destroyed by fire . . . . . 25 January, 1671–72.
Epsom-Wells, produced at Dorset Garden . . . . 2 December, 1672.
   Stationer's Register, 17 February, 1672–73. Term Cata-
    logues, Easter (6 May), 1673, 4to, 1673.
The Tempest; or, The Enchanted Island, an opera, produced at
   Dorset Garden . . . . 30 April, 1674.
   Term Catalogues, Michaelmas (25 November), 1674, 4to,
    1674.
Psyche, produced at Dorset Garden . . . . . 27 February, 1674–75.
   Stationer's Register, 1 August, 1674. Term Catalogues,
    Hilary (15 February), 1675, 4to, 1675.
The Libertine, produced at Dorset Garden . . . . June, 1675.
   Term Catalogues, Hilary (10 February), 1676, 4to, 1676.
The Virtuoso, produced at Dorset Garden . . . . May, 1676.
   Stationer's Register, 1 June, 1676. Term Catalogues,
    Michaelmas (22 November), 1676, 4to, 1676.
The History of Timon of Athens, produced at Dorset Garden . December, 1677, or
                                         January, 1677–78.
   Stationer's Register, 23 February, 1677–78. Licensed for
    printing, 18 February, 1677–78, 4to, 1678.
A True Widow, produced at Dorset Garden . . . . December, 1678.
   Term Catalogues, Easter (May), 1679, 4to, 1679.
The Woman Captain, produced at Dorset Garden . . . September, 1679.
   Term Catalogues, Michaelmas (November), 1679, 4to, 1680.
The Lancashire Witches, after considerable delay, produced at
   Dorset Garden . . . . Autumn, 1681.
   Term Catalogues, Michaelmas (November), 1681.
   "Printed as it was intended (but not allowed) to be
    acted," 4to, 1682.

Dryden's *The Medall*, published . . . . . . March, 1681–82.
Shadwell's *The Medal of John Bayes*, published . . . May, 1682.
Shadwell's *The Satyr to His Muse, by the Author of Absalom and Achitophel*, advertised in *The True Protestant Mercury* . 22–26 July, 1682.
Shadwell's *The Tory-Poets*, published . . . . . 4 September, 1682.
Dryden and Lee's *The Duke of Guise*, produced at Drury Lane. 1 December, 1682.
Shadwell's *Some Reflections Upon the Pretended Parallel in the Play called The Duke of Guise*, published, 4to . . . . 1683.
Sir Charles Sedley gives Shadwell the profits of *Bellamira*, produced at Drury Lane . . . . May, 1687.
Shadwell's *The Tenth Satyr of Juvenal*, licensed for printing . 25 May, 1687.
Published 4to, with Dedication to Sedley . . . 1687.
The Squire of Alsatia, produced at Drury Lane . . . May, 1688.
Term Catalogues, Easter (May), 1688, 4to, 1688.
Shadwell's letter to the Second Duke of Ormonde, thanking him for the election of John Shadwell as Fellow of All Soul's, Oxford . . . . 5 November, 1688.
A Warrant to sware Thomas Shadwell Esqr into the place and quality of Poet-Laureat to his Matie . . . . 9 March, 1688–89.
Bury-Fair, produced at Drury Lane . . . . . April, 1689.
Term Catalogues, Trinity (June), 1689. Printed as "Written by Tho. Shadwell, Servant to His Majesty," 4to, 1689.
Ode for the Birthday of Queen Mary II . . . . . 30 April, 1689.
Shadwell's patent as Poet Laureate drawn up . . . 29 August, 1689.
Ode on the Birthday of William III, 4to, 1690 . . . 4 November, 1689.
The Amorous Bigotte, produced at Drury Lane early in . 1690.
Term Catalogues, Easter (May), 1690, 4to, 1690.
A Song for St. Cecilia's Day . . . . 22 November, 1690.
The Scowrers, produced at Drury Lane . . . . December, 1690.
Term Catalogues, Hilary (February), 1691, 4to, 1691.
Ode for Birthday of Queen Mary II . . . . . . 30 April, 1691.
Votum Perenne . . . . 1 January, 1692.
Letter to the Earl of Dorset with reference to Brady's tragedy, *The Innocent Impostors* . . . . 19 January, 1691–92.
The Innocent Impostors, produced at Drury Lane . . May, 1692.
Term Catalogues, Trinity (June), 1692, 4to, 1692.
Death of Shadwell . . . . 20 November, 1692.
He is buried at S. Luke's, Chelsea Parish Church . . 24 November, 1692.
Probate of Will granted to Mrs. Shadwell . . . 3 December, 1692.
The Volunteers, produced at Drury Lane . . . At the end of November, or very early in December, 1692.
Term Catalogues, Trinity (June), 1693, 4to, 1693.
Anne Shadwell is still alive in . . . . . 1709.
Charles Shadwell dies at Dublin . . . . . 12 August, 1726.
Sir John Shadwell dies . . . . 4 January, 1747.
Sir John Shadwell is buried at Bath Abbey . . . 8 January, 1747.

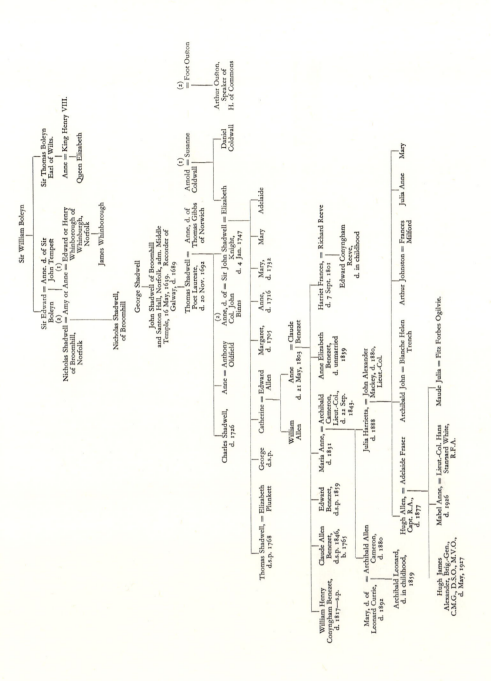

Sir William Boleyn

Sir Edward = Anne, d. of Sir Boleyn | John Tempest (2)(1)

Sir Thomas Boleyn, Earl of Wilts.

Anne = King Henry VIII.

Queen Elizabeth

Nicholas Shadwell = Amy or Anne = Edward or Henry Whinborough of Whinburgh, Norfolk (1) of Broomhill, Norfolk

James Whinborough

Nicholas Shadwell, of Broomhill

George Shadwell

John Shadwell of Broomhill and Santon Hall, Norfolk, adm. Middle Temple, 16 May, 1659. Recorder of Galway, d. 1689

Thomas Shadwell = Anne, d. of Thomas Gibbs of Norwich, Poet Laureate, d. 20 Nov. 1692

Arnold (1) = Susanne Coldwall   (2) = Foot Ouston

Daniel Coldwall

Arthur Ouston, Speaker of H. of Commons

Anne, d. of = Sir John Shadwell = Elizabeth Col. John Knight, Binns (2) d. 4 Jan. 1747

Mary, Anne, Mary, Adelaide
d. 1716 d. 1732

Charles Shadwell, d. 1726

Anne = Anthony Oldfield

Margaret, d. 1795

Anne = Claude d. 21 May, 1803 | Benezet

Anne Elizabeth Benezet, d. unmarried 1859

Harriet Frances, = Richard Reeve d. 7 Sept. 1801

Edward Conyngham Reeve, d. in childhood

Catherine = Edward Allen

George d.s.p.

William Allen

Maria Anne, = Archibald Cameron, d. 1831 Lieut.-Col., d. 22 Sep. 1843.

Julia Harrietta, = John Alexander d. 1888 Mackey, d. 1880, Lieut.-Col.

Archibald John = Blanche Helen Trench

Arthur Johnston = Frances Milford

Julia Anne

Mary

Thomas Shadwell, = Elizabeth Plunkett d.s.p. 1768

William Henry Conyngham Benezet, d. 1817—s.p.

Claude Allen Benezet, d.s.p. 1846, b. 1765

Edward Benezet, d.s.p. 1859

Mary, d. of = Archibald Allen Leonard Currie, Cameron, d. 1892 d. 1880

Archibald Leonard, d. in childhood, 1819

Hugh Allen, = Adelaide Fraser Capt. R.A., d. 1877

Maude Julia = Fitz Forbes Ogilvie.

Mabel Anne, = Lieut.-Col. Hans d. 1926 Stannard White, R.F.A.

Hugh James Alexander, Brig.-Gen., C.M.G., D.S.O., M.V.O., d. May, 1927

Mr. *BRADY*s
SERMON

PREACHED

At the Funeral

OF

THOMAS SHADWELL, Esquire.

Imprimatur,

Novemb. 28.
1692.

Carolus Alston.

A SERMON PREACHED

At the Funeral

O F

THOMAS SHADWELL, Esq;

L A T E

Poet-Laureat, and Historiographer-Royal, who was Interred at *Chelsea*, November 24. 1692.

By *Nicholas Brady*, Minister of St. *Catharine Cree-Church*, and Chaplain to his Grace the Duke of *Ormond*.

Published at the Earnest Request of the Friends of the Deceased.

LONDOON,

Printed for *James Knapton*, at the *Crown* in St. *Paul's* Church-Yard. M DC XC III.

REV. xiv. and part of Verse 13.

Blessed are the dead, which die in the Lord.

The whole Verse runs thus :

And I heard a voice from Heaven, saying unto me, Write, Blessed are the dead which die in the Lord, from henceforth, yea, saith the Spirit, that they may rest from their labours, and their Works do follow them.

IS Death then a Blessing ? Is that King of Terrours an Object of Desire ? Is the common Aversion of human Nature a thing fit to be courted and embraced ? Can the first Curse of God upon Sin and Disobedience become a just Matter of Interest and Advantage ? Is Blessedness the Companion of Rottenness and Corruption ? And does it dwell so meanly and retiredly ? How much mistaken then are the Generality of Mankind, who seek for it in the noisy Tumults of a busie Court, amongst a glittering Collection of Gold and Jewels, in the divertive Society of the Witty, and the Beautiful ; when it is only to be found within the silent Chambers of the Grave, amongst a ruinous Heap of Dust and Ashes, with mouldring Bones, and putrifying Carcases. This is a Paradox so strange, and so surprizing, so hard to Flesh and Blood, so contrary to the Notions which are generally entertained, and so seemingly contradictory in its self ; that it needed no less than a Divine Authority to usher it in, and a Celestial Herald to Proclaim and Recommend it, *And I heard a voice from Heaven, saying unto me, Write, Blessed are the dead.*

But is there no Distinction in the Grave ? no sort of Difference between the Godly and the Wicked ? Is Blessedness the common and indifferent Lot of both ? In vain then do we wish or endeavour to die the Death of the Righteous, and to have our latter end like his : Death will most certainly arrive, and if this Supposition be true, Blessedness will as certainly attend it ; and the foolish Epicure may be justified in his Saying, *Let us eat and drink, for to morrow we die.* This is an Opinion too loose to be admitted, and draws after it a Train of Consequences too fatal to be allowed ; and therefore we find a necessary Condition specified and annexed, by which the Dead must be qualified for Blessedness ; *Blessed are the dead which die in the Lord.*

To *die in the Lord*, is to die in his Fear, and in his Favour ; to die with the Testimony of a good Conscience, in relation to ones self, and with a well grounded Confidence in respect of God ; to have the happy Entertainment, when he casts his Eyes backwards, of a well-spent Life ; and the comfortable Prospect, when he looks forwards, of a Blessed Immortality ; to have those Words continually ringing in his dying Ears, of *Well done, good and faithful servant*, as a due Character of his Life past, *and enter thou into the joy of thy Lord*, as a happy Draught of that which is to come ; to fall asleep, as it were, in the Arms of his Redeemer ; and to be lulled to his long Repose in the Embraces of his Saviour ; to lay down his Life with a certain Assurance of taking it up again, as knowing that it is hid with Christ in God ; to go out of this World with a firm Persuasion of entring into a better ; to have a lively Faith within a dying Body, and a Hope that flourishes under the Decays of Nature ; to have an intire Resignation to the Divine Will, and to put his Death as well as Life into the Hands of God. This is the full and perfect meaning of that short, but comprehensive Expression, *To die in the Lord :* and since we find Blessedness annexed to that Condition, it should forcibly engage us to endeavour its Attainment. *Blessed,* &c.

In my following Discourse therefore upon this Solemn Occasion, I shall insist upon these two Particulars.

(cclix)

SERMON

First, I shall lay down the proper Method which we ought to make use of, in order to attain to the happy Condition, *of dying in the Lord.*

Secondly, I shall prove the thing affirmed in my Text, that *Blessed are the dead which die in the Lord.*

First then, I shall lay down the proper Method which we ought to make use of, in order to attain to the happy Condition of *dying in the Lord.*

1. To *die in the Lord,* is a thing so valueable in it self, and attended with Circumstances so precious and considerable, that we cannot suppose its Purchase to be easie ; but must allow the Price of such a Blessing to bear some Proportion to the Greatness of its Advantages. We cannot therefore promise our selves with any manner of security, that it shall be the Reward of a few sick Prayers, or a Death-bed Repentance ; they who would be certain of *dying in the Lord,* must stedfastly resolve to live in him ; and that whole Life is happily laid out, by which we are assured of so blessed a Conclusion : Some perhaps may flatter themselves, that a happy End is not inconsistent with a wicked Life ; that the Mercy of God will work out their Salvation, even in their own despight ; that they may enjoy the World here, and Heaven hereafter ; that they may live to the Flesh, and yet die in the Lord : But let us not thus deceive our own Souls, God is not thus mocked ; his Mercy is truly infinite, but so are also his Justice and his Truth ; nor will he so far be swayed by that, tho his beloved his darling Attribute, as to forfeit or forego the other two ; there must be some satisfaction made to these, before we can enjoy the Refreshings of the former ; otherwise, this God of Mercy will laugh at our Calamities, and mock when our Fear comes. He, who totally applies himself to the Enjoyments of this Life, and manages his time as if there were no other, can never expect any Comfort or Satisfaction, when he is entring upon a State that he so little thought of : he is tied and wedded to the things of this World, and it is a tearing him from all that he values or esteems, to bring him to that Passage which leads into another. To such a Man Death comes arrayed with all his Pomp of Terrour ; if he looks upon that World which he is about to take leave of, he finds that he is parting with his dearest Companion, the delight of all his Senses, and the Comfort of his Soul : if he looks upon that World which he is about to go into, he has made no Acquaintances there, secured no Interests, engaged no Friendships, to render his future Abode delightful and agreeable : if he is so stupid and inconsiderate, as to have no prospect of the Misery that attends him, yet at best, he sees nothing before him but Darkness and Confusion, *a Land* of Silence *where all things are forgotten.* It is therefore absolutely necessary, that we live here, as Probationers for Heaven and Happiness, if we expect hereafter to be partakers of that Blessedness, which is the Portion of those *dead who die in the Lord.* You have been told already, that to *die in the Lord,* is to die in his Fear, and in his Favour ; But how shall he die in the Fear of the Lord, whose Days have been consumed in the Contempt of his Commandments ? Or how shall he die in the Favour of the Lord, whose Life has been full of rebellious Provocations ? He may die indeed under the Terrours of the Lord, but not in his Fear ; or perhaps flatter'd by his own deceitful Heart, but not favour'd by the Almighty. Indeed could we all *know our End, and the Number of our Days ;* and were every one of us *certified how long he has to live,* it might seem tolerably safe, to devote some part of our Life to Sin and Folly, reserving at the same time a considerable Portion, for the After-Exercises of Piety and Devotion ; we might then for some years indulge our sinful Appetites, and set by so many more for the working out our Salvation : But alas ! we know not how soon Death may seize upon us ; his Arrest may be sudden, surprizing, and unlooked for ; we ought therefore to live in the constant expectation, and be conversant perpetually in our Preparations for it : *Watch ye therefore,* says our Saviour, *for ye know neither the day nor the hour, wherein the Son of Man cometh :* And what will become of us, if our Lord, when he comes, shall find us sleeping ? It will then be in vain to ask, when he will be no more entreated ;

in vain to seek him, when he will not be found ; in vain to knock, when the Gate is shut against us : then if we cry never so much, *Lord, Lord, open unto us ;* we shall receive no other Answer but a positive Denial : *Verily, I say unto you, I know you not, Depart from me ye workers of iniquity.* This Life is the Day wherein we must work ; *the Night* of Death is drawing on apace, *wherein no Man can work ;* and besides the great Danger of being surprized by that, how madly does he proceed, that squanders away the Morning and the Noon of Life, and sets not about his Days work until the Evening ! How comfortless every night must that Man lie down to his necessary Repose, that knows not, but he may wake in another World, and yet finds himself to be unprepared for it ? Can any Man be secure of *dying in the Lord,* that takes no care to go to Bed in his Favour, and yet cannot tell but he may die before he rises ? He that would make sure of so blessed a Condition, should live every Day, as if it were his last ; be always disintangled from the Cares of this World, as if he were then upon taking his leave of it ; have his thoughts still fixed upon a Blessed Eternity, as if he were just launching out into it : for *our Lord may come in a day when we look not for him, and in an hour that we are not aware of ;* and therefore, the only sure Way, not to be taken unprovided, is to be every hour prepared, as if that were it. It is an easie thing to say, I will repent to morrow, I will consider my ways, and fit my self for my end ; but are we sure that to-morrow is our own? And may not our Case be like the rich Man's in the Gospel, whose Soul was required of him that very night ? The Disappointment in this Case is so very dreadful, being not only the loss of a few hours which we proposed to our selves here, but of a joyful Eternity in the World which is to come ; that it will highly concern every reasonable Man, timely to provide against so dismal a Misfortune : and this can be done no better a way, than by a stedfast Faith, and an uniform Obedience.

1. Then, a stedfast Faith is an excellent Preparative, to qualifie us at all times, for *dying in the Lord.*

Faith, says the Apostle, *is the substance of things hoped for, the evidence of things not seen :* by this we depend upon the Promises of God, and settle to our selves a firm assurance of them ; this discloses to us the Secrets of the invisible World, and makes us familiar with that Land of Spirits ; it sets Heaven and Happiness before our Eyes ; *it lifts up the Heads of those eternal Gates, and sets wide open the everlasting Doors ;* it gives us a Relish and Antepast of that Glory which shall one day be revealed, and makes us *taste and see how good the Lord is :* By this, *Stephen* saw the Glory of God, and *Jesus* standing on the Right Hand of the Almighty ; by this, St. *Paul* was rap'd into the third Heaven, and heard and saw such things as were unspeakable ; through this he desired to be dissolved, and to be with Christ ; this made all the Sufferings of Martyrs and Confessors easie to them and delightful ; this supports the Faithful in the Agonies of Death, and makes up in a very great measure, the Blessedness of those *dead which die in the Lord.* But

2. An uniform Obedience is an excellent Preparative, to qualifie us at all times for *dying in the Lord.*

This secures to us those precious Advantages, which Faith but reveals ; and entitles us to the Treasures, which that only discloses : this fits us for the Enjoyment of a Blessed Immortality, and applies to us the Promises of eternal Felicity : that indeed shews us what Heaven is, but this assures us, that it is ours ; that gives us a View of everlasting Happiness, this puts us actually in possession of it. For Christianity, my Brethren, is not a bare Speculation ; it is defined to be a Practical Science ; and the main intent of it is to regulate our Actions. It is true indeed, in order to that it must inform our Understandings ; but if it operates upon us no farther, it only enhances the Heinousness of our Transgressions, by making every offence become a sin against Knowledge. And therefore we find the Holy Apostle, when he compares together the three great Christian Graces, giving the Preference to that which is Practical, to the prejudice of the others which are chiefly Contemplative. *Now remain* (says he) *Faith,*

Hope, Charity, these three : but the greatest of these is Charity. He then, who is always conversant in the Duties of his Profession, always employed in the Exercises of Devotion, and keeps *a Conscience void of offence towards God, and towards man :* he is the Man who, let Death come when it will, is never found dejected or unprovided : *Blessed is that wise and faithful servant, whom his Lord, when he cometh, shall find so doing :* he takes the surest and most infallible way, to secure to himself, whenever he shall die, *the Blessedness of those dead which die in the Lord.*

2. And this leads me to the Consideration of my second General ; namely, to prove the thing affirmed in my Text, that *Blessed are the dead which die in the Lord.*

Death is to be considered under a double Notion ; either as it is a Passage out of this World, or as it is an Entrance into another ; and under each of them, it appears to the unwary Examiner, a matter of Terrour and of Trouble. To leave all the engaging Entertainments, all the agreeable Societies and Diversions, to which we have been accustomed and familiar from our Cradles ; and to pass into a place that we never yet frequented, to go into a Land that we never before travelled, and to enter upon a condition that we never yet experienced ; these Reflections, I say, to such as only dwell upon superficial Appearances, and never pry into the Bottom of Affairs, are strangely frightful and discouraging : but if we will give our selves the useful Labour of considering Matters more strictly and deliberately, we shall find, that let us take it which way we will, to such as *die in the Lord, death is a Blessing.*

First, Then, let us consider Death as a Passage out of this World, and in relation to that Notion of Death we shall find, *That blessed are the dead which die in the Lord.*

A considerable Instance of their Blessedness, or that wherein (as to this particular) it especially consists, is assigned by the Holy Ghost, in the Words immediately consequent to my Text ; *And I heard a voice from Heaven, saying unto me, Write, Blessed are the dead which die in the Lord, from henceforth : Yea, saith the Spirit, that they may rest from their labours.* For the Life of a good Christian is a Life of Labour ; he is born to it, as the Sparks fly upwards ; he is every where beset with Difficulties ; and with many Enemies must he encounter ; the World hates him, because he is not of it ; God often tries him with Temptations and Afflictions, and his Conscience is always keeping him to his Task of *working out his salvation with fear and trembling ;* he is obliged to be constantly upon the Watch ; to bear the Shocks of Satan, and the Contradictions of Sinners ; so that *if in this life only he had hopes, he were of all men the most miserable.* But how joyfully does he welcome the Approaches of his End, by which he shall be freed from the forementioned Troubles ! Death appears to him as pleasing and desirable, as Health, after a dangerous and troublesome Distemper, as Rest after a toilsome and laborious Journey, as Sleep after a tedious and uneasie Watching, as the Port after a stormy and tempestuous Voyage. He had no such intimate Engagements with the World, as may render it unsupportable to part with it ; he has nothing of Earth to hang heavy upon his Soul, to clog its flight, or weigh it downwards to this dull Centre of Corruption ; it is long since that the World and he took leave of one another ; he has a long time been dead to that, having *mortified his Members, which were upon the Earth ;* he can have no Regret for parting with that, of which he never entertained any tolerable good Opinion ; all whose Advantages he has found to be but *Vanity,* and all its Entertainments *Vexation of Spirit :* Nay further, he reflects upon what he is to leave with Comfort and Satisfaction ; he parts with nothing but an inveterate Enemy, who has all his life long been endeavouring to destroy him ; has still put stumbling Blocks in his Way to Heaven and Happiness, and been misleading him from the Paths of everlasting Felicity. Those few good Men which he leaves behind, and to whom his Soul is chiefly linked on this side Heaven, he hopes to see again with ineffable Delight ; and is but going as a Harbinger to prepare their Way : No Ties of Nature or of Blood can biass him, since they are all swallowed up in the Love of his Creator, and in the near expectation of the Fruition of him. Thus the World and the Flesh hang loose about him; his active Soul is just upon the Wing; and he parts from hence as an industrious Traveller from a sorry Inn, where the ill Accommodation made his Stay uneasie, and the opportunity of leaving it, welcom and agreeable. *Blessed therefore are the dead which die in the Lord.* If we look upon Death as a Passage out of this World; for *they rest from their labors.*

But since the Word which is here render'd to rest, does more properly signifie to ease or to refresh; and consequently this Resting does not mean a bare and unactive Cessation from Labour, but a State of perfect Complacency and Satisfaction; I therefore proceed to consider Death.

Secondly, As the entrance into another World, and in relation to that Notion of Death, we shall find, that *Blessed are the dead which die in the Lord.*

A considerable Instance of their Blessedness, or that wherein (as to this particular) it especially consists, is given us by the same Holy Spirit, in the last Words of this Verse, whereof my Text is part: *And I heard a voice from Heaven, saying unto me, Write, Blessed are the dead which die in the Lord, from henceforth, yea, saith the Spirit, that they may rest from their labours, and their works do follow them.*

According to *the Works which we have done in the Body*, so shall we be dealt with in the World which is to come; then shall we receive a suitable Retribution, according to our Actions, whether good or evil. *The Judge of all the Earth will then do Right, and be justified in all his Doings, and his Sayings.* Indeed the ordinary Dispensations of Providence are here so unaccountable, that they scarcely suffice *to justifie the Ways of God to Man*; common Blessings are dispensed indifferently, and *his Sun shines upon the Just and the Unjust*; nay, sometimes, and generally, the Ungodly prosper, and the Men that work Righteousness are miserable and oppressed. But in that World which is to come, eternal Happiness will be entail'd upon the Righteous, and everlasting Tribulation shall be the Portion of the Wicked: Then shall God's Justice appear to act regularly, and either stop the Mouths of all Gainsayers, or open them to confess, That *verily there is a reward for the righteous. Doubtless there is a God that judgeth the Earth.* Certainly all the Blandishments and Flatteries of this World can have nothing so delightful in them, nothing that can so truly affect a rational Soul, as the Prospect of those Joys which are laid up for them which *die in the Lord;* and the Sound of those Words ringing in their dying Ears, *Come ye blessed of my Father, inherit the Kingdom prepared for you, from the foundation of the world.* Then shall their Saviour enumerate their good Actions, and set before their Eyes those *works which follow them*, laying them down as the Reasons of their blessed Entertainment. *For I was an hungred, and ye gave me meat, I was thirsty, and ye gave me drink; I was naked, and ye cloathed me; I was sick and in prison, and ye visited me.* How pleasing and agreeable must the Surprize then be, when they find every Instance of Charity and Compassion, which they formerly extended to their distressed Brethren, accepted and rewarded as fully and effectually, as if it had been performed to Christ himself: *Verily, I say unto you, in as much as ye have done it to the least of these my Brethren, ye have done it unto me.* Then every Action of Piety and Devotion, every Advancement in Godliness and Holiness, every Christian Combat and Struggling with Temptations, every single Act of Faith and Resignation, shall have its due Commendation and particular Regard. How delightful and ravishing will the Prospect be, when all their Virtues shall be thus ranked in order, and attend them jointly to the Throne of Grace, and there present themselves in their Favour and Behalf, as so many Offerings of a *sweet smelling savour!* Then shall their Redeemer know his own *by these their Fruits*, and *confess them before his Father which is in Heaven;* and they shall see face to face *the Holiest of Holies, in whose presence is fullness of joy.* The Scene is so glorious, and so transcendently inviting, that it needs no Foil, no Painter's Art of Shades and darker Colours, to give these brighter ones more Splendor and Vivacity; and therefore it needs not to be set off, by comparing it with the miserable condition of such unhappy Wretches, whose Works are said to go before them unto Judgment : Sense cannot reach the Beauty of it, nor Imagination figure any Resemblance to it ; *for eye hath not seen, nor ear heard, neither hath it enter'd into the heart of man to conceive the things which God has prepared for them that love him. Blessed therefore are the dead which die in the Lord*, if we look upon Death as the Entrance into another World, *For their Works do follow them.*

Into this happy State and Condition, I hope, our deceased Brother is already enter'd ; with whom my Acquaintance was so intimate, during my short Familiarity with him, that it qualified me to know him as well, as those who had conversed with him much longer : and I cannot but do his Memory that Justice, to declare, that during the time of my Acquaintance with him, I found in him a most zealous Affection to the present Government, a great deal of Honesty and Integrity, a real Love of Truth and Sincerity, an inviolable Fidelity and Strictness to his Word, an unalterable Friendship wheresoever he professed it, (and however the World may be mistaken in him) a much deeper Sense of Religion, than many others have, who pretend to it more openly : His natural and acquired Abilities made him sufficiently remarkable to all that he conversed with, and cannot be unknown to any here present, very few being equal to him, in all the becoming Qualities and Accomplishments, which adorn and set off a complete Gentleman : His very Enemies (if he have left any behind him) will give him this Character, at least if they knew him so throughly as I did ; and therefore it is but cold Justice in a Friend, who received from him, during his Life all the Marks of a true Affection which shall make his Memory dear to me, when he is nothing else but Dust and Ashes. His Death seized him suddenly, but could not unprepared, since (to my own certain knowledge) he never took his Dose of *Opium*, but he solemnly recommended himself to God by Prayer, as if he were then about to *resign up his Soul into the Hands of his faithful Creator.* These Considerations give me good Grounds to hope, that *this dead man is blessed ;* because from thence I have reason to believe, that *he died in the Lord.* I should enlarge farther upon his Character, but that he always in his life time disapproved of that Custom upon these Occasions, and most especially in relation to himself, nor should I thus far have infringed his Will in this particular, but that I was willing to inform the World, how much some People have erred in their Opinion of him.

Let us then, in the Name God, so manage our selves, during the Course of this Life, that we may be qualified for the Enjoyment of a better ; that when we shall *go hence and be no more seen,* we may *rest from our labours,* not enter upon greater Miseries, and that *our works which shall follow us,* may recommend, and not impeach us : that so we may have a just Title to *that Blessedness,* which is the portion of those *dead which die in the Lord. To which God, of his infinite Mercy, bring us all through the Merits and Mediation of our Blessed Saviour : to whom with the Father, and the Holy Spirit, be ascribed all Honour, Power, Might, Majesty, and Dominion, henceforth, and for evermore.* Amen.

FINIS.

THE
Sullen Lovers:
OR, THE
IMPERTINENTS.
A
COMEDY,

Acted by
HIS HIGHNESS THE
Duke of YORKES Servants.

Written by
THO. SHADWELL.

Nunc satis est dixisse, Ego mira Poemata pango :
Occupet extremum scabies : mihi turpe relinqui est,
Et, quod non didici, sane nescire fateri.   Hor. de Art. Poet.

In the *SAVOY*,
Printed for *Henry Herringman*, at the Sign of the *Anchor* in the Lower-
Walk of the *New Exchange*, 1668.

Source.

AS Shadwell himself says : " The first hint I receiv'd was from the
report of a Play of *Molieres* of three Acts, called *Les Fascheux*, upon
which I wrote a great part of this before I read that ; and after it
came to my hands, I found so little for my use (having before upon that hint
design'd the fittest Characters I could for my purpose) that I have made
use of but two short Scenes which I inserted afterwards (viz.) the first
Scene in the Second Act between *Stanford* and *Roger*, and *Molieres* story of
Piquette, which I have translated into Back-gammon, both of them being
so vary'd you would not know them. But I freely confess my Theft, and
am asham'd on't, though I have the example of some that never yet wrote
Play without stealing most of it ; and (like men that lye so long, till they
believe themselves) at length, by continual Thieving, reckon their stolne
goods their own too : Which is so ignoble a thing, that I cannot but
believe that he that makes a common practise of stealing other mens Witt,
would, if he could with the same safety, steal any thing else."

Les Fâcheux was produced at the Château de Vaux, 17 August, 1661,
during the fêtes which were held in honour of Louis XIV by Fouquet,
who but a few days later was to be arrested on charges of peculation and
treason and condemned to death, a sentence which was only changed to
perpetual imprisonment at the instant intercession of powerful friends at
court. It is said that owing to a suggestion of Louis XIV himself Molière
in twenty-four hours added the scene (II, vii) of the hunter *Eraste*, who is
a caricature of the marquis de Soyecourt. On the 25 August *Les Fâcheux*
was given at Fontainebleau, and on 4 November of the same year it was
publicly produced at the theatre of the Palais-Royal at Paris. Molière
played *Eraste* ; Du Parc La Montagne ; La Grange Lisandre ; and Mlle.
Molière Orphise.

The play enjoyed forty-four consecutive performances, a notable run
for those days, and was printed February, 1662. It has always been a
favourite in the repertory of the Comédie-Française, and in our time
Monsieur Croué has won a triumph in the rôle of the Poetaster Caritidès.
Émile Faguet has written that *Les Fâcheux* is : " Une *pièce à tiroirs*, c'est-
à-dire une pièce qui ne sert qu'à faire défiler devant le spectateur un
certain nombre d'originaux. . . . Elle est comme un album de caricatures,
et ces caricatures sont merveilleuses. Elles sont si divertissantes qu'on
regretterait bien que le défilé en fût interrompu par ' l'action ' de la pièce
ou simplement par un incident. . . . Les caractères tous poussés au

(3)

burlesque, comme il allait de soi, sont, du reste très justes et vrais." The same criticism might be very justly, and very aptly, applied to Shadwell's *The Sullen Lovers.*

Although, so far as I am aware, it has never before been remarked, it seems to me that Molière for the central theme of *Les Fâcheux* is indebted to Horace, *Sermonum,* I, ix, that piece (*merum sal*) which commences :

> Ibam forte uia Sacra, sicut meus est mos
> nescio quid meditans nugarum, totus in illis.
> accurrit quidam notus mihi nomine tantum,
> arreptaque manu " quid agis, dulcissime rerum ? "

Les Fâcheux has even been transformed into a ballet, June, 1927, and given at the Prince's Theatre, London, with Massine and Tchernichcva. The music was by Aleric.

The Country Gentleman in *The Sullen Lovers,* who is a suitor to Emilia, although comparatively a light sketch, has individuality and differs from such types (good fun though they be) as Crowne's Sir Mannerly Shallow in *The Countrey Wit,* produced at Dorset Garden in January, 1675–6, and his bumpkinly brethren in many another comedy and farce. We are reminded by Emilia's rustic lover of Aretino's Messer Maco in *La Cortigiana,* one of the best Italian comedies before Goldoni. His proverbs may have been suggested by Sancho in *Don Quixote.* In D'Urfey's *The Comical History of Don Quixote* (Parts I, II, produced at Dorset Garden in 1694 ; Part III produced at the same theatre in 1696) Sancho Panca, acted by Dogget, is described as " a dry shreud Country Fellow, Squire to *Don Quixote,* a great Speaker of Proverbs, which he blunders out upon all Occasions, tho never so far from the purpose." Pedrillo in Wieland's *History of Sylvio de Rosalva,* a clever romance satirizing the vogue of the fairy-tale, is a character based upon Sancho. He has the same sententious loquacity, and his mouth also is full of saws and trite proverbs which he cannot refrain from speaking be they relevant or utterly impertinent.

As, however, has been duly emphasized, for Shadwell's contemporaries the personalities gave the allspice to his scenes.

Theatrical History.

SHADWELL'S first comedy *The Sullen Lovers; or, The Impertinents* was produced at Dorset Garden on Saturday, 2 May, 1668, and, chiefly, perhaps, because of the personalities, especially the caricature of Sir Robert Howard, won a great success. Henry Harris created Sir Positive; Smith Stanford; Mrs. Shadwell Emilia; whilst Nokes was Poet Ninny. In his *Diary*, Pepys records:

" At noon with Lord Brouncker in his coach as far as the Temple, and there 'light and to Hercules Pillars, and there dined, and thence to the Duke of York's playhouse, at a little past twelve, to get a good place in the pit, against the new play, and there setting a poor man to keep my place, I out, and spent an hour at Martin's, my bookseller's, and so back again, where I find the house quite full. But I had my place, and by and by the King comes and the Duke of York; and then the play begins, called ' The Sullen Lovers; or, The Impertinents,' having many good humours in it, but the play tedious, and no design at all in it. But a little boy, for a farce, do dance Polichinelli, the best that ever anything was done in the world, by all men's report: most pleased with that, beyond anything in the world, and much beyond all the play."

On Monday, 4 May, Pepys has : " and so to dinner, my sister Michell and I, and thence to the Duke of York's house, and there saw ' The Impertinents ' again, and with less pleasure than before, it being but a very contemptible play, though there are many little witty expressions in it; and the pit did generally say that of it. Thence, going out, Mrs. Pierce called me from the gallery, and there I took her and Mrs. Corbet by coach up and down, and took up Captain Rolt in the street." In spite of Pepys' criticism he none the less went to see the play on the following afternoon, Tuesday, 5 May, for the third time. " At noon home to dinner and Creed with me, and after dinner he and I to the Duke of York's playhouse; and there coming late, he and I up to the balcony-box, where we find my Lady Castlemayne and several great ladies; and there we sat with them, and I saw ' The Impertinents ' once more, now three times, and the three only days it hath been acted. And to see the folly how the house do this day cry up the play more than yesterday ! and I for that reason like it, I find, the better, too; by Sir Positive At-all, I understand, is meant Sir Robert Howard. My Lady (Castelmayne) pretty well pleased with it."

The next day Pepys was at Westminster Hall, " where met with several people and talked with them, and among other things understand that my Lord St. John is meant by Mr. Woodcocke, in ' The Impertinents.' "

Shadwell's play was discussed in every quarter by high and low, and on Friday, 8 May, Pepys, who had to do Admiralty business with the Duke of York notes : " But, Lord ! to see how this play of Sir Positive At-all, in abuse of Sir Robert Howard, do take, all the Duke's and every body's talk being of that, and telling more stories of him, of the like nature, that it is now the town and country talk, and they say, is most exactly true. The Duke of York himself said that of his playing at trap-ball is true and told several other stories of him."

Pepys saw *The Sullen Lovers* again on Wednesday, 24 June, 1668, " to the Duke of York's playhouse, and there saw ' The Impertinents,' a pretty good play." On Saturday, 29 August, of the same year, Henry Harris the actor dined with him, and after dinner he " carried Harris to his play-house, where, though four o'clock, so few people there at ' The Impertinents,' as I went out : and do believe they did not act, though there was my Lord Arlington and his company there. So I out, and met my wife in a coach, and stopped her going thither to meet me ; and took her, and Mercer, and Deb., to Bartholomew Fair." One must remember that the excessive heat of midsummer may well account for the fact that the audience was so scanty on this occasion.

On Wednesday in Easter week, 14 April, 1669, Pepys went " out with my own coach to the Duke of York's play-house, and there saw ' The Impertinents,' a play which pleases me well still ; but it is with great trouble that I now see a play, because of my eyes, the light of the candles making it very troublesome to me. After the play my wife and I towards the park."

In May, 1670, when the English court travelled down to Dover, there to meet the King's sister, the Duchess of Orleans, the actors of Lincoln's Inn Fields were ordered to attend, and one of the plays chosen was Shadwell's comedy.

A performance of *The Sullen Lovers* is recorded 28 July, 1677, when the King was present, but the play did not remain in the repertory of the theatre, and upon a revival at Lincoln's Inn Fields, 5 October, 1703, it was announced as "Not acted 28 years." Powell played Sir Positive "with a Prologue on the death of the Royal Oak Lottery ; and an Epilogue on Maister Observator," a pamphleteer who had attacked the theatre. Since this season Shadwell's first comedy seems entirely to have been laid aside.

T O

The Thrice Noble, High and Puissant Prince

WILLIAM,

Duke, Marquis, and Earl of *NEWCASTLE*, Earl of *Ogle*, Viscount *Mansfield*, Baron of *Bolsover*, of *Ogle*, of *Bertram*, *Bothall*, and *Hepple*, Gentleman of His Majesties Bed-chamber, One of His Majesties most Honourable Privy Councel, Knight of the most noble Order of the Garter, His Majesties Lieutenant of the County and Town of *Nottingham*, and Justice in *Eyre*, *Trent*, *North*, &c.

May it please your Grace,

Had I no particular Obligations to urge me, yet my own Inclinations would prompt me not only to dedicate this to you, but my self to your Graces service : Since you have so much obliged your Countrey both by your Courage, and your Wit, that all men who pretend either to Sword, or Pen, ought to shelter themselves under your Graces Protection : Those Excellencies, as well as the great Obligations I have had the honour to receive from your Grace, are the occasion of this Dedication : And I doubt not, but that Generosity, wherewith your Grace has alwayes succour'd the afflicted, will make you willing (by suffering me to use the honour of your name) to rescue this from the bloody hands of the Criticks, who will not dare to use it roughly, when they see your Graces name in the beginning, that being a stamp sufficient to render it true Coyn, though it be adulterate. That authority that makes you able, and that great Goodness that makes you willing to protect all your servants, may give you frequent troubles of this nature, but I hope your Grace will be pleased to pardon them when they come from,

London, *Sep.* 1.
1668.

My Lord,

Your Graces

Most obliged humble Servant

Tho. Shadwell.

(7)

PREFACE.

Reader,

THE success of this Play, as it was much more then it deserv'd, so was much more than I expected : Especially in this very Critical age, when every man pretends to be a Judge, and some, that never read Three Playes in their lives, and never understood one, are as positive in their Judgement of Plays, as if they were all *Johnsons*. But had I been us'd with all the severity imaginable, I should patiently have submitted to my Fate ; not like the rejected Authors of our time, who, when their Playes are damn'd, will strut, and huff it out, and laugh at the Ignorance of the Age : Or, like some other of our Modern Fopps, that declare they are resolv'd to justifie their Playes with their Swords (though perhaps their Courage is as little as their Wit) such as peep through their loop-holes in the Theatre, to see who looks grum upon their Playes : And if they spy a Gentle Squire making Faces, he poor soul must be *Hector'd* till he likes 'em, while the more stubborn *Bully Rock* damm's, and is safe : Such is their discretion in the Choice of their men. Such Gentlemen as these I must confess had need pretend they cannot Erre. These will huff, and look big upon the success of an ill Play stuff'd full of Songs and Dances, (which have that constraint upon 'em too, that they seldome seem to come in willingly ;) when in such Playes the Composer and the Danceing-Master are the best Poets, and yet the unmerciful Scribler would rob them of all the Honour.

I am so far from valuing my self (as the phrase is) upon this Play, that perhaps no man is a severer Judge of it then my self ; yet if any thing could have made me proud of it, it would have been the great Favour and Countenance it receiv'd from His Majesty and their Royal Highnesses.

But *I* could not perswade my self that they were so favourable to the Play for the Merit of it, but out of a Princely Generosity, to encourage a young beginner, that did what he could to please them, and that otherwise might have been baulk'd for ever : 'Tis to this *I* owe the success of the Play, and am as far from presumption of my own merits in it, as one ought to be who receives an Alms.

The first hint I receiv'd was from the report of a Play of *Molieres* of three Acts, called *Les Fascheux*, upon which I wrote a great part of this before *I* read that ; And after it came to my hands, *I* found so little for my use (having before upon that hint design'd the fittest Characters I could for my purpose) that I have made use of but two short Scenes which

(9)

I inserted afterwards (*viz*) the first Scene in the Second Act between *Stanford* and *Roger*, and *Molieres* story of Piquette, which I have translated into Back-gammon, both of them being so vary'd you would not know them. But I freely confess my Theft, and am asham'd on't, though I have the example of some that never yet wrote Play without stealing most of it; and (like Men that lye so long, till they believe themselves) at length, by continual Thieving, reckon their stolne goods their own too: which is so ignoble a thing, that I cannot but believe that he that makes a common practice of stealing other mens Witt, would, if he could with the same safety, steal any thing else.

I have in this Play, as neer as I could, observ'd the three Unities, of Time, Place, and Action; The time of the Drama does not exceed six houres, the place is in a very narrow Compass, and the Main-Action of the Play, upon which all the rest depend, is the Sullen-Love betwixt *Stanford* and *Emilia*, which kind of Love is onely proper to their Characters: I have here, as often as I could naturally, kept the Scenes unbroken, which (though it be not so much practised, or so well understood, by the *English*) yet among the French-Poets is accomted a great Beauty; but after these frivolous excuses the want of design in the Play has been objected against me: which fault (though I may endeavour a little to extenuate) I dare not absolutely deny: I conceive, with all submission to better Judgments, that no man ought to expect such Intrigues in the little actions of Comedy, as are requir'd in Playes of a higher Nature: but in Playes of Humour, where there are so many Characters as there are in this, there is yet less design to be expected: for, if after I had form'd three or four forward prating Fopps in the Play, I made it full of Plott, and Business; at the latter end, where the turns ought to be many, and suddenly following one another, I must have let fall the humour, which I thought wou'd be pleasanter then intrigues could have been without it; and it would have been easier to me to have made a Plott then to hold up the Humour.

Another Objection, that has been made by some, is, that there is the same thing over and over: which I do not apprehend, unless they blame the unity of the Action; yet *Horace de Arte Poetica*, says,

Sit quod vis, simplex duntaxat, & unum.

Or whether it be the carrying on of the humours to the last, which the same Author directs me to do.

Si quid inexpertum Scenæ committis, & audes
Personam formare novam, Servetur ad Imum
Qualis ab incepto processerit, & sibi constet.

I have endeavour'd to represent variety of Humours (most of the persons of the Play differing in their Characters from one another) which was the practice of *Ben Johnson*, whom I think all Dramatick *Poets* ought to imitate, though none are like to come near; he being the onely person that appears to me to have made perfect Representations of Humane Life, most other Authors that *I* ever read, either have wilde Romantick *Tales* wherein they strein Love and Honour to that Ridiculous height, that it becomes Burlesque; or in their lower Comoedies content themselves with one or two Humours at most, and those not near so perfect Characters as the admirable *Johnson* always made, who never wrote Comedy without seven or eight excellent Humours. I never saw one, except that of *Falstaffe* that was in my judgment comparable to any of *Johnson*'s considerable Humours: You will pardon this digression when I tell you he is the man, of all the World, *I* most passionately admire for his Excellency in Drammatick-*Poetry*.

Though I have known some of late so Insolent to say, that *Ben Johnson* wrote his best *Playes* without Wit; imagining, that all the Wit in *Playes* consisted in bringing two persons upon the Stage to break Jests, and to bob one another, which they call Repartie, not considering that there is more wit and invention requir'd in the finding out good Humor, and Matter proper for it, then in all their smart reparties. For, in the Writing of a Humor, a Man is confin'd not to swerve from the Character, and oblig'd to say nothing but what is proper to it: but in the *Playes* which have been wrote of late, there is no such thing as perfect Character, but the two chief persons are most commonly a Swearing, Drinking, Whoring, Ruffian for a Lover, and an impudent ill-bred *tomrig* for a Mistress, and these are the fine People of the *Play;* and there is that Latitude in this, that almost any thing is proper for them to say; but their chief Subject is bawdy, and profaneness, which they call *brisk writing*, when the most dissolute of Men, that rellish those things well enough in private, are *chok'd* at 'em in publick: and methinks, if there were nothing but the ill Manners of it, it should make Poets avoid that Indecent way of Writing.

But perhaps you may think me as impertinent as any one I represent; that, having so many faults of my own, shou'd take the liberty to judge of others, to impeach my fellow Criminalls: I must confess it is very ungenerous to accuse those that modestly confess their own Errors; but positive Men, that justifie all their faults, are Common Enemies, that no man ought to spare, prejudicial to all Societies they live in, destructive to all Communication, always endeavouring Magisterially to impose upon our Understandings, against the Freedome of Mankind: These ought no more to be suffer'd amongst us, then wild beasts: for no corrections that can be laid upon 'em are of power to reforme 'em; and certainly it was a positive Foole that *Salomon* spoke of, when he said, *bray him in a Mortar, and yet he will retain his folly*.

But I have troubled you too long with this Discourse, and am to aske your pardon for it, and the many faults you will find in the *Play;* and beg you will believe, that whatever I have said of it, was intended not in Justification, but Excuse of it: Look upon it, as it really was, wrote in haste, by a Young Writer, and you will easily pardon it; especially when you know that the best of our Drammatick Writers have wrote very ill *Playes* at first, nay some of 'em have wrote several before they could get one to be Acted; and their best *Playes* were made with great expence of labour and time. Nor can you expect a very Correct *Play,* under a Years pains at the least, from the Wittiest Man of the Nation; It is so difficult a thing to write well in this kind. Men of Quality, that write for their pleasure, will not trouble themselves with exactness in their *Playes;* and those, that write for profit, would find too little incouragement for so much paines as a correct *Play* would require.

Vale.

Prologue.

HOw popular are Poets now a dayes ?
Who can more Men at their first summons raise,
Then many a wealthy home-bred Gentleman,
By all his interest in his Countrey can.
They raise their Friends, but in one day arise
'Gainst one poor Poet, all these Enemies :
For so he has observ'd you alwayes are,
And against all that write maintain a Warr.
What shall he give you composition now ?
Alass, he knows not what you will allow.
He has no cautionary Song, nor Dance,
That might the Treaty of his Peace advance ;
No kinde Romantick Lovers in his Play,
To sigh and whine out passion, such as may
Charm Waitingwomen with Heroick Chime,
And still resolve to live and die in Rhime ;
Such as your Eares with Love, and Honour feast,
And play at Crambo for three houres at least :
That Fight, and wooe, in Verse in the same breath,
And make Similitudes, and Love in Death :
————But if you love a Fool, he bid me say,
He has great choyce to shew you in his Play ;
(To doe you service) I am one to day.
Well Gallants, 'tis his first, Faith, let it goe,
Just as old Gamesters by young Bubbles do :
This first and smaller Stake let him but win,
And for a greater Summ you'll draw him in.
Or use our Poet, as you would a Hare,
Which when she's hunted down, for Sport you spare.
At length take up, and damne no more for shame,
For if you only at the Quarrey aime,
This Critick poaching, will destroy your Game.

(13)

DRAMMATIS PERSONÆ.

Stanford,————— { A Morose Melancholy Man, tormented beyond Measure with the Impertinence of People, and resolved to leave the World to be quit of them.

Lovel,————— { An Ayery young Gentleman, friend to *Stanford*, one that is pleased with, and laughs at the Impertinents, and that which is the others torment, is his recreation.

Sir *Positive At-all*,——— { A foolish Knight, that pretends to understand every thing in the world, and will suffer no man to understand any thing in his Company; so foolishly Positive, that he will never be convinced of an Error, though never so grosse.

Ninny,————— { A conceited Poet, always troubling men with impertinent Discourses of Poetry, and the repetition of his own Verses; in all his Discourse he uses such affected Words, that 'tis as bad as the Canting of a Gypsie.

Woodcock,————— { A Familiar loving Coxcombe, that embraces and kisses all men: So used to his Familiar endearing expressions, that he cannot forbear them in the midst of his Anger.

Huffe,————— { An impudent Cowardly Hector that torments *Stanford* with coming to borrow Money, and is beaten by him.

Roger,————— Stanfords Man.

Father,————— To *Emilia* and *Carolina*.

Country Gent.——— { A Grave ill-bred Coxcombe, that never speaks without a Proverb.

Tim. Scribble,———
Jacob Dash,————— { Two Justices Clerkes.

(14)

DRAMMATIS PERSONÆ

Emilia,——————— Of the same Humour with *Stanford.*

Carolina,——————— Of the same Humour with *Lovel.*

Lady Vaine,——— { A Whore, that takes upon her the name of a Lady, very talkative and impertinently affected in her Language, always pretending to Vertue and Honour.

Luce,——————— *Emilia's* Maid.

Bridget,——————— Lady *Vaines* Maid.

Seargeant with a File of *Musqeeteers,* *Waiters, Fidlers,* &c.

The place of the S C E N E,

L O N D O N.

The Time.

In the Moneth of *March,* 166⅞.

THE
Sullen Lovers:
Or, The
IMPERTINENTS.

ACT I.

Enter Stanford *and* Roger *his Man.*

IN what Unlucky Minute was I born,
   To be tormented thus where e're I go?
   What an Impertinent age is this we live in,
When all the World is grown so troublesome,
That I should envy him that spends his dayes
In some remote and unfrequented Place,
Where none but Bears and Wolves for his Companions,
And never see's the folly of Mankind!
   Rog. Good Sir be patient, let it not disturb you.
   Stanford. Patient——
Thou may'st as well teach patience to a man
That has a fit oth' Collick or the Stone.
   Love. What in a fit agen *Stanford?* now art   (*Enter* Lovel.
Thou as moody as a Poet after his Play is Damn'd.
   Stanf. Oh *Lovel!*   (*Exit* Roger.
I am tormented so beyond my patience
I am resolved to quit the World, and find
Some uninhabited place far from Converse.
Where I may live as free as Nature made me.

(17)

Lov. Why this downright Madness,
Prethee send for a Chirurgeon and open a Veine,
Try what that will do ; for thou wilt be as
Ripe for Bedlum else as a Fanatick.
  Stanf. What would you have me do ?
Where e're I turn me I am baited still
By some importunate Foole's that use me worse,
Then Boyes do Cocks upon Shrove-Tuesday ;
This makes my Life so tedious and unpleasant,
That rather then endure it longer I'le find out
Some place in the *West-Indies,* where I may
See a Man no oftner then a Blazing-Star.
  Lov. Why, thou wilt come to be bound in thy Bed, *Stanford :*
'Thank Heaven I find nothing makes me weary of
My life, thou art scandalous ; Why dost thou abuse
This Age so ? me thinks, it's as pretty an Honest
Drinking Whoring Age as a Man wou'd wish to
Live in.
  Stanf. Sure, *Lovel,* thou wer't born without a Gaule,
Or bear'st thy anger like a useless thing,
That can'st endure to live among such Fooles,
As we are every Day condemn'd to see.
  Lov. Where's the trouble ?
  Stanf. Sure thou art Insensible, or thou woud'st not ask me,
I am more Restless then the Man that has
A Raging Feavor on him ; and like him,
I change my place, thinking to ease my self ; But find
That which should lessen does increase my pain.
  Lov. As how Sir ?
  Stanf. Could any Man have borne but yesterdayes impertinence ;
  Lov. What was that ? for I have not seen you since.
  Stanf. In the morning,
Coming abroad to find you out, (the onely Friend
With whom I can enjoy my self) comes in a brisk
Gay Coxcomb of the Town —— O Lord, Sir, (sayes he)
I am glad I've taken you within, I came on purpose
To tell you the newes, d'ye hear it ? then might I
Reasonably expect to hear of some great Intrigue or
Other ; At the least that the Kings of *France* and *Spain*
Were agreed——Then after he had bid me guess
Four or five times, with a great deal of amazement
Sayes he : Jack-Scatterbrain comes in with ten Guinnys
Last night into the Groom-porters, and

Carry'd away 200; and then Teaz'd me
Half an Hour, to tell me all his Throwes.

    Lov. Now, should I have been pleas'd with this.

    Stanf. You make me Mad to hear you say so.

    Lov. If you are weary of one Company, why don't
You try another? and vary your Companions as often
As your Young Gallants do their Mistresses, or
The Well-bred-Ladies their Servants.

    Stanf. Where e're I go I meet the same affliction : If I go
Into the City, there I find a Company of Fellowes
Selling of their Souls for Two-pence in the Shilling
Profit.

    Lov. You are too Satyricall————

    Stanf. Besides I find the very fools I avoid at this
End of the Town, come thither, some to take
Up Money at Ten in the hundred, what with
Interest and Brokage, as they call it ; others to take
Up Commodities upon Tick, which they sell at half
Value for ready Money, and these Inhumane Rascals
I'th very midst of all their business will fix upon
Me, and I am more Barbarously us'd by e'm, then a
New Poet by a Knot of Critticks.

    Lov. So Sir! go on with your Relation.

    Stanf. The other day, being tyr'd almost to death with the
Impertinence of Fopps that importun'd me ;
For Variety, I ventur'd into a Coffee-house ;
There I found a Company of formal Starch'd Fellows
Talking Gravely, Wisely, and nothing to the purpose ;
And with undaunted Impudence discoursing of the
Right of Empires ; the Management of Peace and War ;
And the great Intrigues of Councils ; when o'my
Conscience you wou'd have sooner took e'm for
Tooth-Drawers then Privy-Counsellors.

    Lov. But why don't you make this
Pleasant to your self and laugh at e'm as I do?

    Stanf. 'Faith Sir, I cannot find the Jest on't.

    Lov. Yet methinks however this should not make me
Uneasie to my self.

    Stanf. Sure, *Lovel,* you have patience more than ever *Stoick* had ;
This damn'd Impertinence makes me resolv'd to fly my Country ; I
can never find one houres refreshment in a Year: If I go to the Theatre,
where all People hope to please themselves ; either I find an Insupportable Play ; or If a good one, ill acted ; or which is worse, so many

troublesome Wits buzzing about my Eares, that I am driven from
thence too.

   Lov. If this torments you so, then change the Scene, and
Go to Court, where Conversation is refin'd.

   Stanf. Why so I do ; but there I find a company of gaudy nothings
That fain would be Courtiers ; that think they are
Hardly dealt withal not to have Imployment too :
Besides, when after all my persecutions, I think
To ease my self at night by sleep, as last night
About eleven or twelve of Clock ; at a solemn
Funeral the Bells set out : That Men should be
Such Owls to keep five thousand
People awake, with Ringing a Peale to him that does not hear it !

   Lov. But 'tis Generously done, especially since in my
Conscience they expect no thanks for their Labour,
Neither from their Dead Friend, nor any one else.

   Stanf. A Curse upon e'm, this was no sooner past, but
About two in the Morning comes the Bell-man,
And in a dismal Tone repeats Worse Rhymes
Then a Cast Poet of the Nursery can make ; after
Him, come those Rogues that wake People with their
Barbarous tunes, and upon their Toting
Instruments make a more Hellish Noise then they
Do at a Play-house, when they flourish for the
Entrance of Witches.

   Lov. All this disturbs not me : but if you are troubled
With this Noise, Why don't you live in the Country ?
There you may be free.

   Stanf. Free ! Yes to be drunk with March Beer, and Wine, worse then
ever was serv'd in at Pye-corner at the eating of Pigs ; and hear no other
Discourse, but of Horses, Dogs, and Hawkes.

   Lov. I wou'd not be of your uneasie disposition for
The World : but granting all this : Cannot the
Women of the Town please you ? methinks
The pretty Devils have Charmes enough to keep me
In the World still without the Danger of being
Felo-de-se.

   Stanf. Women ! O ! name e'm not : They are impertinence
It self, I can scarce endure the sight of e'm.

   Lov. Why thou art stark-mad ; 'faith for my part I
Ne're met with any of the Sex that was kind and
Pretty, but I cou'd bear with her Impertinence.

   Stanf. It cannot be.

Lov. No ! wou'd thoud'st try me :   And bring
Me to a New Woman that's handsom ; If I
Boggl'd at her Impertinence, may I never have
Other to help me at my Necessity, then an Oyster
Wife, or one that cries Ends of Gold and Silver :
Methinks Beauty and Impertinence do well enough
Together.

Stanf. Sure you railly with me all this while, you cannot
Be so stupid to think I have not reason in my
Opinion ; but nothing I have ever told you yet
Has equal'd the persecution of this Day.

Lov. I know whom that concernes——prethee let me
Hear't, that I may laugh a little at those
Monkeys ; The Variety of their folly alwayes
Affords new matter.

Stanf. That it does, to my sad experience ; This morning, just as I was
coming to look for you, Sir Positive At-all, that Fool, that will let no
Man understand any thing in his Company, Arrests me with his Impertinence ; sayes he, with a great deal of Gravity, perhaps I am the Man of
the World that have found out two Plays, that betwixt you and I have a
great deal of Wit in e'm ; Those are, the Silent Woman, and the Scornful
Lady————And if I understand any thing in the World, there's Wit
enough, in both those, to make one good Play, If I had the management of
e'm : For you must know, this is a thing I have thought upon and
consider'd.

Lov. This is the pleasant'st thing I have ever heard

Stanf. May you have enough on't then if you think so :
But this was not all, for notwithstanding I
Granted his Opinion, he forc'd me to stay an
Hour to hear his Impertinent Reasons for't ;
But no sooner, by some happy Accident or
Other, had I got rid of him, but in comes
That familiar Loving Puppy *Woodcock*, that admires
Fooles for Wits, and torments me with a damn'd
Coranto, as he calls it, upon his Violin, which he us'd
So barbarously, I was ready to take it for a
Bag-pipe.

Lov. This would have made me broke my Spleen with
     Laughter.

Stanf. I must be stung with a Tarrantula, before I could laugh at it : but
here my persecution did not end ; For after I had got loose from the other
two, whom should I see as I came along, but that infinite Coxcomb
Poet—*Ninny :* who by force of Arms hales me into his Lodging, and Reads

me there a Confounded Scene in Heroick Verse : so that what with Sir
Positive's Orations, *Woodcocks* squeaking Fiddle, and Poet *Ninny*'s Heroick
Fuſtian, I have a greater Wind-mill in my brain then a New Polititian with
his head full of Reformation ; but as Fate wou'd have it, in came a Dunn,
and out got I and for fear of further Interruption, came back to my
Lodging. *(Enter* Roger.

Roger. O Sir ! here's Poet *Ninny.* *(Enter* Ninny.

Stanf. I ha' but nam'd the Devil, and fee I have rais'd him.

Ninn. Mr. *Lovel,* Your humble Servant.

Lov. Sweet Mr. *Ninny,* I am yours.

Ninn. But dear Mr. *Stanford,* I am infinitely troubled,
That that unmannerly Raskal shou'd come and diſturb
Us juſt now : But you know, Sir, we cannot help the
Impertinence of foolish Idle Fellowes.

Stanf. No, no ! you have convinc'd me sufficiently of that. *(aside.*
How the devil could he follow me ? I think the *(Lovel* and *Ninny* whisper.
Raskal ha's as good a Nose as a Blood-Hound.

Ninn. I have a Copy of Heroick Verses will fit him
I warrant you.

Lov. Read e'm to him, he's a great Judge I can assure you.

Ninn. Sir, I am happy to meet with one that is so great
A judge of Poetry as you are, for it is a miserable
Thing for an Author to expose his things to empty
Giddy-fellowes : and let me tell you, between you and
I, there are seven thousand Fooles to seven Wise Men.

Lov. That so great a Truth should be spoken by one
That I'le swear is none of the seven !

Stanf. Now do you judge *Lovel :* *(enter Woodcock.*
'Slife, another Teazer here ! *Woodcock?*

Wood. Dear *Ninny,* Ah dear *Lovel :* Ah my dear *Jack Stanford,* I am the
happieſt Man in thy Friendship of any Man's upon *(Kiſes them all.*
Earth, Dear *Jack,* I have the greateſt value for thee in the World ; prethee
Kiss me agen dear Heart.

Stanf. Now *Lovel,* Have I reason or not ?

Lov. That you have to Laugh ; this is my recreation.

Stanf. Well ! if I do not leave the World within these three days, May
1 be eternally baited by Sir *Positive, Ninny,* and *Woodcock,* which is a Curse
worse than the worſt of my Enemies Wishes. *(aside.*

Wood. Hay ! Art thou resolv'd to give over the World too
Dear Heart ? There's a Lady that came to Town
Yeſterday that is of the same mind : she told me
So, but I hope she will not, for the truth on't is
Jack, I am in Love with her.

Ninn. Are you so ? but I hope I shall catch her from you for all that.

(aside.

Wood. She sayes she's so troubled with Impertinent People, which, between you and I *Jack*, are so numerous in this Town, that a Man cannot live in quiet for e'm, that she's resolv'd to leave the World to be quit of e'm.

Ninn. Yes, Faith she told me so laſt night as I was reading
A Scene of my Play to her.

Stanf. No doubt she had reason.

Wood. 'Tis your Acquaintance *Ned Lovel, Carolina*'s Siſter, *Emilia*.

Lov. Now *Stanford* I'le oblige you, and bring you
Acquainted with this Lady ; Certainly her humor
Will please you.

Stanf. My Friend torment me too ! Have I not Impertinent
Acquaintance enough already ; but you muſt endeavour
To trouble me with more ?

Wood. Well ! that's an Excellent Coppy of
Verses of thine, Dear *Ninny*. Come on *Jack*,
Thou shalt hear e'm.

Stanf. Hell and Damnation !   (*Offers to go out.*

Ninn. Hold, hold ; You shall hear.
Your sad indifference————(Look you Sir, 'tis upon a
Lady that is indifferent in her Carriage tow'rd me)
Your sad indifference————(I am confident this
Will please you, here are many thoughts I was happy in
And the Choice of words not unpleasant, which you
Know is the greateſt matter of all)—Your sad indifference
So wounds————(Look you, you shall find as much
Soul and Force, and Spirit, and Flame in this, as ever you
Saw in your Life.)

Wood. Come, *Jack*, hear't, it is a moſt admirable piece.

Stanf. Now, *Lovel*, What think you ?   (*Lovel laughs.*
Gentlemen, I have Extraordinary Business,
I muſt leave you.

Wood. No, no, hold ! Faith thou shalt ſtay and hear
His Verses, they are as good as ever were read :
Come, *Ninny*————

Stanf. O Devil ! What have I deserv'd to have this
Inflicted upon me ?

Ninn.   } Your sad indifference so wounds my fair,
Reads. ∫ At once I hope, and do at once despair.
How do you like that, ha ?————
         You do at once both hate and kindness show ;
         And are at once both Kind and Cruel too.

(23)

Wood. O ! Very fine ! Is't not, *Ned?*

Lov. O ! Extreame fine.

Stanf. What the Devil makes you commend these sottish
Verses, That are nothing but a Jingling of Words ?
Let's go.

Ninn. Hold ! hold ! hold ! hear the rest ; hem————

Reads ⎱ At once my hopes you nourish and destroy,
Agen. ⎰ My onely Grief, and yet my onely Joy.
Mark that.

Stanf. O Devil !

Ninn. ⎱ Vertue and Vice at once in you do shine ;
reads. ⎰ Your inclinations are, and are not mine.

Wood. O Admirable ! Didst ever hear any thing so
Fine in thy life Dear Heart ?

Stanf. O how these Curs bait me !

Ninny reads ⎱ At once a storme and calme I do espy,
    agen. ⎰ And do at once a smile and frown descry.
          At once you kindle and put out my flame :
          I cold as Ice, as hot as Charcoal am.
Mark that, Mr. *Stanford,* I was very happy in that
Thought, as I hope to breathe.

Wood. Upon my word, *Jack,* that's a great flight of his.

Rog. Sir, methinks there's as pretty a Soul in't, as a Man shall see in a
Summers Day.

Stanf. What am I condemn'd to ?

Lov. Why do you torment your self thus, methinks nothing can be
pleasanter.

Stanf. Gentlemen, detain me not, I'le stay no longer.

Ninn. Dear Mr. *Stanford,* I ha' just done, if you have any respect in
the World for me, stay and hear the end on't.

Wood. Nay, 'Faith *Jack* thou shalt stay.

Stanf. What's this I endure ?

Ninny ⎱ My Fate at once is gentle and severe,
reads. ⎰ You will not shew your hate, nor Love declare :
          Such safety and such dangers in your eye,
          That I resolve at once to live and die.
There's, Body and Soul, in that Couplet.

Lov. Hey, riddle me riddle me this, but this is the
Fashionable way of writing.

Ninn. What say you, Sir ?   Are they not well ?
You are a great Judge.

Stanf. Pray, Sir, let me go, I am no Judge at all, let me go,
I will not stay.

Sir *Positive*, here ! I had rather   (*Enter Sir* Positive.
Go against an Insurrection of 'Prentices, then
Encounter him.

    Sir *Posit.* Ah Dear *Jack !* Have I found thee ? I would not but have
seen you for twenty pounds : I have made this morning a glorious Corrant,
an immortal Corrant, a Corrant with a Soul in't ; I'le defie all Europe to
make such another : You may talk of your Baptists, your Locks, and your
Banisters ; let me see 'em Mend this : Why here's at least 25 Notes
Compass, Fa, la, la, *&c.* You shall hear.

    Wood. Come, Sir *Positive*, lets hear't.

    Sir *Posit.* With all my heart : Fa, la, la.

    Stanf. Oh Heaven ! Sir *Positive*, though I love Musick,
Yet at present I must tell you,
I am out of Tune,

    Ninn. Out of Tune, Ha, ha, ha,——Now have you said the
Best thing in the World, and do not know it.

    Stanf. Sir *Positive*, I must take my leave of you, I must not lose my
Business for a little Musick.

    Sir *Posit.* Hold, now you talk of Musick——

    Stanf. 'Slife, Sir, I talk of my Business.

    Sir *Posit.* But for Musick, if any Man in *England* gives you a better
account of that then I do, I will give all Mankind leave to spit upon me :
You must know, it's a thing I have thought upon and consider'd, and made
it my business from my Cradle ; besides, I am so naturally a Musician, that
Gamut, A re, Bemi, were the first words I could learn to speak : Do you
like *Baptist*'s way of Composing ?

    Lov. No doubt, Sir, he's a great Master.

    Wood. As ever was born, take that from me.

    Sir *Posit.* Upon my word, *Stanford*, I will make all my Tunes like his—
You shall hear his Vein in this Corrant now.

    Stanf. One trouble upon the neck of another——
When shall I be deliver'd from these Fools ?

    Sir *Posit.* Do but ask *Ninny* there.

    Ninn. Yes doubtless, Sir *Positive* has a great Soul of Musick in him ; he
has great power in Corranto's and Jiggs, and composes all the Musick to
my Playes ; he ha's great power.

    Wood. As any man that ever was born, Dear Heart.

    Sir *Posit.* Come, you shall hear't———

    Stanf. Sir, I beg your pardon ; I'le hear it some other time.

    Sir *Posit.* Pish, pish, Upon my Honour thou shalt stay,
And hear it now.

    Lov. Come, Dear Sir *Positive*, Make us happy.

    Sir *Posit.* Observe ! here's Flame in this Corrant——Fa, la, la.

There's a delicate Note in B Fa Bemi in Alt.
And observe now how it falls down to C. Sol. Fa. Ut.
Fa, la, la————There's Mastery for you.

Stanf. I do not like that part of your Corrant.

Sir *Posit.* It is a prodigious thing, thou shou'dst ever be in my Company, and understand Musick no better ; thou hast found fault with the best part of the Corrant, ask *Woodcock* else.

Wood. By the Lord *Harry*, there is a great deal of
Glory in that part of the Corrant.

Sir *Posit.* Observe here how cunningly it falls out of the Key, Fa, la, *&c.*
And now at last it ends quite out of the Key.

Stanf. Well, well ! it's an Excellent Corrant ; What the Devil
Will you have more ?————Fare you well.

Sir *Posit.* No, no ; Stay but one Minute and you shall hear it
All together. *Ninny*, Do you beat Time————

Wood. Well thought on, do, and I'le dance
To't, Dear Hearts.

Stanf. Now, *Lovel*, what think you ? this Torture's worse than any the
Dutch invented at *Amboyna*.

Sir *Posit.* Here's a Corrant for you, ha ! *Stanford*,
What think'st of this ?

Wood. Think quoth a', I think I danc'd it as well
As any Man in *England*, *Bully-Rock*.

}
Sir Positive *sings.*
Ninny *beats* false
time, & Wood-
cock *Dances to't.*

Lov. Certainly, Sir *Positive*, he dances very finely.

Sir *Posit.* As any Man that ever was born upon two Leggs :
I defie any Man in the World that out-does him ;
For betwixt you and I, I taught him every step he has.

Rog. Upon my Word, *Woodcock*, you have as much power
In Dancing, as any Man in *England*.

Wood. Dear Heart, let me kiss thee ; Gad thou art a great
Judge————Here, drink my Health.

Rog. Ah ! Dear Flattery, How convenient a sin art thou ?   (*aside.*

Ninn. Come, Mr. *Woodcock*, you shall go to the reading of my Play.

Wood. Ay ! Come on, Bully-Rock————   (*Ex.* Nin *and* Wood.

Lov. Come, I'le take pity on you, *Stanford*, and go before, and prepare some place or other, where we may enjoy our selves, and you be free: I'le take your Man along with me, and send him back agen in haste for you ; by that means you may get loose.

Stanf. For Heavens sake make hast, you'l oblige me for ever.
                              (*Exit* Lovel *and* Roger.

Sir *Positive* ! I am sorry I must leave you now ;
I must go speak with a Gentleman that came
From *Flanders* last night.

Sir *Posit. Flanders!* If any Man gives you that account of *Flanders* that I do, I'le suffer Death; You must know I have thought of their Affairs, I have consider'd of the thing throughly, never speak on't more, name it no more, let it not enter into your Thoughts; 'tis a lost Nation, absolutely undone, lost for ever, take that from me: And yet were I with *Castel Rodrigo* but one quarter of an hour, I'de put him in a way to save all yet.

Stanf. This is beyond all sufferance.——Sir *Positive*, I am
So much in haste, that none but your self shou'd
Have staid me of all Mankind.

Sir *Posit.* Mankind! Dost thou know what thou say'st now? Do'st thou talk of Mankind? I am confident thou never so much as thought'st of Mankind in thy life: I'le tell thee, I will give Dogs leave to piss upon me, if any Man understands Mankind better then my self, now you talk of that. I have consider'd all Mankind, I have thought of nothing else but Mankind this Moneth; and I find you may be a Poet, a Musitian, a Painter, a Divine, a Mathematician, a States-man; but betwixt you and I, let me tell you, we are all Mortal.

Stan. Well, they may talk of the Pox, want of Money, and a Scoulding Wife, but they are Heaven to my afflictions.

Enter Bridget.

Bridg. Sir *Positive*, my Lady *Vaine* desires you wou'd come and look upon her Picture that's come this Morning from Master *Lilly*'s.

Sir *Posit.* Why there 'tis now *Stanford*, that people shou'd have no more Judgement, she had as good have thrown her money into the Dirt; 'tis true, I cou'd have made him have made a good picture on't, if I had drawn the Lines for him, but I was not thought worthy; and now you talk of Painting, either I am the greatest Fopp in Nature, or if I do not understand that, I understand nothing in the World: why I will paint with *Lilly*, and draw in little with *Cooper* for 5000 *l.*

Stanf. O intollerable Impertinence! I am afraid he will not go now his Mistress sends for him.

Sir *Posit.* Dear *Stanford!* I must beg thy Excuse——

Stanf. A Curse on him, that's easily granted.   *aside.*

Sir *Posit.* Come, Mistress *Bridget*, I'le go along with you—Dear *Stanford*, take it not unkindly, for I wou'd not leave thee but upon this occasion.

Stanf. A thousand Thanks to the occasion.   *aside.*

Sir *Posit.* But you know a Man must not disoblige his Mistress, *Jack*?

Stanf. Oh no, by no means.

Sir *Posit.* Adieu.   *Ex. Sir Pos.* and *Bridget.*

Stanf. So! this Trouble is over.
  O Fate! how little care you took of me,
  By these Misfortunes I too plainly see.   *Ex.*

ACT II.

Enter Caroline, Lovell.

Car. I Long to bring 'em together, they will be well Match'd; but we must stay a while, for she has been so teaz'd this Morning, she has lock'd her self up in her Chamber.

Lov. Stanford was ready to fall out with me, when I nam'd a new acquaintance to him, and will not be perswaded there is such a Creature as a Woman.
That is not Impertinent.

Car. Emelia is as Cautious as he can be, and wou'd be ready To swound at the sight of a new face, for she will not believe but all mankind are Coxcombs: For Heav'ns sake, *Lovell*, let's surprize them into one anothers Company, we shall have admirable sport.

Lov. Wee'l do't; but, Madam, why shou'd we mind their bus'ness that have enough of our own? What if you and I shou'd play the Fools once in our Lives, and enter into the bonds of Wedlock together?

Car. Fie; fie, 'tis such a constant condition of life, that a Woman had as good be profest in a Nunnery, for she can no sooner get out of one then t'other.

Lov. But with your pardon, Madam, this is somewhat The pleasanter Condition of the Two.

Car. That's according as they use both Conditions; but
Pray Master *Lovell*, bring not this villanous Matrimony
Into dispute any more, lest that they make us desire
It: I have known some men by maintaining a
Heresie in Jest, become of that Opinion in good Earnest.
But do you know that my Lady *Vaine* was here this Morning?

Lov. No, Madam, but what of that?

Car. She told me that of you, will make your Ears tingle.

Lov. Of me, Madam! What was't?

Car. She sayes you are the most inconstant Man, the most perfidious Wretch that e're had breath, and bid me fly you as I wou'd infection.

Lov. What the Devil did she mean by that?

Car. Come, let me know what's betwixt you, I'le
Rack you but I'le know it.

Lov. This Jealousie makes me believe you love me.
That she should be prating her self!   *aside.*
How many Women would be thought honest, if
They could hold their own Tongues?

Car. I am like to have a fine servant of you: but a Lady wou'd have a fine time on't that were to marry you, to stake all the treasures of her Youth and Virginity, which have been preserv'd with so much Care, and Heav'n knows, some trouble too against nothing.

Lov. Faith, Madam, I have e'en as much as I had before, but if you'l be kind, I'le take that Care off your hands, and soon rid you of that trouble.

Car. No, no, go to my Lady *Vaine*, give her your Heart; poor Lady, she wants it too; but for me, I can keep my affliction to my self.

Lov. Dear *Carolina !* name her no more; if you do, I will get drunk immediately : And then I shall have Courage enough to fall aboard her.

Car. Lord! what a loss shall I have? Heav'n fend me patience, or I shall ne're out-live it, to lose so proper a Gentleman; but why should I think to rob her of her due? No, no, now I think on't, to her again, go, go.

Lov. For Heav'ns sake, *Carolina*, do not Tyrannize thus, why, I had rather be kept walking at an ill Play, then endure her Company.

Car. Thus are we, poor Women, despis'd, when we give away our Hearts to ungrateful Men; but Heav'n will punish you.

Lov. Dear *Carolina*, let's leave fooling, and be in down-right Earnest.

Car. I hope, Sir, your Intentions are honourable.

Lov. Madam, Why should you once doubt it ?
My love to you is as pure as the flame that burns upon an Altar :
You are too unjust if you suspect my honour.

Car. Now will you leave fooling ; on my Conscience
He is in earnest.

Lov. As much as the severest Anchorite can be at his Devotions.

Car. O! are you so ? 'its a hard Case; but pray you, Sir, leave off, I had rather hear a silenc'd Parson preach Sedition, than you talk seriously of Love, wou'd you cou'd see how it becomes you; why you look more Comically than an old-fashion'd Fellow singing of *Robin Hood* or *Chevy Chace.*
My Love to you's as pure as the flame that burns upon an Altar !
how scurvily it sounds !

Lov. You are the Cruellest Tyrant alive : Let us be serious a little, I have rallied my self into a passion will ruine me else.

Car. Come, in what posture must I stand to hear you talk formally ?

Lov. On my Conscience 'tis easier to fix quick-silver than your humour, Madam, but if you wou'd enter into Wedlock, I can assure you that will bring you to gravity.

Car. Let me but once more hear you name Marriage, and I protest I'le send for my Lady *Vaine* to you. I tell you again, I will not marry. I love your Conversation, and your humour of all things in the World.
But for Marriage, 'tis good for nothing, but to make Friends fall out.

Lov. Nay, faith, if you be at that, I can do you the same Civility without that Ceremony, as you say it is a kind of formal Thing.

Car. No ! I shall take Example by my Lady *Vaine*, poor Lady, she little thought to be unkindly us'd, I warrant you.

Lov. Again that name !

Car. Besides, if we were Marry'd you might say; faith *Carolina* is a pretty Woman, and has humour good enough, but a pox on't she's my Wife; no, no, I'le have none of that.

Lov. Do you still distrust my Honour ? 'tis unkindly done, but———

Car. Hold, hold, her door opens, step you in there, and you may hear how she entertains the motion.

Enter Emilia *with a Book in her hand.*

Emil. The Wisdom of this *Charles* the fifth was
Wonderful;
Who 'midst of all his Triumphs and his Greatness,
When he had done what Glory had oblig'd him to,
Seeing the Vanity of Mankind, did quit
The pleasures that attend a Monarchs state;
Nay more, that most bewitching thing call'd power,
And left the World, to live an humble life,
Free from the Importunity of Fools : was't not
Wisely done, Sister ?

Car. Yes, no doubt on't, as wisely done to go to a Monastery to shun fools, as to keep Company with Usurers and Brokers to avoid Knaves.

Emil. Thou art a Foolish Girl, I am tormented
With The Impertinence of both Sexes so,
I am resolv'd I'll not stay one Week out of a Nunnery.

Car. O' my Conscience thou art stark out of thy Wits with reading of *Burton's* Melancholly; to a Nunnery to avoyd Impertinence ! where canst thou think to meet with more then there ?

Emil. Now you are too Censorious.

Car. You shou'd like me the better.
But must you needs find relief there ? Doe you
Think that any Women that have sense, or Warmth
Of Blood, as we have, wou'd go into a Nunnery ?

Emil. If I shou'd meet with Fops there too,
I should be irreparably lost : Oh Heaven ! what
Shall I do to ease my self ? rather then
Endure the persecution of those Fools that haunt
Us here. I will go where neither Man nor Woman
Ever came.

Lov. O rare ! *Stanford*, here's juſt thy Counterpart   [*Within.*
To a hair.

Car. Since thou art resolv'd to sequeſter thy self from Company, I'le buy thee a Cage, and hang thee up by the Parrot over the way, thou shalt converse with none but him : I hope he's not Impertinent too ?

Emil. Muſt you torment me too ? fy, Siſter.
What would you have me do ? my Patience
Is not great enough to endure longer, to see
The folly of this age ; Do you judge, after I had been
Sufficiently worry'd by the Lady *Vaine* this Morning,
Whom I was forc'd get rid of, by Telling her, her
Lover my Cozen *Positive* was at her lodging, which
You know is as far as the Pall-Mall.

Car. That *Virtuosa*, as she calls her self, is the pleasanteſt Creature I ever saw : but prethee, Siſter, let me hear none of your fantaſtick Stories, methinks you are as Impertinent as any body.

Emil. It diſtraĉts me to see this folly in things that are intended for reasonable Creatures.

Lov. O *Stanford !* if this Lady does not match thee, the devil's in't.
                                        [*within.*

Car. These Fools you talk of, afford me so much recreation, that I do not know how I should laugh without e'm.

Emil. Thou haſt no sence, they make me weary of the World ! Heav'n ! what shall I do ?

Car. I tell you : *Stanford* hearing of your humour, and admiring it, has a great desire to see you ; before you resolve to leave the world, try how he will please you.

Emil. What a ridiculous thing it is of you to wish me to new Acquaintance, when I am leaving the old ? I am sure He's Impertinent, for all Mankind I have met are so.

Car. Hiſt *Lovell !*

Lov. Your humble Servant, Ladies——   [*Comes out.*

Emil. Is this he ? then farewell.

Lov. Madam ! pray ſtay, and give me the honour of one word with you.

Emil. I knew what he was : My Lady *Vaine* here ?

Enter Lady Vaine *and* Bridget.

L. Vaine. Maſter *Lovell !* your humble servant.

Lov. Your Ladiships humble servant : How I hate the sight of her in presence of my Miſtress !

Car. *Lovell !* for shame be civil to your Miſtress : Let's hear you make Love a little.

L. Vaine. Madam, upon my Reputation there was no such thing ; Sir

Positive was never there, sure some Dirty fellow or other brought a false Message on purpose to rob me of the pleasure of your Ladiships sweet Company: Would he were hang'd for his pains, the passion he has put me in, has put me out of breath. [*To Emilia.*

Lov. Lord! how soon she's put in and put out!

L. Vaine. But, Madam, as soon as ever I found he was not there, I made all possible haste to wait upon you again, for fear your Ladiship shou'd resent my too abrupt departure.

Emil. O Heav'ns! take pity of my afflictions, Madam—

L. Vaine. But the truth on't is, I design'd to spend this day with you, since I can be no where so well satisfi'd as with your Ladiships Converse, a person who is Mistress of so much vertue and honour, which are Treasures I value above the World.

Emil. Why Madam——

L. Vaine. For the truth is so few Ladies have either, that they are things to be valu'd for their rarity.

Emil. Oh Impertinence! Whither will this Eternal tongue of hers carry her?

Lov. This is very pleasant, for her to name Vertue and Honour in my Company. [*aside.*

Emil. Madam! for Heav'ns sake——

L. Vaine. For the truth on't is, Madam, a Lady without Vertue and Honour is altogether as detestable as a Gentleman without Wit or Courage.

Emil. Madam! I am sorry I cannot wait on you longer, I am ingaged to dine abroad.

La. Vain. Where is't, Madam? for I am resolv'd to go along with you.

Emil. Why Madam, you do not know the persons.

La. Vain. That's all one for that, let me alone to make my Apology.

Emil. This is beyond all sufferance.

Car. I hope she will not leave her off so,

Lov. No: if she does, I am mistaken.

La. Vain. Come Madam; Lets go.

Emil. But Madam, I must call at the Exchange first, To buy some trifles there.

La. Vain. O Madam! I'le bring you to my *Milliner*, that Calls himself the *Italian Milliner*, or the Little Exchange; he's better provided then any one in the Exchange.

Emil. I am on the sudden taken ill, and must retire.

La. Vain. Madam, d'ye think, I that am a *Virtuosa* understand no better, then to leave you now you are not well? what's your Distemper? no Woman in *England* was more serviceable among her Neighbours then I with my *Flos Unguentorum*, *Paracelsian* and *Green-Salve*.

Lov. And your *Album Græcum* I warrant you.

La. Vain. That *Album Græcum* was a Salve of my Invention :
But a *propos*, perhaps it may be a fit of the Mother ;
If it be, we muſt burn some *Blew-Inckle*, and *Partridge*
Feathers under your Nose ; or she muſt smell to *Assa fœtida*,
And have some Cold Water with a little Flower to drink :
Ay, ay, 'twill be so ; pray Mr. *Lovel* come and help to hold her.

Emilia. No, no, Madam ; there's no such thing I'le assure you :
I muſt beg leave to go to my Chamber.

La. Vaine. Come Madam, I'le conduɛt you, and be as careful of you
As if you were my Siſter a thousand times.

Emil. Madam ! with your pardon, I desire to be alone, and
Try to reſt.

L. Vaine. Alone ! by no means in the World, Madam, it may
Be very dangerous ; I would not for all the World,
Madam, you should be alone ; suppose you shou'd
Fall into a Fit alone ; I can speak it by Experience,
'Tis dangerous for a Lady to fall into a Fit without
An Able Body by her. Come Madam, I'le Conduɛt you in.

Emilia. How shall I get rid of her ? (*Ex. La. Vaine and* Emilia.

Lovel. Let's in and see when the Fury of this *Dol Comon* will be at an
End.

Carol. Come, come, we shall have the pleasure of seeing my
Siſter Worry'd almoſt to death. (*Exit* Lovell *and* Carolina.

Enter Stanford.

Stanf. I wonder my Man returns not yet.
I thought to have found Mr. *Lovel* here, but
Here's one will do my business. (*Enter* Huffe.

Huffe. Oh Mr. *Stanford !* Have I found you ?

Stanf. Oh Heavens ! Will my punishment never end ?

Huffe. I am the moſt unfortunate Man that ever was born.

Stanf. Why do you trouble me with this ? Am I the
Cause on't ?

Huffe. No ! but I'le tell you, upon my Reputation, I have been Nick't
out of twenty pound Juſt now at *Spierings*, and loſt seven to four, for my
laſt Stake.

Stanf. What the Devil's this to me ? let me go.

Huffe. But Sir, I'le tell you a thing that very nearly concerns you.

Stanf. Some other time ; 'Slife do not diſturb me now.

Huffe. For Heaven's sake hear me, you'l repent it else.

Stanf. Make haſte then, keep me in pain no longer.

Huff. Why, I have found out the fineſt plump fresh Girle,
newly come out of the Country.

(33)

Stanf. Hell and Damnation ! Why do you trouble me with
such trifles ?

Huffe. Trifles, does he call e'm ? Well ! *I* see this won't do : (*Aside.*
But Sir, *I*'le tell you somewhat concerns you more
Nearly ; Sir, it concernes your Honour.

Stanf. My Honour ! Why, who dares call it in question ?

Huffe. Not so, Sir ; but, Do you love Generosity and Honour ?

Stanf. Why do you ask the question ?

Huffe. Why then *I*'le put you in a way to do a very Generous
And Honourable thing.

Stanf. What do you mean by this Impertinence ?

Huffe. If you will relieve an Honest Gentleman in distress,
Lend me two Pieces, you shall have 'em agen within
Four and twenty hours, or may *I* perish.

Stanf. 'Pox on you for an Owl : There take 'em ; I wou'd
I cou'd get rid of all my Impertinents at as cheap
A rate.

Huffe. I give you a thousand thanks.

Stanf. 'Slife ! trouble me no more, be gone !

Huffe. Sir, It were a very ungrateful thing not to
Acknowledge the favour.

Stanf. Away, away, and let your gratitude alone.

Huffe. D'hear, Mr. *Stanford !* upon mine honor *I*'le ⎰ Huff *offers to go*
Return e'm to morrow night without fail. ⎱ *out, and returns.*

Stanf. Curse on you for a Rascal ! (*Ex.* Huffe.
So here's one trouble over !
Well, What's the News ? (*Enter* Roger.

Rog. Do you earnestly desire to know, Sir ?

Stanf. Must I have Impertinence in my own Family too ?

Rog. O ! I am so out of breath, I am not able to speak one word ; but
if I had never so much breath, I cou'd tell you nothing but what you'd be
glad to hear : If I had the winde of an *Irish* Foot-man, nay, of a Non-con-
forming Parson, or——

Stanf. Or, with a Pox to you ! One Similitude more, and I'le
Break that Fooles head of yours.

Roger. Well, Sir, since you are in haste, *I*'le be brief as a Fidler after,
he's paid for scraping, for *I* love to be so in Cases of this Importance, for I
have heard———

Stanf. Out you Dog, a Sentence after your Similitude !
You are as impertinent as a Country Witness.

Roger. I have done Sir, and now I'le tell you in one word :
Hold Sir ! here's a Spider in your Perriwigg.

Stanf. Death, you Rascal ! I'le ram it down your Throat.

Roger. Be patient, Sir : *Seneca* advises to moderate our passions.

Stanf. Hang ye Rascal ! *Seneca* is an Ass in your mouth.
Tell me quickly, or————

Roger. Why Sir, you are so impatient you will not hear me.

Stanf. 'Faith but *I* will speak.

Roger. Not to boast of my diligence, which, though I say it, is as much—

Stanf. You Dogg tell me quickly, or I'le cut your Ears off.

Roger. Why, Mr. *Lovel* wou'd have you come to him ; What wou'd you have ?

Stanf. If I were not in haste, Sirrah, I'de teach you to know your Man, and who you may put your Tricks on, you impudent Raskal.

Rog. Death ! That I shou'd find impertience in $\begin{cases} As \text{ Stanford } is \text{ going} \\ out, \text{ enter Woodcock.} \end{cases}$ others, and not see it in my self.

Wood. Dear *Jack*, thy humble Servant : How dost doe ? My Footman told me, he saw thy Man come in here, which made me believe I shou'd find thee here ; and *I* had not power to stay from thee, my Dear Bully-Rock, for *I* enjoy my self no where so well as in thy Company : Let me kiss thee Dear Heart ; 'Gad *I* had rather kiss thee then any Woman.

Stanf. This is beyond all Example : Oh horrid ! his kindness is a greater persecution than the *In*juries of others.

Wood. I'le tell thee, Dear Heart, I love thee with all my heart : thou art a Man of *S*ence, Dear Rogue, I am infinitely happy in thy Friendship ; for I meet with so many Impertinent silly Fellows every day, that a Man cannot live in quiet for e'm ; Dear Heart. For between you and I, this Town is more pester'd with Idle Fellows, that thrust themselves into Company, than the Country is with Attorny's ; Is it not *Jack ?* (*Exit* Roger.

Stanf. Yes ! I have too much reason to believe you, a Curse on you
(*Aside.*

Wood. Ay, Did not I tell you so *Jack ?* ha ? but this is not my business : Dear Rascal Kiss me, I have a secret to impart to thee, but if it take the least Ayre, I am undone : I have a project in my head shall raise me 20000 *l.* I know you will promise secresie, dear heart.

Stanf. Don't trouble me with it.

Wood. No it concernes thee Man : Why, thou shalt go halfes with me, Dear Heart.

Stanf. For Heaven's sake, Sir, don't trust it with me, I have a faculty of telling all I know : I cannot help it.

Wood. Oh ! Dear Bully-Rock, that Wheadle won't pass. Don't I know thou art a Man of Honour ; and besides, so reserv'd, that thou wilt scarce tell a secret to thy Friend ?

Stanf. Sir *I* am unhappy in your good opinion, this is beyond all sufferance.

Wood. No, Faith, Dear *Jack*, thou deserv'st it ; but my project is this, d'ye see.

Stanf. Well ! I am so tormented with *Impertinent Fellowes*, that I see there is no remedy.

Wood. As I hope to live *Jack*, I am of thy Opinion : the truth on't is, 'tis intollerable, for a man can never be free from these Fooles in this Town ; I like thy resolution so well, that I am the Son of a Whore if I don't go along with thee : Ah how we shall enjoy our selves when we are both together, how we shall despise the rest of the World : Dear Heart !

(*Enter* Roger.

Rog. O, Mr. *Woodcock !* Poet *Ninny* is gone to the *Rose* Tavern, and bid me tell you, he has extraordinary business with you, and begs you wou'd make all possible hast to him.

Wood. O Dear Rascal, kiss me ! thou art the honestest Fellow in the World : Dear *Jack*, I must beg thy pardon for a few minutes, but I hope thou'lt not take it ill, why 'tis about business Dear Heart, you know we must not neglect that.

Stanf. O no Sir, by no means.

Wood. Nay Dear Rogue, be not angry, prethee kiss me ; as I hope to live, I'le return immediately ; Dear *Jack*, thy humble Servant——

(*Exit* Woodcock.

Stanf. This is a lucky Accident.

Rog. Sir, I was fain to sin a little for you, and get rid of him by this lie.

Stanf. Well ! This shall excuse all your former Errors, I'le away, for fear some other fooles shoul'd find me out. (*Exeunt.*

Enter Emilia, La. Vaine (*following her up and down*) *after them* Carolina, Lovel.

Carol. Does she not Tease her bravely, *Lovel ?*

Lov. Admirably ! Oh that *Stanford.* were here ! If't t'were for nothing but to see a fellow-sufferer.

La. Vain. Then Madam, will your Ladyship be pleased to let me wait on you to a Play ? there are two admirable Playes at both Houses ; and let me tell you, Madam, Sir *Positive*, that understands those things as well as any man in *England*, sayes, I am a great Judge.

Emil. Madam, I beseech you ask me no more questions ; I tell you, I had as live stand among the rabble, to see a Jack-pudding eate a Custard, as trouble my self to see a Play.

La. Vain. O Fy Madam ! a young Lady and hate Playes ! why I'le tell you, Madam, at one House there is a huge Two handed Devil, and as brave a Fat Fryer as one would wish to see in a Summers-Day ; and a delicate Machin, as they call it, where one sits and sings as fine a Song : And then

(36)

at t'other house there's a rare Play, with a Jigg in't, would do your heart good to see it; but if there were nothing else in't, you might have your four shillings out in Thunder and Lightning and let me tell you, 'tis as well worth it as one Penny's worth another.

Emil. What have I done?

Stanf. Am I trapan'd into Womens Company? ⎧ *Offers to go out,* Lovell
   Lov. Hold, hold, hold, Madam, here's Mr.⎩ *layes hold of him.*
Stanford desires to kiss your hands.

Emil. I am in that disorder that never Woman was.

La. *Vain.* O Mr. *Lovel!* she's falling into a fit of an Epilepsy: help all to hold her, lend me a Knife to cut her Lace.

Stanf. This is worse than all the rest.

Lovel to La. Vain.] Let me speak with you in the next Room in private.

La. *Vain.* Sir, your most obedient Servant: I shall be glad of any occasion to retire with one, for whom I have so great an affection.

Lov. to Caro.] For Heaven's sake follow me, or I shall be in an ill condition.

Caro. I find you are an Errant Hippocrite, but I'le take you at your word for once.   (*Ex.* Lovel, La. Vaine, *and* Carolina.

Emil. I am the greatest object of pity ⎧ Stanford *and* Emilia *walk up*
that was ever seen: I am never free from⎨ *and down, and take little notice*
these Importunate Fooles.   ⎩ *of one another.*

Stanf. I am not less afflicted, and have as much need of pitty too.

Emil. I find no possibility of relief, but by leaving the World that is so full of folly.

Stanf. Who would live in an Age, when Fooles are Reverenc'd, and Impudence Esteem'd?

Emil. To see a fellow but the other day content with humble Linsey Woolsey, now have variety of Vests, Perriwiggs and Lac'd Linnen.

Stanf. One, that but the other day, could eat but one meal a day, and that at a three-penny Ordinary; now struts in State, and talks of nothing but Shattellin's and Lefronds.

Emil. In so corrupt an Age, when almost all mankind flatter the greatest, and oppress the least; when to be just is to be out of fashion and to betray a friend is lawful Cunning.

Stanf. This is pleasant for her to speak against these things,   (*Aside.*
as if she were not as bad as any one: Who wou'd live in such a treach'rous Age, to see this Gentleman that Courts the t'other Gentleman's Wife, meet him and imbrace him; and swear he loves him above the World: and he poor fool dotes extreamly upon him that does the Injury.

Emil. Now has this Fellow a design to have me think him Wise: (*aside.*
but wisdome and honesty are fool'd out of Countenance.

Stanf. Now the illiterate fool despises Learning.

Emil. Nay, among the learn'd themselves, we find many that are great Schollers by Art, are most abominable Fooles by Nature.

Stanf. This shall not perswade me to believe she is not Impertinent. (*aside.*

Emil. Now the qualifications of a fine Gentleman are to Eate A-la-mode, drink Champaigne, Dance Jiggs, and play at Tennis.

Stanf. To love Dogs, Horses, Hawkes, Dice and Wenches, scorne Wit, break Windows, beat a Constable, ly with his Sempstress, and undoe his Taylor ; it distracts me to think on't.

Emil. Now does he desire to be taken for a discreet fellow, but this will not do. (*Aside.*

Stanf. What relief can I expect in this age, when men take as much pains to make themselves fooles, as others have done to get wisdome ?

Emil. Nay folly is become as natural to all mankind as lust.

Stanf. What shall I do ? Whither shall I turne me to avoid these Fooles ?

Lov. Now let's slip e'm.

Car. We shall have a very fair Course. ⎫ *Enter* La. Vaine,
Emil. O Heavens ! Are they here ? ⎬ Ninny, Lovel,
Stanf. What will become of me ? ⎭ *and* Carolina.

Ninny to ⎰O Madam, I'le tell you ; *Stanford* pray hear once.
Emilia. ⎱'Tis such a thing as never was in the World.

La. *Vain.* Ay, pray Sir hear him, he's as pretty a Wit as any man in this Town, except Sir *Positive* I assure you.

Stanf. What are we condemn'd to ?

Emil. To a worse condition then Galley-slaves.

Ninny. I was with my Bookseller, Madam, with that Heroick Poem, which I presented to your Ladyship, as an earnest of the honour I have for you ; But by the way, he's an *Ignorant* ingrateful Fellow, for betwixt you and *I*, he has got some hundreds of pounds by some Plays and Poems of mine which he has Printed. And let me tell you, some under the Names of *Beaumont* and *Fletcher*, and *Ben. Johnson* too : But what do you think, Madam, I asked the Son of a Whore for this Poem ?

Emil. O Insufferable !

Ninny. What think you *Stanford* ? (*Layes hold on him.*

Stanf. Let me go ; I have no Judgment in these things.

Ninny. But I'le tell you ; there are not above 10 or 12000 Lines in all the Poem : And as I hope to be sav'd, I ask'd him but twelve pence a line one line with another.

La. *Vain.* And really, Sir, that's as reasonable as he can possibly afford e'm, take that from me.

Stanf. O devil ! this is worse then a *Sheerness* Ague : That will give a Man some respit between the Fits.

Ninny. By my Soul, Madam, if he had been my Brother I wou'd not have abated him one penny ; for you must know, there are many hundreds of Lines, that in their Intrinsick value, are worth ten shillings a Line between Father and Son ; and the greatest part of e'm are worth five shillings a Line ; But before *George* very few or none but are worth three shillings a line to the veriest *Jew* in Christendome ; they have that salt, thought, imagination, power, spirit soul, and flame in e'm——ha !

Emil. What does this concern me ?

Ninny. No, but I'le tell you, *Stanford*, prethee hear, as *I* hope for mercy this Impudent Rogue told me he would not give me two shillings for the whole Poem ; an ignorant Puppy, a fellow of all the World *I* design'd to make, for he might have sold these Books for three shillings a piece, and I would have help off with 10000 of 'em, to ten thousand of my particular intimate Friends ; besides, every one that had but heard of my name, which are almost all the King's Subjects, would have brought some ; so that *I* should not have got above six or seven hundred pound, and in a fortnights time have made this fellow an Alderman : That such ignorant Rascalls should be Judges of Wit or Sence !

La. Vaine. Well Sir, we shall never have good World unless the State reforms these abuses.

Ninny. 'Tis very true, Madam, for this a thing is of Consequence to the whole Nation, *Stanford.*

Stanf. What the Devil would you have) Am I the cause of this ?

Ninny. No ! Heav'n forbid I should say so : But Madam, I had forgot another Advantage he had had by this.

Emil. Heav'n defend me ! this puts me beyond all patience.

Ninny. I'le tell you, *Stanford*, prethee mind me a little.

Stanf. Oh now I am undone, ruin'd for ever, Sir *Positive*'s here.

Emil. O intollerable ! [*Enter* Sir Positive.

Sir Posit. ∫ I heard your Ladiship was here, and came to kiss your
to *La. Vain.* ⎰ hand.

Oh *Stanford*, art thou here ? well, how dost Cozin ?
I am glad I have found you all together, I came to
Present my Lady *Vaine* with a Musique I have made,
Which has that invention in't, I say no more but
I have been this Moneth of making it,
And you must know, musique is a thing I value my
Self upon, 'tis a thing I have thought on, and consider'd,
And made my business from my Cradle.

Lov. Come Madam, now they are settl'd in their business, let's Leave e'm.

Car. With all my heart.

Sir *Posit.* Come ! you shall see it.

Emil. Cozen ! Pray let it be another time.

(39)

Sir *Posit.* Nay, nay, never talk of that, you shall see't now,
And let me tell you, I have as much power of Invention
In musique as any man in *England* : Come in.

Stanf. O Heav'n, when shall we be deliver'd } *Enter* Fidlers *and* play a ri-
from these fools ?   } diculous piece of musique.

Sir *Posit.* How do you like it *Stanford*, is it not well ? what say you
Cozin, ha ?

La. Vain. Indeed Sir *Positive*, it's very agreeable.

Sir *Posit.* Upon my honour this honest fellow plaid it with a great deal
of glory, he is a most incomparable Bower, he has the most luscious, the
most luxurious bow-hand of any man in *Europe*, take that from me, and
let me tell you, if any man gives you a better account of the Intrigue of
the Violin, then I do, I am Owl, a Puppy, a Coxcomb, a Logger-head, or
what you will.

Emil. Sure there is Magick in this ; never to be free !

Sir *Posit.* Magick ? why, do you understand Magick ?

Emil. No, no, no, not I Cozen.   O intollerable !

Sir *Posit.* I do ; if you please, talk of something else, leave that to me
why I will discover lost Spoons and Linnen, resolve all horary questions,
nay raise a Devil with Doctor *Faustus* himself, if he were alive.

Ninny to my { *Woodcock* a Poet ? a pimp, is he not ?
Lady *Vaine.* {

Sir *Posit.* Who's that speaks of pimping there ? well ! though I say't,
no man pretends to less than I do ; but I cannot pass this by without
manifest Injury to my self.

Stanf. This Puppy, rather then not be in at all, will declare himself a Pimp.

La. Vain. But Sir, are you such a manner of man ?

Sir *Posit.* Why Madam ? did you never hear of me for this ?

La. Vain. No Sir ! if I had————

Sir *Posit.* If I had—ha, ha, ha,—why Madam, where have you liv'd
all this while ?

La. Vain. O fy upon him, Madam, I shall lose my reputation if I be seen
in his Company.

Sir *Posit.* Well ! the Pimps in this Town are a Company of empty, idle,
insipid, dull fellows, they have no design in 'em.

La. Vain. Sir, *I* am sorry you are such a kind of a Man, but————

Sir *Posit.* Sorry ! well ! if *I* would bend my self to't, I would starve all
these Pimps, they should not eat bread, but I am not thought fit.

La. Vain. Sure you railly all this while.

Sir *Posit.* Railly ! ha, ha, ha.   Why, there is not a Lady of Pleasure
from *Blackwall* to *Tuttle-Fields* that I am not intimately acquainted with,
nay that I do not know the state of her Body from the first entring into
the Calling.

(40)

La. *Vain.* O Madam! I am undone, ruin'd for ever by being in his Company.

Sir *Posit.* Besides, for debauching of Women, Madam, I am the greatest son of a Whore in the World if any one comes near me.

La. *Vain.* Out upon you! if you be such a man, I will have nothing to do with you, see me no more, I must look to my Honour, my Reputation is dearer to me than all the World. I would not have a blemish in my Honour for all the riches of the Earth; this makes me so covetous of your Ladiships Company, a person of so much Vertue and Honour, but for Sir *Positive* I defye him; forbear my presence, you will undoe my Honour for ever.

Sir *Posit.* Oh what have I done?

Emil. O horrid Impertinence!   [*Offers to go out.*

Sir *Posit.* Nay, nay, Dear Cozen stay, and see us friends first. Madam, I beg a thousand pardons: 'Tis true, I said no man in *England* understood pimping better than my self, but I meant the speculative, not the practical part of pimping.

La. *Vain.* O that's something, I assure you; if you had not brought your self off well with your Speculation, I would never have suffer'd you to have Practis'd upon me, for no Woman in *England* values her Honour more than I do.

Enter Bridget.

Bridg. Oh Madam, we must go to the Setting-Dog and Partridge to supper to night, Master *Whiskin* came to invite us, there will be the Blades, and we shall have a Ball.

La. *Vaine.* Will there be none but our own Company?

Bridg. No Madam.

La. *Vaine.* Well! I am resolv'd not to fail, if I can by any means get rid of Sir *Positive*, for I love meat and drink and fiddles, and such merry Gentlemen with all my heart.

Enter Woodcock.

Wood. Your servant, Dear Hearts; Madam
Emilia, I kiss your Hand: Dear *Jack!*

Emil. Nay, now it is time to shift for our selves.

Wood. My Dear Bully-Rock, can I serve thee in any thing?

Stanf. Nay, then fare you well——   [*Emilia* and *Stanford* run out at
                                       several doors, the Imperti-
                                       nents divided follow 'em.

(41)

ACT III.

Enter Stanford, Emilia, *Sir* Positive, *Lady* Vaine, Woodcock *and* Ninny.

Sir *Pos.* NAy then, Cozen, I am an Ass, an Ideot, a Blockhead, and a Rascal, if I don't understand Drammatique Poetry of all things in the World; why this is the onely thing I am esteem'd for in *England*.

Emil. I can hold no longer. *aside.*
This Rudeness of yours amazeth me; 'Tis beyond all Example, must we be perpetually persecuted by you and your Crew? For Heav'ns sake leave me.

Sir *Pos.* Ha, ha, ha, Coz., thou railliest well; 'Tis true, *Woodcock* and *Ninny* will be a little troublesome sometimes; but 'ifaith they are very Honest Fellows, give e'm their due.

Emil. Oh abominable! Worse and worse.

Stanf. to ⎫ Gentlemen! what Obligation have we to endure your
Ninny and ⎬folly any longer? Must we be forc'd to leave the World for
Wood. ⎭ such Importunate Fools as you are?

Ninny. What a Devil ayles he? he's mad; who does he mean by this?

Wood. Nay faith I don't know, I am sure he does not mean me, Dear Heart.

Ninny. Nor me neither; Take that from me.

Wood. Jack, if thou wilt leave the World, I'le go along with thee as I told thee, Dear Heart: but who is't troubles thee now, Bully-Rock?

Stanf. All of ye; ye are a pack of the most insupportable Fools that e're had breath; I had rather be at a Bear-Garden
Then be in your Company.

Ninny. Ha, ha, ha: This is very pleasant 'ifaith: Call the greatest Wits and Authors of the Nation fools! Ha, ha, ha. That's good 'ifaith.

Wood. Nay, perhaps the greatest Men of the Age: You are a great Judge indeed, *&c.*

La. *Vaine.* Nay, Sir *Positive*, e'en leave her, (don't be troublesome) since she desires you: Come, Madam, I'le wait upon you, whither you please: We'el enjoy our selves in private.

Emil. This is worst of all; Do you think I can suffer the Noyse of your Tongue for ever with patience?

La. *Vaine.* O' my Conscience Sir *Positive* she's distracted.

Sir *Posit.* Yes, Madam, If I be a Judge, she is, and I defie any one to deceive me in this.

La. Vaine. It must be so, for she has a vast deal of wit, and great wits you know have always a Mixture of Madness.

Sir *Posit.* Well, Madam! I found that by my self, for I was about three years ago as mad as ever man was: I 'scap'd *Bedlam* very narrowly, 'tis not above a twelve-moneth since my brains were settled again: But come, Madam, I'le wait on your Ladiship, for she do's not deserve the honour of such Company.

La. Vaine. What shall I do to get rid of him? I shall miss my assignation, if I do not.

Sir *Posit.* Come, Madam——

Fare you well! since you are no better Company——

Ex. Sir *Posit.* and La. *Vaine.*

Ninny. So, so, now we shall be a little at rest: For let me tell you, Madam, though Sir *Positive* be a rare man, yet my Lady *Vaine* is a little too talkative, and there can be no greater trouble to one of sence then that.

Emil. You are the most impertinent of all Mankind.

Ninny. Oh Madam! you are pleas'd to say so——

Emil. You are a most abominable fool, and the worst Poet in Christendom: I had rather read the History of *Tom Thumb* then the best of your Poems.

Ninny. Oh Madam! you are pleasant, but this won't pass.

Emil. Such ridiculous insipid Rhimes are you Author of, That I am confident you are that incorrigible Scribler that furnishes the Bell-man of this Ward.

Ninny. Ha, ha, ha, &c. Madam, as I hope to breathe you droll very well, this is the pretty'st humour in the World.

Enter Lovel *and* Carolina.

Stanf. O Heav'n! what will become of me?

Car. Is not this extremly pleasant?

Lov. There was never any thing equal to't.

Emil. Your Verses are such as School-boyes ought to be whipp'd for.

Ninny. This will not stir me, Madam, I know you are not in Earnest.

Emil. And your Playes are below the Dignity of a Mountebanks stage. *Salvator Winter* wou'd have refus'd them.

Ninny. Nay, Madam, never talk of that, I'le shew you a Play I have about me: Come, Madam, wee'l read it, here's the most glorious conceits, the most powerful touches, in a word, 'tis a Play that shall Read and Act with any Play that ever was born, I mean, conceived.

Wood. Come on, *Jack!*

Stanf. Ah! Dear *Lovell,* use some means for my delivery, or I am ruin'd for ever: For if I should go, they would not leave me, they are so barbarously cruel in their persecutions.

(43)

Wood. Nay, never speak of that, Madam, before *George* you will bring your Judgement in question if you condemn *Ninny*'s Playes, Dear Heart.

Emil. Away, you Coxcomb, you are ten times a more ridiculous 'Squire then he's a Poet.

Wood. Ha, ha, ha.   By the Lord *Harry* this is a strange humour of hers as ever I saw in my life : Well, Madam, you will have your frolick, but come, *Ninny,* wee'l e'en take our leaves.

Ninny. Ay, ay, come ; your humble servants.

Wood. Your servant, Dear Hearts, this is the pleasant'st humor in the World.

Ninny. Ay, is't not ? Ha, ha, ha——

Ex. Ninny and Woodcock laughing.

Stanf. O Friend, I have been more inhumanely us'd then ever Bawd was by the fury of the 'Prentices.

Lov. Still I say laugh at 'em as *I* do.

Car. Let's leave 'em, *Lovell,* for they are in such humours, they are onely fit for one anothers Company.

Lov. With all my heart, Madam.——   *Ex.* Lovel & Carolina.

Emil. Well ! *I* will leave the World immediately.

Stanf. Which way do you intend to go ?

Emil. Why do you ask ?

Stanf. That *I* may be sure to take another way.

Emil. Nothing could so soon perswade me to tell you as that.

Stanf. What, are they gone ? they have lock'd the door too !

Emil. I wonder what they leave us alone for.

Stanf. Heav'n knows, unless it be to be troublesome to one another as they have been to us.

Emil. I am sure I have most reason to fear it. ⌈*They walk up and down,*

Stanf. You most reason ? when did you see ⟨ *and take little notice of one*
a man so foolish as a Woman ? ⌊*another.*

Emil. When I see you.

Stanf. No, no, none of our sex will dispute folly with any of yours.

Emil. That's hard, I find nothing but Owls among the best of you; your young men are all positive, forward, conceited Coxcombs ; and your old men all formall nothings, that wou'd have sullen gravity mistaken for wisdom.

Stanf. This is not altogether so much Impertinence as I expected from one of your Sex ; but let me tell you, I have too often suffer'd by Women, not to fear the best of 'em, there being nothing to be found in most of the sex, but vanity, pride, envy and hypocrisie, uncertainty and giddiness of humour ; the furious desires of the young make 'em fit to be seduc'd by the flesh, as the envy and malice of the old prepare 'em to be led away by the Devil.

(44)

Emil. I muſt confess I don't perceive yet that you are altogether so ridiculous as the reſt of Mankind; but let me tell you, I have Reason to fear you will be so; perhaps your impertinence is an Ague that haunts you by fits.

Stanf. That disease in the beſt of Women is quotidian, and if you be not infeſted, you muſt be the moſt Extraordinary Woman in the World.

Emil. I would give Money to see a Man that is not so, as the Rabble do to see a Monſter, since all Men I have ever seen are moſt intolerable Fops : would it not diſtraſt one to see Gentlemen of 5000 *l.* a year write Playes, and as Poets venture their Reputations againſt a Sum of Money, they venture theirs againſt Nothing ?   Others learn Ten years to play o' the Fiddle and to Paint, and at laſt an ordinary Fiddler or Sign-Painter that makes it his business, shall out-do 'em all.

Stanf. This looks like sence ; I find she does underſtand something.
aside.

Emil. Others after twenty or thirty years ſtudy in Philosophy arrive no further than at the Weighing of Carps, the Invention of a travailling Wheel, or the poisoning of a Cat with the oyle of *Tobacco ;* these are your Wits and Virtuoso's.

Stanf. I muſt confess this is not so ill as I expeſted from you ; but it do's not less diſtraſt me to see a young Lady fall in love with a vain empty Fellow not worth a Groat, perhaps for dancing of a Jigge, or singing of a Stanza of fashionable Non-sense : another on the contrary so insatiably covetous, for money, to marry old age, infirmity and diseases, and the same bait that perswades them to Matrimony, shall entice 'em into Adultery.

Emil. This is not so foppish as I believ'd ; yet though this be a great Truth, 'tis a very impertinent thing of you to tell me what I know already.

Stanf. How the Devil should I know that, I am sure not many of your sex are guilty of so much discretion as to discern these things.

Emil. I am sure you have not much, that cannot diſtinguish between those that have and have not.

Stan. I muſt confess I am a little surpriz'd to find a Woman have so little vanity, I could never endure the society of any of the sex better then yours.

Emil. To be plain with you, you are not so troublesome a Fop as *I* have seen.

Stan. What the Devil makes me think this Woman not impertinent ? and yet *I* cannot help it, what an Owl am *I ?*　　　　　*aside.*

Emil. I have been so cruelly tormented, and without intermission too, and this seems some Refreshment to me.

Stan. Why should *I* be catch'd thus ? but I'le keep my folly to my self.
aside.

(45)

I can bear this with a little more patience ; but if you should grow [*To her.*
much Impertinent, I shou'd venture to break open the Doore for my
Liberty, I can assure you.

 Emil. Pray Heaven you don't give me the first occasion.   *to him.*
Well I know not what's the matter, but I like this man strangely ; but,
What a Fool am I ?   *aside.*

 Stan. How like a Woodcock am I insnar'd ! a Curse on *Lovel* for leaving
me alone with her !   [*To himself.*

 Emil. What, do they intend to keep us Prisoners for ever ? [*To him.*

 Stan. I care not how long.   [*Aside.*
I think they intend to deal with us as they do with   [*To her.*
Juries, shut us up till we agree of our Verdict.

 Emil. That would be longer then the Siege of *Troy* lasted.

 Stan. This is not half so bad though as our late persecutions,
That's one Comfort.

 Emil. It fares with me like one upon a Rack, that is a little loossen'd
from his paines ; 'tis pleasure to him when he compares his torments,
though those he has left may be intollerable too.

 Stan. In this we agree, though in nothing else.

 Emil. I wou'd to Heaven we did in all things ;   [*Aside.*
I am tormented with my self, that am forc'd by the Ridiculous Custom of
Women to dissemble, and that way indure my own foppery———
Ah dear *Stanford !*   [*Aside.*

 Stan. How now ! she smil'd, and suddenly check'd the Liberty she took.
                 [*Aside.*

 Emil. O Heaven ! I fear he has discover'd something.   [*Aside.*

 Stan. There must be something in't, I like her very well, but am resolv'd
not to disclose it whate're comes on't ; for, that will make her vain, though
she be not already.   [*aside.*

 Emil. Why don't you break open the door, Sir ?

 Stan. I don't find much reason for't yet.

 Emil. I could find in my heart to give you enough.

 Stan. Nay, I doubt not but 'tis in your Nature. What can the meaning
of this be ? Is there nothing but Riddle in Woman ?   [*aside.*

 Roger. Hold, hold, Mr. *Huffe :* My Master ⌠*Enter* Huffe *and unlocks the*
charg'd me, of all men living to keep you out⟨ *door, and* Roger *after him,*
of his sight.   ⌡ *& lays hold on him.*

 Huffe. Prethee, stand by, you sawcy Coxcomb.

 Roger. Nay, Sir, be not so boisterous ; upon my word you pass no further.

 Huffe. Prethee, dear *Roger,* don't put this upon me.

 Roger. My Master sayes it costs him two pieces a time to be rid of you.

 Huffe. Prethee let me go, and you shall go my halfes.

 Roger. Are you in earnest ?

Huffe. Yes upon my Honour.

Roger. Nay then speed yee, but be sure you sinke nothing.

[*exit* Roger.

Huffe. I warrant you.

Stanf. Is he here! hold, hold, hold, here's your two peices, don't trouble me now.

Huffe. Your humble Servant. I'le return e'm again to morrow without fail: Ha! Do they come so easily? there are more from whence these came: O Sir, I'le tell you, I have had the severest fortune that ever man had.

Stanf. Away, away.

Huffe. For Heaven's sake hear, it's the most prodigious thing you ever heard.

Emil. What will this World come to?

Huffe. I was playing at Back-Gammon for my Dinner, which I won; and from thence we came to five up for half a piece; of the first Set I had three for love, and lost it; of the second I Gammon'd him, and threw Doublets at last, which you know made four, and lost that too; of the third I won never a Game.

Stanf. O Devil! Is this the miraculous thing you would tell me? Farewell.

Huffe. Hold, hold, Sir! you don't hear the end on't.

Stanf. Nor do I desire it, Sir.

Huffe. I'le tell you, Sir, of the fourth Set I was four to two, and for the last game my Tables were fill'd up, and I had born my three odd men, so that you know I had two upon every point.

Emil. O insufferable! though I feel enough my self, yet I cannot but pitty *Stanford*.   [*to her self.*

Stanf. O Damn'd Impertinence! Sir, I tell you, I don't understand Back-Gamon.

Huffe. Not understand Back-Gamon! Sir, that you may understand well what I say, I'll tell you what Back-Gamon is.

Emil. This is worse than t'other: sure *Stanford* has some Charm about him, that I can suffer this rather then leave him.   [*to her self.*

Stanf. I desire none of your Instructions.

Huffe. Well; then, as I was saying, I had just two upon every point, and he had two Men to enter; and as the Devil wou'd have it, my next throw was Size-Ace; he enter'd one of his Men a Size; then, Mr. *Stanford*, to see the Damn'd luck on't, I threw Size-Sinke next, and the very next throw he enter'd upon a Sinke, and having his Game very backward, won the Game, and afterwards he Set so, that I lost every Penny.

Stanf. This will distract me; What the Devil's this to me?

Huffe. No, but did you ever hear the like in your life?

(47)

Stanf. This puts me beyond all patience.

Huffe. But this was not all ; for juſt in the Nick came she that Nurs'd my three laſt Children that were born without Wedlock, and threaten'd to turn e'm upon my hands if I did not pay her. ——'Faith, Mr. *Stanford*, three Pieces more will do my business ; upon my Honour I'le pay you to morrow : Come, will you Communicate ?

Stanf. Yes that, that's fitter for you.————

Huffe. What is that Dear Heart ?

Stanf. 'Tis that, Sir————[*kicks him.*

Huffe. That, Sir, I don't underſtand you ; if you go to that, Sir : There's a business indeed. What do you mean by this ? What would you make a quarrel, Sir ? You'l never leave these tricks : I have told you of e'm often enough. What the Devil do you mean by that ?

Stan. Let this expound my meaning.————   [*Kicks him agen.*

Huffe. 'Slife, Sir, I don't underſtand you ; and ye talk of these things, and these businesses, Sir, I'de have you know, I scorn'd to be kick'd as much as any man breathing, Sir ; and you be at that Sport, your Servant, your Servant, Sir.

Enter Roger *at the Door.*

Roger. Come, Mr. *Huffe*, Divide.

Huffe. Divide ! There's one for you, for two of   {*Gives* Roger
e'm was all I got.   { *a Kick.*

Roger. This you might have kept to your self if you had pleas'd, but D'ye think I'le be serv'd thus ?

Huffe. Let me go.

Roger. I'le not leave you so.——   (*Ex.* Roger *and* Huffe.

Emil. Why don't you go ? the Doores open now, Sir.

Stan. I am afraid I shall light into worse Company.

Emil. O Sir, that's impossible !

Stan. How vain this is of you ! Now would you give me a fair occasion to flatter you, but I can assure you, you shall miss of your design.

Emil. Well, this is an extraordinary man ; I love the very sight [*Aside.* of him : I wonder, Sir, you'll be so foppish to imagine I love to be (*To him.* flatter'd ; I hate flatterers worse then our new Poets.

Stan. What an Owle am I to like this Woman ! sure I am bewitch'd.

Emil. } Well, Sir, Farewell : and yet I would not   { *She offers*
Aside. } leave him.   { *to go out.*

Stan. You'd e'n as good ſtay, Madam, while you are well : You may, perhaps, if you go, incounter some of your Persecutors.

Emil. I'de rather ſtay here then venture that ; my trouble is not here so insupportable.

Stan. She muſt be a rare Woman !   (*Aside.*

Nor perhaps is not like to be, unless it comes from your self : But (*To her.*
I think there's less vanity in you then in moſt women I have seen.

 Emil. This is a moſt excellent person. (*Aside.*

 Stan. Dear *Emilia.* (*Aside.*

O Heaven ! is he here ? (*Enter Sir Positive.*

 Sir Posit. Jack, Hark ye.

 Stan. For Heaven's sake ! I have business.

 Sir Posit. 'Tis all one for that, Sir ; Why I'le tell you.

 Stan. Another time ; I beseech you don't interrupt me now.

 Sir Posit. 'Faith but I muſt interrupt you.

 Emil. What can be the matter he liſtens to him. (*Aside.*

 Stan. 'Slife, Why should you put this upon me now ?

 Sir Posit. If you refuse me, I'le blaſt your Reputation.

 Stan. What shall *I* do ? though this be a Coxcombly Knight, yet the
Puppies ſtout. Are you so cunning in persecuting me, to put a (*To him.*
thing upon me I cannot refuse ? well, Sir, remember this.

 Emil. What can this mean ? (*Aside.*

 Stanf. Come, Sir, I'le follow you, but a Curse upon you for finding
me out : Madam, as soon as I have dispatch'd this business, 'tis possible I
may see you agen.

 Emil. But 'tis not, I'le assure you ; I'le never see the Face of one, that
has so little sence to be seduc'd by such an Ideot as that is.

 Stanf. How ridiculous is this of you, to Judge of a thing before you
know the Bottom on't ?

 Sir *Posit.* Come, *Stanford,* prethee come away. (*Exeunt.*

 Emil. Have I found you ? this Fellow's as bad as any, and without
doubt did but counterfeit his humour, to insinuate himself into my good
opinion. What lucky Accident is this has undeceiv'd me ? I felt a passion
growing in me might else have prov'd dangerous—*Luce.* (*enter* Luce.

 Luce. Madam.

 Emil. Fetch my Hoods and Scarfes,
I'le take a walk in the Fields. (*exit* Luce.

    Enter Lovell *and* Carolina.

 Carol. How Siſter ! What have you loſt your Gallant ?

 Emil. O Siſter, I thank you for locking me up with that Fellow ; well,
the time may come when I may be quit with you. (*exit.*

 Carol. I wonder how the Door came open ; I believe there has been
hard bickering betwixt e'm : but, I find my Siſter is Conqueror, and your
Friend is fled for the same,

 Lov. Fare well he, let us mind our selves. Come, 'Faith Madam, Why
should you and I hover so long about this Matrimony ; Like a Caſt of
Faulcons about a Hern that dare not ſtoop ?

Carol. O Sir, the Quarry does not Countervaile the Danger.

Lov. I'le warrant you, Madam; but let's railly no longer, there is a Parson at Knights-bridge that yoakes all stray People together, we'll to him, he'l dispatch us presently, and send us away as lovingly as any two Fooles that ever yet were condemn'd to Marriage.

Carol. I should be inclinable enough to cast my self upon you; but I am affraid you are gone so far with my Lady *Vaine*, you can never come off with Honour: Besides, I am sure, what e're you say, you cannot so soon forget your kindness to her; and if after we are yoak'd, as you call it, you should draw that way, I should draw another; then our Yoak would go near to Throttle us.

Lovel. Faith some would think it much the easier if 'twere wide enough to draw both wayes: But Madam, Will you never be serious with me?

Carol. I know you cannot love me, she's your delight.

Lov. Yes, yes, I delight in her as I do in the Tooth-Ache; I love her immoderately, as an English Taylor loves a French Taylor that's set up the next door to him.

Carol. Sir, to keep you no longer in suspence, I am resolv'd never to Marry without my Fathers Consent.

Lov. Madam, I'le not despair of obtaining that.

Carol. He has vow'd never to Marry me till he has dispos'd of my Elder Sister.

Lov. Will you assure me to make me happy when that's done?

Carol. I think I may safely promise any thing against that time; for as long as my Sister has these Mellanchollick-Humors, she's far enough from that danger.

Lov. I'le warrant you I'le make a Match yet between *Stanford* and her.

Carol. That's impossible, unless you can alter their Natures; for though neither finds Impertinence in themselves, they'l find it in one another: besides, their very Principles are against all Society.

Lov. Well, Madam, I have a way to make 'em stark mad in love with one another; or at least fetch e'm out of their Sullenness: We will perpetually bait 'em with our Fooles, and by that we shall either plague e'm out of their humour, or at least make their fellow-sufferings be a meanes to endear e'm one to another.　　　　　　　　　　　(*Exeunt.*

Enter Sir Positive, Stanford, *and two* Clerks.

Sir *Posit.* Now will I firke my two *Clerks.*

2. *Clerk.* But Sir, before we engage, I would satisfie my Conscience whether the Cause be just or no.

Stanf. Hang the Cause, we come to fight.

Sir *Posit.* Why I'le tell you the Cause, Sir.

Stanf. By no meanes, Sir *Positive*, we come to fight here, not to tell stories.

Sir *Posit.* Wee'l fight too ; but by your leave I'le tell the Cause first, and you were my Father.

Stanf. Hold, Sir, think upon your Honour, this is no place for Words ; Let your Sword speak your Mind.

Sir *Posit.* Sir, by your Pardon, I am resolv'd to satisfie 'em ; no man in *England* knows how to manage these things better then my self, take that from me.

Stanf. O horrid Impertinence, I fear these Fooles Tongues more than I can their Swords.

Sir *Posit.* Sir, no man in *England* would put up this affront ; Why look you, Sir, for him to sit in the Eighteen pence Gallery, pray mark me, and rail at my Play alowd the first day, and did all that lay in his power to damn it : And let me tell you, Sir, if in any Drammatick Poem there has been such breaks, such Characters, such Figures, such Images, such Heroick Patterns, such Heights, such Flights, such Intrigues, such Surprizes, such Fire, Salt, and Flame, then I am no Judge : I understand nothing in this World.

Stanf. What a Cause his Valour has found out ! and how he Cants too ! What an Owle was I to come along with him ! Sir *Positive* dispatch. Come, come, Gentlemen.

Sir *Posit.* Hold a little————

2. *Clerk.* Why look you Mr. *Timothy*, this is a very honest and ingenious Gentleman for ought I see.

1. *Clerk.* 'Tis true, I sate in the Eighteen Pence Gallery, but I was so far from Railling against your Play, that I cry'd it up as high as I could.

Sir *Posit.* How high did you cry it up ?

1. *Clerk.* Why as high as the upper Gallery, I am sure of that.

Stanf. O Cowardly Currs ! will they never fight ? Ye lye, ye did Rail at his Play.

1. *Clerk.* Sir, I'le hold you twenty pound I dont lie ; Sir, were you there ? Did you hear me ; This is the strangest thing in the World.

Stanf. Will nothing make these Rogues fight ; You are both Rascally Cowards.

2. *Clerk.* 'Tis strange you should say so, you are very uncharitable. Do you know either of us ?

Stanf. Oh insufferable ! what Sons of Whores has he pick'd up, and what an occasion too ?

Sir *Posit.* Why do you say, you did not Raile ? Did not I sit just under you in the Pit ?

2. *Clerk.* Lord ! Who would expect to see a poet in the Pit at his own Play.

Sir *Posit*. Did not you say, Fy upon't, that shall not pass ?

Stanf. Gentlemen either Fight quickly.——sha

Sir *Posit*. Hold, hold, let him speak ; What can you say ? Do Gentlemen Write to oblige the World, and do such as you traduce e'm—ha——

1. *Clerk*. Sir, I'le tell you, you had made a Lady in your Play so unkind to her Lover (who methought was a very honest well meaning Gentleman) to command him to hang himself. Said I then that shall not pass, thinking indeed the Gentleman would not have done it, but indeed did it, then said I, fy upon't that he should be so much over-taken.

Sir *Posit*. Overtaken ! that's good 'ifaith, why you had as good call the Gentleman fool : and 'tis the best Character in all my Play. D'ye think I'le put that up ?

1. *Clerk*. Not I Sir, as I hope to live ; I would not call the Gentleman Fool for all the World, but 'tis strange a man must pay eighteen pence, and must not speak a word for't.

Sir *Posit*. Not when Gentlemen write ; take that from me.

2. *Clerk*. No, I would they would let it alone then.   (*aside*.

Sir Posit. But *Stanford*, it would make an Authour mad to see the Invincible Ignorance of this age, now for him to hang himself at the Command of his Mistress there's the surprize, and I'le be content to hang my self, if ever that was shewn upon a stage before, besides 'twas an Heroick *Cato*-like Action, and there's great Love and Honour to be shewn in a mans hanging himself for his Mistress, take that from me.

Stanf. O horrid ! this Magisterial Coxcomb will defend any thing.

Sir *Posit*. What do you think *Stanford*, you are a great Judge ?

Stanf. I think a Halter is not so honourable as a Ponyard, and therefore not so fit to express Love and Honour with.

Sir *Posit*. Ha, ha, ha, To see your mistake now that's the onely thing in the Play I took pains for, I could have made it otherwise with ease, but I will give you seventeen reasons why a Halter's better than a Ponyard. First, I'le shew you the posture of hanging, look, d'ye mind me ? it is the posture of a Pensive dejected Lover with his hands before him, and his head aside thus.

Stanf. I would you had a Halter, you would demonstrate it more cleerly.

Sir *Posit*. 'Faith, and would I had, I'de shew it you to the life. But secondly——

Stanf. Hold Sir——I am convinced, to our fighting bus'ness agen ; but they have given you full satisfaction,
Let's away——

Sir *Posit*. No, no, hold a little.

Stanf. A Curse on him ! did I leave *Emilia* for this ?

Sir *Posit*. Sir, if you'l set your hand to this Certificate, I'le be satisfy'd, otherwise you must take what follows.

1. *Clerk.* Sir ! with all my heart, I'll do any thing to serve you.

Sir *Posit.* I had this ready on purpose, for I was resolv'd if we had fought, and I had disarm'd him, I'de have made him do't before I'de have given him his life ; how do you write your self ?

1. *Clerk. Timothy Scribble* a Justice of Peace his Clerk.

Sir *Posit.* Here read it, and set your hand to it.

1. *Clerk.* ⎫   I do acknowledge and firmly believe that the Play of Sir
  reads. ⎭ *Positive Att-All* Knight, called the Lady in the Lobster, notwithstanding it was damn'd by the Malice of the Age, shall not onely read, but it shall act with any of *Ben Johnsons*, and *Beaumont*'s and *Fletcher*'s Plays.

Sir *Posit.* Hold, hold ! I'll have *Shakspeares* in, 'slife I had like to have forgot that.

1 *Clerk* ⎫ With all my heart.
  read. ⎭ I do likewise hereby attest that he is no purloiner of other mens Work, the general fame and opinion notwithstanding, and that he is a Poet, Mathematician, Divine, Statesman, Lawyer, Phisitian, Geographer, Musician, and indeed a *Unus in Omnibus* through all Arts and Sciences, and hereunto I have set my hand the   day of

1 *Clerk.* With all my heart.

Sir *Posit.* Come Sir, do you Witness it.

2 *Clerk.* Ay Sir.   *(he sets his hand.*

Sir *Posit.* In presence of *Jacob Dash.*

1 *Clerk.* Look you Sir, I write an indifferent good hand, if you have any occasion to command me, inquire at the Stationers at Furnivals-Inne.—

Stanf. Why you Impudent Rascals ! how dare you come into ⎫ *offers   to*
the Field ? must I be diverted thus long by you ?   ⎭ *kick 'em.*

Sir *Pos.* Hold *Stanford !* I cannot in honour suffer that, now they are my Friends, and after this satisfaction I am bound in honour to defend 'em to the last drop of blood.

Stanf. O intolerable !

1 *Clerk.* Sir ! I pray be not angry ! we did not come into the Field to fight, but Master *Dash* and I came to play a match at Trap-ball for a Dish of Steakes at Gloster hall, and here you found us.

Sir *Pos.* Have you the Confidence to talk of Trap-ball before me ? nay, now you are my Enemies agen : Hark you *Stanford*, I'le play with 'em both for 5000 *l.* why I was so eminent at it when I was a School-boy, that I was call'd *Trap Positive* all over the School.

Stanf. Then farewell good Sir *Positive Trap.*

Sir *Pos.* Dear *Stanford* stay but one quarter of an hour, and you shall see how I'le dishonour 'em both at Trap-ball————They talk of Trap-ball, ha, ha, ha.

Stanf. 'Slife what will become of me : out of the field you inconsiderable Rascals.   *Must* I be diverted thus by you—— (*They run out.*

(*Exeunt omnes.*

Enter Emilia *and her Maid at one Door*, Ninny *and* Woodcock *at t'other*.

Emil. I thought we might have been free here : and here are these Puppy's.

Wood. Let's aboard of 'em, who e're they are, fa, la, la, how now Dear Hearts ? by the L. *Harry* it's pity you should walk without a Couple of Servants, here's a Couple of Bully-Rocks will serve your turn, as well as Two of Buckram, Dear Hearts.

Emil. O Heaven ! (*aside*.

Luce. Gentlemen this is very rude ! we shall have them come shall thank you for't.

Ninny. As I hope to breath Ladies, you look the pretty'st in Vizard Masks of any Ladies in *England*.

Wood. And now you talk of Masks, I'll shew you an admirable Song upon a Vizard Mask, Dear Hearts, of Poet *Ninny*'s making.

Emil. Oh abominable Impudence !

Wood. But I must beg your pardon that I cannot sing it, for I am hoarse already with singing it to the Maids of Honour.

Luce. You sing it to the Maids of Honour ?

Wood. But if I had a Violin here, no man in *England* can express any thing more lusciously upon that then my self, ask *Ninny* else.

Ninny. Yes Ladies ! he has great power upon the Violin, he has the best double Rellish in Gam-ut of any man in *England*, but for the little finger on the left hand no man in *Europe* out does him.

Wood. You may believe him, Dear Hearts, for he's a great Judge of Musick, and as pretty a Poet as ever writ Couplet.

Emil. O horrid ! what's this ? there's no way to scape, but to discover our selves. (*they pull off their masks*.

Ninny. *Emilia*. What shall I do ? I am undone, shee'l never own me agen.

Emil. Farewell you Baboons, and learn better manners.

Wood. 'Slife shee'l take me for a Whore-master, I am nipt in the very blossome of my hopes.

Ninny. For Heav'ns sake, pardon me Madam.

Emil. Let me go.

Wood. No Madam, wee'l wait on your Ladiship home.

Emil. This is worse and Worse.

Enter Huffe.

Huff. Heart ! if I put up this, I'll give him leave to use me worse then a Bayley that arrests in the Inns of Court.

Wood. Why, what's the matter?

Huff. 'Slife kick a man of honour as *I* am! I'le piftoll him pissing againft a Wall.

Luce. Ay then or never to my knowledge.

Wood. What's the business Dear Heart, hah?

Huff. Sir, I'll tele you.

Emil. This is a lucky Occasion. *Ex. Emil., Luce.*

Ninny. Are you gone, I'le follow you? *Ex. Ninny.*

Huff. I had occasion for four or five Pieces to make up a Sum with, and went to borrow it of him, and he like an uncivil fellow as he was————

Wood. What did he?

Huff. Why I did but turn my back, and he like an ill-bred sot, gives me a kick or two of the breech, I'le cut his throat if I should meet him in a Church.

Wood. This will be an ill bus'ness; I am sorry for my Friend *Jack Stan-ford*——— ———for Mafter *Huffes* honour is difturb'd, and I fear (*aside.* hee'l revenge it bloodily, for he underftands Punctilio's to a hair, but I'le endeavour to prevent it however.

Huffe. If he be above ground I'le cutt's throat for't, I'le teach him to use a man of honour thus; if he had pleas'd he might have dealt with me at another rate, as I hope to live I had a fighting Sword by my side near six foot long at that very time, and he to kick a Man. P'shaw. He does not underftand his bus'ness, but I shall find him presently. *Exit Huffe.*

Enter Ninny.

Ninn. Pox on it *Woodcock* she would not let me go with her.

Wood. Prethee, Dear Heart, see if thou canft find *Jack Stanford* in the Fields, while I go and see if I can find him in the Town.

Ninn. What's the matter?

Wood. 'Tis a business concerns his life, Dear Heart, ask no queftions, but if you find him, bring him to the *Sun.* *Exit.*

Ninn. What can this be?

But I'le go see if I can find him out,
So to be sure of what I'me now in doubt.

Fin. Act. tertii.

ACT IV.

Enter Lady Vaine *and* Carolina.

La. *Vaine.* COme Madam, I am not so blind, but I have discover'd something.

Carol. What have you discover'd Madam?

La. *Vaine.* Let me tell you Madam, 'tis not for your honour to give meetings privately to Master *Lovell.*

Carol. Why Madam, if I shou'd, are you concern'd in it?

La. *Vaine.* Yes, Madam, first in my good Wishes to our Ladiship, I would not have the World blame your Conduct, nor that you shou'd have the least blemish in your honour, but that your Fame and Vertue should continue unspotted and undefil'd as your Ladiships Beauty's.

Car. Fear not, Madam, I'le warrant you I'le secure my honour without Instructions.

Enter Lovell *softly, and comes just behind them.*

La. *Vaine.* But, Madam, let me tell you agen, no Woman has really that right in Master *Lovell* that I have: But he's a false Wretch, Madam, he has no Religion in him, if he had any Conscience, or had used to have heard Sermons, he would never have been so wicked and perfidious to a poor Innocent Woman as I am.

Lov. This is very fine i'faith————— (*to himself.*

La. *Vaine.* Madam, he protested all the honourable kindness in the World to me, and has receiv'd Favours from me, I shall not mention at this time, and now he has rais'd the siege from before me, and laid it to your Ladiship.

Car I cannot imagine what you mean by this.

La. *Vaine.* And Madam to confess my Weakness to you, I must needs say, I love him of all men in the World.

Car. Well, Madam, since you do, I'le resigne my Interest in the Gentleman you speak of, here he is.

La. *Vaine.* Oh Heaven! am I betrayed? well, Madam, I shall acquaint your father with your Amour.

Lov. Hold, Madam, if you do, perhaps I may whisper something in *Sir Positive*'s ear.

La. *Vaine.* Sir! you will not be so ungenerous to boast of a Ladies kindness: if he shou'd say the least thing in the World after my unhansome leaving of him just now, it would incense him past reconciliation; what a confusion am I in? *Ex.* La Vaine.

(56)

Lov. Is not this very pleasant, Madam?

Car. I wonder, Sir, after what has now paſt you have the confidence to look me in the face.

Lov. I like this ralliery very well, Madam.

Car. I can assure you, you shall have no reason to think I railly with you.

Lov. Certainly you cannot be in Earneſt.

Car. Upon my word you shall find I am, I will have nothing to do with any man that's engag'd already.

Lov. You amaze me, Madam.

Car. I'le never see you more———

Enter Stanford.

Stanf. O friend! I'm glad I've found you.

Lov. I shall have no opportunity to appease my Miſtress, If I do not get rid of him; but I have a trick for him.   (*aside.*

Stanf. Would this woman were away, that I might acquaint you with the greateſt concernment I ever had.

Lov. Step into that Chamber quickly, and I'le get rid of her, and come to you———

Stanf. With all my heart———   *Exit Stanford.*

Lov. Certainly, Madam, you cannot know this Woman so little as to give her Credit? I'le tell you what she is.

Car. I am very glad I know you so well: Do you think I'le be put off with a Remnant of your Love?

Enter Roger.

Roger. O! Maſter *Lovell!* is my Maſter here? I have loſt him these two houres.

Lov. Ay, ay, but Madam, for Heav'ns sake heare me!

Car. Trouble me no more———   } *Exit* Carolina, Lo-

Rog. Where is this Maſter of mine? I have been } vell *follows her.*
seeking him these two hours, and cannot light of him.

Enter Huffe.

Huffe. Oh *Roger!* where's your Maſter?

Roger. O Sir! you shall excuse me for that.

Huffe. Preethee dear Rogue tell me, 'twill be better for thee.

Rog. No, no, that won't do, you were not so juſt to me laſt time.

Huffe. Upon my honour I was: Why shoud'ſt thou diſtruſt thy friend?

Roger. Come Sir, don't think to Wheadle me at this rate!

Huff. I am a Son of a Whore if I was not juſt to you: but prethee bring

me to him once more : I am sure to get money of him, and may I perish if
I do not give you your share to a farthing.

Roger. Well ! I'le trust you once more : go, and stay for me in the Hall,
and I'le come to you when *I* have found my Master, who is somewhere in
this house.

Huffe. Well ! I'le wait for you—— *Exit.*

Rog. My comfort is, if he gets money I may have my share, if not, he
ventures a kicking agen, and I venture nothing.

Enter Stanford *and* Emilia.

Rog. Oh ! Sir ! I have been seeking you these two houres, and here's
Master *Lovell* in the house.

Stanf. You Rascal, must you trouble me too ? *(offers to strike him.*

Emil. He does not trouble you more then you do me.

Stanf. Now you are like a young hound that runs away on a false scent.

Emil. For Heaven's sake leave me.

Stanf. Nay, This is like a Woman, to condemn a man unheard.

Emil. Must I be for ever pester'd with Impertinent people ?

Stanf. If you were not so your self, you wou'd not think me so ; but she
that has the Yellow Jaundies thinks every thing yellow which she sees.

Emil. Is it possible you can have the impudence to endeavour to justifie
your folly ?

Stanf. Not that I care much for satisfying you, but to vindicate my self
from the unjust aspersion : know it was my honour oblig'd me to go along
with that fool.

Emil. Out of my sight ; Are you one of those Fopps that talk of honour ?

Stanf. Is that a thing so despicable with you ? he ask'd me to be his
second, which I cou'd not in honour refuse.

Emil. Granting that barbarous custom of Duells ; Can any thing be so
ridiculous, as to venture your life for another mans quarrel, right or wrong.

Stanf. I like this Woman more and more, like a sott as I am ; sure there
is Witch-craft in't. *(Aside.*

Emil. But to do the greatest Act of Friendship in the World for the
greatest Owle in Nature.

Enter Huffe.

Huffe. Oh Mr. *Stanford,* I have a business to impart to you.

Stanf. O insufferable ! Have you the Impudence to trouble me agen.

Emil. I know not what's the matter, but I cannot but have some inclination to this fellow yet. *(aside.*

Huffe. I am going into the City, where I shall have the rarest Bubble that
ever man had ; he was set me by a Renegado-Linnen-Draper, that fail'd
last year in his Credit, and has now no other trade but to start the Game,

whil'ſt we pursue the Chace. This is one of those fellows that draw in the Youth of the City into our Decoy, and perpetually walk up and down seeking for a Prey.

Stanf. Be gone! and leave me.

Huffe. But you know a man muſt have a little Gold to show, to bait the Rogues withall.

Stanf. Out, you unreasonable Rascal, I'le send you hence.—— *Drawes.*

Huffe. Nay, 'tis not that *Sir* can fright me, but that I would not diſturb the Lady, I'de make you know.

Stanf. You impudent Villain, I'le send you fur- ⎰ *Follows* Huffe, *and runs*
ther.   ⎱   *away buffing.*

Huff. Nay Sir, your humble Servant and you go to that, Sir; I care as little for a Sword, Sir, as any man upon Earth : I fear your Sword? Who dares say it? your Servant, your Servant————   (*Ex* Huffe.

Emil. This is not altogether so foolish as fighting in Sir *Positive's* Quarrel.

Stanf. Sir *Positives* quarrel! 'twas in effect my own; for I was sure to meet with some impertinent Fellow or other for my Enemy, and was glad of this opportunity to vent my indignation upon one of those many that have tormented me; I had rather fight with them all, then converse with them.

Emil. But you may chuse whether you will do either.

Stanf. Yes, as much as chuse whether I'le breathe or no.

Emil. But how could you be sure to meet with such an one?

Stanf. What Queſtion is that? Is it not above 5000 to one odds?

Emil. ⎱ I am glad he has brought himself well off, for I muſt like him :
aside. ⎰ do what I can, he muſt be a man of sence : I muſt confess, the business is not altogether so ill as I imagin'd.   (*To him.*

Stanf. Now Madam, who is impertinent, you or I?

Emil. You are, to say the same thing twice to me.

Stanf. Well! this is a rare Woman : what a quick apprehension she has! I love her ſtrangely, the more Coxcomb I, that *I* shou'd be drawn in, of all Men living.   (*aside.*

Enter Woodcock.

Wood. O Dear heart, have I met with thee? I have been seeking thee all the Town over.

Stanf. Heart, What's this? I was going in great haſte juſt as you came, adieu.

Wood. Ah dear *Jack*, I have not so little honour as to leave thee in this condition.

Stanf. Good Sir! What condition? *I* am not Drunk, am I?

Wood. No Ga'd, wou'd it were no worse, Dear heart.

Stanf. It cannot be worse, do not trouble me.

Wood. No, I'll tele thee *Jack ; Huffe* threatens thee ʃ *Embraces and kisses*
to cut thy Throat where ever he meets thee ; and *I* ʅ   *him.*
came my Dear Bully Rock to offer thee the Service of my sword and arme.

Stanf. For Heavens sake put not this upon me ; Do you think he that
would be kick'd without resiſtance, dares do any thing ?

Wood. But look you, Dear Heart, Lord this is the ſtrangeſt thing in the
World, you had Ladies with you, and you know it had been an uncivil
thing to have turn'd agen then *Jack :* But now he's resolv'd to have satisfaction, he told me so ; And if I can see as far into a Millſtone as another,
he's no Bully Sandy.

Stanf. Trouble me no more : be gone————————

Wood. Ay, ay, thou doſt this now to try whether I have so little honour
as to quit thee, but it won't pass, my dear Rascall ; kiss me, I'le live and
dye with thee.

Stanf. Sir, let me tell you, this is very rude : and upon my word I have
no quarrel, unless you'l force one upon me.

Emil. Still do I like this man better and better.————   (*Aside.*

Wood. Nay, then I smell a Rat————Farewell *Jack.*
Servant, Dear Hearts.   *Ex.* Woodcock.

Enter Lovel, Carolina, Roger.

Car. But, are you sure my Lady *Vaine* is such a one ?

Lov. Yes, that *I* am, my little peevish Jealous Miſtress.

Car. Yes, yes, I have reason to be jealous of such a Treasure as you are :
But pray, to satisfie a little scruple I have, see her no more.

Stanf. We had beſt change the Scene, I think, what if you shou'd walk
out a little ?

Emil. I care not much if I doe.

Stanf. I cou'd find in my heart to go along with you.

Emil. Yes, and leave me agen for your Honour forsooth.

Stanf. How Devillishly impertinent is this, for you to harp upon one
ſtring ſtill !

Lovel. Let's pursue our design.

Enter Sir Positive.

Car. Agreed : And to our wish here comes my Cozin *Positive.*

Sir *Posit.* Oh ! Have *I* found you ? I'le tell you the pleasant'ſt thing in
the World.

Stanf. Sir, I am juſt now going to a *Lawyer* of the Temple, to ask his
Councell.

Sir *Pos.* P'shaw, p'shaw ; save thy Money, what need'ſt thou do that ?
I'le do't for you ; why I have more Law, then ever *Cooke* upon *Littleton*
had ; you muſt know, *I* am so eminent at that, that the greateſt Lawyers

in *England* come to me for advice in matters of difficulty : Come, state your Case, let's hear't, Come——Hold, hold, Cozen, Whither are you going ?

[*Emilia offers to go out.*

Emil. Let me goe, I am going in haste to bespeak a Seale.

Sir Pos. A Seale ? Why do'st thou know what thou do'st now ? To go about that without my advice : Well, I have given *Symons* and all of e'm such Lessons, as I have made e'm stand in admiration of my Judgment : Do you know that I'le cut a Seale with any Man in *England* for a thousand Pound ?

Roger. I have my Lesson, I'le warrant you I'le do it.   (*exit.*

Emil. O Heav'n !

I must go now to bespeake it ; I am to send it immediately to my Sister at the English Nunnery in *Bruges*.

Sir Pos. Bruges ! ah dear *Bruges ;* now you talk of *Bruges,* I am writing this night to *Castel Rodrigo,* you must know I have thought of their Affaires, and consider'd e'm thoroughly ; and just this very After-noon I have found out such a way for e'm to preserve *Flanders* from the *French,* I defie all Mankind for such an Invention ; and *I* think *I* offer him very fair, if he will let me divide the Government with him, I'le do it ; otherwise if *Flanders* be lost, 'tis none of my fault.

Lov. What is your Design, Sir *Positive ?*

Stanf. That thou should'st be so very foppish to aske questions !

Sir Pos. I'le tell you, I will this year, pray mark me, I will bring 100000 Men in the Field, d'ye see.

Car. But, Where will you have these Men, Cozen ?

Sir Pos. Have e'm, P'shaw p'shaw, let me alone for that ; I tell thee *Stanford,* I will bring 100000 Men into the Field, 60000 in one Compleat body, and 40000 for a flying Army, with which *I* will enter into the very Body of all *France.*

Stanf. O Devil ! I had rather *Flanders* shou'd be lost, then hear any more on't.

Sir Pos. But this would signifie nothing, unless it were done by one that understands the conduct of an Army, which if I do not, let the World Judge : but to satisfie you, I'le tell you what I'le do, pray mark me, *I* will take threescore thousand Spanish Souldiers, and fight with 60000 *French,* and cut e'm off every Man : pray observe one, this is demonstration ; then will I take those very numericall Individual *Frenchmen* I spoke of.

Stanf. What, after you have cut e'm off every man ?

Sir Pos. Pish ; What doest talk Man ? What's matter whether it be before or after, that's not the point ? P'shaw, prethee don't thee trouble thy self for that, I'le do't man ; I will take those very 60000 *French,* and fight with a *Spanish* Army of 100000, and by my extraordinary Conduct destroy e'm all, this is demonstration, nothing can be plainer then this ; by this you may guess whether I may not be a considerable Man to that Nation or no.————Nay, more then that, I'le undertake if I were in *Candia*, the Grand Vizier would sooner expose himself to the fury of the *Janizaries*, then besiege the Town while I were in't.

Emil. I cannot tell whether I am more tormented with Sir *Positive*, or pleas'd with *Stanford*, he is an extraordinary man.   (*Aside.*

Sir *Pos.* But as *I* was saying, Cozen *Emilia ;* I will have 100000 men in the Field, and I will man the Garrisons to the full : besides, pray observe, I will have an infinite store of Provision every where, and pay all my Souldiers to a penny duly.

Car. But where's the Money to do this Cousin ?

Emil. What shall I do ? Whither shall I turn me ?

Stanf. Ah Dear *Emilia !*

Sir *Pos.* Where's the Money ? that's a good one 'Faith———— Prethee dear Cozen do thou mind thy Guittar ; thou dost not understand these things.

Stanf. I am sure I understand you to be the greatest Coxcomb in Nature.

Sir *Pos.* Then I will make you me a League Offensive and Defensive with the King of *England*, the Emperor and Princes of *Germany*, the Kings of *Sweden* and *Denmark*, the Kings of *Portugal* and *Poland*, *Prester John*, and the Great *Cham*, the *States of Holland*, the Grand Duke of *Muscovy*, the *Great Turk*, with two or three Christian Princes more, that shall be nameless ; and if with that Army, Provision and alliance, I do not do the business, I am no Judge, I understand nothing in the World.

Enter Roger.

Roger. O Sir *Positive !* My Lady *Vaine* wou'd speak with you at your Lodging immediately.

Sir *Pos.* Cods my life-kins, *Stanford*, I am heartily sorry I must leave you.

Stanf. So am not I.

Sir *Pos.* I beg your pardon a thousand times. I vow to Gad I wou'd not leave you but upon this occasion.

Emil. How glad am I of the occasion !

Sir *Positive going,* ⎱ Well ! I hope you'l be so kind to believe, that
  returnes in haste. ⎰ nothing but my Duty to my Mistress shou'd have made me part with you thus rudely.

Stanf. O yes ! we do believe it.

Sir *Posit.* But hark you Cozen, and *Stanford*, you must promise me not to take it ill, as I hope to breathe I mean no incivility in the World.

Emil. Oh, no, no, by no meanes.

Sir *Posit.* Your Servant.   (*Exit* Sir Positive.

Carol. Come, *Lovel*, let's follow him, and either prepare him, or find out some others for a fresh incounter.

Lov. Allon's, but be sure, *Roger*, you forget not what I said to you—
(*Ex.* Lov. Carolina.

Rog. I will not, Sir.

Stanf. How Curteously he excus'd himself, for not tormenting us more !

Emil. This is the first good turn my Lady *Vaine* e're did me.

Rog. No, Madam, this was my ingenuity ; I ne'r saw my Lady *Vaine*, nor do I know where she is.   (Sir Positive *Returnes.*

Sir *Posit.* Cozen and Mr. *Stanford*, I have consider'd on't, and I vow to Gad I am so affraid you'l take it ill, that rather then disoblige you, I'le put it off.

Stanf. O no Sir, by no meanes ; 'twould be the rudest thing in the World to disobey your Mistress.

Sir *Posit.* Nay, Faith I see thou art angry now, prethee don't trouble thy selfe, I'le stay with thee.

Stanf. Hell and Damnation ! this is beyond all sufferance.

Emil. Let me advise you by all meanes to go to your Mistress.

Sir *Posit.* Well ! if you won't take it ill, I'le go ; adieu.
(*Exit* Sir Posit.

Enter Woodcock, Serieant, *and* Musqueteeres.

Wood. That's he, seize him.

Serje. Sir, by your leave, you must go to the Captain of the Guard.

Stanf. O intolerable ! What's the matter now ?

Serjeant. I do not know, but I guess 'tis upon a quarrel betwixt you and one Lieutenant *Huffe*.

Stanf. Was ever any thing so unfortunate as this ? Can't you defer't an houre ?

Serje. I am commanded by my Officer and dare not disobey.

Stanf. How loath am I to leave this Woman ! there is something extraordinary in this——Madam, I am willing enough to stay with you, but you see I am forced away :——stay you here *Roger*.
(*Exit with* Serjeant *and* Musqueteeres.

Emil. What an unlucky accident is this ? but my misfortunes never fail me.——   (*Exit.*

Wood. So he's safe, and I have done what I in honour ought to do ; and now honest *Roger*, my dear Bully-Rock, I'le stay with thee, prethee kiss me, thou are the honestest Fellow in the World.

Roger. Sir, I am glad I can repay your Commendations ; I have the best news for ye that ever you heard in your life.

Wood. Me ! What is't Dear Heart ?

Roger. Why, I'le tell you, the Lady *Emilia* is in love with you.

Wood. In love with me, fy, fy ! Pox on't, what a Wheadling Rogue art thou now ? Why should'st thou put this upon thy Friend now ?

(63)

Roger. Sir, this suspition of yours is very injurious : Let me tell you, that, I am sure I have not deserv'd it from you, Sir.

Wood. Nay, I must confess, I have alwayes found thee an honest Fellow, Dear Heart ; but a Pox on't, she can't love me : P'shaw me ? What, what can she see in me to love me for ? no, no.

Roger. Sir, upon my life, it's true.

Wood. Ha, ha, Dear Rascal, kiss me ; the truth on't is, I have thought some such thing a pretty while, but how the Devil com'st thou to find it out, on my Conscience thou art a Witch.

Roger. O Sir ! I am great with her Maid *Luce*, and she told me her Lady fell in love with you for singing, she says you have the sweetest Voice, and the delicatest Method in singing of any man in *England*.

Wood. As Gad shall sa'me, she is a very ingenious Woman ; Dear Dog, Honest Rascal here, here's for thy Newes, I'le go in and give her a song immediately———— *Exit.*

Roger. How greedily he swallows the bait ! But these self-conceited Ideots can never know when they are wheadl'd.

Enter Lovell *and* Ninny.

Nin. P'shaw, p'shaw, ad'au'tre, ad'au'tre, I can't abide you shou'd put your tricks upon me.

Lov. Come, *Ninny*, leave Fooling, you know I scorn it, I have always dealt faithfully with you.

Nin. ⎫ I must confess he has always commended my Poems, that's the
aside. ⎭ truth on't : But I am affraid this is impossible.
don't Wheadle your friend.

Lov. I shall be angry Sir, if you distrust me longer.
You may neglect this opportunity of raising your self,
Do, but perhaps you may never have such another.

Nin. Nay but dear Sir, speak ! are you in Earnest ?

Lov. Doe you intend to affront me ? you had as good give me the lye.

Nin. No, dear Sir, I beg your pardon for that, I believe you,
But how came you to know it ?

Lov. Her Sister *Carolina* told me so, and that she fell in love with you for reading a Copy of your own Verses : she sayes you read Heroick Verse with the best Grace of any man in *England*.

Nin. Before *George* she's in the right of that, but Sir——

Lov. 'Slife ask no more questions, but to her and strike while the Irons hot : have you done your business, *Roger?*

Roger. Most dextrously, Sir.

Lov. Let's away———— *Ex.* Lov. *and* Roger.

Nin. Love me ? I am o'rejoy'd, I am sure I have lov'd her a great while.

Enter Emilia, Woodcock *following her singing.*

Wood. Fa, la, la, la, &c.

Emil. Heav'n! this will diſtraᴄt me; what a vile noise he makes, worse than the Creaking of a Barn door, or a Coach-wheel ungreas'd.

Wood. This is damn'd unlucky, that he shou'd be here to hinder my design: *(aside.*

Nin. What a pox makes him here? But I'le on in my business, Madam, I'le speak you a Copy of Verses of my own that have a great deal of mettle and soul, and flame in 'em.

Emil. But I will not hear 'em, Sir.

Wood. Alas poor fool! he hopes to please her, but it won't do, ha, ha, ha. *(aside.*

Nin. What the Devil can she mean by this, sure she can't be in Earneſt? No, I have found it; Ay, ay, it muſt be so, she wou'd not have me speak before him, because she wou'd not have him take notice of her passion, but what care I—— *(aside.*

(He offers to rehearse.

Wood. Prethee *Ninny* don't trouble the Lady with your Verses.

Ninn. Well, Well! Can't you let it alone——

Wood. Fa, la, la, la, &c.

Emil. What horrid Noise is this you make in my ears? shall I never be free?

Nin. Alas poor Coxcomb! he hopes to please her with his Voice: No, no, he may spare his pains——I am the man. *(aside.*

Wood. What a pox ayles she? She's damnably out of humour, what e'res the matter; I am sure *Roger* wou'd not deceive me of all men: what an Ass am I, that I shou'd not find it? she's affraid my singing will encourage him to trouble her; or else she would not have him perceive her kindness—— *(aside.*

Emil. Sure all the world conspires againſt me this day.

Wood. Fa, la, la, la, &c. }*Wood.* sings all the while

Ninny }*My love to that prodigious height* } Ninny *repeats.*
  reads. } *does rise,*
'Tis worthy of my heart and of your Eyes:
Firſt of my heart, which being subdued by you,
Muſt for that Reason be both ſtrong and true;
Then of your Eyes which Conquerours muſt subdue:
And make 'em be both slaves and freemen too;
Your Eyes which do both dazle, and delight,
And are at once the Joy, and grief of sight.
Love that is worthy of your face and fame
May be a glory, but can be no shame:

(65)

My heart by being o'recome does stronger prove,
Strength makes us yield unto your eyes and Love.
In this my heart is strong, because 'tis weak,
This, though I hold my peace, my Love will speak,
Silence can do more then e're speech did doe,
For humble silence does do more then wooe ;
Under the Rose, which being the sweetest flower
Shows silence in us has then speech more power.

Ninny. Why, what a damn'd Noise does he make ! pox take me Madam, if one can be heard for him ; Can't you let one alone with one's Verses trow ?

Wood. Poor fellow ! alas ! he little thinks why I sing now.   (*aside.*

Ninny. If he thought how pleasant my rehearsing were to her, sure he wou'd not be so rude, but Mum for that.   (*aside.*

Enter Luce.

Luce. O Madam ! your father's come to Town, and has brought a Country Gentleman to come a woing to you : he sent his man before-hand to know if you were within, and one of the servants unluckily inform'd him before I cou'd see him : he says he's the most down-right pladding Gentleman the Countrey can afford.

Emil. What will become of me ? is there no mercy in store for me ?

Wood. Is he coming——nay then—hem———⎫ *They both take hold of*
——hem.   ⎪ *Emilia, and hold her by*

Ninny. I'le make haste before he comes to ⎬*force, and sing and re-*
hinder me.   ⎪ *peat as fast agen as they*

Emil. For Heav'ns sake let me go.   ⎭ *did before.*

Wood. ⎧ Sing ⎫
        {   } together.
Nin. ⎩ Repeat ⎭

Emil. Oh, hold, hold, hold ! I faint if you give not over.

Wood. What a Devil does she mean by this ? *I* am sure she loves me ; but perhaps rather than endure the trouble of his Noise, she's willing to dispense with the pleasure of my Voice.   (*aside.*

Ninny. A poise take this *Woodcock*, that he shou'd anger this Lady, as I hope to live he's a very impertinent fellow, for though she was troubled at him, I perceiv'd she was transported with me.

Emil. It must be so, I must do ill that good may come on't : This Countrey fellow will be the worst plague of all, since he has my fathers Authority to back him, I must be forc'd to subdue my own Nature, and flatter these Coxcombs to get rid of him, for they are so impudent they'l drive him from hence——

Enter Stanford, *and overhears.*

Wood. Madam, let me ask you in private, how did you like my Song, speak boldly Madam, *Ninny* does not hear, Dear heart?

Emil. I muſt needs like it, Sir, or betray my own Judgement.

Wood. Ah, Dear *Roger!* thou art a made man for ever.   (*aside.*
I am the man————

Stanf. What's this I hear?   (*To himself.*

Ninny. How did you like my Verses, Madam?

Emil. So well Sir, that I hope you will let me hear 'em often. What am I reduc'd to?

Stanf. Oh Devil what's this?

Ninny. How happy shall I be? the truth is I did perceive you were troubl'd at *Woodcock's* senseless Songe, how we wou'd enjoy our selves if he were gone!

Stanf. Is it possible I shou'd be deceiv'd so much?

Wood. I'le tell thee, Dear Heart, if thou bee'ſt troubled at *Ninny's* Rimes, upon my honour I'le beat the Rogue.

Enter Father *and* Countrey-Gentleman.

Father. This is she, Sir.

Coun. Gent. Your servant, Madam.

Stanf. 'Death, she is a very Gossip, and Converses with all sort of fools not only with patience, but with pleasure too; how civilly she entertains them! That I shou'd be such an Owl to think there could be a woman not Impertinent, I have not patience to look upon her longer.———   *Ex.*

Wood. It won't do *Ninny*, her father little thinks she's ingag'd, Dear Heart.

Ninny. No, no, her Father little thinks she's ingaged, nor you   (*aside.* neither to whom——ha, ha, ha, it makes me laugh to think how this Countrey Gentleman will be bob'd, *Woodcock.*

Wood. He may go down, *Ninny*, like an Ass as he came, she'l send him down with a flea in's ear, take that from me.

Ninny. What a poise! he does not know she love me, does he? (*aside.*

Wood. Poor Fool! I pity him: ha, ha, ha.

Ninny. So do I, alack, alack.

Coun. Gent. Madam, I am but juſt now come to Town, you see my Boots are dirty ſtill, but I make bold as the saying is.

Emil. More bold then welcome, I assure you Sir.

Coun. Gent. Thank you good sweet Madam; this is the moſt obliging Gentlewoman that ever was———   (*aside.*

Fath. By this he shewes the Impatience of his Love (Daughter).

Wood. Madam, I am a Son of a Whore, if I have not the best song upon that subject, that ever you heard in your life.

Ninny. Before *George* Madam, I'le repeat you a Copy of Verses of my own, ten times better then his Song.

Wood. You are an impudent Coxcomb to say so, Dear Heart, And ye lye, and I am satisfy'd.

Ninny. Do I so, Madam? do but you judge.

Fath. What can this mean? they are both mad.

{ *sing and repeat* } { *together—* }	*Wood.* sings. *My Love is cruel grown,*
Ninny { *I am so impatient for to go to my* repeats. { *Dear.*	*For to leave me all alone,* *Thus for to sing and moan*
That I run headlong without Wit *or fear.*	*Ah woe is me !*
	Peace, Coxcomb, peace
Ninny. What an impertinent Fellow are you.	*(spoke.* *But I'll strive to find*
Woodcock. cannot you let one alone ;	*My Love, though she's unkind* *So far to ease my mind.*
Re { *So great the power of our Love is* peats. { *now,*	*Oh woe is me !*
We can't persuade it reason for to *allow.*	*Hay ho, hay ho, my Love,* *Who so Cruel as* Jenny *to me.*
Strange Miracle of Cytherea's *force,* *For to transform a man into a horse.*	{ *They offer to sing* } { *and repeat again.* }

Fath. Hold, hold, are you both mad, is the Devil in you? if he be, I shall have them will conjure him out of you Come out you Coxcombs, or I'le drive you out.—— *Ex.* Father, Ninny *and* Woodcock.

Coun. Gen. These Gentlemen are as mad are March-Hares, Madam, as the saying is; but to our business, I had not the power as I was a saying, to keep from you longer, Lady, not so much as a pissing while, d'ye see! for Cat will to kind as the saying is.

Luce. Oh Sir, you complement, you are an absolute Countrey Courtier,

Coun. Gent. Who I? alas not I, in sober sadness, we that live in the Countrey are right down d'ye see, we call a Spade a Spade, as the saying is, for our part.

Luce. You doe well Sir, for hypocrisie is an abominable vice.

Coun. Gent. 'Tis indeed to be a Pharisy and carry two faces in a Hood, as the saying is.

Emil. Now I wish my t'other two Fools would come back and drive away this.

Luce. I perceive you are very good at Proverbs, Sir, don't you use to play at that sport with the Countrey Gentlewomen?

Coun. Gent. O yes, I am old dog at that, I am too hard for 'em all at it. d'ye see. *(To* Emilia.
But Madam now we talk of the Countrey, how do you think you can like a Countrey life?

Emil. O rarely! I can't chuse, to fill ones belly with Curds and Cream, and stewd Prunes, to eat Honey-comb, and Rashers of Bacon at poor neighbours Houses, and rise by five a clock in the Morning to look to my dayry.

Coun. Gent. O rare how we shall cotten together, as the saying is! I love a good Huswife with all my heart; but Madam, I have a cast of Hawkes, and five couples of Spaniels too; oh Madam, if you saw my beloved Bitch *Venus,* you would be in love with her, she's the best at a Retrieve of any Bitch in *England,* d'e see.

Emil. Is he here? this is Heaven to me to see him after my late afflictions. *(aside.*

Enter Stanford *and* Roger.

To the Coun. Gent.] Sir I have some bus'ness will engage me half an hour, pray will you avoid my sight in the mean time.

Coun. Gent. I will forsooth, I'le go see my horses fed the while.

Emil. This is a modester Fool then the others I am troubled with, but if my father had been here, I shou'd not so easily have got rid of him————What are you come agen? *(to* Stanford.

Stanf. Ay, ay, too soon I am sure.

Emil. Are you not very foppish that you did stay longer then?

Stanf. This accusation becomes you well indeed.

Emil. Why not Sir?

Stanf. Alas you are not impertinent, no, no, not you!

Emil. I am sure you are: what can this mean?

Stanf. You were never pleas'd with *Woodcocks* damn'd voice yet, nor *Ninny's* ridiculous Poetry, not you?

Emil. Not more, than your self.

Stanf. No, no, you were not pleas'd with them, you did not praise 'em, nor entertain the other Two Fools with kindness, no, not you?

Emil. What a ridiculous thing 'twas of you not to tell me this in one word?
Oh Heaven! are they here?

Stanf. How soon you can counterfeit the humour.

Enter Sir Positive *and Lady* Vaine.

Sir *Pos.* You see, I am as good as my word *Stanford.*
La. *Vaine.* You see, Madam, how ready I am to wait on your Ladiship.
Emil. Ay, to my cost I thank you.

Stanf. She thinks I am so easily bit as to take this for a satisfaction, but I am too old to be deceiv'd agen.   (*aside.*

Enter Lovell *and* Carolina.

Lov. Now Madam to our business, if we don't put 'em out of this humour 'tis strange.

Car. However let's use our lawful Endeavours towards it.

Enter Woodcock *and* Ninny.

Wood. ⎰Sing ⎱
and { } together.
Ninny. ⎱Repeat⎰

Wood. 'Slife Sir, I'le teach you to trouble this Lady with your pitiful rimes.

Ninny. You teach me ? nay, if you provoke me before Company you shall find me a Lion————   (*they draw.*

Wood. Have at you Dear Heart.

Sir *Pos.* Hold *Woodcock !* why shou'd you disparage Poet *Ninny,* He's a man of admirable Parts, and as cunning a fellow, between you and I *Stanford,* I believe he's a Jesuite, but I am sure he is a Jansenist.

Wood. He a Jesuite, that understands neither Greek nor Latine ?

Sir *Pos.* Now he talkes of that *Stanford,* I'll tele thee what a Master I am of those Languages ; I have found out in the Progress of my Study, I must confess with some diligence, four and twenty Greek and Latine words for Black Puddens & Sausages.

Wood. Think to huff me ? I cou'd show you a matter of 200 wounds I got when I was a Volunteer aboard the Cambridge, Dear Heart, wou'd make you swoon to look upon 'em.

Sir *Pos.* Cambridge, well, that Cambridge is a good ship, and do you know, *Stanford,* that I understand a Ship better then any thing in the World ?

Stanf. Do you speak, Madam, you are pleas'd with this————*To* Emilia.

Emil. Methinks you are as troublesome as he.

Sir *Pos.* You may talk of your *Petts* and your *Deanes,* I'le build a Ship with any of e'm for 10000 pound.

Emil. What will become of me ? for if I should goe, they would follow me.

Lovel. This is extreamly well Painted————(*Shewes a picture to* Carolina.

Sir *Posi.* Painted ? Why ? Do you understand Painting ?

Lovel. Not I, Sir.

Sir *Pos.* I do ; if you please leave that to me : 'Tis true, *Michael Angelo, Titian, Raphael, Tintaret,* and *Julio Romano,* and *Paulo Veronese,* were very

(70)

pretty hopeful Men ; but I wou'd you saw a Piece of Mine, I shew'd you my *Magdalen, Emilia,* and I protest I drew that in half an houre.

Emil. O ! What shall I do to get rid of all these Tormenters ?

Stanf. I cannot but like this Woman yet, what ere's the matter : and yet I am sure she is impertinent.   (*aside.*

Sir *Posit.* Let me see, H. H.—Oh Deare ! Hans Holbin, here are Stroakes, here's Mastery ; well, no man in *England* shall deceive me in Hans Holbins hand, take that from me.

La. *Vaine.* ⎱O' my Conscience, Madam, this Gentleman understands
to *Emilia.* ⎰ every thing in the World.

Carol. In good earnest, *Lovel,* that's very pleasant, Hans Holbin ! why 'tis a new Sign for my Landlord, finish'd but yesterday, that cost him a Noble the painting, done by a Fellow that paints Posts and Railes, one *Humphrey Hobson,* and he calls him Hans Holbin.

Roger. Indeed Mr. *Woodcock,* fifty miles in a day was well run.

Wood. 'Ifaith was't, Dear Heart.

Sir *Posit.* Run ? why, Why will you pretend to running in my Company ? you run ! why I have run sixty miles in a day by a Ladies Coach, that I fell in Love withall in the streets, just as she was going out of Town, *Stanford ;* and yet I vow to thee I was not breath'd at all that time.

Lovel ⎱There's Knight Errantry for you, Madam, let any of your
to *Carol.* ⎰Romances match me that now.

Wood. to ⎱ 'Tis true, Madam, Sir *Positive* and Poet *Ninny* are excellent
La. *Vaine.* ⎰ men, and brave Bully-Rocks ; but they must grant, that neither of e'm understand Mathematicks but my self.

Sir *Posit.* Mathematicks ? why, Who'se that talkes of Mathematicks ? Let e'm alone, let e'm alone : Now you shall see, *Stanford.*

Wood. Why, 'twas I Dear Heart.

Sir *Posit.* I Dear Heart, quoth'a ? I don't think you understand the principles on't ; o' my Conscience you are scarce come so far yet as the squaring of the Circle, or finding out the Longitude Mathematicks : Why this is the only thing I value my self upon in the World, Cozen *Emilia.*

Emil. Heav'n ! deliver me.

Stanf. Curse on e'm all—Well, there must be something more in this Woman then *I* imagine.

Ninny to ⎱ No man in *England* plays better upon the Cittern then I do,
Emilia. ⎰ ask *George* my Barbor else, Madam he's a great Judge.

Sir *Pos.* Cittern, Cittern ! Who nam'd a Cittern there ? Who was't ? Who was't ?

Nin. Now am I affraid to speak to him, he does so snub one : 'Twas I and please you, Sir *Positive.*

Sir *Pos.* You talke of a Cittern before me ? when I invented the Instrument.

Lov. Woodcock.——Stand up to him in Mathematicks ; To him.

Wood. Say you so ? well then, by the Lord *Harry*, Sir *Positive*, I do underſtand Mathematicks better than you ; and I lie over againſt the Rose-Tavern in *Coven-Garden*, Dear Heart.

Sir *Pos.* I will juſtify with my Sword, that you underſtand nothing at all on't—— Draw.

Wood. Nay, hold, hold, I have done Bully-Rock, if you be so angry ; but it's a hard case you won't give a man leave to underſtand a little Mathematicks in your Company, Dear Heart.

Sir *Pos.* Pox on't, I have told thee often enough of this, thou wilt ſtill be putting thy self forward to things thou do'ſt not understand.

Emil. This Impudence is beyond all example, and there is no possibility of getting from them.

Car. I'le tell you one thing, Cozen, you cannot underſtand.

Sir *Pos.* I'le be hang'd then.

Car. You cannot cheat at Dice.

Sir *Pos.* Ha, ha ; Why you don't know me sure, you never heard of me.

Lov. Metaphysicks.

Sir *Pos.* Faith, well thought on, *Lovel*, prethee put me in mind of that Presently, if I don't give you that account of Metaphysicks, shall make you ſtare agen, cut my throat : But as I hope to live, *Stanford*, 'tis a ſtrange thing *Carolina* shou'd be so neer a Kin to me, and not know me ! False Dice, I have spent my time very well indeed, if any man out-does me in that ; for your Goade, your High Fullams, and Low Fullams, your Cater-Deuse Ace, and your Size Cater-Deuse, your Sinke Trey Ace, your Barr Cater-Trey, your Barr-Sink-Deuse, your Barr-Sise Ace, and all that, when I have ſtudy'd e'm these sixteen years——Cousin *Emilia*, you know this, don't you ?

Emil. Oh horrid ! What will become of me ?

Stanf. Sure I was miſtaken, for this muſt be a Woman of sence, I love her extreamly, I wou'd I did not.

Sir *Posit.* But what was that *Lovel*, I desir'd you to put me in mind of ?

Lov. Leger-De-Maine.

Sir *Pos.* Good, there 'tis now ; I had thought I had kept that quality to my self of all things in the World : sure the Devil muſt help thee, *Lovel*, How cou'dſt thou come to know that I underſtood Leger-de-maine else ? why, I'll perform all Tricks of Leger-de-maine with any man in *England*, let him be what he will ; For the Cups and Balls, *Jack*-in-a-Pulpit, *St. Andrews*-Cross.

Car. Undoubtedly, *Lovel*, Cardinal *Mazarine* was a great States-man.

Sir *Pos.* States-man do you say ? Cardinal *Mazarine* a States-man ? well, I will say nothing of my self for that ; no, I am no States-man : But : you may please to remember, who was bob'd at *Oſtend*, ha, ha, What say you *Stanford ?*

Emil. O Heavens ! can you contrive no way of escaping ?

Stanf. Let's e'ne try what we can do, for we had better be with one another then with these Fooles.

Sir *Pos.* Betwixt you and I, I was the Man that manag'd all this business againſt him.

La. *Vaine.* Good lack a day, Madam, this Gentleman has a bottomless underſtanding.

Ninny. He's a very rare Man, and has great power and imagination.

Wood. As any Man in Europe, deare Heart.

Sir *Pos.* This very thing has made me so famous all over Europe, that I may be at this inſtant Chiefe Miniſter of State in *Ruſsia*, but the truth on't is, *Stanford*, I expeꝗt that neerer home.

Rog. Jacob Halls a moſt admirable Rope-Dancer, Mr. *Woodcock.*

Sir *Pos.* Honeſt *Roger !* How the Devil cou'dſt thou find me out in that, *Jacob Hall* has told thee, has he not ? I thought he would ha' kept that to himself ; but I taught him, nay, I taught the *Turke* himself.

Lov. Hey, from a States-man to a Rope-Dancer, What a leap was there ?

Car. My Maid is excellent at Paſtry.

Sir *Pos.* Ha, why there 'tis ; now upon my Honour I underſtand this ten times better then any thing I have spoke of yet ! Paſtrey, why, the Devil take me if I would not be content never to eat Pye but of my own making as long as I live ; I'le tell you, when I was but four years old, I had so rich a fancy, and made such extraordinary dirt Pies, that the moſt eminent Cookes in all *London*, wou'd come and observe me, to ſteal from me.

La. *Vaine.* I beseech you, Madam *Emilia*, take notice of Sir *Positive*, he is a Prodigy of underſtanding.

Sir *Pos.* Ah Madam, 'tis your pleasure to say so ; but 'twas this made me skilful in the art of Building, which is the onely Art I am proud of in the World ; I'le tell you *Stanford*, I have seventeen Modells of the City of *London* of my own making, and the worſt of e'm makes *London* an other-guess *London* then 'tis like to be ; but no man in *England* has those Modells of Houses that I have.

Stanf. This affliꝗtion is beyond all example ; why the Devil do'ſt thou provoke him to this ?

Lov. Were it not a ridiculous thing of me not to please my self ?

Stanf. That's true ; but, What will become of us in the mean time ?

Emil. Heaven knows this door's lock'd, and there's no escaping at the other.

Sir *Pos.* I'le tell you, Madam, the other day a damn'd old Rat eat me up a Dining-Roome and Withdrawing-Chamber worth Fifty pound.

Car. A Rat eat up a Dining-Roome and Withdrawing-Room, How cou'd that be?

Emil. O fy, sister, it's no matter how? why Will you ask him?

Sir *Pos.* Why, I make all my modells of Houses in Paste; I vow to Gad I am asham'd to tell you how much it costs me a year in Milk Meale, Eggs and Butter.

La. Vain. Dear Sir *Positive*, I think you understand more then ever *Salomon* did.

Sir *Pos.* No, no, Madam, alass not I, I understand little, but I'll tell you, Madam, what was said of me the other day, by some great persons that shall be nameless.

La. Vain. What was that, Sir?

Sir *Pos.* That I was a man of the most universal knowledge of any man in *England*; but without comparison the best Poet in *Europe*.

Car. —————Now *Lovel* to your post.

Lov. Navigation.
Sir *Pos.* Navigation d'ye talk of?
Car. Geography.
Sir *Pos.* Geography d'ye talk of?
Lov. Astronomy.
Sir *Pos.* Astronomy d'ye talk of?
Car. Palmestry.

Lov. Physick.
Car. Divinity.
Lov. Surgery.
Car. Arithmetick
Lov. Logick.
Car. Cookery.
Lov. Magick.

Lovel *and* Carolina *speak so fast one after another, that Sir* Positive *turns himself first to one, then to another, & has not time to speak to them,*

Sir *Pos.* Hold, hold, hold, hold! Navigation, Geography, Astronomy, Palmestry, Phisick, Divinity, Surgery, Arithmetick, Logick, Cookery and Magick: I'le speak to every one of these in their order; if I don't understand e'm every one in perfection, nay, if I don't Fence, Dance, Ride, Sing, Fight a Duel, speak *French*, Command an Army, play on the Violin, Bag-pipe, Organ, Harp, Hoboy, Sackbut, and double Curtal, speak Spanish, Italian, Greek, Hebrew, Dutch, Welch and Irish, Dance a Jigg, throw the Barr, Swear, Drink, Swagger, Whore, Quarrel, Cuffe, break Windowes, manage Affairs of State, Hunt, Hawke, Shoot, Angle, play at Catt, Stool-ball, Scotch-hope and Trap-ball, Preach, Dispute, make Speeches.————— (*Coughs.* Prethee get me a glass of small beere, *Roger*.

Stanf. Hell and Furies!

Emil. Oh, oh————— (*They run.*

Sir *Pos.* Nay, hold, I have not told you halfe; if I don't do all these, and fifty times more, I am the greatest Owle, Pimp, Monkey, Jack-a-napes, Baboon, Rascal, Oafe, Ignoramus, Logger-head, Cur-dog, Block-head, Buffoone, Jack-pudden, Tony, or what you will; spit upon me, kick me, cuff me, lugg me by the eares, pull me by the Nose, tread upon me, and despise me more than the World now values me. { *Ex.* omnes, *and he goes out talking as fast as he can.*

ACT V.

Enter Emilia, Stanford, *and* Lovel.

Stanf. IF you be my Friend, as you profess to be, you will not deny me this.

Lov. I am your Friend, and would not have you perplex your self with what you see there's no end of ; Can this frowardness relieve you ?

Stanf. Good Sir, none of your Grave advice, I am resolv'd to relieve my self, by abandoning all conversation.

Lov. How can you brook *Emilia*'s company.

Stanf. Pish ! she's not altogether so troublesome : aske me no more Questions.

Lov. Hah ! Does he like her ? Thus farr my Designe thrives : Well ! I'le keep e'm from you a while : But the Hounds are so eager, they'l never endure pole-hunting Long. (*exit.*

Stanf. You hear, Madam, we are not like to be long free from these inhumane persecutors.

Emil. Why will you call e'm so ? you know I am pleas'd with e'm : They are my Recreation, as you were pleas'd to say.

Stanf. No, no ; you have convinc'd me of the Contrary : but, How can you blame me for so easie a Mistake ?

Emil. You are a very fit Man to despise impertinent people : You are !

Stanf. 'Twill be very wisely done to stand muttering here, till the Fooles in the next Room break-in upon you.

Emil. Perhaps as wisely done, as to trust my selfe with you, as you have behav'd your self.

Stanf. If you have no more sense then to stay longer, I shall be assur'd of what I was but jealous of before.

Emil. What would your wisdome have me do now ?

Stanf. The worst of them would not have ask'd such a Question : Who but you would be in doubt, or would not flie as a Thief does from a Hue and Cry ?

Emil. There's no hope of escaping.

Stanf. Now will you in despair of avoiding them, ſtay here, and keep e'm company ?

Emil. 'Twere vain presumption to hope for Liberty by Miracle ; they will no more lose us, then an Attorny will a young Squire that's newly waded into *Law* ; will be sure never to leave him, till he has brought him out of his depth.

Stanf. By this rule you shou'd not resiſt a Man that comes to Ravish you, because he's like to be too ſtrong for you ; but if you did not use the means your honeſty would be no more admir'd in that, then your Wisdome in this.

Emil. Aside. This is a moſt admirable person.———
Where should I go ? (*to him.*

Stanf. I would run into a fire to be quit of e'm.

Emil. Well ! I am content to go along with you, not for your sake, but my own.

Stanf. Perhaps my inclination are not much unlike yours.

Lov. Oh, *Stanford*, I can no longer keep ⎫ *Enter* Lovel, Carol, *Sir* Pos. them from you, 'tis as easie to ſtop a ⎬ Nin. Wood, La. Vaine. Spring-Tide. ⎭

Stanf. Now, Whose fault was this ? a Curse upon your delaying, now 'tis too late to flie.

Sir *Pos.* Doſt talk of flying, Jack ? I'le teach thee to do that with the greateſt ease in the world : 'tis true, I heard of a Coxcomb that broke his neck with the Experiment, but if I had been by him, I wou'd have taught him to have flown with the beſt Goss-Hawke in the World.

Stanf. O Impudence.

Sir *Pos.* And for my own part, for one flight or so, for I will not ſtrain my self for any mans pleasure ; I do't but for my Recreation : I am no mercenary. I will flie at a Herne with the beſt Jer-Faulcon that ever flew ; that's faire.

La. *Vain.* O very Fair as can be ! by all means, Sir, learn of him, hee'l do it.

Sir *Pos.* Do't Madam ? I think so : I tell you all Elements are alike to me, I could live in any one of 'em as well as the Earth : 'Tis nothing but a sordid Earthly Nature in us makes us love the Earth better then any other Element.

Enter Roger.

Emil. I see it is in vain to torment our selves without endeavouring our Liberty.

Stanf. That's cunningly found out.

Rog. Sir, if you can find a way to be rid of Sir *Positive* and my Lady *Vaine*, I'le tell you how to quit your selves of the other.

Emil. We may set 'em one upon another, and by that we may either get rid or (at least) be a little reveng'd of 'em.

Stanf. That may make some amends for your last neglect.

Car. Now they are settl'd in their bus'ness, I'll leave 'em and go to my Tyre woman in Coven-Garden, who has some Excellent new Patterns of Lace for me ; will you please to Squire me along ?

Lov. I hope you have no design upon me : are your ⎫ Emilia *whispers to* intentions honourable ?   ⎭ Woodcock.

Car. Yes indeed are they, I intend no rape upon you.

Lov. Nor any other unlawful way of love.

Car. Leave fooling, and let's away----   *Ex.* Lov. Car.

Sir *Pos.* to La. *Vain.*] *P*'shaw ! I could live in the water so well, that o' my Conscience I am Amphibious, I could catch fish as well as any Cormorant or Otter, nay I can live so long under-water, that (but that I have greater designs on foot here) *I* would go into the West Indies to dive for Sponges and Corals, and if in one year I were not the richest Man that ever went thither I would be hang'd *Jack Stanford*, when I swom over agen.

Stanf. 'Sdeath, I would you were under Water one half hour in the mean time.

Sir *Pos.* Faith I would I were *Jack*, thou woud'st admire to see what pleasure I take in lying under Water an hour or two, especially if the Water be warm !

Stanf. Yes, yes, and you can eat fire too ; can't yee ?

Sir *Pos.* P'shaw ! you admire a man that eats fire among you, one that has a deprav'd pallate, and is not able to taste an Ash from a Oak-Coal, which I can distinguish as well as I can a pickl'd Herring from a Muscle.

Ninny. Eat Fire ? it is Impossible.

Sir *Pos.* You are a Fopp, *I* pity your ignorance, Eat Fire ? why *I*'ll Eat Fire and Brimstone with the Devil himself man, what dost talk of that ?

Wood to *Emilia.*] *I* warrant you, Dear Heart, I'le do't, and yet I am plaguely afraid of Sir *Positive.*

Emil. What am I forc'd to ? Master *Ninny*, you have often profest some kindness to me.

Ninny. And Madam may I never make Couplet agen, if I don't love you better then I do Musick or Poetry.

Emil. And understand me as little————   (*aside.*
I shall soon make trial of you.   (*To him.*

Ninny. And before *George* if I do not serve you !————

Emil. Then be sure the next thing Sir *Positive* pretends to, contradict him in, and be as *Positive* as he is, and by this perhaps you may deserve my kindness.

Ninny. But suppose, Madam, he should draw upon me, and do me a Mischief.

Emil. Maſter *Stanford* and his man will bail you from that.

Ninny. In confidence of this I shall be glad to serve you.

La. *Vain.* I wonder, dear Sir, a man of your incomparable Ability's shou'd want preferment.

Sir *Pos.* Modeſty! modeſty! we that are modeſt men get nothing in this age.

La. *Vain.* Perhaps the World does not know of these things.

Sir *Pos.* Not know! why I was never in Company with any man in my life, but I told him all.

Wood. And no man ever believ'd you, Dear Heart.

Sir *Pos.* As I hope to breathe, *Jack*, this fellow's mad.

Wood. Ne're tell me, Dear Heart, I know you underſtand nothing of all you have pretended to in comparison of me, Dear Heart.

Sir *Pos.* Is not this very pleasant, Madam, ha, ha?

Ninny. Nay, nay, never laugh for the matter, and think to bear up againſt all the World: Do you think I don't think my self a better Poet than you?

Wood. And I a better Musitian?

Sir *Pos.* You Impudent Baboons!

Ninny. Let him alone, let him alone, *Woodcock*.

Wood. Ay, ay, alas I laugh at him: Ha, ha, ha.

Enter Bridget.

Bridg. Madam, the party has ſtay'd for you a good while at the setting-Dog and Partridge.

La. *Vain.* Come, while they dispute, let's go——*Exit La. Vain, Bridg.*
(Emilia *offers to go out.*

Ninn. Nay, Madam, if you don't ſtay to prevent Mischief, I have done: For I find I begin to grow furious, and dare not truſt my own temper.

Sir *Pos.* Have you the Impudence to say you are a better Poet, and you a better Musitian than I am?

Ninn. Ay, ay, and not onely so, but a better Divine, Aſtrologer, Mathematician, Geographer, Seaman——

Wood. A better Physician, Lawyer, States-man, Almanack-maker.

Ninn. Ay, and what shall break your Heart, a better Trap-ball-player too, take notice of that——

Wood. In one word, I underſtand every thing that is or is not to be underſtood, better then you doe: take that from me.

Ninn. And let me tell you, Sir *Positive*, 'tis a very confident thing in you to pretend to underſtand any thing as well as I do.

Sir *Posit.* O Impudence!

(78)

Wood. You underſtand ! How should you come by underſtanding ?
Where had you your Knowledge, Dear Heart ?   P'shaw.

Sir *Posit.* What will this age come to ?

Ninn. Your insolence makes me blush, as I hope to breath, for such an
empty Fellow to talk of Wit or Sense ; p'shaw, prethee hold thy Tongue.

Sir *Posit.* I am amaz'd !

Wood. I tell thee, dear Soul, I love thee so well, I would not have thee
pretend to these things thou doſt not underſtand.

Ninn. Especially before such men as we that do underſtand.

Sir *Posit.* I can hold no longer, ye eternal Dogs, ye Currs, ye Ignorant
Whelps : I'le sacrifice ye, let me go : if there be no more Sons of Whores
in *England*, I'le murder 'em.

Stanf. Bear up to him, I'le prevent all Injuries.

Ninn. Nay then, Sir, never fret and fume for the matter ; Look you,
Sir, pray what can you do better then I ?

Wood. Or I either ? Let's hear't, Dear Heart.

Sir *Posit.* Hear it, you Rascals ? I'le rout an Army with my single
Valour : I'le burn a whole Fleet at three Leagues diſtance : I'le make
Ships go all over the World without sales : I'le plow up rocks ſteep as
the *Alps* in duſt, and lave the Tyrrhene Waters into Clouds, (as my
Friend *Cateline* says.)

Ninny. 'Pshaw ! you ! I'le pluck bright Honour from the pale-fac'd
Moon, (as my Friend Hot-Spur sayes) what do you think of that ?

Emil. Certainly ; he's diſtraⅽted ! this is some revenge.

Sir *Posit.* This single head of mine shall be the balance of Chriſtendom :
And by the ſtrength of this I'le undermine all Commonwealths, deſtroy
all Monarchies, and write Heroick Plays : ye dogs, let me see either of
you do that.

Stanf. This is raving madness.

Ninny. Wou'd I were well rid of him, I tremble every joynt of me.

Sir *Posit.* With this right hand I'le pluck up Kingdoms by the Roots,
depopulate whole Nations, burn Cities, murder Matrons, and ravish
sucking Infants ; you Currs, can you do this ?

Rog. But, Sir, in the midſt of your fury, my Lady *Vaine* is gone away
with a Gentleman.

Sir *Posit.* Ah dear *Roger*, which way did she go ? shew me quickly,
I'le bring her back, and she shall see me take satisfaⅽtion of these
Rascals.——

Ex. Sir Posit. *and* Roger.

Wood. I'm glad you are gone, Sir, my heart was at my mouth, did I
not do the business rarely, my pretty Rogue ? How canſt thou reward
me for this ? hah ?

Emil. Unfortunate Woman ! What am I reduc'd to ? If you will go immediately to *Oxford* Kates, and stay for me in the great Room there, I will not fail to come to you in a little time, and let you know how sensible I am of this favour; go, go instantly, and make no words on't.

Wood. I fly, Madam. O dear Roger! I have catch'd her, O Rogue! I'll provide a parson immediately : dear son of a Whore, let me kiss thee. [*Ex.*

Stanf. I shall have a better Opinion of her Wit then ever I had, if she gets rid of this brace of *Jack-Puddens*.

Ninny. Ay, Madam, you see what danger I have undergone : I am onely unhappy I have lost no bloud in the service : for as a Noble Author sayes,

—— *It would have been to me both loss and gain.*

But shall I hope for any favour from you ?

Emil. Let not *Stanford* perceive any thing; go and stay for me at *Oxford* Kates in the great Roome, and there we may freely speak our Minds.

Ninny. And will you not fail to come ?

Emil. No, no, but whatever happens, remove not till I come to you : away, away, we are observ'd.

Ninny. O admirable Fortune! Sure I was born with a Caul on my Head, and wrapt in my Mothers Smock, the Ladies do so love me. *Exit.*

Emil. I would these two Fools were oblig'd to stay there till I came to 'em.

Stanf. Now I hope you will take warning, and stay here no longer, where they may find you out, unless you take pleasure in 'em.

Emil. Where can I find a place of safe retreat ?

Rog. I have a Sister lives in Coven-Garden, a Tyre-woman, where at this time of night you may be private : if you please, command the House.

Enter Sir Positive.

Emil. Make haste then! O Heav'n, is he return'd ?

Sir *Pos.* Pox on't, I can't find my Mistress; where are these Rogues ?

Stanf. My Lady *Vaine* is return'd, and *Ninny* and *Woodcock* are with her in the next room.

Sir *Pos.* Say you so ? I'le in, and first make the Puppy's recant their errours, and then murder 'em in presence of my Mistress.

Stanf. So! you are fast.   *Locks the door.*   [*Ex.*

Emil. Come away, away!   *Ex.* Stanf. Emil. Rog.

Sir *Pos. within.* *Stanford*, open the door, are you mad? hey *Stanford!* Cozen *Emilia!* open the door.

Enter Lady Vaine *and* Bridget.

La. Vaine. What, is the house empty ? —— 'Twas an unlucky thing That the Gentlemen should go before we came.

Bridg. You may thank Sir *Positive*, would he were far enough for me for keeping you Ladiship so long.

Sir *Pos. Stanford! Emilia!* open the door there! help, help, help!

La. *Vaine.* That's his voyce! what can be the matter? the Key is in the door, I'll in and see ———————   *She unlocks the door.*

Enter Sir Positive.

Sir *Pos.* O Madam! your humble servant! If *I* don't murder *Stanford*, may *I* never have any share in your Ladiships favour.

La. *Vaine.* Did he lock you in?

Sir *Pos.* Yes, Madam; for which with this Blade that is inur'd to slaughter will *I* slice him into Attoms.

La. *Vaine.* No, sweet Sir *Positive* reſtrain your passion, such a fellow as he *deserves to be toss'd in a blanket.*

Sir *Pos.* No, no, never talk of that, Madam! Such a Revenge is below me, but *I* have a Pen that will bite, and I'le do it vigorously. And yet the Rogue has done me a kindness: For if he had not lock'd me up, I had miss'd of your Ladiship.

La. *Vaine.* Sir, upon my honour, I intended not to have ſtay'd from you!

Sir *Pos.* But Madam, the loss of you has put me into that fright, that *I* desire to make sure of you.

La. *Vaine.* As how, good Sir?

Sir *Pos.* To marry you this Night.

La. *Vaine.* That's short Warning.

Sir *Pos.* But Madam, I have had your Promise these three days, and that's long enough to expeƈt performance.

Bridg. Madam, e'en take him at his Word.

La. *Vaine.* But how shall I answer that to my Friend in the Countrey?

Bridg. Ne're trouble your self for that, Madam, 'tis fashionable to have a servant as well as a husband, and besides the pleasure of a Gallant, there will be another, which is no small one to some women, of deceiving your husband.

La. *Vaine.* Thou art in the right, Wench: Besides the failing of this assignation has set me so a Gogg, I would very unwillingly lye alone to night.

Sir *Pos.* Come Madam, I see you are consulting: I'le send for a Parson shall soon finish the debate.

La. *Vaine.* Well Sir! your Intentions are so honourable, I submit to you.

Sir *Pos.* O intollerable happiness! Let's dispatch it immediately in this house.

La. *Vaine.* No Sir! I'le carry you to a more private place.

Sir *Pos.* Come Madam, I'le wait on you.———————   *(Exeunt.*

Enter Lovell, Carolina.

Car. Now I have dispatch'd this important bus'ness of woman-kind, which is making themselves fine, we may return.

Lov. To the place from whence we came, and from thence to the place of Execution, if you please : I'le have a Levite ready.

Car. No Sir, I know you are too true a Son of the Church to venture that after the Canonical hour.

Lov. I am not so formal to observe a Method in any thing ; besides, Marriage being at best unseasonable, can never be less then now.

Car. To speak gravely ; let us first take the advice of our pillows : since sleep being a great setler of the brain, may be an Enemy to Marriage, for one wou'd think that few in their right Wits wou'd undertake so unseasonable an action, as you call it.

Lov. Must people then be tam'd into Marriage ? as they man Hawks with watching.

Enter Stanford, Emilia, Roger.

Car. What's here ? my Sister with *Stanford?*

Emil. How unlucky is this, my Sister, and an idle fellow with her ?

Stanf. Ne're trouble your self, if your Sister be not a Fopp, He's none I'le assure you.

Emil. You are a very Competent Judge indeed,

Car. How now Sister, can you with all your gravity steal away by night with a Gentleman ?

Lov. Come *Stanford*, there's Love betwixt you ; for nothing else can make men and women so shame-fac'd as to seek out private places.

Car. Come Sister, if it be so, ne're mince the matter, 'tis the way of all flesh.

Lov. And we are so far onward on that way, that if you don't make haste, you will scarce overtake us.

Car. Come, confess, *Emilia*, what brought you hither ?

Emil. I came to fly from Impertinence, and *I* have found it here.

Car. That will not bring you off Sister : for if you did not like this Gentleman very well, you wou'd fly from him as soon as any Man.

Stanf. For my part, I onely came to defend her from Assaults at this time o'night.

Lov. If you had not an extraordinary value for her, you would not play the Knight-Errant to my knowledge : Is not this dissimulation of yours very ridiculous ?

Stanf. I must needs confess I never saw any Woman I dislik'd less.

Car. And, What say you Sister of this Gentleman ?

Emil. To give the Devil his due, I have met with less affliction from him then from other men.

Car. Nay, then in good earneſt it muſt be a match.

Emil. That's wiſely propos'd of you to me, that am immediately leaving the World.

Stanf. ⎱Pox on her ! how she pleases me.———————(*Aside.*
to *Emil.* ⎰Why, Who intends to ſtay behind ?

Car. If you negleſt this opportunity, Siſter, you'l ne're be so well match'd agen.

Stanf. 'Twill not be so pleasant to go alone as you imagine.

Car. No, no, take hands and march along I say.

Emil. That wou'd be much to the advantage of my honour.

Lov. I'le send for one shall satisfie that scruple, Madam.

Emil. The remedy is almoſt as bad as the disease.

Stanf. Perhaps if you consider it, 'twill be your wiseſt course.

Emil. No doubt I shou'd have an admirable Companion of you, as you think.

Bar. I find you have so grert a passion for the *Country Gentleman* my Father has provided for you, you will never be perswaded to be false to him.

Emil. He will be the greateſt plague of all : What shall I do to be rid of him ?

Car. There is but one way, Siſter ; E'ne dispose of your self to that honeſt Gentlemen, to have and to hold.

Stanf. 'Twill be very discreetly done, not to quit your self of this Country Fellow, and the reſt of your Fooles, now it is in your power.

Lov. Faith, Madam, be perswaded and joyn hands.

Stanf. The truth is, I think we cannot do better then to leave the World together : 'twill be very uncomfortable wandring in desarts for you alone.

Emil. If I shou'd be so mad as to Joyn hands with you, 'twould not be so much an Argument of Kindness to you, as Love to my self ; since at beſt I am forc'd to chuse the leaſt of two great Evils, either to be quite alone, or to have ill Company.

Lov. This will end in Marriage I see.

Emil. O no ! I dare not think of that, if he should grow troublesome, then 'twould be out of my power to caſt him off.

Stanf. Why there's no necessity we should be such Puppies as the reſt of Men and Wives are, if we fall out, to live together, and quarrel on.

Emil. The Conditions of Wedlock are the same to all.

Stanf. Whatsoever the Publick Conditions are, our private ones shall be, if either grows a Fopp, the other shall have liberty to part.

Emil. I muſt confess that's reasonable.

Lov. Away *Roger*, and fetch a Canonical Gentleman.

Rog. I will, Sir.

Lov. Faith, Madam, you have taken great paines, Was't for your self or me you did it ?

Car. You have a very civil opinion of your self I see.

Enter Roger.

Rog. O Sir ! yonder's Sir *Positive* and my Lady *Vaine* just alighted at the Door, with the man you sent for.

Emil. O undone ! ruin'd for ever !

Stanf. 'Slife you Rascal, did not you tell me I might be private here ?

Rog. Pray Sir do not fret, but make your escape out at the back doore.

Stanf. Away, away ! quickly, for Heavens sake !

Lov. Come, Madam ! let's follow e'm————————(*Exeunt omnes.*

Enter Ninny *and* Woodcock.

Nin. Will you never leave ones roome a little ? I tell you I am busie.

Wood. So am I, and 'tis my roome, deare heart, let me tell you that.

Nin. Before *George*, *Woodcock*, 'tis very Impertinent to trouble one thus.

Wood. So 'tis, *Ninny*, I wonder you'l do it ; for my part, a man that had the least Soul of Poetry in him, would scorne to do this.

Ninny. What ! Do you say I have not a Soul of Poetry in me ? I don't love to commend my self *Woodcock ;* but now I am forc't to't, I must tell you, I have six times as much power in me, as you have.

Wood. You lye dear heart ?

Ninny. Why, you lye then, to tell me that I lye, so you doe.

Wood. You are a Son of a Whore, dear heart, to tell me I lye.

Ninny. You are a Son of a Whore as well as my self, to tell me so, and you go to that.

Wood. I, I, you may say your pleasure ; but have a care Bully Rock, for if you give me the least affront, I'le break your Pate, take that from me.

Ninny. I'le take it from no man : If you do, I'le break yours agen man, for all you are so briefe : 'Slife, one shan't speak to you one of these days, you are grown so purdy.

Wood. Well ! well ! Dear Heart !

Ninny. Well ! well too ! and you go to that, if you be so fierce : But I'de faine know what occasion there is for you and I to quarrel now.

Wood. Ay, what indeed dear heart ? Therefore, prethee Dear Soul kiss me ; Dear Rogue, if thou lov'st me, go out of my Roome.

Ninny. No, good sweet *Woodcock* now, go thee, I'le do as much for thee another time, as I hope to Live.

Wood. Dear Curr I love thee ; but prethee excuse me, *I* have a Mistress to meet in this very Room ; Therefore dear pretty *Ninny* leave me.

Ninny. Cods my Life kins to see the luck on't : May I never versify agen if I am not here upon the same occasion : I'le give thee five Guynnys if thou'lt leave me : I shall spare e'm well enough when I have got her.
(aside.

Wood. I'd have you know, *Ninny*, I scorn your Guinnys : Alas, poor Fool, he little thinks I shall be in a better Condition to spare fifty then he can five : Why then, in short, let me tell you I am to be marry'd within this halfe hour, in this very Roome, dear heart.

Ninny. This is prodigious ! may I never have Play take agen if I am not to be marry'd here within this halfe hour, and to a very great Fortune too.

Wood. So is mine, Bully Rock !

Ninny. Dear *Woodcock*, let's reconcile this business here ; I have two Dice, he that throws most, stayes : then am I sure to be too hard for him that way, for I can nap a Six a-yard.
(aside.

Wood. No, not I : by the Lord *Harry*, I'le not trust a business of that Concernment to Fortune.

Ninny. Nay, then Sir, I will keep my Roome, I was first in't.

Wood. By that rule, you shou'd go first out.

Ninny. 'Tis not you can turn me out.

Wood. Say you so ? I'le try that.
(Draw, and fight at distance.

Ninny. At your own peril !

Wood. Can't you stand a little ? Why do you go back so, dear heart ?

Ninny. Let me alone, I know what I do in going back, I have the Law on my side, and if I kill you it will be found *se defendendo*.

Wood. Ay, ay, Have you murd'rous Intentions, dear heart ? If you do kill me, I will declare upon my Death-bed, That you had Malice in your heart, dear heart.

Ninny. Who I ? as I hope to be sav'd I scorn your Words : I Malice ; do your worst : I am better known then so : I am not so outragious : pray hear me a Word : You know we Authors and Ingenious Men have a great many Enemies.

Wood. We have so.

Ninny. At this rate we may kill one another : And a Pox on them they'd be glad on it ; and for my part *I* would not dye to please any of 'em.

Wood. Nor *I* neither ; therefore prethee leave me my Roome, to prevent danger.

Ninny. I am not so base : but, if you will, let us lay down these dangerous Engines of Blood, and Contend a safer way, by the way of Cuffe and Kick.

Wood. Ay, ay, with all my heart ; what a Pox care *I* : come, come, you shall see *I* dare do any thing, since you are resolv'd to try me. (*Enter two*
(*Servants, and part 'em, and Ex.*

Enter Stanford, Lovel, Carolina, Emilia, Roger.

Stanf. Here we are in as much danger as ever : Could any thing be so Foppish as returning to the place from whence we fled ?

Emil. 'Tis a sweet time of night to go on upon the Ramble.

Car. We are safe enough from any body but my Father ; and we cannot be troubled with him long : 'tis his hour of going to Bed.

Emil. How shall we despose of the Country Fellow, if he should return ?

Rog. Let me alone ; I'le find a Trick for him : I liv'd in the same Town with him, and know him to be a down-right credulous man, that will swallow any thing.

Enter Father *and* Countryman.

Stanf. Now see what you have brought your self to.

Fath. Come, Daughter, What think you of my choice of a Husband, He's extreme rich ; and, Is he not a very accomplish'd Gentleman, hah ;

Emil. There's a Fellow indeed, why he has not Soul enough for a Cock-Chicken.

Fath. You are a foolish froward Girle thus to despise your happiness ; I'le tell you, either resolve to Marry him to morrow morning————

Lov. Heark you Sir ! if you will take my advice, be not so hasty : you know young Ladies are alwayes Coy, and out of their little knowledge of the World, are apt to refuse that which may prove their greatest happiness.

Fath. What would you have me do with one that is so obstinate ?

Car. If you please, take some milder way : let us withdraw, and wee'l all help to perswade her : You know it is not proper to be done before him.

Fath. I'le be ruled in this : but if perswasions will not do, force shall.

Car. Be sure you seeme pliant to his Commands, it may advance our design.

Fath. Sir, we'll wait on you agen presently. (*Ex. all but* Cou. G. *&* Rog.

Coun. Gent. Your Servant Sir !——honest *Roger*, in sober sadness I am glad to see you well ; I had almost forgot you.

Rog. And how does your sweet Sister Madam *Dorothy ?*

Coun. Gent. O brave and lusty, as sound as a Roach, as they say.

Rog. I heard your Worship was Knighted.

Coun. Gent. No not I *Roger :* I am not ambitious of that : As the excellent Proverb sayes : Honour will buy no Beefe.

Rog. Now we are alone, Sir, I am oblig'd to tell you, I am sorry to see one, whom I so much honour'd, so ill us'd.

Coun. Gent. Pish ! it's no matter man ! I care not for Knight-hood one pin of my slieve, as the saying is.

Rog. Sir, I mean something concernes your Worship nearer.

Cou. Gent. Nearer ! What can that be ?

Rog. I muſt beg your pardon for that ; *I* may be ruin'd for my endeavours to serve you.

Cou. Gent. What, would any of your Town-Gallants bob me of my Miſtress ?

Rog. That were too good newes for you to be true.

Cou. Gent. Thank you for nothing : Is this the honour you have for me, to wish me the loss of a Miſtress worth 10000 *l* d'ye see ? udds nigs that's a good one indeed.

Rog. 10000 *l.* Ha, ha, ha, ; would she had it for her own sake and yours too !

Cou. Gent. Faith are you there with your Bears ? nay then I have brought my Hoggs to a fair Market.

Rog. If she had had one of those thousands, my Maſter would have Marry'd her long e're this ; Sir, I have alwayes honour'd you, and could not in Conscience but tell you this, and now it is in your power to ruine me.

Cou. Gent. Nay, *I*'le be as silent as a Dormous, but is it possible ?——

Rog. Nay, do not believe me if you please ; but *I* have discharg'd my duty ; and, if you Marry her, the Inconvenience will be yours not mine : Besides, if she had that Fortune you speak of, which she has as much as I have ; What good would it do you in the end ? She'l ne'r be perswaded to live in the Country, you muſt keep her in Town, with her Coach and six Horses, Pages and Lacquies : And she muſt visit the Playes, the Park, and the Mulberry-Garden.

Cou. Gent. O Lamen-table ! this were the way to get a pair of Hornes bigger than the Staggs head in my Hall has : but, if I were Marry'd to her, I'd get her into the Country as sure as a Gun.

Rog. If you shou'd, you'd have every week this Earle, that Lord, this Knight, and that Gentleman of her kindred come to take the fresh Aire ; and to Hunt and Hawke with you in the time of year.

Cou. Gent. Why they wou'd eat me out of House and Home, as the saying is.

Rog. They would despise your Beife and Mutton : You muſt keep a couple of French Cookes ; and eate nothing but Potages, Fricases, and Raguſts, your Champinions, Coxcombes and Pallats, your Andoilles, your Langue de porceau, your Bisks and your Olio's.

Cou. Gent. What are all these, several sorts of Sweet Meats ?

Rog. O, no Sir ! these muſt be your conſtant food, and every Dish will coſt you a Piece ; and, Will this be done with a small Portion of a Thousand Pound ?

Coun. Gent. I shou'd soon bring a Noble to Nine-pence then, as they say.

Rog. Then you must have your Quails, Ruffs, Gnates, Godwitts, Plover, Dotrills, Wheat-Eare, Cock of the Wood, and a hundred sorts of Fowles : besides, they would scorn your Ale and Cider, and March-Beer ; you must have your Sellar full of Champaign, Chablee, Burgundy, and Remedy Wines ; But Mum, Sir, if you love me.

Enter Father, Stanf. Emil. Carol. Lov.

Fath. Come, Sir, I have brought my Daughter to be obedient to my Commands, and I would have you prepare to be Marry'd to morrow morning.

Coun. Gent. I shall faile you, d'ye see.

Fath. What is't you say ?

Coun. Gent. I shan't be so civil, as the saying is.

Fath. This is madness.

Coun. Gent. No, Sir, no ; There's no catching old Birds with Chaffe. Fare-you-well.

Fath. D'hear Sir !

Coun. Gent. No, Sir, fare ye well——I am no Bubble, as they say. *Exit.*

Fath. I am amaz'd ! I'le after him, and inquire into the business ; I must not lose this Son-in-Law.   *Exit.*

Lovel. The Rogue has done it dexterously !

Enter Roger.

Rog. Come, Sir, here's a Parson in the next Roome, dispatch, while the old Gentleman's out of the House.   (*They are going out.*

Enter Woodcock.

Stanf. 'Slife, *Woodcock's* here ! I'le cut his Throat.

Emil. Pray none of your Hectoring here, to Alarm the House.

Wood. How now, Dear Heart ! Why did not you come to me as you promis'd ?

Emil. For Heavens sake go up into the Room two pair of Stairs, and I'le steal from hence, and give you an Account : Make haste.

Lov. Come let's in before we be interrupted agen.   (*Ex.* Wood.

Enter Ninny.

Nin. Hi'st, Madam ; before *George* 'twas unkindly done, not to remember your assignation just now.

Emil. You'l spoil all : I could not get loose ; run into the garden, there's a back door : I'le come to you immediately ; make haste, we are observ'd.

Nin. O ho ! this is something.

Stanf. This Woman has a soul.   *Exeunt omnes.*

Enter Huffe *drunk.*

Huffe. *I* have pursu'd him into this house, that has abus'd me so basely behind my back ; and by this Whiniard, and by the spirit of Gun-powder, I'le sacrifice him to my fury : Come out you son of a Whore.

Enter Stanford, *and the rest after him ;* Stanford *presses upon* Huffe, *and he falls.*

Stanf. That this Puppy shou'd provoke me to draw upon him, that is so drunk he cannot stand.

Huffe. That's a mistake ; not so drunk yet, but if I had stood soberly to't, I should have been run through the Lungs before this.   (*To himself.*

Enter Sir Positive *and Lady* Vaine.

Emil. Is there no end of our affliction ?

Sir *Pos.* Dear Cozen and *Jack Stanford*, give me Joy, I am Marry'd to a Lady that is the greatest Pattern of Wit, and the greatest Example of Vertue that this Age hath produc'd, and for her face look upon't, look upon it I say ! she's a beauty, take that from me, what say you *Stanford ?*
(*flourish within.*

Stanf. Yes, yes, she's cursedly handsome.

La. *Vain.* If my glass does not flatter me, you are not deceiv'd in your Judgment, dear Sir.

Sir *Pos.* Here I have brought Fiddles to rejoyce with you *Jack* and Cousin, since I know you love mirth as well as I do.

Enter Woodcock.

Wood. I had waited for thee my dear Miss, if this unexpected Musick had not brought me hither.

Enter Ninny.

Ninny. How now ? what Fiddles are these ?

Sir *Pos.* You dogs, are you here ? now, Madam, you shall see how I'le chastise these fellows that wou'd be Wits.

Wood. Hold, dear Rogue ! why should'st thou be angry ? upon my honour I did but droll with thee, for by the Lord *Harry* I take thee to be one of the pillars of the Nation, Dear Heart !

Sir *Pos.* O, do you so ?

Ninny. Dear Sir *Positive*, I beg your pardon a thousand times, for my part I believe there never was a man of that prodigious understanding that you have.

Sir *Pos.* Do you so ? I knew it was impossible they shou'd be in Earnest, but do you hear ? have a care of being *Positive* another time, a man would think you might learn more Modesty of me.

(89)

Wood. Come, Dear Heart, art thou here ? prethee kiss me, and lets be friends for all our late Cuffing : What need we care for a douce or two of the Chops, Bully-Rock ?

Ninny. Nay, for my part, I value it as little as you do, and you go to that.

Enter Father *and* Countrey Gentleman.

Fath. What Ryot's this in my house ? at this time o' night ?

Sir Pos. Riot ! do you understand what a Riot is in Law ? I'll telle you : for no man in this Nation has committed more then I have.

Fath. Tell me not of Law, Sir ; what mean these Fiddles, I say, at this time o'night ?

Sir Pos. Unckle, they are mine : I am marry'd to this Lady, and resolve to be merry in your house before we go to Bed.

Fath. Is that it ? give you Joy, your Cozin *Emilia* and this Gentleman will not be long after ye.

Stanf. Sir, you are mistaken, your Daughter had dispos'd herself in another place.

Wood. How the Devil did he know that, *Ninny ?*

Ninny. He little thinks where she has bestow'd her self, ha, ha, ha.

Wood. No, no, nor thee neither, dear Rogue, ha, ha, ha.

Ninny. Well honest *Woodcock*, I think I may trust thee, thou art my Friend : I am the man she has made choice of, and thou shalt be my Brideman.

Wood. Ha, ha, ha, poor whelp ! how he will find himself bobb'd immediately ! that this Coxcomb should not find all this while that I am the man ! (*aside.*

Fath. It cannot be ; what without my Knowledge or Consent ?

Wood. Ay, ay, she's dispos'd on ; Dear Heart.

Ninny. Ay, ay, she's dispos'd on.

Fath. To whom ?

Stanf.	⎫	⎧ To me.
Wood.	⎬	⎨ To me.
Ninny.	⎭	⎩ To me.

Fath. How now, to all three ?

Car. Sir, she has taken Master *Stanford*, and I Master *Lovell*, as sure as a Parson can make us.

Fath. What do I hear ?

Car. Sir, I beseech you be not offended, their Births and Fortunes are not unequal to ours, and if they were, 'twere too late for it to be redrest.

Fath. Is this true ?

Emil. Yes, Sir, perhaps too true ? (*To Stanford.*

Wood. Am I fool'd after all this ? well, I say no more, Dear Hearts.

Ninny. Well, let the Nation sink or swim an it will for me : hence forward instead of Heroick Verse, hereafter I will shew all my power, and soul and flame, and mettle in Lampoon, I durst have sworn she had lov'd me.

Fath. Well! Heaven bless you together, since you have don't.

Coun. Gent. So Sir, I see my Cakes dough, as they say; but I hope you'l pay the Charges of my Journey, d'ye see.

Sir *Pos.* Well Cozins, I am glad of your good Fortunes, and for my own part, if I understand any thing in the world, I am happy in this Lady.

La. *Vain.* Sir! you are pleas'd to Complement.

Enter Luce.

Luce. Sir *Positive*, here's a Letter was left for you, it comes out of the Countrey.

Sir *Posit.* } *SIr Positive, I am inform'd, but know not how to believe it,*
reads. } *that you intend to marry one that calls her self my Lady Vaine: The respect I have for your family urges me to tell you she is a Counterfeit Lady, and is at present my Mistress, by whom I have had one child, and I believe she's half gone of another, all the Fortune she has is what I allow her.* I have seen enough, how am I perplex'd? read *Lovell.*

Fath. Come Master *Woodcock* and Master *Ninny*, notwithstanding you are displeas'd let's have your Company a little longer.

Wood. Nay for my part, Dear Heart, I do not care what becomes of me.

Ninny. Nor I neither as little as any man.

Lov. Don't betray your self to the Company.   *(To Sir Positive.)*

Sir *Pos.* Well! this is the first thing in the World that I have met with which I did not understand: but I am resolv'd, I'le not acknowledge that: Master *Lovell*, I knew well enough what I did when I marry'd her, He's a wise man that marry's a harlot, he's on the surest side, who but an Ass would marry at uncertainty?

Lov. What will not a *Positive* Coxcomb defend?

Car. Since we are all agreed: in stead of a grand Dance according to the laudable Custome of Weddings, I have found out a little Comical Gentleman to entertain you with.

Enter a Boy in the habit of Pugenello, *and traverses the Stage, takes his Chair, and sits down, then Dances a Jigg.*

Emil. No Wedding day was ever so troublesome as this has been to me.

Stanf. Make haste and quit the Trouble.

> *Now to some distant desart let's repair:*
> *And there put off all our unhappy Care,*
> *There certainly that freedom we must find,*
> *Which is deny'd to us among Mankind.*   Exeunt omnes.

FINIS.

(91)

EPILOGUE

PHysicians tells us, that in every Age
Some one particular Disease does rage,
The Scurvey once, and what you call the Gout,
But Heaven be prais'd their Reign is almost out;
Yet a worse malady than both is bred,
For Poetry now reigneth in their stead:
The Itch of Writing Plays, the more's the pity,
At once has seiz'd the Town, the Court, and City.
Among'st the rest, the Poet of this day
By meer infection has produc'd a Play.
Once his hot fit was strong when he was bold
To write, but while you judge he's in the Cold;
Yet pray consider, few of you but may
Be given up so far to write a Play:
If not for his, for your own sakes be kind,
And give that mercy which you hope to find.

THE END.

THE
ROYAL
Shepherdess.

A
TRAGI-COMEDY,

Acted

By His Highness the Duke of York's
SERVANTS.

Non Quivis videt immodulata Poemata Judex.

Hor. de arte Poet.

LONDON,

Printed for *Henry Herringman*, at the Sign of the Blew-
Anchor in the Lower Walk of the *New-Exchange,* 1669.

Source

THE original play of John Fountain, which Shadwell has altered for the stage, was printed as " THE | Revvards of Vertue; | A | COMEDIE. | *rule* | By | *J. F.* Gent. | *rule*, printer's design, *rule*. | LONDON, | Printed by *Ja. Cottrel*, for *Hen. Fletcher* at the | three Gilt Cups in St. *Pauls* Church- | yard, 1661. | " Of John Fountain practically nothing is known save what Shadwell relates in his address " To the Reader " prefixed to *The Royal Shepherdess*. That he was a deep student leading a retired life is obvious, and *The Rewards of Vertue* certainly reads better in the closet than it would appear upon the theatre. Fountain was dead before 1668.

Shadwell has very fairly acknowledged his part. He has aptly curtailed the lengthier speeches, and not ill adjusted the comic underplot, such as it is. As he points out the only song in the original is " Thus from the Prison to the Throne," and Pepys tells us that the music and dancing much helped the performance.

Upon the whole I find *The Rewards of Vertue* a moderate library piece, somewhat academic and betraying the amateur, writ by one who had a feeling for poetry but without much fire or flame.

From a practical point of view, that is so far as acting is concerned, I conceive that Shadwell has improved his original in a very efficient and capable manner, and after all such, no more, was his definite object and intention.

Theatrical History

THIS romantic Pastoral was produced at Lincoln's Inn Fields on Thursday, 25 February, 1668-9. Pepys, who was present at the first performance, records: "At noon home and eat a bit myself, and then followed my wife and girls to the Duke of York's house, and there before one, but the house infinite full, where, by and by, the King and Court come, it being a new play, or an old one new vamped, by Shadwell, called 'The Royall Shepherdesse;' but the silliest for words and design, and everything, that ever I saw in my whole life, there being nothing in the world pleasing in it, but a good martial dance of pikemen, when Harris and another do handle their pikes in a dance to admiration; but never less satisfied with a play in my life." The next day Pepys took his wife to the King's playhouse to see Fletcher's *The Faithful Shepherdess*. "But, Lord! what an empty house, there not being, as I could tell the people, so many as to make up above £10 in the whole house! The being of a new play at the other house, I suppose, being the cause, though it be so silly a play that I wonder how there should be enough people to go thither two days together, and not leave more to fill this house." We must not take these trenchant criticisms too seriously, for Pepys was thoroughly ill-tempered, suffering both from his eyes and from an influenza cold, two complaints which would make the happiest man dour and cantankerous.

Downes having noted the production of Davenant's *The Man's the Master* adds: "This being the last New Play that was acted in *Lincoln's-Inn-Fields*, yet there were sundry others done there, from 1662, till the time they left that House: As, *Love's Kingdom*, wrote by Mr. *Fleckno*; *The Royal Shepherdess*, by Mr. *Shadwell*; *Two Fools well met*, by Mr. *Lodwick Carlile*; the *Coffee-House* by Mr. *Sincerf*; *All Plot*; or, *The Disguises*; by Mr. *Stroude*: All which expired the third day, save *The Royal Shepherdess*, which liv'd six."

Langbaine tells us that *The Royal Shepherdess* was "acted with good Applause." No doubt it remained in the theatrical repertory for some years, but we have no notice of any special revivals.

Yet the rococo pastoral play was a type popular enough on the Restoration stage, and we have such examples as Settle's *Pastor Fido*, produced at Dorset Garden in the winter of 1676; *The Constant Nymph; or, The Rambling Shepheard*, Dorset Garden, June, 1677; and Mrs. Behn's *The Young King* produced at the same theatre in the spring of 1679.

TO THE
READER.

READER,

THis Play, before I took it in hand, was wrote by one Mr. *Fountain* of *Devonshire ;* a Gentleman that had too many good Parts, that any man should take a Measure of him by that, which he wrote as a slight diversion from his more serious Studies. The esteem I had for him living, and the value I had for his memory being dead, made me unwilling that any thing of his should be obscur'd : And if, in exposing this, I have done any injury to his Reputation, it was an error of my Understanding, and no fault of my Will.

This (being never by him intended for Action) was wrote in single Scenes (without that connexion which the Incomparable *Johnson* first taught the Stage) and had also many long, uninterrupted Soliloquies, some of fifty lines together, which perhaps might give some delight in the reading, but could afford little diversion to the Hearers. Yet finding many things in the Play, which I confess pleas'd me, I thought it might, with some pains, be made a pleasant entertainment for the Audience.

I have added little to the Story, onely have represented that in Action, which was expressed by him in long Narrations : For we find (though the French do often relate the most considerable Actions in their Plays, especially in their Tragedies) the English will not be content without seeing such Actions done, and this is one of those many things, that make our English Plays so much exceed the French : But this was long ago observed by *Horace :*

> *Segnius irritant animos demissa per aurem,*
> *Quam quæ sunt oculis subjecta fidelibus.*

I have endeavour'd to carry on those few Humors, which were but begun by him ; and (to satisfie the Concupiscence as Mr. *Johnson* call's it, of Jigge and Song) I designed as fit occasions for them as I could, there being in the former Play but one short Song which is the last but one.

Where it is possible, I have kept the Scenes unbroken, and with as proper a connexion as I could. What I have besides added I need not tell you, being I fear so much worse than his, that you will easily distinguish it.

I shall say little more of the Play, but that the Rules of Morality and good Manners are strictly observed in it: (Vertue being exalted, and Vice depressed) and perhaps it might have been better received had neither been done in it: for I find, it pleases most to see Vice incouraged, by bringing the Characters of debauch'd People upon the Stage, and making them pass for fine Gentlemen, who openly profess Swearing, Drinking, Whoring, breaking Windows, beating Constables, &c. and that is esteem'd, among us, a Gentile gayety of Humour, which is contrary to the Customs and Laws of all civilized Nations. But it is said, by some, that this pleases the people, and a Poets business is only to endeavour that: But he that debases himself to think of nothing but pleasing the Rabble, loses the dignity of a Poet, and becomes as little as a Jugler, or a Rope-Dancer; who please more then he can do: but the Office of a Poet is,

Simul & jucunda, & idonea dicere vitæ.

Which (if the Poets of our age would observe it) would render 'em as usefull to a Commonwealth as any profession whatsoever.

But I have too long troubled you with a Discourse of this Play, which (let me say what I will of it) you will judge of as you please: But if you consider, after such an Infinite number of Playes, when

(*Nil intentatum nostri liquere Poetæ.*)

How difficult it is to write even an indifferent one: (as none but those that cannot write think it easie) Methinks it were but an ordinary piece of Humanity to pardon those Errors you find in Playes, especially, since they are committed by those who endeavour to please you, which is the aim among the rest of

Your Servant

Tho. Shadwell.

PROLOGUE.

ONE of the Poets (as they safely may
When th' Authour's dead) has stollen a whole Play :
Not like some petty Thieves that can endure
To steall small things to keep their Hands in ure.
He swears he'l die for something : In our times
Small Faults are scorn'd, the Great are worthy Crimes,
Onely for Noble Sparks, who think it fit
That the base Vulgar should mean Crimes commit.
—But 'tis your fault Poets such Thieves are grown,
For that injurious mercy you have shown,
To some great malefactors heretofore
Has, for each Thief you've pardon'd, made Ten more.
—This for the bold Purloiner of the Play,
'Tis fit I something too of that should say :
It is a Vertuous Play, you will confess,
Where Vicious men meet their deserv'd success.
Not like our Modern ones, where still we find,
Poets are onely to the Ruffians kind ;
And give them still the Ladies in the Play,
But 'faith their Ladies are as bad as they.
They call 'em Ayery, Witty, Brisk, and Wild,
But, with their Favours, those are terms too mild.
—But (what is better yet than all the rest)
In all this Play, there's not one Baudy jest,
To make the Ladies bite their Lips, and then
To be applauded by the Genilemen.
Baudy, what e're in private 'tis, is here not fit,
'Tis to Assemblies Sawciness, not Wit.
But yet we vow'd, (if it were to be had
For Love or Money) we'd have what's as bad ;
We've stuff'd in Dances, and we have Songs too
As senceless, as were ever sung to you.
If all these things will not support our Play,
Then Gallants you may damn it, yes you may ;
But if you do, you'l suffer such a Curse—
Our Poet swears he'll write one Ten times worse.

Dramatis Personæ.

BAsilius,   King,
   Theander   Prince.
   Endymion   A worthy Lord of small Fortune.
Pyrrhus   A Creature of the Kings.
Neander   A vain, cowardly, vicious, effeminate Lord
Geron   An old Jealous Fop that has married a young Wife.
Priest.———

Queen.———
Cleantha   Niece to the King.
Evadne   Servant to the Queen.
Urania   One that was a Shepherdess, and preferr'd by the Prince to wait on *Cleantha*.
Phronesia   A vain foolish Woman, Wife to *Geron*.
Cleopatra   Mother to *Urania*; conceal'd by the name of *Parthenia*.

Messengers, *Officers*, Shepherds, and *Shepherdesses*, Nymphs and *Satyrs*, Priests of *Mars*, &c.

SCENE *ARCADIA*.

THE
Royal Shepherdesse

THE FIRST ACT.

Enter Pyrrhus, Endymion, Neander.

Pyr. BEliev't my Lords, they say the Prince does Wonders.
    Nean. They say he kills a world of men indeed ;
    But 'faith I think the wonder had been greater
If he had made but half so many live.
    Endy. Perchance, my Lord, you'd have him turn Physitian,
    Nean. Rather than Butcher, 'tis the Nobler Trade.
    Endy. But they are his Enemies he kills,
Men that offend, and do deserve to die.
    Nean. O ! then I think you'l praise the Hangman next,
You give a definition of his Trade.
    Pyrr. If I do not mistake your humour, Sir.
You were never taken with this dying.
It is a thing does marr a Courtier much.
    Nean. 'Thank Heav'n, I am not yet so mad to wish for't ;
Let Broken-Merchants, and the busie Rout
That durt the Streets, when their designs miscarry,
Cry that there's nothing Certain in this World,
I think there's less in that which is to come :
Here I'm sure of something, I'm a Lord,
And live with men : But to be turn'd a grazing
In the *Elizian-Fields* (that Men do talk of)
Among Philosophers, n'ere could make a Legg.
    Endy. Fie, fie, *Neander !* this is too prophane,
And relisheth far more of Beast than Man.
    Nean. My Lord, I ask you Pardon, I'd forgot
You are a Virtuoso : 'Tis my Lord *Pyrrhus*
That makes me wander from my Argument,

By putting me in Mind o' th' World to come,
(A Theam indeed on which few men speak sence.)
  Endy. My Lord! you take too great a Liberty.
  Nean. I am sure you do, to give such mighty Names
To killing men : why Celebrate the Plague :
What General ever did destroy like that ;
Or study Glorious Titles for old age,
That kills all those whom nothing else can kill.
  Pyrr. The honour of our Country lies at stake.
  Nean. Honour! The Fools Paradise, a bait
For Coxcombs that are poor, and cannot have
Pleasure and Ease ; but sell their Wretched lives
(That are not worth the keeping) for that Trifle
Honour ; the breath of a few Giddy People :
Well, I shall leave you to your mighty thoughts,
And make a Visit to a Mistress, which I think
Concerns us more than broken Pates for honour.
Adieu—————   *Ex. Neander.*
  Pyrr. 'Tis a vain Lord!
  Endy. He's too prophane, and Chooseth to buy Wit
At the expence of Friends, Religion,
And all but Ladies smiles ; which he more values
Than Honest men do the kind looks of Heaven.
  Pyrr. And hates nothing, like Reputation won
By Armes : he hates all Deities for *Mars*'s sake,
And swears that Generals onely famous grow
By Valiant Friends, or Cowardly Enemies,
Or, what is worse, by some mean piece of Chance.
  Endy. The truth is, 'tis odd to observe
How little, Princes, and great Generals
Contribute oft-times to the fame they Win ;
How often have we known, that bravest Men,
With too short Armes, have fought with fatal Stars :
And have endeavoured, with their dearest blood,
To get renown, and with such glorious actions,
As the great Hero's have been fam'd for less :
And yet have fallen by Vulgar hands at last,
Among the Sacrifices of their own Swords,
No more Remembred than poor Villagers,
Whose Ashes sleep beneath the Common Flowers
That every Meadow wears, whilst other men,
With trembling hands, have caught a Victory,
And, on pale fore-heads, worn triumphant Bayes.

Pyrr. I have observ'd it often.

Endy. Besides I have thought,
A Thousand times in time of War, when we
Lift up our hands to Heaven for Victory,
Suppose, some Virgin Shepherdess (whose Soul
Is Chast, and Clean as the Cold Spring where she
Quenches all her Thirst) being told of Enemies
That seek to fright the long enjoy'd Peace
Of our Arcadia hence, should straight repair
To some small Fane, and there on humble Knees,
Lift up her trembling hands unto the Gods,
And beg their help ; 'Tis possible to think
Heaven will not suffer her to weep in vain,
But grant her wish——
And so, in the next action happens out,
(The Gods still using means) the Enemy
May be defeated, the glory of all this
Is attributed to the General,
And none but he's spoke Loud off for the Act,
Whilst she, (from whose so unaffected Tears
His Laurel sprung) for ever dwells unknown.

Pyrr. Your Lordship does not doubt the Princes Merit ?

Endy. By no means :
I know the Prince a Man of that vast Soul,
That flesh did never Circumscribe a Greater.
All that I say, is what I've thought upon
Some hours of sweet Retirement, when I've sate,
And viewed the fleeting State of poor Mankind,
A thing too giddy to be understood.

Pyrr. Indeed the Prince does more then give us hopes
Arcadia shall Command those Provinces,
Who lately thought our long and happy Peace
Had soften'd so our Minds, that now we were
Fit to be Lorded over by their Wills :
But strange it is, to see the King so little
Joy'd with the news, that still he bears a Face
More troubled than *Sicilian* Seas in storms.

Pyrr. 'Tis for the Love of that poor Shepherdess,
The Prince not Ten months since took from a Cottage
As he was a Hunting, and gave the fair
Cleantha for a Present.

Endy. aside. Alas ! my poor *Urania* ! how doth
Thy harder Fortune vindicate my Choice ?

(105)

Who now dares say *Endymion* loves too low,
When he loves her that can make Princes die?
No more, no more, we must scorn Cottages,
Those are the Rocks from whence our Jewels come.
Gold breeds in barren Hills, the brightest Stars
Shine o're the poorer Regions of the North.

Enter King.

Pyrr. Here comes the King! *Endymion*, pray retire,
It is not fit you should be privy to his Thoughts.
  Endy. I'le try if I can hear what resolution
The Kings enrag'd Passion makes him take.   [*He retires.*
  King. Pyrrhus! how thrives my Love? I have
Intrusted you with all I am, and all I wish for.
  Pyrr. Sir, I have already done,
What Language and Rewards have power to do.
  King. And what return am I to hope for then?
  Pyrr. There's little hope: This Ermin will not be
Perswaded from the whiteness she so loves.
  King. Poor Country Girl, where can she find Words
Or Resolution when you do assault her?
  Pyrr. When I first
Mention'd the business to her, all alone,
Poor soul she blush'd, as if already she
Had done some harm by hearing of me speak:
Whilst from her pretty Eyes two Fountains run
(So true, so Native) down her fairest Cheeks,
As if she thought her self oblig'd to weep
That all the World was not as good as she.
  Endym. Heaven! how does this Carriage please me!
  King. This Modesty of hers inflames me more,
As springs are hottest in the coldest weather.
  Pyrr. Her Tears so innocently begg'd my pity,
That I was straight turn'd over to her side,
And had forgot the Cause for which I strove:
Till rallying agen, I once more gave
A new assault, and urg'd her to answer:
All her reply was, No: then humbly pray'd me,
Not to be Cruel to a poor weak Maid,
Who had not had anything, in all the World,
To give her value but her Innocence;
With such success as this I often have
Assail'd her Vertue.

King. Ah *Pyrrhus!* where will this Tyrant end? shall I
Still be Priest, and Sacrifice, and Altar too,
Unto a Passion, I can satisfie,
But never conquer? What poor things are Kings?
What poorer things are Nations to obey
Him whom a petty Passion does Command?
Heav'n! why was man made so ridiculous?

Pyrr. Your Majesty sayes that of your self,
Which were Impiety in any else,
But once to think.

King. Men but Flatter me.
Oh Fate! why were not Kings made more than men?
Or why will people have us to be more?
Alas! we govern others, but our selves
We cannot rule, like to our Eyes, that see
All other things, but Cannot see themselves.

Pyrr. Sir, do not discompose your self; you may
Soon Quench this mighty Flame, and where your Prayers
Have not prevail'd, your Power may Command:
Who in *Arcadia* dares resist your Will?

Endym. O Villain! This will make thee Chief among
The damn'd in Hell.

King. But stay! when this poor Maid
Shall Call on Vertue, and the Gods to keep
Her Body, they too weakly have Expos'd,
Shall I (whom Men call sacred and divine,
And look on as deriv'd from Ancestors
Who have not Tombs, but Altars) without shame,
And thousand blushes, dare with ruder force,
To drive poor Vertue from her Cleanest Temple?
And use that power, the Gods have given me
O're others, but to offend them how I please;
By Heav'n I will not.——But I die——O I am Mortal——

Pyrr. Sir, you'r a King; But Love's a Deity
Must be obey'd by all. Resolve to try
Whether *Urania* will Love or Die?

Endym. Heav'n! what do I hear?

King. O unruly passion! whither will it hurry me?
I must submit; Use all your subtilties
T' entice her to comply with my desires;
But if allurements fail, she must be forc'd,
And let me know my Fate within this hour:
Farewell.

(107)

Pyr. Sir, I shall be diligent in obeying all your Commands. [*Exit King·*

Enter Endymion *from behind the Arbour.*

Endym. And I'le reward your diligence.
Pyrr. What does this posture mean ?
Endym. Wert thou not sear'd in Wickedness, thou wouldst
Not ask ; That thou maist know thy Crime I'le write it
In thy own blood, draw quickly, or I'le Kill thee
Without defence.
   Pyrr. I am amaz'd, but if you long for action,
Come on, I have a Sword that will employ you.

They fight, Endym. *gets* Pyrr. *down,*
with his Sword at his breast.

[*Enter* Cleantha *and* Urania.

Endym. Now Villain !
Clean. Hold, hold ! *Endymion.*
Endym. Madam ! I obey.
Go ! thank the Princess *Cleantha* for your Life !
And look you use it better than you have done.
   Uran. Madam ! he bleeds, I'le try to bind up his wounds.
   Endym. No dear *Urania !* 'tis but a scratch, but were
It ne're so deep, one touch of that fair hand
Were a sufficient Balsome.
   Clean. O fie *Urania !* how unhandy art thou ?
Sir, let me practice my little skill in Surgery
Upon you.   *She tears her Handkercher and binds up his wounds.*
   Endym. This is an honour Princes should receive
Upon their Knees : I beseech your Highness
Do not humble your self so far ; it is
So slight it does not need a Miracle, for so
Ought your Assistance to be valu'd, Madam,
Urania's skill in this would be sufficient.
   Clean. Your Courage makes that seem slight, which others
Would think dang'rous, I'le bind it up.
   Endym. How I am confounded with this favour ?
Your Highness does dispence your Charity
As the Gods do to us ; not for reward of Merit,
But for Pity, so to inhaunce the value of their mercy.
   Clean. This Modesty is too much, *Endymion.*   'Tis
Ingratitude to Heaven, when it disclaims
Those Vertuous Endowments it has given you.
But what was the occasion of this Quarrel ?

(108)

Enter Evadne.

Evad. The Queen desires your Highness
To come to her instantly.

Clean. Come then, *Endymion*, tell me as you go.

Endym. I will obey your Highness.——

Clean. But, my Lord, *Pyrrhus* may tell the King of this, and it may be
your Ruine ; 'twill not be safe for you to appear.

Endym. Madam ! he will be unwilling to meet his own ruine, to procure
mine ; he has drawn blood within the Court, which your Highness knows
by an indispensable Law is death in *Arcadia ;* hee'l not betray himself.

Clean. My Lord 'tis true, Let's to the Queen——

[*Exeunt all, but* Evadne.

Enter Neander.

Nean. How does this Minute transport my soul with Joy, to have the
blessed priviledge to be with fair *Evadne ?*

Evad. I am glad it makes some body happy.

Nean. With her who has my Heart.——

Evad. Have I it ? pray my Lord take it agen.
I would not be troubled with keeping such a Bawble for the World.

Nean. She whom great Nature (now grown wanton) made to look upon,
and scorn her other Works.

Evad. My Lord *Neander !* I see you are resolv'd not to study to no
purpose, you will have out your Complement, let me say what I please :
but I must take liberty to leave you in the middle of it.

Nean. Nay, Madam, I beseech you be not so unkind.

Evad. Nay now I have put you out of your Complement ; I care not if
I stay a little longer.

Nean. Madam ! you are Cruel ! how do you Kill ?

Evad. Kill, *Neander ?* No sure then you would not be so near me.

Nean. I ne're could fear death from so fair a hand as yours.

Evad. I believe indeed, my Lord, you fear death least from the hands of
a Woman, which is the Reason you chuse to stay here at Court among the
Ladies, rather than go to War with the Prince.

Nean. Madam !——You Ladies have a Priviledge.

Evad. Yes, my Lord, it's sometimes a priviledge to speak Truth.

Nean. 'Faith Madam, you may say what you please.

Evad. Pardon me, my Lord, it would please me much better if I could
say you were in the War in *Thessaly.*

Nean. Truly, Madam, I could give you very good reasons why I went
not to the War with the Prince.

Evad. I believe you can, and so can every body else that knows your
Lordship : The first and Chiefest reason was a certain tenderness you have

for the preservation of your Person, some scandalous people stick not to call it fear.

Nean. Do not judge so Madam ; I can assure you it was for very different reasons.

Evad. You will give very much satisfaction to the World, if you say what they are.

Nean. Why then, to tell you the truth, Madam, I am somewhat troubled with Corns that I cannot without pain wear a riding Boot : and then I am strangely subject to the Tooth-ach, which makes me very unfit to lie in the Field, which indeed were the two main Reasons made me refuse the War.

Evad. What pity 'tis so brave a Mind should be so unluckily hindred from showing it self.

Nean. I perceive you railly, Madam.

Evad. I see Sir, you are a Man of quick apprehension.   (*Enter Priest.*

Priest. How now Daughter ? what do you here ? my Lord, I do not desire your Lordship should make any addresses to my Daughter, her Fortune is too humble for your thoughts.

Nean. Your Servant, Madam.

[*Aside*] Pox on this Formal Priest.——   *Exit.*

Priest. Well now *Evadne*, my dear Child, thou art
Come forth upon the Worlds great Stage, and it
Must be my care first to advise thee, then
To pray for thee : Yet thou art innocent,
(Oh maist thou still be so my Child) yet know'st not
Ought but the holy practices of cells,
Where vertuous Matrons have instructed thee.

Evad. But now the Scene is chang'd, the Queens Commands
Have brought me to the Court to wait on her ;
The employment truly noble : and I have
In her the brightest pattern of true vertue
That all the world can boast of.

Priest. But thou'lt find
Few more besides whose wandring paths are safe :
Those of thy Sex thou'lt find so strangely vain,
That they think they have wash'd, and patch'd, and curl'd
Themselves ev'n into little Deities :
They do believe that wanton men speak truth,
When to consume those hours, they care not for,
They tell 'em that their Eyes are more then Stars.
And that they have a killing power, with
A great deal of such amorous fustian.

Evad. They're very credulous that believe 'em sure.

Priest. Then, by degrees, they strangely cheat themselves,

Poor souls, into the fond belief that they
Not only are fairest, but wisest too :
And now they are attain'd to that degree,
All must admire, but none must merit them,
Till ruggid time, too old to complement,
Takes from 'em all those little Ornaments
Which wanton Nature had adorn'd them with ;
And then they do Awake, the Dream is done,
The Market falls, and some distressed Knight,
Unenvied, bears away what all had Courted.

 Evad. This is the common Fate of our poor Sex,
When they have great opinions of themselves.

 Priest. Therefore *Evadne*, let me pray thee still
Keep thy best jewel, thy Humility :
If thou wearest better Cloaths, alas consider,
Each little flower, that does in Meadows grow,
Is better clad than thee, yet is not proud.

 Evad. I will endeavour to obey you in all.

 Priest. Hence maist thou shun the common vice of Courts,
Scorn and contempt of others, which oft have
A nobler Vertue, though a meaner Fortune.
For know, *Evadne*, that this lower World,
In which we live, is not distributed
According to mens Merits : the Gods preserve
That Justice for those nobler Regions, which
Themselves inhabit : here the mighty are
Like mighty Mountains, high, but seldom fertile.
The richest soyl is in low Valleys found :
Devotion often weeps, in humble cells,
Whilst under-guilded Roofs profaneness sings.

 Evad. I have consider'd often this sad truth.

 Priest. This is the World, *Evadne*, but to come
To what I've else to say ; thy next Temptation
Will be to love ; Know thou wilt surely have
Enow to Court thee : Some 'cause 'tis the Mode,
Others, because they've nothing else to say,
And Wisest Men because they think me rich :
But know my Child ! to Marry is
The greatest Action of our Lives, and merits
The greatest of our Cares : but above all I warn thee
Against *Neander*.
He's a Vicious, Profane, and Idle Person,
One, that would make me hate the name of Father,

Should he but call me so? Well, *Evadne*,
Pray Meditate on what I've said to you,
I'le leave you to your thoughts———   [*Ex. Priest.*

Enter Phronesia.

Evad. What in tears, *Phronesia?* what's the matter?
Phro. O Madam! have a care of Marriage, I give you warning of it.
Evad. What is the old man Jealous still? It may be you give him cause.
Phro. No other Cause but that I am with Child, and he distrusts himself.
Evad. Why did he marry you then?
Phro. Nay I cannot tell not I.
Evad. Why don't you ask him?
Phro. I have.
Evad. And what sayes he?
Phro. He told me———
Evad. What?———
Phro. O Madam! you cannot imagine his wicked Intentions———
Evad. What does he say?
Phro. He told me he marry'd me onely to keep me honest, like an old
Villanous Tyrant as he is.
Evad. But now it seems he is convinc'd 'tis more than he can do.
Phro. Every one best knows his own abilities; But why should he do
that to me of all Women? Marry me to keep me honest? out upon him,
I defie him and his wicked Intentions.
Evad. Indeed it is a hard Case.
Phro. Ay, Madam, is it not? would you be willing to be us'd so?
Besides, Madam, no man in the Court offers to speak to me, but he thinks
'tis Love.
Evad. He thinks you are so handsome, perhaps, that it is impossible for
any man to look upon you without being smitten.
Phro. That may be something, as you say, Madam, but I will never put
up this Injury: Marry me to keep me honest, quoth 'a?
I'le never endure it, while I ha' breath:——See Madam——where he
comes——do but observe him.

Enter Geron.

Ger. I have brought my self into a sweet condition, like an old fool as
I am, why could not I remember how many I had Cuckolded my self, and
to think I should not be serv'd in the same kind, were to suppose neither
Wickedness, nor Justice in the World.
Phro. Look, Madam upon this Mischievous Count'nance.
Geron *to himself.* How could I imagine that any of these sort of Women
would keep themselves honest three minutes, when they fear'd neither the

danger of taking Savin, nor a great Belly? Heaven! what a Condition am I in!——now do I plainly perceive the pain that poor Children indure at the coming of their Teeth, by the coming of my Horns——Oh *Phronesia*! are you there?

Phro. Yes! you old Fumbling Sot, I am here.——

Evad. Fare you well. *Ex. Evadne.*

Ger. O wicked *Phronesia*! how have you us'd me? whom have you appointed now to do me the Courtesie?—my Lord *Pirrhus*—he is of a black Complexion, and that never fails;—My Lord *Endymion*'s a Poet forsooth, and prevails with Sonnets;——and for my Lord *Neander*,—the Priest convinc'd him the other day, that Adultery was a very great Sin, and that's reason enough for him to lie at Rack and Manger; I am sure my head must ake for't.

Phro. Let it ake on, you old Fop, you marry'd me to keep me honest, did you? I'le honest you; I will go instantly and meet 'em all three. [*Exit.*

Ger. But I'le follow you close at the heels, and prevent your recreation!—

If any Man be weary of his life,
Let him at Threescore marry such a Wife. [*Exeunt.*

The End of the First Act.

THE SECOND ACT.

Enter Pyrrhus *and* Urania.

Pyrr. COme fair *Urania*, think upon the honour
　　　To be a Mistress to a King, sounds it not Well?
　　　Uran. It is an Honour I should not envy her
That sought my ruine! I will ne're forsake
My Vertue, for a little outward splendor.
　　Pyrr. Is Love a Vice *Urania?* why did Nature
Make us all Vicious, when she did immerse
Love in the very beings of all Creatures:
Go search the Universe, and shew me there
What but affrighted man is not as free
To satisfie his Love as Thirst or Hunger;
Beasts ne're dispute the Lawfulness of what is
Natural.
　　Uran. 'Tis well, my Lord, when you intend
Unlawful Loves to instance not in men

(113)

But Beasts———but let me ever be
Of that affrighted Number that follow vertue.
   Pyrr. Come, come, *Urania !* Love, like men, was free,
E'er Pow'r and Laws had taught 'em both the use
Of Chains and Fetters : Nature ne're Confin'd
Her Noblest Creature to the Narrow'st Prison,
Nor gave him Inclinations to torment him.
   Uran. But, since those Laws are made, I will obey.
   Pyrr. But when thy Prince, *Urania* (who in right
Abridges all thy other Liberties)
Shall offer to restore thee this, thou maist
As freely take it as thou might'st the rest.
   Uran. But all the power he has can never cancel
That obligation which I owe to Heaven.
   Pyrr. Nay, now my work is almost at an end,
When Women come to argue once the thing
It is a kind of yielding.
   Uran. Ah my Lord,
Pray add not injury to my Misfortune,
But know, that all the baits you lay before me,
Shall ne're allure me to put off that true
Content I have in being Innocent.
   Pyrr. Well ! I perceive you make me toil in vain ;
You fool your self, not me ; pray hear your doom :
The King's resolv'd to leave you but this Choice
Either to Love, or die ; to be the subject
Of his Revenge, or Pleasure ; answer quickly,
And answer Wisely ; for believ't, *Urania,*
If you refuse his Love, this hour's your last.
   Uran. Sure Sir, the King's more just.
   Pyrr. By Heaven, it's true.
   Uran. Then Heav'ns more merciful ; Unfortunate,
Unfortunate *Urania !* what canst thou do ?
   Pyrr. What ? thou canst grant the Kings desires and live :
Come, be brief, here's one at hand will have small
Pity on you.
   Uran. Oh, my Lord, pity me, pity a distrest Maid.   *[Kneels and weeps.*
   Pyrr. Pity your self, and pity a Prince that loves you :
Come, do not cast away your self ; you'r young,
And, if you please, may have many years to live,
(And pleasant Ones) be wise e're it be too late.
   Uran. My Lord ! what shall I do ?
   Pyrr. Why, love the King———

Uran. And muſt I lose my innocence ?
Pyrr. Come rise,
Urania live, the King will ſtrait be with you———   *Ex. Pyrrhus.*
  Uran. Wretched *Urania.*
I am undone, for evermore undone ;
Loſt to the World, or Innocence ; my choice
Is either to be wicked, or to die.
Oh Heaven ! what black, what fatal Star
Gave sad Misfortune at my birth ?
How happy had I been had I ſtill dwelt
With those who wear poor Cloaths, and honour vertue ?
Whose pure Chaſt Loves made Love a Deity !
What will my Mother say when she shall hear
Urania is not Innocent ? and what
Will my brave Lover think ; who ne'er approach'd me
But with a Flame as pure, as that which burns
On holy *Veſta's* Altars ; no, no, die
Unfortunate, but chaſte *Urania,*
Never be thrifty of that blood, which muſt
But serve to blush that it preserv'd it self.

        Enter Endymion.

  Endym. Ah, dear *Urania !* why these tears ?
  Uran. Oh, my Lord, *Urania* is undone !
  Endym. Not so because *Endymion* lives ; Know
Urania's ruine never can be writ
But with *Endymion's* blood——
  Uran. Undone beyond
All your relief, because to help me is
To be a Traytor now.
  Endym. If to assiſt
My Queen, be to rebel, then let me wear
The glorious name of 'Traytor.
  Uran. Ah, my Lord, you know not what I mean.
  Endym. Yes, yes, (my Dear)
'Tis that for which I had rewarded *Pyrrhus,*
(Had not *Cleantha* then call'd back my hand.)
  Uran. I muſt this very hour consent, or die.
  Endym. Have comfort ; I will help you yet, but know,
My dear *Urania,* I have lov'd thee long,
And with a holy Flame, my Sighs and Tears
Have been as pure, as are those Gales and Springs
Which in *Elizium* do refresh the bleſt :

And yet thou haſt not pitty'd him that loves thee,
Even though thou be'ſt as gentle, and as soft
As morning dew juſt melting into Ayre.
   Uran. What shall I serve you in, my Lord?
   Endym. Permit
Me to enjoy the Title of your servant,
And pay my fire with equal flames again.
   Uran. My Lord, I were ingrateful if I should not.
   Endym. Then be not so, (but to be short) I fear
The Kings approach, and therefore if thou'lt promise
This night to sleep within my armes (being firſt
Authoriz'd by *Hymens* Prieſt)
I'll free thee from the Kings unlawful Love.
   Uran. What's to be done in this sad Exigence?——   *aside.*
(*To him*) My Lord, I will, but satisfie me, how?
   Endym. You muſt appoint the King to meet you there,
In yonder Grotto, and oblige him to
The Language, and the time of Love, soft Whispers,
And the Night; and I'le prepare
Some other Woman to supply your place;
This will gain time till to morrow, when
I'le own you to the King to be my Wife,
Then the respeſt to all my Loyal services
Will make him quench his now Unruly Passion.
   Uran. Ah, who will be so wicked as to meet him?
   Endym. Enow, ne're fear it.
   Uran. Sure 'tis impossible!
What Woman would consent to such an Act?
   Endym. Ten thousand, Madam!
   Uran. But they shall not for me,
I'll rather chuse a Thousand times to die,
Than own a wretched Life, sav'd at the rate
Of so much infamy.
   Endym. Come, be content,
Chaſte soul; I'le do what you shall well approve;
My dear, I muſt retire, I fear the King:
Now aſt thy part, and then confide in me;
Be happy, fair *Urania*, I am bleſt
That my employment is to do thee service.   [*Ex. Endymion.*
   Uran. Ah, dear *Endymion!* how could I weep
If tears were able but to wash away
The blackness of my Crime? now thou haſt thought
To lead me from the Labyrinth of my Woes,

The next thing I muſt think muſt be to cheat
All thy Innocent expeĉtations, which
Are every of them Honours to my self,
And Condescentions in thy noble Soul ;
I muſt endeavour at this very time
To fruſtrate all thy hopes, and cannot help it.———   *weeps.*

Enter King.

 King. And why with Showres allay you thus your Beams ?
Uran. These Tears and more are due to my Misfortunes.
 King. How's this, *Pyrrhus* told me you had consented.
 Uran. With what Face can I say yes to the King ?
Tho' I but feign consent, and mean to cheat him.———   *aside.*
It is immodeſt ſure———It cannot fit
A Womans Mouth.
 King. Are you not yet resolv'd ?
What means this doubt ? Consent to my desires,
And you shall live ador'd and fear'd by all ;
The Kingdom shall rejoyce at all your smiles,
And tremble at your frowns : but if you do not——
 Uran. Is there no other way to save my life ?
 King. Come, do not trifle thus to tempt my rage.
 Uran. Good Sir, be not angry ; I will.
 King. My dear *Urania !* now be happy, let's withdraw.
This place is much too publick for our Love———
 Uran. Let me not lose all Modeſty at once.
But let Sin take possession by degrees,
I have some sparks of Vertue yet remaining,
Which will require some time to quench.
 King. I am impatient of delays, in this
My Expeĉtation makes each hour a day ;
Come follow me, and be obedient.
 Uran. Stay but till night, my guilty blushes may
Be hid in darkness then, a season fit
For aĉtions that may shame the wicked doers.
 King. This, though it be hard to grant, I'le not deny.
 Uran. And I beseech your Majeſty let's Whisper so
That none may over-hear us when we meet ;
I am now afraid of every little thing
That looks like danger.
 King. Fear not ; none shall hear us.
 Uran. I have one thing more, but 'tis the chief of all.
 King. Name it *Urania,* what e're it be :

(117)

After this boon of thine, there's not a thing
In all the World I can deny thee.
  Uran. *Endymion* oft has made Addresses to me ;
And has been still repuls'd, which makes him have
Such wary Eyes upon me, that I fear
I cannot be secure, but by his absence :
I beseech your Majesty, let him be sent
So far from Court, that he cannot return
Until to morrow morning at the soonest :
This Sir, upon my Knees, I beg you'l grant.
  King. Rise, and ask something worth my giving.
  Uran. I think this so ; pray, Sir, deny me not.
  King. I'll instantly perform what you enjoin——   *Ex. King.*
  Uran. Thus, thus, I must reward the brave *Endymion ;*
Thus my Engagement to him is made void ;
But I will recompence him with my Tears,
That's all the Expiation I can make.

Enter Neander *meeting her going out.*

  Nean. Madam, your most obedient Servant.
  Uran. Sir, I beseech you let me go.——
  Nean. How am I confounded with your Beauty ?——
  Uran. I am not now dispos'd for Mirth,——
  Nean. So absolute that Nature seem'd to have collected
        All her scatter'd strength———
  Uran. My Lord——
  Nean. To shew it in one perfect piece.
  Uran. Detain me not——
  Nean. And has e're since been idle——
  Uran. My Lord, the Princess expects me !
  Nean. As if she had done enough in making you.———
  Uran. I cannot stay.——
  Nean. Such an accomplish'd beauty, that——
  Uran. What means this rudeness ?——
  Nean. She seems to have out-done her self.——
  Uran. Why *Neander ?*———
  Nean. In this incomparable Model.——
  Uran. What torment's this ?
  Nean. She has shown such admirable skill.——
  Uran. Oh ! what Immodesty is this ?——
  Nean. That all submit to your Victorious Eyes.—
  Uran. What have I done you shou'd affront me thus ?——
  Nean. Which do like Lightning dazle——

(118)

Uran. For Heav'ns sake let me go ?——
Nean. Whose high insinuating pow'r is such——
Uran. I am oblig'd to you, Sir, Fare you well. [*She gets loose, he follows her.*
Nean. It melts the Soul, though it does not
Touch the body.—— *Ex. Urania.*
So! now 'tis out; I had been most abominably heart burnt if I had kept
it in; This Love Passion, if I had not vented it as it rose, would have
swell'd me as much as a Fit of the Mother.
Here comes *Evadne?*

Enter Evadne.

What can I say to her? 'Slife, I have spent all my Stock already.——
Dearest *Evadne*, fairest Murdress, thou hast
Slain *Neander* with thy pretty Eyes. *Embraces her.*
Evad. And do you apprehend me for it, Sir?
Nean. That flower in your bosome is far happier than I; That fain
would live, and you to kill it place it in your bosome: I would fain live
too, and you to kill me, thence will keep me out.
Evad. Here's such killing and slaying at Court,
That you had as good have gone to War with the Prince, for ought I see.
Nean. A death from your fair hand, I wou'd embrace.
Evad. Ay, this kind of dying put's a man to no pain, but to be run
through the Lungs, or shot through the Body, is mighty inconvenient.
Nean. Ay, 'faith is it.——
Evad. But 'tis honourable.
Nean. For my part, I cannot possibly find what honour there is in having
Oylet-holes made in a man's body: 'Slife a Man's body is not made to see
through, is it? and yet I know some Duelling Coxcombs so often run
through, as if their Bodies were intended Thorough-fares for Swords.——
Evad. But I hope you have more prudence then to venture that danger.
Nean. If I be run through, may I be pickl'd up, when I am dead, like a
Sturgeon, & be serv'd up to the Table of an old Mangy Usurer.
Evad. I will say this in your Commendations, that when danger presents
it self, I believe there is not a Man in all *Arcadia* so active as your self, I
mean so swift of Foot.
Nean. Not so, Madam, indifferent, indifferent!
Evad. But suppose, Sir, I should stand in need of a Champion.
Nean. O Madam! your Eyes will revenge your Quarrels.
Evad. Or they must be unreveng'd for you!
Nean. Nay, Madam, in a Ladies Cause I can be a Lyon.
Evad. When you meet with a Lamb.
Nean. Nay, Madam! I have Courage, but I must confess,

(119)

'Tis a thing a man may better spare than any of his
Goods and Chattels.

Evad. Yes, yes, you have Courage, witness the going to
The War when you were commanded!

Nean. It was not want of that; but who the Devil, that had a plentifull
Estate, like me, and might live among these pretty Ladies at the Court,
would go to lie without Sheets, with Stones and Blocks for Pillows, and
be most honourably Lowsie, and damnably maul'd, for a company of
ungratefull Fellows, that live Luxuriously at home, and laugh at the
Honourable Affairs abroad? and when they have done, they value these
mighty Men of War, just as a man does a Creditor that Duns him for
Money lent, which he never intended to pay.

Enter Geron.

Evad. What would this old jealous Fop have?

Ger. Nay, now I will not hang my self yet: I'le be reveng'd on this Lord
first—My Lord—

Nean. Pox o' this Rogue, how I scorn any one that's below me,
What say you, *Geron?*

(*Geron* aside.) Furies pursue him.
How does your Lordship?

Nean. Very well! how does your Lady?

Ger. 'Tis he has done it, a Curse on him.   *Aside.*

Nean. Why, how now? what do you Conjure? what is the matter?

Ger. I need not Conjure, I know the Father now.   [*To himself.*

Nean. Why, what do'st thou mutter, man?

Ger. My Lord! why shou'd you ask for my Wife?

Nean. Because I am Civil.

Ger. Because I am a Cuckold.   [*Aside.*

Nean. Pox on thee, why do'st thou speak out?

Evad. Your Servant, my Lord, suppose by this time my Lord *Endymion*
has left the Queen.

Nean. I beseech you let me wait on your Ladyship.   [*Exeunt.*

Ger. This is the man! 'tis he; Why should he ask for my Wife?
Suppose I have a Wife, what's that to him, must he needs be asking for
her presently? This Rascal *Neander*, this Villain that I dare not say any
thing to; not because he's Valiant, for then it would not grieve me, I but
because he's a Lord, which he could no more help, than I can that I am a
Cuckold: Here's another Lord too.

Enter Endymion.

Endym. O *Geron!* how is it with you?

Ger. Your Servant, my Lord.

Endym. How does *Phronesia?*

Ger. Here's another, what two Lords to make one Cuckold?

Endym. What, are you mute? has any misfortune befaln your Wife?

Ger. Too much has befaln me I am sure: 'sDeath I am Cuckolded and laught at too: you do not well, my Lord, to use me thus.

Endym. You make me wonder, *Geron!* what, are you distracted?

Ger. And you have made me a Cuckold among you, I am sure; a sweet one, I thank you for't.   [*To himself.*

    Enter a Page, *and delivers a Letter to* Endymion, *at which*
          he withdraws a little.

Ger. My Lord, I take my leave: you have bus'ness———
(*Aside.*) A Curse on you all.   [*Ex. Geron.*

             Endymion reads.

My Lord,

WE *are informed that there happen'd last night a Mutiny in our Castle at* Argos: *It is our pleasure therefore immediately on sight thereof, you take a convenient Number of our Light-horse, and go thither, and use your best Endeavours to appease it, and bring with you the principal Actors therein, to receive such punishment as their Crimes shall deserve.*

                        Basilius Rex.

Where will not Misfortune find me out?
Sure Fortune has more Eyes than those that say
She has none; Else how could she still hit
The self-same mark.———
This night, when I suppos'd within thy Armes,
Thy Armes, thy dear, to have scorn'd all the World,
To have pity'd Monarchs, and look'd down on Kings,
Thus to be hurry'd thence?——but stay!——I sin,
I sin like all the World, who never think
That every other part is well, if but
One Finger pains them.   I am happy that
I have gain'd her Love, which can no more
Change than a Star his Course, or Fate
Her everlasting Laws; and I'me to fail
But one night of my Promise;——but that night
Is a whole Age,——yet I must go.——O Heaven!——
I dare not go to take my leave of her:
One look of hers would tempt me to Rebellion.
Here she comes! Heaven! what shall I do?

Enter Cleantha *and* Urania.

Clean. My Lord!
In what Condition did you leave the Queen,
That she's retir'd at this unusual hour?
   Endym. Madam, her Majesty was very well; but thoughtful!——
(*Aside.*) How is my Loyalty already shaken———
I cannot longer endure the shock——I'le write to her.
To excuse my absence.——Your Highness humble Servant,
Your servant, Madam.   [*Ex. Endymion.*
   Clean. He seem'd as if he had disorder in his
Thoughts, and yet methinks it did become him too.   [*She sighs.*
   Uran. Why does your Highness thus afflict your self?
   Clean. Wretched *Cleantha!* yet too Fortunate
In that which Fools call Happiness; O Fate!
Why do'st thou thus abuse the World, to make
Some high, some low; yet every one alike
Unhappy? what e're our stations be,
We meet in this sad Center——Misery.
   Uran. Madam, you are more happy then you think you are.
   Clean. Those whom Fate does destine to such Plagues,
As would break forth through private windows, it
Does place in Mighty Palaces, and with
External splendor hides their Inward griefs
From Common-peoples Eyes, while they, poor Souls,
Admire what (did they understand) they'd pity.
   Uran. How many that behold your Highness walk,
Attended by the proudest Youths of *Greece*,
And Gayer much than Tulips in the Spring,
Do think you, every Minute, happier far
Then Cowards, Condemn'd, are when their Pardons read,
And Every Lady in *Arcadia*,
But wretched, when compar'd to your bright Fortune.
   Clean. Whilst poor *Cleantha*, at that very time,
Envy's some Village Maid, that Russet wears,
(The Livery of those Sheep she does attend)
And freely favours the poor Swain she loves,
And sleeps at night——*Cleantha's* oft admir'd,
And her great Titles reckon'd up, whilst she,
Does in her Closet, weep she is not less.
Poor *Endymion!* how little dar'st thou think
My Thoughts; or I dare say them to thee?
   Uran. Should *Endymion* speak,
You then would hate him for his Confidence,

A Crime of which he never can be guilty.
  Clean. Nay, should he speak, in that he would forfeit
The very thing I love him for, that rest
He finds in the *Elizium* of his thoughts,
And those true satisfactions which he takes
In being all the World unto himself.

Enter Evadne *and* Neander.

  Evad. Sir, I beseech you do not follow me,
It would incense my Father much against me
If he shou'd see you.
  Nean. Madam, never mind.
What old Gray people in their Wisdom talk of,
They'd Cross us out of envy to our youth ;
For when the Wine of Love is drawn out of 'em,
They live some years by its Vinegar, spight.
  Clean. Poor Lady, how she's pester'd with yon gaudy Nothing.

Enter Phronesia *and after* Geron.

  Phor. O Madam ! we shall have a Ball to night,
The Queen will entertain his Majesty, and desires your Highness to be ready.
  Clean. I attend her pleasure.
  Ger. Hell take that Clogg of mine ; how over-joy'd she is to have an
opportunity to show her self, and lay baits for young Gudgeons ?
  Nean. Let me Consider how I may look amiably in the sight ⎤ *He puls out*
of these Ladies ; let me see, a Patch or two here, and a little ⎬ *of his Pocket*
more red here——very well ; this Face of mine cannot chuse ⎪ *a Looking-*
but charm them ! ⎦ *Glass.*
  Ger. Well Minion, there's a Ball ; but let me but see you dare to look
upon any man but my self there, and by all the villanies of thy Sex, I'le
tear thy flesh from thy bones, and hang thy Skeleton up in a Physick-
School.   *[She shrinks from him.*
  Clean. What now, *Geron,* what in passion with your Wife ?
  Ger. O no : and' please your Highness I cannot be angry with any one
I love so well.
  Phor. Ah, Madam ; he threats to tear my flesh from my bones, and't
please your Highness.
  Clean. Geron ! Do you know before whom you do this ?
  Ger. Certainly, my dear, thou art distracted, how com'st thou to mistake
thy self so ; Madam I have a great tenderness for her as I have for my own
eyes, Heaven knows.
  Nean. They deserve much alike ; his Eyes are Blood-shot, Rhumatick
and Blind, and his Wife Ugly, Insolent and Froward.

(123)

Ger. If thou knew'ſt, my dear *Phronesia*, how great a value I have for thee, thou would'ſt not thus have injur'd me.

Clean. So, this is well ; but *Urania* and *Evadne*, let us go wait upon the Queen : *Neander*, ſtay thou here.　　　　　　*Ex. Clean. Uran. Evad.*

Nean. I like not that so well, I love this *Evadne* most abominably.

Ger. Prithee, my dear, harbour not so ill thoughts of thy loving Husband till death, *Geron*——you Strumpet, I'le make you know what 'tis to use me thus.

Phor. My Lord *Neander* help, or this old Wizard will murder me ; Avant *Belzebub.*

Nean. Hold *Geron !*

Here's a Fellow I may show my Valour on ;　　　　　　　　　　[*Aside.*
He is old, and cowardly : Oh, that all Hectors had the
Same discretion in the choice of their men that I have,
They would not be so often beaten as they are ;　Now
Will I prove as good a Knight Errant as the beſt of 'em,
And rescue this diſtress'd Lady.

Ger. Huswife, to morrow will come——

Phor. My Lord ! 'Pray take my part againſt this wicked old Jealous, Toothless, Impotent Fellow.

Nean. Do you hear, Sir ; do but dare to think of injuring this Lady, and I will take you, and slice you, and salt you, and broyl you upon a Grid-Iron, as they do a Neck of Mutton ; Rogue, I will, look for't : Now methinks I huffe as bravely as the beſt of 'em all ; when I find no resiſtance.

Ger. A curse on him ; without queſtion this is he that has done me the injury : If I cannot get my Wife with Child, muſt he do't for me with a Murrain to him ?

Nean. What's that you mutter, Sir : Come immediately and Reverence this Lady, or by my Courage, (which 'thank Heaven he thinks too great to queſtion) and by the Soul of my Friend *Alexander*, I'le make as many holes in thy old muſty Body, as there are in the inside of a Dove-house.

Ger. I muſt do't ; I may be cut off else in the flower of my age.

Nean. D'you hear, Sir, when I say the word, make your honour to her.

Phro. Ay, my Lord, teach him his duty to me.

Ger. Alas ! your Lordship miſtakes me, she is a moſt admirable Lady ; I hold her next my heart.

Nean. Come, do't then, and look you serve her, and adore her, d'ye hear, Sir.

Ger. My deareſt pretty Duckling, thy moſt humble servant to command——

Phro. Ay, this is as it should be.——

Ger. (*with a kind look*). Muſt you have your Stallions, and your Bravo's too, you moſt abominable Strumpet ; I will cut your throat infallibly.

Phor. Ah, my Lord, he threatens me again; I beseech your Lordship give him due correction for his Insolence.

Ger. This is insufferable, that a Man must be affraid to chastise his own Wife for fear of her blustering Gallants.

Nean. You Hell-hound, come and be Friends with her, and kiss her instantly, or thou shalt not draw thy perfidious breath two minutes longer.——Peace, peace, the Queen's a coming, Sir, I'le think of you another time!

Enter Priest *and* Queen.

Priest. Madam, I hope your Majesty will, in this
Slight trouble, still preserve that noble Temper
Which hitherto has guided all your actions.
The Sin is but in *Embrio*, yet we'll stifle it
Before it is brought forth; you have found
The Intention, and may well prevent the act.

Qu. I cannot but resent the injury,
My Lord intends to do himself, and me:
Poor Prince! I pity him, and oh that Heaven
Wou'd do so too, and vouchafe one beam
To his benighted Breast, to let him see
How mean a thing it is, softly to creep, at
Cowardly Midnight, to his bed of sin:
But I am resolv'd to hide my resentments,
And design'd this little Entertainment for that
Purpose——Here comes the King.

Enter King *and* Pyrrhus.

Pyrr. Sir! *Urania* assures me she will not
Fail as soon as the Dance is over.

King. Go you, and see yon *Grotto* then prepar'd.

Pyrr. It shall be fitted for the Scene of Love.
I shall make haste to wait on your Commands.

King. Then all I have to do is to make some fair
Pretence to the Queen for my absence:
How does my Queen? what, no more Company?

Queen. I need none, now I have found my Lord, who is to me all
Company.

King. She still obliges me so, I cannot think
Of my *Urania's* Love, but with regret.

Queen. Will your Majesty please to sit and see this Entry.
King. With all my heart.   ⎰ *Dance with Gittars*
Queen. How does this please you, Sir?   ⎱ *and Castanietta's.*

King. I am a little disorder'd on the sudden : I am not well.
Queen. Heav'n guard you, Sir, what is the matter?
King. 'Tis not much, but I hope this Nights reſt will make Me well.
Queen. Sure, Sir, you do not well to tarry here.
King. I do not, Madam; I'le retire : Good night.
Queen. Nay, give me leave, Sir, to attend you.
King. No! I will not draw you from the Entertainment this pleasant
Evening may afford you, Madam.
Queen. Alas! dear Sir! you injure me to think that that same Evening
that gives pain to you ; can give me pleasure.
King. My dear! I am not sick.
I onely am a little indispos'd.
I'le beg your pardon to retire this night,
But pray ſtay you, and take no further care,
Till at your own appartment I see you
To morrow morning.
Queen. Sir! your will is ſtill my Law.
King. Once more good Night————   *Exit.*
Queen. Poor Prince! now little do'ſt thou think
How soon thou art to meet with her thou fly'ſt,
That wife that ſtill has been so conſtant!
Oh! how ridiculous
Juſt Heaven does make the wayes of men,
When they forsake the wayes of Vertue.
This brave Prince,
(At whose Victorious Armies Greece now trembles)
When he contrives inglorious actions, shall
At the same time, be pity'd by his servants,
And a poor Girl shall up-braid him, in
Contriving to preserve him vertuous :
How do men ravel back to Child-hood, when
They cease to be thy Children, sacred Vertue!
And need the Care of every little person,
That what they call for, may not do 'em harm.
Prieſt. Not to be subject to temptation is
A priviledge onely had in th' other World,
And yet I hope, Madam, what you design
Will him from his intended Crime defend,
Use you the means, and Heaven will crown the End.   *Exeunt.*

The End of the Second Act.

THE THIRD ACT.

Enter King *and* Pyrrhus.

King. GOod morrow, my Lord.
  Pyrr. A good day to your Majesty.
  A day as pleasant as your night has been.
King. Ah, *Pyrrhus !* I wish it indeed.
 Pyrr. I hope your Majesty has been well enough diverted
This night———
 King. Yes, my Lord, tho' not as you suppose,
I've been diverted from those wild desires
That made me first injure my self, and then
Unlord my Confident, but I have ask'd pardon
Of Heaven, and my own Majesty, and now
I beg it too from you, my Loyal *Pyrrhus ;*
Forgive me that I have profan'd thy faith,
By such Commands that thou art bound to ask
Blest Heav'n forgiveness for thy Loyalty.
 Pyrr. Your Majesty I hope will give me leave
To wonder at this Change, and understand it,
When you shall please to think me fit for't.
 King. I'le tell thee all———when now the Night
Grew blak enough to hide a sculking action,
I softly stole
To yonder Grotto, through the Upper Walks,
And there found my *Urania ;* but I found her,
I found her, *Pyrrhus*, not a Mistress, but
A Goddess rather, which made me to be,
No more her Lover, but her Worshipper :
She onely whisper'd to me as she promis'd,
Yet never heard I any voice so loud,
And tho' her Words were gentler far than those
That holy Priests do speak to dying Saints ;
Yet never Thunder signify'd so much.
 Pyrr. 'Plague of her whispering, if this Change be true,
I am in a sweet Condition———   *Aside.*
 King. And what did make still more impression on me,
Methought her whispers were my injur'd Queens,
Her manner just like hers, and when she urg'd

(127)

(Among a thousand things) the injury
I did the faithfull'st Princess in the World,
Who now suppos'd me sick, and was perchance
Upon her knees off'ring up holy Vows
For him who mock'd both Heav'n, and her.
 Pyrr. This is very fine I'faith !
 King. When she urg'd this, and wept, and spake so like
My poor deluded Queen, *Pyrrhus,* I trembled,
And my hot raging blood straight turn'd to Ice,
I being perswaded that it was her Angel
Spoke through *Urania's* Lips, who for her sake
Took Care of me as something she much Lov'd.
 Pyrr. aside. These are unhappy qualmes for me, I have
No way to keep his favour now, for I am sure
I am good for nothing Else, but what he last
Employ'd me in ; but how did you leave her, Sir ?
 King. Urania still is Chaste, but how do'st think
I shall reward her for this vertuous Action ?
 Pyrr. A Curse on her———*Aside*
There are ten thousand ways, Sir.
 King. No, no, for this I must undo her now.
 Pyrr. You make me wonder, Sir.
 King. You know she told me,
Endymion was her Servant (a rare man)
That can love Vertue where he sees her poor ;
And I shall be constrain'd to banish him
To some remoter Island, unless he'll be
(Which I much doubt) content to marry her,
Within few dayes.
 Pyrr. This is all news.
 King. It is :
But *Pyrrhus,* thou art worthy of my secrets,
And therefore know, I've lately learnt *Cleantha,*
Loves nothing but *Endymion :* tho' she has
(Thou know'st) a Prince that courts her high in Birth,
And Fortune too : One worthy of our alliance,
The Prince of *Macedon,* who by his Father was
Engag'd to marry the King of *Thraces* eldest Daughter :
But that was hindered by the late rebellion
Where the pious King of *Thrace* by his inhumane
Subjects was basely murder'd, and his Queen and two
Daughters forc'd to fly for their safety, and never
Since were heard of.

Pyrr. The great *Cleopatra*, with her Eldest, who was grown,
A Woman, and another who was a little Child.
   King. The same : But since the loss of all these Princesses,
The Prince's affections have engag'd him here ;
That was his Fathers Choice, but this his own ;
Yet she slights all his Addresses, and last night
I was inform'd 'twas onely for the sake
Of this *Endymion*, the certainty
I hope to know from our good Priest, whom I
Employ'd to sound her resolutions,
Whence I shall soon discern *Endymion*'s Fate.
   Pyrr. But does *Endymion* know *Cleantha* loves him ?
   King. I am told he does not : all that can be gather'd
Is but from some few words, she was by chance
O'reheard to say unto her self, too big
For her own breasts Confinement, and too secret
It seems for any others Ear.
But heark ! what's yonder ?   *[Trumpet within.*
   Pyrr. I believe *Endymion* is return'd
   King. Go and enquire the News of him ; I must to' th'
Queen, the Shepherds are to entertain me here in this
Adjoyning Grove with some of our *Arcadian* sports,
As they do once a Month : but here's my Niece.

Enter Cleantha.

Niece ! A good morning to you.————
What makes you abroad so early ?
   Clean. To take the pleasant ayre of this Garden.
   King. Much good may it do you ; I'le leave you to your thoughts.
   Clean. Heaven bless you————   *Ex.* King.
————when Ev'ry thing is green
Must poor *Cleantha* only wither, and never
Know a Spring ? Was I made onely high
Like *Rhodope*, and *Hæmus*, or the Alps,
To dwell with everlasting Winter ? to wear Snow,
When every Valley is adorn'd with Roses ?
Well I must die, then I may also be
Happy as other Folks ; the Grave looks Wistly,
Like my Fortune, there I shall not see
Poor Villagers more blest in Love then I,
And there I shall be able to make appear
Cleantha and *Endymion* Equall are ;
Then possibly some of *Cleantha*'s Earth

(129)

May prove a little Flower, and look fresher
Then when it was a part of a great Princess.

Enter Urania.

Uran. Madam! the Queen expects your Highness.
Clean. I'll wait on her————   *Ex.* Cleantha.
Uran. *Endymion* is return'd! what shall I do?
To be at once both Just and Civil too.
If I could satisfie *Endymion's* Love,
I shou'd unjust to great *Theander* prove;
That Prince who to so mean a thing as I,
(Bred in a little Cottage) did bestow
His Noble Heart, which is a Present fit
For any Princess fruitful *Greece* can boast of:
From whom if I could give my Love, I would not.
Why did I give my Promise then last night?
And yet the Generous *Endymion*
Will sure forgive me when he knows the Cause:
He's here; Heaven forgive me, what I'm forc'd to.

Enter Endymion.

Endym. Madam! I come upon my Knees to beg your pardon.
Uran. My Lord, it is not well to mock me further,
You have deluded me enough already:
Thus we that are so easie to bestow
Our Love, the greatest Treasure we possess,
Are still neglected by ungrateful men;
But I had thought to have found more truth in you.
Endym. Madam! 'twas my allegiance forc'd me from you.
Uran. Those men, who dare offer such injuries,
Never want boldness to excuse their Crimes.
Endym. Had I refus'd t'obey my Kings Command,
You could not think me Worthy of your Love.
Uran. (*aside.*) He speaks a truth, I ought, but dare not own,
What a fond Fool was I to be so forward
In trusting a Court Lord, to believe
You e're would marry one of mean Fortune.
Endym. Dear *Urania*, I appeal to' th' Gods
Who are honour'd when they'r witnesses to truth.
Uran. Make no more Vows, I am not to be deceiv'd agen,
I was too foolish to believe your last: Farewel, my Lord.
(*Aside.*) The Powers above forgive me.   *Ex.* Uran.
Endym. How much unlike *Urania* is this passion?
Who us'd to be all Calm and gentle still:

(130)

And sure would be so, did not my unlucky
Stars, that never meant me good, incline
Her to this Anger.——

Enter Neander.

Nean. Your Servant, my Lord!

Endym. 'Curse on this vain Fop——   [*Ex.* Endym.

Nean. Are you so stout? Farewel——Well! I wonder whom the Devil
intends I shall marry with? I have been a Servant, as they call't; that is,
I have ly'd, sworn, and spent Money upon every Lady about the Court,
and still am as far from having one of them as the very'st Evnuch is; nay,
more, for they say, Evnuchs have a Trick now a-dayes to please the
Ladies Exceedingly:——I was in most hopes of *Evadne*, and love her best:
but the old Priest forbids her to see me, or speak with me; here she comes!
——I will force her to hear me——

Enter Evande *in haste.*

Dear Apple of my Eye! why this haste; thou hast wounded me, and then
thou fly'st me.

Evad. There is a sufficient reason for't.

Nean. Must then *Neander* die?

Evad. My reason is obedience.

Nean. Obedience to a Priest! we have liv'd to a fine age to be govern'd
by that Tribe i'faith.

Evad. That Priest is my Father.

Nean. Ay, and an incomparable father too! that will Chuse no Husband
for you but a heavy headed Fool, that is afraid to swear, thinks most old
Women Witches, and believes that dead folks walk.

Evad. Let me go! why do I talk with this vain piece of Frippery.

Nean. Well, I perceive you will hear no more of your ser- [*Ex.* Evadne.
vant——   What Sot in all *Arcadia*, but this old ball'd Hackney Priest,
would not marry his Daughter to my Estate, tho' I were the arrantest
Coxcomb in *Greece*? So he might have said his Daughter my Lady, such
a one, and talk of her Gentlemen Ushers, her Pages, and her Women, who
would care whether her Husband were a Philosopher or no? Poor *Evadne*,
thy mother dy'd too soon for thee; she, good Woman, would have made
a hard shift to have sat at the upper end of my Lord *Neander*'s Table, to
have had occasion to have made up a fine Mouth, and have said to *Evadne*,
Daughter, you don't help my Lord, *&c.* well! I'le be aveng'd on some
body for this.

Enter Geron.

Ger. For my Wife, I have secur'd her under two double Locks and Keys;
the Devil's in't if she breaks Prison now: I'le keep her from these publick

Meetings : She, like a Strumpet, was mad to be at this Entertainment of the Shepherds.

Nean. Here's a Fellow in a worse condition with a Wife, then I am for want of one.

Ger. Hell take this Lord ! must I still see him where e're I go——My Lord, your most obedient Servant.

Nean. Geron ! how is it ?

Ger. How is what ? but let it be how it will, I care not.

Nean. How does your Wife ?

Ger. Furies seize this damn'd Lord !—— *Aside.*
My honour'd Lord ! my Wife is at your Lordship's service. 'Plague on him, he has made, I believe, too bold with her already—— Is she here —— I shall be undone, Cuckolded, abus'd ; what will become of me ? I am sure I lock'd her fast.

> *Enter* King, Queen, Clean. Uran. Evad. Phro. Endym. Priest,
> (*and all the Court.*)

Queen. Geron ! let me once more hear of this ill usage of your Wife, and I'le banish you the Court.

Ger. A Curse on her, must she appeal to the Queen too.

King. Have you spoke with the Princess.

Priest. I have Sir, and when I prest her to it, she confest to me she lov'd *Endymion* tho' at first she was unwilling to own it.

King. What a misfortune is this to me : some speedy Care must be taken——But come let us take our places, and hear what these Shepherds will afford us.

Queen. I am infinitely pleas'd with 'em, they are
The happi'est innocent'st people in the World.

SCENE draws, the Shepherds and Shepherdesses are discover'd lying under the Shades of Trees, at the appearance of the King and Court ; one arises and sings as follows, *In Stilo recitativo.*

I.

SHepherds awake, the God of day does rise,
Bedeck'd with all the Glories of the Skyes,
And round about scatters his heat and light,
And dazles all our sight.

{ Here they rise, and bow to the King and
Court, and one sings on.

(132)

In vain the Persians, *heretofore,*
Did their dull God of light adore,
Since we have one can give us more :
By whose bright influence, we enjoy
(What other Nations toyle for long)
Life without Labour ; full of Joy,
And free from all Oppressors wrong.

Cho. *{Here our own proper Flocks of Sheep*
of 2. *{We may in pleasant safety keep.*

Here a perpetual Spring does cloath the Earth,
And makes it fruitful with each seasons birth.
In this fair Climate every day
Is fresh and green as May,
And here no beauty can decay.

Cho.
of 3.
{Thus, thus live we
{As the Elements free
{Each day and each night
{Is Crown'd with delight
{Without either Envy or Strife
{This is the Jolly Shepherds life.

2.

Free from all Cares in pleasant Shades,
And fragrant Bowres, we spend the day ;
(Bowers which no Heat, nor Cold invades,
Which all the year are fresh and gay)
Each does his loving Mate imbrace,
And in soft pleasures melts the hours away,
So innocently that no Face
Of Nymph or Shepherd can a guilt betray :
And having Ease, the Nurse of Poetry,
We sing the Stories of our Loves,
As Chaste as Turtle-Doves,
Free from all Fear and Jealousie,
From every envious Eye :
For every Man possesses but his own,
No Shepherd sighs, nor Shepherdess does frown :
No Ambition here is found,
But to be Crown'd
Lord or Lady of the May ;

(133)

And on the Solemn Day,
For Singing to have praise
Or for inditing to deserve the Bayes.
Thus, thus live we, &c.

3.

In the Cool Evening, on the Lawns we play,
And merrily pass our time away.
We dance, and run, and pipe, and sing,
And Wraſtle in a Ring.
For some gawdy Wreaths of Flowers,
Cropt from the fruitful Fields, and Bowers,
By some pretty Nymphs compos'd,
By their fair hands to be dispos'd,
To those ambitious Shepherds, who
With Vertuous Emulation ſtrive to do
What may deserve the Garlands, and (obtain'd)
Are prouder far than Princes that have gain'd)
In fight their Valours prize,
Or over ſtubborn Nations Victories ;
Whil'ſt in the adjoyning Grove the Nightingale
Does tell her mournful Tale,
And does our Pleasures greet,
With each Note,
So sweet, so sweet, so sweet
From her pretty jugging, jugging throat.
It does each Breaſt inspire
With loving heat and with Poetick Fire.
Thus, thus live we, &c.

4.

We live aloof from Deſtiny,
(That only quarrells with the Great)
And in this Calm Retreat,
(Content with Nature uncorrupted) we
From ſplendid miſeries of Courts are free ;
From pomp, and noise, from pride, and fear,
From factions, from divisions cleer,
Free from brave beggery, smiling ſtrife,
This is indeed a Life :
No flaws in Titles vex our Cares,
Nor quarrel we for what's our own,
No noise of War invades our Eares,

We suffer not the Rage of Sword, or Gown.
Our little Cabans stronger are,
Than Palaces, to keep out woes ;
Nor ever take we Care
To fortify 'gainst any Foes,
But little showres of rain, or hail,
Which seldom do this place assail.
Thus, thus live we, &c.

Here the Shepherds and Shepherdesses take hands round, and Dance, as they sing the following Song, and at the end of the Song they fall into the Figure they must dance in.

I.

THus all our Life long we are frolick and gay,
And, instead of Court-Revels, we merrily play
At Trap, and at Keels, and at Barlibreak run,
At Goff, and at Stool-ball, and when we have done
Cho. { *These Innocent Sports, we laugh, and lie down,*
And to each pretty Lass we give a green-Gown.

2.

We teach our little Dogs to fetch and to carry
The Partridge, the Hare, and the Pheasants our Quarry :
The nimble Squirrels with Cudgells we chase,
And the little pretty Lark we betray with a Glass,
And when we have done, we laugh and lie down,
And to each pretty, &c.

3.

About the May-pole we dance all around,
And with Garlands of Pinks, and of Roses are Crown'd ;
Our little kind Tributes we cheerfully pay
To the gay Lord, and to the bright Lady of the May.
And when we have done, &c.

4.

With our delicate Nymphs we kiss and we toy,
What all others but Dream of, we daily enjoy ;
With our sweet-hearts we dally so long till we find
Their pretty Eyes say that their hearts are grown kind :

And when we have done, we laugh and lie down,
And to each pretty Lass we give a green Gown.

Enter a Messenger.

King. What means this Messenger?
Mess. Great Sir, *Theander* now has gain'd in *Thessaly*
A perfect Conquest over all our Enemies,
Having o'rethrown them in one fatal Battle,
He has reduc'd them to obedience.
 King. The Powers above be prais'd:
Let me know the Particulars.
 Uran. (*to her self.*) How am I transported with this happy News!
My heart is yet too narrow for my joy:
My prayers were heard, the brave *Theander's* safe,
And comes in Triumph too.
 Mess. He bid me say,
He will be here to morrow e're night, and then he'l
Give your Majesty a full account of all the War.
 Uran. (*to her self.*) And shall I see the God-like man to morrow?
Let me contain my self a little.
 Endym. Madam! are you resolv'd still to persist in Cruelty?
 Uran. Endymion, forgive me.——   *Aside.*
Sir, I acquainted you with my resolutions.
 King. This Evening we will Celebrate the Victory,
And give the Gods our thanks and praises for't.
         Exeunt all but Urania *and* Cleantha.
 Uran. I am privately told by *Evadne*, that her Father
Has discover'd your Highness's Love to the King,
And that the King has secretly resolv'd to banish
Endymion.
 Clean. O Gods! banish *Endymion*: desire *Evadne* to come
To me.
 Uran. I will——   *Ex.* Urania.
 Clean. Wretched *Cleantha*! is thy Love a crime,
A crime to him thou lov'st? must it be ruine
To a person, if thou but affect'st him?
Have I some Plague that I must thus destroy,
Whom I embrace? or is my Destiny
Grown Paradoxical, and proves my Love
To be true Hatred?——
O Death! thou art not half so Cruel yet,
In thy destructions of the Prosp'rous,
As in not killing Wretches that would die.

Enter Endymion.

Endym. *Urania* does not well to treat me thus :
I took no leave of her, but I have told her
The reasons why my Love forbad it me,
Yet she persiſts in Cruelty.
   Clean. He's here———
His Count'nance betokens grief.
   Endym. To be thus angry and accuse me of
Slighting a poor deluded Maid
In spight of all my Vows of Love to her———
The Princess ſtill is Gracious to me :
I had beſt intreat her to perswade my now
Provok'd *Urania*———She's here ;
But she's alone, I dare not interrupt her Thoughts.
   Clean. Good morrow, My Lord.
   Endym. Your Pardon, Madam, if unthought of, I
Have rush'd on your Retirement.
   Clean. Your Presence will better it.
'Pray what News from *Argos ?*
   Endym. Madam, the report was brought laſt night to *Court*
Had nothing in't of truth : I found all quiet,
But only for the diſturbance which we made
Our selves by our Arrival in the Night.
   Clean. I am glad my Lord your danger was no more.
   Endym. You oblige me, Madam, to undergo
Much greater danger for your Highness then
This could have prov'd.
   Clean. My Lord ! you have already
Serv'd me beyond what I can recompence.
   Endym. Madam ! t'has been your Highness's pleasure ſtill
To honour with too great respeɕts the little
Merits of your mean Servant, who's advanc'd
When numbred in the loweſt rank of those
That have been Fortunate to do you service.
   Clean. You add ſtill to my debts, my Lord, yet are
No ways injurious, since you make me rich
In having such a Noble Creditor :
But pray, my Lord, tell me, (as one concern'd
Much in your Fortunes) what's the Cause
Your Lordship has not worn of late that reſt
Upon your looks which heretofore appear'd.

Endym. Madam, it is for you to wear that rest who are
Plac'd in that upper Region where there is
No Wind, but a little Bark, i'th midst
Of a great Sea, subject to every Wave,
And every gust of Wind, can ne're pretend
To this blest 'State.
    Clean. My Lord ; you have som griefs that are particular.
    Endym. For my troubles, Madam,
Alas ! their objects would appear so small
To your great Eye, you'd think I did affront you,
Shou'd I dare say them to you.   Could the Lyon
In his Midnight-walks hear some poor Worms
Complain for want of little drops of dew,
What pity could that noble Creature have,
Who never wanted small things, for those poor
Ambitions ? yet these are their concernments,
And but for want of these they pine and die.
    Clean. I hope my Lord what is your Trouble may
Not be augmented by my knowing it,
Else I shall never think ought small that can
So much affect you, nor beneath my Cure
To seek to remedy what gives you pain.
    Endym. Great Princess ! you undo me with your Honours :
My blood turns all to blushes, Madam ;
I must obey your Highnesse's Commands,
And thank you for 'em too since in your knowledge
Of what afflicts me is my Remedy.
    Clean. What will he tell me, Heav'n, he knows I love him.   [*Aside.*
    Endym. Madam, I long have lov'd———
    Clean. Lov'd whom ?
    Endym. The fair *Urania* who attends your Highness.
    Clean. }Forgive me poor *Endymion* when I say
    aside. ∫What I of all the World ought least to say :
Indeed, my Lord, I never could have guess'd———   *To him.*
Your Melancholly had so mean a Cause :
I could not think you would so far dishonour
Your Family and Name to love
So low a person.
    Endym. Madam ! I well know
Urania was a Shepherdess, and born
In a low Cottage, 'mongst those little people
Whom honour seldom visits, but yet she,
Like to a Star mistaken of its Sphear,

Grew so conspicuous 'mongst those dimmer Lights,
That brave *Theander* had no sooner spy'd her,
But he became all Wonder, and thought her a fit
Present for your Highness, an Advancement
Few Families can boast of.

   Clean. But her Birth is mean.

   Endym. You cast your eyes upon her from the height
Of Birth, and Fortune too, and see her low :
Whil'st that some other Princess born as high
But not under so happy Stars, may think
Her Birth more Noble, 'cause more free, and less
Subject to Fate.

   Clean. Wretched *Cleantha !* now *Endymion* sayes
Thou art unhappy——But
My Passion is now authoriz'd, and I
Must speak : tell me, my Lord, and truly too,
Should I make it my Care to Chuse you a Mistress
Fair as *Urania*, and as vertuous too,
Extracted from a Family would give
Lustre to yours, although it were as mean
As hers you court now : Say, would you not leave
Urania who does seem to slight
All your Respects for her.

   Endym. Should your Highness condescend to chuse
A Torment for me, it were Impudence
In me to chuse ought else : but that's all blest
Which is so like *Urania.*

   Clean. So like to her ?
Her Birth is very low ; perhaps her Mind
As low as that.

   Endym. Madam ! *Urania* may
Find thousands of more Merit than
The poor *Endymion,* who durst never measure
Himself but by the Passion he had for her.

   Clean. Sure 'twas his modesty, he might have thriven
Much better, possibly, had his Ambition
Been greater much——they oftentimes take more pains
Who look for Pins, than those who look for starrs.

   Endym. Those who look for Stars, must be provided
With Arts and Glasses, and such costly things
As humble men must be content to want.

   Clean. For Stars of greatest Magnitude you need
Onely to fix your eyes, and they'l appear

By their own light, and all you have to do
Is to receive those beams they cast upon you.
    Endym. ⎰ What can this mean?——But, Madam, 'tis hard,
    aside. ⎱ To fix our eyes aright upon that part
Of Heaven where those Stars inhabit, if
We have not some directions first.
    Clean. Indeed, those, who look downwards, ought to be directed
To look above them, to the highest Sphear;
(For there they are) then I am apt to think
Their task would not prove hard——my Lord, I blush
Thus to instruct you in Astronomy.
    Endym. I am lost in wonder :——   *Aside.*
Madam, 'tis not strange
If I'm proud of what you blush at, but
I am sure your unbounded wit to morrow
Will with much greater reason quite deny it.
    Clean. My Lord, you think no woman can be constant
To what she sayes a days, but your *Urania :*
But till you have try'd, pray have more Charity,
You'l after have more Faith : my Lord, Farewell :
The Gods forgive my breach of Modesty——   *Aside.*
    Endym. What have I heard !
Was't not enough to lose my dear *Urania,*
Unless I also did adore the hand
That snatch'd her from me, *Cleantha* Loves *Endymion ;*
But Fool it cannot be ; ne're may I know
Her noble Breast harbour a thought so low.——   *Exeunt.*

The End of the Third Act.

THE FOURTH ACT.

Enter Neander.

Nean. I Was (at least in my own conceit) in probability of winning the sweet *Evadne :* and now, that not onely her ugly Father, but the Queen too should forbid her to see me or speak to me ; it is what I cannot, will not bear : Though Fate it self say, I shall do it, I am resolv'd that old grey Priest and his Mistress the Queen, shall be the subjects of my Revenge : and yet I am not ambitious to show my Valour so far, as to be hang'd for't neither——I think I ha't; If I can do this, 'twill be the sweetest part of my Revenge, to live, and tread, and spit upon their Graves: I have sent for *Geron* a Rogue fit for my purpose, for he is Covetous to Extremity, and I have Gold to bribe him, and which is lucky above my Wishes, the Priest and Queen have check'd him lately, and countenanc'd his Wife against him, which torments him so, that I believe he would be glad to be hang'd on any terms.——Here he is.

Enter Geron.

Ger. Consume him, he's here——

Nean. Dear *Geron*, let him embrace thee that
Perhaps is thy best Friend.

Ger. Perhaps, with a Curse to him—— *Aside.*
No, my Lord, you are a Friend to my Wife.

Nean. Geron! give me your hand.

Ger. Wou'd I had your Heart's blood.—— *Aside.*

Nean. Give me your Hand, *Geron.*

Ger. My good Lord! you do me too much honour.

Nean. I beg your pardon heartily that I presum'd to
Count'nance your ugly, impertinent, ill-natur'd, vain
Wife against you, you that are so worthy an honest Knight;
It was Ignorance of her, and you made me do it. I protest it was.

Ger. What the Devil does he mean by this?—— *Aside.*

Nean. Upon my Honour, *Geron*, it was; had I not been a stranger to
her ill Qualities.

Ger. I am afraid you know 'em too well—— *Aside.*

Nean. I should never have encourag'd her in her Insolence to you.

Ger. What does all this tend to?—— *Aside.*

Nean. For I am well satisfy'd, a Man, especially an old Man that has had experience of the vanity of the World, ought to have an absolute Dominion over his Wife.

Ger. My Lord, this is a Truth! I would you had acknowledg'd sooner; for my abominable Wife, instead of being humbled, is encourag'd by the Court.

Nean. I know though too late now, your Wife is froward, Foolish, petulant, wanton, proud, expensive, disobedient, ungrateful.——

Ger. 'Tis too true; but a Plague on him, I am afraid he has Made shift with her with all these faults——my good Lord——

Nean. What sayes my dear Friend, give me leave to call you so: *(aside.)* whom I would not give two Drachma's to save from a Gibbet.

Ger. I would fain be satisfi'd of one scruple.

Nean. Speak it.

Ger. I beseech your Lordship be not angry——

Nean. My dear *Geron*, I cannot be with thee.

Ger. My Lord! were you never a little familiar or so with——

Nean. Whom?

Ger. My Wife, my Lord, in private; I mean in a Civil way.

Nean. I am not to interpret your meaning, but upon my honour I was never alone with her in my life, nor ever will I be if I can avoid it———

Ger. Is your Lordship in earnest?

Nean. Upon my Honour, *Geron*.

Ger. Honour, that's a word for some, who call themselves men of Honour to borrow Money with; it is a tenure they Mortgage, as often as they do their Lands, and forfeit the Mortgage too; and yet they wou'd have both their Honours and Estates pass for Security, as if there were no incumbrance upon either.

Nean. Do'st thou distrust me, Friend? I could never endure her, she's so ugly, so abominably ugly.

Ger. So ugly, my Lord, I did not think you wou'd have abus'd my Wife thus; so ugly, I'de have your Lordship know there is not her fellow in the Court——'Pox on her she's but too handsome for me.

Nean. Nay, 'prethee, *Geron*, be not offended; my Nature is so just to all my Friends, that their Wives, though ne're so beautiful appear to me deform'd; and if thou doubtest my Friendship, make tryal of me, let me know how I can serve thee.

Ger. I humbly thank your Lordship———Sure he must be in earnest; but I'le try: My Lord, you have an Interest here, the Queen and Priest have given me so severe Rebukes about my damnable Wife, that they have encourag'd her to be ten times more troublesome and insolent than ever, my life is now become a Torment to me.

Nean. And wilt thou tamely put up this injury?

Ger. I would it were in my power to help it.

Nean. It is man———

Ger. What sayes your Lordship.

Nean. It shall be, and I'le joyn with thee in the Revenge.

Ger. Now do I hope he'll plot some Treason, that I may accuse him, and beg his Estate for't.

Nean. I will propound to him, but if I see him waver in the buis'ness, I'le make the first accusation, and hang him for't. *Geron*, in short, I am not injur'd less then you; the Queen and Priest have crost me in my Love, and kept the fair *Evadne* from my embraces, the onely thing I hop'd for pleasure in.

Ger. My Lord I know the story.

Nean. If you will joyn with me and help me to Effect my Revenge, you will not only be reveng'd your self, but I will give you twenty Talents to boot.

Ger. Twenty Talents ! a delicious sum, how I could embrace 'em.

Nean. We may contrive some way to make the King jealous of the Priest and Queen, thou know'st the Queen extreamly favours that old Priest.

Ger. 'Tis for his Piety she esteems him so.

Nean. Piety ! hang him !————but however we may design it so ; that that piety may look like Treason.

Ger. As how, my Lord ?

Nean. Let us contrive some private meeting for them in yonder Grotto that may look suspitiously, then bring the King to see it ; joyn with me, and thou shalt have the Talents, man.

Ger. I am very fearful ; but Twenty Talents !————a Revenge To boot ————ha !————I'le venture it.

Nean. Have courage man————
Which Heaven knows is a thing I neither have, nor desire to have. [*Aside.*

Ger. Your Lordship has prevail'd, and now I'le put you in a way : As I was watching my Wives haunts, I overheard the Queen and *Endymion*, saying, that the King had forc'd *Urania* to appoint a private meeting with him in the Grotto, and the Queen resolv'd to supply her place, to keep the King from his intended Crime.

Nean. What then ?

Ger. We may feign a Tale to the Queen, that the King has this Night resum'd his desires, and that *Urania* has promis'd it in earnest.

Nean. But *Urania* will contradict that————

Ger. No ; she ask'd the Princess liberty to leave the Court a day or two for some private business or other, and is now absent.

Nean. Excellent, *Geron* ! but how shall we carry this story ?

Ger. My Wife ; who shall still be ignorant of the matter.

Nean. Admirably invented : thou shalt have the Talents ; besides, if thy Wife shou'd discover thee or me, if she be question'd, we'l face her down in't and she shall hang for't.

Ger. That Argument prevails with me more then the Talents : whether she betrays us or no, we'l do that, my Lord.

Nean. With all my heart, Excellent *Geron* : for the Priest, thou shalt go to him, and subtilly perswade him, that the Queen has made an appointment to meet me in the Grotto, and that I to avoid suspition am to be in Womans Cloaths.

Ger. My Lord, he'll ne're believe it.

Nean. Do thou confirm it by ten thousand Oaths.

Ger. That will be dang'rous.

Nean. Not at all : But think on the Talents, and the death of thy Wife, man : Thou mai'st perswade the Priest to meet her to prevent it in a Womans loose habit, and then bring the King to see them.

Ger. But the Priest will soon undeceive the King.

Nean. No, no, fear not that, the King will be so inrag'd: 'tis ten to one he kills 'em both without examination; if not, you and I, who will be the first Accusers will swear 'em both down in't; think upon Revenge and Profit.

Ger. My Lord! I'le do't about the time of this Evening Sacrifice for the Victory of *Theander*.

Enter Endymion *with a Guard.*

Ger. What means this?
Nean. O *Endymion*'s banish'd.
And this Guard is to convey him out of the
Kings Dominions; let him be hang'd and
He will————let us about our business——   *Ex.* Geron *and* Nean.
Endym. May I not see the Princess for
Whom I am banish'd before I go?
Officer. No, no, along, Sir.
1. *Sould.* 'Pray, Sir, go a little faster.
2. *Sould.* Prithee, let the Gentleman alone, soft
And fair goes far, and the Gentleman
Considers he has far to go.
Endym. Farewel then, brave *Cleantha,* may'st thou never
Once think *Endymion* suffers for thy sake:
And farewel, dear *Urania,* I will love thee
On those hard Rocks I now must dwell upon.
Officer. What's this muttering? Along, Sir.
2. *Sould.* Good Gentleman! he's loath to leave the Princess
I warrant him.

Enter Cleantha.

1. *Sould.* Here she comes.
Endym. The Princess!——Great Princess, pardon
My glorious sufferings; forgive me that   [*Kneels.*
I ever saw the Light, or liv'd a Minute:
That you are injur'd thus by him whose being
Is not worth your meanest thought.
Clean. Ah, my Lord, affront me not:
Rise, brave *Endymion!* 'Tis my misfortune:
Thou art too low already.
Endym. Fortune made me low to be advanc'd by a hand
More Worthy than her own.   [*Rises.*
Clean. My Noble Lord!
I have undone you! what can I give you now
In recompence of Liberty, and all

The pleasures you must loose
In a sad banishment, for her who onely
Can be afflicted at your sufferings.
 Endym. Madam, you have Enough to give to pay
So mean a debt, if you will call it one
A thousand times.
 Clean. Name it, and take it, dear
Endymion, though it be my life.
 Endym. Madam !
Then grant me this request : use every art
To make your Hours as blest as I shall pray
They may be many ; and never let a Thought
E're represent to your remembrance more
Unfortunate *Endymion :* then shall I be
Among the desolations of my Fortune
Happy, to think the brave *Cleantha's* happy,
And wears a Crown, and lives ador'd : what then
Tho' I live in an obscure banishment.
 Offic. Sir, this is what was forbidden us to permit you ;
You must away, Sir————   *Takes him by the Arm.*
 Clean. Impudent Villain, dar'st thou interrupt a person I am talking with.
 Offic. Yes, Madam, when I have the Kings Commands to do it.
 Endym. Madam ; these persons do their Duty, they are the
Hands of Fate, that pull me from you——Sacred Princess,
All that is bliss attend you—— *He kneeles to kiss her Hand.*
 Clean. My Lord, Farewell !
Take this Ring and remember me :
Know that *Cleantha* loves you, and will never
Be happy till *Endymion* makes her so.
 Endym. I cannot doubt but Heaven will prosper what
Is so like it self : blest Princess, take my prayers,
Heav'n thinks not fit to entrust me with ought else.
 Clean. Farewell, and with thee all my happiness !
 Offic. Come, Sir, when will you go ?
 Endym. Thus Fate directs me, what I now must do,
To serve my Shepherdess, and Princess too.
Endymion falls ; but to the first he dies
A Lover, to the last, a Sacrifice———— *Ex. Endymion with Guards.*
 Clean. Heaven ! Heaven ! where was thy mercy then,
When thou mad'st Life so great a pain, and Death
A Sin ? Did'st thou Create great Souls but to
Affront them with thy greater power ?
If by my power

With the King I cannot get him recall'd,
I am resolv'd privately to follow him ; and spend
My dayes with him that has my heart.

Enter Phronesia.

Phro. Madam ! why does your Highness thus submit to grief,
Clean. Have I not reason for't ?
Phro. Madam, your Highness shou'd study to forget
Endymion now.
Clean. Forget him (foolish Woman) I sooner shall
Forget that I have Eyes, forget I have
A Memory ! Shall brave *Endymion* live
In banishment for me, and I forget him ?
Sure thou would'st mind me of him, if I shou'd.
Phro. Well, Madam, I wish your Highness does not
Remember him too much ; I am glad you are
Alive yet for my part.
Clean. Indeed I speak, and do the offices of life,
But say, *Phronesia ;*
Did'st never see a Tree cut down i'the Spring
A while put forth his Buds and Leaves, as if
He'd been alive untill that sap was spent
Which he had suck'd from his life-giving Root,
And then he wither'd ?

Enter King and Queen.

King. How do you, Niece ?
Queen. We are come to visit you in the absence of your Lover.
Clean. Your Majesties do always do me honour.
Queen. Indeed you ought to thank those who do you honour,
When you forget to do it your self.
King. *Cleantha !* you are too wise, I hope, to be
Afflicted at *Endymion's* banishment.
Clean. Sir ! what so e're my Troubles are, as they
Are my own, so I shall endeavour not
To make 'em any others.
King. You ought to look to the Justice of
The Action, and be satisfi'd
Clean. Indeed there's little Mercy in't ; if that be
Most Just, that is most Cruel, this is so
King. The action I have done is just : I thought it so,
And I have done it, and you must be patient.
Clean. Your Majesty may please to know, that I shall

(146)

Have that regard to my self, as not to suffer
My impatience to be troublesome to others.
   King. You grieve for *Endymion,* when all *Arcadia*
Rejoyces at the Victory of
Theander, which this Evening we shall Celebrate
With Sacrifices, and with other Rites, for whom
We will prepare a publick Triumph :
Compose your self, and let not others see
Your shame.
   Clean. My Shame they ne're   [*Aside.*
Shall see ; call it my Glory, so it is.

Enter Pyrrhus.

   Pyrr. Sir, the Sacrifice is ready for the
Altar, and the Priests wait your Royal presence
For the Execution.
   King. Niece ! think on what I've said, and follow us. [*Ex.* King *and* Pyrr.
   Queen. Come, dear *Cleantha,* 'prithee be not sad,
The Prince of *Macedon* will be fitter for
Your noble Blood which is deriv'd from Kings.
   Clean. And some other will be fitter for him
Then I, unless he likes a broken heart.
Besides, the Prince is Contracted already to
The Queen of *Thrace's* eldest Daughter.
   Queen. She is long since dead.
   Clean. Who can tell that, Madam ; I am apt to believe
If she had her Kingdom yet, the Prince would find
Her out.

Enter Phronesia.

   Queen. What News with you ?
   Phro. News that does import your Majesty————   *Whisper.*

Enter Geron.

   Ger. Madam ! The Queen and your Highness are expected at the Temple ;
this will be a night of Joy.
   Clean. That brings me nought but sorrow ; the name of joy
Is odious to me, since *Endymion's* gone.
   Queen. Art thou sure of this *Phronesia ?*
   Phro. Yes, Madam, doubt it not.
   Queen. The Gods amend all once more, I'le prevent it :
But first I'le to the Temple ; Come *Cleantha.*
   Ger. What have you told the Queen
What I enjoyn'd you ?

(147)

Phro. I have, and she is resolv'd to Circumvent him: Come to the Temple, haste.——— *Ex. Phron.*

Ger. Thus far it goes well; I have with many Oaths and Protestations confirm'd the Priest in the belief that *Neander* in Womans Cloaths is this night to meet the Queen: it takes admirably——The Talents are my own, and this wife of mine is dead already.

The Scene changes to the Temple.

After the Sacrifice, there is a Consort of Martial Musick, and two or three of the *Salii* or Priests of *Mars* sing as follows.

I.

ALL *Praises to the God of War,*
    Who in our Battels gives Success,
    By whom we now Victorious *are,*
Who does not onely us with Conquests *bless,*
    But 'tis his Pow'r that gives us Peace.
Arcadia *now may safely that enjoy,*
    Thessalians *cannot that destroy :*
For brave Theander *has our Foes opprest,*
And by his Noble Toyls procur'd our Rest.

2.

In vain they did their Heedless Force oppose,
Against such Courage and such Conduct too,
Such as requir'd more strong and numerous Foes
Fit for his Noble fury to subdue.
    Oh how he thunder'd in the Van,
Godlike he threaten'd, and did more than man :
        His Glorious Rage did then impart
        A Flame into the coldest heart ;
All by his great Example did appear,
To slight their Dangers, and disclaim their Fear.
He ought to none his Laurel to submit,
But to our Patron Mars *the Cause of it.*

3.

Now the Armies meet, and vigorously engage,
(Each man reaking with Sweat, with Blood besmear'd)
The boist'rous Seas in all their Wildest Rage
Were ne're so rough as then that Field appear'd.

(148)

The Clangor of the Trumpets sounds,
The roaring Drums thunder aloud ;
Some howl with anguish of their Wounds
Whilst others hollow in the Crowd.
A Cloud of Arrows Flyes, Spears, Javelings break,
Horses by neighing do their Courage speak ;
The Clattering Swords against the Shields rebound,
And all this Noise the Ecchoing Hills resound.

4.

This dreadful Valley over-flows with blood,
Streaming from Fountains of fresh bleeding veins,
Horses with Humane-gore make up the Flood,
And undistinguish'd with their Purple stains,
    Besmear the Valley every where
While brave Theander *void of fear,*
    So generously fought,
That he at length the rash Thessalians *taught*
    That all resistance was but vain,
    And could of him nothing obtain,
    But serv'd but to prolong their pain.
Then they themselves and useless Weapons yield,
With all the Spoils and Trophies of the Field.

Cho. $\begin{cases} \textit{Thus brave Theander has our Foes opprest,} \\ \textit{And by his Noble Toyls procur'd our Rest} \end{cases}$

Martiall Dance.

King. 'Tis very well ! Come, Madam.
Queen. Sir, I must have some few Minutes discourse with
This good Priest, and then I'le wait on you.
King. Haste then, do not defer your joy ; I'm sure
It cannot trouble you to see this Night dedicated
To your belov'd *Theander*.
Queen. My joy is rather too intemperate : $\begin{cases} \textit{Exit King, manent} \\ \textit{Queen and Priest.} \end{cases}$
Poor Prince, little dost thou think I am
Acquainted with thy Guilt, and thy too great
Unkindness ! O holy Father ! this night the King
Afresh has kindled his foul Lust, he has
Once more tempted *Urania*, and I hear
She is seduc'd in earnest, and this day has seem'd
To leave the Court on purpose to avoid
Suspition.

(149)

Priest. Ye Gods that I should ever live to see
The Queen that was so spotless in her Honour
Perverted thus : what Fury or Devil does this ?
   Queen. Sir, 'Pray give me your wise Councel as you
Still have done.
   Priest. What an abject thing dissimulation is ? below
One of her birth to suffer, much less use.
   Queen. Father ! what say you !
   Priest. I know too well already what she'l do——   *Aside.*
I'le try her——Madam, do as you did before ;
And though you cannot cure this feavourish Love,
Anticipate all further Crimes.
   Queen. I did resolve to do it.
   Priest. I knew that but too well already ; the
Gods forgive you : with *Neander* too the
Vainest Trifle of the Court ? how am I afflicted !
   Queen. Well, Sir, I'le away, and strive to hide my resentment,
The better to carry on my design
   Priest. Heaven bless you, Madam—— *to her* ——   *Exit Queen.*
(*To him-* ⎱ And make you see your Crime
  self.) ⎰ In it's own horrid shape e're you attempt it,
And yet she bears it with so much assurance,
I could believe her Innocent, yet why
Should *Geron* dare to invoke all the Gods
To testifie it ; if it be false, what can
Provoke him to this Villany ? If true,
She never will acknowledge it to me
What e're it be ; 'tis worth my venturing
To be undeceiv'd.   *Ex.*

THE THIRD SCENE.

Enter King, Geron *and* Pyrrhus.

   King. Is't possible ? my Queen an Adultress ?
It cannot be : Be sure, Sir, if you accuse her
Falsly, ye shall not onely die, but
Linger out a wretched life in Torments.
   Ger. Sir ! if I lye, let me have what death
The witty'st cruelty can invent.
   Pyrr. I am amaz'd ! the Queen and Priest
In Womans Cloathes ? strange Circumstance
To meet in the Grotto, this Night ? Sure 'tis
Impossible.

Ger. Sir, I am content do dye fort, if you see not your
Self all this to Night.
    King. In the mean time, you'l be content to be secur'd ?
    Ger. Sir with all my heart.
    King. Guard ! take *Geron* and secure him till further order.

Enter Guard, and seizes him.

    Pyrr. Sir ! this dreadful news amazes me !
    King. Ah, *Pyrrhus !* in this very Grotto
I met *Urania,* and forgot the Queen,
Tho' then I thought her faithful,
And as free from any Carnal thoughts
As are departed Souls in th' other world.
    Pyrr. The Gods grant this meeting prove no worse
Than that did.
    King. O Heav'n ! methinks I see 'em already in their Luſt, yet sure it
cannot be ; if I find this Accusation false, it had been better for this fellow
he never had been born.
    Pyrr. Sir, you may yet prevent it.
    King. I may for this time, but I will not harbour
That Devil Jealousie within my Breaſt
For all this World can give me : I am resolv'd
To see the certainty my self : and if
It prove untrue, my Queen shall live with freedom,
As she has ever done, in all my thoughts,
And her Accuser fall her Sacrifice :
But if she can forget her former Vertue,
I can take as much pleasure to see her blood
Drop from the fatal Sword, as e're I did
To see it blushing on her Cheek, when firſt
I thought her modeſt.
Look ! where they come———

Enter Queen and Prieſt.

Let us withdraw ; it may be we shall
Discover something.
    Prieſt. And nothing is more Common
Then this, which is not thought a sin, because
It seems an Impulse of Nature.
    King. Hear'ſt thou, *Pyrrhus ?* I am diſtraԑed !
    Queen. The King.
    Prieſt. All happiness attend your Majeſty.
    King. I muſt contain ! how do you, Madam ?

Queen. Always happy whil'st your Majesty is so.
King. And what are you discoursing of?
Queen. Nothing! but good with this good person sure.
King. What's that you talk of which is not Sin
Because an impulse of Nature?——
Queen. What do you mean, Sir?
Priest. I know not how we came by Chance to speak
How little wantonness is thought a sin,
Because it seemeth an impulse of Nature.
Whereas the Vertuous still fix their Eyes
On the Command, not the Temptation,
And think't enough, if what Heaven gives as Law
Be Possible, although not Natural.
(*Aside.*) I would I had no cause to have said it to her.
King. 'Tis well put off——I shall never hold——   *Aside.*
To hear this Hypocrite——I must leave you——
Queen. I'le wait upon your Majesty! if it may not be a trouble.
King. To you it may be——   *Ex. King*
Queen. I see he's unwilling to disappoint *Urania*——   *Ex. Queen*
Priest. No, she's rather unwilling to disappoint *Neander*——well, for
all her cunning, I'le prevent her, my Lord, Farewell——   *Ex. Priest*
Pyrr. If I dar'd to disobey my Prince, I could prevent
This Tragedy, but what Kings
Please to Command requires obedience, not
Examination: when they once have judg'd,
'Tis want of Judgement if we dare judge too——

Enter King.

King. Pyrrhus! I had forgot one thing, thou
Know'st the Prince is expected here to morrow,
And I believe he'l be here early too: it will
Be necessary his coming be retarded,
Till the business be done, that I may know
With what face to receive him, after
All the glorious Actions he has done, I
Would not for a World he should arrive
Before the Examination be over.
Pyrr. It will be an unhappy entertainment for his Highness:
Would your Majesty have me go my self?
King. If thou canst handsomely do it, and be back early in the Morning;
it is but riding all Night; in the Morning I shall want you.
Pyrr. I shall do it with much Ease, if it be your Majesties pleasure.
King. I leave you to frame an Excuse to the Prince.

Pyrr. I'le go immediately ; I hope I shall meet better news to morrow——*Ex.*

King. I fear it :
Thus we with them in plotting do consent ;
But they plot Crimes, and we plot Punishment :
And little think they in how small a time,
Poor Fools, my Justice shall o'retake their Crime.
Men were too happy if they understood,
There is no safety but in being Good.——   *Ex.*

The End of the Fourth Act.

THE FIFTH ACT.

Enter Basilius Rex.

King. UNfortunate *Basilius !* yet durst I judge
Those happy Essences that dwell in light ;
And cannot err : I should be apt to say
My Punishment exceeds my Crime : for that
Went never further then th' intention, and

Enter Pyrrhus.

My suff'rance is real——*Pyrrhus* undone !
My Eyes are witnesses ; I saw them both
Enter the Grotto.
   Pyrr. The Priest in Womans cloaths !
   King. All's true ; The Queen has been already
Examin'd by the Councel : all she sayes
Is that she's Innocent ; but will not say
The cause which mov'd her to an action so
Suspected, tho' she dye for't : But such, *Pyrrhus,*
Are never Innocent, who are asham'd
To vindicate their Deeds, when their Lives
Are at Stake.
   Pyrr. Your Majesty was not present ?
   King. No, I leave them totally to Justice, I shall
Make the Law their Judge.
   Pyrr. But, Sir ! what says the Priest ?
   King. I now expect to hear th' Examination,

(153)

It has been very long, two hours at least :
It's bad enough for certain ; here it comes !

Enter a Lord of the Councel.

My Lord, you have been long ; but I expect
No good ; and therefore care not if you had
Been longer.
   Lord. Sir, before I can satisfie your expectations,
I must humbly pray you will be pleas'd to pardon
The intreating your Answer to a Question
On which all we have done depends.
   King. What's that ?
   Lord. I may seem too insolent : but the whole Truth
Of all the Examination does depend
Upon't ; that is, Whether your Majesty
Did not one night Command a little Lady,
That waits on the Princess, one *Urania*,
To attend you in that Grotto, where
The Queen and Priest were seiz'd on.
   King. I did.
   Lord. And she was there ?
   King. She was.
   Lord. Is your Majesty assur'd it was she, or might it be the Queen ?
   King. Ha !——her whispers were like the Queens : *Pyrrhus* knows I
told him so.
   Lord. Be happy then great Prince ;
Your Queen is Innocent ; your Priest is holy,
And *Geron* and *Neander* onely are
The Criminals.
   King. Are you assur'd of this ?
   Lord. Yes, Sir ; it was the Hellish contrivance of
Geron and *Neander* brought them both together.
   King. Why did not the Queen reveal this ?
   Lord. She rather would have dy'd than have disclos'd
Your Summons to *Urania*, which with your Majesties
Pardon, she's pleas'd to call your dishonour.
   King. My Lord, it was ; but pray relieve my Wonder,
And tell me the whole Story.
   Lord. Sir, in this Confession of *Geron* and *Neander*, and *Phronesia*,
which we, (having found them Tripping in some part of the Story) by
threatning Tortures, have extored from 'em : Your Majesty may fully
read the story of the innocence of the Queen and Priest, and of the guilt
of these Barbarous Wretches.

King. Bles't Heaven ! how are thy ways juſt like thy Orbes,
Involv'd within each other : yet ſtill we find
Thy Judgements are like Comets that do blaze,
And fright, but die withall, whil'ſt all thy Mercies
Are like the Stars which oft-times are obscur'd,
But ſtill remain the same behind the Clouds.
    Pyrr. May all your doubts and fears thus terminate.
    Lord. Thus are you shaken to be more confirm'd.
    King. Send for *Urania, Pyrrhus !* she shall wear
This day the juſt rewards of Virtue ; I
Will visit my brave Queen, who rather chose
To die unjuſtly as a Criminal
Than I should juſtly be so term'd,
For which I will proclaim my Fault, since she
Will have the Glory of concealing it.

Enter Evadne.

    Evad. The King seems pleas'd, as he has reason.
    King. My Lord ! let the Councel remove
Into the Hall, where before all the Court
I'le bring my Queen in Triumph there to hear
Her base Accusers sentenc'd.——   *Ex. all but* Evadne.
    Evad. I was told I should find *Cleantha* here——
Why did I beg to leave my Cell ?
(Where I did never injure any one)
To see this place, and in so little time
To do more mischief than whole Generations
Can parallel ? how much
Had it been better I had ever dwelt
In those Retirements, where small Sins seem great,
And great Devotions small, then to be here
Where the blood of Queens and Prieſts had like
To have been sacrific'd to the Malice of
Wicked men ? (had not the Gods taken the Cause
Into their hands.)——Madam, the

Enter Cleantha.

Queen commanded me to wait on your
Highness, with the good news of her Innocence
Being fully clear'd.
    Clean. I did not expeƈt no less : the Gods had been
Unjuſt to have left such Vertue in diſtress,
They had injur'd too themselves, as well as her :

(155)

For should such Innocence as hers not be
Protected : their Altars would be empty,
'Tis Justice makes 'em Deities.   I should be
O'rejoy'd at this, if any thing could make
Me so, when my *Endymion* mourns.

 Evad. Madam, I beseech you moderate your Grief,
At least conceal it in this time of joy ;
The Queen desires your company too : your Highness
Therefore will do well to hide your Passion.

 Clean. As well may Flames of greatest Cities be
Conceal'd from neighbouring Villages, as I
Can hide my Love and Grief : but I will wait
Upon her Majesty : she knows my Afflictions
But too well already.——   *Exeunt.*

Enter at the other door Marshall with a Guard, and Neander, Geron,
and Phronesia.

 Marsh. Come away, make haste, is it fit the King and Councel should
stay for you, or you for them ?

 Nean. They may let my business alone if they please : I am not in such
haste to have it dispatch'd.

 Ger. Well ! I shall be hang'd ; but I hope you shall be hang'd with me,
my damn'd Wife.

 Phro. No, you old Rascal, I am with Child you Villain, all the Court
knows that well enough ; I shall be spar'd, for I have an interest among
them.

 Ger. Ay, too much ! 'tis that has brought me to this.

 Marsh. Come on, or I'le make you come on ; what are you muttering
there ? my Lord, come on.

 Nean. Well, well ! Lord, you are so chollerick, you won't give a man
leave to say his Pray'rs a little, that never did before.

 Marsh. Come on.——   *Exeunt.*

Enter Lords of the Councel, and seat themselves, a Guard of Souldiers with
  Neander, Geron *and* Phronesia, *conducting them to the Bar, then the*
  King leading his Queen Crown'd, with a Royal Robe on her, after them the
  Priest, Cleantha *and Attendants.*

T*Hus from the Prison to the Throne*
   Virtue comes to claim her own,
     And now appears
Upon the Throne a Star,
Who lately at the Bar

Stood with no other Jewels but her Tears,
     Great Queen,
     Great Queen.
Who ever was so well content
To suffer, and be Innocent,
To suffer, and be Innocent.

   Enter a Gentleman leading Urania.

 King. The fair *Urania,* Madam I must this day
Do honour to this Virgin ; and since it is
To Noble Natures a more pleasing task
To give Rewards to Vertue, then Punishments
To Vice ; I'le in the first place shew
How lovely Justice looks when we are good,
And onely Sin makes her seem terrible.
 Urania ! come near.
 Gent. Ah, great King !
Urania's place I fear will be nearer
The Bar, than the Throne.
 Clean. How's this ?
 King. What mean'st thou ?
 Gent. See, Sir, see,
Those Cheeks that lately Beauty wore, now pale
With guilt.
 King. Her Crime !
 Gent. She is with Child.
 Clean. It is impossible ; she cannot dissemble so much Vertue,
I'le engage my Life she's Innocent.
 King. How know you this ?
 Gent. Sir, being sent in haste by my Lord *Pyrrhus,*
To bring her to your Majesty, by chance
I learn'd of one o' th' Servants of the Princess
Near to what place he thought she was :
I made Enquiry there, at a small House
I was acquainted at ; the Woman told me,
She thought she I enquir'd for was in the house,
And asking of me many Circumstances,
She told me it was surely she : but told me too,
As a great Secret, That she was with Child,
But that she said she was Marry'd ;
As did her Mother who this morning left her.
At this I went to *Urania,* who confes't it,

But would not tell me who her Husband was,
And was very loth to come with me, though
I told her, your Majesty had sent for her.

   King. And is this truth, *Urania?*

   1. *Lord.* Speak to the King.

   Uran. 'Tis true.

   King. And who's your Husband?

   Lord. Be not asham'd to name your Husband, Madam,
'Twill be your shame if you name none.

   Uran. I am not asham'd to name him, but affraid———

   King. Who is't, speak?

   Uran. I dare not disobey, and by my Lord
Am authoriz'd to name him, when
My Honour shall be question'd, who's more tender
Of that, then of his own.

   1. *Lord.* Name him!

   Uran. It is the Great *Theander?*

   Queen. The Prince!

   King. What are you marri'd to the Prince!
Marri'd to *Theander?*———   *Rises in a Fury.*

   Uran. O pardon me, Great King,
That I refus'd not to be taken from
A Cottage, to the bosome of a Prince,
On such Conditions as we dar'd to call
The Gods to Witness.

   King. Whether she be his Wife,
Or onely dares affirm it, though she were
More to me then my Eyes, she should
Die e're I sleep.

   Clean. Upon my Knees I beg,
Great Sir, you will recall this hasty Sentence;
It is the Prince's fault, not hers.

   King. I will hear
No Intercessions——by the Honour of a King,
I swear it.——The Prince in some few hours
Will be in Town;——if what she sayes be false,
This news shall be his welcome: but if true,
'Tis fit his coming be too late to save her.

   Uran. Ah, Great Prince, pity the distress'd who has
No friend to pleade her Cause; all I affirm
Is Truth; *Theander* is my Witness, see   *{ Takes a Letter out*
That Noble Name; this I receiv'd from him   *{ of her bosome.*
Not three dayes since.   *King reads it and gives it to the Queen.*

King. 'Tis so ; but know *Urania !*
My Crown would prove too heavy for your off-spring,
Fit onely for Cottages ; it will behove you to
Prepare for death this day within Two hours.
  Queen. Sir hold !
  Clean. I beseech your Majesty———
  King. I charge you on your Loyalty to hold ;
I swear again this day within two hours
I'le see her head off ; Marshall take her hence,
Let all things be prepar'd.
  Uran. Is there no Mercy then ? Heav'n help me !
Nothing lies heavy on me but the thoughts of
Parting with *Theander.*
  Clean. Poor *Urania !* I'le follow, and speak some comfort
To her to prepare her for her Death.
  King. My Lords, had not this Accident befaln me
I had been too blest : Wise Heav'n does see't as fit
In all our Joyes, to give us some allayes,
As in our sorrows Comforts : when our Sayls
Are fill'd with happy'st Winds, then we need most
Some heaviness to ballast us : I am afflicted
For poor *Urania ;*———but the Gods have sure
Rewards in death for those who fall, not for
Their Crimes, but through a kind of sad necessity.
Bring in the rest of the Pris'ners.
  1. *Lord.* This Sentence on *Urania* is severe.
  2. *Lord.* But Just ; for by our Law, whoever marries the Heir to the
Crown, without the Consent of King and Councel, is to suffer death.

Enter Marshall, with Geron, Neander, *and* Phronesia.

  King. I am to proceed now to a far more willing Task :
The sentencing of those most wicked persons at the Bar.
  Nean. Sir ! for Heavens sake, mercy, mercy, I beg it on my
Knees ! O spare my life.
  1. *Lord.* Silence.
  Nean. Upon my Honour, Sir.———
  King. So great a Villain, and talk of Honour.
  Nean. O spare me ! I am not fit to die ! mercy, mercy———
  King. You'r more unfit to live ; I do adjudge you———
  Nean. Hold, hold, great Sir !
  2. *Lord.* Stop his Mouth till the Sentence be past.
  King. Neander, I condemn to lose his Head to morrow, which I will
have plac'd over his Lodgings. Take him away.

Nean. Oh! that ever I was born to see this day!——oh, oh——

[*Ex. Marsh. and* Neander.

Ger. Must I be cut off in the Flower of my Age! mercy,
Mercy, Sir, I was provok'd by my Lord *Neander.*   [*Marshall returns.*

King. Peace Hell-hound! I do adjudge *Geron* to be hang'd, then cut in
pieces to morrow, and to be cast among Dogs to be devour'd.

1. *Lord.* Take him hence.

Ger. Oh, oh! yet if that Strumpet be condemn'd too,
'Twill be some comfort to me.——   *Ex. Marsh. with* Geron.

Phro. What will become of me?

King. For *Phronesia!*

Phro. O Sir! I am with Child, I am with Child: I beseech you, Sir, kill
not that within me, make me not Miscarry.

2. *Lord.* Woman be silent.

Phro. A Woman, and be silent, it is impossible, I must speak; I cannot
die, I must not die, I cannot indure it.

King. You shall not die, but suffer perpetual Banishment; what she
did was by Command from her Husband.

Phro. 'Thank your Majesty! I am glad to live, if it were for
Nothing but to see my Husband die.

King. Thus now I hope to expiate the thoughts
I've had of my chaste Queen, and Holy Priest,
Through these mens wickedness; and teach the World
That such who dare be Traytors to their King,
Do on themselves the certain'st ruine bring.

Queen. I pity those poor Wretches!

King. Come, Madam;
I must now go to see that done which will
Be much the saddest sight I ever saw,
But the Prince will be so suddenly in Town,
I must see it dispatch'd forthwith.——   *Exeunt omnes.*

Enter Neander, Geron, *and* Phronesia *in Prison.*

Nean. My Head cut off? I have not patience to think on't! Oh
Miserable, wretched man! Oh my head!

Phro. Your Lordship will not look so gracefully without a Head, though
it be none of the best.

Nean. Peace, wicked Woman!

Ger. O vile Woman! 'tis you that have brought me to this! must I
be cut in pieces?

Phro. Truly, loving Husband, you must, and be given to Doggs too,
but they'll have but ill Commons of you; you will be mighty tough;
besides, you have so many diseases, that if you were divided into as many

pieces as there are hairs in your Beard, each Morsel would own a several Malady : for my part, I would not advise any Dog that I have a kindness for, to taste of you, for fear of endangering his health.

Ger. O thou abominable filthy Hag, if thou wert to be serv'd so first, it would not trouble me.

Phro. O Sir, you would have drawn me in, but I shall live to tread upon your Grave ! you know it were ill manners for me to be hang'd before my Husband ! but how does your Lordship ? will you have some Greek-wine to comfort your cold stomach, you'l die with the fear on't else before to morrow morning ; but I beseech you, my Lord, do not forget, if you do live till then, to have a Nose-gay, and a pair of white Gloves, with clean Linnen too, for the Execution ! Men of quality are always very cleanly when they go to be hang'd.

Nean. O ! what will become of me ? I shall never be able to endure it. Oh ! you old cowardly Sot ! this comes of your confessing ; Rogue.

Ger. This may thank your villainous design, with a Curse to you, I was onely drawn in.

Nean. You deserv'd to be hang'd, Rascal, and will be so.

Ger. 'Twill be some comfort to me to have a Lord suffer with me, but 'twould be more honour to me, if that Lord were a wiser man.

Nean. O ! you old Dog ! that I could come at you.

Ger. That I could poyson you with my breath, but that 'twould put you out of your pain, which is your immoderate fear.

Enter Priest.

Priest. Peace be here !

Phro. You come as seasonably as can be, for the Traytors are at Civil War.

Priest. Away, Woman, and interrupt them not.

Phro. I will not take my leave on you, for I intend to see my dear Husband again, at least before you be cut into Messes, Farewell.——

Priest. I am now come to speak to you as dying men.   *Ex.* Phro.

Nean. Ay, ay, you old Rascal *Geron*, whom may that thank ?

Ger. A villainous Lord that corrupted a poor innocent man as I was : a Curse on him for drawing me in.

Nean. A curse upon an old Cowardly Rogue, to let his fear betray us.

Priest. Come, 'tis not now a season to quarrel with one another, but to make peace with the Gods : I am come to prepare you for your deaths, and first, *Neander*, I begin with you.

Nean. 'Pray, Sir, begin with him, he needs it most ! he has always been the most perfidious, impious Wretch.

Ger. I need it most ? I scorn to be prepar'd any more then your self, if you go to that, with that ugly, pocky Whore-masters face of your own.

Nean. Sir, it's no matter what he sayes ; he has as much malice to good men, as Whores have to honest Women.

Priest. I must first begin with you my Lord.

Ger. Look there, he knows who has most need on't.

Nean. Peace, Wisard, peace ! do you say this to me ?

Priest. Peace, stupid Wretches, I command you : and confess, and repent of your most horrid Crimes.

Nean. Well, Sir, I have done ; and I do confess from the bottom of my heart—O you old dry, raw-bon'd, wretched, decrepit Cuckold you, to bring me to this.

Priest. Heav'n ! what impiety is this ?

Ger. Ay, Sir ! you see his Devotion ? O ! Villainous wicked man.

Priest. Sir ! hold your Tongue ! my Lord, 'tis time now to be sensible of your sad condition.

Ger. Ay, Sir ! so it is, if you knew as much as I do of his wickedness, you'd say so.

Nean. Well, Sir ! I do confess, I'le torment the Rogue.　　　　[*Aside.* I have many sins to repent of——First——I have been naught with that old Fellow's Wife.

Priest. The Gods forgive you.

Ger. What do I hear ? Hell and Furies !

Priest. Do you repent of it ?

Nean. Yes, Sir ; it was a horrid Crime.

Ger. O Villain ! I'le be reveng'd of him ! it was a horrid Crime indeed ; 'twas Incest, for he is my Son, about five or six and twenty years ago, his Mother and I were a little familiar.

Priest. O impious men ! you are too near of kin in wickedness.

Nean. He like a Villain brought his Wife to me, and drew me in ; Oh wretched Pimp !

Priest. Hard-hearted Wretches, will nothing awake you ?

Enter Marshall.

Marsh. Sir, *Urania* is just ready to go to Execution, and you are expected to assist her.

Priest. Poor Lady ; I'le wait on her ! Gentlemen consider your turns are next—　　　　　　　　　　　　　　　*Ex. Priest and Marshall.*

Nean.⎱
Ger.⎰O ! what will become of me ?　　　　　　　[*They roar aloud.*

Nean. What will become of you you Rascal ; what will become of me, I am a Lord, you old Dog.

Ger. A Villainous Wretch, what care I for a Lord : what will become of me !

[*Exeunt* Geron *and* Neander.

Enter Urania (*in White, with Guards ; Musicians cloath'd in White, and other Attendants in a solemn Procession*) *led between two Gentlemen in Mourning : As they go this Song is sung, to a solemn Tune.*

L*Overs Lament, Lament this fatal day,*
When Beauties sweetest Bud is snatch'd away :
Unhappy Nymph, that could so wretched prove,
To suffer so for such a Noble Love :
A Love which was her Glory, not Offence :
The Gods will sure reward such Innocence,
Within those ever springing Groves, where she
Shall from disasters in her Love be free ;
Whither her Lov'd Theander *shall repair*
In her Eternal Joy, to claim his share.

There appears a Scaffold cover'd with Black, and Urania *led between two Gentlemen in Black : The King looks to see the Execution* [*above*].

King. Poor *Urania !* did I not fear the Prince's coming,
I could not see so sad a Spectacle : but I'le retire a little.

> 2. *Gent. lead up* Urania *to the Scaffold, and she having wip'd her Eyes, speaks to the people*,

Uran. Did any thing but my own Innocence
Lie now at stake, I should not dare to speak,
Before so many Persons, (but though I
Must quite dispair of Mercy in this World,
I hope I may find Charity, and that
The good will credit a poor dying Person,
Altho' she bring no Witness but her Vows :
All I am now condemn'd for, is my Birth,
Which seems indeed a Misery, but not
A Crime ; for if it were, I could not help it :
My Poverty must be reliev'd with Death.
But though I can
Find no forgiveness in the world, I am glad
I find it in my self : I freely can
Forgive who e're have injur'd me, and this
Is some ease to me, though perchance the living
Do little heed the pardons of the dead.
Gent. Poor Lady, my heart mourns for her.
Uran. I do not know I e're did harm to any,

Onely my Lord *Endymion* I did once
Delude to save my life, would Heav'n I had not ;
But he is merciful to others, though
He has met with little for himself.
    Evad. If pitty poor *Urania* could do thee good,
Thou haſt enough on't.
    Uran. I do confess I'm marri'd to the Prince ;
But he will witness for me 'twas th' effect
Of his own Choice : I never presum'd
To think it till he told me it should be so ;
Since when how faithful I have been to him,
Witness ! Oh ! Heaven ! and all those Powers that dare
Acquit whom Kings condemn ; and tho' for this
I now muſt suffer death, I cannot wish
I had not don't, since 'twas the Prince's pleasure,
Whom to contradict, to me were worse then death.
    Gent. Alas ! I pity her, her Case is too severe.
    Uran. And yet I feel
That Death is bitter, 'tis an Enemy
Looks cruelly on those who have no friends :
'Tis hard to undergo the greateſt Task alone ;
But 'tis my Fate, and Heaven muſt be obey'd——
——'Tis a long hazard that we run in death,
And a short warning rather does diſturb
Then fit us for it ; were't not for this,
I could be well content to close these Eyes
That have of late beheld so little pleasure.
    Marsh. She draws Tears from my Eyes ; I was not wont
To be so soft.
    Uran. But I too long
Detain you with Complaints, whose business is
To see me die : Live happy, brave *Theander,*
May all thy Sorrows die with thy *Urania,*
And all those Joyes live with thee which she took
In thy Contents.——May'ſt thou be happy in
A Princess, great as thy own Merits, bright
As thy own Eyes, and vertuous as
Are all thy Thoughts ; and may she honour thee
As truly as thy poor *Urania* did.
    Execu. Are you ready, Madam ?
    Uran. Who is this ?
    Gent. Madam, 'tis your Deſtiny.
    Uran. O, it is he.

Sir, you can instruct me what I am to do ;
I never yet saw any body die.

 Gent. Madam, you must kneel.

 Uran. How will he strike?

 Gent. With all the mercy that he can.

 Execu. When you have ended all you have to say,
Pray kneel with your Face that way, and give
Some sign when I shall strike.

 Uran. I will.

 Evad. I cannot stay to see't ; Farewell, dear *Urania.*——   *Ex.* Evad.

 Uran. When I am dead, pray, Sirs, suffer none
But my Mother to fit me for my Grave ;
She will be careful of me, she will pay
Holy devotions for me, and bedew
With pious Tears that face she still has lov'd :
And may the Gods give comforts in her sorrows,
And all those Stars which have been hard to me
Be merciful to her——May my misfortune
Work in her onely a more true content
In the low Sphere she so securely moves in.

 Execu. I think she'll ne're a done prating, they all keep such a coile when they come to die : Wou'd the King wou'd please to forbid all Speeches upon Scaffolds.

 Uran. Sirs ! Farewel, pray present
My humble Service to my Noble Princess,
With thanks for all her Favours, in my life,
And Charity in death——bless'd Gods assist me.——   *Kneels.*
Pray expect the Sign.

 Execu. I shall.——

   Enter in haste Parthenia, *Urania's Mother.*

 Parth. Stay, stay the fatal Blow.

 King. What's this?

 Parth. A miserable Mother come to save her onely Child.

 King. Executioner, do your Office. [*One of the Gent. layes hold of the*

 Parth. Great King, dread Sovereign, hear,   *Executioner.*
Hear a distress'd Mother, hear for their sakes
That at your death must hear you.

 King. What will you say?

 Parth. My Child is innocent.

 King. Do your Office Executioner.

 Parth. O stay, stay, Great King, *Urania* is
A Princess born, her Father was a King.

King. What say you ?
Parth. Urania's Father was a King.
Great, but Unfortunate, the King of *Thrace.*
    King. It is impossible, the King of *Thrace ?*
And what are you ?
    Parth. Great King, I'm now your Subject,
My name *Parthenia,* and my habitation
A little Cottage : but I once was known
By the name of *Cleopatra,* and was Wife
To *Pyrocles* the vertuous Prince of *Thrace.*
Of whom all that remains besides his Fame
Is this poor Child, for whom I beg your mercy,
Not to extinguish with one stroke all that
The strokes of Fate have left among the ruines
Of a late glorious Family.
    King. Her Language !
Bespeaks her something else than her Habit :
'Tis strange——but how do you make this good
Which you affirm ?——how came you to *Arcadia ?*
    Parth. Will your Majesty be pleas'd to hear my Story ?
I shall be brief.
    King. Speak on !
But if you speak not truth, you shall partake
Your Daughters Fate.
    Parth. Let it be so !
I shall not now repeat the long misfortunes
Of my unhappy Prince by that dire War
His Rebel Subjects rais'd against him through
His too great Goodness : These reports enough
Already have afflicted all good Ears,
And all good Hearts : I onely now shall tell you
When he had acted out his Tragedy——
    King. That we have all heard.
    Parth. Next they came
To his Relations ; how they did betray
And butcher diverse of them, all have heard,
And I have felt ; I having then remaining
Of all my Children but two Daughters, whereof
One being 14 years of age, was before our ruine
Contracted to the Prince of *Macedon* (and is since dead ;)
The other, this poor Child (then but some few months old)
And knowing how soon Kingdoms
Grow weary of th'Unfortunate,

Resolv'd for safety to retire
To some small place, such as my narrow Fortune
Could make my own, and there to buy my peace
With my obscurity, hither then I came,
Invited by the peace of this bless'd Region,
And purchas'd the small Cottage where I live,
And learn'd to change a Scepter for a Sheep-hook,
And thus I bred my Child.
  King. But ſtay!
Is't probable in all that time you should not
Acquaint *Urania* with her Birth?
  Parth. I never did,
Not willing to diſturb those sweet contents
She took in being all she hop'd to be;
And all she underſtood, she felt no care;
And with more pleasure govern'd her small Flock,
Then her unhappy Father his great Kingdom.
  King. Pyrrhus! She does not speak amiss, and has
Methinks the look and meen of a Woman of Quality.
  Parth. But Heaven that oft
Affronts the higheſt probabilities,
And gratifies by wayes that were never thought of;
In this low Ebb, when all my hopes were grown
More proſtrate than my Fortune, does begin
To dawn upon me, and inſtruct me, those
Are neerer it, who kneel in humble Cells,
Than such as ſtand on Tiptoe on high Towers.
For now *Theander* makes *Urania* more
A Princess, then a Kingdom could, by courting
Her as a Shepherdess, and shews the World,
That more then Chance conduc'd to her Greatness.
  King. Why did you not tell *Theander* the whole truth?
  Parth. Sir, he marry'd her at Court, and I knew not of it
Till he was gone to the War in *Thessaly*:
For witness of all this, I do invoke
Those Pow'rs, who never teſtifie untruths;
And here produce those small Remains of Greatness
Misfortune yet hath left me; See, Sir, here   {*She shews several*
That so fam'd Jewel which so many Kings   {*rich Jewels.*
Of *Thrace* have worn, and with such veneration
Have ſtill preserv'd on an old Prophesie, that
This should preserve the *Thracian* Family.
  King. Pyrrhus! 'tis all true! Go tell the Queen and Princess this: [*Ex.*
        (167)   *Pyrr.*

I need no Testimony but those words,
All Queens might blush to hear from Cottagers,
But is it possible so mean a place
So long should hold great *Cleopatra* ?
 Parth. Know, great Prince (and know it too
From one who has experimented Greatness)
When I had satisfi'd my self in my
Endeavours of regaining my lost Rights,
And saw 'em all unprosperous, (as if
Heaven long enough had given one Family
The priviledge to govern others)
I was as well content to be the first
Must learn to act with common People,
As he who first was call'd from them to rule.
 King. Great Queen,
The Prophesie is now fulfill'd, That Jewel
Will serve to satisfy the World as much
Of all you say, as your own Words have me :
And thus preserves the *Thracian* Family,—— *Embraces* Urania.
Dear Daughter ! still be happy and forgive
Our ignorance ; I cannot love thee better
Then at that very time I did condemn thee,
I could as well have sentenc'd my two Eyes ;
And pardon me, dear Sister, if I first—— *Salutes* Cleopatra.
Ask'd pardon where I most did need it.
Call the Queen, and tell *Cleantha Urania* is alive.
 Parth. Now, my dear Daughter, thou art safe within my Arms.
 Uran. Madam, it onely did belong to you
Who gave me life, thus to preserve it too—— *Trumpets within.*
 King. What's this ?
 Gent. The Prince is come.
 King. What will *Theander* say, to see his dear *Urania*
Thus attir'd at his return ?
 Uran. He'l say you'r mercifull.

   Enter Queen, Cleantha, *and* Pyrrhus.

 King. Madam, see here Great *Cleopatra*
And call her Sister ; take, *Cleantha* !
Her thou hast wept for : *Pyrrhus* has told you all.

    Enter Theander.

My Son ! never more welcome ! never { *The Prince fixes his*
Did more Joy spring from more sorrow. { *Eyes on* Urania.

Thean. Bless me, dread Sir !
What Scene does entertain me ?   Are your Joyes
Exprest by Sacrifice ?
  King.   *Theander,* take,
Take thy *Urania,* and wonder not
At any thing but her.
  Thean. My Triumphs are more dreadful than my Conquests.
  Queen. My Son, be happy
In thy best Choice ; let not thy wonder make
Us longer languish.
  Thean. Madam, I'le believe,
And hope in time to understand——dear Cozen——   { *Goes to salute*
 Clean. Sir, when you first have done   { Cleantha.
Your Duty to the Queen of *Thrace,* your Mother,
Then to your *Urania,* I shall be thankful for
The honour you too early wou'd vouchsafe me.
  Thean. I must obey what Heaven knows when
I shall understand.———   *Salutes* Cleopatra.
This is an earlier Tribute than I thought———   *To* Urania.
To pay your Lips : (my dear *Urania*) But why
Do'st thou conspire to my distraction ? why
This Habit, and why these Tears ?
  King. Heav'n bless you both !
And may your Loves increase still with your days :
May you be fresh as Spring, as Autumn fruitful,
And know no Winter of adversity ;
And may the Gods that have done Wonders in your Loves
Do Wonders in the effects of it.
  Thean. Sure this is all a Vision ! am I awake ?

Enter Priest.

 Priest. A day full of Wonders !
 King. A day all Miracle !
How mercifull is Heaven ; who would be bad
When Vertue's thus rewarded in distress ?
  Thean. Couzen, your pardon,——   *Salutes* Cleantha.
Happy is this meeting ;——   *To all.*
I am oblig'd for all the Joy I see
Start out of Sorrow now at my Return.
  Clean. Heav'n give you Joy of your *Urania.*
  Thean. You have oblig'd me, Madam, that you have
Dealt so gently with your Servant.

Clean. She ne're had been esteem'd so, had you thought
Me worthy of your Councel, Sir ; but now I shall endeavour
To repay her all
Those services I have receiv'd from her.

 Thean. She is still your Servant, Cozen.

 Clean. (*aside.*) How can there be such Joy, when brave
Endymion lives in unjust Banishment ?

 Thean. I long to ease my wonder, and to know
The story of great *Cleopatra*, how
She has been so long obscur'd to all the World
But to her self.

 King. Wee'l find a Scene for that,
Less like the Face of sorrow, ('tis enough.
Urania is a Princess) and had Fortune
In ought but in her blindness been like Justice
Had worn the Crown of *Thrace*, onely my Daughter
My dear *Urania*, ask me on this place,
I so have injur'd thee, what I shall do
To expiate my Ignorance of thy Worth,
Ask what thou wilt, I'le not deny it.

 Uran. I want not a Request, had I but merit
And Confidence to ask it.

 King. If you do not ask it, you choose the perfect way
To disoblige me.

 Uran. It is *Endymion*'s Liberty ; pardon, Sir, the boldness
You'r pleas'd to give me, and the Gratitude
I hope I ne're shall lose.

 King. You have my Word, do with it what you please,
I'll give you Order for't.

 Thean. Your pardom, Sir,
If your Commands already are obey'd,
Endymion is return'd, I met him e're
He was imbarqu'd, and having been inform'd,
From my *Urania* of all his Cares for her,
I stay'd him, hoping from your Goodness to
Obtain his Pardon, for the Love *Cleantha*
So truly bears him. I have no more to say
Against it than against my own I had
For my *Urania* when I thought her less :
And since the Gods have made her Great for me,
'Twill be but gratitude in me to do
Some of their business for them, and reward
So brave a Vertue as *Endymion* owns,

And make him great for his *Cleantha* too.
   Clean. Is *Endymion* return'd ? O happy hour !
   Thean. The War in *Thessaly* has found an happy end,
And there I've left
Those hands that made that Scepter stoop, who, now,
Want but a Scene to do new wonders in,
And this may prove rebellious *Thrace*, if you,
Sir, think fit I wear that Crown *Urania* gives me ;
In this Conquest, the brave *Endymion*
Shall be my second ; what shall I not expect from
Such vertue and such valour when they meet ?
   King. I have of late receiv'd such mercies, that
I cannot think of any thing which looks
Like Cruelty. Therefore wonder not
All that you ask so soon is granted you,
Cleantha ; Take then your *Endymion ;* be
More blest in him than Greatness e're could make you.
   Queen. And now you'r doing works of mercy, Sir,
I beg for the sake of this glorious day
Which is a day of mercy to us all,
That *Geron* and *Neander* may not die,
But suffer Banishment for life.
   King. What you propose has much of Piety ;
I'le not deny't : and now I've one request
To you my honour'd Priest, your leave
That *Pyrrhus* my best Confident may serve
The fair *Evadne.*
   Priest. You oblige me Sir to make me see
My poor *Evadne* is so much your care,
It shall be mine ; she still shall think that best
Your Majesty is pleas'd to chuse for her.

Enter Endymion.

   Thean. *Endymion !* why so slowly to thy Joyes ?   } *Kneels and kisses*
Reap here the fruits of Gratitude and Mercy.   } *Cleantha's hand.*
   Clean. Welcome my Lord.
   Queen. My Lord, you'r welcome from your Banishment.
   King. You've onely now this Ladies leave to ask
For any thing you'd have.
   Endym. I am happy in your Royal mercy, Sir,
And hope in time to be so too in hers.
Madam, I hope your Highness has the Charity
To pardon your poor Servant, who was the

(171)

Unwilling occasion of so much injury
To so Noble a Princess.
   Clean. You need not fear
Your Sentence, when *Cleantha* is your Judge.
   King. Let us all away, and satisfie our selves with what
We have so long travail'd with, and let the World
Learn from this story, Those that are vertuous
Cannot be long in Clouds ; Innocence conceal'd is the
Stoln pleasure of the Gods, which never ends
In shame as that of Men does oft times, but
Like the Sun breaks forth, when he has
Gratifi'd another World, and to our Eyes appears
More Glorious through his late obscurity.
   Priest. The Impious here a while may find some Rest,
But in the End the good are only blest.   *Ex. omnes.*

FINIS.

Epilogue.

AS a young Merchant who had scap'd of late
   The wrack of all his Wealth, and his own Fate,
When that comes home which he had giv'n for lost,
Would fain preserve what had so dearly cost:
With other Men he ventures little shares
In other Bottoms, but not all his Wares;
Preserving still wherewith to put to Sea
Again, if what he has ventur'd Shipwrackt be.
So our Adventurer, who not long since past
Through these most dang'rous Seas with storms o'recast,
And brought his little Vessel home at last:
Unwilling now to meet another shock,
Has in this Bottom ventur'd some small stock:
Which if you suffer to come safely home,
It may encourage him for time to come;
But if you sink this Vessel, yet he will
Keep on a little Trade a going still.
He sayes you cannot break him, if you do,
But (whatsoe're he sayes) I beg that you
To us will be good natur'd but this day,
And pardon all the Errors in our Play.

The Humorists;

A

COMEDY.

ACTED

By his **ROYAL HIGHNESSES**

Servants.

Written

By **THO. SHADWELL**,

Of the Middle Temple.

——*Quis iniquæ*
Tam patiens urbis tam ferreus ut teneat se.

LONDON,

Printed for *Henry Herringman*, at the Sign of the *Blew Anchor* in the *Lower Walk* of the *New Exchange*. 1671.

Source.

THE incidents in *The Humorists* seem to be original, in fact, the play depends far more upon the juxtaposition of characters, or rather humours, than upon any intrigue. It is certainly a sufficiently realistic picture of town life in 1670. Crazy can hardly have suggested Florio in Crowne's *City Politiques*, produced at Drury Lane in January 1682–3, since Florio is merely feigning to be dying of the diseases his vices brought upon him, whilst Mr. Crazy is really afflicted. With Crazy, however, may be compared the French valet Dufoy in Etherege's *The Comical Revenge ; or, Love in a Tub*, produced at Lincoln's Inn Fields in 1664. In D'Urfey's *The Fond Husband ; or, The Plotting Sisters*, produced at Dorset Garden in the spring of 1676, and long one of the most popular of his comedies, Cordelia and Sir Roger visiting young Sneak at his lodging find him in a night-gown with an Apothecary in attendance, and the lady, moreover, discovers that a sweating-chair is part of his furniture. " 'Tis a Mathematical Engine they use at Cambridge," blusters Sir Roger trying to pass it off, but the nature of the disease from which the hapless undergraduate is suffering is only too thoroughly exposed. Perhaps Sneak owes something to Sir Roger in *The Scornful Lady*, but although undeniably amusing, he stands far below that immortal figure. The return of a husband supposed dead, who disguises himself, and thus is able to keep an eye on his wife's lewdness is an old story. It forms the main theme of Steele's *The Funeral ; or, Grief A-la-mode*, produced at Drury Lane in the winter of 1701, although in this comedy Lord Brumpton, who is supposed dead is concealed, and not in masquerade. It is perhaps worth noting that in a very different play Southerne's *The Fatal Marriage ; or, The Innocent Adultery*, produced at Drury Lane in 1693–4, Biron, the husband of Isabella who returns, is reported to have been killed at Candia, where it was said that Sir Richard Loveyouth fell.

Theatrical History.

*T*HE *Humorists* was produced at Lincoln's Inn Fields early in 1671, probably January or February. Shadwell complains that it "came upon the Stage with all the disadvantages imaginable." He had had to make drastic alterations, presumably during rehearsals. None the less a certain party, who may have been friends of Sir Robert Howard resenting the caricature of Sir Positive At-all, formed a clique, which was resolved to damn the play. Moreover, the actors were, in the jargon of to-day, " fluffy " ; or in Shadwell's neater phrase " extremely imperfect in the Action of it." The first performance was anything but a success, and perhaps it would hardly have survived had not Mrs. Johnson introduced various dances which attracted large audiences, who at last began to receive the comedy with some share of applause. Charles II also liked it, and by these recommendations " the poor Play's life was prolonged." In spite of all it seems never to have been a great favourite, and there are no records of any particular revival, so we are probably safe in surmising that in a few years it fell out of the usual repertory.

A dramatic entertainment entitled *The Humourists* was acted at Drury Lane in 1754, but has not been printed. James Cobb's farce *The Humorist*, produced with considerable success at Drury Lane in 1785, has nothing in common with Shadwell's comedy.

To the most Illustrious Princess

M A R G A R E T

D U T C H E S S

O F

NEWCASTLE.

May it please your Grace,

THE *favourable Reception my* Impertinents *found from your Excellent Lord, and my Noble* Patron, *and the great mercy your* Grace *has for all offenders of this kind, have made me presume humbly to lay this* Comedy *at your feet : for none can, better than your* Grace, *protect this mangled, persecuted Play from the fury of its Enemies and Detractors, who by your admirable Endowments of Nature and Art, have made all Mankind your Friends and Admirers. You have not been content only to surmount all your own Sex in the excellent Qualities of a Lady and a Wife, but you must overcome all ours in wit and understanding. All our Sex have reason to envy you, and your own to be proud of you, which by you have obtained an absolute Victory over us. It were a vain thing in me to endeavour to commend those excellent Pieces that have fallen from your* Graces *Pen, since all the* World *does. And this is not intended for a Panegyrick, but a Dedication, which I humbly desire your* Grace *to pardon.*

The Play was intended a Satyr against Vice and Folly, and to whom is it more properly to be presented than to your Grace ? *who are, above all your Sex, so eminent in Wit and Vertue. I have been more obliged by my Lord* Duke *than by any man, and to whom can I shew my gratitude better than to your* Grace, *that are so excellent a part of him ? But, Madam, this trifle of mine is a very unsuitable return to be made for his favours and the Noble Present of all your excellent Books. But I hope your* Grace *will forgive me, when you consider, that the Interest of all*

(181)

Poets is to fly for protection to Welbecke ; *which will never fail to be their Sanctuary, so long as there you are pleased so nobly to patronize Poesie, and so happily practise it. That will still be the onely place where they will find encouragement that do well, and pardon that do ill ; and of the latter of these no Man has more need than*

Madam,

Your Graces

Most humble and obedient

Servant

Tho. Shadwell.

Preface.

THis Play (besides the Errors in the writing of it) came upon the Stage with all the disadvantages imaginable : First, I was forced, after I had finish'd it, to blot out the main design of it ; finding, that, contrary to my intention, it had given offence. The second disadvantage was, that notwithstanding I had (to the great prejudice of the Play) given satisfaction to all the exceptions made against it, it met with the clamorous opposition of a numerous party, bandied against it, and resolved, as much as they could, to damn it, right or wrong, before they had heard or seen a word on't. The last, and not the least, was, that the *Actors* (though since they have done me some right) at first were extreamly imperfect in the Action of it. The least of these had been enough to have spoil'd a very good Comedy, much more such a one as mine. The last (*viz.*) imperfect Action, had like to have destroy'd *She would if she could,* which I think (and I have the Authority of some of the best Judges in *England* for't) is the best Comedy that has been written since the Restauration of the Stage : And even that, for the imperfect representation of it at first, received such prejudice, that, had it not been for the favour of the *Court,* in all probability it had never got up again, and it suffers for it ; in a great measure to this very day. This of mine, after all these blows, had fall'n beyond Redemption, had it not been revived, after the second day, by her kindness (which I can never enough acknowledge) who, for four days together, beautified it with the most excellent *Dancings* that ever has been seen upon the Stage. This drew my enemies, as well as friends, till it was something better acted, understood, and liked, than at first : By this means the poor Play's life was prolonged, and, I hope, will live in spight of Malice ; if not upon the Stage, at least in Print.

Yet do not think I will defend all the faults of it : Before it was alter'd I could better have answer'd for it : Yet, as it is, I hope it will not wholly displease you in the reading. I should not say so much for it, if I did not find so much undeserved malice against it.

My design was in it, to reprehend some of the Vices and Follies of the Age, which I take to be the most proper, and most useful way of writing Comedy. If I do not perform this well enough, let not my endavors be blam'd.

Here I must take leave to dissent from those, who seem to insinuate that the ultimate end of a Poet is to delight, without correction or in-

(183)

struction : Methinks a Poet should never acknowledge this, for it makes him of as little use to Mankind as a Fidler, or Dancing-Master, who delights the fancy onely, without improving the Judgement.

Horace, the best Judge of Poetry, found other business for a Poet.

> *Pectus præceptis format amicis,*
> *Asperitatis & Invidiæ, corrector & Iræ,*
> *Recte facta refert, orientia tempora notis*
> *Instruit Exemplis :*

I confess, a Poet ought to do all that he can, decently to please, that so he may instruct. To adorn his Images of *Vertue* so delightfully to affect people with a secret veneration of it in others, and an emulation to practice it in themselves : And to render their Figures of *Vice* and *Folly* so ugly and detestable, to make People hate and despise them, not only in others, but (if it be possible) in their dear selves. And in this latter, I think Comedy more useful than Tragedy ; because the Vices and Follies in *Courts* (as they are too tender to be touch'd) so they concern but a few ; whereas the Cheats, Villanies, and troublesome Follies, in the common conversation of the World, are of concernment to all the Body of Mankind.

And a Poet can no more justly be censured for ill nature, in detesting such *Knaveries*, and troublesom impertinencies, as are an imposition on all good Men, and a disturbance of Societies in general, than the most vigilant of our Judges can be thought so, for detesting Robbers and High-way-men, who are hanged, not for the sake of the money they take (for of what value can that be to the life of a man) but for interrupting common communication, and disturbing Society in general. For the sake of good men, ill should be punished ; and 'tis ill nature to the first, not to punish the last. A man cannot truly love a good man, that does not hate a bad one ; nor a Wiseman, that does not hate a Fool ; this love and hatred are correlatives, and the one necessarily implies the other. I must confess it were ill nature, and below a man, to fall upon the natural imperfections of men, as of Lunaticks, Ideots, or men born monstrous. But these can never be made the proper subject of a Satyr, but the affected vanities, and the artificial fopperies of men, which, (sometimes even contrary to their natures) they take pains to acquire, are the proper subject of a Satyr.

And for the reformation of Fopps and Knaves, I think Comedy most useful, because to render Vices and Fopperies very ridiculous, is much a greater punishment than Tragedy can inflict upon 'em. There we do but subject 'em to hatred, or at worst to death ; here we make them live to be despised and laugh'd at, which certainly makes more impression upon men, than even death can do.

Again, I confess a Poet ought to endeavour to please, and by this way of writing may please, as well as by any way whatsoever, (if he writes it well) when he does

Simul & Jucunda & idonea dicere vitæ.

Men of Wit and Honour, and the best Judges (and such as cannot be touch'd by Satyr) are extreamly delighted with it ; and for the rest

Odi profanum vulgus & Arceo.

The rabble of little People, are more pleas'd with *Jack-Puddings* being soundly kick'd, or having a Custard handsomely thrown in his face, than with all the wit in Plays : and the higher sort of Rabble (as there may be a rabble of very fine people in this illiterate Age) are more pleased with the extravagant and unnatural actions the trifles, and fripperies of a Play, or the trappings and ornaments of Nonsense, than with all the wit in the world.

This is one reason why we put our Fopps into extravagant, and unnatural habits ; it being a cheap way of conforming to the understanding of those brisk, gay Sparks, that judge of Wit or Folly by the Habit ; that being indeed the only measure they can take in judging of Mankind, who are Criticks in nothing but a Dress.

Extraordinary pleasure was taken of old, in the Habits of the Actors, without reference to sense, which *Horace* observes, and reprehends in his Epistle to *Augustus*

Garganum mugire putes nemus, aut Mare Tuscum,
Tanto cum strepitu ludi spectantur, & Artes,
Divitiæque peregrinæ, quibus oblitus actor,
Cum stetit in scena, concurrit dextera Lævæ,
Dixit adhuc aliquid ! nil sane, quid placet ergo ?

But for a Poet to think (without wit or good humor, under such a Habit) to please men of sense, is a presumption inexcusable. If I be guilty of this, it is an error of my understanding, not of my will. But I challenge the most clamorous and violent of my Enemies (who would have the Town believe that every thing I write, is too nearly reflecting upon persons) to accuse me, with truth, of representing the real Actions, or using the peculiar, affected phrases, or manner of speech of any one particular Man, or Woman living.

I cannot indeed create a new Language, but the Phantastick Phrases, used in any Play of mine, are not appropriate to any one *Fop*, but applicable to many.

Good men, and men of sence, can never be represented but to their advantage, nor can the Characters of Fools, Knaves, Whores, or Cowards (who are the people I deal most with in Comedies) concern any that are

(185)

not eminently so : Nor will any apply to themselves what I write in this kind, that have but the wit, or honesty, to think tolerably well of themselves.

But it has been objected, that good men, and men of sence enough, may have blind-sides, that are liable to reprehension, and that such men should be represented upon a Stage, is intollerable.

'Tis true, excellent men may have errors, but they are not known by them, but by their excellencies : their prudence overcomes all gross follies, or conceals the less vanities, that are unavoidable Concomitants of humane nature ; or if some little errors do escape 'em, and are known, they are the least part of those men, and they are not distinguished in the world by them, but by their perfections ; so that (if such blind-sides, or errors be represented) they do not reflect upon them, but upon such on whom these are predominant ; and that receive such a Biass from 'em, that it turns 'em wholly from the wayes of Wisdom or Morality.

And even this representation, does not reflect upon any particular man, but upon very many of the same kind : For if a man should bring such a humor upon the Stage (if there be such a humor in the world) as only belongs to one, or two persons, it would not be understood by the Audience, but would be thought (for the singularity of it) wholly unnatural, and would be no jest to them neither.

But I have had the fortune to have had a general humor (in a Play of mine) applied to three, or four men (whose persons I never saw, or humors ever heard of) till the Play was acted.

As long as men wrest the Writings of Poets to their own corrupted sense, and with their Clamors prevail too, you must never look for a good Comedy of Humour, for a humor (being the representation of some extravagance of Mankind) cannot but in some thing resemble some man, or other, or it is monstrous, and unnatural.

After this restraint upon Poets, there is little scope left, unless we retrieve the exploded Barbarismes of Fool, Devil, Giant, or Monster, or translate French Farces, which, with all the wit of the English, added to them, can scarce be made tollerable.

Mr. *Johnson*, I believe, was very unjustly taxed for personating particular men, but it will ever be the fate of them, that write the humours of the *Town*, especially in a foolish, and vicious Age. Pardon me (*Reader*) that I name him in the same Page with my self ; who pretend to nothing more, than to joyn with all men of sense and learning in admiration of him ; which, I think, I do not out of a true understanding of him ; and for this I would not value my self. Yet by extolling his way of writing, I cannot but insinuate to you that I can practise it ; though I would if I could, a thousand times sooner than any mans.

And here I must make a little digression, and take liberty to dissent from my particular friend, for whom I have a very great respect, and whose Writings I extreamly admire ; and though I will not say his is the best way of Writing, yet, I am sure, his manner of Writing it is much the best that ever was. And I may say of him, as was said of a Celebrated Poet, *Cui unquam Poetarum magis proprium fuit subito æstro incalescere ? Quis, ubi incaluit, fortius, & fælicius debacchatur.* His Verse is smother and deeper, his thoughts more quick and surprising, his raptures more mettled and higher ; and he has more of that in his writing, which *Plato* calls σώφρονα μανίαν, than any other Heroick Poet. And those who shall go about to imitate him, will be found to flutter, and make a noise, but never rise. Yet (after all this) I cannot think it impudent in him, or any Man to endeavour to imitate Mr. *Johnson,* whom he confesses to have fewer failings than all the English Poets, which implies he was the most perfect, and best Poet ; and why should not we endeavour to imitate him ? because we cannot arrive to his excellence ? 'Tis true we cannot, but this is no more an argument, than for a Soldier (who considers with himself he cannot be so great a one as *Julius Cæsar*) to run from his Colours, and be none ; or to speak of a less thing, why should any man study *Mathematicks* after *Archimedes, &c.* This Principle would be an obstruction to the progress of all learning and knowledge in the world. Men of all Professions ought certainly to follow the best in theirs-theirs, and let not endeavours be blamed, if they go as far as they can in the right way, though they be unsuccessful, and attain not their ends. If Mr. *Johnson* be the most faultless Poet, I am so far from thinking it impudence to endeavour to imitate him, that it would rather (in my opinion) seem impudence in me not to do it

I cannot be of their opinion who think he wanted wit, I am sure, if he did, he was so far from being the most faultless, that he was the most faulty Poet of his time, but it may be answered, that his Writings were correct, though he wanted fire ; but I think flat and dull things are as incorrect, and shew as little Judgment in the Author, nay less than sprightly and mettled Nonsense does. But I think he had more true Wit than any of his Contemporaries ; that other men had sometimes things that seemed more fiery than his, was because they were placed with so many sordid and mean things about them, that they made a greater show.

> *Inter quæ verbum emicuit, si forte, decorum,*
> *Si versus paulo concinnor, unus, & alter,*
> *Injuste totum ducit, venditque Poema.*

Nor can I think, to the writing of his humors (which were not only the follies, but vices and subtilties of men) that wit was not required, but judgment ; where by the way, they speak as if judgment were a less thing than wit. But certainly it was meant otherwise by nature, who subjected wit to the government of judgment, which is the noblest faculty of the mind. Fancy rough-draws, but judgement smooths and finishes ; nay judgment does indeed comprehend wit, for no man can have that who has not wit. In fancy madmen equal, if not excell all others, and one may as well say, that one of those mad men is as good a man, as a temperate wise man, as that one of the very fanciful Plays (admired most by Women) can be so good a Play as one of *Johnson*'s correct, and well-govern'd Comedies.

The reason given by some, why *Johnson* needed not wit in writing humor, is, because humor is the effect of observation, and observation the effect of judgment ; but observation is as much necessary in all other Plays, as in Comedies of humor : For first, even in the highest Tragedies, where the Scene lies in Courts, the Poet must have observed the Customs of Courts, and the manner of conversing there, or he will commit many indecencies, and make his Persons too rough and ill-bred for a Court.

Besides Characters in Plays being Representations of the Vertues or Vices, Passions or Affections of Mankind, since there are no more new Vertues or Vices ; Passions or Affections, the Idea's of these can no other way be receiv'd into the imagination of a Poet, but either from the Conversation or Writings of Men. After a Poet has formed a Character (as suppose of an Ambitious Man) his design is certainly to write it naturally, and he has no other rule to guid him in this, but to compare him with other men of that kind, that either he has heard of, or conversed with in the world, or read of in Books (and even this reading of Books is conversing with men) nay more ; (besides judging of his Character) the Poet can fancy nothing of it, but what must spring from the Observation he has made of Men or Books.

If this argument (that the enemies of humor use) be meant in this sense, that a Poet, in the writing of a Fools Character, needs but have a man sit to him, and have his words and actions taken ; in this case there is no need of wit. But 'tis most certain that if we should do so, no one fool (though the best about the Town) could appear pleasantly upon the Stage, he would be there too dull a Fool, and must be helped out with a great deal of wit in the Author. I scruple not to call it so, First, because 'tis not your down-right Fool that is a fit Character for a Play, but like Sir *John Dawe* and Sir *Amorous la Foole*, your witty, brisk, airy *Fopps* that are *Entreprennants*. Besides wit in the Writer, (I think, without any Authority for it) may be said to be the invention of remote and pleasant thoughts of what kind soever ; and there is as much occasion for such imaginations in the writing of a Curious Coxcomb's part, as in writing the greatest Hero's ; and that which may be Folly in the Speaker, may be so remote and pleasant, to require a great deal of wit in the Writer. The most Excellent *Johnson* put wit into the mouths of the meanest of his people, and which, is infinitely difficult, made it proper for 'em. And I once heard a Person, of the greatest Wit and Judgement of the Age, say, that *Bartholomew Fair* (which consists most of low persons) is one of the Wittiest Plays in the World. If there be no wit required in the rendering Folly ridiculous, or Vice odious, we must accuse *Juvenal* the best Satyrist, and wittiest Man of all the Latine Writers, for want of it.

I should not say so much of Mr. *Johnson* (whose Merit sufficiently justifies him to all Men of Sense) but that I think my self a little obliged to vindicate the Opinion I publickly declared, in my *Epilogue* to this *Play;* which I did upon mature consideration, and with a full satisfaction in my Judgement, and not out of a bare affected vanity of being thought his Admirer.

I have only one word more, to trouble you with, concerning this Trifle of my own, which is, that as it is at present, it is wholly my own, without borrowing a tittle from any man; which I confess is too bold an attempt for so young a Writer; for (let it seem what it will) a Comedy of humor (that is not borrowed) is the hardest thing to write well; and a way of writing, of which a man can never be certain.

> *Creditur, ex medio quia res accessit, habere*
> *Sudoris minimum, sed habet comœdia tanto*
> *Plus oneris, quanto veniæ minus.*

That which (besides judging truly of Mankind) makes Comedy more difficult, is that the faults are naked and bare to most people, but the wit of it understood, or valued, but by few. Wonder not then if a man of ten times my parts, miscarries in the attempt.

I shall say no more of this of mine, but that the Humors are new (how well chosen I leave to you to judge) and all the words and Actions of the Persons in the Play, are always sutable to the Characters I have given of them; and, in all the Play, I have gone according to that definition of humor, which I have given you in my *Epilogue*, in these words:

> *A Humor is the Biasse of the Mind,*
> *By which, with violence, 'tis one way inclin'd.*
> *It makes our actions lean on one side still;*
> *And, in all Changes, that way bends the Will.*

Vale.

PROLOGUE.

Written by a Gentleman of Quality.

Since you are all resolv'd to be severe,
  To laugh and rail at every thing you hear,
  I know not why a Prologue should forbear
First, we declare against the wary Wit,
Who having had the luck of one good hit
Dares not appear again before the Pit.
Some have done well, yet to remove all doubt,
Men must fight more than once to be thought stout :
Others are too much in a scribling vein,
As if they had a looseness in the brain :
These catch at every little slight occasion,
As our Gay empty Sparks at each new Fashion :
Perptually they fumble for the Bayes,
With Poems, Songs, Lampoons, and long dull Playes.
A man would wonder what the Devil they meant,
(Like ill-nos'd Currs that only foil the scent)
To mangle Plots, and they'l as boldly do't ;
As our Sir Martin undertakes the Lute.
Now for the Women——
The little Fools into extreams are got,
Either they are stone cold, or scalding hot.
Some peevish and ill-bred, are kind to none ;
Others stark mad, in love with all the Town.
The famous Eater had his Worm to feed,
These Rampants have a hungry Worm indeed.
And as his ravenous Stomack made him get
Tripes, Livers, and the coursest sort of Meat,
Our craving Damosels, rather than stand out,
With any raw-bone Coxcombs run about ;
Making no difference of Size or Age,
From the grim Hector to the beardless Page.
Learn little ones, for shame learn to be wise,
And not so very rank, nor yet so nice.
Who buryes all his Wealth, and never lends,
Is more a wretch than he that wildly spends.
And she who is so coy to fancy no man,
Is yet a viler thing than she that's common.
If you will own your selves concern'd you may,
And for a Saucy Prologue damn the Play.

Dramatis Personæ.

Crazy. ONe that is in Pox, in Debt, and all the Misfortunes that can be, and in the midſt of all, in love with moſt Women, and thinks moſt Women in love with him.

Drybob. A Fantaſtick Coxcomb, that makes it his business to speak fine things and wit as he thinks; and alwayes takes notice, or makes others take notice of any thing he thinks well said.

Briſk. A Brisk ayery, fantaſtick, singing, dancing Coxcomb, that sets up for a well-bred Man and a Man of honour, but miſtakes in every thing, and values himself only upon the vanity and foppery of Gentlemen.

Raymund. A Gentleman of wit and honour, in love with *Theodosia*.

Sir *Richard* Loveyouth. } Husband to the Lady *Loveyouth*, supposed dead.

Sneake. A young Parson, Fellow of a Colledge, Chaplain to the Lady *Loveyouth*, one that speaks nothing but Fuſtian with Greek and Latine, in love with *Bridget*.

Pullin. A French Surgeon, originally a Barber.

Lady Loveyouth. } A vain amorous Lady, mad for a Husband, jealous of *Theodosia*, in love with *Raymund*.

Theodosia. A witty ayery young Lady, of a great fortune, committed to the government of Lady *Loveyouth* her Aunt, persecuted with the love of *Crazy*, *Brisk*, and *Drybob*, whom she mimicks and abuses, in love with *Raymund*.

Bridget. Woman to the Lady *Loveyouth*.

Mrs. *Errant*. One that sells old Gowns, Petticoats, Laces, French Fans and Toys, Jessumine Gloves, and a running Bawd.

Striker. A Habberdashers Wife, a' vain fantaſtick Strumpet, very fond and jealous of *Crazy*.

Friske. A vain Wench of the Town, debauch'd and kept by *Briske*.

Servants, Attendants, Fidlers, Bayliffs.

SCENE *LONDON*, in the Year, 1670.

Duration of the Scene 24 hours.

(191)

THE

HUMORISTS.

THE FIRST ACT.

Enter Crazy *in a Night-Gown and Cap.*

Crazy. OH this Surgeon! this damn'd Surgeon, will this Villanous Quack never come to me? Oh this Plaister on my Neck! It gnaws more than *Aqua-Fortis:* this abominable Rascal has mistaken sure, and given me the same Caustick he appli'd to my Shins, when they were open'd last.

Enter Mrs. Errant.

Errant. Good morrow sweet Mr. *Crazy.*

Craz. Good morrow Mrs. *Errant.*

Errant. How does the pain in your Head?

Craz. Oh I am on the Rack; No Primitive Christian under *Dioclesian* ever suffer'd so much as I do under this Rascal: This Villain, that like a Hangman destroys Mankind, and has the Law for't. Oh abominable Quacks! that devour more than all the Diseases would do, were they let alone, which they pretend to cure.

Errant. Ay, but Sir, yours is a French Surgeon, and who so fit to cure the French Disease as a French-Surgeon?

Crazy. Yes, as one poyson expels another; but if this Rogue should cure me, he can cure me of nothing but what he has given me himself; 'twas nothing, when I put my self into his hands; he brought it to what it is, and I think I must deal with him as they do that are bitten with a Viper, crush the Rogues Head and apply it to the part, for if I do not kill him, he'l be the death of me.

Errant. It may be Sir, he favours the Disease for his Countrey's sake.

Craz. A Curse on these French Cheats, they begin to be as rife amongst us, as their Countrey Disease, and do almost as much mischief too: No Corner without French Taylors, Weavers, Milliners, Strong-Water-Men,

(193)

Perfumers, and Surgeons : but muſt I be such a fantaſtick Sot as to be cheated by them? Could not I make use of my own Countrey-men, that are famous all over the World for cheating one another?

Errant. I am heartily sorry Sir, for you could not have been ill in so unseasonable a time.

Craz. Oh! why Mrs. *Errant*, what's the matter?

Errant. Do you think he could not mend you, and patch you up to hold together a little for the present?

Craz. Why Mrs. *Errant*? Oh death! what's this I feel?

Errant. I was with Mrs. *Striker* the Habberdashers Wife, this Morning, to sell some of my little French Toys, as Fans, Points, that had been worn a little, and Jessamine Gloves; but chiefly a Maid of Honours Old Gown, that fitted her to a hair; and a delicate white Mantou: and a pair of the neateſt little Shoes that had been worn two or three days by a Countess, that bewitched the very heart of her.

Craz. Well! and how does my dear *Striker*? Does she not desire to see me poor heart. . . . Oh what a twinge was that?

Errant. She does moſt impatiently wait the good hour, that she may ſteal from her Husband and give you a meeting at the White-Hart at *Hammersmith.*

Craz. Alas! dear soul! I know she loves me entirely. Oh my Shinne! 'tis there now: sweet Mrs. *Errant* sit down, and do me the favour to chafe it a little.   [*She sits down and rubs his Shins, he makes sowre faces.*

Enter Raymund.

Raym. Ha, ha, ha! this is pleasant, 'faith; this Itinerant Habber-dasher of small Wares, is a Ranger of the Game, a very Bawd-Errant . . . chafing of his Shins too! ha, ha, ha . . . but how could I think any of that Profession could be otherwise, procuring lies so in their way, they cannot avoid it.

Craz. She is a moſt delicate person, I love her infinitely, and I believe she has no unkindness for me.

Raym. Ah brave *Crazy!* do'ſt thou hold up thy humor ſtill? Art thou ſtill in love with all Women?

Craz. 'Faith *Raymund* I cannot but have an affeċtion, nay a veneration for the whole Sex yet.

Raym. I'll swear all Women ought to believe thou lov'ſt 'em, for thou haſt suffer'd more for them than all Knight Errants in Romances ever did. I'll say that for thee, and thou haſt as much Passive-Valour as to Pill and Bolus, as any man in Chriſtendom.

Errant. It shews him to be a person of much generosity and honour.

Craz. Perhaps there is not a truer Lover of the Sex than my self among Mankind. . . . Oh my Shoulders!

Raym. Thou haſt reason, witness that twinge else : well certainly so much Love and Pox never met together in one Man since the Creation. Nor 'faith do know which is the more tolerable Disease of the two.

Craz. Prethe *Raymund* no more of this Raillery.

Errant. Do not scandalize Mr. *Crazy* so ; the Venom of his Disease is all gone, this is but a Rheum, a meer Rheum.

Raym. Why thou Villain *Crazy*, wilt thou never leave wheedling Women thus ?

Craz. Prethee leave off ; I tell thee 'tis no more.

Raym. Why what impudence is this ? If thou goeſt on in this, thou art not fit to go loose, I will have a Red Cross set upon thy Door : Why don't I know thou haſt taken Bushels of Pills and Bolus's enough to purge all the Corporations in the King's Dominions.

Craz. You make good use of your time, to get Drunk so soon in a Morning.

Raym. Haſt thou not rais'd the price of *Sarsaperilla*, and *Guiacum* all over the the Town. The Drugſters are very ungrateful Fellows, if they do not give thee a Pension for the good thou haſt done to their Trade.

Craz. Mind him not Mrs. *Errant*, he's lewdly drunk.

Errant. I proteſt, Sir, he's the leaſt in my thoughts.

Raym. Why thou Sot thou, doſt thou talk of Love, and say thou haſt no Pox ; Why, I will not give Six Moneths Purchase for an Eſtate during the term of thy Natural Nose ! I shall live to see thee snuffle worse than a Scotch Bagpipe that has got a flaw in the Bellows.

Craz. Let him alone, let him alone ! This is a way he has with him.

Errant. He's a very uncivil man, let me tell you that.

Raym. Why haſt thou not for these seven years observ'd thy Seasons, like the Swallow or the Cuckoe ; with them thou ſtir'ſt abroad in the Summer, and with them retir'ſt in the Winter ; why, thou art a kind of Vegetable, that peep'ſt out thy head at the coming of the Spring, and Shrink'ſt it in again at the approach of the Winter ; while we that drink *Burgundy*, like Bay-trees, are green, and flourish all the year.

Craz. Why, haſt thou the confidence to compare Wine to Beauty ?

Errant. Ay, I thought what a proper man you were.

Craz. Wine, that makes you swell'd like Trumpetters with pimpl'd Faces ; and Eyes ſtaring like Pigs half roaſted, prominent Bellies, perish'd Lungs, tainted Breaths, parch'd Livers, decay'd Nerves, perpetual Feavers, Dropsies, Gouts, Palsies, and a Complication of more Diseases than you drink Healths.

Raym. With what ease can I return upon thee ; Women, that bring you to sore Eyes, weaken'd Hamms, Sciatica's, falling Noses, and Rheums, *Crazy.*

Errant. Now out upon you for a base man, to revile Women thus.

Raym. But then Wine, the Bond of human Society, that makes us free as absolute Princes, rich without covetousness, merry, valiant, witty, generous, and wise without allay; that inspires us far above the level of humane Thoughts, and affords us diviner Raptures than the deities of old did to their Prophets in their Extasies.

Craz. But then Beauty, Heaven's brightest Image, the thing which all the World desires and fights for; the Spur to Honour and all Glorious Actions, without which, no Dominion would have been priz'd, or Hero ever heard of; the most gentle, sweet, delicate, soft thing——

Errant. O dear Mr. *Crazy*! Go thy ways, thou art a sweet Man.   *(She claps* Crazy *on the Shoulders.*

Craz. O Death! What have you done? You have murder'd me; oh, you have struck me just upon a Callous Node, do you think I have a body of Iron?

Errant. Sir, I beg your pardon, I had quite forgot it, this Rheum is very violent.

Craz. Oh, oh.

Raym. The most sweet, delicate, gentle soft thing, go on *Crazy*.

Craz. The most delicate, sweet, gentle, soft——Oh Devil what do I endure?

Enter Pullin the *French Surgeon.*

Pullin. Good morr, Good morre.

Craz. Oh, Oh!

Pul. 'Tis ver vel, come to our Business, ve vil proceed to de operation.

Craz. Oh my Neck and Shoulders.

Pull. Yes, yes, I vas ver vel assure of dat; it vil put you to de pain indeed; but if dere be such tinge in *Englande* for draw, den I am no Syrigin indeed.

Craz. Oh you damn'd eternal Son of a Whore Quack!

Pull. Cacque morbleu! Vat is Cacque? I know ver vel vat is Son for a Whore, but vat is Cacque vertu-bleu I can no tell.

Raym. 'Tis a certain Rascal that cheats a man both of his money and health.

Craz. Just such a Rascal as you are.

Pull. Begar, you are mistake, Cacque is no French vard; it is for the Damn'd Syrigin-English. Mais vat is de matre vid you?

Raym. Damn'd English Surgion! Why you impudent Villain, did not you when you came first into *England*, ride upon a Milch Ass, and did not you maintain your self by selling her Milk to people in Consumptions, till you set up for an abominable Barber, but for the damn'd roughness of your hand, and the filthy noisomness of your breath, could get no Customers; and then were fain to set up with six penny worth of Diaculum

(196)

and a Collection of rotten Pippins, and pretended only to the Cure of Broken Heads; and had you any other Customers for a year together, than the Cudgel-Players of *Moor-fields*, or now and then a Drawer that was wounded with a Quart Pot.

Pull. I am amaze, vat is de businesse?

Errant. Sir, I must make bold to take my leave.

Craz. Your Servant sweet Mrs. *Errant*, present my service to *Theodosia*, and let her know I have a passion for her, you understand me.

Errant. Fear it not, Sir———   [*Exit* Errant.]

Pull. Ver vel, you make de jest of me.

Raym. Was not the next thing you arriv'd at, the inestimable secret of Brimstone and Butter for the Cure of the Itch, and had you any one Receipt more?

Pull. 'Tis ver vel indeed Mr. *Crazy!* I am come to be abuse.

Craz. Why, have you the impudence to deny this? Good Mounseur *Pullin*, do not I remember when you first set up for the Cure of this Disease you pretend to, with only Two pound of Turpentine and a little China, a few Hermodactyles, a pound or two of *Sarsaparilla*, and *Guiacum ;* Two Glyster-bags, and one Syringe: Could all thy wealth arrive at more Materials than these?

Raym. I must confess, since, you have learn'd some little experience, by Marrying an unsound English Strumpet, that was Pepper'd by some of your Ambassadors Footmen; she, by the many Courses she has gone thorow, has taught you something.

Pull. Tete bleu, dat I shoule be dus affronte.

Raym. If you had been good for any thing, there were Diseases enough in your own Country, to maintain you, without coming to us, with a Pox to you.

Pull. O Jernie, vat is dis? I have cure ten thousand Gentlemen of de Clappe in *Paris*, and to be abuse !———

Craz. Am not I oblig'd to you then, that you would not cure one in *England?* for *Raymund*, now there is not a Woman here, I confess to you, he has not wholly cur'd me; but on my Conscience I can do a Woman no hurt.

Pull. I am assure dat all de Operators for de Clapp in *England*, can no do so much as I do to cure you.

Raym. Why, hast thou not been longer in curing him than a *Chancery* Suit is depending?

Craz. Did not I put my self into your hands when it was first a *Gonorrhea virulenta?* Did not you by youe damn'd French Tricks, your Styptick-Injections, and your Turpentine-Clysters, suffer me to be Chorde, to come to Caruncles, to the Phymasii, Caries, Pubii, Bubones, Herniæ.

Raym. Nay, have you not driven his Enemy out of the open Field, where he might have been easily conquer'd, into his Strong Holds and Garisons.

Pull. Ver vel, ver vel.

Craz. Is there any one Symptome which I have not had?—Oh— have I not had your *Carbuncula, Acbrocordones, Mermecii, Thymi,* all sorts of Ulcers superficial and profound, Callous, Cancerous, Fistilous.

Raym. Hey-brave *Crazy!* Thou hast terms enough to set up two reasonable Mountebanks.

Craz. Have I not had your *Pustulæ, Crustatæ,* and *Sine Crustis Verucæ, Cristæ, Tophi, Ossis, Caries, Chyronya, Telephia, Phagadenia, Disepulotica.*

Raym. What art thou going to raise the Devil with these hard words?

Pull. Vel! and have I no cure all dese? Have I no given you de sweate, not in a damn'd English Tub or Hot-house, but I have taught you to sweat in de Cradle, and vid Spirit of Vine in de Pape Lanthorn, *a la Francois,* and taught you de use of de Baine *d'Alexandre.*

Craz. And has all this done any thing but driven him to his Winter Quarters, where he domineers as much as ever; Oh I have him here.

Raym. You have given him so many Bolus's in Leaf-Gold, that the loathsomness of 'em, has made his Stomach turn at a Twenty shillings piece, and that's the reason he never carries any in his Pocket.

Craz. Do you hear that Rascal? I have been cheated enough by you; but I'll bilk your Cribbidge for you.

Pull. But assure de Law will give de remede.

Craz. And that thou mayst be curst sufficiently for this, mayst thou be as long in Law as I have been in Physick.

Raym. Prethee curse him to purpose, may he be choak'd with Bolus's, drown'd in Dyet-drink, or smother'd in a Privy-house, that he may dye by that Excrement by which he liv'd.

Pull. Diable, no curse me, give de Madiction to the Dam Whore.

Craz. O Impudence! I protest to you *Raymund,* she is as pretty a civil young Lady, and between you and I, a Person of Honour?

Raym. She was a very Pocky Person of Honour.

Craz. And on my Conscience and Soul, loved me as passionately as any young Lady in *England.*

Raym. Besides, if she were a Whore, her Calling [*To* Pullin.] is to give it, and yours to cure it, Sirrah.

Craz. Shall I suffer so excellent, so virtuous a Person, to be traduc'd by your foul Mouth, you Rascal: Get you gone, you Dogge.——*Kicks him.*

Pull. O vat is dis? Elp, Elp—vel, vel, dere is de Law for do me Justice—— *Ex.* Pullin.

Enter Footman.

Footman. Sir, here's a Lady alighted out of a Coach, and coming up hither.

(198)

Craz. 'Slife a Lady! give me my Hat and Peruke, quick, quick, prethee *Raymund* help me quickly, that I may appear well before her.

Raym. If thou canſt appear no better than thou art, she'll not like thee very well.

Craz. So, so! you say I am not in favour with the Ladies.

Enter Mrs. Striker.

Striker. Your humble Servant sweet Mr. *Crazy*, I have juſt broke loose from my Husband, and come to kiss your hands. Oh, cry you mercy, you have a Stranger with you; I proteſt if I had known it, I would not have been so bold.

Raym. Though I be a stranger, Madam, I am ready to be as well acquainted with you as you please.

Craz. Dear Madam *Striker* ſtay a little, this is a Friend of mine, you may truſt him——You see *Raymund*, alas, I am no body with the Ladies, not I. This is a Person of honour.

Raym. No doubt on't.

Strik. Sir, I beseech you misconſtrue not my innocent intentions, I heard Mr. *Crazy* was not well, or I should not have seen him.

Craz. If I were not, I should be oblig'd to my diſtemper, were it the Gout, and be very loath to part with it, to be depriv'd of the honour of seeing you, but I am very well.

Friske. Your Servant sweet Mr. *Crazy*, I heard you were not well.

Enter Mrs. Friske.

Raym. Another! They flock about this Fellow, as Ravens do about a sick man for the reversion of Carrion.

Strik. How came she here tro? I do not like this Mr. *Crazy*.

Frisk. Your Servant Madam *Striker*.

Strik. Your servant Madam *Friske*.   [*Raym. takes* Striker *aside.*

Craz. Really, Madam *Friske*, this is such a favour as will make me eternally indebted to you——but I am so well, as I intended to come and kiss your hands.

Frisk. But how came she here I wonder?

Raym. Pray Madam, do me the favour to tell me who she is?

Strik. Sir, I'll inform you presently. Truly Mr. *Crazy*, this is not civil, to be so familiar with such a one as she is in my presence; I thought for my part, that I had been enough for any one person.

Frisk. Mr. *Crazy*, one word with you; I wonder for my part Madam Flirts should have no more breeding than to interrupt us.

Strik. Why I'll tell you Sir, what she is, she is a person of mean descent; I think her Father was at firſt a Journy-man Taylor or some such thing: She was debaucht by one Mr. *Briske* an Inns-of-Court-

Gentleman, and I am sure 'twas well for her, she was so; for before that she went in Paragon and Pattens: for my part I would not be known to be in her company for more than I'll speak of.

Raym. This is pleasant.

Strik. Pray Mr. *Crazy* favour me with one word; Lord, Madam *Friske*, cannot you let one speak a word with ones Friend?

Frisk. Your friend, alas poor soul, sure I may pretend to as much interest in him as you can.

Strik. How's this? you pretend!

Craz. No *Raymund*, I have no share in the Ladies favours, not I! Do you see how jealous the poor things are of me, poor Hearts! Oh my Shoulders! they are both Persons of Quality—— But Madam *Striker*, pray mistrust not my affection.

Raym. Pray Madam, let me beg the favour to know who she is?

Frisk. She! why she's a pitiful Habberdashers Wife, her Husband's a poor sneaking Cuckold; she has a very ill reputation, for my part I don't care for being seen in her Company, that's the truth on't.

Raym. That's very well.

Frisk. She used to appear in a scurvy *Fleetstreet* Dress, but now she comes into the Pit at the Play-House, and makes brisk Repartees to young Sparks.

Strik. What to have such a scandalous Woman as she come to your Chamber; truly if it were not here, I should have soon left her company. One may have one Friend I confess, or so; but to have two or three club for one, I scorn her.

Raym. I see there are Punctilio's of Honour among Whores as well as Bullies.

Frisk. But pray Mr. *Crazy*, come hither; you do not tell me how you like my new Petticoat here?

Strik. Lord, Madam *Friske*, why how should he like it, 'tis but an ordinary slight thing; for my part I do not like it at all.

Frisk. No matter what you say, as long as one does.

Raym. Who's that one, *Crazy*?   [*Jogs him*]

Craz. 'Slife you hurt my Arm; but that one is I, man, that thou should'st not find it.

Strik. But pray Mr. *Crazy* how do you like this Point about my Neck?

Craz. 'Tis a very pretty Ornament, but you give an Ornament to that.

Frisk. That! 'tis a foolish Counterfeit-Point.

Strik. I come, come; I come by my things honestly.

Frisk. Ay, and I as honestly as you too; but pray how do you like this Ruby upon my Finger?

Craz. 'Tis very glorious indeed.

Strik. Is not this a very pretty Locket?

Frisk. Let me see what's a Clock; 'tis juſt Eleven———

Strik. 'Tis a quarter paſt by mine.

Frisk. Yours! Ay I think so; yours is a scurvy Silver Watch, and does not go right.

Strik. Good lack a day, a Silver Watch! why it should go with any Gold Watch in Town for 20 *l.*

Frisk. Yes, yes; 'tis very like a Silver Watch can go as well as a Gold one; ha, ha, ha———

Raym. Hey! they use him as if they were bidding from him by Candles ends.

Strik. Alas poor silly Creature.

Raym. But Madam *Friske,* from whence came all these fine things?

Frisk. Ha, ha, there is a way that we have Sir.

Strik. But Mr. *Crazy,* I muſt of necessity leave you; my Husband will be come home: but I'll see you agen.

Craz. I am sorry you muſt make me unhappy so soon, but have you a Coach?

Strik. Yes, I have a Hackney waiting below.

Frisk. O fie! a Hackney! I hate 'em all they are so uneasie: I have a Coach with a Coronet waits for me.

Strik. Ay, ay, there's some could borrow Lords Coaches too, if they would do as others do, Madam *Friske,* let me tell you that.

Frisk. I don't know, Madam *Striker,* but I believe they would if they could.

Strik. Well, well, I like a Hackney; but 'tis no matter, Mr. *Crazy,* your servant——— *[Exit.*

Frisk. I muſt be gone Sir too.

Craz. Will you eclipse me so soon?

Frisk. Indeed I beg your pardon for eclipsing of you, but I cannot help it at present; your servant——— *[Exit.*

Craz. Have you such Ladies as these come to visit you?

Raym. No Sir, I keep no such ill Company.

Craz. Company! Why they are Persons of Honour.

Raym. Yes, yes, I know Habberdashers Wives, and Taylors Daughters, are Persons of Honour; fare you well, fare you well, and keep your Persons of Honour to your self.

Craz. But do yee hear Sir?

Raym. No Sir, no; no wheadles upon me, I am to dine at *Chatolins* with some Persons of Honour——Adiew. *[Exit.*

Craz. 'Sdeath! how unlucky is this, he should discover it, Boy.

[Enter Boy.

Boy. Sir.

Craz. Come in and dress me: Oh my head and shoulders—— *[Exit.*

(201)

THE SECOND ACT.

Enter Raymund *and* Footman.

Raym. I wonder my Lady *Loveyouths* Woman appears not yet; this was the time appointed! if 'twere an assignation for her self, she would be more punctual: Waiting Women have always the Grace to keep touch for that. Sirra, Go tell Mrs. *Bridget* I am here.

Foot. I will Sir————— [*Ex.*

Raym. I am very uneasie, till I hear an Account from her of my Letter to *Theodosia*, Excellent *Theodosia*! I have fought many opportunities to make my passion known to her; and upon her receiving it, depends my life or death.

Enter Bridget *and* Footman.

Oh Mrs. *Bridget* your servant————
Come! you are my little Genius from whom I expect nothing but good; what's my doom?

Bridget. Why Sir, she read your Letter, and whether she would not trust me, being a Servant to her Aunt, or what it was, I know not; but methought your Letter did not seem so agreeable as I expected.

Raym. He's a faint Souldier that gives off for one repulse, if she were as hard to be taken as *Candia*, I'll not raise the Siege: but you are my dear Confident, do me the honour to receive this little earnest of my Gratitude: I must confess it is too small a Present. And yet enough to make a Waiting Woman betray her Countrey, were it in her power.
[*Aside.*

Bridget. Really Sir, you make me blush.

Raym. No more, no more; but dear Mrs. *Bridget*, can you tell me why your Lady so narrowly watches me, that I could never yet have opportunity to speak to her Niece?

Bridget. Well! there is nothing I can keep from you; the truth is, my Lady loves you most passionately and desires no such Rivals as her Niece, I warrant you.

Raym. Prethee don't rally with me, but tell me————

Bridg. You are strangely dull, if you perceive it not your self; does she not admit those that have less fortunes, as Mr. *Drybob* and Mr. *Briske* to make love to her, and yet bars you of that liberty: Can this be any thing but her love to you?

Raym. It is impossible.

Bridg. Well, it shall all out; the truth on't is, she can neither think nor talk of any thing but Mr. *Raymund* in her very sleep; she embraces me when I lie with her, and calls me Mr. *Raymund;* I remember once she did it so eagerly, I protest I was afraid of a Rape.

Raym. If this be true she tells me, I must disguise my love to her Niece, or I shall be sure to lose her.

Bridg. My Lady, Sir you know, has a great Estate, besides her Jointure, and has the disposal of *Theodosia* absolutely given her by her Brothers Will.

Raym. What unlucky Devil design'd this to cross me.

Bridg. If you please to consider, 'twould be no ill bargain for you; I should be very glad of the honour to serve you in it.

Raym. But I have heard she is not yet assur'd of the death of her husband, indeed I have been told he parted from her about three years since upon some discontent, and never since was heard of.

Bridg. Yes Sir, my Lady heard of him from *Venice*, from whence about two years since, he went to the War at *Candia*, and we having never heard from him since, conclude him dead.

Raym. 'Tis very probable, she is employ'd by her Lady, I must not trust her.   [*Aside.*
It must be so, I see there is no way to come to the Niece, but by the Aunt——Wonder not that I am surpriz'd at this News, since it is a happiness too great for my belief.

Bridg. Do you think it a happiness?

Raym. So great, that I am doubly paid for the loss of *Theodosia*, in gaining so excellent a Lady as my Lady *Loveyouth;* and I'll assure you there I should have made my first address, but that I heard she had made a Vow of Widdowhood.

Bridg. And did you believe that Vow Sir?

Raym. No I warrant you. I would as soon credit a Knight of   [*Aside.* the Post, as a protesting Widdow. Dear Mrs. *Bridget* let me entrust you with my love to your Lady, since it concerns me so nearly.

Bridg. Sir, I shall be very glad of this occasion, and can the more easily promise you my assistance in it; since Mr. *Sneake*, whom I have no small power over, can perswade my Lady to any thing.

Raym. Is't he that speaks nothing but Greek or Latine, or English Fustian? He's Fellow of a Colledge, if I mistake not.

Bridg. The same Sir.

Raym. Indeed I have heard he is a Well-wisher to you. But he's out of Town——

Bridg. He will be in Town this Afternoon, I had an Epistle from him, which tells me so, which perhaps is one of the pleasant'st you ever read.

Raym. What's this?

A Letter.

Perdurant and inconcussed Mistriss,

T Is not only my Solamen, but the Celsitude of my felicity, that the transpiration of our Chast Flames of Sympathetick Amity, are mutually continuate; whose perpetuity no Snake hair'd destiny nor Furies-Furiband, nor the ghastly Ghosts of Central Nigritude, with all their dam'd infernal Powers, can e'r evert, renode, or dissolve——

Why this is conjuring.

Bridg. O Lord Sir, yonder comes Mr. *Drybob*; walk off I beseech you, I must not be seen with you.——   [*Ex.* Raymund.

Enter Mr. Drybob *with a little French Dog under his Arm.*

Dryb. Well, I know some Sots, that are still presenting their Mistresses rich Rings and Lockets, till they spend more than their Portions in the wooing of them; but let 'em match me for a Present. Here's a pretty French Dog shall charm the Heart of *Theodosia*. This is as new a Present, it may be, as can be thought on besides, really 'tis very pretty and fantastick.

Bridg. What has this Fopp got under his Arm?

Dryb. Besides, this Dog I stole from my Mother, who lov'd him as well as if she had whelp'd him her self; and I can say so many fine ingenious pretty things upon him too, besides a Song that I have made of him, that shall bewitch her certainly.

Bridg. How now Mr. *Drybob*, Why are you designing some Reformation i'th Government, you are so studious?

Dryb. Oh Mrs. *Bridget*, your Servant! my little Factor in Love! ha! I think that was no ill expression of mine; but what news of the Cargo of my Love, which I intrusted you with? Will it turn to account? I think by the way, that thought of mine was well enough? Oh what thinkst thou?

Bridg. O admirably well said!

Dryb. Nay, it may be I do say as many fine things in a year, as e'r a Wit of 'em all; but let that alone.

Bridg. I think so, you are the Chief of all the Wits.

Dryb. I! no alas, not I; I know they will have me one amongst them, do what I can, but deuce take me, if I care much for the Name on't. Indeed I do value my self upon Reperty a little that's the truth on't, and not lie to you, I must confess I am very happy in that; but alas! who can help it?

Bridg. But what have you got under your Arm, Sir?

Dryb. A pretty little French Dog, which I intend to sacrifice to my Mistriss; Sacrifice! observe that word———hum, ha.

Bridg. What Sir, shall he die for your Mistriss?

Dryb. I thank you for that, ha! ne'r a Dog in Christendom shall have the honour to die for my Mistriss, I intend to do that my self, if there be occasion for't.

Bridg. How then Sir?

Dryb. I intend to present him to her delicate Alabaster hands, as an Hieroglyphick of my Affection, Hieroglyphick? ha, ha, well, I am amaz'd to think how these Thoughts come into my head. I am, as to matters of Jests, as my Friend *Ovid* was in Verses, *Quicquid conabor dicere*—— now as I hope to live, this came into my head before I was aware on't.

Bridg. Good lack, 'tis wonderful.

Dryb. Nay, faith, 'tis strange, as thou sayst, but would I might ne'r stir out of this place, if it was not *ex tempore*, I protest and vow, as I am an honest man it was.

Bridg. It is impossible.

Dryb. Nay, prethee, dear Mrs. *Bridget*, believe now, deuce take me, if it was not; but faith I think Hieroglyphick was very pretty and Catechrestical,——hum.

Bridg. Sir, If you please, I'll sacrifice this Dog to my Lady *Theodosia.*——

Dryb. No, I beg your pardon, I will my self make an Oblation of him to her, as I do of this little Tribute of a Purse to you.

Bridg. Your humble Servant, Sir.

If this Trade holds, I shall get as much by Bribery as e'r a Magistrate in the Nation can——

Dryb. But pray how does *Theodosia* receive or entertain my Love? no, no, my Flame, my Flame? ay Flame: that's well enough exprest too, hah.

Bridg. Very well Sir; and yet I must tell you, you have a very dang'rous Rival, one Mr. *Crazy.*

Dryb. He, pshaw,! a pox on him, he has no wit; a damn'd dull fellow, he cannot break a jest in an hour: but may I have the liberty go and caress my Mistress.

Bridg. No Sir, at present she is not visible.

Dryb. Visible! ha, ha, ha, very prettily said upon my Life and Soul; well I see thou art happy in thy thoughts sometimes as well as I am.

[*Bell rings.*

Bridg. Hold Sir, I hear my Ladies Bell! I am call'd, adieu.

Dryb. Adieu—my dear Love Factor, as I said before.

Enter Crazy.

Here comes *Crazy*, ha, ha, he is my Rival, pox on him; I fear him not; no, no, *Theodosia* has judgement to distinguish between a dull Fellow and a man of parts. Hold, I must conceal my Dog.

Craz. I am your Servant Mr. *Drybob.*

Drybob. O Sir, your humble——but whither are you marching with so galliard and facetious a Countenance, as if you intended this day to storm Ladies hearts——hah.

Craz. Ha, ha! Faith to tell thee the truth, I am going to visit a Lady, a Person of Honour.

Dryb. By what Name or Title dignify'd or distinguish'd?

Craz. Well, honest *Drybob*, thou art my loving Friend; I'll bring thee to her: She is upon my honour, the most delicate bewitching Person: and I think I may say without vanity, has some affection for me.

Dryb. He little thinks I am his Rival. Pox on me, if he be not one of the dullest fellows. I could find in my heart to write against him, and I'll be hang'd, if in a Moneths time I did not write his head off.

Craz. On my soul and conscience she is one of the most ingenious and judicious Ladies——and in good earnest I don't use to be mistaken in these things. I could tell you many symptomes of her Affection.

Dryb. Symptomes of Affection; to give the Devil his due, that's not amiss; but I'de be hang'd if I did not break his heart with Reperties in half an hour for all this; poor Sot.

Craz. As Sir, I'le tell you some.

Enter Bayliffs *and arrest* Crazy.

Bayl. Mr. *Craz.* I arrest you.

Craz. Arrest me! at whose Suit? Hold, hold, hands off. Oh you hurt my Callous Node.

Bayl. Do not tell us of this and that, I Arrest you at the Suit of Monsieur *Pullin* the French Surgeon. Come away.

Dryb. Let me go.——————[*Craz. lays hold on* Drybob.

Craz. Prethee, dear *Drybob* bail me.

Dryb. Hold *Crazy*, do not name me, I was bound with a wit for a sum of Money, and 'tis come to an Execution, as most of their Debts do; and there is a Warrant out against me—I dare not stay——[*Breaks loose.*

Craz. O I am undone, beyond redemption.

Dryb. So, so, *Crazy* is catch'd as sure as a Rat in a Trap.

Craz. O my Shoulders! I am murder'd——[*They tug and hale him.*

Enter Mrs. Errant.

Errant. Help, help, here, will you kill Mr. *Crazy*? Help, help.

Bayl. Out you Strumpet, what do you come to make a rescue?

[*Kick her.*

Errand. Murder, Murder, help, help.

Craz. Good, honest, worthy, loving, pretty, dear, good-natur'd Gentlemen stay but a moment.

Bayl. No Sir, no ; come along———

Craz. Nay, Dear Hearts, Dear Souls, I have no Money, but here is a Ring I had at the Funeral of my Unkle, take that to let me have the honour to speak with that Lady.

Bayl. Nay, I'll be glad for my part to do any Civility I can for a Gentleman.

Errant. What's the matter, Sir, are you arrested ? I'll fetch you bayl.

Craz. No, it is no matter for that ; but dear Mrs. *Errant* thou art my life and soul, prethee tell me, how dost thou find *Theodosia* inclin'd, dost thou think she loves me.

Errant. Without question she has some kindess for you, she confest to me you were one of the wittiest persons.

Craz. No alas, not so neither.

Errant. And one of the handsomest Gentlemen she ever saw.

Craz. Nay, fie, fie, that was a little too much faith, she's a very judicious Woman.

Errant. But you have a dangerous Rival, one Mr. *Drybob.*

Craz. He alas ! Alas !

Bayl. Come Sir, we can stay no longer.

Craz. Hold but a little, but one minute.

Enter Raymund.

Raym. How now *Crazy ?* Are they hurrying thee to base durance, and contagious prison ?

Craz. Yes *Raymund,* at the Suit of *Pullin* the French Surgeon.

Raym. Stay ye Dogs.

Bayl. Who are you ? What would you rescue our pris'ner from us ? then have at you.

Raym. How now Rascals ?   *They fight.*

Errant. Hey brave Mr. *Crazy,* Hey brave Mr. *Raymund :* So Sir, now you are at liberty, I'll take my leave ; I'm in haste to go to Mrs. *Striker* the Habberdashers Wife.

Craz. And wilt thou remember me dear Mrs. *Errant ?*

Errant. Ay, ay, I warrant you.

Craz. Your most obliged Servant———   [*Exit* Errant.

Raym. Come on *Crazy,* thou behav'st thy self bravely.

Craz. O Sir, I should have fought better, but for some damn'd Pustles upon my Arm, and some Acrochordones upon my right Shoulder ; but really Mr. *Raymund* this is such a deliverance, that nothing can shew my Gratitude, but to bring you to see a Person of Honour hard by.

Raym. What, a Habberdashers Wife and a Journeyman Taylors Daughter——

Craz. Nay, prethee *Raymund*, no fooling; I'll tell thee who 'tis, 'tis *Theodosia;* I hope she is a Person of Honour, Sir.

Raym. Are you acquainted with her?

Craz. Acquainted! yes, yes! I shan't say much, but it may be—— but I am a fool for speaking——yet thou art my Friend, she commends me extreamly, and says I am the wittiest Gentleman, and the finest Person, and if I may with modesty tell thee, I have some assurances of her kindness.

Raym. Death, if I did not know the vanity of this Rascal, this would strangely move me.

Craz. But why do I talk, you'll not believe I am in favour with the Ladies, but I'll bring you to her, and convince you.

Raym. Come on Sir, I'll go with you.   *Exeunt.*

Enter Lady Loveyouth *and* Theodosia.

La. Lovey. Come, come, Gentlewoman, deny it not to me: I perceive your Inclinations well enough: but pray let me advise you not to set your thoughts upon Mr. *Raymund*.

Theo. What's your reason, Madam?

La. Lovey. My reason, Minx! Come, come, there's something in't that is not fit to tell you.

Theo. I understand the mystery well enough, but I will set my Heart upon him in spight of her ravenous Ladyship, that would make him her Prey.

Lady Lovey. Besides, he's a wild young Gentleman.

Theo. And you would have the taming of him.   [*Aside.*

Lady Lovey. I believe he'll dispose of himself in another place too I'll assure you——This insolent Girl would come in competition with me forsooth. Do not I allow you three Suiters, that's enough for any reasonable Woman one would think.

Theo. And three such too! Madam!

Lady Lovey. Such, I'll assure you, Mr. *Crazy*, Mr. *Briske*, and Mr. *Drybob*, are three as agreeable persons, and as pretty Sparks perhaps.——

Theo. And as well match'd as any three Baboons in *Europe*, why, Madam, I would as soon Marry a Drill as one of them. The little Gentleman a Horseback, that leads the Bears to persecution, is a Prince to any of them.

La. Love. Ay, ay, I know her drift, she would rob me of Mr. *Raymund*, but if I have any prevailing Charms remaining in these Eyes of mine, she shall not.

Theo. They Husbands, why a Nunnery were more tolerable, to be mew'd up with none but musty old Women, or your melancholy young

Eaters of Chalk. I had rather be kept waking at a Conventicle than hear the name of them.

La. Lovey. You are a foolish Girle! I protest they are pretty Gallants and Wits of the Town.

Theo. Gallants and Wits! Buffoons and Jack-puddens; rather condemn me to a little City Shop-keeper, with whom I may never have new Gown and Handkercher, but half a year behind the Fashion; where I may be bred to rail against the Ladies of the Court, among my publick She Neighbours, and to mince and simper at an Up-sitting or a Christning.

La. Love. Ay, ay, go on, go on.

Theo. To live all the Week in a melancholy Back-room, and on Sunday go to Church with my Husband in a broad Hat, strutting before me, and the Fore-man of the Shop having me in one hand, and a huge Boss'd Bible, as big as I am, in the other.

La. Love. Good Mrs. Dis-dain make much of them, for I'll assure you, you are like to have no other; I'll look to you for Mr. *Raymund* I promise you.

Theo. No other! why I had rather marry a Countrey Justice, that lives in a Hall-place, two mile from a Town; that's too covetous to keep a Coach, and too jealous to suffer me to come to *London* : that makes me rise by five a Clock in the morning to look to my Dairy, and to receive Geese and Capons as Bribes to his Worship for Justice.

La. Love. How your Tongue runs?

Theo. Or when I have a Holyday, to have the liberty to walk two mile to fill my Belly with Stew'd Prunes or Rashers of Bacon at a poor Neighbours-house.

La. Love. Good Mrs. Nimble Chops they are fit for your betters.

Theo. Yes, for your Ladyship, why don't you chuse one of them.

La. Love. So I would, Mrs. Malepert, had I not vow'd to live a Widdow.

Theo. A Widdow, that keeps a Vow against Marriage, were a more monstrous Creature than the Fish taken at *Greenwich*.

Enter Bridget.

La. Love. How now Sauce Box! Oh *Bridget* where hast thou been?

Bridg. Oh Madam, I have News for your Ladyship, that I hope will not be unpleasant.

La. Love. For me? what is't?

Bridg. From Mr. *Raymund*, Madam.

Theo. How's this?

La. Love. From Mr. *Raymund*, alas, what can that be?

Bridg. Madam, I'll tell it in your Ladyships Ear.

La. Love. Nay, nay, pray speak it out————well he's an excellent person————   [*Aside.*

Bridg. Madam, he told me, he had an extraordinary passion for your Ladyship.

Theo. What says she ?   [*Aside.*

La. Love. For me ! O my dear *Raymund*, I am sure I have for thee———— What did you say *Bridget*, I did not mind it ?

Bridg. That Mr. *Raymund* had a very great passion for your Ladyship, and I am sure he loves your Ladyship most violently.

Theo. Can I endure to hear this ?

La. Love. Me, fie, fie, why sure he did not tell thee so ? I am transported at this happy News————   [*Aside.*

Bridg. I'll assure your Ladyship he did, and but that I would not take money to betray your Ladyships affections, offer'd me good round Fees, to be his Advocate.

Theo. Perfidious Man !

La. Love. I told you Gentlewoman he had dispos'd himself in another place.

Theo. But Madam, you are resolv'd to live a Widdow.

La. Love. I know not, I am as unwilling to marry as any body ; but you know where Marriages are made, alas, there's no resisting of our Fate. How I am o'rjoy'd that I shall get him from this confident Girl ! who would be my Rival.

Enter Crazy *and* Raymund.

Theo. Here he comes, that I could breath infection on him.

La. Love. Good lack ! he's here, and I am not half in order. *Bridget* you have drest me so carelessly to day.

Craz. Ladies your most humble Servant, I make bold to introduce a Friend of mine.

Raym. Prethee peace, I can introduce my self.

La. Love. He is very welcome upon his own account.

Raym. Madam, you infinitely oblige me.

Craz. Dear Madam, I kiss your fair hands.

Theo. Dear Sir, 'tis very civilly done of you.

Craz. Alas Madam ! but I make bold to present this worthy Friend of mine.

Raym. Pox o' this Coxcomb————   [*Aside.* Madam, I hope you will do me the Honour to receive my duty from my self——Ha ! what means this scorn ?   [*Turns away from him.*

La. Love. I knew 'twould vex her to see him make his applications to me.

Craz. Prethee *Raymund* don't be troubled at her aversion, you know

I told you before I was the only person in her affection; Faith I was afraid she wou'd use you thus.

Raym. Curse on this Fool. I will find some means to put a Ticket I have into her hand, that will try her farther.

La. Love. Sir, my Niece is a foolish ill-bred Girle, that knows not how to value a Gentleman; but I hope you will be so just to me, to believe you are to me most welcome.

Raym. If you knew how much I desir'd to be so to you, of all your Sex, I fear I should be less.

La. Love. No Sir, I should not be so uncivil.

Raym. 'Slife! she comes on faster than I have occasion for her. Madam, I beseech you, Let the violence of my passion excuse me, when I presume to tell you that I have so long suffer'd by your Charming Eyes, that I can no longer keep my passion in; 'tis now too head-strong for me.

La. Love. Oh, he's a rare person—— [*Aside.*

Theo. This is an affliction which nothing can surpass but the love of this Coxcomb.

Craz. Well! 'tis most evident, she has a passion for me, but who can help it.

Raym. Kill not a young Gentleman at first dash, Madam, 'tis too inhumane.

La. Love. Sir, I hope you intend nothing but honorable.

Raym. Injure me not to suspect my honour.

La. Love. No Sir, by no means. Indeed I heard something of this from my Maid,

Raym. But I am now come to present my heart with my own hands.

La. Love. Sir, If you please, let us retire a little and discourse of this business.

Craz. Madam! I humbly demand your pardon, I perceive your aversion to *Raymund* does disturb you a little, had I known it, I would not have brought him; and yet faith he's a very honest Fellow.

Theo. Do not believe so ill of me, to think any thing can give me a disturbance while you are present.

Craz. Ah Madam, I kiss your fair hands; you are so obliging, really I know not how to deserve it.

Theo. This conceited Ass can never know when he is abus'd.

Enter Drybob.

Drybob. Ladies! Your most obedient humble Footstool, I take the liberty to pay my devoir here.

La. Love. You are welcome, sweet Mr. *Drybob.*

Drybob. Dear sweet Lady, your Vassal couchant.   *Raymund,* servant
Raymund. How now *Crazy?*
   Crazy. How I despise this Fool?
   La. Love. But Sir, what were you saying, these Gentlemen inter-
rupted us.
   Theo. I will conceal my resentment, if *Raymund* should perceive it,
'twould make him more insolent.
   Drybob. Madam, You see I am a bold man, that dare venture to
come within Eye-shot of you.   It may be *Crazy* that was not ill said.
But Madam, I would adventure any danger to atchieve a Kiss of your
fair hand.   Mind that *Crazy.*
   Theo. Sir, you have conferr'd a favour on me, that I cannot be worthy
of, tho' I should sacrifice all my endeavours to merit it.
   Craz. This Coxcomb does not find that she abuses him.
   Drybob. Dear Spark of Beauty, you are very pleasurable ; but I swear
Madam by the Tip of your Ear, that I love you most immaculately,
There again *Crazy*————   [*Kicks his Shins*
   Craz. Death, this Rogue has murder'd me !   Oh my Shins, a Pox
of his fine Sayings.
   Drybob. And as Hieroglyphick of that affection, I present you with
this little French Dog to be Servant to your little Bitch.
   Craz. What an Employment has he found   [Theo *gives the Dog to*
out to be Pimp to a Bitch.   Bridget, *who carries*
   Theo. Really Sir, it is a Dog of a very elegant   *him away.*
composure.
   Drybob. Admirably well said, I protest and vow, Madam, is it not,
Crazy.   I know 'twould take her strangely ; but what does this dull
Sot hope for, that does not say two good things in a day.   But I beseech
you, Madam, how does your little Domestick Animal your Bitch.   Mark
that Crazy.   [*Kicks him.*
   Craz. 'Slife can't a man stand in quiet for this Rascal, if he be so
damnable witty I'll draw upon him.
   Theo. Really Sir, the poor Creature, by reason of a great Defluxion
of Rheum, has sore Eyes and keeps her Chamber.
   Drybob. This Lady has an admirable wit, pox on me Madam, if I
am not extreamly afflicted for the indisposition of her body.

Enter Bridget.

   Bridg. Madam, here's one from Mrs. *Errant*————
   La. Love. Sir, I take my leave of you at present, but shall wait on you
immediately.   [*Exit* La. Love.
   Raym. Your humble Servant, this is a happy opportunity.   Madam,
I beg the honour of you to hear me one word.

Theo. No Sir, I have heard too much already.

Raym. Hah! this anger of hers is no ill sign.

Craz. Prethee *Raymund*, for my sake, don't trouble thy self for this; Alas, I told thee this before. That Coxcomb may be allow'd to be abus'd.

Drybob. *Raymund*, thou seest this Lady is most abstemiously squeamish, and yet that damn'd dull Fellow *Crazy* does most pertinaciously caress her. Poor Sot, I pity him.

Enter La. Loveyouth *and* Bridget.

La. Love. Sir, I am now return'd, if you please to the point.

Raym. Pox of all impatient Widdows.

Drybob. Let me see, I forgot something I was to say of this Dog that was worth Diamonds.

Craz. Madam, This is a very Impertinent Fellow, but I could wish we were alone, that we might enjoy our selves.

Theo. That were too great a happiness for me.

Craz. No Madam, you deserve a great deal more.

Drybob. Oh I have it.

Craz. Now is this Villain going to break a jest, and I dare not stand near him.

Drybob. Madam, I must confess the Dog was not born in *France*, but of French Parents upon my honour, and is of as ancient a Family, and has as good blood running in his Veins (no dispraise) as ere a Dog in *France*. But *Raymund*, I'll shew the Song I made of this Present, that may be is well enough.

Raym. Most excellent.

Drybob. Ay is't not brisk, I am asham'd to give it to my Mistriss, prethee do thou.

Raym. With all my heart. Madam, Mr.   [*Changes it, and puts a* *Drybob* desires to present this to you.   *Ticket into her hands*

Theo. He might ha' don't himself. Ha! what's this?   [*She views it.*

She reads,

MAdam, The love I make to your Aunt, is only acted by me, finding I can never come to an opportunity of revealing my passion to you, till by pretending love to her I have remov'd all jealousies; you see at present she watches me so narrowly, that I can find no occasion to tell you how much I honour you, who am entirely yours

Raymund.

Forgive my unjust suspicion, this is a happy turn.

Drybob. Come, Madam, I see it pleases you; if you please, Madam, pronounce it with an audible voice, that this little Audience may communicate.

La. Love. Ay, do so Niece. I have seen very pretty things of Mr. *Drybob*'s; or if you will I'll read it, give it me.

Theo. Heaven! what shall I do?

Raym. Madam, I fear you are not us'd to the hand, give me leave———— [*Changes it for the Song.*

Theo. But I hope Mr. *Drybob* will be pleased to give it breath, and utter it harmoniously.

Dribob. My mellodious Pipes are a little obstructed, but to serve you, I will chant it forth incontinently, hem, hem, but Madam, I want a Theorbo to pitch my voice.

La. Love. Will not a Gittar serve?

Dribob. It will in some measure supply the defect.

La. Love. Bridget go fetch one———— [*Ex. and brings a Gittar.*

Dribob. Now *Raymund* observe. *Crazy* listen carefully, Methinks it should break this Fools heart to see how kindly I am us'd.——Hem, hem.

Sings.

> *I hope it is your pleasure*
> *To accept of this Dog for a Treasure,*
> *From him that loves you beyond all measure*
>   *Which may mystically shew*
>   *What to your Eies I owe.*
> *That of your affection I have put on the Clog,*
> *And am your most humble Servant and Dog.*
> *With a Bow, Wow, Wow,* &c.

Ha, how do you like that *Chorus*, faith I think it is very new.

Raym. 'Tis so, and in my judgement has as much sense as most *Chorus*'s.

Drybob. Is it not very brisk and facetious, hah?

Craz. It is so, but in good truth I did not take you for a Dog before.

Drybob. Now for a Reparty to knock down this Coxcomb, with hum——Death it will not do. Pox on't, I us'd to be more present to my self.

Craz. Madam, I beseech you let's retire from this impertinent Ass.

Theo. Yes, with a more impertinent one.

Drybob. Now I have it, ha, ha, ha, though I am a Dog, I am not the Son of a Bitch *Crazy*, ha, ha, ha.

Craz. Why Sir, who is? [*Bustles up to him.*

Dribob. Nay Sir, I say nothing, Mum is the Italian *tu quoque* word.

Craz. But Sir, let me tell you, if you be a Dog, and not the Son of a Bitch, you are not lawfully begotten.

Dribob. Ha, ha, pox on me, if it be not well said; prethee let me kiss thee for that. O my Conscience my Company makes thee witty.

La. Love. Sir, since I find you are so honourable, if you please we'll withdraw.

(214)

Raym. 'Sdeath I have plung'd my self over head and ears before I was aware on't.———   [*Exit* Raym. La. Loveyouth.

Theo. My Termagant Aunt has no mercy on her Lover.

Craz. Sir, notwithstanding your mirth, I hope you are ready to give me satisfaction for the affront.

Dribob. This dull insipid Fellow takes a witty reparty for an affront, but I'll bear up to him. Sir, if you talk of satisfaction, the world knows I am ready to attend any mans motion in that way.

Theo. Gentlemen, I must retire a while.

Craz. I hope I shall have the honour to wait on you.

Dribob. Madam I'll wait on you.

Theo. How shall I rid my self of these Fopps?

Craz. You wait on her?

Dribob. Yes Sir, I, for all you Sir. Lord, Sir, you are so hasty.

Craz. Do not be impertinent, to intrude upon a Ladies privacy.

Dribob. Peace Coxcomb, peace. Come, Madam, I'll wait on you, I vow this Fop makes me very merry.

Craz. Prethee stand by and learn more manners.

Dribob. Alas, Madam, mind him not.

Theo. Farewel Gentlemen———   [*Exit.*

Dribob. Keep you back then, if you go to that———[*Exeunt.*

THE THIRD ACT.

Enter Crazy *and* Drybob *with their Swords drawn.*

Craz. COme, come, have you made your Will?

Drybob. Yes, yes, don't you trouble your your self for that, I have it always ready upon these occasions.

Craz. If you have not, your Estate by being unsetled, may come to be divided among the Lawyers, after I have kill'd you.

Drybob. Sweet Mr. *Crazy*, don't think to fright me, for I am a Rhinoceros, if I care any more for you than I do for a Feather of a Shuttlecock.

Craz. This will not fright the Rogue.———   [*Aside.*
Under Favour, I will run you thorow the Lungs immediately.

Drybob. He shall not out-huffe me———   [*Aside.*
Look you, Sir, I am no Man to be frighted, though you look as big as a Dutch Trumpeter; and I think that's well enough said too.

Craz. I am no Gentleman, if I do not stick you to the ground the first Pass.

Drybob. I am the Son of a Corn-cutter if I do not rip up your Puddens instantly. Death this Rogue looks like a very *Bussy d' Ambois.*

Craz. Come on Sir, have at you—— yet if you will resign *Theodosia,* I care not, if I be contented with a Leg or an Arm; not that I believe you have an interest; but for form-sake.

Drybob. Resign my Mistriss! ha, ha, if I should, do you think she would marry a Fellow with a Face that look'd like a squeez'd Turnip; and I think there's a Satyrical Bob upon you.

Craz. I must try some other way.

Drybob. Why you look already as sowrely as the Picture of a stabb'd *Lucrece.* I shall break the Rogues Heart with these Bobs.

> [*Craz. beats* Drybob's *Sword out of his hand before he is aware on't.*]

Craz. Now Sir, pray quickly.

Drybob. Hold, hold, I cannot pray very well, but I can run as well as most men in the Nation, which will serve my turn better at this time——

> *Runs.*

Craz. Are you so nimble, I shall overtake you; S'life this Rogue has run his Heats at *New Market,* I think——

> [Drybob *Runs round the Stage, and* Crazy *after him*——

Drybob. This is a lucky opportunity.

> [*Craz. Lets fall one of the Swords.*
> [Drybob *takes it up and fights.*

Enter Mrs. Friske *passing slowly over the Stage.*

Craz. Hold, hold, I say; I'll spare your Life two Minutes, till I wait upon you, Lady.

Drybob. You spare my life! I scorn your words; but I will in mercy let you take your leave of her; since 'tis the last time you shall ever see her.

Friske. Ah——What's here, a Sword drawn—— *Shrieks.*

Craz. Be not afraid, Madam *Frisk;* I am fighting with a simple Fellow here for your Honour.

Friske. For my Honour? I was going to Mr. *Brisk's* Lodging, I'll call him to help you.

Craz. By no means. Dear Madam *Friske* let me kiss but this fair hand, and that will inspire me to kill twenty such Rascals in an Afternoon. ——But where shall I have the Honour to wait upon you by and by?

Friske. Put up your Sword then, I will be at my Lodging within a quarter of an hour, and I shall have never a Friend with me.

Drybob. What will you ne'r have done there?

Craz. Madam, I will but run this Fellow thorow the Body a little, and I'll not fail to wait on you.

Drybob. If I fall on now, I shall come off with Honour, for she'll be sure to call some body to part us.   [*Runs at* Crazy.

Friske. Help, help, Mr. *Briske.*   Oh help, help Mr. *Briske.*

Craz. Stand your ground you Coxcomb, do you think   [*Fight,* and I am bound to fight you by the mile.   Craz. *drives* Dryb. *back.*

Enter Mr. Briske *and* Friske.

Brisk. Where are they ?

Friske. There, I dare not ſtay to look on them——   [*Exit.*

Brisk. Hold, hold ! What a pox ails you ? Hold, hold, you Wits can never agree among your selves ; you are not so ſtrong a party, that you should need to deſtroy one another, you are fighting here as fiercely as *Guy of Warwick* and *Colbrand* the Dane.

Dribob. Faith *Jack Briske* that's a pretty thought of thine, ha, ha.

Brisk. Put up, for shame, put up, and be *Pilades* and *Oreſtes,* what was your quarrel ? I am afraid you do not underſtand these nice points of honour.   Let me hear, how was it ?

Craz. He had the insolence obliquely to give me the name of *Son of a Bitch.*

Dribob. I proteſt and vow he gave me the ignominious appellation of a Dog, like a Damn'd Cynick Phyloſopher.

Brisk. Why look you, here's your miſtake already : Why, I was call'd Son of a Whore at *Chatolins* laſt night, and what do you think I did ?

Craz. According to the Laws of honour I make no queſtion.

Dribob. P'shaw, you underſtand those things no more than a Coſter-monger.

Brisk. Pish, you are out, you are out ! Lord, Lord, To see the fault of mens Education.   I'll tell you——when he call'd me Son of a Whore, I ev'n took him up roundly, and told him flat and plain I scorn'd his words.   Now by this means I put this Rogue out of his Road ; the Sot knew not what to reply, I took such a new way offronting him.

Craz. This fellow is no better than a Coxcomb.

Drybob. I am the Son of a Squirrel, if this was not mighty pretty and exotick.

Brisk. Ay, was't not, I knew I should vex the heart of him with this affront, and upon my honour it incens'd him so divilishly, that ha, ha, ha ——he gave me three as good sufficient subſtantial kicks as a man would wish to see in a Summers day, ha, ha, ha.

Drybob. But what didſt thou reply to the Kicks, *Jack,* ha ?

Brisk. Why faith when he kick'd me, I told him very smartly, I scorn'd such ill-bred Sots from my heart, and that I thought him as much below me as the fellow that cries Tinder-boxes and Mouse-traps ; and then Sung a Corant of *Berkenshawes* in D'sol, re, fa, la, la, la.

(217)

Drybob. By *Gayland, Ben. Buker,* and *Daffaletta,* most judiciously manag'd.

Brisk. At this he was amaz'd, and said I was a Stoick, but I Sung on, fa, la, la, la, which by the way is an excellent Corant, thou shalt hear't, fa la, la.

Drybob. In good faith it is a very merry and luscious Corant.

Brisk. But come, my dear friends, embrace, embrace.

Craz. Sir, under favour, I do no more care for him, than I do for one of your Operators for Teeth.

Drybob. Nor I for you, any more than for one of those obstreperous wide-mouth'd Rogues that cry Spratts, which I think by the way, is another-guess Thought than yours, ha, ha.

Brisk. Come, upon my honour you shall embrace, and I will bring you to my Mistriss, and we'll have Fiddles and dance too.

Craz. Nay, if there by a Lady in the Case, I submit.

Drybob. And what care I, no body shall bee too hard for me in kindness.

Craz. Your Servant, Mr. *Drybob.*

Drybob. Your humble Servant, Mr. *Crazy.*

Brisk. So come, let's go to my Mistriss, fa la, la, la.

Craz. This was a lucky rancounter.——— *Exeunt.*

Enter Bridget *and* Sneake.

Bridg. Good Mr. *Sneake,* you will overset me with Learning, you smell so strong of the University.

Sneak. Truly Mrs. *Bridget,* by the interposition of an Opacous distance between those Luminaries your Eyes and my self, I have suffer'd a *Deliquium, viz.* an Eclipse.

Brid. You have not, I deny your Major.

Sneak. I could delucidate this by way of illustration, but I confess Metaphors, are not argumentive ; but your Eyes, I say, are like the Birds in the *Hyrcinian Groves,* which by the refulgency of their Wings did guide the wandring Traveller, and enlighten the most Opacous tenebrosity.

Bridg. So much for this time, yonder comes a stranger, we will retire.

Sneak. I am your Servant in any thing within the Sphere of my Activity.

Enter Sir Richard Loveyouth *in disguise.*

Bridg. Who's this——— [*Ex.*

Sneak. You shall have conference with her, I will cause her to approach incontinently.

Sir Rich. What Coxcomb have we got here? well, this disguise and my long absence will secure me from my Wives knowledge, I am resolv'd to try her farther. 'Tis possible that impertinence, that vanity and

frowardness, that made me leave her, by this time may have forsaken her
——Here she comes, I'll observe her.

Enter La. Loveyouth.

Madam, Are you my Lady *Loveyouth?*

La. Love. I am, Would you have any thing with me?

Sir Rich. I am the unhappy Messenger of ill news to your Ladyship.

La. Love. Ill news? What can that be?

Sir Rich. Your Husband, Sir *Richard Loveyouth.*

La. Love. My Husband! What of him? I hope he is not living yet.

Sir Rich. Madam, he is dead.

La. Love. Dead! And how dy'd he?

Sir Rich. He was kill'd in *Candia,* in that fatal Sally made by the French upon the Turks.

La. Love. Art thou sure of it?

Sir Rich. This is very fine.   [*Aside.*

Madam, I brought off his Body, having then the honour to be his Servant, and to confirm what I say, behold this Ring of his.

La. Love. It is so; but I will not afflict my self farther, we must all die; the grief that was due to his Memory, I believing him dead, have paid already.

Sir Rich. A very short liv'd grief, I thank her for't. Ha! I have a way to make discoveries of her, that may be cause of a Divorce, which Heaven send me. Madam, the death of my Master has put me out of employment, and if your Ladyship has any vacant place, I beg to serve you, I will do it faithfully.

La. Love. You speak very seasonably; for my Gentleman-Usher dy'd last week for love of my Shoomakers Daughter, you shall succeed him.

Sir Rich. A worthy Employment———   [*Aside.*

Madam, I humbly Thank you.

La. Love. Much good may it do you, and as a beginning of your Service, pray go into the next room, and desire Mr. *Raymund,* a handsom worthy Gentleman, that waits there to come to me.

Sir Rich. I will Madam——A very good beginning——   [*Aside.*

Enter Raymund *and Sir* Richard.

La. Lov. Now Mr. *Raymund* I am assur'd of my Husband's death.

Raym. How Madam?

La. Lov. This honest fellow whom I have entertain'd into my Service, saw him dead. Pray tell him you Sir.

Sir Rich. O Devil! What's this?——   [*Aside.*

'Tis too true Sir.

La. Lov. And now Sir, I take the liberty to tell you, I can no longer be refractory to your honourable desires.

Enter Bridget *with a Letter.*

Bridg. Sir, Here's a Letter for you left by a Porter; who said, it requir'd no Answer, and is gone.

Raym. For me, what can it be?

La. Lov. Where's my Niece?

Bridg. In her Chamber, Madam.

La. Lov. If she offers to intrude upon Mr. *Raymund* and my self; tell her we are busie.

Bridg. I will Madam.

La. Lov. And do you hear?

Raym. Shall I believe my Senses?

Reads.

I *Cannot but be sensible of the honour you do me in your Professions of kindness to me, and since this Paper cannot blush, I presume to tell you what nothing but the restraint I suffer could force me to; which is, that your Person and your Passion are esteem'd by.*

You may trust this Bearer. Theodosia.

Ah my dear *Theodosia.*

Enter Theodosia.

La. Lov. How now Minx? What makes you sawcily intrude upon Mr. *Raymund* and me?

Theo. A certain curiosity of doing things that are forbidden me.

La. Lov. 'Tis very well; but pray gape not after him. You may if you please call him Uncle: In the mean time get you in.

Raym. Curse on her impertinent Jealousie.
Madam, I have too short a time to tell you how I am transported at your Letter.

Theo. Pray take care, we are spy'd; talk with *Bridget*, I am assur'd of her Faith to me.

La. Lov. Good lack! Niece, you might have spoken lowd, Mr. *Raymund* would have trusted me; but pray get you to your Chamber.

Theo. Well Aunt I shall be quit with you—— [*Ex.*

La. Lov. Hark you *Robin.* [*Whisper Sir* Rich.

Raym. Mrs. *Bridget,* since *Theodosia* has intrusted you, you must not refuse to bring me privately into her Chamber this Night.

Bridg. I shall be glad to serve you, but my Lady will discover it.

Raym. Let me alone to manage that; I'll dispose of her that she shall never know of it.

La. *Lov.* Mr. *Raymund* I beg your pardon; but if you please at present we will with-draw.

Raym. I'll wait on your Ladyship.

Enter Crazy, Brisk, *and* Drybob.

Brisk. Ah Madam! Your Ladyships humble Servant.

La. Lov. Gentlemen your Servant.

Brisk. Where is your Niece?

La. Lov. I'll send her to you—— [*Ex.* La. Lov. Raym. *and* Bridget.

Brisk. Now, you shall see my Mistriss.

Dryb. This is a very good Jest, i'faith, *Crazy*; his Mistriss.

Craz. That Men should understand themselves no better?

Brisk. Fa, la, la, la, that's an excellent Corant; really I must confess *Grabu* is a very pretty hopeful Man, but *Berkenshaw* is a rare fellow, [*Walks* give him his due, fa, la, la, for he can teach men to compose, *about combing* that are deaf, dumb, and blind. *his Peruke.*

Dryb. This is a good, pretty, apish, docible Fellow; really he might have made a very pretty Barber-Surgeon, if he had been put out in time : but it arrides me extreamly, to think how he will be bob'd?

Craz. Yes, yes, he will be bob'd; that men should be so mistaken.

Dryb. Ay, on my Conscience and Soul, the Palat of his Judgement is down; and by the way, how dost like that Metaphor, or rather *Catachresis*?

Craz. Oh admirably.

Brisk. Drybob.

Craz. While these Coxcombs are in discourse, I'll privately go in and see my Mistriss—— [*Ex.* Craz.

Brisk. Here's a Perriwig, no Flax in the World can be whiter; how delicately it appears by this Colour'd Hanging, and let me advise you ever while you live, if you have a fair Peruke, get by a Green or some dark colour'd Hanging or Curtain, if there be one in the Room. Oh it sets it off admirably.

Dryb. A very Metaphysical Notion.

Brisk. And be sure if your Eye brows be not black, to black 'em soundly; ah your Black Eye-brow is you fashionable Eye-brow. I hate Rogues that wear Eyebrows that are out of fashion.

Dryb. By the Soul of *Gresham* a most Phylosophical Invention.

Brisk. Thou't scarce believe it, but upon my Honour, two Ladies fell in love with me one day at the King's Play-house, and are in a desperate condition at this very time, for this Perywig.

Dryb. But why are you so cruel?

Brisk. Alas! if I should mind every Lady that falls in love with me, I should have a fine time on't indeed.

Dryb. *Stultorum omnia plena !* I am the spurious issue of a Fishmonger ; if a more conceited Puppy ever presented himself to my Eyes.

Brisk. I had three several Suits in one year, won me three very ingenious quick-spirited, and very pretty merry conceited Ladies, as any are within the Walls of *Europe.* You must know I do value my self upon my Cloaths, and the judicious wearing of 'em.

Dryb. Nay, certainly you are a most compleat and polite Gentleman in the opinion of at least two besides your self.

Brisk. No, no ; but I'll tell thee an honest fellow of my acquaintance, by imitating one of my Suits, got himself a Widdow of 3000 *l.* a year Peny Rent.

Enter Crazy *and* Theodosia.

Craz. Pray Madam, let me advise you, don't run your self into trouble with these Puppies, but let us enjoy our selves in private.

Theo. Sir, I must obey my Aunt, 'tis not for want of Inclination to your sweet Society, I assure you.

Brisk. Ah, my Queen Regent, I salute the hem of your Garment.

Theo. I cannot without a blush, allow the humility of the Address.

Dryb. Thou shalt see *Crazy* how she'll abuse him, for I am the Son of a Bum-Baily if she has not the most exuberant and luxureous expressions that every enter'd the concave of this Ear.

Craz. This Fool *Drybob*, has no more understanding than a Gander.

Brisk. By the Coat of our Family, which is an Ass Rampant, a very ancient and honourable one, I am ready to venture my life under the Banner of your Beauty ; and honour you so, that I would, oh 'tis incomparable, 'tis incomprehensible———

Theo. By my Grandfather's Spur-leather, which was in those dayes worn by very Honourable Persons, you oblige me so immoderately : That oh——'tis admirable, 'tis inexpressible !

Craz. How I blush for this fellow !

Brisk. Come, Madam, let's be frolick, Galliard, and extraordinary brisk, fa, la, la, la.

Theo. Sir, I cannot behold the lines of that Face, but I am provok'd to Mirth, fa, la, la, la.

Brisk. Look you there *Drybob* and *Crazy*, look ye——

Craz. Madam, I am so interrupted by these Fellows, that I have not time to tell you that I feed a Flame within, which so torments me.

Dryb. Pox on't, that's stole out of a Play.

Craz. What then, that's lawful ; 'tis a shifting Age for Wit, and every body lies upon the Catch.

Brisk. O Madam, where were you, that I miss'd you last night at the Park ?

Theo. Did you shine there laſt Night?

Brisk. Madam, I did; For after I had pranc'd before your Window upon my Roan Nag, in Honour to my Love,——
Did you see me Madam?

Theo. O Sir, my Eyes met you in your Career, by the same Token you had a Muskatoon and Piſtols.

Brisk. I had so Madam, and my Man carry'd a skrew'd-Gun, that I bought at *Brussels*; for I alwayes love to do things *en Cavalier*; but thus equipp'd, I went to take the Air in the Park, and immediately all the Ladies and Persons of Quality left the Tour and came about me, and were moſt imcomparably pleas'd with the Fashion; so that I am resolv'd next time to go with Back, Breaſt, and Headpiece.   [*Floriſh.*

Theo. Moſt acutely imagin'd.

Brisk. But hark you Madam, yonder are my Fiddles: I bespoke 'em, and pray let me have the honour to dance with you; it may be you will like my manner well enough.

Dryb. But we want Women.

Craʒ. I'll supply that, Madam, immediately.

Brisk. Prethee do, and make haſte *Crazy.*

Craʒ. Now will I be reveng'd upon *Briske*, and bring his own Strumpet hither.——   [*Ex.* Crazy

Enter Lady Loveyouth *and* Raymund.

Raym. You muſt not deny me this Evening some private Conference with you.

La. Lov. But how shall I keep it from the knowledge of my Niece?

Raym. I'll tell you, Madam, If you please to walk in the Garden, I'll come in at the Back-door and wait on you there, where we will confer about our mutual happiness.

La. Lov. I will not fail——

Brisk. My Honourable Aunt that shall be, I adore your Shoeſtrings.

La. Lov. O Lord Sir, your Servant. Come on Mr. *Raymund,* let's hear you break a Jeſt, and put these two Wits out of Countenance.

Theo. Methinks Mr. *Dryobob* is a notable Man.

Brisk. Ay, Madam, as far as Inns-of-Court breeding; but alas, we are above those things.

Raym. Are you above Inns-of-Court breeding?

Brisk. Yes, that I am, Sir, what's that to you?

Raym. Why it is not Six Moneths since you us'd to keep company with none but Clerks, and call for your Three pence in Beef at *Hercules Pillars,* or at the *Harrow* in *Chancery lane;* where the whole Company us'd to fall out about the dividing of Three half-pence: When every Night you us'd to drink Ale, and put Law Cases as long as you could see.

Brisk. You are merry, Sir.

Dryb. And where you us'd——

Raym. Nor is it five Moneths since I saw you strut most Majestically in the Hall, and inveagle a third man at Six-penny In and In, and by the help of a dozen men, chastize one poor Topper or Palmer; where I have seen you most magnanimously assist at the pumping of a Bawd, or the washing and trimming of a Baily.

Dryb. Where I have seen you?——

Brisk. Is this your breeding?

Dryb. A pox on't a man cannot speak for you.

Brisk. But Sir, I'd have you know I was as well esteem'd there as any man that ever eat Loyns of Mutton dry-rosted yet, and danc'd as well at the Revels too.

Dryb. I have seen you there, how you——

Brisk. And let me tell you that at *Christmas*, when we were to have had a Prince, I was as fair for preferment as any man there.

Dryb. Yes, and I can tell you——

Brisk. But the Government, by reason of some civil dissentions, fell that *Christmas* to a Common-wealth; but alas I am above these things.

Dryb. Above 'em!——I'll tell you——

Raym. Why this to me?

Dryb. Pox of these uncivil fellows, they won't let a man break a jest among 'em; and Madam, I am the Son of a Baboon, if stoppage of Wit be not as great a pain to me as stoppage of Urine.

Raym. Have not I seen you within these three Moneths lolling out of *Mundens* with a Glass of Windy-Bottle-Ale in one hand, and a Pipe of *Mundungus* in the other; and out of a brisk gay humour, drinking to Passengers in the Street.

Brisk. 'Tis well Sir, I hope you will give me satisfaction for these affronts?

Raym. Yes, as much as you dare ask.

Brisk. Then blood will ensue.

Enter Crazy *and* Friske.

Craz. Madam, here is one Lady.

Brisk. Death this Rogue has undone me! *Friske* here! *Theodosia* will for ever disown me——

Raym. What's the matter *Briske?* are you Planet struck. *Crazy*, I could hugge thee for this.

La. Love. We need your assistance in a Dance, Madam.

Frisk. Your Servant sweet Madam; Lord, Mr. *Brisk*, you need not be so strange.

Brisk. Ah Cosin, your Servant.

Theo. Is she your Cosin Sir?

Frisk. Mr. *Brisk* is none of my Cosin, I assure your Ladyship; he is my Servant, nay perhaps there is a little nearer relation betwixt us.

Theo. How's this Sir?

Brisk. 'Slife, this She Devil will ruin me! Alas, Madam, she's merry, she drolls; but come let's dance and put these things out of our heads. Come in Minnim and Crotchet and fegue your Violins away, fa, la, la, la.

Enter Mrs. Striker.

Craz. O Heaven! who's here, I am undone. [*He goes to thrust her away.*

Brisk. This is a Revenge beyond my expectation, stand by *Crazy;* whither do you put the Lady? Come in Mrs. *Striker;* here's a Mistress of *Crazy's* will serve to make up the number of Dancers, Madam.

Craz. Prethee begone, if thou lov'st me.

Striker. Come Mr. *Crazy,* this won't pass upon me.
Your Ladiships most obedient Servant—— [*To* Theod.

Raym. Bear up *Crazy,* you know she's a Person of Honour.

Craz. Come Fiddles strike up, pray Madam, let's dance. [*They Dance.*

Brisk. Now Sir, I hope you are ready to give me satisfaction.

Raym. I am Sir.

Brisk. Follow me then. Ladies, I have an inexorable business calls me away at present——Servant, your Servant.

Raym. Ladies, I'll wait on you agen instantly; Mrs. *Bridget* prethee forget not what I said to you, we shall have excellent sport. [*Ex.* Raym.

Bridg. I warrant you I'll do't Sir.

La. Love. Now he's gone, I'll retire; Ladies and Gentlemen your
Servant—— [*Ex.*

Frisk. O me, Madam, why does not your Ladyship frequent the Mulberry-Garden oftner: I vow we had the pleasant'st Divertisement there last Night.

Strik. Ay, I was there, Madam *Frisk,* and [Craz. *whispers* Bridget.
the Garden was very full, Madam, of Gentlemen and Ladies, that made love together till Twelve a Clock at Night, the prettily'st: I vow 'twould do ones heart good to see them.

Theo. Why that's a time for Cats to make love in, not Men and Women.

Frisk. Well Madam, there was a Lord, that shall be nameless, would needs come and proffer his service to me.

Strik. I know who that was; alas, he'll do that to any body, Madam *Friske.*

Frisk. Lord, you are so troubl'd, I warrant you, Madam *Striker.*

Dryb. to Bridg. But art thou sure thy Mistress loves me?

Bridg. Why she cannot rest for you.

(225)

Dryb. But she's so pester'd with these Fools *Brisk* and *Crazy*, that I can have no time to caress her.

Bridg. I'll tell you a way to get privately into her Chamber this Night.

Frisk. But Madam, this Lord took me by the hand and kiss'd it, and told me it was as sweet as Roses and soft as Jelly of Quinces.

Theo. Or he might have said as sweet as Frankinsence, or as soft as the Pappe of an Apple.

Strik. Alas, Madam, that's nothing; I assure your Ladyship, he has said the same thing to me twenty times.

Frisk. For my part, Madam *Striker*, I do not think you know him.

Strik. Lord, Madam *Friske*, you are always detracting from one, I am sure I saw him last Night, and he told me, Madam, he honour'd the ground I trod upon, and made me abundance of the rarest Complements, and I said a number of the pretty'st things to him: if I could remember, I'd tell 'em your Ladyship, you shou'd be judge of them, Madam.

Dryb. Dear Mrs. *Bridget* accept of this little Present, I'll not fail to do it—Ladies I have an exorbitant affair causes me at present to bestow my absence upon you, but I'll be sure not to fail you—— [*Exit.*

Theo. What means this foolish Fellow?

Bridg. Pray Mr. *Crazy* let me beg a word with you. [*Whisper.*

Frisk. I'll tell you, Madam, now she talks thus, there was another Person of Quality came to me, and told me I was a pretty Nymph, and he was a Satyr, and invited me to drink a Bottle of Rhenish and Sugar, and I protest and vow he would not drink one drop, till I had dipt my Finger in the Glass.

Theo. It seems he lov'd to drink with a Tost——

Strik. Pish! that's nothing, I assure you a Person of Quality, that treated me, would not drink a drop of Wine, till I had wash'd my hands in the Glass, now she talks of that, hah.

Theo. What ridiculous vain Wenches are these?

Frisk. Pish! mind her not Madam, but I vow, now she puts me in mind on't, a Gentleman t'other day play'd the Wagg with me, and would needs pull my Shoe off my Foot and drink it full of Wine; upon my word he did now.

Craz. to *Bridg.* Faith, as thou say'st, I believe she loves me; but why would she not tell me this her self?

Bridg. She had no opportunity, but she charg'd me to desire you to come in at her Window this Night as I tell you.

Craz. And upon my honour I'll do't, wer't as high as *Pauls.* Ladies my occasions invite me hence, and I shall be glad to wait on you.

Strik. Madam, I humbly covet the honour of your further acquaintance.

Frisk. I hope your Ladyship will not deny me that honour.

Frisk and *Strik*. Your humble Servant, Madam.

Theo. Your humble Servant, Ladies.

Craz. Madam, I'll not fail you upon my honour.——   [*Exit*.

Theo. What means this fellow, *Bridget?* what trick have you put upon these two Coxcombs, that they both tell me they will not fail me?

Bridg. Madam, Mr. *Raymund* designs this Night privately to wait on you, and that he may not be interrupted, has appointed my Lady to wait for him in the Garden; and I to get rid of this brace of Widgeons, have appointed each of 'em to get in at your Window by Ladders privately this Night.

Theo. How then shall I see *Raymund* in my Chamber without discovery?

Bridg. Madam, I have appointed them to come to a wrong Window, but were it the right Window, they being to come both at one time, would disappoint one another.

Theo. That's not unpleasant, we may have good sport. 'Tis possible they may be taken by the Watch, and apprehended for House-breakers; but come along with me.——   [*Ex. Ambo*.

THE FOURTH ACT.

Enter Raymund *and* Briske *in a Tavern*.

Raym. COme out Sir, and fight, if you have a maw to't: I am ready, I thought you would have brought me into the Field, and you bring me into a Tavern.

Brisk. Nay prethee dear Rogue, let's stay a little and debate the business over a Bottle of Wine first: Look you, here's to you.

Raym. Must I stay, till by the strength of Terse Claret, you have whet your self into courage?

Brisk. But look you, dear *Raymund*, the Case is this——

Raym. No more words, I am ready.

Brisk. Now I think on't better, we must adjourn the Combat, for 'tis grown dark, and we cannot see to kill one another.

Raym. Come I warrant you we can see one anothers Bodies, and that's enough.

Brisk. Ay, but I have sworn never to fight, but when I can see to parrie.

Raym. I'll take away that objection; here are Candles in the Room, and I'll bolt the Door, that no Drawer shall come to part us.

Brisk. Fie *Raymund*, is that like men of honour, fight in a Tavern? why 'tis like the Bullies man.

Raym. None of your foolish punctilio's here, draw.

Brisk. Well, ha, ha, ha, I have consider'd on't, and Gad thou art a very honest fellow, I have that affection for thee, that the Devil take me if I fight with thee.

Raym. Why did you call me out then?

Brisk. Come, pox on't, put up; I must confess I have rashly embarqu'd my self in a most prejudicial affair, but thou art a man of honour, and I will not fight with thee.

Raym. Are you not a Coward?

Brisk. Ha, ha, honest *Raymund*, thou art a very merry fellow, I'll give thee leave to say what thou wilt.

Raym. I need not ask the question.

Brisk. Well faith, I will not fight with thee, say what thou wilt, but upon my honour I'll give thee this Diamond Ring and my Roan Nag, if thou'lt oblige me in one thing.

Raym. In what can that be?

Brisk. You know my Mistriss will think I ought in honour to fight; and if you will do me the favour to make her believe you fought with me, I'll tell her you disarm'd me, and by this means I shall save honour, and you will get it and for ever oblige me.

Raym. Faith I had best take 'em for sport sake, though I return 'em again.   [*Aside.*

Brisk. Prethee, dear *Raymund* do; I'll do as much for thee upon my honour.

Raym. Would you have a Gentleman lie for you?

Brisk. Why I'll lie for you agen man, when you will; what do you talk of that?

Raym. Not I Sir.

Brisk. Let me see, I have thought upon a way to save that; look you, we'll fight a little in jest; and I'll let you disarm me. Here, prethee take the Ring, and do't; and I'll send for my Roan Nag immediately.

Raym. Come Sir, to oblige you I will, Draw then.——

Brisk. Honest *Raymund*, I am thy dear Servant.——

Raym. Come on, come, have at you——

Brisk. Hold, hold man——hold——

Raym. What's the matter?

Brisk. How shall I be sure you won't fight in earnest?

Raym. I give my word for't.

Brisk. But Gad now I think on't, I won't trust you, if you wou'd give me your Bond; I don't know how the Devil may tempt you:

Besides, who knows, but your foot may slip, and you may run me thorow the Body.

Raym. What an immoderate Coward is this?

Brisk. Faith, thou had'st as good tell her so without this Experiment!

Raym. But there must appear some signs of fighting, or she'll not believe it.

Brisk. Why I'll tear my Band and my Shirt, and run my self thorow the Coat.

Raym. But there must be some sign of blood.

Brisk. Pox on't, how shall we contrive that?

Raym. Why take your Sword, and run your self thorow the Arm.

Brisk. Thank you for that i'faith, I have known men have dy'd of that.

Raym. Fie, Fie! 'tis nothing; I'll do't my self then.

Brisk. Hold, hold, 'Slife you may prick an Artery and bleed to death, and then I shall be hang'd for that.

Raym. That's well thought on! O incomparable Coward!

Brisk. 'Twill do as well if my Shirt be bloody at the hand, and I'll venture to prick my fingar for that; and to run thorow my Coat.

Raym. Well, as you will; but do't as you go along.

Brisk. Dear *Raymund* kiss me, you have obliged me so, that I am a Son of a Scavenger, if I die without issue, I'll make you my Heir: but if you love me, not a word of all this.

Raym. I warrant you. Drawer to pay.

Brisk. Prethee, by no means, Gad I'll treat thee dear Rogue; 'tis all mine. Come on, dear *Raymund,* let's go——   [*Exeunt.*

Enter Crazy *with a Ladder.*

Craz. This is the Window Mrs. *Bridget* appointed to get in at, so, now for my Climbing.——   [*Sets down the Ladder.*
How I shall laugh at my two foolish Rivals, *Brisk* and *Drybob,* poor Puppies' that they could not find all this while how *Theodosia* abuses them.

Enter Drybob *with a Ladder.*

Dryb. This is the Window, my expectation is on Tiptoes, as I may so say, but let me fix my portable pair of Stairs.   [*Sets it upon* Crazy.

Craz. Heaven! what will become of me? This is some Villain coming to commit Burglary.

Dryb. Pox take me, if I know what is the matter; it cannot be the Wall that yields thus.

Craz. 'Slife if it should be a Thief, he'll cut my Throat, lest I should discover him; what shall I do?

Dryb. Well, let what will come on't, though I precipitate my fate, I will ſtorm this inchanted Caſtle.

Craz. Who e'r he be, I am sure I'll not suffer him to come up; if he be a mortal man, I'll try if he has a Neck to spare, for I am resolv'd to break one for him—— *[Turns the Ladder.*

Dryb. 'Slife! what's this, am I to be turn'd off and executed for Love-felony before my time? what can this mean? I have got no hurt yet: it may be 'twas the corner of the Balcony I set my Ladder againſt: I'll make one experiment more: so now, 'tis faſt. *[Goes up a little.*

Craz. Theodosia, Theodosia, open your Window.

Dryb. The Ladder ſtands very faſt now, I will once more enterprize this honorable action, though *Belzebub* himself ſtood in my way—— *Theodosia* open your Window, 'tis I my Dear.

Craz. Death, what will become of me, this muſt be the Devil, a Man would have broke his Neck.

O Heaven! yonder is a Light coming towards us. I shall be ruin'd if I don't shift for my self.

Dryb. If I be discover'd by you *Ignis fatuus* or Lanthorn, I shall be undone for ever, I muſt try to make an escape.

Enter Raymund *and* Brisk, Boy *with a Light and Fiddles; and beat them as they come down the Ladder.*

Brisk. Come on my dear Friend, ſtrike up my Men of Noise; How now! what's here? Thieves with Ladders at my Miſtrisses Window, I'll mall 'em.

Raym. How now Villains——*Bridget* has done this admirably. *[They beat them off.*

Brisk. 'Slife *Raymund*, if I had not come, I might have loſt my Miſtriss out of this Window; for on my Conscience these Rogues came with a felonious intention: but come let's in and give 'em an account of it: and Fiddles make way for us.

Raym. Come on: But how shall I get rid of this Fool, I muſt think of some way.

Enter Bridget *with a Candle.*

Bridget. O Gentlemen! what's the cause of this uproar?

Brisk. Oh, Mrs. *Bridget*, I have made bold to beat a couple of Rascals, that were going to commit Felony, without the benefit of the Clergy; but I'll go and wait upon my Miſtriss—— *[Exit.*

Raym. Oh, Mrs. *Bridget*, 'twas *Crazy* and *Drybob*, our Plot is spoil'd; I shall be diverted by them from seeing my Miſtriss.

Bridg. No, no, let me alone, I'll dispose of 'em another way.

Raym. Adieu—— *[Ex. Raym.*

Enter Crazy *from behind the Door.*

Craz. Oh I am beaten, bruis'd and lam'd so, that I had rather have been twice flux'd than have endur'd it; my Bones are as loose as the Skeletons in the Physick School: Oh my Head and Shoulders! Mrs. *Bridget* I kiss your hands, and rest your humble Servant *Crazy*.

Brid. Sir, I find you are defeated by some ill accident or other, but I'll put you in another way to be secure. The Lady *Theodosia* is in that passion for you, that I fear she will discover her self.

Craz. Poor heart! I know she loves me; but I hope she will be so discreet as to conceal her passion; but here was another with a Ladder climbing up to the Window, or I had got in.

Brid. Another! that's impossible; but lest you should be suspected, take away your Ladder, and set it against the Garden Wall, and I will appoint your Mistriss to receive you there; if you will venture to come over to her; and there shall be a Parson ready to joyn you in the Banquetting house: make haste, lest you be surpriz'd, and come to us instantly.

Craz. Dear Mrs. *Bridget* take this, I flie, I flie.—— [*Ex. with a Ladder.*

Enter Drybob.

Dryb. O Mrs. *Bridget!* Are you there? I have been beaten more severely than ever Turk was by *Tamberlain;* which by the way is no ill comparison, hah?

Bridg. I have heard so; but take up your Ladder and be gone, and lay it down on the back side of the house and come to us presently, and I will design an easier assignation for you; haste, lest you be discover'd.

Dryb. Dear Mrs. *Bridget* take this Ring, I'll be with you instantly.
[*Ex. with a Ladder.*

Bridg. Go your wayes you brace of Baboons, and be still the subject of all Farces—— [*Ex.* Bridget.

Enter Raymund, Brisk, La. Loveyouth, Theodosia, Bridget.

La. Love. Is it possible! Thieves coming in at my Window! Heaven! how I tremble!

Bridg. Truly Madam, they were as sufficiently beaten as your Ladiship can wish.

Theo. That's some revenge for the trouble their impertinence has given me, but I am afraid these Coxcombs will hinder Mr. *Raymunds* Visit.

Bridg. Fear not that, Madam.

Raym. Be not apprehensive Madam, for the Rascals are too well satisfied for their pains to attempt any more.

Enter Crazy, *and after* Drybob.

Craz. Ladies and Gentlemen, your humble Servant.

Dryb. Dear friends, your Slave; I am in one word the Enemy to all your Foes.

Brisk. Oh are you here ! I'll tell you as I was coming in to give my Mistriss a Serenade, a couple of Felonious Rascals were with two Ladders climbing in at a Window of the House; but I think I have so bruis'd the Dogs, they'll scarce be fit for climbing this Week agen.

Craz. A plague on't, I feel it in my bones, but I must dissemble it.

Dryb. Pox on them, the Rogues laid on as if they had been threshing for Twelve Pence a day.

Craz. But is it possible ?

Brisk. Yes, I assure you as this Blade doth testifie.

Dryb. Why, what impudent Rogues were these *Crazy.*

Craz. 'Death, that I must be forced to call my self so.—— [*Aside.* If I had been there I would have mall'd the Villains.

Dryb. For my part I don't wish I had been there, for my extraordinary passion would have made me had the blood of the Rogues; that's certain ——O pox of their heavy hands.

Raym. He has been fighting, Madam, that's the truth on't; pray take notice on't.

Briske. I wonder, *Raymund*, no body takes notice of my torn Band, my bloody Sleeve, and my Coat being run thorow, I think they are all blind.

La. Lov. Good lack, Mr. *Briske*, you're bloody, and your Band's torn.

Briske. Ha ! Bloody say you ?

Raym. Pray hold up the humor, Madam.

Theo. I protest, Sir, you fright me, what dangers have you run your self into ?

Briske. Alas, Madam, this is nothing, a trifle, a trifle.

Bridg. Your Coat's run through, you have been fighting.

Brisk. My Coat run thorough ! Where, Where ? ha, ha, 'tis so.

Dryb. A pox on him this damn'd Bully *Heildibrand* was flesh'd, and would needs shew his Valour upon my Shoulders.

La. Lov. Are you wounded Sir ?

Briske. 'Pshaw, Madam, this, alas, alas, I beseech you take no notice of this; 'pshaw, a slight thing, a toy, fa, la, la, la.

Bridg. Shall I go for a Surgeon !

Briske. No, I thank you, he'd discover the trick on; no't, no, by no means; alas, you make so much on't : I am us'd to these things, 'pshaw, this is nothing; Pray call in the Fiddles, come, come; let us be very merry, fa, la, la.

Theo. Sweet Mr. *Briske* do me the favour to tell me the occasion of this ?

Briske. Nothing, nothing, Madam, alas, alas,——

La. Love. Assure your self I'll not fail to wait for you in the Garden.

Raym. I hope your Ladyship doubts not me.

Briske. Faith Madam, if you will needs have it, I made bold to call Mr. *Raymund* to an account for some words that passed before you ; and upon my Honour, Madam, he's a very gallant fellow.

Raym. Nay, I beseech you Mr. *Brisk.*

Briske. Nay, Gad it shall all out, he fought like Thunder and Lightning, and I muſt confess it was my fortune to be disarm'd, Madam ; but I hope I loſt no Honour, since 'twas by so brave a fellow, whom for his generosity I embrace. Dear Friend, you have oblig'd me for ever. Come Fiddles ſtrike up, I have provided a very honeſt fellow to dance.

[*A Jig is Danc'd.*

Raym. Madam, I'll not fail to wait on you, your humble Servant.——

Ex.

Dryb. Madam, I hope you will be punctual.

Theo. Truſt me, Sir.

Dryb. Adieu to all.—— [*Ex.*

Craʒ. Madam, I'll inſtantly go and prepare to wait on you, you'll fail not.

Theo. I shall not be so injurious to my self.

Craʒ. I humbly kiss your hands. Madam, your Ladyships moſt humble Servant.—— [*Ex.*

La. Lov. Good night, sweet Mr. *Crazy* ; Mr. *Brisk,* I pray be pleas'd to favor me with your absence.

Theo. Pray do, and get a Surgeon to dress you, and to Morrow I shall be ready to receive a Visit.

Briske. Ladies your Servant, Servant, Ladies, fa, la, la, la.——

[*Ex. Brisk.*

La. Lov. Pray Gentlewoman go up into your Chamber.

Theo. Madam, I'll obey——

La. Lov. Be sure you do.—— [*Ex. La.* Lov. *and* Bridg.

Theo. Go thy ways, my dear Aunt, and meditate on what thou'lt ne'r enjoy——If my Uncle, after all this report of his being kill'd should appear again, when she has, as she thinks, made sure of another Husband, it would be no ill Farce.

Enter Raymund.

Raym. Now, now, my Incomparable *Theodosia.*
I am bleſt with the opportunity I have so long sought for to caſt my self

at your feet, and to tell you, that it belongs to you to make my life for ever happy or miserable.

Theo. You may with justice enough accuse me of levity, in so suddenly granting it; but I hope you have so much honour, to impute my easiness somewhat to the slavery I suffer, though I have no disesteem of you.

Raym. Madam, It is so much to my advantage, that I shall never enquire the Cause, only let me beg of you, since our fortune is like to allow us so few of those opportunities, that we may make what use we can of this.

Theo. I have so absolute a confidence in your honour, that I yield to your conduct in this affair, and desire nothing more than to be redeem'd from the foolish Tyrany of my Aunt.

Enter Bridget.

Bridg. I have left my Lady in the Garden, most impatiently expecting you Mr. *Raymund.* But pray Madam, if you love me, retire into your Chamber, lest any of the Servants should unluckily see you, and inform your Aunt.

Theo. 'Tis no ill advice.

Raym. But how have you dispos'd of *Drybob* and *Crazy.*

Bridg. O they are safe enough, Sir;   [*Exeunt.*

Enter La. Lovey, *in the Garden.*

La. Lovey. Sure the passion he has for me, will not suffer him to stay long, the Story of Thieves at my window, has put me into such a fright, that nothing but Love could engage me to walk here alone.

Enter Crazy *looking over the Wall.*

Craz. The Coast is clear on this side, if my Mistriss be but in the Garden, I am safe——My Dear.

La. Lovey. Here I am.

Craz. Now I come, wer't as high as *Grantham-steeple !* Death I have broke both my Shins: I am murder'd: Oh, I see these leaps are not for men that have flux'd thrice.

La. Lov. How Mr. *Raymund !* Have you hurt your self?

Craz. Did you expect *Raymund* here? I am not he.

Enter Drybob *looking over the Wall.*

Dryb. Now for my leap of Honour.   [*Noise crying Thieves*

La Love. Oh Heaven! Thieves, Thieves, Help, Help.

Craz. Death what do I here?

Dryb. Thieves! I shall be apprehended for a House-breaker.

Craz. Where shall I hide my self? I would not be discover'd for the World.

Dryb. I am astonished like the Head of a Gorgon; what shall I do to abscond a little, I shall be apprehended for a Thief else.

Craz. 'Tis very dark, where shall I hide my self?

Dryb. What Devilish mistake is this? Pox o' this damn'd post, I am sure I had like to have got a most Diabolical fall with running against it.   [*They run against one another.*

Craz. Death what was that I run against, what an unfortunate fellow am I, to be thus disappointed, just as I thought to have been sure of my Mistriss? but my comfort is, I know she loves me.

Dryb. What a Devilish Catastrophe is this?——
                                    [*Groping, lights upon his hands.*

Craz. O horrid! Sure this House is haunted, which way can I scape?

Dryb. If this be the Devil that touch'd me, I don't like his slie Tricks to fright a man thus; wou'd he would be as civil as the *Wiltshire* Devil was; and beat a Drum, to give a man notice where he is, that I might avoid him, unless he were better company.

Craz. What's here? her amazement hath made her leave open the Door of the House, I'll in there, there's more safety yet than here——
                                    [*Goes in.*

Dryb. Ha, I saw one enter at that Door, I'll follow and apprehend him; and his attachment will secure me.——   [*Ex.*

Enter Crazy.

Craz. What Door is this? I'll e'en hide my self here till this bustle be over.

Enter Drybob.

Noise within. Lights here, follow, follow.

Dryb. If I could but conceal my self till they are past, I might easily insinuate my self into *Theodosia's* Chamber. What's here? This I believe leads into the Cellar, I will descend and lie in Ambush there.—— [*Ex.*

Enter Servants with Torches, Spits, and Fireforks, Mr. Sneak, *and Sir* Richard.

1. *Serv.* Come, now we have muster'd up our forces, let's into the Garden.

Sir Rich. Ay, come let's see who this Devil is my Lady speaks of; we shall find more than one I believe.

2 *Serv.* I believe we shall find them to be Thieves.

1 *Serv.* If it be the Devil, Mr. Parson, we'll turn you loose to him, you take pay to fight against him; we are but Volunteers.

Sneak. If he dares approach I will conquer him Syllogistically in Mood and figure, and conjure him down with
Barbara, Celarent, Darii, Ferioque, Darapti.
Cesare, Camestres, &c.

2. Serv. Hold, hold, s'life this is the way to raise him.

1 Serv. I think your best way is to take the great Bible in the Hall and fling at his Head : that will knock him down certainly.

Sir Rich. Come, let's in quickly, if they be Thieves, they'l escape else.——

1 Serv. The Cellar Door is open, if there be any body there, we'll lock it and secure 'em—— [*Ex.*

Enter Bridget *with a Candle.*

Bridg. How unlucky is this! this has marr'd all our design; my Lady has found Mr. *Raymund* and her Niece, we are undone beyond redemption.

Enter La. Loveyouth, Raymund, *and* Theodosia.

La. Love. False and ungrateful man, did I for this, so soon bestow upon you my too credulous heart, so early to betray me; O unheard of Villany.

Raym. Madam, pray hear me.

La. Love. No, thou vile treacherous man, I will hear no more, Hast thou the impudence to excuse it! Oh heaven! I am lost for ever. But for you, you most abominable Creature, to undermine me thus : Take leave of liberty, henceforwards your Chamber shall be your Prison, till I have dispos'd of you to another Person, I assure you.

Theo. Then Madam, you force me to declare my self sooner than my Modesty would give me leave; this Gentleman is mine while I have breath; nothing but death shall part us.

Raym. And Madam, that minute that I am false to you, may all the plagues that e'r afflicted yet mankind fall on me.

La. Love. In what a miserable condition am I? but Mr. *Raymund* I cannot believe this, sure this is some enterlude.

Raym. Madam, it is a truth I'll die for, though Madam, I am oblig'd to beg your Ladishyps pardon for making you a property.

La. Love. O impudence! Come Mistriss into your Chamber quickly, I'll be your Keeper.

Raym. Madam, we will be pris'ners together.

La. Love. Out of my Doors, you Villain, or I will have those that shall chastise your insolence with death.

Raym. Madam, I have not so mean a soul, to be frighted from protecting my Mistriss.

(236)

Theo. Sir, Let me entreat you to leave me, and assure your self we will not long be separated.

Raym. But Madam, 'twill be dangerous to leave you to her fury.

Theo. Sir, Let me beg you will not dispute it further, but be gone; if you should make more noise in this business, it might call my honour in question.

Raym. Madam, I must obey, and I have a way to free you instantly, 'tis this.

La. Love. Away no more discourses——[*Ex.* La. Loveyouth *and* Theodosia.

Raym. Well a desperate disease must have a desperate Cure; Mrs. *Bridget* I have a way this moment to secure my Mistriss.

Bridg. O Sir, I am in that fright for you.

La. Love. within. Bridget come up quickly.

Bridg. O Sir, I am call'd, I must away.

Raym. I have not time to tell you; but desire *Theodosia*, what ever happens not to be frighted, I'll about it instantly.

Enter Servants, *Sir* Richard, Sneak,——

1 *Serv.* My Lady was frighted with nothing.

2 *Serv.* If any body had been there, the Walls are so high on the inside, they could not have 'scap'd.

1 *Serv.* Ha, here's one, seize him.

Raym. Seize me, you Rascals; have at you.   [*They fight, and* Raym.

Sneak. Nay, now you are in Combat,   *beats them off.*
I'll leave you——   [*Exit.*

2 *Serv.* This a Thief, I am sure he fights like a Devil.

Sir *Rich.* 'Tis Mr. *Raymund*, did you not know him.

1 *Serv.* A pox on him, was't he? but let's to my Lady, and give her an account.——   [*Exeunt.*

Enter Crazy *and* Drybob *in the Cellar.*

Craz. I hear a bustling here about the Cellar that frights me horribly! This is a most unfortunate Night.

Dryb. O that I were out of this Hellish Place! if ever I had to do with Love and Honour more, would I were an Eunuch in the Turks *Seraglio.*——
Oh Heaven, who's that there?

Craz. 'Tis a man by his asking that Question, and may be one of the House.

Dryb. Who are you in the Name of Wonder? O how I dissolve!

Craz. I am the Devil.

Dryb. The Devil! oh he's come to fetch me away for my whoring and my drinking.

Craz. Mortal thou art my due.

Dryb. That may be, but he's a damn'd impatient Devil to dun before his day.

Craz. Come into my Arms.

Within. Fire, fire, fire.

Craz. O Heaven, what shall we do?

Dryb. 'Slife fire! Oh Heaven! how shall we get out?

Craz. groping. Which is the way out? The Door's lock'd, what shall I do? They'll not mind us if we call; we shall be burnt.

Dryb. What are you a Devil, and afraid of your own Element? Methinks a Devil out of the Fire should be like a Fish out of the Water.

Within. Fire, fire, fire.

Both. Help, help, here, fire, murder, help.

Enter Servants above.

1 *Serv*. What noise was that below?

Both. Help, help.

2 *Serv*. Oh oh, have we caught you? They are the Thieves.

1 *Serv*. That's well, ſtay there; you Dogs, if the House be burnt, I'll assure you, you shall be burnt with it.

Craz. O help, help, 'tis *Crazy*.

Dryb. *Crazy!* a Curse on you for frighting me; help, 'tis I *Drybob*.

Craz. We'll see if we can get out at the Window. Well this is a judgement upon me for acting the Devil.—— [*Exeunt*.

Enter Servants *running up and down.*

1 *Serv*. More hands, water quickly, and we shall quench it inſtantly.

2 *Serv*. 'Tis ſtrange how the Coach-house should be fir'd.——[*Exeunt*.

Enter Raymund *and* Theodosia.

Theo. This was an excellent Stratagem, Sir, and with little or no danger.

Raym. Come Madam, while your Aunt is seeing the fire quench'd on the back-side, let us escape at the fore-door.—— [*Exeunt*.

Enter La. Loveyouth, Bridget, *Sir* Richard, Sneak, *and* Servants.

La. Love. So, Heaven be thanked, all danger's paſt; How could this fire happen? This has been a night of wonder.

Sneak. I will dilucidate it to you, you saw a Spirit in the Garden, Madam.

La. Love. I did, I think, to my great aſtonishment; I have not yet recover'd the fright.

(238)

Sneak. Look you, Madam, These Philosophers aver, that all Spirits are transported through the Air in their several and respective Vehicles; now this was infernal, and had a Bituminous Vehicle, which by a violent Motion against the Coach-House, as it were by Collision, did generate this Flame, which had like to have caus'd this Conflagration.

Sir *Rich.* A pox o' this Fustian Rascal.

Bridg. Come, Madam, it must be some Thieves design to rifle your house.

1 *Serv.* We have some of the Thieves safe in the Cellar, they shall suffer for it.

La. Love. In the Cellar, fetch 'em up quickly; by them we may discover something. Go see where my Niece is *Bridget.* [*Ex.* Bridget.

2 *Serv.* Come along you Rascals.

Enter Servants *haling* Crazy *and* Drybob.

1 *Serv.* Come out you Sons of Bitches.

La. Love. Who are these Mr. *Crazy* and Mr. *Drybob*? this is as strange as all the rest.

Craz. Madam, I kiss your fair hands.

Dryb. Pish, that's a vile old phrase. I am an humble Servant of your Footmans.

La. Love. Sure this is Enchantment! How came you two in the Cellar?

Enter Bridget.

Dryb. Madam, I will most expeditiously inform you.

La. Love. How now, where's my Niece?

Bridg. Madam, She's gone! fled away! I have been in every Room of the House and cannot find her.

Sir *Rich.* Gone! What can this mean?

La. Love. Gone! I am undone! Ruin'd for ever! What shall I do?

Sir *Rich.* She undone! Oh invincible impudence!

Dryb. What imports this transport of yours, Madam?

La. Love. You and I and all of us are abus'd! betray'd! this false Wretch, this base Villain *Raymund*, has stol'n away my Niece.

Sir *Rich.* I see *Raymund* is a man of honour. This pleases me.

Craz. Madam, do not fear that, to my knowledge there is a person in the world, she is more than half engag'd to. No, no, she cares not for *Raymund*, take that from me.

La. Love. Flatter not your self, 'tis true, 'tis true.

Dryb. Raymund! I'll assure you Madam, she us'd to simper more favourably upon me than upon any man, and gad if the truth were known, she thinks me all the Nine Worthies, compar'd to him.

La. Love. Come Gentlemen, Let's in and hear the Story, while I send for a Warrant to search for my Niece; I'll have her dead or alive.

[*Exeunt Omnes.*

THE FIFTH ACT.

Enter La. Loveyouth, Bridget, *and Sir* Richard.

La. Love. NO News of either *Raymund* or *Theodosia?*

Sir *Rich.* All possible search has been made after 'em both laſt night and this morning, and they are neither to be found.

La. Love. How am I confounded with this disaſter; yet I have it in my head to be reveng'd on 'em both.

Sir *Rich.* Your Ladyship was too credulous to truſt him so soon.

La. Love. And *Robin*, he's a dirty person thus to desert me; but I'll be quit with him, and that Jig-em-bob my Niece.

Bridg. How Madam?

La. Love. Why, I will immediately settle my Eſtate, to which she is Heir, for want of lawful issue of my Body, on my Cosin *Richard*, and to plague *Raymund* I will marry another; for I am resolved to play at a small game rather than ſtand out.

Sir *Rich.* Oh unparallel'd impudence! I'll try her farther: Madam, what think you of Mr. *Crazy*, he is no unfit man for a Husband?

La. Love. Why really I believe he is a good natur'd Person and a Child of Honour, the softness and gentleness of his Amorous Nature is admirable; but do you think he will have any sprinklings of affection for me.

Sir *Rich.* 'Sdeath! what do I hear?

Bridg. Sprinklings, Madam? He will have a whole Flood of Love for you.

La. Lov. Why truly, he is a pretty hopeful Man, and I have no aversion to, but rather a concern for him; you shall see, *Bridget*; I am a Woman easie to command my Passions; but in the mean time send for a Scrivener, and bid him bring a Blank Conveyance with him: for though I do resolve to make Mr. *Crazy* my Husband, yet I will dispose of my Eſtate, as prudent Widdows are wont to do.

Sir Rich. 'Slife! Now 'tis time to appear! I shall be finely us'd else by this Villanous Woman. I'll into the Town and prepare for't.

Enter Servant.

Serv. Madam, Mr. *Crazy* is coming to wait on you.

La. Lov. Tell him I am retir'd. *Bridget*, I'll leave thee to sound him as to a point of this Concern—— [*Ex.*

Bridg. This is pleasant, I'll observe him.

Enter Crazy, *stumbles and falls.*

Craz. Murder, Murder. O Heaven! What shall I do? I have hurt my self just upon the Shin-bone, that was exfoliated: I have spoil'd my Arm: I fell just upon that part of my Arm, where is a Callous Node upon the *Periostium.*

Bridg. What's the matter, Sir?

Craz. I have hurt my self a little with the fall; besides, I am in a little disorder for the loss of *Theodosia;* sure some base fellow has forc'd her hence; for I am sure she lov'd me most extreamly. 'Sdeath I have spilt my bottle of Diet-drink in my Pocket, and spoil'd all my Almonds and Raisins.

Bridg. Flatter not your self Mr. *Crazy;* she loves you not.

Craz. Prethee do not put this upon me; ha, ha, ha. I am sure no Man had those favourable smiles from her that I received. Oh! that twinge.

Bridg. Come, the truth is, Sir, she is fled away with Mr. *Raymund.*

Craz. Lord, Mrs. *Bridget!* all this won't do; as if I did not know when a Woman loves me?

Bridg. You may please to slight it; but to my knowledge she is marry'd to Mr. *Raymund.*

Craz. Is it true?

Bridg. Too true for you.——

Craz. I am ruin'd beyond redemption, I am for ever disappointed both of Love and Money.

Bridg. There is another Person in the World that's worth your Love, and has a Fortune equal to *Theodosia.*

Craz. Dear Soul, thou dost eternally oblige me! but prethee who is't? Oh, oh, prethee tell me.

Bridg. My Lady *Loveyouth.*

Craz. Ha, ha, ha, well really she is a fine person, and I am extreamly deceiv'd, if she has not a violent and most predominant Passion for me.

Bridg. Sir, you are not deceiv'd.

Craz. I think not——I would forgive a Woman that can deceive me in that point.——But where is she?

Bridg. In her Chamber, where I am sure you would be no unwelcome person.

Craz. This is very lucky, by this means I shall be fully reveng'd for the most perfidious Apostacy of *Theodosia,* and with this ample fortune patch up my own ruinous condition.

Bridg. No more, Sir, but go to my Lady while she is in this humor.

Craz. I am happy beyond expression in your Friendship; Alas, I know this poor thing loves me dearly; and gad she shall be no loser by it: I will go immediately and kiss my Ladies hand; but in the mean time receive this little piece of my Gratitude.

Bridg. Your humble Servant, Sir.

Craz. Sweet dear Rogue, I kiss thy pretty hand.——   [*Ex.*
                              Enter Drybob.

Dryb. How now?
Is the stray Lady return'd home?

Bridg. No Sir, there's no news of her?

Dryb. I am the unlawful Off-spring of a Jugler, if ever Man of Honour encounter'd such a Crocodile; and yet let me not live, if she had not the most pretty harmonious strain of Wit with her that ever tempted a judicious Ear.

Bridg. But she is false——She is false.

Dryb. Really I begin to conjecture it, yet she has so many predominant perfections with her, which I did adore; that I can scarce invite this into my belief: Invite it——'faith that's well enough too.

Bridg. 'Tis too true.

Dryb. Well she is gone, adieu to her; yet really she had the prettiest Figures, and the choicest Phrases in her ordinary Conferences: there are not better in *Pharamond,* or *Cleopatra.*

Bridg. I am glad to see you so indifferent.

Dryb. Not so indifferent: Gad I admire the sharpness of her Ingenuity ——But I'll tell thee the truth, I have sent my Man to a little *Rosicrucian,* or *Stargazer;* to enquire of my Star how she comes thus to start from her Sphere: start from her Sphere, that is well now, that is well.

Bridg. And when will he return?

Dryb. I expect him at every pulse of my Watch; and by the way, is not that prettily said?——hum——but I hope I shall recover her, and yet if I lose her, I am a Rat-catcher if I have not as many Mistrisses as I can turn my self to: Faith I have abundance of Ladies that would think themselves happy to enjoy me: but I cannot be in all places at once: yet in good faith I wish my self an Ubiquitary for their Love, as I am an honest Man.

Within. Bridget.

Bridg. I am call'd, adieu Sir——   [*Ex.* Bridget.

Enter Mr. Briske.

Brisk. How now! What's the news? Has *Raymund* stole away *Theodosia*——ha.

Dryb. Ay pox on him, he, or some damn'd Robber as bad as he, that I fear by this time have committed Burglary upon her Body.

Brisk. And shall I be thus cheated of my Mistriss?

Dryb. Your Mistriss——ha, ha, ha, you speak as freely of her, as if you were acquainted ever since the Deluge with her.

Brisk. Why, had you any pretence to her?

Dryb. Yes Sir, that I had, and perhaps no man receiv'd larger testimonies of her innate Affection.

Brisk. Oh impudence! Why sure you don't pretend to be a man fit for Ladies Conversation! What Charms have you to attract 'em? Ha, ha, ha, you——

Dryb. What Charms quoth he? Is any man in *Europe* more notorious among Ladies, or valu'd for his pregnant parts, than *Drybob*? My manner of speaking, if it were nothing else, is enough to intoxicate Ladies affections. No Orator in Christendom adorns his Language with those Flowers that I do, or is enrich'd with more plentiful Discourse.

Frisk. *Ad autre Monsieur ad autre.*

Dryb. Ne'r tell me, Sir, The Ladies of the Town are so exorbitantly pleas'd with my manner of speaking, that I have been often set upon a Table to speak *ex tempore* to a whole Room full, and have ravish'd 'em all for half an hour together; and this I have got by University Learning and Travelling.

Brisk. Fiddle, faddle on your Travelling and University.

Dryb. Ha, ha, ha, I protest you make me smile.

Brisk. You talk of Ladies, I am a man that still flourish in the Spring, of all the Fashions, and in such variety, that upon my honour 'tis not a fortnight since the publishing of my last new Suit.

Dryb. Publishing! Pox o' this Rogue! How came he to light upon that pretty expression.—— [*Aside.*

Brisk. You visit Ladies! Gad I spend more Money in a year to keep my self sweet, than thy revenue comes to.

Dryb. I am the Son of a *Lancashire* Witch, if thou art not an arrant stinking Fellow then; but what do such people signifie but to maintain Fools, Whores, Mercers, Barbers and Fidlers.

Brisk. Look you Sir, I care not a farthing for your frumps; What can you do? I can Sing, or walk a *Corant* with any man in *Europe*, fa, la, la, la.

Dryb. As I hope ever to live to eat Woodcocks, this is a most stupendious Baboon. Pshaw, what d'ee talk of this? Can you break a Jest, or

(243)

make a Reperte to render your self acceptable to Persons ? That ought to be the business of all Gentlemen, to take all opportunities of shewing their parts, and complying with Company.

Brisk. Break Jests! Pshaw, no man in *Europe* better; but I have other ways to catch Ladies. Look you, no Man appears better upon a Bench in the Playhouse, when I stand up to expose my Person between the Acts; I take out my Comb, and with a *bonne mien Comb* my Periwig to the Tune the Fiddles play: thus, look you, fa, la, la, la.

Dryb. 'Pshaw, I bear my self at another rate; I sit in judgement upon Playes with my Hat thus; with a Brow wrinckl'd like a wither'd Pear-mayne; which Gad is a very pretty Thought, take notice of that: But by this posture am I become more dreadful to the Poets and Players then.—— What, let me see, pox on't hum. This is the first time that ever I wanted a Simile in my life.

Enter La. Loveyouth *and* Crazy.

Craz. Madam, I am transported with your Favours.

La. Lovey. Why in earnest, Sir, I take you for a Person of Generosity, and I cannot but comply with your honourable affections.

Craz. Madam, I humbly kiss your Foot, I will immediately go and prepare for the perfection of my happiness.

La. Lovey. Why truly Sir, it is something too suddain and temerarious, but you have so absolute an Ascendant over me, that I cannot signify any thing as to point of Repulse.

Craz. I make bold to take my leave for some few moments.

Enter Raymund *in disguise, and* Bridget.

La. Lovey. Have you brought a Deed with you ?

Raym. Yes Madam, such a one as will fit you to a Hair.

La. Lovey. Let us in and read it.—— [*Ex.* La. Lov. *and* Raym.

Brisk. Pox on't Mrs. *Bridget,* thou know'st well enough what's become of *Theodosia,* prethee tell me.

Bridg. Well, to you I must confess I do, since she gave me Commission to do it; and Sir, the report of Mr. *Raymund's* stealing her is false: She still preserves her Love to you, you are the Man she resolves to live and die with.

Brisk. Dear Rogue, bring me to her; faith I was amaz'd to think she should leave me, and betray her self to *Raymund,* a fellow that never wore a noble and polite Garniture or a White Periwig; one that has not a bit of Interest at *Chatolins,* or ever eat a good Fricacy, Sup, or Rogust in his life; but prethee bring me to her.

Bridg. Go immediately to your Lodging, you shall hear from me.

Brisk. Adieu, Servant *Drybob.*

Dryb. Pray will you oblige my understanding, to reveal to it this Mystery.

Bridg. 'Tis all for you, in short, *Theodosia* has employ'd me to tell you, that to avoid the importunity of *Crazy* and *Briske,* she fled away; but for you she has still the same Honour and Esteem which you deserve.

Dryb. In good faith this thought was no stranger to my imagination.

Bridg. I have sent him away, that he might not pry into our actions. Hark, my Lady is coming; go instantly and walk in the Piazza, I will send to you suddainly.

Dryb. I will, I will—— [*Ex.* Dryb.

Bridg. I have a plot in this mischievous head of mine, if it takes, shall prove no ill farce.

Enter La. Loveyouth *and* Raymund.

La. Lovey. What are the Gentlemen gone?
Pray call a Servant or two to be witnesses of this Deed of Gift of all my Estate to my Cosin *Richard* after my decease.

Bridg. Yes, Madam.—— [*Ex.*

Raym. Remember Mrs. *Bridget.*

La. Lovey. Now I shall fit *Theodosia* for a punishment for all her villany, by this Deed, shall I not?

Raym. Yes, Madam,——better than you imagine.

Enter Servant *and* Bridget.

La. Lov. Oh are you come, Come, are you ready?

Raym. I will put on the Wax, Madam, here's a Deed will match it, and ready fill'd up to my purpose; I have chang'd it without discovery. ——Come Madam [*She sets her hand to it.*

La. Lov. I declare this as my Act and Deed. Come witness it. So,——here *Bridget,* take my Key and lock it up.

Bridg. Yes, it shall be kept safe.——from you I assure you.——[*Aside.*

La. Lov. There's for your pains; does that content you? [*Ex.*

Raym. Yes, Madam, I am contented.—— [*Ex.* La. Lov.
Or all the World can never make me so, to have obtain'd my *Theodosia,* is a Happiness so great, that I could think of nothing beyond that; nor should I have done this, had it not been for her: for I in her have all I e'er would aim at.

Bridget *returns.*

Bridg. There Sir, there's the Deed.

Raym. Dear Mrs. *Bridget,* you have oblig'd me beyond a Recompence.

Bridg. Now you are Marry'd to her and have the Writing, pray let the Lady *Theodosia* come hither instantly, I have more Irons in the Fire, and need her assistance.

Raym. 'Tis well, I'll not fail to tell her.   [*Ex.* Raym.

Enter Sneake.

Sneak. Now, Dear Madam *Bridget*, Let our Flames incorporate, and by the Mysterious Union of a Conjugal Knot, beyond the Gordian, too strong for the *Macedonian* Steel to rescind.

Bridg. Shall I never learn to understand you, pray help me to a *Clavis*.

Sneak. The meaning of it is, I would make you my Spouse.

Bridg. What? would you lose your Fellowship.

Sneak. I would to that, as they say—*Nuncium remittere;* for I am presented to a Benefice worth six on't.

Bridg. You have Reason, I shall deny you nothing that's reasonable, upon condition you will do one thing for me.

Sneak. 'Tis very well, I shall not deny it.

   Post varios Casus post tot discrimina rerum.

   Tendimus in Latium——

Bridg. You must first Marry Mr. *Brisk* and Mr. *Drybob*, as I shall direct you, but the Ladies will not be known, therefore you must Marry 'em in Vizor Masks.

Sneak. I will, since you command make no hæsitation or dilatory scruple.

Bridg. Pray be gone, I see one coming I must speak with; well, this Plot if it takes, will produce no unpleasant Effects.   [*Ex.* Sneake. Oh Madam!

Enter Theodosia.

I am heartily glad your Plot succeeded so well.

Theo. Dear *Bridget* I owe a great deal of it to thee.

Bridg. I am happy that I could serve you; but now I have a design of my own, in which I beg your Ladyships assistance.

Theo. You may be assur'd of that, what is it?

Bridg. I have perswaded each of the Coxcombs *Briske* and *Drybob*, that you fled to reserve your self for him; and each has so good an opinion of himself, that I found it no hard matter.

Theo. What can this produce to your advantage?

Bridg. Madam, I'll tell you.

Enter Striker *and* Friske.——

Friske. Good lack, Madam *Striker*, Who thought to have seen you here?

Strik. Why, Madam *Friske*? I hope I may be as welcome here as you can.

Frisk. I do not know that neither.

Strik. Madam, your Ladyships most Obedient Servant.

Theo. Madam, your Ladyships most Affectionate Servant.

Frisk. Madam, your Ladyships most obliged Servant.

Theo. Madam, your Ladyships most faithful and devoted Servant.

Strik. Madam, I have weighty occasion invites me to kiss your Ladyships hands this Forenoon.

Frisk. And I one of no less consequence, I assure your Ladyship.

Theo. I hope your Ladyships will do me the Honour to pronounce both your occasions.

Strik. } Madam, Mine is.
Frisk. }

Strik. I wonder you have no more breeding than to interrupt one.

Frisk. Marry come up Mrs. *Habberdasher!* Do you think my Breeding inferiour to yours? I am sure I was bred at a very pretty dancing School hard by, and you talk of that.

Strik. Good Mistriss Gigg-em-bob! your breeding, ha, ha, I am sure my Husband Marry'd me from *Hackney* School, where there was a number of substantial Citizens Daughters; your Breeding——

Frisk. Good Mrs. Gill-flirts we live in a fine age, if a little Paltry Citizens Wife shall compare her self with a Person of my Quality, i'faith.

Strik. Thy Quality Mrs. Kick up——

Theo. Nay, pray Ladies! Pray keep the Peace. Come, have but a little patience, and I will give Audience to both; but no more contention, I am in haste Mrs. *Striker.*

Strik. Madam, I have done; and my Business is this: I protest I am almost asham'd to tell you; but it must out: Mr. *Crazy* has long since engag'd his Heart to me, and I mine to him, and therefore I think, Madam, your Ladyship ought not to encourage the falshood of any Ladies Servant, to listen to any proffers of affection from him.

Theo. Why, you are marry'd! Your Servant.

Strik. Ay, ay, by that time your Ladyship has been marry'd a year or two, you'll soon find the necessity of a Gallant as well as I; besides, my husband's in a Consumption, heaven be prais'd he cannot live long.

Theo. Madam, upon my word I will not rob you of your Jewel, I freely resign him to you.

Frisk. What! will you never have done? Madam, Does your Ladyship know that Mr. *Briske* is my Servant.

Theo. Yes, yes, and know (and know what you would have) and I have found out a way to get you marry'd to this Servant too, or to another as good.

Frisk. I humbly thank your Ladyship; indeed I had rather have another, and besides variety in the Case, I shall be then at once provided with a Husband for a Gallant.

Theo. Pray take this Key, and go up two pair of Stairs to a Chamber on your Left hand, and stay there till further order. I warrant you I'll please you; but at present you must leave me: Be gone.

Strik. Madam, I humbly take my leave of your Ladyship, your Servant——

Frisk. Your Servant, Madam, I am gone,——   [*To* Theo.

Theo. Your Ladyships humble Servant, I'll to my Chamber *Bridget*, and I'll warrant thee to effect thy design.

Strik. Why sure, you han't the confidence to take place of me, have you Mrs. Whirliwigg.

Frisk. Prethee Pusse be quiet, I know what I do.

Strik. Avoid you Strumpet, I am the Mother of Children.

Frisk. Then stay there thou grave Matron.——   [*Ex.*

Strik. She has got it, well, I was never so affronted in my life, I could tear her Heart out: I'll be reveng'd if I live——   [*Ex.* Striker.

Theo. Stay here! I'll send for the brace of Oafs.

Bridg. I will Madam.——

Enter Crazy, Parson, *and* Footman.

Craz. Sweet Mrs. *Bridget*, I am thy most obliged Servant, I have found out Mr. *Sneake*, and brought him here along with me, to compleat my happiness in joyning me to your Lady; and upon my Honour, the whole remainder of my life and love shall be at thy service.

Bridg. I am glad it was in my power to oblige my Lady in so fine a Person.

Craz. Not so neither, yet I will be bold to say she will not be altogether unhappy in a Husband. Boy, I had forgot, go home, and bring me a Bottle of my Dyet-drink, or I shall eat no Dinner to day. Come Sir——   [*Ex.* Craz. *and* Sneak.

Enter Raymund.

Raym. Where's my dear *Theodosia?*

Bridg. She'll instantly be here; now Sir, I have time to wish you all Happiness.

Raym. I thank you, but 'tis a superfluous wish, I have it all already; nothing is yet behind but to make peace with my Lady *Loveyouth*, whom I really have used ill; and to reward your kindness, in earnest of which, you must receive this small present.

Bridg. Sir, I am already too well rewarded, the honour of serving you carries that along with it.

Raym. You are too kind; but what possibilities is there of reconciling me to your Lady.

Bridg. She is now pretty well appeas'd, and has made choice of another for a Husband.

Enter Theodosia.

Raym. Who's that?

My dearest *Theodosia,* I am so happy in thy love, that 'tis beyond the power of Fortune to oblige me more; I can now look down on those I once have envy'd, and scorn all pleasures in the world but thee.

Theo. I can sooner distrust my self than your honour, and cannot but be very easie to believe what I like so well; though my own want of merit would perswade me to the contrary.

Raym. I find the wisest have still less knowledge of themselves than of others, or you would value more what all Men do; your Beauty, Wit, and Vertue, are so admirable, that Nature could have added nothing to you; nor is there one Charm in all the rest of your Sex, that can one moment divide my thoughts from you.

Theo. I have so great a belief in your constancy and truth, your words can ne'r confirm me more; therefore let us leave this, and think of some attonement to my Aunt: for my part I know none better than helping her to another for a Husband if we can: for she longs more for one, than a Son and Heir of one and twenty does for the death of his Father.

Bridg. Madam, She does not want that, for she and Mr. *Crazy* have resolv'd, he to be reveng'd of you, and she to be reveng'd of Mr. *Raymund,* to couple in the Bonds of Wedlock.

Theo. 'Tis pity to forbid the Banes.

Raym. To *Crazy!* What has she a mind to practise Physick and Surgery?

Enter Drybob *and* Briske.

Theo. O! yonder comes *Drybob* and *Briske.*

Pray Mr. *Raymund* avoid the room, and enter not till I give you your cue——   [*Ex.* Raymund.

Brisk. I am come, Madam, according to appointment, and understand your resolutions are to live and dye with *Jack Briske.*

Theo. I will no longer conceal my affections! I am so ill us'd by my Aunt, that if you think fit, I will immediately consent to be your Wife; Mr. *Sneake* shall do it for us.

Briske. How am I exalted! Dear Madam, let it be instantly.

Theo. But I must hide my face, or he'll discover me to my Aunt, and we may be prevented for this time.

Briske. 'Slife, I have thought on't, you shall put on a Vizor Mask.

Dryb. What! will you engross the Ladies Ear?

Theo. Pray go and expect me suddenly.

Briske. Farewel *Drybob*, ha, ha, ha! poor sneaking fellow.　　[*Ex.*

Theo. Mr. *Drybob*, I will not blush to own my affection to you.

Dryb. I hope, Madam, you need not.

Enter Sir *Richard.*

Theo. Yonder comes one I must speak with, pray go with *Bridget;* I have entrusted her with the rest : I will be with you suddainly.

Dryb. Come, my Dear *Bridget*, I flie as quick as thought.

　　　　　　　　　　　　　　　　[*Ex.* Drybob *and* Bridget.

Sir Rich. Madam, I beseech you where's my Lady?

Theo. Oh she's Marry'd to *Crazy* since I saw you ; she has made quick dispatch I assure you.

Sir. Rich. 'Sdeath and Hell Marry'd! Is this truth, Madam?

Theo. Ay Sir, but what's the Cause that makes you so concern'd at it?

Sir Rich. Have I not reason? Do you know this Face?

　　　　　　　　　　　　　　　　　　[*Pulls off his disguise.*

Theo. O Heaven! my Uncle Sir *Richard Loveyouth.*

Sir Rich. Cease your wonder Niece, you see the Story of my death was feign'd.

Theo. My dear Uncle! I am infinitely happy to see you once more in this place. This was a happy change.

Sir *Rich.* Niece I rejoyce no less to see thee ; thou art improv'd in beauty since I saw thee : but this abominable Woman I for ever banish from my thoughts.

Theo. But pray Sir, what made you keep your disguise so long after your return?

Sir *Rich.* I'll tell you Niece, but hold I hear some coming hither ; I'll withdraw and acquaint you with it.

Theo. Come Sir, and I'll bring you to one that will be glad to see you.——　　　　　　　　　　　　　　　　　　　[*Exeunt.*

Enter Crazy, L. Loveyouth, *and two* Servants.

Craz. Now, my dear Lady, I am happy beyond my wishes.

La. Love. Sir, I beseech you be not the worse opiniated of me, for your easie Conquest ; for I have long had an inclination for you.

Enter Sneak, Drybob, *and* Friske, Briske *and* Bridget.
(Friske *and* Bridget *masked.*)

How now? whom have we here?

Brisk. Madam! your Servant, ha, ha, ha, you little think where *Theodosia* is?

La. Love. Name her not, vile Creature, to run away with *Raymund.*

Dryb. No, no, she did not run away with him.   With *Raymund* quoth she? no, no.

Brisk. What does this Fool mean? ha, ha, ha.

L. Love. Not marry'd to *Raymund!* how unlucky is this? that I should fool my self into marrying this fellow? I might yet have captivated Mr. *Raymund.*

Sneak. Gentlemen, are you both satisfi'd with your marriage?

Dryb. Ay, ay,

Brisk. Ay, ay.   Come, my dear *Theodosia,* unmask thy self, and keep 'em no longer in suspence.

Bridg. Sir, I obey you——   [*She unmask.*

Brisk. 'Sdeath and Hell! Who's this! *Bridget?*

All. *Bridget*——ha, ha, ha.

Sneak. O *tempora!* O *mores!* Would you serve me thus? I shall not live to endure it, I shall suddenly expire, and Ἐνς θανοντος γᾶει μιθητω πῦρι.

Dryb. Now *Briske,* thou hast marry'd the Chamber-maid, I'll prefer thee; I told thee the Mistriss was for my turn: Prethee my dear unmask, ha! Who's this?

Frisk. Even as you see Sir——   [*Friske unmaskes.*

Dryb. Death, Fire-brands, Devils, Damnation! What's this!

Brisk. My old Mistriss? Prethee *Drybob* be patient, thou wilt have a Son and Heir of mine shortly; and prethee for my sake take care and see him well educated.

Craz. How now Gentlemen, are you bob'd?

Enter Raymund *and* Theodosia.

Raym. Madam, We are come to beg your approbation of our Marriage; I humbly beg your pardon for the irregular means I us'd: Pray Madam turn not from us, but give us your consent; since 'tis now too late to prevent it.

La. Lov. Avoid my presence thou impudent fellow, I'll have thee kick'd.

Enter Mrs. Striker *and whispers Mrs.* Bridget.

Craz. Poor fellows, methinks you look as scurvily as if you were mounting the Pillory with Papers on your backs.

Strik. Marry'd say you? Ah false man! have you us'd me thus? Did I for this yield up my honour to you, and you promis'd me to marry me after the death of my Husband, who is in a deep Consumption! Ah villainous man! I will have thee kick'd and beaten.

Raym. Drybob, Tell him his Wife has made over all her Estate.

Dryb. Yet this condition of mine is as good as marrying a Widow that has made over her Estate, as you have done.

Craz. Is this true, Madam?

La. Love. I must confess I did it to defeat my ungracious Niece of her Inheritance.

Dryb. }
Brisk. } Give you joy good Mr. *Crazy.*

Raym. Madam, your Ladyship is mistaken, it is a Deed of Gift of all your Estate, after your decease, to *Theodosia:* I have it here.

Theo. Madam, I thank your Ladyship; I shall study to deserve it.

La. Lov. Am I thus cozen'd and abus'd.

Craz. 'Tis I am cozen'd and abus'd.

Strik. Go thy ways thou vile man, thou art serv'd right for thy falshood to me.

Craz. I'll be reveng'd of her—— [*Aside.*
I must tell you, Madam, you are not less disappointed than I am; for I must ingeniously confess I am very much visited with the Pox.

Dryb. Pox on him for a Rascal; visited is a very pretty word there i'faith.

La. Love. O Heaven! I am undone for ever; this is a most unspeakable disappointment to a Lady! O miserable unfortunate Woman that I am.

Enter Sir Richard.

Sir *Rich.* What's the matter Madam?

La. Love. Oh I have just now cast my self upon that diseas'd impotent fellow, that walking Hospital *Crazy.*

Sir *Rich.* Now, Madam, d'e wish your other Husband alive in *Candia.*

La. Love. No, not so neither; but would I were as fair rid of this Husband, as I was of him.

Sir *Rich.* So! I am beholding to her! [*Aside.*
I have a way to rid you of this Husband.

La. Love. If you have, you shall command my person and my purse.

Sir *Rich.* And you shall know that I'll command 'em both. [*Discovers himself.*

Omn. Sir *Richard Loveyouth* alive.

La. Love. O Heaven! I am ruin'd for ever, there is now no dissembling! all my misfortunes are compleated now.

Craz. I am glad you are come to take your Wife again.

Sir *Rich.* Fond Woman, thy foolishness and vanity, and thy impertinent contentions with me, caus'd my three years absence; and shall make me still continue a stranger to your Conversation: yet you shall never want what'er befits your Quality: upon the rest of all the Company let no Cloud appear to day.

(252)

Brisk. You are a happy man *Crazy.*

Dryb. You have had ill luck with honest Women, *Crazy,* you had e'en as good stick to Whores.

Craz. I have had worse luck with them I am sure, yet this is better than marrying a Chamber-maid, or Wench big with Child, Gentlemen.

Sir *Rich.* Sir I am a stranger to your repute, and think my self much honoured in the relation I have to you.

Raym. Sir, the honour is wholly on my side.

Sir *Rich.* Come Gentlemen, I am inform'd of all your Stories, and 'tis wisdom in you to be content, with what you can't redress.

Sir *Rich.* I shall ne'r have Children, I therefore here declare my Niece my Heir.

Theo. Sir, I can return nothing but my thanks.

Sir *Rich.* This day, Sir, I dedicate to my fair Niece and you.

Raym. You do me too much honour.

Sir *Rich.* Come Gentlemen and Ladies, Let's be merry; we'll have Musick, we'll begin this days jollity with a Dance.

Craz. Sweet Madam *Striker,* receive me into your favour; for upon my honour, tho' I marry'd her, I intended to reserve the whole stock of my affection for thee.

Strik. Get thee gone, thou wicked fellow, I will have none of thee; thou hast declar'd thou hast the Disease: Get thee gone, I tell thee I will have thee kick'd.

Sir *Rich.* Come Gentlemen, joyn in a Dance.　　　　　　　*[Dance.* So, 'tis well.

> All happiness to both, and may you be,
> From discontents of Marriage ever free;
> May all your life be one continued peace,
> And may your Loves each day and hour encrease——

　　　　　　　　　　　　　　　　　　　　　　　[Ex. Omnes.

EPILOGUE.

THE *Mighty Prince of Poets, Learned* BEN,
Who alone div'd into the Minds of Men :
Saw all their wandrings, all their follies knew,
And all their vain fantastick passions drew,
In Images so lively and so true ;
That there each Humorist himself might view,
Yet onely lash'd the Errors of the Times,
And ne'r expos'd the Persons, but the Crimes :
And never car'd for private frowns, when he
Did but chastise publick iniquitie,
He fear'd no Pimp, no Pick-pocket, or Drab ;
He fear'd no Bravo, *nor no Ruffian's Stab.*
'Twas he alone true Humors understood.
And with great Wit and Judgment made them good.
A Humor is the Byas of the Mind,
By which with violence 'tis one way inclin'd :
It makes our Actions lean on one side still,
And in all Changes that way bends the Will.
This——
He only knew and represented right.
Thus none but Mighty Johnson *e'r could write.*
Expect not then, since that most flourishing Age,
Of BEN, *to see true Humor on the Stage.*
All that have since been writ, if they be scan'd,
Are but faint Copies from that Master's Hand.
Our Poet now, amongst those petty things,
Alas, his too weak trifling humors brings.
As much beneath the worst in Johnson's *Plays.*
As his great Merit is about our praise.
For could he imitate that great Author right,
He would with ease all Poets else out-write.
But to out-go all other men, would be
O Noble BEN! *less than to follow thee.*
Gallants you see how hard it is to write,
Forgive all faults the Poet meant to night :
Since if he sinn'd, 'twas made for your delight.
Pray let this find——

(254)

As good success, tho' it be very bad,
As any damn'd successful Play e'r had.
Yet if you hiss, he knows not where the harm is,
He'll not defend his Nonsence Vi & Armis.
But this poor Play has been so torn before.
That all your Cruelty can't wound it more.

FINIS.

TEXTUAL NOTES

The Sullen Lovers

p. 1.   *The Sullen Lovers :* THE | Sullen Lovers : | OR, THE | IMPERTINENTS. | A | COMEDY | Acted by His Highness the Duke of *YORK'S* | Servants. | *rule* | Written by | *THO.* SHADWELL. | *rule* | *Nunc satis est dixisse, Ego mira Poemata pango : Occupet extremum scabies : mihi turpe relinqui est,* | *Et, quod non didici, sane nescire fateri.* | Hor. de Art. Poet. | *double rule* | LONDON | Printed for *Henry Herringman* at the Sign of the *Anchor* in the | Lower-Walk of the *New-Exchange.* 1670. |

p. 1.   *Acted.* 1693 : Acted at the | *Theatre Royal* | By Their Majesties Servants. | *rule* | Written by | Tho. Shadwell. *Laur.* | *rule* | [Horatian quotation.] | *double rule* | LONDON. | Printed for *H. Herringman,* and sold by R. *Bently, F. Saunders, J. Knap* | *ton,* and D. *Brown.* 1693. |

p. 7, l. 7.   *Councel.* 1693 : Council.
p. 7, l. 7.   *noble.* 1693 : Noble.
p. 7, l. 13.   *Countrey.* 1693 : Country.
p. 7, l. 16.   *always.* 1693 : always.
p. 9, l. 3.   *more then.* 1693 : than.
p. 9, l. 6.   *Playes.* 1693 : Plays.
p. 9, l. 7.   *Judgement.* 1693 : Judgment.
p. 9, l. 17.   *damm's.* 1693 : damn's.
p. 9, l. 18.   *Erre.* 1670 ; 1693 : Err.
p. 10, l. 7.   *stolne.* 1693 : stoln.
p. 10, l. 9.   *Witt.* 1693 : Wit.
p. 10, l. 11.   *neer.* 1693 : near.
p. 10, l. 15.   *onely.* 1693 : only.
p. 10, l. 18.   *accomted.* 1693 : accounted.
p. 10, l. 26.   *Plott.* 1693 : Plot.
p. 11, l. 5.   *strein.* 1693 : strain.
p. 11, l. 6.   *Comœdies.* 1693 : Comedies.
p. 11, l. 12.   *Drammatick-Poetry.* 1693 : Dramatick Poetry.
p. 11, l. 28.   *chok'd.* 1693 : shock'd.
p. 11, l. 29.   *'em.* 4to., 1 : e'm.
p. 11, l. 33.   *Criminalls.* 1693 : Criminals.
p. 11, l. 34.   *Errors.* 1693 : Errours.
p. 11, l. 39.   *corrections.* 1693 : correction.
p. 11, l. 40.   *'em.* 4to, 1 : e'm.
p. 12, l. 12.   *incouragement.* 1693 : encouragement.
p. 13, l. 9.   *Warr.* 1693 : *War.*
p. 13, l. 23.   *choyce.* 1693 : *choice.*
p. 14, l. 1.   *Drammatis.* 1693 : Dramatis.
p. 14, l. 6.   *Ayery.* 1693 : Aiery.
p. 14, l. 31.   *Clerkes.* 1693 : Clarks.
p. 15, l. 5.   *Vertue.* 1693 : Virtue.
p. 15, l. 14.   *Moneth.* 1693 : Month.
p. 17, l. 11.   *dayes.* 1693 : days.
p. 18, l. 4.   *Bedlum.* 1670 ; 1693 : Bedlam.
p. 18, l. 19.   *Gaule.* 1693 : Gall.

p. 18, l. 26. *Feavor.* 1693 : Fever.
p. 18, l. 30. *borne.* 1693 : born.
p. 18, l. 36. *I came.* 1693 : I come.
p. 18, l. 42. *Guinnys.* 1693 : Guineys.
p. 21, l. 43. *Reads me.* 1693 : read me.
p. 23, l. 1. *all that. (aside.* 1693 omits *(aside.*
p. 23, l. 43. *Cruel too.* 4to, 1, misprints : two.
p. 24, l. 37. *in that Couplet.* 1670 ; 1693 : in that laſt Couplet.
p. 24, l. 38. *riddle me riddle me this.* 1693 : riddle my riddle.
p. 25, l. 1. *here !* 1693 misprints : hear !
p. 25, l. 4. *I would not but have.* 1693 omits " but," thus altering the whole sense.
p. 26, l. 40. *Exit Lovel and Roger.* 1693 : *Exeunt.*
p. 28, l. 10. *can be.* 1693 omits " be."
p. 28, l. 12. *Lovell.* The spelling now varies between *Lovel* and *Lovell.*
p. 28, l. 31. *She sayes.* 1693 : She says.
p. 29, l. 12. *ne're out-live.* 1693 : ne'er out-live.
p. 29, l. 30. *Chevy Chace.* 1693 : *Chevy Chase.*
p. 30, l. 9. *distruſt.* 1693 : miſtruſt.
p. 30, l. 30. *Melancholly.* 1670 ; 1693 : Melancholy.
p. 31, l. 6. *fy, Siſter.* 1693 : Fie, Siſter.
p. 31, l. 12. *Cozen.* 1693 : Cousin.
p. 31, l. 33. *farewell.* 1693 : farewel.
p. 32, l. 1. *Dirty fellow.* 1693 : dirty Fellow.
p. 32, l. 12. *vertue.* 1693 : Virtue.
p. 32, l. 24. *ingag'd.* 1693 : engag'd.
p. 33, l. 3. *Blew-Inckle.* 1693 : *Blew Inckele.*
p. 33, l. 4. *Assa fœtida.* 4to, 1 : *Asra foetida.*
p. 33, l. 20. *Dol Comon.* 1693 : *Dol Common.*
p. 34, l. 23. *honor.* 1693 misprints : Houour.
p. 35, l. 12. *Raskal.* 1693 : Rascal.
p. 35, l. 27. *Attorny's.* 1693 : Attorneys.
p. 35, l. 32. *Ayre.* 1693 : Air.
p. 35, l. 35. *halfes.* 1693 : halfs.
p. 36, l. 16. *thou'lt.* 1693 : thou't.
p. 36, l. 26. *find me out.* 4to, 1, 1668, here has catch-word SCENE, at the end of page 24.
    But page 25 commences : " *Enter* Emilia. . . ." It will be noticed
    that, although there is a ſtage-direction " (*Exeunt*) ", Stanford, who has
    said " Ile away " as the scene is now arranged remains on the ſtage.
    It would appear that a scene has dropped out at this point, and his
    re-entry has not been marked when the play was revised with this
    omission for the press.
p. 37, l. 3. *four Shillings.* 1693 : 4s.
p. 37, l. 6. *trapan'd.* 1693 : trepan'd.
p. 37, l. 18. *Hippocrite.* 1693 : Hypocrite.
p. 37, l. 23. *pitty.* 1693 : pity.
p. 38, l. 2. *Schollers.* 1693 : Scholars.
p. 39, l. 17. *Rascalls.* 1693 : Rascals.
p. 39, l. 31. *Cozin.* 1693 : Cousin.
p. 41, l. 37. *Impertinents divided follow.* 1693 : *Impertinents divide and follow.*
p. 42, l. 4. *Ideot.* 1693 : Idiot.
p. 42, l. 12. *Coz.* 1693 : Cousin.
p. 42, l. 35. *Noyse.* 1693 : Noise.

p. 44, l. 26.   *troublesome.*   1693 : troublesom.
p. 44, l. 35.   *formall.*   1693 : formal.
p. 45, l. 12.   *Fiddler.*   1693 : Fidler.
p. 47, l. 30.   *Back-Gamon.*   1693 : Back-Gammon.
p. 47, l. 39.   *Size-Sinke.*   1693 : Size-Cinque.
p. 47, l. 40.   *Sinke.*   1693 : Cinque.
p. 48, l. 27.   *Doores.*   1693 : Doors.
p. 48, l. 35.   *Owle.*   1693 : Owl.
p. 49, l. 15.   *Puppies.*   1693 : Puppy's.
p. 49, l. 31.   *Scarfes.*   1693 : Scarffs.
p. 50, l. 1.   *Countervaile.*   1693 : countervail.
p. 50, l. 3.   *yoakes.*   1693 : yokes.
p. 50, l. 15.   *Tooth-Ache.*   So 1670.   4to, 1, has : Tooch-Ache.   1693 : Tooth-Ach.
p. 50, l. 25.   *Mellanchollick-Humors.*   1693 misprints : Melanchoickl-Humours.
p. 50, l. 38.   *firke.*   1693 : firk.
p. 51, l. 16.   *breaks.*   1693 : Breaks.
p. 51, l. 20.   *Valour.*   1693 : Valor.
p. 51, l. 27.   *Railling.*   1693 : Railing.
p. 51, l. 30.   *Currs.*   1693 : Curs.
p. 52, l. 37.   *bus'ness.*   1693 : business.
p. 52, l. 37.   agen.   1693 : again.
p. 53, l. 8.   *Att-All.*   1693 : At-All.
p. 53, l. 9.   *onely.*   1693 : only.
p. 53, l. 17.   *Statesman.*   1693 : States man.
p. 53, l. 35.   *Steakes.*   1693 : Stakes.
p. 53, l. 35.   *Gloſter.*   1693 : Gloceſter.
p. 54, l. 1.   *of me :.*   1693 : of me ?
p. 55, l. 7.   *Ex. Emil.*   1693 : *Ex. Emelia.*
p. 55, l. 33.   *I'me.*   1693 : I'm.
p. 55, l. 34.   *Fin. Aĉt. tertii.*   1693 omits.
p. 56, l. 32.   *father.*   1693 : Father.
p. 56, l. 36.   *unhansome.*   1693 : unhandsom.
p. 57, l. 27.   *houres.*   1693 : hours.
p. 58, l. 25.   *Fopps.*   1693 : Fops.
p. 58, l. 28.   *Duells.*   1693 : Duels.
p. 58, l. 31.   *Witch-craft.*   1693 : Witchcraft.
p. 58, l. 35.   agen.   1693 : agen ?
p. 59, l. 1.   *Chace.*   1693 : Chase.
p. 59, l. 6.   *withall.*   1693 : wittall.
p. 59, l. 9.   *I'de.*   1693 : I'd.
p. 59, l. 22.   *breathe.*   1693 : breath.
p. 59, l. 41.   *Ga'd.*   1670; 1693 : Gad.
p. 60, l. 9.   *Millſtone.*   1693 : Milſtone.
p. 60, l. 33.   *Cozin.*   1693 : Cousin.
p. 60, l. 39.   *Cooke.*   1693 : *Coke.*
p. 61, l. 2.   *Cozen.*   1693 : Cousin.
p. 61, l. 4.   *Scale.*   1693 : Scal.
p. 61, l. 15.   *Caſtel Rodrigo.*   1693 : *Caſtel Roderigo.*
p. 61, l. 17.   *for e'm.*   1693 : for them.
p. 61, l. 22.   *aske.*   1693 : ask.
p. 61, l. 35.   *Souldiers.*   1693 : Soldiers.
p. 61, l. 37.   *numericall.*   1693 : numerical.

p. 63, l. 10.   *affraid.*   1693 : afraid.
p. 63, l. 20.   *Musqueteers.*   1693 : Musquetiers.
p. 65, l. 25.   *ayles.*   1693 : ails.
p. 66, l. 2.   *Strength.*   1693 misprints : *Strenght.*
p. 66, l. 32.   *Voice. (aside.*   1693 omits : *(aside.*
p. 67, l. 4.   *Judgement.*   1693 : Judgment.
p. 67, l. 18.   *Countrey-Gentleman.*   1693 : Countrey Gendleman.
p. 67, l. 39.   *ever was—(aside.*   1693 omits : *(aside.*
p. 68, l. 20.   *persuade.*   1693 : perswade.
p. 69, l. 8.   *dayry.*   1693 : dairy.
p. 69, l. 10.   *Hawkes.*   1693 : Hawks.
p. 70, l. 23.   *Black puddens & Sausages.*   1693 : Black-puddings and Sausages.
p. 70, l. 33.   *any of e'm.*   1693 : any of them.
p. 71, l. 6.   *Oh Deare !*   1693 : Oh Dear !
p. 71, l. 37.   *Barbor.*   1693 : Barber.
p. 72, l. 4.   *Coven-Garden.*   1693 : *Covent-Garden.*
p. 72, l. 25.   *Size Cater-Deuse.*   1693 : Sise Cater-Deuse.
p. 72, l. 25.   *Sink Trey Ace.*   1693 : Cinque Trey Ace.
p. 72, l. 34.   *Leger-De-Maine.*   1693 : Leger de main.
p. 73, l. 26.   *Cookes.*   1693 : Cooks.
p. 73, l. 32.   *Modells.*   1693 : Models.
p. 74, l. 3.   *ask.*   1693 : Asks.
p. 75, l. 26.   *Fooles.*   1693 : Fools.
p. 76, l. 4.   *Attorny.*   1693 : Attorney.
p. 76, l. 9.   *Wisdome.*   1693 : Wisdom.
p. 76, l. 27.   *flight.*   1693 misprints : fight.
p. 76, l. 29.   *Jer-Faulcon.*   1693 : Jer-Falcon.
p. 77, l. 5.   *Tyre woman.*   1693 : Tire-woman.
p. 77, l. 5.   *Coven Garden.*   1693 : *Covent-Garden.*
p. 77, l. 16.   *Sponges.*   1693 : Spunges.
p. 77, l. 24.   *yee ?*   1693 : ye ?
p. 77, l. 36.   *agen.*   1693 : again.
p. 78, l. 5.   *Ability's.*   1693 : Abilities.
p. 78, l. 25.   *ſtay'd.*   1693 : ſtai'd.
p. 78, l. 34.   *States-man.*   1693 : Statesman.
p. 79, l. 10.   *Currs.*   1693 : Curs.
p. 81, l. 34.   *a Gogg.*   1693 : agog.
p. 83, l. 40.   *Fopp.*   1693 : Fop.
p. 84, l. 14.   *roome.*   1693 : Room.
p. 85, l. 14.   *ſtayes.*   1693 : ſtays.
p. 85, l. 23.   *dear heart.*   1693 : Dear Heart.
p. 87, l. 13.   *Hoggs.*   1693 : Hogs.
p. 87, l. 18.   *Dormous.*   1693 : Dormouse.
p. 87, l. 26.   *Lamen-table.*   1693 : Lamentable.
p. 87, l. 36.   *Coxcombes.*   1693 : Coxcombs.
p. 88, l. 1.   *Gnates.*   1693 : Gnats.
p. 88, l. 18.   *inquire.*   1693 : enquire.
p. 88, l. 20.   *done it dexterously.*   1693 omits " it."
p. 89, l. 13.   *Cozen.*   1693 : Cousin.
p. 90, l. 6.   *Ryot's.*   1693 : Riot's.
p. 90, l. 23.   *bobb'd.*   1693 : bob'd.
p. 91, l. 8.   *Complement.*   1693 : Compliment.

The Royal Shepherdesse

p. 93, l. 7.   *Duke of York's Servants.* 4to, 1691, has: " As it is Acted | By Their Majeſties | Servants. *rule* | Written By | Thomas Shadwell, Laur. | " *rule* | [Horatian quotation] | *double rule.* |

p. 93, l. 12.   *Herringman:* " and are to be Sold by *Francis Saunders,* | at the *Blue-Anchor* in the Lower Walk of the *New-Exchange ;* and | *James Knapton,* at the *Crown* in St. *Paul's* Church-Yard. 1691. | "

p. 99, l. 6.   *Man.* 1691 has : Man, throughout.

p. 99, l. 10.   *error.* 1691 : errour.

p. 100, l. 10.   *gayety.* 1691 : gaiety.

p. 101, l. 22.   *Ayery.* 1691 : *Airy.*

p. 103, l. 3.   *The Firſt Act.* 1691 : Act I, and so Act II, etc.

p. 103, l. 9.   *Physitian.* 1691 : Physician.

p. 104, l. 20.   *Chooseth.* 1691 : choseth.

p. 106, l. 10.   *I'le.* 1691 : I'll, throughout.

p. 108, l. 25.   *Handkercher.* 1691 : *Handkerchief.*

p. 109, l. 15.   *priviledge.* 1691 : privilege.

p. 113, l. 19.   *The End of the Firſt Act.* 1691 omits.

p. 114, l. 34.   *Kings.* 1691 : King's.

p. 114, l. 37.   *diſtreſt.* 1691 : diſtress'd.

p. 115, l. 18.   *Vnfortunate.* 1691 : Unfortunate.

p. 116, l. 1.   *pitty'd.* 1691 : pitti'd.

p. 117, l. 8.   *Showres.* 1691 : showers.

p. 119, l. 15.   *bosome.* 1691 : Bosom.

p. 119, l. 31.   *& be.* 1691 : and be.

p. 121, l. 24.   *within thy Armes.* 1691 : within my Arms.

p. 124, l. 9.   *Lord Neander.* 1691 : Lord *Nean.*

p. 125, l. 3.   *affraid.* 1691 : afraid.

p. 125, l. 40.   *Rhumatick.* 1691 : Rumatick.

p. 126, l. 15.   *appartment.* 1691 : apartment.

p. 126, l. 40.   *The End of the Second Act.* 1691 omits.

p. 129, l. 41.   *Equall.* 1691 : equal.

p. 130, l. 27.   *forc'd.* 1691 : forc't.

p. 131, l. 10.   *Evnuch.* 1691 : Eunuch.

p. 132, l. 33.   *Skyes.* 1691 : *Skies.*

p. 140, l. 28.   *The End of the Third Act.* 1691 omits.

p. 143, l. 9.   *suſpitiously.* 1691 : suspiciously.

p. 143, l. 41.   *mai'ſt.* 1691 : may'ſt.

p. 144, l. 25.   *loath.* 1691 : loth.

p. 150, l. 29.   *The Third Scene.* 1691 : SCENE III.

p. 151, l. 1.   *dye fort.* 1691 : die for't.

p. 153, l. 10.   *The End of the Fourth Act.* 1691 omits.

p. 154, l. 3.   *Councel.* 1691 : *Council.*

p. 155, l. 4.   *withall.* 1691 : with all.

p. 156, l. 10.   *Flames.* 1691 : Frames.

p. 156, l. 15.   *Marshall.* 1691 : *Marshal.*

p. 157, l. 39.   *Marry'd.* 1691 : marri'd.

p. 159, l. 19.   *Sayls.* 1691 : Sails.

(263)

p. 160, l. 16.   *indure.*   1691 : endure.
p. 160, l. 40.   *Doggs.*   1691 : Dogs.
p. 162, l. 5.   *Wisard.*   1691 : Wizard.
p. 167, l. 19.   *meen.*   1691 : mien.
p. 167, l. 40.   *Prophesie.*   1691 : Prophecy.
p. 172, l. 16.   *FINIS.*   1691 places at the end of the Epilogue.

The Humorists

p. 175, l. 9.   *Of the Middle Temple.* 1691 omits and gives : *Poet Laureat,* and *Historiographer-Royal. rule* | Quotation from Journal | *rule.* |
p. 175, l. 13.   *Herringman.* 1691 : " and are to be Sold by *Francis Saunders* | at the *Blew Anchor* in the *Lower Walk* of the *New Exchange,* | and *James Knapton* at the *Crown* in *St. Pauls Church-yard.* 1691. | "
p. 183, l. 11.   *extreamly.*   1691 : extremely.
p. 183, l. 34.   *endeavors.*   1691 : endeavours.
p. 184, l. 23.   *High-way-men.*   1691 : Highway-men.
p. 184, l. 29.   *Wiseman.*   1691 : Wise man.
p. 184, l. 40.   *despised.*   1691 : dispis'd.
p. 185, l. 7.   *Jack-Puddings.*   1691 : *Jack-Puddens.*
p. 186, l. 26.   *Clamors.*   1691 : Clamours.
p. 187, l. 11.   *think it impudent.*   1691 : think it Impudence.
p. 188, l. 6.   *fancyful.*   1691 : Fanciful.
p. 190, l. 36.   *buryes.*   1691 : *buries.*
p. 191, l. 10.   *Brisk.* In 1691 the speech-prefix varies at random between *Brisk* and *Briske.*
p. 191, l. 10.   *ayery.*   1691 : airy.
p. 194, l. 12.   *Honours.*   1691 : Honors.
p. 194, l. 22.   *Shinne.*   1691 : Shin.
p. 195, l. 4.   *Prethe.*   1691 : Prethee.
p. 195, l. 35.   *Trumpetters.*   1691 : Trumpeters.
p. 195, l. 36.   *half roasted.*   1691 : halfe roasted.
p. 196, l. 22.   *morre.*   1691 : Morr.
p. 196, l. 31.   *vertu-bleu.*   1691 : vortue-bleu.
p. 197, l. 3.   *Moor-fields.*   1691 : *Moorfields.*
p. 197, l. 5.   *businesse.*   1691 : business.
p. 197, l. 35.   *Clapp.*   1691 : Clappe.
p. 198, l. 38.   *Dogge.*   1691 : Dog.
p. 202, l. 1.   *The Second Act.*   1691 : *Act II.*
p. 203, l. 36.   *Latine.*   1691 : Latin.
p. 204, l. 16.   *fantastick.*   1691 : fantastique.
p. 204, l. 35.   *Reperty.*   1691 : Repertee.
p. 205, l. 16.   *Nay, prethee.*   1691 : Nay, I prethee.
p. 206, l. 39.   [*Kick her.*   1691 : [*Kicks her.*
p. 207, l. 34.   *Habberdashers.*   1691 : Haberdashers.
p. 208, l. 32.   *Lady Lovey. Such.*   1691 misprints : *Lady Tovey.* Such.
p. 209, l. 3.   *Girle.*   1691 : Girl.
p. 209, l. 16.   *Dis-dain.*   1691 : Disdain.

p. 209, l. 29. *Ladyship.* 1691 : Ladiship.
p. 211, l. 39. *Drybob.* 1691 varies with Dribob.
p. 213, l. 9. *Widdows.* 1691 : Widows.
p. 215, l. 22. *The Third Act.* 1691 : Act III.
p. 215, l. 32. *run you thorow the Lungs.* 1691 : run you under the Lungs.
p. 216, l. 10. *as sowrely.* 1691 : as sower.
p. 216, l. 19. *New Market.* 1691 : *Newmarket.*
p. 217, l. 20. *Phylosopher.* 1691 : Philosopher.
p. 217, l. 35. *divillishly.* 1691 : divelishly.
p. 218, l. 14. *Fiddles.* 1691 : Fidles.
p. 218, l. 21. *Sneake.* 1691 varies between " Sneak " and " Sneake."
p. 221, l. 20. *Palat.* 1691 : Palate.
p. 222, l. 11. *Peny Rent.* 1691 : Penny Rent.
p. 224, l. 38. *hugge.* 1691 : hug.
p. 226, l. 7. *Pappe.* 1691 : Pap.
p. 227, l. 18. *The Fourth Act.* 1691 : *Act IV.*
p. 229, l. 1. *thorow.* 1691 : through.
p. 229, l. 7. *thorow my Coat.* 1691 : thorough my Coat.
p. 232, l. 16. *mall.* 1691 : maull.
p. 234, l. 12. *Tyrany.* 1691 : Tyranny.
p. 235, l. 40. *Volunteers.* 1691 : Voluntiers.
p. 240, l. 4. *The Fifth Act.* 1691 : Act V.
p. 241, l. 25. *marry'd.* 1691 : Married.
p. 242, l. 33. *Sphere : start from her Sphere, that is.* 1691 here reads : " Sphere, that is,"
in error omitting the repetition.
p. 244, l. 10. *wrinckl'd.* 1691 : wrinkl'd.
p. 244, l. 34. *die.* 1691 : dye.
p. 246, l. 22. *hæsitation.* 1691 : hesitation.
p. 247, l. 31. *Ladies Servant.* 1691 : Ladys Servant.
p. 250, l. 9. *flie.* 1691 : fly.
p. 254, l. 11. *iniquitie.* 1691 : *iniquity.*

EXPLANATORY NOTES

The Sullen Lovers

p. 1. NUNC SATIS EST DIXISSE. Horace, *Ars Poetica*, 416–18.

p. 7. WILLIAM, DUKE . . . OF NEWCASTLE. 1592–1676. For his patronage of Shadwell see the Introduction.

p. 9. GRUM. Surly, morose. So in Wycherley's *The Gentleman Dancing-Master*, produced at Dorset Garden, March, 1672, I, 1, Monsieur says : " Your *Englis*, for want of Wit, drive everything to a serious grum quarrel." Cf. Lucy's air (xi) in Fielding's farce *An Old Man Taught Wisdom*, produced at Drury Lane, 1734 :

> Oh, dear papa, don't look so grum ;
> Forgive me, and be good.

p. 9. BULLY-ROCK. A powerful bravo ; a truculent hectoring fellow. Cf. Urquhart's *Rabelais* (1653), I, l. iv : " Ye Bully-rocks and rogues." Also, the Epilogue spoken by Mrs. Mary Lee to Otway's *Alcibiades*, produced at Dorset Garden in 1675 (probably September) :

> *Now who sayes Poets don't in blood delight ?*
> *'Tis true, the varlets care not much to fight ;*
> *But faith they claw it off when e're they write ;*
> *Are bully Rocks not of the common size ;*
> *Kill ye men faster than* Domitian *flyes.*

Dictionary of the Canting Crew gives : " *Bully-rock*, a Hector, or Bravo." Cotton, *Compleat Gamester*, 1674, p. 9, mentions " *Bully-Huffs* and *Bully-Rocks* " as synonyms for desperadoes frequenting gambling-dens.

p. 9. SONGS AND DANCES. The chief ingredients (according to the opposition) of the heroic play. As Mr. Bayes laid down : You must ever interlard your Playes with Songs, Ghosts, and Dances, if you mean to—a—" " Pit, Box, and Gallery, Mr. *Bayes*," finishes off Johnson neatly. In Otway's *Friendship in Fashion*, produced at Dorset Garden, April, 1678, they discuss the new tragedy, and Saunter grumbles : " I did not like it neither for my part ; there was never a Song in it, ha ! " " No," chimes in Caper, " nor so much as a Dance." Malagene delivers the verdict : " Oh, 'tis impossible it should take, if there were neither Song nor Dance in it."

p. 9. HIS MAJESTY. Pepys tells us that both the King and the Duke of York were present at the first performance, Saturday, 2 May, 1668. The King was also present on Monday, 4 May. On 8 May Pepys notes : " Lord ! to see how this play of Sir Positive At-all, in abuse of Sir Robert Howard, do take, all the Duke's and everybody's talk being of that, and telling more stories of him, of the like nature that it is now the town and country talk." 28 July, 1677, the King was present again at *The Sullen Lovers*.

p. 9. LES FASCHEUX. Molière's comédie-ballet (*à tiroirs*) was produced at Vaux, 17 August, 1661, and eight days later at Fontainebleau with an additional scene, that of the hunter Dorante. On 4 November it was given at the Palais-Royal, Paris. The piece was acted forty-four times successively, and printed in February, 662.

(269)

p. 10. STANFORD AND ROGER. In the French, II, 3, Eraste, and La Montagne. Molière played Eraste, Du Parc the servant.

p. 10. PIQUETTE. In the French, II, 2. Alcippe is the gambler who torments Eraste with his long-winded tale of the cards.

p. 10. SIT QUOD VIS. *Ars Poetica*, l. 23. Si quid inexpertum, l. 125–7.

p. 11. LOVE AND HONOUR. The conflict between passionate love and exalted honour is often the whole theme of a heroic tragedy, a complex debated in nicest detail with the utmost refinements of casuistry. Buckingham did not overlook these quandaries in *The Rehearsal*, produced at the Theatre Royal, 7 December, 1671, when Mr. Bayes says : " Here, now, Mr. *Johnson*, you shall see a combat betwixt Love and Honour. An ancient Author has made a whole Play on't ; but I have dispatch'd it all in this Scene." The famous episode of Prince Volscius and the boots follows (Act IV). The " ancient Author " is Davenant, whose *Love and Honour*, 4to, 1649, originally acted at the Blackfriars, was revived with great splendour 21 October, 1661. In Sir Richard Fanshawe's translation of Hurtado de Mendoza, *Querer por solo querer* (4to, 1671), Act III, we have :

> *Felisbravo.*   Love, and Honour, pull two ways ;
> And I stand doubtful which to take :
> " To Arabia," Honour says,
> Love says : " No ; thy stay here make."

p. 11. REPARTIE. Perhaps Shadwell is particularly aiming at Dryden's dialogue, as the Ruffian and Tomrig may be his angry names for Celadon and Florimel, the delightful lovers, in *The Maiden Queen*.

p. 11. BRAY HIM. " Though thou shouldest bray a fool in a mortar among wheat with a pestle, yet will not his foolishness depart from him." *Proverbs*, xxvii, 22 (A.V.).

p. 13. CRAMBO. Capping verses. Valentine in *Love for Love* (I, 1) avows his intention of writing a play, and instructs Jeremy : " You are witty, you Rogue, I shall want your help ;—I'll have you learn to make Couplets, to tag the Ends of Acts ; d'ye hear, get the Maids to Crambo in an Evening and learn the knack of Rhiming."

p. 14. NINNY. A satire upon Edward Howard, fifth son of Thomas, Earl of Berkshire, who was indeed a prime butt for the wits of the day. Rochester has some scathing verses *On Poet Ninny*. Of Howard's seven plays four have come down to us, and although Pepys considered *The Change of Crowns*, produced at the Theatre Royal, Monday, 15 April, 1667, but not printed, " a great play and serious," which " took very much," it must be confessed that the four pieces we possess from the poet's pen are extraordinarily wooden and uninspired. In the British Museum copy of the quarto, 1668, a contemporary hand has written against Ninny, *Edward Howard*.

p. 14. WOODCOCK. Pepys, Wednesday, 6 May, 1668 : " To Westminster Hall, where met with several people and talked with them, and among other things understand that my Lord St. John is meant by Mr. Woodcocke, in ' The Impertinents.' " Oliver St. John, born about 1598, was called to the Bar as a member of Lincoln's Inn, 1626 ; M.P. for Totnes, 1640 ; Solicitor-General, January, 1640–1 ; Chief Justice of the Common Pleas 1648, and afterwards Lord Chief Justice of the Upper Bench. He died 31 December, 1673. His first wife, Johanna Altham, was aunt to Oliver Cromwell and to John Hampden. His second wife was Elizabeth Cromwell, first cousin to Oliver.

Marvell, *Farther Instructions to a Painter*, (*Satires*, ed. G. A. Aitken, p. 64), writes :

> Whilst Positive walks, like Woodcock in the Park,
> Contriving projects with a brewer's clerk.

Captain E. Thompson, who edited Marvell, has a note : " Sir Robert Howard, and Sir William Bucknell, the brewer." Aitken suggests that Woodcock is Sir Thomas Woodcock, M.P. for Lewes, and Deputy-Governor of Windsor Castle. In the *Flagellum Parliamentarium* he is said to have had a pension of £200 a year. 26 November, 1670, Marvell wrote : " Those that took the Customs, etc., at £600,000 are now struck off again, and Sir Robert Howard, Bucknell, and the brewers, have them as formerly projected."

p. 14. COUNTRY GENT. So in D'Urfey's *Don Quixote*, Parts I and II produced in 1694; Sancho, acted by Dogget in Part I and by Underhill in Part II, is described as " a dry shrewd Country Fellow, Squire to *Don Quixote*, a great Speaker of Proverbs, which he blunders out upon all Occasions, tho never so far from the purpose."

p. 15. LADY VAINE. A satirical portrait of Susanna Uphill, the actress of the Theatre Royal. Evelyn alludes to her when (18 October, 1666) he gives as a reason for his shunning the " publiq theaters " " fowle and undecent women now (and never till now) permitted to appeare and act, who inflaming severall young noblemen and gallants, became their misses, and to some their wives ; witness ye Earl of Oxford, Sir R. Howard, Prince Rupert, the Earle of Dorset, and another greater person than any of them, who fell into their snares, to ye reproach of their noble families."

The author of a pamphlet attacking Sir Robert Howard, *A Seasonable Argument to persuade all the Grand Juries in England to petition for a new Parliament*, 1677, says : " Many other places and boons he has had, but his whore *Uphill* spends all, and now refuses to marry him." Although, according to Downes, Mrs. Uphill had been one of Killigrew's earliest actresses, we find her name in printed casts only set to small rôles such as Erotion, an attendant in Dryden's *Tyrannick Love ; or, The Royal Martyr*, produced at the Theatre Royal, May, 1669 ; Artemis, a court lady, in *Marriage A-la-Mode*, produced at Lincoln's Inn Fields, Easter, 1672 ; Syllana, in Lee's *The Tragedy of Nero*, Drury Lane, May, 1674.

p. 18. FANATICK. A very common word in the latter half of the seventeenth century. It was invariably applied to Nonconformists, and always in a hostile or derisive sense. It is thus used by Archbishop Maxwell as early as 1644, and Fuller, in his *Mixt Contemplations* (1660), has : " A new word coined, within few months, called fanatics . . . seemeth well . . . proportioned to signify . . . the sectaries of our age."

p. 18. COCKS UPON SHROVE TUESDAY. This abominable cruelty was practised at Shrovetide and especially permitted at the old grammar schools. The unfortunate bird was tied by a short cord to a stake, and it was pelted with sticks until killed outright by the blows. The wretches who indulged this villainy stood at a marked distance, and paid a trifling sum, a penny or three halfpence, for three *shies*. Tumult and outrage accompanied this barbarity, and decent people feared to pass near the place where it was practised. Cockfights were also common on this day, and at many large schools the masters received a small tax from the boys known as a *cock-penny*.

p. 18.   BLAZING STAR. Cf. Oldham *Thirteenth Satyr of Juvenal, imitated*, written April, 1682 :

> Then Knave and Villain, things unheard of were,
> Scarce in a Century did one appear,
> And he more gaz'd at than a Blazing Star.

p. 18.   KINGS OF FRANCE AND SPAIN WERE AGREED.   Philip IV of Spain had died 17 September, 1665, leaving by his second wife, Mariana of Austria, an infant son, Charles II.   The late king's will had appointed Mariana Regent. Although Louis XIV had upon his marriage (June, 1660) with Maria Teresa, the daughter of King Philip by Isabel of Bourbon, renounced all claim in his wife's right of succeeding to any territory of the Spanish crown, he now set this renunciation at nought and demanded as his due Flanders, Brabant, and Franche Comté.   The Emperor Leopold consented that Louis should take possession of Flanders, upon the secret condition that he himself, in the event of the death of Charles II, might without let annex Spain to his own dominions.   The French army, with Louis at its head, Turenne commanding under him, entered Flanders in May, 1667.   Several towns were captured, and in the following year the Prince of Condé with ease reduced the whole of Franche Comté.   England, Holland, and Sweden, however, interfered as mediators ; and a peace was concluded 2 May, 1668, at Aix-la-Chapelle.   Pepys, Saturday, 18 July, notes : " They say the King of France is making a war again, in Flanders with the King of Spain ; the King of Spain refusing to give him all that he says was promised him in the treaty."

p. 18.   GROOM-PORTER'S.   The Groom-Porter was an Officer of the Royal Household, abolished under George III, whose duties, at least from the sixteenth century, were to regulate all matters connected with gaming in the precincts of the court, to furnish cards and dice, etc., and to decide such disputes as arose during play.   Cf. *The Alchemist*, acted in 1610, III, 4 :

> He will winne you
> By unresistable lucke, within this fortnight,
> Inough to buy a baronie.   They will set him
> Upmost, at the groome-porters, all the Christmasse.

Also Otway's *Friendship in Fashion*, produced at Dorset Garden, April, 1678, where Malagene says : " I ran to the Groom-Porter's last Night, and lost my Money."   Pepys, who on Wednesday, 1 January, 1667–8, went " to see the manner of the gaming at the Groome-Porter's," has a lively description of the scene.

p. 20.   CAST POET OF THE NURSERY.   The Nursery was a training theatre for boys and girls intended for the stage.   Established under Royal Letters Patent, 30 March, 1664, it is frequently alluded to in contemporary literature.   It seems that there was only one Nursery, although, as it not infrequently changed its quarters, it is sometimes asserted that two Nurseries existed simultaneously.   The Nursery was originally in Hatton Garden.   About 1668 it was transferred to Vere Street, and thence finally to the Barbican. Mr. W. J. Laurence, in his exhaustive history of *Restoration Stage Nurseries*, shows that Wilkinson's oft-engraved view of the supposed Fortune Theatre is none other than this Golden Lane Nursery on the site of the old Fortune Theatre.   Pepys speaks with unwonted contempt of performances at the Nursery.   Monday, 24 February, 1667–8, he saw *The Spanish Tragedy* at the Nursery, "where the house is better and the musique better than we looked for, and the acting not much worse, because I expected as bad as could be : and I was not much mistaken, for it was so." The next day he repaired again to the Nursery, "and there saw them act a comedy, a pastorall, 'The Faythful Shepherd,' having the curiosity to see whether they do a comedy better than a tragedy ; but they do it both alike, in the meanest manner, that I was sick of it." There is subtle point in Mr. Bayes' declaration : "I'm resolv'd hereafter, to bind my thoughts wholly for the service of the *Nursery*, and mump your proud Players, I gad" (*The Rehearsal*, II, 2). Oldham has the following couplet :—

> Then slighted by the very Nursery,
> Mayest thou at last be forced to starve like me.

p. 20.   ENTRANCE OF WITCHES. In particular allusion to *Macbeth*, which having been tinkered at by Davenant with special elaboration of the witch scenes and, as Downes says, "being drest in all it's Finery, as new Cloath's, new Scenes, Machines, as flyings for the Witches," "Recompenc'd double the Expense." This is all burlesqued in Duffett's extraordinary epilogue to his farce *The Empress of Morocco*, produced at Drury Lane in the spring of 1674. Here we have : "EPILOGUE Being a new Fancy, after the old and most surprising way of MACBETH Perform'd with new, and costly MACHINES." During the course of this fantastic puppetry "Three Witches fly over the Pit Riding upon Besomes," and "*Heccate* descends over the Stage in a Glorious Charriott adorn'd with Pictures of Hell and Devils, and made of a large Wicker Basket." There is much topical and gross parody, when all the witches cry "Huff! no more !" Thereupon "*a Hellish noise is heard within*," Heccate is called away, and a trio by Three Witches concludes this extravaganza.

p. 20.   MARCH BEER. A potent beer brewed in March. Lithgow, *Travels* (1632), III, 106, speaks of : "Strong *March*-Ale surpassing fine Aqua-vitae." Tom Brown, *Last Observator* (1704) in *Collected Poems*, 1705, has : "Hast with thee brought some . . . Protestant March-Beer, to raise my Fancy ?"

p. 20.   PYE-CORNER. West Smithfield, between Giltspur Street and Smithfield ; now the Smithfield end of Giltspur Street. Stow (p. 139) has : "Pie Corner, a place so called of such a sign, sometime a fair Inn for receipt of travellers, but now divided into tenements." Strype, Book III (p. 283), mentions : "Pye corner—noted chiefly for Cook's Shops and Pigs drest there during Bartholomew Fair." There are numberless jests and allusions.

p. 21.   A DAMN'D CORANTO. A tune in triple time used for accompanying the dance, coranto. The coranto, literally "running" dance, was a lively French measure, to which there are many allusions, *e.g.*, Shakespeares "swift Carranto's," *Henry V*, III, v (1599). Sir John Hawkins, *History of Music* (1776), IV, 111, i, 387, explains : "The Coranto . . . is a melody or air consisting of three crotchets in a bar, but moving by quavers."

p. 21.   TARRANTULA. The bite of this spider, a large wolf-spider of Southern Europe, was fabled to cause extraordinary effects, such as laughter, dancing, singing. T. Hoby in his translation of Baldassare Castiglione's *Courtyer* (1561, ed. 1577) speaks of "Them that are bitten with a Tarantula," and has a marginal note : "A kind of spiders, which being diuers of nature cause diuers effectes, some after their biting fal a singing, some laugh, [etc.]."

p. 23.   YOUR SAD INDIFFERENCE. These verses not unpleasantly burlesque the paradoxes so common in heroic tragedy, especially in scenes of stichomythia.

p. 24. RIDDLE ME RIDDLE. Answer my question. A very old catch-phrase. *Riddle me a* (or *my*) *riddle.* So in Davenant's *Man's the Master*, produced at Lincoln's Inn Fields, March, 1667–8, III, 1, where Jodelet says : "Riddle my riddle, what's this ? " The expression is often reduplicated, *riddle me, riddle me ;* whence the fanciful variant *riddle-me-ree, riddlemeree*, which came to mean "any rigmarole," "nonsense." Many nursery riddles of yore begin :

> Riddle me, riddle me, riddle-me-ree,
> And oh ! how I wonder what this can be. . . .

p. 25. AN INSURRECTION OF 'PRENTICES. On Shrove Tuesday in each year, as also during Eastertide, it was customary for the apprentices of the metropolis to avail themselves of their holidays by assembling in large numbers and making organised assaults upon notorious houses of ill fame, which they sacked and even demolished. In Middleton's *Inner Temple Masque* (4to, 1619), we have :

> " Stand forth, Shrove Tuesday, one a' the silenc'st brick-layers ;
> 'Tis in your charge to pull down bawdy-houses."

So Duffett's skit *The Mock Tempest* (4to, 1674) opens with a formidable attack by the mobile upon a brothel. And in Marmion's *Holland's Leaguer*, acted at Salisbury Court, December, 1631, Act IV, 3, which scene is the exterior of the Leaguer :

> " Good sir, let's think on some revenge ! call up
> The gentlemen 'prentices and make a Shrove Tuesday."

Holland's Leaguer was a celebrated brothel, which stood where is now Holland Street, Blackfriars. The fourth act of the play passes chiefly before this house, which is sometimes called a castle or a fort. The first scene of *The Mock Tempest* may be aptly compared with Marmion.

Pepys, 24 March (Easter Tuesday), 1667–8, gives a long account of " the tumult at the other end of the town, about Moore-fields, among the 'prentices, taking the liberty of these holydays to pull down bawdy-houses." There was a dangerous riot, and the military had to be called out under the command of Lord Craven. When several of the 'prentices were imprisoned in the Clerkenwell Bridewell " the rest did come and break open the prison and release them," giving out that they were for pulling down the bawdy-houses, " which is one of the greatest grievances of the nation." When this was reported to Charles he said : " Why, why, do they go to them, then ? " Which certainly seems an extremely pertinent query, although Pepys thought it " a very poor, cold, insipid answer." The following morning Pepys found the Duke of York and all with him " full of the talk of the 'prentices, who are not yet (put) down, though the guards and the militia of the town have been in armes all this night and the night before. . . . Some blood hath been spilt, but a great many houses pulled down ; and among others, the Duke of York was mighty merry at that of Damaris Page's, the great bawd of the seamen ; . . . it was said how these idle fellows have had the confidence to say that they did ill in contenting themselves in pulling down the little bawdy-houses, and did not go and pull down the great bawdy-house at Whitehall." Eight of the leaders in these riots were captured and condemned to death. On 9 May four were drawn, hanged, and quartered at Tyburn, two of their heads being fixed upon London Bridge (*The London Gazette*, No. 259). See also " The Tryals of such persons as under the notion of London Apprentices were tumultuously assembled in Moore Fields, under colour of pulling down bawdyhouses," 4to, 1668. A number of lampoons appeared, and Evelyn, 2 April, remarks : " Amongst other libertine libels there was one now printed, and thrown about, a bold petition of the poore whores to Lady Castlemaine," and Pepys, four days later, writes : " I do hear that my Lady Castlemaine is horribly vexed at the late libell, the petition of the poore whores about the town, whose houses were pulled down the other day. I have got one of them, but it is not very witty, but devilish severe against her and the King ; and I wonder how it durst be printed and spread abroad." This pasquil is entitled : " The Poor-Whores Petition to the Most Splendid, Illustrious, Serene, and Eminent Lady of Pleasure, the Countess of Castlemaine, etc. The Humble Petition of the Undone Company of poore distressed Whores, Bawds, Pimps, and Panders, etc." It is " Signed by Us Madam Cresswell and Damaris Page, in behalf of our Sisters and Fellow-Sufferers (in this day of our Calamity) . . . this present 25th day of March, 1668." A very few days after appeared " The Gracious ANSWER of the Most Illustrious Lady of Pleasure, the Countess of Castlem . . . To the Poor-Whores Petition." This commences : " Right Trusty and Well-beloved Madam Cresswell and Damaris Page with the rest of the Suffering Sisterhood . . ." and concludes " CASTLEM . . . Given at our Closset in King Street, Westminster, Die Veneris, April 24 1668." These two remarkable documents may be seen in full in Steiman's *Memoir of Barbara, Duchess of Cleveland*, 1871, pp. 100–111.

p. 25.   YOUR BAPTISTS, YOUR LOCKS, YOUR BANISTERS. Baptist is Giovanni Baptista Draghi, an Italian musician who settled in London about the middle of the seventeenth century. On Tuesday, 12 February, 1666–7, Pepys notes : " With Lord Bruncker by coach to his house, there to hear some Italian musique ; and here we met Tom Killigrew, Sir Robert Murray, and the Italian Signor Baptista, who hath composed a play in Italian for the Opera, which T. Killigrew do intend to have up ; and here he did sing one of the acts. He himself is the poet as well as the musician, which is very much." Draghi on the death of Lock in 1677 succeeded him as organist to Queen Catharine. He excelled as a player on the harpsichord. In 1675 he composed the act-tunes and some other instrumental music to Shadwell's *Psyche*. In 1687, for the celebration of S. Cecilia's Day, he set Dryden's splendid ode to music. In 1706 he contributed part of the music to D'Urfey's comic opera *Wonders in the Sun*.

   Matthew Locke, born at Exeter, *circa* 1630, one of the most famous of English musicians, whose name will always be generally associated with his music for *Macbeth*. He died in August, 1677.

   John Banister, born in 1630, after some study in France, was appointed leader of the king's band. *The State Papers*, 1663, note : " Mr. Banister appointed to be chief of His Majesty's violins." Banister is said to be the first to establish lucrative concerts in London. He died 3 October, 1679.

p. 25.   GAMUT, A RE, BEMI. Gamut is the " Great Scale " (arranged by Guido of Arezzo) comprising the seven hexachords or partial scales and consisting of all the recognized notes used in mediæval music ; hence in later use the whole series of notes recognized by musicians.

   A re, an obsolete musical term, which in Guido Aretino's arrangement was the name of the note A in those hexachords (the first, fourth, and seventh) in which it coincided with the second lowest note, sung to the syllable *re*.

B is in England the seventh note of the scale of C major. A *Burlesque* of 1450 has: "Every clarke . . . seythe that a-re gothe before be-my." Morley, Introduction to Music, 1597, explains: "Every keye hath but one cleife except b fa, b mi."

p. 25. JIGGS. Edward Howard (Ninny) in his preface to *The Women's Conquest*, 4to, 1671, alludes to the "Scenes, Machines, Habits, Jiggs, and Dances" which found their way even into tragedies, and in his first Prologue he makes Edward Angel say: "We are to act a farce to-day that has sixteen Mimics in it . . . with two and thirty Dances and Jiggs à la mode." D'Urfey in the Epilogue to *The Injur'd Princess*, produced at Drury Lane in 1682, avows:

> *The way to please you is easie if we knew't,*
> *A Jigg, a Song, a Rhyme or two will do't.*

p. 26. DOWN TO C. SOL. FA. UT. C is the first note or key-note of the "natural" major scale. Cf. *The Taming of the Shrew* (1596), III, 1: "C fa vt, that loues with all affection." *Sol* is the fifth note of Guido Aretine's hexachords; the note G in the natural scale of C major. Playford, *Skill in Music* (1662, ed. 1674), explains: "*Ut* and *Re* are changed now into *Sol* and *La*."

p. 26. AMBOYNA. The wholesale arrests in 1622, on the pretence of a plot being hatched by them, of the English merchants at Amboyna (one of the Molucca islands), their tortures and murder by the Dutch, caused intense excitement, but the atrocity, though deeply resented by King James, was in the end left unavenged. There is a contemporary pamphlet *A True Relation of the unjust, cruel, and barbarous Proceedings against the English at* Amboyna *in the East Indies by the Netherlandish Governor there*. Cf. Fletcher's *The Fair Maid of the Inn*, licensed January, 1626, IV, where Forobosco says to the Clown: I'll send thee . . . to Amboyna i'th' East-Indies, for pepper

> To bake it.
> *Clown.* To Amboyna? so I might
> Be pepper'd.

In Shirley's *Honoria and Mammon*, I, Conquest upbraids Alamode:

> sell thy countrymen
> To as many persecutions as the devil,
> Or Dutchmen, had invented at Amboyna!

Dryden's tragedy *Amboyna* produced at Lincoln's Inn Fields in 1673 with Hart, Mohun, Kynaston, and Mrs. Marshall in the cast, was written in war time to inflame the nation against the Dutch. It seems to me a very fine and pathetic drama. The head title reads "Amboyna, or the Cruelties of the Dutch to the English Merchants."

p. 27. CASTEL RODRIGO. The Marquis of Castel Rodrigo, the Spanish governor of the Netherlands. 21 May, 1667, Louis XIV had crossed the border with an army of 50,000 men, and in three months a long line of frontier fortresses fell into French hands.

p. 27. WE ARE ALL MORTAL. A sharp hit at Sir Robert Howard's poem *Against the Fear of Death*. Dryden in his *Defence of an Essay of Dramatique Poesie*, prefixed to the second quarto, 1668, of *The Indian Emperour* (and not reprinted in the author's lifetime), which is a retort upon Howard's criticisms in the preface to *The Great Favourite*, writes in pursuit of an argument concerning the unity of place: "The Stage being one place cannot be two. This, indeed, is as great a Secret, as that we are all mortal," thus smartly alluding to Howard's poem.

p. 27. LILLY . . . COOPER. Sir Peter Lely (1618–1680), the famous painter of the beauties at the court of Charles II. Originally hung in Windsor Castle, they now adorn Hampton Court. Cf. Pope, *Imitations of Horace*, I, 149–50:

> Lely on animated Canvas stole
> The sleepy eye, that spoke the melting soul.

Samuel Cooper, 1609–1672, the eminent miniaturist, whom Pepys calls the "great limner in little." (2 January, 1661–2) Horace Walpole highly praises this artist as "the first who gave the strength and freedom of oil to miniature." A "Picture in little" was the common term for a miniature. Cf. *The Country-Wife*, IV, 3, where Old Lady Squeamish cries to Horner: "Prithee kiss her, and I'll give you her Picture in little, that you admir'd so last night, prythee do," and he answers: "Well, nothing but that could bribe me, I love a woman only in Effigie, and good painting."

p. 29. SILENC'D PARSON. Silenced by the Act of Uniformity, May, 1662, when every beneficed clergyman was ordered to use the services of the *Book of Common Prayer* under pain of deprivation. Rather than conform nearly two thousand ministers went forth from their cures on Sunday, 24 August, 1662, S. Bartholomew's Day. The Conventicle Act of 1664 made it illegal for more than five persons to assemble for a service not in accordance with Anglican discipline, and the Five Mile Act, October, 1665, forbade Nonconformist ministers to come within that distance of any city or corporate town. They were silenced, then, from their chief exercise, preaching, and were no longer able in windy sermons to disseminate "the poisonous principles of schism and rebellion." Cf. for the phrase Dryden's *St. Martin Mar-all*, produced at Lincoln Inn Fields, Thursday, 15 August, 1667, II, where the Landlord being discovered and afraid to speak, Sir Martin bawls: "Have you no Tongue, you Rascal?" and Sir John tartly comments: "Sure 'tis some silenc'd Minister: he grows so fat he cannot speak." One of Butler's "Characters" is *A Silenc'd Presbyterian*.

p. 29. ROBIN HOOD OR CHEVY CHASE. Two of the most popular old ballads, sung at every cottage fireside. One version of *Robin Hood* is found in Ravenscroft's *Pammelia*, 1609. It commences:

> Robin Hood, Robin Hood, said little John,
>   Come dance before the Queen a
> In a redde Petticote and a greene Jacket
>   A white hose and a greene a.

"The old Song of *Chevy-Chase* is the favourite Ballad of the common People of *England*; and *Ben Johnson* used to say he had rather have been the Author of it than of all his Works." Addison, *Spectator*, Monday, 21 May, 1711 (LXX.). Percy in his *Reliques* remarks that Addison is mistaken as to the antiquity of the common-received copy, which is Elizabethan, and probably written after Sir Philip Sidney's eulogium of the old song; perhaps in consequence of it. Percy gives the text of "the genuine antique poem," but see Skeat, *Specimens of English Literature*, for a correction of various errors.

p. 30.   CHARLES THE FIFTH. This great emperor having requested the German
electors to accept his abdication and elect Ferdinand his successor, this was
done after some delay 28 February, 1558. In 1555 he had already con-
vened the Estates of the Netherlands and in their presence transferred the
government to his son Philip. Three months later (16 January, 1556) he
resigned the Spanish crown to his son, but even so it was September, 1556,
before he was able to withdraw to his long-chosen place of retirement in
Spain, the Hieronymite monastery of S. Jerome of Yuste, situated in a
sequestered valley near Placencia, in Estremadura. Even then he could
not actually enter enclosure until 8 February, 1557. Here he did not in
detail follow the conventual life, although the greater part of his day was
spent in religious exercises and the practice of ascetic austerities. He
expired, owing to a fever, on 21 September, 1558, in the fifty-ninth year of
his age.

p. 32.   I'M RESOLV'D TO GO ALONG WITH YOU. So in Otway's *Friendship in Fashion*,
produced at Dorset Garden, April, 1678, I, Malagene refuses to leave
Truman and Valentine. "'Tis time we were going," says Truman to his
friend. "What, to Dinner?" chips in Malagene, "I'le make a third Man
—where shall it be?" "Sir," answers Truman, "I am sorry, we must
beg your Excuse this Time, for we are both engag'd." "Whoo!" pertly
ripostes Malagene, "prithee that's all one, I am sure I know the Company;
I'le go along at a Venture." He is finally got rid of by being falsely informed they are going to fight a duel.

p. 32.   THE EXCHANGE. The New Exchange was a kind of bazaar on the south
side of the Strand, built out of the stables of Durham House, the site of the
present Adelphi. The first stone was laid 10th June, 1608, and the new
building was named by James I "Britain's Burse." It was an immensely
popular resort, and there are innumerable references to its shops, its semp-
stresses and haberdashers. Langbaine tells us that Thomas Duffett, the
writer of burlesques, was, "before he became a poet, a Milliner in the New
Exchange."

I have counted more than one hundred allusions to the New Exchange in
Pepys, *e.g.*, Saturday, 22 September, 1660: "From thence by coach home (by
the way at the New Exchange I bought a pair of short black stockings to
wear over a pair of silk ones for mourning; and here I met with The.
Turner and Joyce, buying of things to go into mourning too for the Duke
(of Gloucester) which is now the mode of all the ladies in town)." Saturday,
20 April, 1661: "With Mr. Creed to the Exchange and bought some
things, as gloves and bandstrings, etc." Wednesday, 6 May, 1668: "Thence
by water to the New Exchange, where bought a pair of shoestrings."
The New Exchange was demolished in 1737.

In many plays we find scenes laid in the New Exchange. Sir George
Etherege's *She wou'd if she cou'd*, produced at Lincoln's Inn Fields, Thursday,
6 February, 1668, has "Act III, scene 1. Scene, the New Exchange.
Mistress Trincket *sitting in a Shop. People passing by as in the Exchange. Mrs.
Trinc.* What d'ye buy? what d'ye lack, Gentlemen? Gloves, Ribbons, and
Essences: Ribbons, Gloves, and Essences?" Among the Dramatis Personæ
are "*Mrs.* Gazette *and Mrs.* Trincket, *Two Exchange Women.*" Again, among
the Dramatis Personae of Carlile's *The Fortune-Hunters ; or, Two Fools well
met*, produced at Drury Lane in 1689, are "Mr. *Spruce*, an *Exchange-man*,"
acted by Nokes, and "Mrs. *Spruce*, the *Exchange-man's* wife," acted by
Frances Maria Knight. Act II, scene 2, "*The Exchange. Discovers Mrs.*

Spruce *in her Shop.*" Presently Sophia and Maria enter, whereupon " Mrs.
Spruce. Ribbonds or Gloves, Madam ; Gloves or Ribbonds." In Otway's
The Atheist, Dorset Garden, autumn of 1683, the Second Act opens in the
New Exchange, and Mrs. Furnish, *an Exchange-Woman* (Mrs. Osborn),
calls : " Gloves or Ribbands, Sirs ? Very good Gloves or Ribbands,
Choice of fine Essences." So in Pierre Corneille's comedy, *La Galerie du
Palais, ou, L'amie Rivale* (1635), the scene is laid in the Palace Gallery, which
was very similar to the New Exchange, and in his *Examen* Corneille says :
" J'ai donc pris ce titre de la Galerie du Palais, parce que la promesse de ce
spectacle extraordinaire, & agréable pour sa naïveté, devoit exciter vrai-
semblablement la curiositè des auditeurs ; & ç'a été pour leur plaire plus
d'une fois, que j'ai fait paroître ce même spectacle à la fin du Quatrième
acte, où il est entièrement inutile, & n'est renoué avec celui du premier que
par des valets, qui viennent prendre dans les boutiques ce que leurs maîtres
y avoient acheté, ou voir si les marchands ont reçules nippes qu'ils atten-
doient. Cette espèce de renouement lui étoit nécessaire, afin qu'il ne fût
pas tout-à-fait hors d'oeuvre. La rencontre que j'y fais faire d'Aronte &
de Florice est ce qui le fixe particulièrement en ce lieu-là, & sans cet accident
il eût été aussi propre à la fin du second ou du troisième, qu'en la place
qu'il occupe. Sans cet agrèment la pièce auroit été très régulière pour
l'unité du lieu & la liaison des scènes, qui n'est interrompue que par-là."
Among the characters of the comedy are, Le Libraire du Palais, Le Mercier
du Palais, La Lingère du Palais. Act I, 4, *On tire un rideau, & l'on voit le
Libraire, la Lingère, & le Mercier, chacun dans sa boutique.* Scene VI commences : *Hippolyte, à la Lingère.* Madame, montrez-nous quelques collets
d'ouvrage.

> *La Lingère.* Je vous en vais montrer des toutes les façons.
> *Dorimant, au Libraire.* Ce visage vaut mieux que toutes vos chansons.
> *La Lingère, à Hippolyte.* Voilâ du point d'esprit, de Genes, et d'Espagne.
> *Hippolyte.* Ceci n'est guère bon qu'à des gens de campagne.
> *La Lingère.* Voyez bien, s'il en est deux pareils dans Paris.
> *Hippolyte.* Ne les vantez point tant, & dites-nous le prix.
> *La Lingère.* Quand vous aurez choisi.

p. 32. FLOS UNGUENTORUM, PARACELSIAN, AND GREEN-SALVE. Flos unguentorum,
or Ointment of Roses, a common salve.
   Paracelsian, Lily of Paracelsus. Tincture of Flowers of Antimony.
" Excellent in the black Jaundis, Gout, Dropsy," prescribes the *Compleat
Chymical Dispensatory* of W. Rowland (translated from the Latin of Dr.
Joannes Schroeder), folio, 1669, p. 238.
   Green-Salve, or Green Butter, a stimulant, for which see Rowland's
work, Book II, c. 87 (p. 146).

p. 32. ALBUM GRAECUM. The excrement of dogs and some other animals which
from exposure to air and weather becomes whitened like chalk. It was
formerly much used in medicines. Cf. Mrs. Behn's *The Rover*, Part II,
produced at Dorset Garden in 1680, V, 3, where Fatherfool, who has been
" mall'd and beaten," begs Harlequin : " Procure a little Album Graecum
for my Backside."

p. 33. A FIT OF THE MOTHER. Hysteria. Cf. Webster's play upon the phrase, *The
Dutchesse of Malfy,* 4to, 1623, II :

> *Duchess.* Shall I sound under thy fingers ? I am
>   So troubled with the mother !
> *Bosola [aside].* I feare to[o] much.

p. 33. **BLUE INCKLE.** Incle is linen thread or yarn which was woven into a tape, once very commonly used. It burned or smouldered with a pungent smell, and so was used as feathers for reviving persons from a swoon.

p. 33. **DOL COMON.** The virago colleague of Subtle and Face in *The Alchemist*. Mrs. Corey was famous in this rôle, and teste Pepys was actually often known as Dol Common.

p. 33. **NICK'T.** To nick is a slang term for " to cheat " ; " to rook." So " *Nickum*, a Sharper." *Dictionary of the Canting Crew*.

p. 33. **SPIERINGS.** A notorious gaming-house. Cf. Cotton, *Compleat Gamester*, 1674, p. 9, where, speaking of " *Bully-Huffs* and *Bully-Rocks*," he says : "We need no other testimony to confirm the danger of associating with these Anthropophagi or Man-Eaters, than *Lincoln's-Inn-Fields*, whilst *Speerings Ordinary* was kept in Bell-Yard."

p. 34. **PIECES.** The piece is an English gold coin, originally applied to the *unite* of James I, and afterwards to a sovereign or a guinea, as each was the current coin. *The Dictionary of the Canting Crew*, circa 1700, explains the slang *Job* as " a Guinea, Twenty Shillings, or a Piece." Chambers, 1727–41, has " *Coin*, Guinea or Piece."

p. 35. **SENECA.** *Les Fâcheux*, II, 3 :

> *La Montagne.* Ah ! il faut modérer un peu ses passions ;
> Et Sénèque . . .
>
> *Eraste.*   Sénèque est un sot dans ta bouche.

Shadwell has slightly misunderstood the French. La Montagne was going on with some wise saw, attributed to Seneca, upon whom most of the well-worn apophthegms were fathered at random, and Eraste cuts him short in the midst of his moralizing before he has had time to give vent to the Senecan adage.

p. 36. **ROSE-TAVERN.** Covent Garden, afterwards known as Will's Coffee-House, after William Urwin, the landlord. It was greatly resorted to by literary men, and here Dryden had his own chair reserved. The Rose was on the west side of Bow Street, and at the corner of Russell Street. After the theatre the critics were wont to flock here, and Mrs. Behn in her preface to *The Luckey Chance*, 4to, 1687, complains : " A Wit of the Town, a Friend of mine at *Wills* Coffee House, the first Night of the Play, cry'd it down as much as in him lay, who before had read it and assured me he never saw a prettier Comedy." There are continual references to Will's. On Wednesday, 3 February, 1663–4, Pepys looked in there for a space and saw " Dryden the poet (I knew at Cambridge), and all the wits of the town, and Harris the player."

p. 36. **JACK-PUDDING EAT A CUSTARD.** The sobriquet *Jack-Pudding* for a Merry-Andrew, which is used by Milton, *Defence of the People of England*, I, was much in vogue in literature at the end of the seventeenth century, and is a favourite term with Shadwell. The Jack-Pudding was originally the servant to the quack or mountebank at a fair, and he attracted the rustic by the grossest tricks, such as eating a posset and slobbering it all over his face and clothes with many a hiccup and grimace. Addison, *Spectator*, Tuesday 24 April, 1711 (XLVII), speaks of these " Drolls, whom the common People of all Countries admire. . . . I mean those circumforaneous Wits whom every Nation calls by the Name of that Dish of Meat which it loves best. In *Holland* they are termed *Pickled Herrings ;* in *France* Jean Potages *;* in *Italy*, Maccaronies *;* and in *Great Britain*, Jack Puddings."

p. 36.   A DELICATE MACHIN. Flecknoe in *A Short Discourse of the English Stage*
           appended to *Love's Kingdom*, 12mo, 1664, declares : " Scenes and Machines
           . . . are no new Invention, our Masks and some of our Playes in former
           times (though not so ordinary) having had as good, or rather better than
           any we have now." This judgement is, perhaps, conservatively pre-
           judiced, for Monconys, writing as early as 22 May, 1663, of the Theatre
           Royal in Bridges Street, remarks that " *les changements de Théâtre et les
           machines sont fort ingénieusement inventées et exécutées.*" Chappuzeau in 1667
           (*L'Europe vivante*) considered that the English theatre " *réussit admirablement
           dans la machine, et . . . va maintenant du pair avec les Italiens.*" It was frequent
           for one to sit and sing in a machine, and Buckingham in *The Rehearsal*, V,
           parodies this when Prince Pretty-man exclaims :

> Behold, with wonder, yonder comes from far
> A God-like Cloud, and a triumphant Carr :
> In which, our two right Kings sit one by one,
> With Virgins Vests, and Laurel Garlands on.

           And immediately : " *The two right Kings of* Brentford *descend in the Clouds,
           singing, in white garments ; and three Fidlers sitting before them, in green.*" In
           Settle's *Cambyses, King of Persia*, acted 1666–7, two glorious spirits descend
           in clouds with a song.

p. 37.   FOUR SHILLINGS. The price of admission to the boxes. Cf. Dryden's Epilogue
           (*Intended to have been spoken to the Play before it was forbidden last summer*) to
           The Duke of Guise, which was to have been produced in July, 1682, but
           banned and postponed until the following November, where the poet,
           having commented on the rowdiness of the pit, especially at political plays,
           continues :

> This makes our Boxes full ; for men of Sense
> Pay their four Shillings in their own Defence :
> That safe behind the Ladies they may stay,
> Peep o'er the Fan, and judge the bloody Fray.

p. 37.   LINSEY WOOLSEY. A textile material woven from a mixture of wool and flax,
           used for rough and inferior clothes. Cf. Nashe, *Lenten Stuffe* (1599): " I
           had as lieue haue . . . no cloathes rather then wear linsey woolsey."

p. 37.   SHATTELIN'S AND LAFRONDS. There are many references to these famous
           ordinaries. Cf. Pepys, Friday, 15 March, 1667–8: " At noon all of us to
           Chatelin's, the French house in Covent Garden, to dinner—Brouncker,
           J. Minnes, W. Pen, T. Harvey, and myself : and there had a dinner cost us
           8*s.* 6*d.* a-piece, a damned base dinner, which did not please us at all, so that
           I am not fond of this house at all but do rather choose the Beare." Yet
           Chatelin's was very fashionable. On Wednesday, 22 April, 1668, Pepys
           thought to have met Mr. Pierce and his wife, and Knepp ; but " met their
           servant coming to bring me to Chatelin's, the French house in Covent
           Garden, and there with musick and good company, . . . and here mighty
           merry till ten at night. . . . This night the Duke of Monmouth and a great
           many blades were at Chatelin's." In a Prologue which appears in *Covent
           Garden Drollery* (1672), and later seems to have been spoken before D'Urfey's
           The Fool Turn'd Critick, 4to, 1678, we have :

> Next these we welcome such as briskly dine
> At *Locket's*, at *Gifford's*, or with *Shatiline*.

Warner in Dryden's *St. Martin Mar-all*, produced Saturday, 15 August, 1667, IV, speaks of "Wine from *Shatling* and *La-fronds*." In Sedley's *The Mulberry-Garden*, produced at the King's House, Monday, 18 May, 1668, Act IV, Modish says: "Leave your *Chaste Ling* And *La-Fronds*, dine with my Lord such a One one day, my Lady What d'you call 'um another."

p. 38. SLIP 'EM, *i.e.*, let Ninny and Lady Vaine loose upon Stanford and Emilia.

p. 38. HEROICK POEM. Probably in allusion to Edward Howard's *The British Princes. An Heroick Poem.* 8vo, 1669 (Term Catalogues, May, 1669). Extracts, at least, had no doubt been circulated in manuscript.

p. 38. SHEERNESS AGUE. Many details concerning Sheerness will be found in Pepys. The yard and fortifications were designed and first "staked out" by Sir Bernard de Gomme, see the *Diary*, 24 March, 1667.

p. 39. SOUL, AND FLAME. In the Epistle Dedicatory, to the Duchess of Monmouth, which precedes *The Indian Emperour*, 4to, 1667, Dryden speaks of this tragedy as, in his own judgment, "written with more Flame than Art."

p. 40. HORARY QUESTIONS. Horoscopes and planetary schemes. Thus the Second Part of John Middleton's *Practical Astrology*, 8vo, 1679: "Sheweth the resolution of all manner of Horary questions which concern the life of man, his estate, brethren, or short Journeys; if the Querent shall ever have children; of sicknesses, and how to find the nature and kind of the disease; also concerning marriages, Law-suits, etc. Together with several examples of Celestial figures created for horary questions."

p. 40. BLACKWALL TO TUTTLE-FIELDS. "To Poplar adjoineth Blackwall, a notable harbour for ships, so called because it is a *wall* of the Thames, and distinguished by the additional term Black, from the black shrubs which grow on it, as on Blackheath, which is opposite to it on the other side of the river." Dr. Woodward and Styrpe, in Styrpe's *Appendix*, vol. II, p. 102. From an early date Blackwall was a great place for ships, ship-building, and docks.

Tothill Fields (Tuttle Fields) comprised that portion of land between Tothill Street, Pimlico, and the river Thames. In early times it was the scene of jousts and tournaments, later duels often took place here.

p. 41. SETTING-DOG AND PARTRIDGE. This well-known ordinary was in Fleet Street. It is mentioned in *The Country-Wife*, I, where the gallants discuss where to dine.

> *Sparkish.* Come, but where do we dine?
> *Horner.* Ev'n where you will.
> *Sparkish.* At *Chateline's.*
> *Dorilant.* Yes, if you will.
> *Sparkish.* Or at the *Cock.*
> *Dorilant.* Yes, if you please.
> *Sparkish.* Or at the *Dog* and *Partridge.*
> *Horner.* Ay, if you have a mind to't, for we shall dine at neither.

Cf. Butler's *Characters* (Thyer's edition, 1759), *A Pimp:* "He is the Whores Jackal, that hunts out Treats for them all Day, and at Night has his Share in a Tavern-Supper, or a Treat at the *Setting Dog and Partridge*, a very significant Sign, like the Brokers *Bird in Hand*." The Setting Dog and Partridge was much frequented by Etherege and Sedley; the latter of whom Charles Montague calls its "Darling Son" (Add. MS. 28644, f. 57b.). Etherege wrote to Jephson: "I expect to see my Lord Carlingford in his way to Vienna, then you may be sure all the remains of the Dog and Partridge will be remembered," 27 February/8 March, 1687–8. Radcliffe in his *News from Hell* says that Etherege is lost

> for writing superfine,
> With words correct in every Line :
> And one that does presume to say,
> A Plot's too gross for any Play :
> Comedy should be clean and neat,
> As Gentlemen do talk and eat.
> So what he writes is but Translation,
> From Dog and Pa[r]tridge conversation.

p. 41. SEVERAL DOORS. The permanent proscenium doors on opposite sides of the stage.

p. 42. GREAT JUDGE INDEED, ETC. The " etc." is, of course, for the actor to fill in the line with " gag." Cf. *The Adventures of Five Hours*, 4to, 1671, Act I, where as the Servants separate all cry : " Your Servant, your servant, &c." In Act II, 2, of Henry Carey's *Hanging and Marriage*, produced at Lincoln's Inn Fields, March, 1721–22, where Mother Stubble enters bawling out " Aw law ! What shall I do ? what shall I do ? &c." The stage direction is " *A great deal more of this stuff.*"

p. 43. SALVATOR WINTER. The mountebank master of a contemporary puppet show.

p. 43. READ AND ACT. One of Edward Howard's favourite expressions. Cf. *The Rehearsal*, I, 1, where Bayes says his play shall " read, and write, and act, and plot, and shew, ay, and pit, box and gallery, I gad, with any play in *Europe*." *The Key to the Rehearsal* (1709) explains that these were favourite expressions of the Hon. Edward Howard at his rehearsals.

p. 44. BAWD WAS. On a Shrove Tuesday (or Easter Tuesday), when the 'prentice lads were wont to attack the brothels and maul the bawds and common whores. Pepys, 24 March, 1667–8, gives a long account of " the tumult at the other end of the town, about Moore-fields, among the 'prentices, taking the liberty of these holydays to pull down bawdy-houses."

p. 45. STUDY IN PHILOSOPHY. A hit at the newly formed Royal Society, which later Shadwell satirizes in *The Virtuoso*.

p. 46. A WOODCOCK. Proverbial for its silliness. Cf. *The Taming of the Shrew*, I, 11, " O ! this woodcock what an ass it is ! "

p. 46. YOU SHALL GO MY HALFES. This old story is of an Oriental origin, and is found in the Italian novelists.

p. 49. THE PUPPY'S STOUT. Sir Robert Howard, in spite of his whimsicality and encyclopædic pretensions, was well known for his quixotic ideals and heroism. It is probable that by the name Bilboa, which stood for Bayes in the first sketch of *The Rehearsal*, Howard was intended, and not Davenant, as Malone thought.

p. 50. COUNTERVAILE. To countervail is to compensate for; to be equivalent to; to balance.

p. 50. KNIGHT'S-BRIDGE. This hamlet long retained its suburban character, and in 1629 an ancient chapel of the Holy Trinity once attached to a lazar-house was erected into the district chapel for the hamlet. Marriages and baptisms were frequently performed here, probably because of the very retired nature of the church. Twenty volumes of registers, some few being duplicates, dating from 1658 to 1752, are still preserved. Knightsbridge Chapel was rebuilt about 1628–9, during Laud's episcopate.

p. 50. DISPOS'D OF MY ELDER SISTER. One may remember *The Taming of the Shrew*, I :

> *Baptista.* Gentlemen, importune me no further,
> For how I firmly am resolv'd you know ;
> That is, not to bestow my youngest daughter
> Before I have a husband for the elder.

p. 51. EIGHTEEN PENCE GALLERY. The middle gallery, which seems to have been divided into boxes. Friday, 29 November, 1661, Pepys notes : " Thence Sir W. Pen and I to the Theatre, but it was so full that we could hardly get any room, so he went up into one of the boxes, and I into the 18*d.* places, and there saw ' Love at first sight,' a play of Mr. [Thomas] Killigrew's, and the first time that it hath been acted since before the troubles." Lowe (*Thomas Betterton*, p. 19) says : " I think it probable that these upper boxes were situated only at the sides of the middle gallery, and that the centre space was simply arranged in benches like the pit, as is the case in the third gallery of the Théâtre Français." In Wycherley's *The Country-Wife*, produced at the Theatre Royal January, 1674–5, I, Horner banters Pinchwife : " I saw you yesterday in the eighteen penny place with a pretty Country-wench." This was Mrs. Pinchwife, who a little later complains of her visit to the play, since she and her husband " sate amongst ugly People : he wou'd not let me come near the Gentry, who sate under us, so that I cou'd not see' em." The Honourable John Stafford in his Epilogue to Southerne's *The Disappointment ; or, The Mother in Fashion*, produced at Drury Lane in the spring of 1684, fervently exclaims :

> Let all the Boxes, *Phoebus*, find thy grace,
> And ah ! preserve thy eighteen penny place !

p. 51. UPPER GALLERY. The shilling gallery, a humble if lofty position. It is generally referred to with sarcasm or banter. Thus Dryden in his Prologue to Tate's *The Loyal General*, produced at Dorset Garden in the winter of 1679, advises the rowdy pit :

> Remove your Benches, you apostate Pit,
> And take Above, twelve penny-worth of Wit.

p. 53. THE LADY IN THE LOBSTER. The lady is the calcareous structure in the stomach of a lobster, serving for the trituration of its food ; fancifully supposed to resemble the outline of a seated female figure. Swift, *The Battle of the Books*, 1704, uses the phrase : " Like the Lady in a Lobster." Farley, *London Art of Cookery*, Tenth Edition, 1804, p. 47 : " Take out their bodies, and what is called the lady."

p. 53. TRAP-BALL. " A game in which a ball placed upon one end (slightly hollowed) of a trap is thrown into the air by the batsman striking the other end with his bat, with which he then hits the ball away." *N.E.D.* Pepys, 8 May, 1668, notes : " Lord ! to see how this play of Sir Positive At-all, in abuse of Sir Robert Howard, do take, all the Duke's and every body's Talk being of that, and telling more stories of him, of the like nature, that is now town and country Talk, and, they say, is most exactly true. The Duke of York himself said that of his playing at trap-ball is true, and told several other stories of him." In Duffett's skit *The Mock-Tempest*, produced at the Theatre Royal in the winter of 1674, Hypolito asks Prospero : " Will it play at Bullet [bowls] with me ? " " Ay and Cat," is the answer, " and Trap-Ball too."

p. 54.   TWO OF BUCKRAM. *Henry IV*, II, iv, Falstaff's "Two I am sure I have paid, two rogues in buckram suits."

p. 59.   I'LE PISTOLL HIM PISSING. Cf. Otway's *The Cheats of Scapin*, II, where it is said of the supposed Bully: "Two he shot pissing against the Wall."

p. 60.   COKE UPON LITTLETON. Littleton, the famous English lawyer, was a judge of the Court of Common Pleas in the reign of Edward IV. His *Treatise of Tenures*, although the interest is now mainly historical and antiquarian, must always be considered a classic of jurisprudence. He died 23 August, 1481, and is buried in Worcester Cathedral. Sir Edward Coke was born 1 February, 1551–2, and died 3 September, 1634. His great work is the *Institutes*, a comment of amplest length upon Littleton's *Treatise of Tenures*, often quoted and constantly referred to as "Coke Littleton."

p. 61.   SYMONS. Abraham Simon, 1622 ?–1692 ? Elder brother of the famous medallist Thomas Simon. He was a skilful modeller in wax and seal-cutter. At the Restoration he modelled a portrait of Charles II for one hundred "broads." However, he lost court favour by his impertinence to the Duke of York. Evelyn (*Diary*, 8 June, 1653) calls him: "fantastical Simons, who had the talent for embossing so to the life."

p. 62.   CANDIA. Formerly the chief city of Crete. Founded by the Saracens in the ninth century, and fortified by the Genoese in the twelfth, it was greatly extended and strengthened by the Venetians in the thirteenth, fourteenth, and fifteenth centuries. It was besieged by the Turks under Ahmad Kiuprili in 1666 ; and in spite of a most heroic defence, in which the Venetians lost 30,000 in killed and wounded, maintained by the great Venetian general Francesco Morosi with the aid of thousands of volunteers who flocked to the service of the Republic from all countries, in September, 1669, the defenders were obliged to capitulate, and the whole isle of Crete, with the exception of the coast fortresses Suda, Spinalonga, and Karabusa, passed from Western to Ottoman rule.

p. 62.   PRESTER JOHN, AND THE GREAT CHAM. Prester (priest) John was a supposed Christian priest and king in Abyssinia or some Eastern country in the Middle Ages. Cham is an obsolete form of Khan, the Emperor of China in the Middle Ages.

p. 64.   AD AU'TRE, AD AU'TRE. An affected phrase very fashionable in the mouths of those who inclined towards Frenchified speech. Cf. Dryden: *Marriage A-la-Mode*, produced at Lincoln's Inn Fields Easter, 1672, where Melantha says: "I regarded him, I know not how to express it in our dull *Sicilian* Language, *d'un air enjoué ;* and said nothing but *ad autre, ad autre*, and that it was all *grimace*, and would not pass upon me."

p. 66.   UNDER THE ROSE. Early modern Dutch, *onder de roose*. M.L.G. *under du rosen*. G. *unter du Rose*. The phrase, which is possibly of German origin, is found early, *e.g.*, *State Papers, Henry VIII*, 1546, XI, 200 : "The sayde questyon were asked with lysence, and that yt shoulde remayn under the rosse, that is to say, to remayn under the bourde, and no more to be rehearsyd." Although perhaps not quite so common to-day as formerly, *under the rose* has yet persisted.

p. 66.   PLADDING. Northamptonshire and other dialects. "Pladding" or "ploading," which means "clumsy-gaited ; waddling ; walking heavily ; awkward." The word is connected with "to plod along," "plodding."

p. 67.   BOB'D. "Cheated, Trick'd, Disappointed, or Baulk'd." *Dictionary of the Canting Crew.*

p. 67. A POISE. Poise, pize, which was vulgarly used in various imprecatory expressions, is a word of uncertain origin. It has been well suggested that it may be an arbitrary substitute for Pest or Pox, which latter came into common speech *circa* 1600. Pize is a favourite word with old Bellair in Etherege's *The Man of Mode*, 4to, 1676. Cf. Duffett's *The Mock-Tempest*, produced at the Theatre Royal in the winter of 1674, II, 2, where Alonzo says: "Fortune has cheated me of all, pize on her." "A pize take 'em, meer Outsides: Hang your side-box Beaus," exclaims Sir Sampson in *Love for Love*, V, 1.

p. 68. MAD AS MARCH-HARES. During March, the breeding season, hares are notably wilder, hence the simile which occurs in Chaucer, The Freres Tale, 1327 (Skeat): "For thogh this Sumnour wood were as an hare." Skelton, *Garland of Laurel*, 632, has: "As mad as a March hare he ran like a scut"; and *Replication against Certayne Young Scholars*, (1520) 35: "I saye, thou madde March hare." In Dryden's *The Kind Keeper*, V, Limberham cries to Brainsick: "Now are you as mad as a *March* Hare." The March Hare of *Alice in Wonderland* is immortal.

p. 68. A PISSING WHILE. Cf. *The Plain-Dealer*, produced at Drury Lane in the winter of 1676, III, where Widow Blackacre cries to Manly: "Stay but a making Water while (as one may say), and I'll be with you again."

p. 68. CALL A SPADE A SPADE. Cf. *The Poetaster*, V, iii (satirizing Marston and Dekker):

> *Rampe up, my genius ; be not retrograde :*
> *But boldly nominate a Spade, a Spade.*

p. 70. CAMBRIDGE. This famous ship is mentioned by Pepys Friday, 14 June, 1667: "And this morning also, some of the Cambridge's men come up from Portsmouth, by order from Sir Fretchville Hollis, who boasted to us the other day that he had sent for 50, and would be hanged if 100 did not come up who would do as much as twice the number of other men: I say some of them, instead of being at work at Deptford, where they were intended, do come to the office this morning to demand the payment of their tickets; for otherwise, they would, they said, do no more work; and are, as I understand from every body that has to do with them, the most debauched, damning, swearing rogues that ever were in the Navy, just like their prophane commander."

p. 70. YOUR PETTS AND YOUR DEANS. The great shipbuilding family of Pett was chiefly connected with the growth of the English navy from the reign of Henry VIII to that of William III. Peter Pett, who is mentioned by Pepys as Commissioner Pett, was the fifth son of Phineas Pett, "Master Shipwright to James I," and was born in 1610. There are many details concerning him in the *Diary*. Christopher Pett, of Woolwich, who is also repeatedly referred to by Pepys, was the eleventh child of Phineas Pett, and was born 14 May, 1620.

Anthony Deane, eldest son of Anthony Deane, mariner, of Harwich, Essex, was born about 1638, and was celebrated as a shipbuilder. He was appointed to Woolwich dockyard at the Restoration, and was subsequently master shipwright at Harwich in 1664, and at Portsmouth in 1668. In 1672 he was Commissioner of the Navy at Portsmouth, and in 1675 Comptroller of the Victualling, being knighted about that time. He was M.P. for Shoreham in 1678, and for Harwich in 1679 and 1685 (with Pepys), and elected Fellow of the Royal Society in 1681. He died in Charterhouse

Square in 1721. See Duckett's *Naval Commissioners*, 1889, p. 71. There are very many allusions to him in Pepys.

p. 71. NOBLE. A gold coin first minted by Edward III and worth 6s. 8d. or 10s. *London Gazette*, No. 5207/3, 1714, has: "John Meeres of Gosport . . . was . . . Fined Twenty Nobles." The proverb "to bring one's noble to ninepence," or, "One's noble is not worth ninepence," survived until the end of the nineteenth century.

p. 71. CITTERN. Or Cithern, an instrument of the guitar kind, but strung with wire, and played with a plectrum or quill. It was commonly kept in barbers' shops for the use of customers, and often had a grotesquely carved head. The Tyrolese form of the instrument, which is known of recent years in England, is generally called the Zither. Cf. Wycherley's *Hero and Leander*, 1669, speaking of Leander, the young barber:

> For he wore Nails as long as Bill of Bittern,
> For what ? to scrape Teeth, and to play on Cittern.

p. 72. ROSE-TAVERN. Afterwards known as Will's Coffee-House, after William Urwin, the landlord. It was on the west side of Bow Street, and at the corner of Russell Street. See note *supra*, p. 280, on p. 36.

p. 72. GOADE, YOUR HIGH FULLAMS. Cf. Chapman, *Monsieur d'Olive* (1606), IV, 1, where Pacque, showing a set of dice, describes them as : "The Goade, the Fulham, and the stop-kater-tre." Grosart, *Greene's Works*, X, p. 288, describes a goad as a false die "scooped out on one side or more." Dekker in the *Bellman of London* mentions *gourds* or *goads* and *fulhams* in his list of the names of false dice.

A *Fullam*, conjectured to be derived from *Fulham*, once a notorious resort of gamesters, was a die basely loaded at one corner. A High Fullam was loaded so as to secure a cast of 4, 5, or 6 ; a Low Fullam to secure a cast of 1, 2, or 3. Cf. *The Merry Wives of Windsor*, I, 3, where Pistol says : "Gourd and fullam holds, And high and low beguile the rich and poor ;" also Cotton's *Compleat Gamester*, 1674, where the false dice are described.

p. 73. JACOB HALL. The famous rope-dancer, whose name is perhaps chiefly remembered on account of his intrigue with the Duchess of Cleveland. On Saturday, 29 August, 1668, at Bartholomew Fair, Pepys admired "Jacob Hall's dancing of the ropes ; a thing worth seeing, and mightily followed." On Monday, 21 September of the same year, he went to Southwark Fair : "To Jacob Hall's dancing on the ropes, where I saw such action as I never saw before, and mightily worth seeing ; and here took acquaintance with a fellow that carried me to a tavern, whither come the musick of this booth, and by and by Jacob Hall himself, with whom I had a mind to speak, to hear whether he had ever any mischief by falls in his time. He told me, 'Yes, many ; but never to the breaking of a limb': he seems a mighty strong man." Count Hamilton says of Hall that "sa disposition et sa force charmoient en public : on vouloit voir ce qui c'étoit en particulier : car on lui trouvoit dans son habit d'exercise toute une autre conformation, et bien d'autres jambes que celles du fortuné Germain. Le voltigeur ne trompa point les conjectures de la Castelmaine, à ce que prétendoient celles du public, et ce que publioient maints couplets de chansons, beaucoup plus a l'honneur du danseur, que de la Comtesse : mais elle se mit bien au-dessus de tous ces petits bruits, et n'en parut que plus belle." In fact, she rewarded her lover with a salary, and permitted a painting to be taken wherein she is represented at full length, in ermine robe, and head adorned with plume of feathers, sitting near a table and playing on the violin, he leaning over her playing on the guitar. There are two other portraits of Jacob ; one represents him with a comb in his hand, in the other—a Van Oost, engraved in mezzo-tinto by de Brunne, and in stipple by Shencker, Freeman, and Scriven, and often reproduced—the comb lies on a table.

One of the many items in a silversmith's bill of 1674, an elaborate bed-stead for Nell Gwyn, is " Paid for iacob haalle dansing upon yᵉ robbe [rope] of Weyer Worck, £1 10." In another bill there is a charge " for yᵉ cleensing of Jacobs halle of weyer worck."

p. 73. THE TURKE. Evelyn in his *Diary*, 1657, has the following entry : " 15th September. Going to London with some company, we stept in to see a famous rope-dauncer, call'd *the Turk*. I saw even to astonishment ye agilitie with which he perform'd ; he walk'd barefooted, taking hold by his toes only of a rope almost perpendicular, and without so much as touching it with his hands ; he daunc'd blindfold on ye high rope, and with a boy of 12 yeares old tied to one of his feete about twenty foote beneath him, dangling as he daunc'd, yet he mov'd as nimbly as if it had ben but a feather. Lastly he stood on his head on ye top of a very high mast, daunc'd on a small rope that was very slack, and finally flew downe ye perpendicular, on his breast, his head foremost, his legs and arms ex-tended with divers other activities."

The same author in his *Numismata*, folio, 1697, p. 277, mentions : " extra-ordinary *Zanis* and *Farcers*, *Scaramuccios*, *Trivelin*, *Harlequin*, *Pulchinello* and such as excel in slight of hand ; the late Famous *Funamble Turk*, *Jack-Adams*, and the *Dutch-Woman* Tumbler."

p. 73. AN OTHER-GUESS LONDON. It must be borne in mind that London was being rebuilt after the Great Fire of September, 1666.

p. 74. SACKBUT, AND DOUBLE CURTAL. The Sackbut was a bass trumpet with a slide like that of a trombone for altering the pitch. The word is now generally familiar through *Daniel* iii, where the *A.V.* employs it in a mis-translation of the Aramaic sabbekā. The Vulgate correctly turns it by sambuca, a stringed instrument.

The curtal, or double curtal, is an obsolete musical instrument. Stainer and Barrett, *Musical Terms*, 1888, give : " *Courtaut, Cortaud, Corthal*, an ancient instrument of the bassoon kind." Cf. E. Ward, *Hudibras Redivivus*, 1706, V, 24 : " With Voice as hoarse as a double Curtal."

p. 74. CATT, STOOL-BALL, SCOTCH HOPE. Cat, variants of which are still played in our seminaries, games I have myself watched, is more usually known as Tip-cat, where a piece of wood tapering at one end is hit with the cat-stick and so made to spring, and then driven away by a smart side-stroke. John Taylor (Water Poet) in his *Journey into Wales*, 1652, speaks of " The . . . laudable games of trapp, catt, stool-ball, reckt, etc."

Stool-ball is an old country game, something resembling cricket, often played by the lads and wenches at Easter, when a tansy was the stake. It still persists in rural places, and is a favourite with women and children, especially in Sussex. See Herrick, *Hesperides*, 1648, No. 692 (Lawrence and Bullen, II, p. 45), *Stool-Ball :*

> At stool-ball, Lucia, let us play
> For sugar-cakes and wine :
> Or for a tansy let us pay,
> The loss, or thine, or mine.

Poor Robin's Almanack, 1677, 19 April, has:

> Young men and maids Now very brisk
> At Barley-break and stool-ball frisk.

The Encyclopædia of Sports (1898), II, describes the modern variety of stool-ball.

Scotch hope. Hopscotch; there are innumerable allusions to this childish game. *Poor Robin,* 1677: " The time when school-boys should play at Scotch-hoppers."

p. 74.   TONY. *The Dictionary of the Canting Crew, circa* 1700, defines: " *Tony,* a silly Fellow, or Ninny." It has been suggested that the word may be derived from Middleton's famous tragedy *The Changeling* (1623), I, 2, where Antonio, disguised as an idiot, gives his name to the play. When he is brought to the asylum, " What is his name ? " asks the doctor's man. " His name is Antonio," comes the reply. " Marry, we use but half to him, only Tony." " Tony, Tony, 'tis enough, and a very good name for a fool. What's your name, Tony ? " In Dryden's *Sir Martin Mar-all,* produced at the Duke's House, Saturday, 15 August, 1667, V, the Landlord, acted by Priest, enters " disguised like a Tony," that is as a zany, a clown.

p. 75.   POLE-HUNTING, where the hounds and young dogs are kept at bay by men with poles and staves, so that the pack becomes more eager.

p. 75.   COXCOMB. Icarus, the son of Daedalus. Ovid, Metamorphoses, VIII, 183–235, tells the story. The boy flew too near the sun

> rapidi uicinia Solis
> Mollit odoratas pennarum uincula ceras.
> Tabuerant cerae : Nudos quatit ille lacertos :
> Remigioque carens non ullas percipit auras.
> Oraque caerulea patrium clamantia nomen
> Excipiuntur aqua.

Ovid repeats the same legend, *De Arte Amandi,* II, 21–96.

p. 77.   EAT FIRE. A favourite trick at rustic fairs and revels to attract the vulgar. Thus Hogarth in his *Southwark Fair* shows us upon an elevated stage a mountebank, who is devouring fire to the vast amusement of the wondering spectators, amongst whom his attendant merry-Andrew busily dispenses his infallible nostrums. Cf. Evelyn's *Diary,* 8 October, 1672 :

> " My Lady Sunderland . . . made me stay dinner at Leicester-House, and afterwards sent for Richardson, the famous fire-eater. He devoured brimstone on glowing coals before us, chewing and swallowing them ; . . . then taking a live coal on his tongue, he put on it a raw oyster, the coal was blown on with bellows till it flamed and sparkled in his mouth, and so remained till the oyster gaped and was quite boiled. Then he melted pitch and wax with sulphur, which he drank down, as it flamed ; I saw it flaming in his mouth, a good while."

p. 79.   LAVE THE TYRRHENE WATERS INTO CLOUDS. *Catiline,* Act I, being the fifth line of Catiline's first speech.

p. 79.   I'LL PLUCK BRIGHT HONOUR. I *Henry IV,* 1, 3, ll. 201–2. *Henry the Fourth* was a favourite play in the Restoration repertory. Both parts were the monopoly of Killigrew's company at the Theatre Royal. In *Mr. Tur-*

bulent ; Or, The Melanchollicks, 4to, 1682 (reissued 1685 as *The Factious Citizen, Or, the Melancholy Visioner*) a madman cries :

I'll pull down Honour from the pale-fac'd Moon,
And break the Wheels of the all-circling Sun.

p. 80.   OXFORD KATE'S. The Cock in Bow Street, Covent Garden, one of the best-known houses of the day. In the summer of 1663 it acquired great notoriety as the scene of the debaucheries of Lord Buckhurst, Sir Charles Sedley, and Sir Thomas Ogle. Wednesday, 1 July, 1663, Pepys notes : " Mr. Batten telling us of a late triall of Sir Charles Sydly the other day, before my Lord Chief Justice Foster and the whole bench, for his debauchery a little while since at Oxford Kate's, coming in open day into the Balcone and showed his nakedness." Dr. Johnson relates the episode in his *Lives of the Poets*, Sackville, Lord Dorset : " Sackville, who was then Lord Buckhurst, with Sir Charles Sedley and Sir Thomas Ogle, got drunk at the Cock, in Bow Street, by Covent Garden, and going into the balcony exposed themselves to the populace in very indecent postures." The story is also told by Anthony à Wood. There are very many references to the Cock, Oxford Kate's. In the Fifth Act of Wycherley's *The Plain Dealer*, produced at the Theatre Royal in the winter of 1676, " *The Scene changes to the* Cock *in* Bow-street. *A Table and Bottles.*" A little later Widow Blackacre comes in with two Knights of the Post (false bails ; sharking pettifoggers), and when the waiter promises her a more private room, she reassures them : " You are safe enough, Gentlemen, for I have been private in this house ere now, upon other occasions, when I was something younger."

p. 80.   A NOBLE AUTHOR. The Earl of Orrery, *The Black Prince*, produced at the Theatre Royal Saturday, 19 October, 1667 ; folio, 1669 ; III, where King John of France says :

A happy Planet at his Birth did Reign ;
A seeming Loss brings him a double Gain.

p. 80.   CAUL ON MY HEAD. Walker, *Paraemiologia*, 1672, gives " Fortune's darling " as the equivalent of this phrase. The French say : " Il est né coiffé." In Swift's *Polite Conversation* Lady Answerall remarks : " No, Mr. Neverout, I believe you were born with a caul on your head, you are such a favourite among the ladies."

Ramsay, *Scottish Proverbs*, tells us that the Scots have a superstitious custom of receiving a child when it comes to the world in its mother's shift, if a male, believing that this usage will make him well beloved among women. " He has been rowed in his mother's sack-tail." In Rowley's *A Match at Midnight*, 4to, 1633, IV, when Moll, mistaking Randall, promises to marry him, he cries : " Sure, Randalls was wrapped in mother's smock." Cf. also Davenport's *The City Nightcap*, 4to., 1661, II, where Francisco thinks he has gained Dorothea, and exclaims : " Fortunate Francis, that was wrapped in's mother's smock."

p. 81.   TOSS'D IN A BLANKET. As Mavis says in *The Silent Woman*, V : " We'll have our men blanket them in the hall. . . . I'd have the bridegroom blanketted too."

p. 82.   LEVITE. A clergyman. The word, which is very common, was used in a somewhat jocular or even disparaging sense. Cf. Glapthorne's *Wit in a Conftable*, 4to, 1640, IV, 1 :

> There shall a little Levite
> Meet you and give you to the lawful bed.

Also *The Scornful Lady*, IV, 1, where Abigail, alluding to Sir Roger the Curate, says :

> My little Levite hath forsaken me.

In *The Old Batchelour*, IV, when Barnaby suggefts that in Fondlewife's absence from home : " I could have brought young Mr. *Prig*, to have kept my Miftress Company," the old man angrily retorts : " I say let him not come near my Doors, I say he is a wanton young *Levite*, and pampereth himself with Dainties, that he may look lovely in the Eyes of Women."
In reference to *Judges*, xvii, 12, " Levite " often particularly denoted a domeftic chaplain.

p. 82. THE CANONICAL HOUR. So in *The Country-Wife*, III, 1, Sparkish urges Alithea, " Pray let us go to Church before the Canonical hour is paft," and later he remonftrates : " Come, Madam, 'tis e'ne twelve a Clock, and my Mother charg'd me never to be married out of the Canonical hours." Cf. *The Way of the World*, I, Mirabell : *Betty*, what says your Clock ? *Betty*. Turn'd of the laft Canonical Hour, Sir. *Mirabell*. How pertinently the Jade answers me ! Ha ! almoft one a Clock ! [*Looking on his watch.*]

p. 84. PURDY. An Eaft Anglian, particularly Suffolk, dialect term, with the meaning " surly ; ill-humoured ; proud." Wright cites a Suffolk quotation : " A fare so big and so purdy tha's no speaken tew 'em."

p. 85. NAP A SIX A YARD. " Nap or knap, or cog a die is the slurring it out of ones fingers." Holme, *Armoury* (1688), III, xvi. *The Dictionary of the Canting Crew*, circa 1700, explains : " *Nap*, by Cheating with the Dice to secure one's chance."

p. 86. IN SOBER SADNESS. This is a very puritanical expression. Thus in Mrs. Behn's *The Roundheads, or, The Good Old Cause*, produced at Dorset Garden in the late winter of 1681, III, 2, Ananias Goggle, the sanctified Lay Elder of Clement's Parish, unctuously asseverates to Lady Desbro : " In sober sadness the place inviteth." It should be noted that all the Country Gentle-man's Talk is old-fashioned and obsolete.

p. 87. LOSS OF A MISTRESS. The hint of this scene between the Country-Gentleman and Roger was perhaps taken from Philippe Quinault's *L'Amant indiscret, ou le Maître étourdi*, produced at the Hotel de Bourgogne in 1654, but not printed until ten years later, Rouen and Paris, 12mo, 1664. It even more closely resembles *Monsieur de Pourceaugnac*, II, 4. Molière's comedy was firft played at Chambord in September, 1669, and at Paris, Palais-Royal, 15 November of the same year. That is to say, the public production was some eighteen months after *The Sullen Lovers*.

p. 87. UDDS NIGS. A ridiculous old oath. In Dryden's *The Kind Keeper, or, Mr. Limberham*, produced at Dorset Garden in March, 1677-8 ; 4to, 1680 ; IV, 1, when Mrs. Saintly, the hypocritical fanatic, is making amorous advances of the moft obvious kind to young Woodall, he banters her : " You will not swear, I hope ? " " *Uds Niggers*, but I will ; and that so loud, that Mr. *Limberham* shall hear me." " *Uds Niggers*, I confess, is a very dreadful Oath," he laughingly replies. " You cou'd lye naturally before, as you are a Fanatick : If you can swear such Rappers too, there's hope of you : you may be a Woman of the World in time." In Rowley's *A Match at Mid-night*, 4to, 1633, II, 1, Alexander, introducing Sue Shortheels the whore to his silly brother Tim, grandiloquently proclaims : " Lindabride's her name," upon which Tim gasps out : " Niggers, I have read of her in the Mirror of Knighthood." In D'Urfey's *Don Quixote*, Part I, produced at Dorset Garden in 1694, I, Mary the Buxom, Sancho's rude, clownish, hoyden daughter, seizing hold of her father, bawls out : " Gadsniggers, I'll hold fast by this Arm." " Uds Niggers Noggers," swears Simpkin in *The Humours of Simpkin*, ed. 1673.

p. 87. MULBERRY GARDEN. On the site of the present Buckingham Palace and gardens. Originally a garden of mulberry trees, planted by James I in 1609 with the intention of cultivating the manufacture of English silks. Wednesday, 20 May, 1668, Pepys " walked over the Park to the Mulberry-Garden, where I never was before ; and find it a very silly place, worse than Spring-garden, and but little company, and those a rascally, whoring, roguing sort of people, only a wilderness here, that is somewhat pretty, but rude." On Monday, 5 April, 1669, Mr. Sheres treated Pepys, his wife, and Betty Turner, with a Spanish Olio, " a very noble dish," at the Mulberry Garden. This place of entertainment seems to have for a time enjoyed a fresh vogue owing to Sir Charles Sedley's comedy *The Mulberry-Garden*, produced at the Theatre Royal, Monday, 18 May, 1668. Since Sir Charles was " so reputed a wit, all the world " did " expect great matters." In truth, the play, which borrows something from *L'école des maris*, although not uninteresting, may hardly be compared with the more lively vein of Etherege, and certainly as a presentation of manners falls far below Shadwell himself.

p. 87. CHAMPINIONS. A name originally applied, as in French, to mushrooms and fungi generally, but in the seventeenth and eighteenth centuries to edible mushrooms. Martyn, *Rousseau's Botany*, 1794, xxxii, 501, speaks of : " A Champignon, or common eatable mushroom."

p. 87. ANDOILLES. Explained by Cotgrave (1611) as : " A big hogges gut stuffed with small guts (and other intrailes) cut into small pieces and seasoned with pepper and salt." Phillips, 1706, has : " *Andouille*, a kind of Chitterling, made either of Hogs or Calues Guts."

p. 87. NOBLE TO NINEPENCE. See note *supra* on p. 71.

p. 87. BISKS. French, *bisque*, crayfish soup. Also a rich soup made by boiling down birds. Stapylton's *Juvenal*, 1647, p. 267 : " Beccafico . . . one of the greatest rarities they [the Italians] can put into a bisk or olio." Bailey, *Cookery*, 1731, defines " Bisk, Bisque, a rich kind of pottage, made of Quails, Capons, fat Pullets, and more especially of pigeons roasted."

p. 88. RUFFS, GNATES. The ruff is the male of a bird of the sandpiper family, his female being the reeve. Ruffs were accounted a great delicacy. So in Dryden's *The Wild Gallant*, 4to, 1669, I, old Justice Trice the *gourmand* boasts : " I have a delicate dish of Ruffs to dinner." In Wycherley's *The Gentleman Dancing-Master*, Dorset Garden, March, 1672 ; 4to, 1672 ; I, Mrs. Flirt, ordering a luxurious supper, especially bespeaks " Some Ruffes."
The gnate, or more commonly knot, is a very similar bird, which was highly esteemed by epicures as a delicate dish.

p. 88. MARCH-BEER. A particularly potent ale, so called because brewed in the month of March.

p. 88. REMEDY WINES. Mr. Morton Shand, a high authority upon the history of wines and vintages, writes to me as follows : " My own belief is that this probably refers either to the progenitors of those dangerous proprietary liquids known as 'Tonic Wines'; or to what the French call 'Vins médecins' or 'vins de Remède'; i.e. stout-bodied dark-coloured wines used for blending with thinner growths so as to enable the latter to sell and keep. Classic instances of 'vins de remède' were Cahors and Gaillac, and, more recently, the Spanish Benecarlo."

p. 91. HE'S A WISE MAN THAT MARRIES A HARLOT. The same sentiment occurs in the Song contributed by Congreve to Dryden's last play, *Love Triumphant; or, Nature will Prevail*, produced at Drury Lane in 1693, Act V, 1. The first stanza runs :

> *How happy's the Husband, whose Wife has been try'd !*
> *Not damn'd to the Bed of an ignorant Bride !*
> *Secure of what's left, he ne'er misses the rest,*
> *But where there's enough, supposes a Feast ;*
> *So foreknowing the Cheat,*
> *He escapes the Deceit,*
> *And in spite of the Curse resolves to be blest.*

Sancho, a foolish coxcomb, acted by Dogget, has married a jilt, Dalinda (Mrs. Mountford), and the nuptials are interrupted by the entrance of Ynez, the nurse (Mrs. Kent), with a boy and girl, Dalinda's children.

The Royal Shepherdesse

p. 93. NON QUIVIS. Horace. *Ars poetica*, 263.
p. 99. MR. FOUNTAIN. " John Fountain, A Gentleman who flourish'd in *Devonshire* at the time of his Majesty King *Charles* the Second his Return ; and was the Author of a single Play nam'd, *Reward of Virtue*, a Comedy, printed in 4°, *Lond.* 1661. This Play was not design'd for the Stage by the Author ; but about eight Years after the first printing, Mr. *Fountain* being dead, it was reviv'd with Alterations, by Mr. *Shadwell*, and acted with good applause, under the Title of *The Royal Shepherdess*." Langbaine.
p. 99. CONNEXION. " The stage is so supplied with persons, that it is never empty all the time ; he that enters the second, has business with him who was on before ; and before the second quits the stage, a third appears who has business with him. This Corneille calls la liaison des scènes, the continuity or joining of the scenes ; and 'tis a good mark of a well-contrived play, when all the persons are known to each other, and every one of them has some affairs with all the rest." Dryden: *An Essay of Dramatick Poesie*. Cf. Corneille's *Discours des Trois Unités* : " La liaison des scènes qui unit toutes les actions particulières de chaque acte l'une avec l'autre." Also : " Un acteur occupant une fois le théâtre, aucun n'y doit entrer qui n'ait sujet de parler à lui. Surtout lorsqu'un acteur entre deux fois dans un acte, il doit absolument ou faire juger qu'il reviendra bientôt quand il sort la première fois, ou donner raison en rentrant pourquoi il revient sitôt."
p. 99. SEGNIUS IRRITANT. Horace, *Ars Poetica*, 180–1.
p. 99. CONCUPISCENCE . . . OF JIGG AND SONG. Shadwell's reference is probably to the Induction to *Bartholomew Fair*, the passage attacking *The Winter's Tale* and *The Tempest* (folio, 1631, sig. A6) : " Hee is loth to make Nature

afraid in his *Playes*, like those that beget *Tales, Tempests*, and such like *Droleries*, to mix his head with other mens heeles; let the concupiscence of *Ligges* and *Dances* raigne as strong as it will amongst you." But Jonson also used the phrase earlier in the address " To the Reader " prefixed to the 1612 quarto of *The Alchemist*. " To the Reader. If thou beest more, thou art an undertaker, and then I trust thee. If thou art one that tak'st up, and but a pretender, beware at what hands thou receiv'st thy commoditie; for thou wert never more fair in the way to be cos'ned than in this age, in poetry, especially in playes; wherein, now, the concupiscence of jigges and daunces so raigneth, as to runne away from nature, and be afraid of her, is the onely point of art that tickles the spectators." It should be noted that there are variants in this passage. Some copies of the 1612 quarto read instead of " jigges and daunces " " Daunces and Antikes."

p. 100.   BREAKING WINDOWS. One of the favourite entertainments of the fine young gentleman of the day. In the Prologue to *The Wild Gallant*, as revived at the Theatre Royal, Dryden writes of the raw country squire :

>   led by the renown
> Of *Whetstones Park*, he comes at length to Town
> Where enter'd by some School-fellow or Friend,
> He grows to break Glass-Windows in the end.

p. 100.   SIMUL & JUCUNDA. Horace, *Ars Poetica*, 334.

p. 100.   NIL INTENTATUM. Horace, *Ars Poetica*, 285.

p. 101.   IN URE. In use; practice. Cf. *The Country-Wife*, III, where Horner says : " A Man drinks often with a Fool, as he tosses with a Marker, only to keep his hand in ure." Also Mrs. Behn's *The City-Heiress; or, Sir Timothy Treat-all*, produced at Dorset Garden in the spring of 1682 (4to, 1692), II, 2, where Wilding says to his mistress : " *Diana*, thou shalt have a good opportunity to lye, dissemble, and jilt in abundance to keep thy hand in ure."

p. 103.   MAKE A LEGG. A very common phrase meaning to bow. It persisted as late as *Edwin Drood*, c. XVIII : " ' I beg pardon,' said Mr. Datchery, making a leg."

p. 113.   SAVIN. *Juniperus Sabina*. A small bushy evergreen shrub, the dry tops of which were used medicinally. Savin is strongly poisonous. It possesses emmenagogic properties, and hence was a common means of procuring abortion. A MS. *Satire on the Players*, c. 1682–3, thus attacks Mrs. Sarah Cook, the well-known actress :—

> Impudent *Sarah* thinks she's praised by all,
> Mistaken Drab, back to thy Mother's stall,
> And let true Savin whom thou hast proved so well; ⎫
> 'Tis a rare thing that belly will not swell,   ⎬
> Though swived and swived and as debauched as hell. ⎭

Dryden in his translation of Juvenal (1693), VI, 773–6, writes :

> Such is the Pow'r of Herbs; such Arts they use
> To make them Barren, or their Fruit to lose.
> But thou, whatever Slops she will have bought,
> Be thankful, and supply the deadly Draught :
> Help her to make Manslaughter; let her bleed,
> And never want for Savin at her need.
> For, if she holds till her nine Months be run,
> Thou may'st be Father to an *Æthiop's* Son.

p. 113. RACK AND MANGER. To lie at rack and manger is a frequent phrase for " to live in the midst of plenty ; to want nothing." Cf. Mrs. Behn's *The Feigned Curtezans ; or, a Night's Intrigue*, Dorset Garden, 1679, III, where Sir Signal says :

> *No Happiness like that atchiev'd with Danger,*
> *—Which once o'ercome—I lie at Rack and Manger.*

p. 119. FIT OF THE MOTHER. Hysteria. As in *King Lear*, 1605, II, 4 :

> O how this Mother swels vp toward my heart !
> *Historica passio*, downe thou climing sorrow.

Cf. Also Otway's *The Souldiers Fortune*, produced at Dorset Garden early in 1680, I, where Lady Dunce says : " One kiss of him were enough to cure the fits of the Mother, 'tis worse than *Asa foetida*."

p. 119. OYLET-HOLES. Eyelet holes. An oylet-hole is a small round hole worked in cloth for the purposes of fastening, etc.

p. 120. HONOURABLY LOWSIE. With Neander's speech one may compare the description of Otway when he returned from his military life on the Continent in the spring of 1679. " He returned from Flanders scabbed and lowsie, as 'twas reported," says Antony à Wood. In *A Trial of the Poets for the Bays* Buckingham and Rochester write :

> Tom Otway came next, Tom Shadwell's dear Zany,
> And swears, for heroics, he writes best of any :
> Don Carlos his pockets so amply had fill'd,
> That his mange was quite cur'd, and his lice were all kill'd.

p. 123. CLOGG. Shadwell was thinking of Captain Otter's famous sentiment " A wife is a scurvy clogdogdo," *Silent Woman*, IV.

p. 129. RHODOPE AND HAEMUS. Rhodope is one of the highest ranges of mountains in Thrace. Hæmus is also a lofty chain of Thracian mountains. Shadwell probably had in mind Ovid, *Metamorphoseon*, X, 76–77, the story of Orpheus :

> Esse deos Erebi crudeles, questus in altam
> Se recipit Rhodopen, pulsumque Aquilonibus Haemon.

p. 135. TRAP. See note on *The Sullen Lovers*, on p. 53.

p. 135. KEELS. Kales ; kayles ; a kind of ninepins or skittles. The word is a provincialism. Mrs. Bray, *Tradition of Devonshire*, 1830, II, 170, notes : " Kales . . . This is our provincial name for . . . nine-pins or skittles." Cf. Ben Jonson, *Chloridia*, 1633, " All the furies are at a game called nine-pins or keils."

p. 135. BARLIBREAK. Barleybreak is an old country game, originally played by half a dozen, in couples. One couple, who stood in a middle spot called " hell," had to catch the other couples. These were hand in hand, but if hard pressed could " break " away. The couple caught took their place as catchers. Suckling has a famous poem which commences :

> Love, Reason, Hate, did once bespeak
> Three mates to play at barley-break. . . .

There are innumerable references to this pastime.

p. 135. GOFF. Or " goaf " ; golf. The *N.E.D.* quotes this passage.

p. 135. STOOLBALL. See note *ante* on p. 74.

p. 135. WE GIVE A GREEN-GOWN. To give a woman a green gown is to roll her, in sport, upon the grass so that her gown is stained with green. Cf. Robert Greene's *George a Greene, the Pinner of Wakefield* (1599), where Jenkin says : " Madge pointed to meete me in your wheate-close. And first I saluted her with a greene gowne, and after fell as hard a-wooing as if the Priest had bin at our backs to haue married vs." *The Dictionary of the Canting Crew* (*circa* 1700) has : " *Green gown.* A throwing of young Lasses on the Grass and Kissing them." Cf. Wycherley's " *A* SONG *to* Phillis ; *who was angry that her* Lover *gave her a* Green-Gown, *calling him* Rude *and* Ill-manner'd *for it.*" This commences :

> Why *Phillis !* shou'd you Rudeness call
> My throwing you, so gently down ?
> Had I not given Thee the Fall,
> Thou Reason hadst, to call me Clown ;
> Since though I fell on top of Thee,
> My Fall, not thine, it term'd shou'd be.

p. 135. THE GAY LORD. William Horman, *Vulgaria*, 4to, London, 1519 (p. 279), says : " It is the custom that every year we shall have a May-king " (rex uernalis).

p. 148. SALII, *i.e.*, the Leapers, Jumpers. A college of priests at Rome, dedicated by Numa to the service of Mars, who, armed and bearing the sacred shields (*ancilia*), upon which the prosperity of Rome was declared to depend, with songs and dances, made solemn processions every year, in the first half of March, about the city and its sanctuaries. Their songs, being in an obsolete language, were almost unintelligible in the classical period. Varro, who died B.C. 27, *De Lingua Latina*, says : " Salii a salitando, quod facere in Comitio in sacris quotannis et solent et debent." Cf. also Ovid, *Fasti*, III, 260 *sqq.* ; and Livy, I, xx.

p. 148. MARTIALL DANCE. So much admired by Pepys at the first performance : " A good martial dance of pikemen, where Harris and another do handle their pikes in a dance to admiration."

p. 161. NOSE-GAY. A man going to be hanged was always finely dressed—if he could afford it—and provided with clean white gloves, and a bright bouquet of flowers. Henri Misson, who travelled in England about 1718, has left some entertaining experiences, and he tells us : " He that is to be hanged, or otherwise executed, first takes care to get himself shaved and handsomely dressed ; either in Mourning, or in the Dress of a Bridegroom. This done, he sets his Friends at Work to get him Leave to be buried, and to carry his Coffin with him, which is easily obtained. When his Suit of Clothes, his Night Gown, his Gloves, Hat, Periwig, Nosegay, Coffin, Flannel Dress for his Corps, and all those things are bought and prepared, the main Point is taken Care of, His Mind at Peace, and then he thinks of his Conscience."

p. 163. [*ABOVE.*] The King appeared in one of the balconies which were set over the permanent proscenium doors, forming part of the architecture of a Restoration theatre. These balconies were not unlike regular boxes. They are sometimes termed windows. In Mrs. Behn's *The Rover*, Part I, produced at Dorset Garden in the spring of 1676-7, II, 1, we have a stage direction : *Enter two Bravoes, and hang up a great Picture of* Angelica's, *against the Balcony, and two little ones at each side of the Door.* Presently : *Enter* Angelica *and* Moretta *in the Balcony, and draw a Silk Curtain.* Also Ravenscroft's *The London Cuckolds*, produced at the same theatre in the winter of 1681, V,

Enter Ramble *above in the Balcony*. He cries: "Which way shall I get down? I must venture to hang by my hands and then drop from the Balcony." He accordingly thus descends. There are innumerable references to these balconies, frequently as "at a window" or "above," and they proved extremely serviceable to contemporary dramatists in their comedies of intrigue. Mr. W. J. Lawrence in *The Elizabethan Playhouse and other Studies*, First Series (pp. 173–4), aptly writes: "No dramatist of the time had a better sense of the theatre than Mrs. Behn, and none made more adroit employment of the balconies."

The Humorists

p. 175.   THE HUMORISTS. The Jonsonian theories of "humours" adopted by Shadwell are discussed in the Introduction.

p. 175.   — QUIS INIQUAE. Juvenal, I, 30–1.

p. 181.   MARGARET, DUTCHESS OF NEWCASTLE. 1624?–1674. The youngest daughter of Sir Thomas Lucas, in 1643 appointed maid of honour to Queen Henrietta Maria, whom she accompanied to Paris. Here she met William Cavendish, Marquis, and subsequently Duke, of Newcastle, then a widower, and their marriage took place in 1645. From Paris they went to Rotterdam, and thence to Antwerp. At the Restoration her husband returned to England, whither, after she had despatched his affairs, she followed him. 16 March, 1664, the Marquis was created Duke of Newcastle and Earl of Ogle. This happy couple devoted the rest of their life to the service of letters. The Duchess died in London and was buried at Westminster 7 January, 1673–4. She has left a large number of works, including two folio volumes of plays, 1662 (21 plays) and 1668 (5 plays). However fantastic, and indeed extravagant, the pieces written by this "Thrice Noble, Illustrious and Excellent Princess," they are not without a vein of true poetry, and both she and her noble husband deserve all honour for their patronage of literature.

p. 182.   WELBECKE. Welbeck Abbey, now the seat of the Duke of Portland, situate some eight miles from Mansfield, Notts. This Premonstratensian house was founded in the reign of Henry II by Thomas the Cuckeney. King Charles I was royally welcomed here in 1633 by William Cavendish, then Earl (afterwards Duke) of Newcastle, for which occasion Ben Jonson wrote his masque *The King's Entertainment at Welbeck, in Nottinghamshire, at his going to Scotland*, 1633. Welbeck Abbey is a large battlemented house, lying in a hollow near the margin of the lake.

p. 183.   IMPERFECT IN THE ACTION. Dr. James Drake published his comedy *The Sham Lawyer; or, The Lucky Extravagant*, 4to, 1697, "As It Was Damnably Acted at the *Theatre Royal* in *Drury Lane*."

p. 183.   SHE WOULD, IF SHE COULD. Cf. Pepys, Thursday, 6 February, 1667-8: "My wife being gone before, I to the Duke of York's playhouse; where a new play of Etherige's, called 'She Would if She Could'; and though I was there by two o'clock, there was 1000 people put back that could not have room in the pit: and I at last, because my wife was there, made shift to get into the 18*d*. box, and there saw ; but, Lord ! how full was the house, and how silly the play, there being nothing in the world good in it, and few people pleased in it. The King was there ; but I sat mightily behind, and could see but little, and hear not all. The play being done, I into the pit to look [for] my wife, and it being dark and raining, I to look my wife out, but could not find her ; and so staid going between the two doors and through the pit an hour and half, I think, after the play was done ; the people staying there till the rain was over, and to talk with one another. And, among the rest, here was the Duke of Buckingham to-day openly sat in the pit ; and there I found him with my Lord Buckhurst, and Sidly, and Etherige, the poet ; the last of whom I did hear mightily find fault with the actors, that they were out of humour, and had not their parts perfect, and that Harris did do nothing, nor could so much as sing a ketch in it ; and so was mightily concerned : while all the rest did, through the whole pit, blame the play as a silly, dull thing, though there was something very roguish and witty ; but the design of the play, and end, mighty insipid." Shadwell's own wife acted in the comedy. Downes notes : " *She wou'd if she cou'd*, wrote by *Sir George Etheridge ; Courtall*, acted by Mr. *Smith ;* Freeman, Mr. *Young ;* Sir *Joslin*, Mr. *Harris ;* Sir *Oliver*, Mr. *Nokes ; Ariana*, Mrs. *Jennings ; Gatty*, Mrs. *Davies ;* Lady *Cochwood*, Mrs. *Shadwell ;* It took well, but inferior to *Love in a Tub*."

Dennis in the Epistle Dedicatory to *The Comical Gallant*, a sorry version of *The Merry Wives of Windsor*, 4to, 1702, remarks that " the only Play that ever Mr. *Cowley* writ, was barbarously treated the first night," and " *She wou'd if she cou'd* met with no better usage from the People at first, tho at the same time it was esteem'd by the Men of Sense, for the trueness of some of its Characters, and the purity and freeness and easie grace of its Dialogue. I need not say, that both those Plays have been since acted with a general applause."

p. 183. MOST EXCELLENT DANCINGS. Probably by Mrs. Johnston, who danced the Jigg in *Epsom Wells*. Mrs. Davies had left the theatre.

p. 184. PECTUS PRAECEPTIS. Horace, *Epistularum*, II, 1, 128–130.

p. 184. —SIMUL & JUCUNDA. Horace, *Ars Poetica*, 334.

p. 184. ODI PROFANUM. Horace, *Carminum*, III, 1, 1.

p. 184. GARGANUM MUGIRE. *Epistularum*, II, 1, 202–6.

p. 186. PERSONATING PARTICULAR MEN. Even a short discussion of Jonson's satirical introduction upon the stage of his contemporaries would require a long essay, but very briefly we might note that in *The Case is Altered* (1598) Antonio Balladino is generally held to be Anthony Monday ; Mr. H. C. Hart identified Juniper with Gabriel Harvey and Onion with Thomas Nashe. Mr. Matthew, " the towne-gel," in *Every Man in his Humour* (acted in 1598), is said to be an attack on Samuel Daniel. Penniman insists that Daniel is also Fastidious Brisk in *Every Man out of his Humour* (1599), Thomas Lodge is Fungoso, and, according to Mr. Hart, Puntarvolo is Sir Walter Raleigh. Aubrey, on the authority of Dr. John Pell, informs us that Carlo Buffone was " one Charles Chester, . . . a bold impertent fellowe, . . . a perpetuall talker " (Aubrey, *Lives*, ed. by A. Clark, 1898, vol. II, p. 184). In *Cynthia's Revels*, acted 1600, Amorphus is often supposed to be Raleigh, and Asotus Lodge. It should, however, be mentioned that Penniman considers Monday to be the original Puntarvolo and Amorphus. In *The Poetaster*, acted 1601, Crispinus is Marston, Demetrius Dekker, and Tucca a Captain Hannam, of whom nothing is known. Sir Politique Would-bee in *Volpone*, acted in 1605, is clearly Sir Henry Wotton, an admirable portraiture. Fleay considered that Sir John Daw in *Epicoene*, acted in 1610, was Sir John Harrington. He also maintains (a doubtful opinion) that Lanthorn Leatherhead in *Bartholomew Fair*, acted in 1614, is Inigo Jones, who, however, is certainly scarified as In-and-in Medley, the cooper, *architectonicus professor*, *A Tale of a Tub*, acted in 1633.

p. 187. MY PARTICULAR FRIEND. John Dryden, with whom Shadwell was then on good terms.

p. 187. FEWER FAILINGS. "As for *Johnson*, . . . I think him the most learned and judicious Writer which any theatre ever had." Dryden, *Of Dramatick Poesie, an essay*. 4to, 1668.

p. 187. INTER QUAE VERBUM. Horace, *Epistularum*, II, 1, 73–5.

p. 188. ENTREPRENNANS. Cf. Dryden's *Marriage A-la-Mode*, produced at Lincoln's Inn Fields about Easter, 1672, 4to, 1673, IV, 3, where Melantha banters Doralice, who is disguised as a boy : " And you, I imagine, are my young Master, whom your Mother durst not trust upon Salt-water, but left you to be your own Tutor at fourteen, to be very brisk and *entreprenant*, to endeavour to be debauch'd ere you have learn'd the knack on it."

p. 189. CREDITUR, EX MEDIO. Horace, *Epistularum*, II, 1, 168–170.

p. 190. SIR MARTIN. In allusion to the famous scene in Dryden's *Sir Martin Mar-all*, produced at the Duke's Theatre Thursday, 15 August, 1667, 4to, 1668, Act V, where Mrs. Millisent insists that her lover shall serenade her, and as he is unable to play or sing, he appears at the window making as if he played a lute, whilst the music is in truth supplied by his man, who is concealed. A little bell is rung as a signal for him to stop, but after the song is done and the music has ceased, in spite of the warning, he "*continues fumbling, and gazing on his Mistress*," who thus discovers the trick, and cries : "Methinks he plays and sings still, and yet we cannot hear him—Play louder, Sir *Martin*, that we may have the Fruits on't. . . . Ah ! ah ! have I found you out, Sir ? Now as I live and breathe, this is pleasant, *Rose*—his Man play'd and sung for him, and he, it seems, did not know when he should give over." The scene is founded upon an episode in Charles Sorel's *La vraie Histoire Comique de Francion* (1622), Book VII, where a similar misadventure befalls the amorous count during his wooing of the doctor's daughter.

There are very many references to this scene in contemporary literature, *e.g.*, *The Country-Wife*, I, where Harcourt says of Sparkish : "The Rogue will not let us enjoy one another, but ravishes our conversation, though he signifies no more to't, than *Sir Martin Mar-all's* gaping, and auker'd thrumming upon the Lute, does to his Man's Voice and Musick." Also Oldham, *A Satyr, In Imitation of the Third of Juvenal* (1682) :

> Commend his Voice and Singing, tho' he bray
> Worse than *Sir Martin-Marr-all* in the play.

Addison writes in *The Spectator*, No. 5, Tuesday, 6 March, 1711 : "I perceived that the Sparrows were to act the part of Singing Birds in a delightful Grove : though upon a nearer Enquiry I found the Sparrows put the same Trick upon the Audience that *Sir Martin Mar-all* practised upon his Mistress ; for, though they flew in Sight, the Musick proceeded from a Consort of Flagellets and Bird-calls which was planted behind the Scenes."

p. 191. DRYBOB. A dry bob is a sharp rap or blow, but one that does not actually break the skin. Hence it is used to denote a bitter taunt.

Cf. *An Allusion to Horace*, "The Tenth Satire of the First Book" (ascribed to Rochester) :

> D(ryden), in vain try'd this nice way of Wit,
> For he to be a tearing *Blade* thought fit,
> To give the Ladies a dry Bawdy bob,
> And thus he got the name of Poet *Squab*.

p. 191.   PULLIN. One may compare Monsieur Turboon, the French doctor in Mrs. Behn's *Sir Patient Fancy*, Dorset Garden, January, 1678, who cries : " I have not kill'd above my five or six this Week," and when Brunswick ejaculates : "How, Sir, kill'd ? " snaps him up with " Kill'd, Sir ! ever whilst you live, especially those who have the grand *Verole*." D'Urfey in *The Richmond Heiress*, Drury Lane, 1693, has " Dr. Guiacum, An opinionated Chemical Doctor, a great Pretender to cure Lunaticks and Claps." Ravenscroft's *The Anatomist*, with Underhill's part accentuated as a caricature of the French, held the stage for many years as a farce. Blakes excelled as the Doctor.

p. 191.   JESSAMINE-GLOVES. Jasmine was often used to perfume gloves. Edmund Howes, who continued Stowe's *Chronicle*, says that sweet or perfumed gloves were first brought into England by the Earl of Oxford on his return from Italy, in the fifteenth year of Queen Elizabeth, during whose reign, and long afterwards, they were very fashionable. Autolycus in *The Winter's Tale* has among his wares " Gloves as sweet as damask roses." Saturday, 27 October, 1666, Mrs. Picra and Mrs. May Knapp dined with Pepys : " Towards evening I took them out to the New Exchange, and there my wife bought things, and I did give each of them a pair of Jesimy plain gloves, and another of white." In *The Plain-Dealer*, produced at Drury Lane in the winter of 1676, II, Manly asks Olivia : " Was it a well-trimm'd Glove, or the scent of it that charm'd you ? " In *The Man of Mode* Sir Fopling Flutter's gloves are " Orangerii," and going to the theatre he was " almost poison'd with a pair of Cordivant Gloves " worn by his neighbour. Thereupon Mrs. Loveit sympathizingly exclaims : " Oh ! filthy Cordivant, how I hate the Smell ! " In *The Kind Keeper* Mrs. Tricksy remarks to Limberham : " I have been looking over the last Present of *Orange* Gloves you made me ; and methinks I do not like the Scent.—O Lord, Mr. *Woodall*, did you bring those you wear from *Paris* ? " " Mine are *Roman*, Madam," replied Woodall, to which the lady answered, " The Scent I love, of all the World."

p. 193.   DIOCLESIAN. This persecutor of the Church was born A.D. 245 and died 313. His reign lasted from 284–305, when he abdicated and withdrew to Salona, where he lived in magnificent seclusion. His name will be for ever associated with the last and most terrible of the ten persecutions of the early Church, although the guilt is almost wholly due to Galerius, and the cruelties continued unabated for at least seven years after Diocletian had retired to private life.

p. 193.   FRENCH DISEASE. Syphilis is said to have appeared at Naples in 1495, whence it spread like wildfire all over Europe. It was from the beginning known as the *mal franzese*, owing to its ravages in the army of Charles VIII. Some contemporary observations concerning the rapid spread of the disease in Italy, its symptoms, and its cure, are contained in Matarazzo's *Cronaca di Perugia* (*Arch. Stor. It.* vol. XVI, Part II, pp. 32–36), and in Portovenere

(*Arch. St.* vol. VI, Part II, p. 338). One of the earliest works issued from the Aldine Press in 1497 was the *Libellus de Epidemia quam uulgo morbum Gallicum uocant*. It was written by Nicolao Leoniceno, and dedicated to the Count Francesco della Mirandola. The fine epic *Syphilis*, by Geronimo Fracastoro, should be read on account of its elegant Latinity. There is an English translation by Nahum Tate, which was printed in the third volume of Dryden's *Miscellany*, 8vo, 1693. The disease seems to have been indigenous in America. Authoritative accounts are Rosenbaum's *Geschichte der Luſtseuche im alterthum*, Halle, 1845, and Von Hirsch's *Hiſtoriſch-geographiſche Pathologie*, Erlangen, 1860.

p. 193. FRENCH TAYLORS. One may compare Johnson's *London*, 1738 :

> *London*, the needy villain's general home,
> The common-sewer of *Paris* and of *Rome*,
> With eager thirſt, by folly or by fate,
> Sucks in the dregs of each corrupted ſtate.
> Forgive my transports on a theme like this—
> I cannot bear a *French* Metropolis.

> All that at home no more can beg or ſteal,
> Or like a gibbet better than a wheel ;
> Hiss'd from the ſtage, or hooted from the court,
> Their air, their dress, their politics import ;
> Obsequious, artful, voluble, and gay,
> On *Britain's* fond credulity they prey.
> No gainful trade their induſtry can 'scape.
> They sing, they dance, clean shoes, or cure a clap :
> All sciences a faſting *Monsieur* knows,
> And bid him go to hell, to hell he goes.

p. 194. POINTS. Thread lace made wholly with the needle, and often lace generally. Ray, *Travels*, 1673, says : "Venice is noted . . . for Needle-work Laces called Points." Cf. also Butler, *Remains* (1680, ed. 1759), I, 148 :

> To know the Age and Pedigrees
> Of Poynts of Flandres or Venise.

p. 194. HAMMERSMITH. Then a country village. The White Hart, an ancient hoſtelry, was swept away in 1841.

p. 194. GAME. In *Bartholomew Fair*, produced 31 October, 1614, punk Alice is " mistress o' the game." Cf. *Troilus and Cressida* (1606), IV, v :

> O ! these encounterers, so glib of tongue,
> That give a coaſting welcome ere it comes,
> And wide unclasp the tables of their thoughts
> To every tickling reader, set them down
> For skittish spoils of opportunity
> And daughters of the game.

p. 194. BOLUS : (βῶλος, a clod of earth). A mass of medicine exhibited in the form of a large pill. *Willis' Rem. Med. Works* (1681) : "*Bolus*, is a medicine made up into a thick subſtance to be swallow'd not liquid, but taken on a knives point." The word is often used somewhat contemptuously.

p. 195. RED CROSS. As was officially painted upon the door of a house afflicted with the plague. So in Killigrew's *The Parson's Wedding*, folio, 1663, general title 1664, IV, 3, when the pest is suspected at the Widow's house, Mistress Pleasant, her niece, cries : "I am not ambitious of a Red-cross upon the door."

p. 195. SARSAPARILLA AND GUIACUM. Sarsaparilla is the root of various species of the *Smilax* family, native to tropical America. It contains an essential oil and several extractive principles, and is diuretic, tonic, and alterative. It is used, says Dr. Gould, in tertiary syphilis, scrofula, and similar diseases.

Guaiacum, Lignum uitae. The heart of the tree, and also the oleoresin of *Guaiacum officinale* and *Guaiacum sanctum*, a prompt diaphoretic, expectorant, and alterative. Formerly much used as an antisyphilitic. Fracastoro concludes his poem *Syphilis* with a panegyric of the tree Hyacus, Guaiacum.

p. 195. BAY-TREES. In allusion to *Psalm* xxxvii, 35 : I have seen the wicked in great power, and spreading himself like a green bay tree (A.V.).

p. 195. WINE TO BEAUTY ? Cf. the two characters in Ravenscroft's comedy *The London Cuckolds*, produced at the Duke of York's theatre in the winter of 1681. Mr. Townly, a Gentleman of the times, careless of Women, but fortunate, acted by Joseph Williams, is a hard drinker ; whilst Mr. Ramble, a great Designer on Ladies, but unsuccessful in his Intrigues, acted by William Smith, prefers his amours to the bottle.

p. 195. PIMPL'D FACES. Crazy's Diatribe against drinking may be paralleled with the denunciation in Chaucer's *The Pardoner's Tale*, especially the particular passage that commences :

> A lecherous thing is wyn, and dronkenesse
> Is ful of stryving and of wrecchednesse.

Chaucer's moral reflections and much of the language are borrowed from the *De Contemptu Mundi, siue de miseria conditionis humanae, libri III*, an ascetical treatise by Pope Innocent III, written whilst he lived in retirement during the pontificate (1191–8) of Celestine III. See Reinlein, *Papst Innocenz der dritte und seine Schrift "De contemptu mundi."* Chaucer had made a translation, which is lost, of this tractate.

p. 196. CALLOUS NODE. A hard, oblong, indurated swelling or tumour. Syphilitic nodes are the localized swellings on bones due to syphilitic periostitis.

p. 196. MORBLEU. An altered form of Mort Dieu, an oath. Frequent in the Restoration dramatists, and generally given comically to French speakers.

p. 196. DIACULUM. A popular variant of Diachylum. Originally the name of a kind of ointment composed of vegetable juices ; then a common term for leadplaster, *emplastrum plumbi*, an adhesive plaster made by boiling together litharge (lead oxide), olive oil, and water ; prepared on sheets of linen as a sticking-plaster which adheres when heated. So Boyle, *New Exp. Phys. Mech.* (1660), mentions : "Proem 8. The Common Plaister call'd Diachylon."

p. 197. CUDGEL-PLAYERS OF MOORFIELDS. Moorfields was first drained in 1527 ; laid out into walks in 1606, and finally built upon late in the reign of Charles II. It has been swallowed up in Finsbury Square and the adjoining localities. The district became famous for its musters and promenades ; the laundresses and bleachers ; the cudgel-players and popular amusements ; the bookstalls and balladmongers. 28 June, 1661, Pepys notes : "Went to Moorfields, and there walked, and stood and saw the wrestling, which I never saw so much of before, between the north and west countrymen."

p. 197. TURPENTINE. Terebinthia. The oleoresin obtained from yellow pine, *Pinus australis*, and other species. It was formerly much used as an antisyphilitic.

Cf. Massinger and Dekker, *The Virgin-Martyr*, 4to., 1622, III, 3, where Spungius says: " We are justly plagued, therefore, for running from our mistress." To which Hircius replies: " Thou didst ; I did not : Yet I had run too but that one gave me turpentine pills, and that staid my running."

p. 197. HERMODACTYLES. The root or bulb of *Colchicum uariegatum* or *Colchicum autumnale ;* also of *Iris tuberosa.* It was formerly prized in medicine, but now is little used, except in India. Willis (1681) speaks of : " *Hermodactyls.* Mercuries fingers, white and red."

p. 197. TETE BLEU, *i.e.*, Tete Dieu. So in *The Gentleman Dancing-Master* Monsieur constantly swears " testè bleu."

p. 197. JERNIE. Jarni = jarndieu = je renie Dieu. A blasphemous oath. In Etherege's *The Comical Revenge*, produced in 1664, the French valet, Dufoy, is continually swearing, *Jernie*, I, 1 : " begar he did striké, braké my Headé, Jernie." Also Monsieur La Prate in D'Urfey's *Love for Money*, produced in the winter of 1689, II, 2 : " Ah Jernie, Vat a Filthy place is this." To Jernie actually became a verb, as Butler in his *Satire on our Ridiculous Imitation of the French :*

> T'adorn their English with French scraps,
> And give their very language claps,
> To jernie rightly.

p. 197. STYPTICK-INJECTIONS. Styptic, στυπτικός, astringent. An injection causing vascular contraction of the blood-vessels.

p. 197. TURPENTINE-CLYSTERS. A clyster is an enema.

p. 197. CHORDEE. A painful inflammatory downward curving of the penis.

p. 197. CARUNCLES. A caruncle is a small fleshy excrescence ; in pathology the word was formerly applied to a stricture. Becket in *Philosophical Transactions*, XXXI, 51 (1720), speaks of : " A Caruncle in the Urethra."

p. 197. PHYMASII. Phimosis is a contraction of the orifice of the prepuce, so that it cannot be retracted. φίμωσις = muzzling.

p. 197. BUBONES. A bubo is inflammation and swelling of a lymphatic gland, properly and generally of the groin, and usually following chancroid, gonorrhœa, or syphilitic infection.

p. 198. ACHROCORDONES. An acrochordon is an excrescence on the skin with a slender base ; a tumor which hangs by a pedicle. Hoblyn's *Dictionary of Medical Terms.*

p. 198. MERMECII. Myrmecia ; μυρμήκιον. Sessile tumors or growths, especially occurring on the palm of the hand and sole of the foot. " Distinguished from ἀκροχόρδονες, pedunculate tumors ; they are so called because they give rise to *formication*," Hoblyn. Formication is a sensation of *creeping* in a limb, or on the surface of the body, occasioned by pressure or some affection of a nerve.

p. 198. THYMI. An old term for condyloma (κονδύλωμα, a swelling), a tumor of the pudendum. The term is also applied to syphilitic patches and discolorations.

p. 198. PUSTULAE. Pustules or blebs.

p. 198. CRUSTATAE = scabby.

p. 198. VERUCAE. Verrucæ = syphilitic condylomata.

p. 198. CRISTAE, affecting the ucrumontanum, a longitudinal ridge on the floor of the canal of the male urethra.

p. 198. TOPHI. Tophus, a swelling which particularly affects a bone or the periosteum.

p. 198. OSSIS, a hard formation.

p.198. CHYRONYA. An old name for scabies. The itch-mite, Sarcoptes scabei, was
termed Chyron.

p. 198. TELEPHIA, obstinate sores.

p. 198. PHAGADENIA. Phagadena, a spreading and destructive ulceration, often
obstinately and rapidly disintegrating soft parts: gangrene.

p. 198. DISEPULOTICA. Ulcers and sores.

p. 198. TUB OR HOT-HOUSE. Cf. the Epilogue to Mrs. Behn's *The Luckey Chance ; or,
An Alderman's Bargain* (produced at Drury Lane in the winter of 1686),
spoken by Betterton: *'Tis Bulkers give, and Tubs must cure your pain.* (A
Bulker was the lowest kind of whore, one that would lie down on a bulk
to any man.) A patient suffering from the *lues uenerea* was disciplined by
long and severe sweating in a heated tub, which, combined with a mer-
curial treatment and strict abstinence, was formerly considered an excellent
remedy for the disease. Cf. *Measure for Measure*, III, 2, "Troth, sir, she
has eaten up all her beef, and she is herself in the tub." Also *Timon of
Athens*, IV, 3 :

> Be a whore still ; they love thee not that use thee ;
> Give them diseases, leaving with thee their lust.
> Make use of thy salt hours ; season the slaves
> For tubs and baths ; bring down rose-cheeked youth
> To the tub-fast and the diet.

The "Cradle" and the "*Baine d'Alexandre*" were particular sudorific
treatments prescribed to sufferers. There is extant a letter of Rochester's,
July, 1678, which refers to a house in Leather Lane, Hatton Garden, where
Henry Savile was undergoing a medicinal course of this kind.

p. 198. BILK YOUR CRIBBIDGE. The verb *bilk* was at first a technical term in the game
of Cribbage, where it is interchanged with *balk ;* hence the conjecture that
it may have originated in a mincing pronunciation of this term. To bilk a
cribbage is to balk or spoil any one's score in his crib. J. Williams (A.
Pasquin), *Cribbage* (1791): "Bilking the Crib of your adversary is a very
essential part of the game of Cribbage."

p. 199. TRO ? Trow, used elliptically for *I trow* or *I trow you*, and almost equal to
"May I ask ?" Sometimes *I trow* = "I ween," "I suppose." Cf. Hey-
wood, *A Challenge for Beauty* (1636), I : "How came you by them tro ?
Honestly ?"

p. 200. PARAGON. A kind of double camlet, a stuff much used for dress and upholstery
in the seventeenth and early eighteenth centuries. So Pepys, Thursday, 8
March, 1659–60, notes : "Took my wife by land to Paternoster Row, to
buy some Paragon for a petticoat." *Flemings in Oxford* (O.H.S.), 1678, I,
255 : "7 yards & an halfe of black Paragon for a [Undergraduate's]
Gowne."

p. 201. BIDDING FROM HIM. Auctions were held in which bids were received so long
as a small piece of candle burned, the last bid before the candle went out
securing the article. Cf. Pepys, Wednesday, 3 September, 1662 : "We
met and sold the Weymouth, Successe, and Fellowship hulkes, where
pleasant to see how backward men are at first to bid ; and yet when the
candle is going out, how they bawl and dispute afterwards who bid the
most first." Cf. also Mrs. Behn's *The Younger Brother*, produced at Drury
Lane in the winter of 1696, II, 1, where Lady Youthly is bargaining with
Sir Rowland to marry his son George, and the knight cries : "My House
will be besieged by all the Widows in Town ; I shall get more by shewing

him, than the *Rhinoceros*. Gad, I'll sell the young Rogue by Inch of Candle, before he's debauch'd and spoil'd in this leud Town."

p. 203. KNIGHT OF THE POST. "A Mercenary common Swearer, a Proſtitute to every Cause, an Irish Evidence." *Diſtionary of the Canting Crew.*

p. 205. QUICQUID. Ovid. *Triſtia*, X, 26. The quotation is, perhaps purposely, in-correſt. The line runs : *Et, quod tentabam dicere, uersus erat.*

p. 205. CATECHRESTICAL. Catachresis is the improper, or unnaturally artificial, employment of a word.

p. 207. A RING I HAD AT THE FUNERAL. To diſtribute rings at a funeral was a very general cuſtom, and indeed persiſted among old-fashioned people until comparatively recent years. Pepys often mentions the diſtribution of Mourning rings. Wednesday, 3 July, 1661, he notes : " This day my Lady Batten and my wife were at the burial of a daughter of Sir John Lawson's, and had rings for themselves and their husbands." Also Friday, 15 May, 1668 : " To Sir Thomas Teddiman's burial, where moſt people belonging to the sea were. And here we had rings." There is a very long liſt of persons to whom " Rings and Mourning were presented upon the occasion of Mr. Pepys' death and funeral," 26 May, 1703.

p. 207. BASE DURANCE. These are Piſtol's words, *II King Henry IV*, v, 5. This quotation has not been collected in the *Shakeſpeare Alluſion Books.*

p. 208. DRILL. A drill-maſter. The reference to the leading of " the Bears to persecu-tion " is to bear-baiting, which ruffianism ſtill persiſted.

p. 209. EATERS OF CHALK. A morbid symptom of green-sickness, an anæmic disease which moſtly affeſts young women about the age of puberty. This chlorosis is usually associated with menſtrual abnormality, generally suppression. There is present well-marked neuraſthenia, with, at times, hyſterical mani-feſtations. The appetite is disordered, and R. James, *Introduſtion to Moufet's Health's Improvement* (1746), alludes to " The Mischief that young Girls do themselves who are inclined to . . . the green Sickness, by Taking great Quantities of Chalk, Lime, and other Absorbents."

p. 209. UPSITTING. An upsitting was the occasion upon which a woman firſt sat up to receive company after her confinement. Cf. Brome's *A Jovial Crew*, aſted at the Cockpit in 1641, Aſt II, where Oldrents says :

We will have such a lying in, and such
A Chriſtning ; such up-sitting and Ghossipping !

p. 209. HUGE BOSS'D BIBLE. It was the duty of a prentice to carry the Family Bible to church and to take notes of the sermon.

p. 209. MRS. DIS-DAIN. There is no allusion, I think, to *Much Ado about Nothing*, I, " my dear Lady Disdain."

p. 209. FISH TAKEN AT GREENWICH. Greenwich seems to have been regarded as a sort of show-town for rarities and monſtrosities. On 18 June, 1657, Evelyn notes : " At Greenwich I saw a sort of catt brought from the Eaſt Indies, shap'd and snouted much like the Egyptian racoon, in yᵉ body like a monkey, and so footed ; . . . it was exceedingly nimble, gentle, and purr'd as dos ye catt." Probably a mocock. It is hardly possible to ascer-tain what kind of fish this was which attraſted curious crowds to Greenwich, where it was shown in the spring of 1670. A few years later, in 1683, the *London Gazette* informs us : " A perfeſt mermaid was, by the laſt great wind, driven ashore near Greenwich, with her comb in one hand and her looking-glass in the other. She seemed to be of the countenance of a moſt fair and beautiful woman, with her arms crossed, weeping out many pearly

(305)

drops of salt tears ; and afterwards she, gently turning herself upon her back, swam away without being seen any more." In 1749, a riobiscay from Russia was being exhibited.

p. 212. PIMP TO A BITCH. In Otway's *The Souldiers Fortune*, produced at Dorset Garden early in 1680, I, 1, Beaugard describes Sir Jolly Jumble as " one that is never so happy as when he is bringing good people together and promoting civil understanding betwixt the sexes : Nay, rather than want employment, he will go from one end of the Town to t'other to procure my Lords little Dog to be civil to my Ladies little languishing Bitch."

p. 216. PUDDENS. The bowels, guts, entrails. Still in dialect use and in several counties written " pudden." In J. E. Brogden's *Provincial Words and Expressions current in Lincolnshire* (1866) we have : " He slit open the poor fellow's belly, and let out the puddings." It should be noted that Norfolk, Shadwell's own county, uses " pudden " (so spelled) in this sense.

p. 216. BUSSY D'AMBOIS. Louis de Clermont, Bussy d'Amboise, was born in 1549 of a noble house. He followed the profession of arms and by his bravery and accomplishments won the favour of Monsieur, the Duke of Anjou, brother of Henri III. He was for a while governor of Anjou. In the course of his amours with Françoise de Maridort, wife of the Comte de Monsoreau, a trap was laid for him by the cuckold, and on the night of 18 August, 1579, he was assassinated by the Comte's retainers. Bussy had a *liaison* with Margareute de Valois, who wrote of him that there was not " en ce siècle-là de son sexe et de sa qualité rien de semblable en valeur, reputation, grace, et esprit." Bussy seems to have made an extraordinary impression upon the seventeenth century as a Don Juan, a caballero, a " Rupert of Hentzau " of his day. Chapman's two tragedies *Bussy d'Ambois* (1607) and *The Revenge of Bussy d'Ambois* (4to, 1613) were famous. In Restoration days Charles Hart won great renown as Bussy (*Bussy d'Ambois*), and is celebrated both by Dryden and D'Urfey. According to the latter, indeed, the drama " lay buried in Mr. *Hart's* Grave." Yet he altered it with some success. His version was acted in the spring of 1690–1, and Mountfort, who was very reluctant, but was finally persuaded, took the title-rôle.

p. 217. COLBRAND. The Danish giant, slain, in the presence of King Athelstan, by Sir Guy of Warwick, who had just returned from a pilgrimage, still in his palmer's weeds with a hermit's staff in his hand. The combat is described by Drayton, *Polyolbion*, XII.

p. 217. BERKENSHAW. John Berchinshaw, an Irishman, translated the *Elementale Musicum*, 8vo, 1664, and in 1672 issued a prospectus of a complete system of music, but it is doubtful if the book ever appeared. In the Pepysian library is a thin folio volume entitled *Mr. Berchinshaw's Two Parts to be sung (severally) with ye ordinary Church Tunes of the Singing Psalms.* Evelyn mentions him in his *Diary* 3 August, 1664, and describes him as " that rare artist who invented a mathematical way of composure very extraordinary, true as to the exact rules of art, but without much harmonie." A John Birchenshaw was buried in the cloisters of Westminster Abbey 14 May, 1681, but it is not certain that this was the teacher of music. There are many references in Pepys' *Diary* to Mr. Berkenshaw.

p. 218. GAYLAND. Three Moorish chiefs. The English first entered Tangier during an upheaval in the history of Morocco. In 1662 Er Rasheed II, one of the Shareefian race, whom the English knew as " the great Taffiletta," was fighting for supremacy against his brother Mohammed, whom he killed in battle in 1664. Among the supporters of Mohammed against "the great Taffiletta" was Said Abdulla ibn Ahmed ben ibn Ali Ghalain, whom the English called "Gayland" or "Guyland." He was an ambitious man who hoped to carve out for himself a kingdom in Northern Fez; but he had no right to the title often accorded him, "Emperor or Prince of West Barbary." When the English garrison was landing at Tangier this formidable chieftain was fortunately engaged in a war of his own against a "Saint" of Salli, Benboukir, whom the English called "Ben Bowcar" or "Ben Buker." Ghalain seemed willing to come to terms with the Earl of Peterburgh, the first English governor of Tangier, but his actions soon proved him at heart a foe. Several difficult years followed. In 1665 Ghalain found himself hard pressed both by the "Great Taffiletta" and his old foe Benboukir. Before long he proposed to send an ambassador to London "to greet in my name my beloved friend the King of Great Britain." The position was critical, as Ghalain was treacherous, but to the English Er Rasheed II would prove a more terrible opponent. Eventually Ghalain fell in a battle near Alcazar, being defeated by Taffiletta's brother, Mulai Ismail.

These events were much talked of in England, and "Gayland" is mentioned with interest by Pepys. In 1664 was published "A Description of Tangier, The Country and People adjoyning with An Account of the Person and Government of GAYLAND, The present Usurper of the Kingdome of FEZ." There is a frontispiece *A Guyland alias Gayland the Present Usurper of the Kingdome of Fez.* This is a Moorish warrior on horseback, not unskilfully designed. Monette's *Histoire des Conquestes de Monley Archy, Connu sous le Nom de Roy de Tafilet*, 1683, and Miss E. M. G. Ronte's *Tangier, 1661–1684*, may be read for ample accounts of this history.

In Settle's heroic tragedy *The Empress of Morocco*, Morena is the daughter of Taffalet. *The Heir of Morocco, With the Death of Gayland*, which may be regarded as a kind of sequel, is entirely unhistorical. It was produced at Drury Lane in the spring of 1682, with Clarke as Gayland; Griffin Albuzeiden, King of Algiers; and Mrs. Cox, Artemira, the princess.

p. 218. HYRCINIAN. Diodorus Siculus, XVII, 75, speaking of Hyrcania says: "'Ἔστι δὲ καὶ ζῶον κατὰ τὴν χώραν ἐπτερώμενον, ὃ καλεῖται μὲν ἀνθρηδών, λειπόμενον δὲ μεγέθει μελίττης, μεγίστην ἔχει τὴν ἐπιφάνειαν· ἐπινεμόμενον γὰρ τὴν ὀρεινὴν αὕτη παντοῖα δρέπεται, καὶ ταῖς κοιλάσι πέτραις καὶ τοῖς κεραυνοβόλοις τῶν δένδρων ἐνδιατρίβον κηροπλαστεῖ, καὶ κατασκευάξει χόμα διάφορον τῇ γλυκύτητι, τοῦ παρ' ἡμῖν μέλιτος οὐ πολὺ λειπόμενον."

p. 221. GRABU. Louis Grabu or Grebus, Master of the King's Music. He was a pupil of the famous Robert Cambert. The "Warrant to Edward, Earl of Manchester, to swear in — Grabu as Master of the English Chamber Music" is dated 12 November, 1666, *Calendar of State Papers*, 1666–7, p. 256. Pepys, Wednesday, 20 February, 1666–7, remarks: "They Talk also how the King's viallin, Bannister, is mad that the King hath a Frenchman come to be chief of some part of the King's musique, at which the Duke of York made great mirth." Grabu composed the music to Dryden's *Albion and Albanius*, operatic allegory, produced at Dorset Garden 3 June, 1685. Unluckily it failed, owing to the political situation, since on the sixth night news arrived in London of the landing of Monmouth.

p. 221. GRESHAM. Sir Thomas Gresham, 1519?–1579, whose College, to which upon his wife's death his own residence, Gresham House, was to be devoted, became the first home of the Royal Society.

p. 222. PENNY RENT. Rent paid (or received) in money; cash income; revenue. When Don Diego in *The Gentleman Dancing-Master* is displeased with Monsieur he cries: "He shall never marry my Daughter look you, *Don Diego*, though he be my own Sister's Son, and has two thousand five hundred seventy three pound sterling twelve shillings and two pence a year Penny-rent, Segonaramentè."

p. 222. GALLIARD. Brisk; lively; gay. Cf. Chaucer, *The Cokes Tale*, 3:

> Gaillard he was as goldfinche in the shawe.

p. 223. MUSKATOON. A musketoon is a kind of musket, short and with a large bore. Cf. Otway's *The Atheist*, II, 1, where Portia says: "Ill-lookt Rogues . . . stand Centinel up and down the house with Musquetoons and Blunder-busses."

p. 223. SKREW'D GUN. A gun furnished with a screwed barrel, *i.e.*, one having a helically grooved bore. Evelyn in his *Diary*, 1646, at Geneva speaks of "excellent screw'd guns" being among the staple commodities of that town.

p. 223. TOUR. The Ring in Hyde Park. This favourite ride and promenade was laid out in the reign of Charles I. There are innumerable allusions to so modish and frequented a rendezvous. Thus in the Prologue, spoken by Jevon, to Mrs. Behn's *The Luckey Chance ; or, An Alderman's Bargain*, produced at Drury Lane in the winter of 1686, we have:

> *the Mall, the Ring, the Pit is full*
> *And every Coffee-House still swarms with Fool.*

Cf. also Dorset's *Verses on Dorinda* (1680) :—

> Wilt thou still sparkle in the Box,
> Still ogle in the Ring ?

p. 223. HERCULES PILLARS. Fleet Street, on the south side, at the corner of *Hercules' Pillars Alley*, opposite S. Dunstan's church. It was a tavern of considerable repute in the seventeenth century. The Bear and Harrow was actually in Butcher Row, Strand, the Chancery Lane district. It was here that Nathaniel Lee died in 1692.

p. 224. SIX-PENNY IN AND IN. In and In was a gambling game played by three persons with four dice; the player who threw *in and in* took all the stake. The throw *in and in* is made with four dice, when these all fall alike or as two doubles. A full description of the game is given in Cotton's *Compleat Gamester*, 1680, p. 117.

p. 224. TOPPER OR PALMER. A topper is one who "tops," and to "top" at dice is to retain one of the dice at the top of the box by some unfair manipulation. *Dictionary Canting Crew*, circa 1700, has: "*Top*, to Cheat or Trick any one; also to Insult. *What do you Top upon me ?* do you stick a little Wax to the Dice to keep them together, to get the Chance ?"
   Palmer. Phillips, 1700, explains: "*Palmer* . . . one that deceitfully cozens or cogs at Cards or Dice, by keeping some of them in his Hand unseen." Cf. Dryden, *The Kind Keeper ; or, Mr. Limberham*, produced at Dorset Garden in March, 1677–8; 4to, 1680; IV, 1: where Mrs. Termagant says: "I feel the young Rascal kicking already like his Father—Oh, there's an Elbow thrusting out : I think in my Conscience he's Palming

and Topping in my Belly; and practising for a Livelihood before he comes into the World."

"Another way the Rook hath to cheat, is first by *Palming*, that is he puts one Dye into the Box and keeps the other in the hollow of his little finger, which noting what is uppermost when he takes him up, the same shall be when he throws the other Dye, and which runs doubtfully any cast. Observe this, that the bottom and top of all Dice are seven, so that if it be 4 above, it must be a 3 at bottom; so 5 and 2. 6 and 1. Secondly by *Topping*, and that is when they take up both Dice and seem to put them in the Box, and shaking the Box you would think them both there, by reason of the ratling occasioned with the screwing of the Box, whereas one of them is at the top of the Box, between his two forefingers, or secur'd by thrusting a forefinger into the Box." Cotton, *Compleat Gamester*, 1674, p. 14.

p. 224. MUNDENS. A coffee-house in Fleet Street, much frequented by young Templars and cits.

p. 224. MUNDUNGUS. Shag or rank tobacco. Cf. Sir Robert Howard's *The Committee*, folio, 1665, II: A Pipe of the worst Mundungus. In Mrs. Behn's *The Widow Ranter*, II, 2, Ranter calls Dullman "A walking Chimney, ever smoking with nasty Mundungus." Johnson in his *Dictionary* (1755) has: "Mundungus. Stinking tobacco. A cant word."

p. 224. PLANET STRUCK. Dazed and confounded. Cf. Dryden's *The Wild Gallant*, 4to, 1669, II, where Sir Timorous is unable to speak through shyness and Constance rallies him: "What, are you planet struck? Look you, my Lord, the Gentleman's tongue-tied."

p. 225. FEGUE. To fegue is to beat or drive, or to use any motion with an idea of speed. In *The Rehearsal*, Theatre Royal, 7 December, 1671, Actus II, Scaena 4, the Physician remarks: "When a knotty point comes I lay my head close to it, with a snuff-box in my hand, and then I fegue it away, i' faith." Sir Walter Scott uses this phrase in his journal, adding "as Mr. Bayes says." Cf. also Wycherley's *Love in a Wood*, produced at the Theatre Royal in the autumn of 1671, I, 2, where Sir Simon says:

No treat, sweet words, good meen, but sly Intrigue,
That must at length, the jilting Widow fegue.

p. 226. RHENISH. White Rhenish wine was regarded as a delicate beverage, fitted for ladies, and is often contrasted with the manlier and more robust Burgundy.

p. 226. DIPT MY FINGER. So in Dryden's *The Kind Keeper*, produced at Dorset Garden in March, 1677-8, I, Aldo says: "He drank thy Health five times, *supernaculum*, to my Son *Brain-sick;* and dipt my Daughter *Pleasance's* little Finger, to make it go down more glibly."

p. 226. SHOE. This silly piece of affected gallantry has been repeated, if not imitated, to-day, and probably on more occasions than one, when a lady's satin shoe was filled with champagne and drunk by one of her admirers. Nor are we to suppose that the draught was taken as an emetic.

p. 227. TERSE CLARET. The origin of the word "terse" seems obscure. It may be from the adjective "terse," or more probably from Thiers, a wine-producing district in France. The word is very common, and often stands as a synonym for the wine. Cf. *Timon, A Satyr*, by Buckingham and Rochester:

Our own plain Fare, and the best Terse the Bull
Affords, I'll give you, and your Bellies full.

Compare also Sedley's *Bellamira, or The Mistress*, produced at Drury Lane in May, 1687, II, 1, where the roistering old Merryman says : " I am so full, I should spill terse at every jolt."

p. 232. HEILDIBRAND. A peer of the Charlemagne cycle. His exploits won him a famous name, and in the chap-book stories he is the type of a somewhat truculent valour.

p. 234. GRANTHAM-STEEPLE. The old local proverb says : " 'Tis height makes Grantham steeple stand awry." Alan B. Cheales in his *Proverbial Folk Lore* quotes :

O Grantham ! Grantham ! these wonders are thine,
A lofty steeple and a living sign.

It is explained that a hive of bees once served as the sign of an inn.

p. 235. WILTSHIRE DEVIL. The famous Drummer of Tedworth. Tedworth, a small village in Wiltshire, was for a while the most talked-of spot in England, and a very Mecca for those interested in the supernatural. The phenomena which commenced in April, 1661, appear to have continued intermittently until April, 1663, and there seems reason to think that they even were renewed at a later date. Mr. Mompesson, of Tedworth, had handed over to the village constable on a charge of vagrancy a wandering drummer, who was annoying the whole village. This man escaped, and a few weeks afterwards Mr. Mompesson's house was much disturbed with knockings and loud drummings. In fact, it was a case of poltergeist hauntings. Amongst others Joseph Glanvill visited the scene and has left us some valuable notes upon the disturbances. For a full account of this very curious case see *The Geography of Witchcraft*, by the present editor, pp. 271–3. Pepys, Monday, 15 June, 1663, writes : " Both at and after dinner we had great discourses of the nature and power of spirits, and whether they can animate dead bodies ; in all which my Lord Sandwich is very scepticall. He says the greatest warrants that ever he had to believe any, is the present appearing of the Devil in Wiltshire, much of late talked of, and, they say, very true ; but my Lord observes, that though he do answer to any tune that you will play to him upon another drum, yet one tune he tried to play and could not ; which makes him suspect the whole ; and I think it is a good argument." I think it is a very superficial argument. It may be remembered that Addison's comedy *The Drummer, or The Haunted House*, produced at Drury Lane in March, 1715–16, which I have seen acted with applause, and have enjoyed more on the stage than in the reading, was largely founded upon the story of Tedworth. The play was published anonymously in 1716, and later reissued with a long preface by Steele in 1722.

p. 236. BARBARA, CELARENT. The scholastic mnemonic lines for figures and moods of the syllogism.

p. 236. A PROPERTY. Cf. *The Way of the World*, V, when Foible is discovered, and endeavours to explain : " Pray do but hear me, *Madam*, he could not marry your Ladyship, *Madam*—No indeed his Marriage was to have been void in Law ; for he was marry'd to me first, to secure your Ladyship. He could not have bedded your Ladyship ; for if he had consummated with your Ladyship, he must have run the risque of the Law, and been put upon his *Clergy*—Yes indeed, I enquir'd of the Law in that case before I would meddle or make." " What, then," bursts out the infuriated Lady, " I have been your Property, have I ? I have been convenient to you, it seems, . . . I have been Broker for you ? What, have you made a passive Bawd of me ? "

p. 239.   NINE WORTHIES. Three Gentiles : Hector, Alexander, Julius Cæsar ; Three
Jews : Joshua, David, Judas Maccabæus ; Three Christians : Arthur,
Charlemagne, Godfrey of Bouillon.

p. 240.   JIG-EM-BOB. Jiggumbob (cf. thingumbob), more often a trinket, as a humorous
formation from Jig. It is rarely applied to a person. In Beaumont and
Fletchers *The Coxcomb* (1613), IV, 7, Mercury's Mother says of the jewel
Viola proffers her : " What Giggombob have we here ? "

p. 241.   EXFOLIATED. Exfoliation is the lamellar (or other) separation of bone or other
tissue from the living structure as in Dry Necrosis, and other diseases.

p. 241.   PERIOSTIUM. Periosteum. A fibrous membrane that invests the surfaces of
bones, except at the points of tendinous and ligamentous attachment, and
on the articular surfaces, where cartilage is substituted. At the attachment
of tendons the periosteum blends with the fibres of the tendons. The
periosteum consists of two layers, an ectal, fibrous, and an ental, osteo-
genetic layer. The periosteum serves as a medium for the attachment of
tendons, and as a means of nourishment and regeneration of bone.

p. 241.   DIET-DRINK. A highly medicated beverage, especially used by venereal
patients. Cf. Duffett's farce *The Mock-Tempest*, 4to, 1675, I, 1, where when
the brothel is being stormed Hectorio, the bully, cries : " 'Sdeath, our
Ammunition's spent, the dear dear dyet-drink's gone." In Etherege's *The
Comical Revenge*, 4to, 1664, IV, 6, Betty says that Dufoy's illness was known
by the discovery of " a Bottle of Diet-Drink he brought and hid behind the
stairs." Gideon Harvey, *Little Venus Unmask'd*, 1685, recommends the
" Grand Diet," Article xviii, Patients are enjoined " to Dine upon Meat
rotten Roasted, and Sup upon Biscuits and Raisins." In his *Great Venus
Unmask'd*, 1672, p. 152, he lays down that as diet " ordinary biscuit, Naples
biscuit, or crusty thorow-baked bread is much approved of : which with a
few Raisins are to afford the Patient his supper."

p. 242.   PHARAMOND. This heroic romance is in twelve volumes. Seven volumes
were written by Gautier de Costes, Seigneur de la Calprenède, 1610–1663.
The remaining five volumes were the work of Pierre d'Hortigues, Sieur
de Vaumorière, 1610–1693. This continuation is considered to be of equal
merit with the original volumes. The romance turns on the love of King
Pharamond for the beautiful Rosemonde, daughter of a Cimbrian monarch.
There is an English translation of Pharamond by J. Phillips, London, folio,
1677. Nathaniel Lee's tragedy *Theodosius, or, The Force of Love*, which was
produced at Dorset Garden in 1680, is to some extent founded upon this
romance. One may see the History of Varannes, Part III, Book III, of
Martian, Part VII, Book I ; of Theodosius, Part VII, Book III.

    Cleopatra, the work of La Calprenède, was first published in parts, of
which the earliest appeared in 1646, and when completed, the whole was
printed in 12 octavo volumes. An English translation by Robert Loveday
was published in London, folio, 1669. Several English romantic dramas
have been founded upon episodes in *Cleopatra* ; for example, Lee's *Gloriana,
or, The Court of Augustus Cæsar* ; Mrs. Behn's *The Young King, or, The
Mistake*.

p. 242.   ROSICRUCIAN. It should be remembered that a firm belief in Astrology and
Divination by the stars persisted very late. The famous William Lilly had
many clients of all ranks and degrees. Astrologers are often satirized in
contemporary drama, *e.g.*, Mopus in Wilson's *The Cheats* ; Mr. Gazer in
The Counterfeit Bridegroom, or, The Defeated Widow ; Forsight in *Love for
Love* ; and very many more. One may also instance the scene in Farquhar's

The Recruiting Officer, produced at Drury Lane in April, 1706, where Kite is disguised as a conjuror, and both rich and poor come to learn the future. Even to-day Astrologers and Horoscopers advertise widely in appropriate journals.

p. 243. LANCASHIRE WITCH. Shadwell's allusion, especially in view of his later play, should be noted.

p. 244. UPON A BENCH. Cf. the Prologue, spoken by Mohun, to the Second Part of Dryden's *The Conquest of Granada*:

> But, as when Vizard Masque appears in Pit,
> Straight every Man who thinks himself a Wit
> Perks up ; and, managing his Comb with grace,
> With his white Wig sets off his Nut-brown Face;
> That done, bears up to th' prize, and views each limb,
> To know her by her Rigging and her Trimm ;
> Then, the whole noise of Fops to wagers go,
> —*Pox on her*, 't must be she ; and *Damm'ee no*.

There are many allusions to fops standing on the seats of the Pit. The Prologue, spoken by Mountford, to Dryden's *Cleomenes, the Spartan Heroe*, produced at Drury Lane in April, 1692, commences :

> I think, or hope at least, the Coast is clear ;
> That none but Men of Wit and Sense are here ;
> That our Bear-Garden Friends are all away,
> Who bounce with Hands and Feet, and cry, Play, Play,
> Who, to save Coach-Hire, trudge along the Street,
> Then print our matted Seats with dirty Feet ;
> Who, while we speak, make Love to Orange-Wenches,
> And between Acts stand strutting on the Benches.

p. 244. PERMAIN. The name of a variety of apple, of which there are many sub-varieties. Mortimer, *Husbandry*, 1707 (ed. 1721), II, 287, tells us : " The Russet Pearmain . . . partakes both of the Russeting and Pearmain in colour and taste, the one side being generally Russet, and the other streak'd like a Pearmain."

p. 244. CHATOLINS. " The French house in Covent Garden." *Vide* note on p. 37.

p. 244. ROGUST. Ragoût.

p. 245. PIAZZA. An open arcade on the north and east sides of Covent Garden Market Place. It was built by Inigo Jones, *circa* 1633–4, and for well-nigh a century remained a fashionable promenade. Scene II, Act IV, of *The Souldiers Fortune* is the Piazza at midnight. There are innumerable references. In *The Country-Wife*, 1675, IV, Sparkish says : " I keep my wedding at my Aunts in the *Piazza*." Cf. Brome, *The Covent Garden Weeded* (8vo, 1658), I, 1, where Cockbrayne says : " Yond magnificent Peece, the *Piazzo*, will excell that at Venice, by hearsay (I ne're travell'd)."

p. 246. GORDIAN. Gordius, an ancient king of Phrygia, was originally a peasant. Disturbances had broken out in Phrygia, and the Oracle declared that a waggon would bring a king who should restore peace. Whilst the people were deliberating, Gordius, with his wife and son, suddenly appeared in his rustic cart, and was acknowledged as king. He dedicated his cart to Zeus, in the Acropolis of Gordium. The pole was fastened to the yoke by a knot of bark ; and the Oracle announced that whosoever should untie this knot should be lord of Asia. Alexander the Great cut the knot with his sword,

and applied the Oracle to himself. Plutarch, *Alexander*, 13 ; Quintus
Curtius, III, i, 15.

p. 246.　NUNCIUM REMITTERE. To renounce. *Uirtuti nuntium remittere ;* Cicero,
Epistulaead Familiares, XV, 16, 3.

p. 246.　POST VARIOS. Vergil, *Æneid*, I, 204–5.

p. 247.　HACKNEY SCHOOL. Hackney was long famous for its boarding-schools. On
Sunday afternoon, 21 April, 1667, Pepys and his wife visited Hackney
Church, " where very full, and found much difficulty to get pews. . . .
That which we went chiefly to see was the young ladies of the schools,
whereof there is great store, very pretty." In Tom Brown's *Letters from the
Dead to the Living*, " Madam Creswell to Moll Quarles " writes : " I had a
parcel of as honest, religious girls about me as ever pious matron had under
her tuition at a *Hackney* boarding-school."

p. 251.　O TEMPORA ! O MORES ! Cicero, *In Catilinam Oratio Prima*, II.

p. 251.　Ἐυς θανοντος. Rather Ἐμοῦ θανόντος γαῖα μιχθήτω πυρί, upon which Professor Bensly has obliged me with the following note :

" The earliest extant reference to this much-quoted line is in Cicero,
De Finibus, 3, 19, 64. Quoniamque illa uox inhumana et scelerata ducitur
eorum, qui negant se recusare, quo minus, ipsis mortuis, terrarum omnium
deflagratio consequatur (quod uulgari quodam uersu Graeco pronuntiari
solet), certe uerum est, etiam iis, qui aliquando futuri sint, esse propter ipsos
consulendum.

The ' uulgaris quidam uersus Graecus ' to which Cicero alludes is found
in Suetonius, *Nero*, 38, Dicente quodam in sermone communi : Ἐμοῦ
θανόντος γαῖα μιχθήτω πυρί, ' Immo,' inquit, ' ἐμοῦ ζῶντος,' planeque ita
fecit.

Dio Cassius, 58, 23, puts the quotation in the mouth of the emperor
Tiberius :

Λέγεται γοῦν πολλάκις μὲν ἀναφθέγξασθαι τοῦτο δή τὸ ἀρχαῖον ' ἐμοῦ
θανόντος γαῖα μιχθήτω πυρί,' πολλάκις δὲ καὶ τὸν Πρίαμον μακαρίσαι ὅτι
ἄρδην μετὰ τῆς πατρίδος καὶ μετὰ τῆς βασιλείας ἀπώλετο.

Stobæus, *Anthologia*, 2, 7 (6), 13 (7), has the same line followed by this
other

Οὐδὲν μέλει μοι· τἀμὰ γὰρ καλῶς ἔχει.

The two lines are included in Nauck's *Tragicorum Graecorum Fragmenta*,
where they are Fragment 573 of the *adespota*. It does not seem certain that
the two lines are part of a single quotation. In the prose extract given by
Stobæus in which they occur it is possible for them to be independent
citations.

It has been conjectured that the lines may be taken from the *Bellerophon*
of Euripides."